TRADE SECRET LITIGATION & PROTECTION

A Practice Guide to the DTSA and the CUTSA

THE INTELLECTUAL PROPERTY SECTION OF
THE CALIFORNIA LAWYERS ASSOCIATION

Co-Editors:
Randall E. Kay
Rebecca Edelson
Robert Milligan

TRADE SECRET LITIGATION & PROTECTION:
A Practice Guide to the DTSA and the CUTSA

CLA books may be purchased for educational, business, or sales promotional use. For information, please contact: info@calawyers.org

Intellectual Property Law Section
400 Capitol Mall, Suite 650
Sacramento, CA 95814
calawyers.org

This volume may be cited as:

Randall E. Kay, Rebecca Edelson, and Robert Milligan, eds., TRADE SECRET LITIGATION & PROTECTION (California Lawyers Association 2022)

PREFACE
March 2022

This is an exciting time for those who work with trade secrets. The passage of the Defend Trade Secrets Act in 2016 brought renewed attention to trade secrets as an important form of intellectual property protection. In recent years we have seen more trade secret lawsuits brought in federal courts, state courts, and arbitration forums. We hope that this practice guide helps trade secret owners and everyone else involved in protecting and litigating trade secrets.

We appreciate and want to recognize the assistance of many people who volunteered their time for this treatise:

- The Executive Committee of the Intellectual Property of the California Lawyers Association.
- All of the contributing authors: Michael J. Allan, David Almeling, Travis J. Anderson, Michael Bandemer, Janet Craycroft, Kevin D. DeBré, Seth M. Gerber, Bradley C. Graveline, Steven P. Hollman, Angelique Kaounis, Seong H. Kim, Mark Leonard, Catherine ("Cathy") Lui, M. Alim Malik, Elizabeth McBride, James D. McNairy, Joanna R. Mendoza, Philip H.R. Nevinny, Anthony J. Orler, Michael E. Pappas, Puya Partow-Navid, John V. Picone III, Kent R. Raygor, Tenaya Rodewald, D. Joshua Salinas, Benjamin D. Scheibe, Cary D. Sullivan, Mikela T. Sutrina, Keith R. Szeliga, James D. Vaughn, Gabrielle Walker, and Dylan W. Wiseman.
- Our contributing editors and reviewers for the treatise: Warren Dranit, Shelby Hogan, Angelique Kaounis, Jonathan Lurie, and Ashley N. Smith.
- Additional talented attorneys and law clerks who volunteered their valuable time to further the preparation of this treatise: Emily Abbey, Jordan B. Arakawa, Adam A. Bartolanzo, Jenna G. Crawford, James V. Fazio, Christopher E. Hodge, Nicholas A. Hodges, Rebecca L. Mackin, Megan McKnelly, Kazim A. Naqvi, Joseph C. Peacock, Angela Reid, Elizabeth M. Rowe, James G. Stinehart, and Jennifer Wilson.

- Our firms who encouraged us to devote the time to create this treatise: Jones Day, Sheppard Mullin, and Seyfarth Shaw.

- Others who provided assistance to us: John Buelter from the California Lawyers Association, Courtney Kenney (publishing & project management), and Barbara L. Friedman.

With great appreciation to all,

Rebecca ("Bec") Edelson

Randall E. Kay

Robert Milligan

BIOGRAPHIES

CO-EDITORS AND AUTHORS

Rebecca ("Bec") Edelson is a partner in the Intellectual Property and Litigation Practice Groups in Sheppard Mullin Richter & Hampton LLP's Los Angeles (Century City) office and leads the firm's trade secret practice. Ms. Edelson's litigation practice emphasizes intellectual property and other complex business disputes, with a particular focus on trade secrets and injunctions. She has broad experience in all phases of state and federal litigation, including provisional remedies, pre-trial development, discovery and motion practice, trials, writs, and appeals. She also counsels businesses on protecting their proprietary rights and information outside the litigation context. Clients value her ability to see the big picture, hone in on the strategic options, and then focus on the best path to achieve the desired outcome. Ms. Edelson has represented clients in diverse industries, including the financial, medical technology, biotech, aircraft, database, toy, fashion, jewelry, retail, entertainment, and travel and leisure industries. Ms. Edelson previously served as the Chair of the Executive Committee of the Intellectual Property Section of the State Bar of California and is also a past chair of its Trade Secrets Standing Committee. She also previously served as Vice Chair of the Federation of Defense and Corporate Counsel's Intellectual Property Section. Ms. Edelson is a recipient of the Century City Chamber of Commerce's Women of Achievement award in the area of law. She contributed to an English language handbook on trade secret litigation in the United States created for the Ministry of Commerce of the People's Republic of China. She frequently lectures and publishes articles on trade secret protection and litigation strategies.

Randall E. Kay is a California trial lawyer with over thirty years of experience in trade secret litigation. Randy has represented leading technology and life sciences companies in some of the most notable and sizable trade secret lawsuits of the past decade. Randy's representations involve trade secrets for technological and scientific inventions in telecommunications, semiconductors, computerized technologies, medical devices, biotech and pharmaceuticals. Randy represented the plaintiffs in two of the first lawsuits filed under the DTSA where the courts exercised extraterritorial jurisdiction over foreign actors accused of misappropriation abroad. Randy has particular expertise in handling trade secret lawsuits stemming from failed collaborations. Randy handles trade secret cases through injunctions, summary judgments, jury verdicts, arbitrations and appeals. He also has experience in handling co-pending civil and criminal trade secret lawsuits. The Legal 500 selected Randy as a Leading Lawyer for trade secret litigation and the National Law Journal named Randy as an Intellectual Property Trailblazer. The Daily Journal has named Randy a Top Intellectual Property Lawyer and Top Trade Secrets Lawyer on numerous occasions, and it selected one of Randy's trade secret defense wins as a Top Defense Verdict of the Year. The California Superior Court recognized Randy as an expert witness on trade secret litigation. Randy, a partner with Jones Day, also represents clients in patent, copyright and trademark litigation, as well as licensing disputes and unfair competition matters.

Robert B. Milligan co-chairs Seyfarth Shaw LLP's Trade Secrets, Computer Fraud & Non-Competes practice group. His practice primarily focuses on trade secret, non-compete, and data theft/protection litigation, investigations, and transactional work. Robert represents multinational companies in a variety of key industries in trade secrets and restrictive covenant litigation and routinely provides valuable transactional advice on how to best protect valuable intellectual property assets in significant business transactions. He is a recognized national leader in trade secrets law serving on the prestigious Sedona Conference for Trade Secrets Working Group and serving as a Chair of the California Lawyer Association's Trade Secrets Interest Group. He previously served in similar positions for the ABA and ITechLaw. Clients frequently turn to Robert for his practical and effective advice to address their trade secret and non-compete issues, including conducting internal investigations, trade secret audits, and drafting relevant agreements and policies. In the past few years alone, he has obtained numerous injunctions in several high profile "bet-the-company" matters involving high level executives and has also defeated numerous requests for injunctive relief in similar type matters. Robert is a leading industry expert on trade secret and non-compete matters and is often interviewed by the media concerning high profile and significant trade secret matters. He played a leading role on the ABA Intellectual Property Section, and he was instrumental in drafting an ABA resolution in support of the passage of Defend Trade Secrets Act, which were credited by Congress in its ultimate passage. He is the Editor in Chief of the firm's award winning trade secrets blog, www.tradesecretslaw.com, and he coordinates the firm's popular trade secrets webinar series, which produces regular timely content on significant trade secret issues. He also played a leading role as a founding member of the Sedona Group's Trade Secret Working Group and recently served as Senior Editor of the Sedona Group's paper "Protecting Trade Secrets throughout the Employment Life Cycle." More information about Robert Milligan can be found at www.seyfarth.com/people/robert-b-milligan.html

CONTRIBUTING EDITORS AND AUTHORS

Michael J. Allan serves as Chair of the Copyright and Trademark Practice Groups at Steptoe & Johnson LLP. Mr. Allan has a broad practice that involves the prosecution and defense of various intellectual property rights on behalf of his clients in the software, pharmaceutical, fashion, music, entertainment, and financial services industries. He appears regularly in federal district and appellate courts throughout the country, as well as the International Trade Commission (ITC) and the Trademark Trial and Appeal Board (TTAB). Mr. Allan's trade secret practice involves litigation and counseling. He has tried bet-the-company trade secret cases in courts throughout the country. He also regularly advises clients on developing trade secret protection and compliance programs designed to help clients guard their trade secrets and avoid litigation. He has been named a Trailblazer by the National Law Journal and an MVP in IP by Law360 for his work on cutting edge intellectual property litigation.

David Almeling is one of the country's leading attorneys in trade secret law. Legal 500 describes him as one of the "key figures in the trade secrets space," IAM Patent 1000 calls him a "trade secret authority" and "one of the country's best trade secret litigators," he has taught trade secret law at UC Berkeley Law School for the last few years, and he has testified before Congress on safeguarding trade secrets. His book, Trade Secret Law and Corporate Strategy, is now in its third edition. David has represented clients in countless matters that span the full range of trade secret and employee mobility issues, from advising on protection programs to investigating alleged thefts to litigating trade secret cases in state and federal court.

Travis J. Anderson is a litigation partner of Sheppard Mullin Richter & Hampton LLP in the Labor and Employment and Business Trial Practice Groups in the firm's San Diego (Del Mar) office. He is the Editor of the firm's Trade Secrets Law Blog: www.tradesecretslawblog.com, and a frequent writer and presenter on trade secret law and restrictive covenants. He handles complex trade secret, business and employment disputes. He has litigated numerous high stakes matters from inception through trial and arbitration for businesses, business owners, employers, executives and retailers. Travis has been repeatedly selected as a Super Lawyers' Rising Star.

Michael Bandemer, CPA, CMA, CITP, EnCE, CFF is a Managing Director and Practice Leader with Berkeley Research Group, LLC, and specializes in digital forensics, e-discovery and corporate investigations. Mr. Bandemer has served as the leading expert in hundreds of investigations involving the theft of trade secrets and other intellectual property in California and across the United States. Mr. Bandemer has provided qualified expert testimony as a computer forensics and e-discovery expert in both federal and state courts and has served as a court appointed expert, third-party forensic neutral, and as a 30(b)(6) Corporate Representative. He has performed or supervised the forensic collection and analysis of electronically stored information (ESI) from corporate networks, databases, personal computers (Mac and PC), phones, tablets, external storage devices, social media, archives, cloud storage, and other data sources. Mr. Bandemer is currently a chapter President and International Board Member for the High-Tech Crime Investigation Association. He is a frequent speaker on the use of digital evidence in the investigation of trade secret thefts and presentation at trial.

Janet Craycroft is Assoc. General Counsel, Director of Legal Practice Excellence, Chief Learning Officer for the Law & Policy group for Intel Corporation in Santa Clara, California. Ms. Craycroft has represented companies as both outside counsel and in house counsel in trade secret matters in both state and federal court. Her trade secret matters have included civil litigation, trade secret misappropriation investigations, and government prosecution of trade secret theft. Prior to Intel, Ms. Craycroft was a partner with Gray Cary Ware & Freidenrich LLP. She was also a litigation associate with Wilson, Sonsini, Goodrich & Rosati. Ms. Craycroft served as Chair of the Trade Secret Law Committee of the AIPLA. She also served on the Patent Discovery Committee, U.S. District Court, EDTX, for the Hon. T. John Ward. She is a past president of Stanford Professional Women. Ms. Craycroft received her A.B. from Stanford University and J.D. from Santa Clara University.

Kevin D. DeBré is a partner with Stubbs Alderton and Markiles, LLP in the Los Angeles area and is the Chair of the firm's Intellectual Property and Technology Transactions Practice Group. Mr. DeBré specializes in intellectual property-related transactions, including software licensing, research and development collaborations, university licensing and technology transfer agreements, and product sourcing and distribution arrangements and in strategic planning of intellectual property protection. Mr. DeBré was the founder and Chair of the Licensing Interest Group of the California State Bar IP Section. He is a frequent speaker on intellectual property protection, licensing and monetization. After graduating from UC Hastings College of the Law, Mr. DeBré served as a judicial law clerk for Honorable John G. Davies, United States District Court for the Central District of California.

Seth M. Gerber is a partner with Morgan, Lewis & Bockius LLP in Century City, California. His trial practice focuses on trade secrets and non-compete litigation. Mr. Gerber has practiced extensively in both state and federal courts, and he has jury and bench trial, arbitration, and appellate experience. Mr. Gerber has been recognized by the Daily Journal as one of California's "Top Trade Secrets Lawyers." He has also been recommended by Legal 500 for Trade Secrets and recognized in The Best Lawyers in America (commercial litigation), and as a Southern California "Super Lawyer." Mr. Gerber is the leader of the Morgan Lewis IP Trade Secrets Working Group and his trial victories were featured by Law360 when Morgan Lewis was named "Employment Group of the Year." Mr. Gerber is also a member of the drafting team for the Sedona Conference, Working Group 12, on the topic of Cross-Border Trade Secret issues.

Bradley C. Graveline is a partner in Sheppard Mullin's Intellectual Property and Litigation Practice Groups. Brad is a nationally recognized first chair trial lawyer with more than 25 years' experience litigating intellectual property cases, including trade secrets, patents and trademarks. His practice focuses on trade secret advice and litigation, patent litigation, intellectual property advice, cannabis, trademarks and other commercial litigation. Brad litigates intellectual property cases involving a wide array of technologies, including pharmaceuticals, biologics, medical devices, nutrition supplements, security screening systems, computer software and wireless communications. Brad has extensive experience working with experts at all stages of litigation -- searching for and retaining appropriate experts (including liability and damages experts); preparing expert reports; preparing experts for depositions; taking and defending expert depositions; preparing experts for trial; and conducting direct and cross examination of experts at trial. Brad's clients have included Snap, Inc., HTC, Walmart, Stryker, TaylorMade, and the American Medical Association.

Steven P. Hollman is a Co-Head of the Trade Secrets Group at Sheppard, Mullin, Richter & Hampton, LLP and is a partner in the firm's Intellectual Property and Business Trials Practice Groups. In his 38 years of complex business litigation practice, he has focused on trade secret, trademark, patent, copyright and advertising disputes in federal courts around the country and in Section 337 proceedings before the U.S. International Trade Commission. In over 65 trials or contested evidentiary hearings, Steve has used the trial lawyer's art of narrative-building, story-telling and persuasive argument to achieve outstanding results. SHollman@sheppardmullin.com | sheppardmullin.com/shollman

Angelique Kaounis is Of Counsel in the Century City office of Gibson, Dunn & Crutcher where she practices in the Firm's Litigation Department, with a focus on intellectual property and technology-related issues. As an experienced litigator, she has successfully represented clients in state and federal court, arbitration, and mediation, in pre-trial, trial, and appellate proceedings, including in trade secret, antitrust and unfair competition, business tort, and breach of contract cases. Ms. Kaounis represents diverse clients, including Fortune 100 companies, in the high-tech, entertainment, financial, and health care industries. Ms. Kaounis is also a Chair of the IP Section's Trade Secrets Interest Group. Ms. Kaounis received her J.D. from the University of Pennsylvania Law School and her B.A., magna cum laude from Rutgers College. Ms. Kaounis has been honored numerous times by Law & Politics and Los Angeles magazines as one of Southern California's "Rising Stars."

Seong H. Kim is a Senior Vice President and Head of Foreign Legal Affairs at Samsung Display Co., LTD. Before that, he was a partner in the Intellectual Property and Litigation Practice Groups at Sheppard Mullin Richter & Hampton, LLP, and partner at an Am-Law 100 law firm, where he served as an Executive Committee member, as Head of Korea Commercial Litigation Practice Group, and Co-Managing Partner of that firm's Los Angeles and Century City offices. Over the course of his career, Mr. Kim has obtained judgments and settlements totaling billions of dollars and handled trade secret disputes involving billions of dollars. He has been recognized for his expertise by Chambers and Partners, Legal 500, Benchmark Litigation, IAM Patent 1000, etc. Mr. Kim is also an Adjunct Professor at University of Southern California, Gould School of Law, and University of California, Irvine, School of Law, where he teaches Advanced Trial Techniques.

Mark Leonard is the former General Counsel for Jelly Belly Candy Company where, from July 2015 to December 2021, he was responsible for all company litigation and all legal matters related to global brand protection, intellectual property, data privacy and security, e-commerce, licensing, marketing, international distribution, and ingredient and packaging regulatory compliance. Prior to joining Jelly Belly Mark was in private practice at Davis & Leonard LLP, a boutique intellectual property litigation and transactional firm he co-founded in Sacramento in 2003. Mark is a former chair of the California Lawyer Association's Intellectual Property Law Section and currently serves as the IP Section's representative on the CLA Board of Representatives as well as Vice-Chair of the IP Section's Legislation Interest Group.

Catherine ("Cathy") Lui is a partner in Orrick Herrington & Sutcliffe's Complex Litigation and Dispute Resolution Group. Cathy is based in the San Francisco office. Cathy's practice is focused on trying complex commercial and trade secrets litigation. For her achievements, Legal500 recognized her as a "Next Gen Lawyer" in Trade Secrets from 2019-2021. In addition, the National Asian Pacific American Bar Association honored Cathy as a 2019 Best Lawyer Under 40; this award recognized Cathy's excellence in her practice and her service to her community. Cathy is also very involved in diversity, equity, and inclusion initiatives. She previously co-led the firm's Asian American Affinity Group and served as Orrick's 2020 Leadership Council on Legal Diversity Fellow.

M. Alim Malik is the President of Jackson Tidus at its principal office in Irvine, California. He is the Chair of the Litigation and Employment Departments. He was educated at Oxford University and Harvard Law School. He is admitted to the California Bar and as a Barrister (Gray's Inn, UK). His State and Federal practice includes copyright claims in computer software, trademark/trade name protection, domain name disputes, trade secret disputes, employee mobility issues, IP ownership disputes and complex business litigation. He has been an Adjunct Professor of Law at Chapman University's Dale E. Fowler School of Law. Mr. Malik presented on the "Intellectual Property Aspects of the Draft Hague Convention on Jurisdiction and the Recognition of Foreign Judgments in Civil and Commercial Matters" at the Center For International Studies, Salzburg, Austria, and has spoken widely on Cyber risk management strategies for businesses.

Elizabeth McBride is Vice President at Applied Materials, leading Global Litigation and the Office of Compliance, which includes Ethics & Compliance, Privacy & Data Governance, and Trade. She currently leads risk management programs while overseeing complex investigations and litigation around the world. She plays a key role in shaping corporate strategy on global risk and compliance, including intellectual property protection, cybersecurity, employee mobility, cross-border data governance, trade, and anti-corruption. She is deeply committed to cross-functional partnerships focused on sustainable programs, policy, and controls, and is passionate about building diverse and high performing teams that collaborate to solve complex problems and enable the business.

Prior to joining Applied Materials, Ms. McBride was an IP litigator at Orrick, Herrington & Sutcliffe. Her practice focused on trade secret, copyright, and patent litigation involving complex technologies in high-stakes cases at both the trial and appellate court levels. Ms. McBride spent her early career in public policy, as a research associate at The Urban Institute, where she analyzed and evaluated state and federal justice policy and programming. She also clerked in the United States Attorney's Office, Criminal Division, in the Northern District of California. Ms. McBride graduated from Princeton University and earned her J.D. at Stanford University.

James D. McNairy is a Shareholder of Boutin Jones Inc. He leads the firm's Trade Secrets and Employee Mobility practice. Jim specializes in the protection and enforcement of intellectual property rights, with an emphasis on trade secrets, most often in matters also involving non-compete, computer fraud, unfair competition, and related business tort claims. He has represented Fortune 500 companies in some of their most challenging and significant engagements in these areas. He frequently writes and presents on trade secrets issues.

Joanna R. Mendoza is an intellectual property attorney whose practice has included litigation and transactional matters relating to: copyright, trademark and patent disputes; trade secret misappropriation; copyright and trademark registration; Trademark Trial and Appeal Board proceedings; WIPO/ICANN domain name dispute resolution proceedings; Independent Film and Television Alliance (IFTA) arbitrations; licensing and other technology transfer instruments; film and television production transactions; entity formation; general business transactions and matters related to entertainment law transactions. Ms. Mendoza graduated from U.C. Berkeley School of Law in 1990. In 2019 she closed her practice to take up traveling nearly full-time.

Philip H.R. Nevinny is Senior Counsel for Live Nation Entertainment, the world's leading live entertainment company, supporting Live Nation Concerts, the largest provider of live entertainment globally, promoting more than 40,000 shows and 100+ festivals annually for nearly 4,000 artists in over 40 countries. In his role at Live Nation, Mr. Nevinny supports all aspects of presenting concerts, including venue development and operation, production, vendor services, labor and employment, corporate transactions, talent and touring contracts, venue rentals, co-promotions, booking agreements, music licensing, marketing and promotion, copyright, trademark, and trade secrets. Given the proprietary nature of Live Nation's business and know-how, Mr. Nevinny regularly advises on and negotiates Non-Disclosure Agreements, and on the protection and maintenance of his client's trade secrets. Shortly prior to taking his position at Live Nation, Mr. Nevinny was co-counsel for the plaintiff in a trade secret trial in which the jury unanimously awarded his client $2,800,000 in damages for trade secret misappropriation under the California Uniform Trade Secrets Act, and thereafter obtained a royalty on defendant's sales. Mr. Nevinny previously was General Counsel for LMN Ventures, an early-stage venture capital firm that invests in entrepreneurs who are focused on creating ground-breaking businesses that are clean, green, health, wellness, fitness or education-oriented. Mr. Nevinny, who has practiced extensively in both state and federal courts, also has substantial trial and appellate experience. Prior to taking on his in-house duties, Mr. Nevinny was in private practice specializing in general business litigation, intellectual property matters, real estate, and a variety of business transactions, such as corporate formations, acquisitions, restructuring, joint ventures, financings, and offerings. He has also been a member of the State Bar of California Intellectual Property Section Standing Committee on Trade Secrets. Mr. Nevinny is a graduate of Columbia University, and Boston College Law School.

Anthony J. Orler is an attorney with Arent Fox, LLP in Los Angeles, California. Mr. Orler focuses his practice on foreign and domestic patent prosecution, trade secret counseling, and intellectual property licensing. Mr. Orler specializes in intellectual property issues related to materials science, semiconductor and alloyed materials and processing, satellite and terrestrial communications systems, and digital signal processing. Mr. Orler holds several United States and foreign patents and is an Adjunct Professor of Law at Loyola Law School in Los Angeles, California. Mr. Orler has represented

Fortune 50 companies and nationally recognized universities, and his clients include three Nobel Laureates. Mr. Orler was also Counsel of Record, amici curiae, in *Demore v. Kim*, 123 S.Ct. 1708 (2003), where his brief was cited by Justice Souter in one of the Opinions of the Court.

Michael E. Pappas routinely represents clients in litigation involving employee mobility and restraints and advises clients about best practices with respect to trade secret, confidential and proprietary information. He was counsel to the plaintiff and cross defendant in *Whyte v. Schlage Lock Company*, 101 Cal.App.4th 1443 (2002), a leading case concerning the "inevitable disclosure doctrine" in trade secret law. Mike is a principal of Lesnick Prince & Pappas LLP, a litigation and bankruptcy boutique in Los Angeles, California. In addition to his trade secrets practice, Mike represents clients in complex commercial disputes, including matters involving distribution, franchising, marketing, competition, trademarks, insurance coverage, partnership dissolution, real estate, creditors' rights and general business law.

Puya Partow-Navid is a Partner at Seyfarth Shaw LLP. His practice is focused on preparing and prosecuting patent applications, providing litigation support, and preparing opinions regarding infringement analysis, patent validity and freedom to operate. He has experience in prosecuting U.S. and foreign patents for various hardware and software technologies, such as wireless devices, wireless communication networks (e.g., LTE, 5G), neural networks (e.g., machine learning, computer vision, autonomous vehicles), e-commerce platforms, and portable shelters. Puya also assists clients in other areas of IP. This includes drafting and responding to cease and desist letters, reviewing watch notices, researching infringements, assisting with assignments, reviewing clearance reports, providing IP diligence for mergers and acquisitions, and prosecuting trademark applications. Previously, Puya was a software quality assurance engineer at Symantec Corporation where he helped develop major consumer products, such as Norton AntiVirus and Norton Internet Security. For additional information, please visit Puya's firm bio: www.seyfarth.com/people/puya-partow-navid.html

John V. Picone III is the Co-Chair of Hopkins & Carley's Litigation Department and its IP Practice Group. Mr. Picone's practice involves intellectual property generally with an emphasis on trade secret cases involving complex technology. He has other legal experience as San Benito County Panel Public Defender and lead special prosecutor, San Benito County District Attorney's Office. His other experience includes decorated service as a Naval Aviator stationed at the Naval Air Station, Moffett Field, California, flying the U.S. Navy's P-3 "Orion" aircraft. Mr. Picone was voted one of the "Best Commercial Litigators" in Silicon Valley by Bay Area Lawyer magazine. Mr. Picone received his J.D. from Santa Clara University and was an Emery Scholar, a B.T. Collins Scholar, and participated in the Santa Clara Law Review. He earned his M.A., summa cum laude, from San Jose State University, and his B.A., with faculty honors, from Trinity College in Connecticut.

Kent R. Raygor is a partner with Sheppard Mullin Richter & Hampton LLP in Los Angeles, CA. He specializes in intellectual property, constitutional, media law, and entertainment litigation. He has litigated numerous trade secret misappropriation cases, including to summary judgment and trial.

Tenaya Rodewald is a partner with Sheppard Mullin Richter and Hampton LLP's Litigation and Privacy and Cybersecurity practices. She specializes in intellectual property, media law, defamation defense and First Amendment litigation, and counsels clients on EU and US privacy law compliance. She represents clients in a broad array of intellectual property matters, including high tech and software trade secret and copyright disputes. She is also a nationally-recognized media and First Amendment lawyer, and was awarded American Lawyer's 2020 Tony Mauro Media Lawyer award (part of American Lawyer's annual industry awards) and the James Madison Freedom of Information Award from the Society of Professional Journalists, NorCal Chapter. Tenaya received her J.D. from NYU School of Law and a Ph.D. in Neuroscience from U.C. San Diego. Her scientific background gives her a unique ability to master technical information and allows her to play a critical role in technology and trade secret litigation.

D. Joshua Salinas is an attorney at Seyfarth Shaw LLP in Los Angeles, where he practices commercial litigation with a focus on trade secrets, employee mobility, unfair competition, blockchain technology, and computer fraud. Mr. Salinas authors annual updates to chapters in the Continuing Education of the Bar's Trade Secrets Practice in California treatise (Chapter 4A, Audits and Chapter 11, Litigation) and Thomson Reuters' Data Security and Privacy Law treatise. He has also spoken in the areas of trade secret protection strategies, social media, and blockchain technology, and is a regular contributor to his firm's law blog, Trading Secrets (tradesecretslaw.com). Mr. Salinas received his J.D. from California Western School of Law with an honors concentration in Intellectual Property, Telecommunications, and Technology Regulation. He also completed the Blockchain Unlocked Executive Academy at U.C. Berkeley Law.

Benjamin D. Scheibe has been a partner at Ellis George Cipollone Ross O'Brien Annaguey LLP in Los Angeles, California since 1986. He is a business litigator and trial attorney who concentrates his practice in the areas of complex business disputes, trade secret misappropriation, and other intellectual property rights. Mr. Scheibe's work in the area of trade secrets and intellectual property has spanned many different industries and businesses, from Fortune 500 companies to entrepreneurial "mom and pop" businesses, and includes obtaining and defending on appeal a $28 million trade secrets judgment. Mr. Scheibe speaks and writes regularly on trade secret law and business litigation. He served as the Project Coordinator for California Business Litigation, the attorney's practice book published by Continuing Education of the Bar, and co-authored Chapter 4 of that text, entitled "Trade Secrets." Mr. Scheibe is the former Chair of the Trade Secrets Standing Committee of the State Bar's Intellectual Property Section and has also served as both the Chair and Vice-Chair of the American Bar Association's Committee on Intellectual Property, Tort, and Insurance Practice Section, as well as on the Boards of Governors of the Association of Business Trial Lawyers and the Beverly Hills Bar Association.

Cary D. Sullivan is a litigation partner at Jones Day, where his practice focuses on high-stakes trials and trade secrets. With nearly 20 years of experience, Cary has represented public and private companies in trade secrets disputes around the globe, including multi-billion dollar disputes and cases that have helped define the limits of extraterritorial application of the federal Defend Trade Secrets Act. Cary has handled trade secrets disputes in numerous industries and in numerous contexts, ranging from failed collaborations to employee theft to international conspiracies. He has tried multiple cases to verdict and has found that preparing cases for trial is often the best way to resolve them short of trial.

Mikela T. Sutrina is a partner in Sheppard Mullin's Labor and Employment Practice Group. Mikela defends employers in state and federal court, as well as before federal, state and local administrative agencies in matters of discrimination, harassment, retaliation, wrongful termination, whistleblower actions, and breach of contract, especially as it relates to restrictive covenant agreements and misappropriation of trade secrets. Mikela both prosecutes and defends actions involving trade secret misappropriation, unfair competition and the enforcement of restrictive covenants across the country. Mikela aggressively advocates for her clients and the protection of their assets and information. Mikela also regularly counsels employers on restrictive covenant agreements and trade secret protection, including performing audits on these key issues to identify weaknesses and craft solutions to meet her clients' needs.

Keith R. Szeliga is a partner in the Government Contracts group of Sheppard Mullin's Washington, DC office. Keith represents clients ranging from small businesses to the nation's largest defense contractors in a broad range of government contracts matters including bid protests, claims, prime/sub disputes, audits, investigations, and compliance counseling. Keith has specialized expertise in advising clients regarding the protection and enforcement of IP rights, drafting and negotiating IP licenses, and developing IP strategies relating to government contracts, and lectures frequently on these topics. Keith has been recognized as a Leading Lawyer by Chambers, a Recommended Lawyer in the Legal 500 United States, and named to Who's Who Legal: Public Procurement. More information about Keith's practice is available here: www.sheppardmullin.com/kszeliga.

James D. Vaughn is a Managing Director with iDiscovery Solutions, Inc. in Orange County, California. Mr. Vaughn specializes in digital forensic investigations involving allegations of trade secret misappropriation and other intellectual property theft. He has provided live testimony more than 80 times in state and federal court, and on behalf of plaintiffs, defendants and as a forensic neutral. His experience includes trials, arbitrations, depositions, evidentiary and motion hearings. Mr. Vaughn is frequently called upon to speak at conferences, CLE events, law firms and other venues because of his in-depth industry knowledge and expertise. He regularly presents on topics involving eDiscovery issues, as well as sub-sets of eDiscovery such as mobile device forensics, social media collections and cloud computing. As part of Mr. Vaughn's desire to educate thought leaders and others in trade secret investigations, he is an active member of Sedona Conference Trade Secrets - Working Group 12.

Gabrielle Walker is an experienced commercial counsel with a proven track record of building and leading top-tier, highly successful global commercial legal teams, negotiating collaboratively with customers and vendors to successfully close deals, and working closely with executive leadership and cross-functional teams to drive revenue and increase efficiency. She is known for her positive attitude, collaboration and mentoring. Gabrielle currently leads the NA/ANZ Go-To-Market Legal team at Contentful, Inc.

Dylan W. Wiseman is the Co-Chair of Buchalter's Trade Secret and Employee Mobility Practice Group. For over 25 years, Mr. Wiseman has focused exclusively on intellectual property protection, including representing employers in cases involving trade secrets and employee mobility. Mr. Wiseman also defends businesses accused of engaging in trade secret misappropriation and acts of unfair competition. Mr. Wiseman has extensive jury trial experience. He has been lead trial counsel in several complex-designated unfair competition jury trials. *The Daily Journal* named Mr. Wiseman among California's 2021 Top Trade Secrets Lawyers. In 2021, he co-authored *Template Civil Jury Instructions Under the Defend Trade Secrets Act*, which was published in the Intellectual Property &

Technology Law Journal. He has taught numerous classes on trade secret litigation for the State Bar and other professional organizations, and has a podcast about trade secret issues. Mr. Wiseman is resident in Buchalter's San Francisco and Sacramento offices.

TABLE OF CONTENTS

Chapter 10 HANDLING TRADE SECRETS DURING THE LITIGATION PROCESS

Chapter 23 SPOLIATION SANCTIONS IN TRADE SECRETS CASES

Chapter 24 WORKING WITH EXPERTS IN TRADE SECRETS CASES

Appendix A COMMENTARY ON THE CALIFORNIA TRADE SECRETS JURY INSTRUCTIONS

Appendix B MODEL NON-DISCLOSURE AGREEMENT

Chapter 1
WHAT IS A TRADE SECRET?
By: Randall E. Kay, Esq.

---

§ 1.01 Demystifying Trade Secrets

Mystery surrounds the makeup of many trade secrets—understandably so. By their nature, trade secrets are not publicly known. Companies often do not have formal written descriptions of their own trade secrets. When ownership and misappropriation disputes arise, though, the precise nature of the claimed trade secrets takes center stage.

Some fundamental questions regarding trade secrets include:

- What is a trade secret?
- How does one define a trade secret?
- How does one identify a trade secret?
- How does one protect a trade secret?
- How can one guard against theft of a trade secret?

This chapter answers these questions.

§ 1.02 Laws Governing Trade Secret Practice in California

Both state and federal laws govern trade secret protection. Under California law, the California Civil Code and Code of Civil Procedure contain the statutes governing civil trade secret practice. The Defend Trade Secrets Act governs federal civil claims. Criminal trade secret law is governed both by the California Penal Code and the federal Economic Espionage Act.

Trade secret laws applicable in California include:

- The California Uniform Trade Secrets Act (CUTSA) effective as of January 1, 1985. Cal. Civ. Code §§ 3426.1-3426.11, added by Statutes of 1984, ch. 1724, § 1; Cal. Assemb. B. 501 (Harris);
- The Defend Trade Secrets Act (DTSA) effective as of May 11, 2016. 18 U.S.C. §§ 1831-1839 (2016) (enacted as an amendment to the already existing Economic Espionage Act to provide for civil actions);
- Court decisions applying the CUTSA and the DTSA;
- Court decisions applying pre-CUTSA law that do not conflict with the CUTSA. (To the extent pre-CUTSA court decisions conflict with the CUTSA, the CUTSA controls. *See Am. Credit Indem. Co. v. Sacks*, 213 Cal. App. 3d 622, 630 (1989));
- Section 2019.210 of the California Code of Civil Procedure;
- Section 499c of the California Penal Code;

- The federal Economic Espionage Act. 18 U.S.C. §§ 1831-1839 (2016);
- Rules 2.550—2.551 of the California Rules of Court;

and

- Sections 1060-1063 of the California Evidence Code.

In addition to the foregoing authorities, resources for California trade secret law include:

- The Judicial Council's California Civil Instructions (CACI) contain recommended jury instructions for use in civil trade secret cases. The CACI instructions for trade secret cases are reprinted in Appendix A to this practice guide;
- Legislative history for the CUTSA, including the Model Uniform Trade Secrets Act, the various versions of the bill that became California law, documents generated during California Assembly deliberations and California Senate deliberations, and communications with then-California governor Deukmejian;
- Legislative history for the DTSA;
- Unpublished or uncitable court opinions which, although not precedent, indicate how some courts have addressed and handled trade secret issues;

and

- The American Law Institute's Restatement (First) of Torts, section 757, comment (b) (1939) (which preceded the UTSA in the evolution of California trade secret law) and the Restatement (Third) of Unfair Competition, sections 39-45 (1995).

This chapter discusses the scope and practical application of California trade secret law by reviewing the statutory definition of a trade secret, assessing how court decisions have defined trade secrets, and considering how the defining characteristics of trade secrets may be used to protect intellectual property.

§ 1.03 Defining a Trade Secret in Civil Litigation

A. The California Civil Code Definition

> "Trade secret" means information, including a formula, pattern, compilation, program, device, method, technique, or process, that: (1) Derives independent economic value, actual or potential, from not being generally known to the public or to other persons who can obtain economic value from its disclosure or use; and (2) Is the subject of efforts that are reasonable under the circumstances to maintain its secrecy.

Cal. Civ. Code § 3426.1(d). Under section 3426.1, trade secret holders must establish that what they are claiming was misappropriated satisfies these elements of a trade secret:

- **Information.** The trade secret must be information that can be described with sufficient particularity to separate it from matters of general knowledge in the trade.
- **Value from being unknown.** The information must have actual or potential independent economic value.
- **Not generally known.** The information's value must come from not being generally known.
- **Secrecy measures.** Efforts to maintain the secrecy of the information must be deemed reasonable under the circumstances.

Analyzing these elements is the key to determining the existence of a protectable trade secret under California law.

B. Definition of Trade Secret Under the DTSA

A plaintiff must prove that it owns a legally protectable trade secret. The term "owner," with respect to a trade secret, means the person or entity in whom or in which rightful legal or equitable title to, or license in, the trade secret is reposed. 18 U.S.C. § 1839(4); *HealthBanc Int'l v. Synergy Worldwide, Inc.*, 208 F. Supp. 3d 1193, 1201 (D. Utah 2016).

The DTSA defines a "trade secret" broadly and with reference to many examples of the types of information capable of protection:

> [T]he term "trade secret" means all forms and types of financial, business, scientific, technical, economic, or engineering information, including patterns, plans, compilations, program devices, formulas, designs, prototypes, methods, techniques, processes, procedures, programs, or codes, whether tangible or intangible, and whether or how stored, compiled, or memorialized physically, electronically, graphically, photographically, or in writing if—
>
> (A) the owner thereof has taken reasonable measures to keep such information secret; and
>
> (B) the information derives independent economic value, actual or potential, from not being generally known to, and not being readily ascertainable through proper means by, another person who can obtain economic value from the disclosure or use of the information;

18 U.S.C. § 1839(3). Thus, the definition identifies two overarching categories of trade secret information: (a) information of a commercial nature (financial, business and economic information); and (b) information of an industrial nature (scientific, technical and engineering information). The definition also lists thirteen examples of the information types, such as patterns, formulas, methods, and techniques—all of which are familiar under other trade secret laws.

C. Key Words and Phrases in the Statutory Definition

Dissecting the words and phrases in the California definition of "trade secret" illustrates the many facts for which plaintiffs need to marshal evidence and defendants need to challenge. Key words and phrases to analyze are:

- **Information:**
  formula
  pattern
  compilation
  program
  device
  method
  technique
  process
  including

- **Derives value:**
  independent
  economic
  actual
  or
  potential

- **Not generally known:**
  to the public
  or
  to other persons
  who can obtain economic value from
  disclosure
  or
  use

- **Secrecy:**
  reasonable
  efforts
  maintain
  secrecy

A trade secret holder must establish each of the elements in the definition in order to have a protectable trade secret.

1. "Information"—What Information Qualifies as a Trade Secret?

Many different types of information can constitute protectable trade secrets. Types of trade secret information range from ideas and design concepts to source code and computer algorithms, customer lists, software programs and recipes. A classic trade secret that has lasted for over a century is the formula for Coca-Cola. The Coca-Cola Company has maintained the recipe for this soft drink as a trade secret, just as Kentucky Fried Chicken has kept its original recipe blend of eleven herbs and spices as a trade secret.

The court in *Silvaco Data Systems v. Intel Corp.*, 184 Cal. App. 4th 210 (2010), *disapproved of on other grounds by Kwikset Corp. v. Superior Court*, 51 Cal. 4th 310 (2011), contrasted trade secret rights with patent rights, observing that trade secret law may apply to secret information that tends to communicate an idea or fact to another. *Id.* at 220-21 ("Indeed a trade secret may consist of something we would not ordinarily consider an *idea* (a conceptual datum) at all, but more a *fact* (an empirical datum), such as a customer's preferences, or the location of a mineral deposit.") (emphasis in original). Ideas and design concepts can constitute protectable trade secret information so long as they meet all the other elements for trade secret protection. *Altavion, Inc. v. Konica Minolta Sys. Lab.*, 226 Cal. App. 4th 26, 53-56 (2014).

a. Specifically Recognized Types of Information

The California definition of a trade secret provides that the basic building block of a trade secret is information. The CUTSA definition identifies, by way of example, the following eight types of trade secret information:

- Formula, pattern, compilation, program, device, method, technique, and process.

These eight types of information are expressly recognized as protectable under California's UTSA, subject to satisfaction of the remaining criteria.

The Defend Trade Secrets Act identifies similar types of information as trade secret:

- All forms and types of financial, business, scientific, technical, economic, or engineering information, including patterns, plans, compilations, program devices, formulas, designs, prototypes, methods, techniques, processes, procedures, programs, or codes.

b. "Other" Types of Information

The CUTSA provides eight examples of trade secret information that are protectable subject matter under trade secret law. The CUTSA states " 'Trade secret' means information, *including* a formula, pattern . . ." (emphasis added). Cal. Civ. Code § 3426.1(d). The term "including" signifies that information, in addition to the eight specifically identified examples, may also receive trade secret protection. *Am. Paper & Packaging Prods., Inc. v. Kirgan*, 183 Cal. App. 3d 1318, 1323-24 (1986). For example, customer lists are often regarded as subject to trade secret protection. Although customer lists may sometimes be considered compilations, they could also constitute another recognized type of information subject to trade secret protection. *Id.*; *Morlife, Inc. v. Perry*, 56 Cal. App. 4th 1514, 1521 (1997).

The word "including" in the trade secret statutes provides legitimacy to claims that any kind of information—not just the eight enumerated types of information—can constitute a trade secret. Trade secret information can include all kinds of knowledge, facts, data, communications, and intelligence.

c. Types of Information Recognized as Trade Secrets by the Courts

Published court decisions provide judicial interpretation of trade secret claims. Courts have found many types of information that can constitute legally protectable trade secrets (subject to the trade secret holder satisfying all of the statutory requirements). The following types of information can constitute trade secrets under California law (or, at a minimum, have survived pretrial challenges by demurrer, motion to dismiss, or motion for summary judgment). While some of the referenced court decisions were decided prior to California's enactment of the UTSA, the courts' reasoning remains persuasive.

- **Advertising strategies, plans, and techniques including advertising allowances.** *Whyte v. Schlage Lock Co.*, 101 Cal. App. 4th 1443, 1455-56 (2002).

- **Business strategies and methods.** *Morton v. Rank Am., Inc.*, 812 F. Supp. 1062, 1073-74 (C.D. Cal. 1993) (denying motion to dismiss in a suit by Hard Rock Cafe restaurant claimants against Planet Hollywood restaurants asserting trade secret rights in supplier lists, "negative" research, financial information, operational information, marketing strategies and methods, advertising and promotion information, merchandising, financing sources, and related information).

- **Combinations of generally known elements.** *O2 Micro Int'l Ltd. v. Monolithic Power Sys.*, 420 F. Supp. 2d 1070, 1089 (N.D. Cal. 2006) (affirming a jury verdict that declared a combination of generally known transformer wires, turns and bays—when combined in a novel way—constituted a trade secret); *UniRAM Tech., Inc. v. Taiwan Semiconductor Mfg. Co.*, No. C-04-1268 VRW, 2007 WL 2572223, at *2-6 (N.D. Cal. Sept. 5, 2007) (detailed discussion of combination trade secrets); *SkinMedica, Inc. v. Histogen, Inc.*, 869 F. Supp. 2d 1176, 1196 (S.D. Cal. 2012) (holding that, even if most or all elements of a method are generally known individually, the combination of elements, taken together, may constitute a protectable trade secret); *In re Bio-Response, Inc.*, Nos. C-92-3036-DLJ, NC-92-1114, 4-89-04159-N-3, 1993 WL 87213, at *5 (N.D. Cal. Mar. 16, 1993) (involving a malicious prosecution case relating to underlying misappropriation case, stating "a trade secret may consist of a combination of generally known elements"); *Cybertek Computer Prods., Inc. v. Whitfield*, 203 U.S.P.Q. (BNA) 1020, 1024 (Cal. Super. Ct. 1977) (applying Restatement of Torts definition of trade secret to a pre-CUTSA case involving a computer system consisting of an entire bundle or combination of concepts as developed and used by plaintiff); *Copper Harbor Co., Inc. v. Cent. Garden & Pet Co.*, No. A149709, Nos. A150381 and A150381, 2019 WL 2296224, *9 (Cal. Ct. App. May 30, 2019) (affirming the jury's finding of a combination trade secret consisting of a continuously stirred tank reactor, temperature control, pH control, and low-shear mixing).

• **Compilations of information for disk storage devices and data modules.** *Forro Precision, Inc. v. IBM Corp.*, 673 F.2d 1045, 1057 (9th Cir. 1982) (affirming misappropriation verdict based on engineering drawings and blueprints constituting compilations of information).

• **Construction project information.** *San Jose Constr. v. S.B.C.C., Inc.*, 155 Cal. App. 4th 1528, 1537-39 (2007) (claimed trade secret compilation included project budgets, proposals, correspondence between owner and architect, bids, estimating documents, subcontractor requests for information and special reports).

• **Contact Lists.** *Main St. Partners & Assocs. Inc. v. Precision Asset Mgmt. Corp.*, No. B281567, 2018 WL 3425047, *6 (Cal. Ct. App. July 16, 2018) (determining at pleadings stage that contact lists identifying secondary purchasers in real estate transactions could constitute protectable trade secrets if those contacts were not generally known in the industry).

• **Cost information.** *Whyte*, 101 Cal. App. 4th at 1455-56 (distinguishing trade secret cost information from commonly used industry formulas for setting prices, which are not trade secrets); *Cutera, Inc. v. Lutronic Aesthetics, Inc.*, 444 F. Supp. 3d 1198, 1205-1206 (E.D. Cal. 2020) (manufacturing, vendor and labor costs qualify as a trade secret under the DTSA and the CUTSA at temporary restraining order stage).

• **Customer lists and customer information.** *Cutera, Inc. v. Lutronic Aesthetics, Inc.*, 444 F. Supp.3d 1198, 1205-06 (E.D. Cal. 2020) (current and prospective customer contact information can constitute trade secrets under the DTSA and CUTSA); *Brocade Commc'ns Sys., Inc. v. A10 Networks, Inc.*, 873 F. Supp. 2d 1192, 1214 (N.D. Cal. 2012); *Reeves v. Hanlon*, 33 Cal. 4th 1140, 1155-56 (2004); *Lillge v. Verity*, No. C 07-02748, 2008 WL 906466, at *5 (N.D. Cal. Apr. 1, 2008); *Morlife*, 56 Cal. App. 4th at 1520-24; *Hall, Mahar & Assocs. Ins. Servs., Inc. v. Sanborn & Churton Ins. Servs., Inc.*, No. G051572, 2016 WL 6872958, *5 (Cal. Ct. App. Nov. 22, 2016) (insurance company's client information considered trade secrets when containing policy, contact and plan information); *ABBA Rubber Co. v. Seaquist*, 235 Cal. App. 3d 1, 18-20 (1991); *Courtesy Temp. Serv., Inc. v. Camacho*, 222 Cal. App. 3d 1278, 1286-88 (1990) (information regarding potential customers not interested in the relevant services can constitute trade secret information); *Am. Credit Indem. Co. v. Sacks*, 213 Cal. App. 3d 622, 630-31 (1989); *Am. Loan Corp. v. Cal. Commercial Corp.*, 211 Cal. App. 2d 515, 522-23 (1963); *Peerless Oakland Laundry Co. v. Hickman*, 205 Cal. App. 2d 556, 559-60 (1962) (customer likes, dislikes, and needs is "the very kind of information which so often spells the difference between success and failure in a business based on service"); *Alex Foods, Inc. v. Metcalfe*, 137 Cal. App. 2d 415, 423-24 (1955).

• **Data.** *Masonite Corp. v. County of Mendocino Air Quality Mgmt. Dist.*, 42 Cal. App. 4th 436, 449 (1996) (deeming "emission factors" data as trade secret information, as compared to public "emission data"); *Masonite Corp. v. Superior Court*, 25 Cal. App. 4th 1045, 1054-56 (1994).

• **Databases.** *MAI Sys. Corp. v. Peak Computer, Inc.*, 991 F.2d 511, 520-23 (9th Cir. 1993) (affirming summary judgment on misappropriation claim and permanent injunction prohibiting use and disclosure of trade secret customer database).

- **Design concepts.** *Cisco Sys., Inc. v. Chung*, No. 19-CV-07562-PJH, 2020 WL 4505509, *4 (N.D. Cal. Aug. 5, 2020) (design specifications and schematics adequately pled as trade secrets); *Altavion*, 226 Cal. App. 4th at 59-61 (design concepts underlying digital stamping technology protectable as trade secrets when only disclosed under nondisclosure agreement).

- **Employee lists.** *Medipro Med. Staffing, LLC v. Certified Nursing Registry, Inc.*, No. B294391, 2021 WL 387879, *9 (Cal. Ct. App. Feb. 4, 2021) (affirming judgment on jury verdict finding that nurse registry containing names, credentials, shift preferences, and pay rates constitutes a trade secret); *Hilderman v. Enea TekSci, Inc.*, 551 F. Supp. 2d 1183, 1202 (S.D. Cal. 2008) (denying defendant's summary judgment motion because a triable issue existed regarding use of trade secrets in solicitation of engineers).

- **Engineering drawings and blueprints.** *Forro Precision*, 673 F.2d at 1057.

- **Idea for device for converting brain waves to audible form.** *Sinclair v. Aquarius Elecs., Inc.*, 42 Cal. App. 3d 216, 221-22 (1974) (involving device disclosed under confidentiality agreement).

- **Ideas for digital stamping technology**. *Altavion*, 226 Cal. App. 4th at 53-56 (broadly stating that ideas are protectable as trade secrets and affirming bench trial finding of misappropriation of design concepts and ideas).

- **Information in one's head or memory.** *Morlife*, 56 Cal. App. 4th at 1522 (stating that trade secret information need not be in writing). Courts recognize, however, that they "cannot compel a man who changes employers to wipe clean the slate of his memory." *Futurecraft Corp. v. Clary Corp.*, 205 Cal. App. 2d 279, 288 (1962) (citations omitted).

- **Information regarding prototypes for speech technology for verbally-impaired people to communicate with computer-generated digitized speech.** *Speech Tech. Assocs. v. Adaptive Commc'n Sys.*, No. C-88-2392-VRW, 1994 WL 449032, at *1, 9-10 (N.D. Cal. Aug. 16, 1994).

- **Insurance premium and renewal date information.** *Liberty Mut. Ins. Co. v. Arthur J. Gallagher & Co.*, No. C94-3384 MHP, 1994 WL 715613, at *5-6 (N.D. Cal. Dec. 19, 1994).

- **Manufacturing processes.** *Maxwell Alarm Screen Mfg. Co. v. Protective Serv. Corp.*, 218 U.S.P.Q. (BNA) 580, 581 (C.D. Cal. 1982); *Copper Harbor*, Nos. A149709 and A150381, 2019 WL 2296224 at *9.

- **Marketing research, strategies, plans, and techniques, such as marketing concessions.** *Whyte*, 101 Cal. App. 4th at 1455-56; *Ansett Aircraft Spares & Servs., Inc. v. Cue*, No. B272100, 2018 WL 2425713, *4-5 (Cal. Ct. App. May 30, 2018) (affirming jury finding that inventory management and marketing agreement regarding aircraft spare parts met requirements as protectable trade secret).

- **Methods of producing die-cut masks and overlapping discs in machinery.** *By-Buk Co. v. Printed Cellophane Tape Co.*, 163 Cal. App. 2d 157, 166 (1958) (involving information learned through employment relationship imposing confidentiality).

- **Methods for teaching meditation.** *Art of Living Found. v. Does 1-10*, 102 U.S.P.Q.2d 1820, 1836 (N.D. Cal. 2012) (finding that methods for teaching meditation through instructional courses may be protectable trade secrets, even if the meditation exercises themselves are publicly known).

- **Negative research.** *Courtesy Temp.*, 222 Cal. App. 3d at 1287-88 (recognizing that knowing which customers have not purchased services deserves protection as trade secret information).

- **Payment terms.** *Whyte*, 101 Cal. App. 4th at 1455.

- **Pricing information, including pricing concessions, volume rebates and rebate incentives.** *Whyte*, 101 Cal. App. 4th at 1455; *Hilderman*, 551 F. Supp. 2d at 1200 (ruling at summary judgment that triable issue of fact existed whether specific pricing for engineers' hourly rates at different rates for different customers constituted trade secret information); *Cutera, Inc.*, 444 F. Supp. 3d at 1205-1206.

- **Product concepts**. *Mattel, Inc. v. MGA Entm't, Inc.*, 782 F. Supp. 2d 911, 962 (C.D. Cal. 2011) (stating that concepts for unreleased products can merit trade secret protection, and rejecting defendant's motion for summary judgment that fashion doll concepts are not trade secrets).

- **Product plans and designs.** *Vacco Indus., Inc. v. Van Den Berg*, 5 Cal. App. 4th 34, 41-42, 50-51 (1992) (protecting plans for military, aerospace, petrochemical, and nuclear power industries, including manufacturing and engineering technology).

- **Production techniques and methods and manufacturing processes.** *Components for Research, Inc. v. Isolation Prods., Inc.*, 241 Cal. App. 2d 726, 728-29 (1966).

- **Production techniques which permit commercially feasible manufacture.** *Maxwell Alarm*, 218 U.S.P.Q. (BNA) at 581.

- **Profit margins.** *Whyte*, 101 Cal. App. 4th at 1455.

- **Promotional discounts.** *Whyte*, 101 Cal. App. 4th at 1455.

- **Religious materials.** *Bridge Publ'ns, Inc. v. Vien*, 827 F. Supp. 629, 632-33 (S.D. Cal. 1993) (granting summary judgment for trade secret holder who demonstrated that defendant instructor misappropriated plaintiff's religious materials which had economic value and had been subject of reasonable secrecy efforts).

- **Software.** *Pixion, Inc. v. PlaceWare, Inc.*, 421 F. Supp. 2d 1233, 1243, 1245 (N.D. Cal. 2005), *aff'd*, 177 F. App'x 85 (Fed. Cir. 2006) (denying defendant's motion for summary judgment on asserted trade secret for aspects of plaintiff's multi-speed architecture for a computer conference system); *Bus. Sols. LLC v. Ganatra*, No. SA CV 18-1426-DOC(KESx), 2020 WL 1279209, *3-5 (C.D. Cal. Jan. 22, 2020) (finding that screenshots of software constituted trade secrets under the CUTSA and the DTSA because one screenshot included pictures of a phone with confidential product information, such as names, origination dates, order identifications and more and the other screenshot included a picture of a computer screen showing customer information); *Vermont Microsys. v. Autodesk, Inc.*, 88 F.3d 142, 147-49 (2d Cir. 1996) (applying California law and finding that the architecture of display list drivers and source code algorithms for computer aided design (CAD) software qualified as trade secrets); *MAI Sys.*, 991 F.2d at 522-23 (generally recognizing "computer software" as qualifying for trade secret protection, but reversing summary judgment in plaintiff's favor because plaintiff failed to identify the trade secrets with specificity); *S.O.S., Inc. v. Payday, Inc.*, 886 F.2d 1081, 1089-90 (9th Cir. 1989) (alleged misappropriation of source code; reversing summary judgment in defendant's favor and remanding for further proceedings).

- **Strategic plans.** *Whyte*, 101 Cal. App. 4th at 1456.

- **Suppliers' identities.** *Citizens of Humanity, LLC v. Costco Wholesale Corp.*, No. B204117, 2009 WL 323622 (Cal. Ct. App. Feb. 11, 2009).

- **Technical know-how.** *Whyte*, 101 Cal. App. 4th at 1456 (referring to technical know-how as the quintessential trade secret).

- **Technical specifications.** *Forro Precision*, 673 F.2d at 1049-50, 1056-57.

- **User name and passcode for subscription-based website.** *Therapeutic Research Faculty v. NBTY, Inc.*, 488 F. Supp. 2d 991, 999 (E.D. Cal. 2007).

d. Types of Information Failing to Qualify as Trade Secrets in Court

Some information, such as patented inventions, can never have trade secret status. Other types of information may or may not qualify for trade secret protection depending on all the facts and circumstances. For example, some customer lists qualify for trade secret protection while other customer lists do not. Trade secret rights depend upon the nature of a particular customer list and whether the trade secret holder can demonstrate all of the criteria necessary for protection (information, value, unknown, and secret).

California courts have held that—at least in particular instances—the following types of information failed to constitute protectable trade secrets:

- **Business forms and procedures.** *Scott v. Snelling & Snelling, Inc.*, 732 F. Supp. 1034, 1045 (N.D. Cal. 1990) (granting summary judgment to counterdefendants because trade secret claimant failed to demonstrate that forms and procedures derived independent economic value; accused party presented proof that forms and procedures were widely used in the industry).

- **Client names and addresses.** *Payward, Inc. v. Runyon*, No. 20-CV-02130-MMC, 2020 WL 5642612, *2-3 (N.D. Cal. Sept. 22, 2020) (determining that a physical address is not a trade secret despite reasonable security concerns for failure to allege how competitors would gain an economic advantage); *Moss, Adams & Co. v. Shilling*, 179 Cal. App. 3d 124, 128-29 (1986) (holding former employees who showed that client names and addresses were already known to them not liable for trade secret misappropriation; no protection for addresses deemed easily obtainable through normal resources such as telephone directories).

- **Contact people at prospective customers.** *Liberty Mut.*, 1994 WL 715613, at *5 (considering that names of contact people could be obtained by a simple phone call).

- **Course materials, training materials, and instruction techniques.** *Self Directed Placement Corp. v. Control Data Corp.*, 908 F.2d 462, 465-66 (9th Cir. 1990) (finding course for unemployed and under-employed individuals regarding how to obtain employment, alleged trade secrets of beginning the course on a Wednesday, having a surprise cocktail party prior to the normal ending time on the last day of class, and conducting dress rehearsals for job interviews on the last day of class were in the public domain or were common techniques that would be used in any course, and noting that more than 30,000 students had attended the courses without any secrecy agreement).

- **Customer identity.** *AMN Healthcare, Inc. v. Aya Healthcare Servs., Inc.*, 28 Cal. App. 5th 923, 946 (2018) (rejecting travel nurses' contact information as a trade secret due to the information being known to the defendant competitor before the alleged misappropriation and very general in nature information); *Gemini Aluminum Corp. v. Cal. Custom Shapes, Inc.*, 95 Cal. App. 4th 1249, 1263 (2002) (finding no actual or potential economic value in the identity of customer who owed plaintiff $326,219.21 and who filed for bankruptcy).

- **Customer lists known in the trade.** *Scott*, 732 F. Supp. at 1044-45 (finding customers of a temporary personnel service—large and small companies—are not trade secret because they are easily discoverable through public sources); *Am. Paper & Packaging*, 183 Cal. App. 3d at 1326; *Cont'l Car-Na-Var Corp. v. Moseley*, 24 Cal. 2d 104, 108-09 (1944).

- **Design features.** *Futurecraft*, 205 Cal. App. 2d at 289-90 (finding design features revealed by product on the market not protectable). *But see Altavion*, 226 Cal. App. 4th at 59-61.

- **Die drawings.** *Gemini Aluminum*, 95 Cal. App. 4th at 1263 (finding die drawings used for customer who filed for bankruptcy lacked economic value).

- **Digital collectibles.** *Founder Starcoin, Inc. v. Launch Labs, Inc.*, No-18-CV-972 JLS (MDD), 2018 WL 3343790, *5-8 (S.D. Cal. July 9, 2018) (finding that the idea of digital collectibles based on a celebrity's likeness did not constitute a trade secret under the DTSA or CUTSA; no showing that it was not generally known) ("Marrying the concept of celebrity licensing with blockchain technology appears, on its face, to be unremarkable, obvious, and general knowledge").

- **Distributor lists.** *Stilwell Dev. Inc. v. Chen*, 11 U.S.P.Q.2d (BNA) 1328, 1331 (C.D. Cal. 1989) (awarding attorneys' fees to prevailing defendant following directed verdict on trade secret claim; no showing that the distributor list had been subject to secrecy efforts).

- **Functional features of device.** *Stilwell Dev.*, 11 U.S.P.Q.2d (BNA) at 1331 (finding features in device sold to general public not trade secret).

- **Improvements to fortune telling cards.** *Walker v. Univ. Books, Inc.*, 602 F.2d 859, 865 (9th Cir. 1979) (pre-CUTSA case applying Restatement) (affirming summary judgment for defendant based on finding that improvements to cards at issue—use of higher quality stock, brighter colors, rounded corners, red borders, larger hexagrams on card faces, and a higher quality container—were vague, obvious, and unprotectable as trade secrets).

- **Information from reverse engineering products.** *VSL Corp. v. Gen. Techs., Inc.*, 44 U.S.P.Q.2d (BNA) 1301, 1302 (N.D. Cal. 1997) (noting proof that information was not secret included showing that it reverse engineered its product using samples lawfully obtained from job-site dumpsters); *People v. Gopal*, 171 Cal. App. 3d 524, 533 (1985) (noting in criminal case that "'reverse engineering' is an accepted and lawful practice in industry. It involves starting with a known product and working backwards to discover the process by which it was developed and manufactured") (citing *Kewanee Oil Co. v. Bicron Corp.*, 416 U.S. 470, 476 (1974)) (note that the *Gopal* decision pre-dates the current criminal law definition of a trade secret).

- **Job requirements.** *Metro Traffic Control, Inc. v. Shadow Traffic Network*, 22 Cal. App. 4th 853, 861-63 (1994) (deeming job requirements regarding quality, sound, and personality of radio anchors as nothing more than unprotectable job classifications).

- **Lecture materials including seminar manual.** *Oral Vision, Inc. v. Encompass, Inc.*, No. C 94-20430-JW, 1995 WL 66790, at *1 (N.D. Cal. Feb. 10, 1995) (finding plaintiff failed to show that materials were not readily, properly available such as through public access).

- **Patented inventions.** *Stutz Motor Car of Am., Inc. v. Reebok Int'l, Ltd.*, 909 F. Supp. 1353, 1359-61 (C.D. Cal. 1995), *aff'd mem.*, 113 F.3d 1258 (Fed. Cir. 1997) (holding invention loses trade secret status as of date of patent issuance, but trade secret claim can still exist for period prior to patent issuance).

- **Pesticide spray reports.** *Uribe v. Howie*, 19 Cal. App. 3d 194, 209-10 (1971) (pre-CUTSA case) (applying law of the Restatement of Torts; reports submitted to county agricultural commissioner pursuant to statutory requirements not trade secret).

- **Process for manufacturing diodes.** *Diodes, Inc. v. Franzen*, 260 Cal. App. 2d 244, 251 (1968) (affirming judgment of dismissal for complaint which deemed to speak in "circumlocutions and innuendoes" rather than direct and detailed statement of metallurgical process for manufacturing diodes).

- **Process for coating and lacquering door knobs and locks.** *Gate-Way, Inc. v. Wilson*, 94 Cal. App. 2d 706, 707-10 (1949) (affirming finding that process deemed in the public domain).

- **Proposal methods and pricing estimates.** *Rigging Int'l Maint. Co. v. Gwin*, 128 Cal. App. 3d 594, 611 (1982); *Aetna Bldg. Maint. Co. v. West*, 39 Cal. 2d 198, 206 (1952) (pre-CUTSA case) (plaintiff failed to show proof that method was secret).

- **Real estate listings and related financing commitment and prospective purchaser information.** *Cal Francisco Inv. Corp. v. Vrionis*, 14 Cal. App. 3d 318, 320-23 (1971) (pre-CUTSA case) (dismissing plaintiff's complaint for failure to show that real estate listings were subject to trade secret protection, finding that plaintiff did not plead that information gave plaintiff a competitive advantage, and considering public policy favoring employee mobility).

- **Religious materials or scriptures.** *Religious Tech. Ctr. v. Wollersheim*, 796 F.2d 1076, 1090-91 (9th Cir. 1986) (deeming materials to have spiritual value but not economic value).

- **Salary information.** *GAB Bus. Servs. v. Lindsey & Newsom Claim Servs., Inc.*, 83 Cal. App. 4th 409, 428-29 (2000), *disapproved of on other grounds*, *Reeves v. Hanlon*, 33 Cal. 4th 1140 (2004) (affirming jury finding that salary information lacked independent economic value). For contrary authority, *see Bancroft-Whitney Co. v. Glen*, 64 Cal. 2d 327, 350-51 (1966) (pre-CUTSA case) (finding list of salaries paid to corporate employees constitutes "confidential information").

- **Sales telemarketing scripts and pitch materials.** *In re Providian Credit Card Cases*, 96 Cal. App. 4th 292, 304-05 (2002) (use of sales telemarketing scripts foreclosed any potential trade secret status even if disclosure was in piecemeal fashion.: "The scripts were sales pitches, and once they have been used, sales pitches are not treated as trade secrets.") (note that holding assumes the sales pitch was not pursuant to a nondisclosure agreement).

- **Software design features, functions and characteristics.** *Agency Solutions.com LLC v. Trizetto Grp.*, Inc., 819 F. Supp. 2d 1001, 1016-17 (E.D. Cal. 2011) (information in workflow process charts does not constitute a trade secret when manifested in how the software functions); *Silvaco*, 184 Cal. App. 4th 210, 221-22 (the distinctive characteristics of software product design cannot constitute trade secrets as they are evident to anyone running the finished program; to the extent the product discloses the underlying software design, the design itself lacks trade secret protection as well).

- **Technical know-how.** *Calendar Research. LLC v. StubHub, Inc.*, No. 2:17-CV-04062-SVW-SS, 2020 WL 4390391, *4-5 (C.D. Cal. May 13, 2020) (determining at summary judgment that technical know-how and learnings of a mobile application's ability to go "viral" were not trade secret because they are "nebulous concepts that, unless clearly defined, encounter the long-standing tension between employment law and the trade secrets doctrine"); *Cinebase Software, Inc. v. Media Guar. Trust, Inc.*, No. C98-1100 FMS, 1998 WL 661465, at *12 (N.D. Cal. Sept. 22, 1998) (stating technical know-how for what does and does not work in the process of designing digital media management software "too nebulous").

- **Temporary employee lists.** *Scott*, 732 F. Supp. at 1045 (showing of evidence by accused party that it developed its lists independently and that industry functions such that temporary employees typically list themselves with multiple agencies in nonexclusive manner).

- **Workers' compensation premiums and renewal dates.** *Liberty Mut.*, 1994 WL 715613, at *5 (deeming workers' compensation insurance information available in several directories commonly used in the insurance business, as opposed to premium and renewal dates for other lines of insurance where such information is not publicly available).

2. "Value"—When Is Information Valuable?

For information to constitute a trade secret, it must derive actual or potential "independent economic value" from not being generally known. The CUTSA and the DTSA statutes expressly provide that value can be either actual or potential. In other words, a trade secret must have current or future value. If the economic value to information was solely in the past, for example, because the information has become public, then it does not currently have value from a trade secret perspective. Furthermore, the value must be economic. Noneconomic qualities, such as information that has a spiritual, sentimental, or historic value, is insufficient for trade secret protection. *See Religious Tech. Ctr., Church of Scientology Int'l, Inc. v. Scott*, 869 F.2d 1306, 1309-10 (9th Cir. 1989); *Religious Tech. v. Wollersheim*, 796 F. 2d at 1090-91 (spiritual value insufficient; CUTSA requires economic value).

For information to constitute a trade secret, the information must derive "independent economic value, actual or potential, from not being generally known to the public or to other persons who can obtain *economic value from its disclosure or use*." Cal. Civ. Code § 3426.1(d); Cal. Penal Code § 499c (emphasis added).

The following decisions address whether information has the requisite economic value to constitute a trade secret.

a. Court Findings That Information Has Economic Value

Courts have held that the following types of trade secrets have met the independent economic value requirement:

- **Advertising and marketing strategies.** *Whyte*, 101 Cal. App. 4th at 1456 (holding that advertising and marketing strategies had independent economic value because they would allow a competitor to predict and counter the trade secret holder's advertising and marketing).

- **Combination of generally known elements.** *Copper Harbor,* Nos. A149709 and A150381, 2019 WL 2296224 at *9 (deeming a manufacturing process comprised of multiple elements had economic value because the process itself had more value than individual elements).

- **Construction project information.** *San Jose Constr.*, 155 Cal. App. 4th at 1537-39 (finding that trade secret compilation of construction information derived independent economic value as having the information provided a distinct advantage over competitors).

- **Customer database.** *MAI Sys.*, 991 F.2d at 521 (determining that information in a customer database had economic value because it would allow a competitor to direct its sales efforts to those potential customers that were already using the plaintiff company's computer system).

- **Customer information and customer list.** *Courtesy Temp.*, 222 Cal. App. 3d at 1287-88 (finding that the nature and character of customer information such as billing rates, key contacts, specialized requirements, and markup rates were sophisticated and irrefutably of commercial value).

The court in *Morlife*, 56 Cal. App. 4th at 1521-22, explained its rationale for finding that customer information can have economic value. The *Morlife* court addressed economic value of a customer list in the context of a claim that former employees had used the plaintiff's customer lists in competition with the plaintiff trade secret holder. The court stated that for a customer list to have economic value, it means that the secrecy of the information provides a business with a "substantial business advantage," that disclosure of the information would allow a competitor to direct its sales efforts to those customers who have already shown a willingness to use a unique type of service or product as opposed to a list of people who only might be interested, and that its use enables a former employee to solicit both more selectively and more effectively. *Id.* at 1522 (citing *Klamath-Orleans Lumber, Inc. v. Miller*, 87 Cal. App. 3d 458, 465-66 (1978) and *Courtesy Temp.*, 222 Cal. App. 3d at 1287-88); *see also Allergan, Inc. v. Merz Pharm.*, No. SACV 11-446 AG, 2012 WL 781705, at *10 (C.D. Cal. Mar. 9, 2012).

In *ABBA Rubber*, 235 Cal. App. 3d at 18-20, the court held that the plaintiff established the "economic value" requirement by proof that the customer list, which was not generally known by competitors, contains information revealing businesses that use the goods or services which competitors sell. Conversely, the court noted that if it is known to the competitors that the customers buy the goods or services at issue—even though it is not known that the customers buy from the plaintiff—then there is no economic value to the plaintiff's customer list. *Id.* at 19.

The court in *American Credit*, 213 Cal. App. 3d at 630-31, found that a customer list had economic value on the ground that the list allowed a competitor to direct sales efforts to the elite 6.5% of potential customers predisposed to purchase credit insurance.

- **Design documents and diagrams**. *Cisco Sys., Inc. v. Chung*, No. 19-CV-07562-PJH, 2020 WL 4505509, *7 (N.D. Cal. Aug. 5, 2020) (finding that design documents and hardware diagrams had independent economic value due to the "careful orchestration" that allowed the plaintiff to manufacture at a competitive cost).

- **Marketing information.** *Cinebase Software*, 1998 WL 661465, at *12 (holding that marketing information such as client lists, analyses of potential clients, and marketing plans had independent economic value from not being generally known).

- **Pricing policies.** *Whyte*, 101 Cal. App. 4th at 1455 (determining that information regarding a company's pricing policies has independent economic value because it would be valuable to a competitor to set prices which meet or undercut the trade secret holder's pricing; however, publicly known pricing information would not be subject to trade secret protection).

- **Product concepts.** *Mattel*, 782 F. Supp. 2d at 962 (stating that concepts for unreleased products can have value independent from the products they eventually inspire, as shown by manufacturer's investment in "a tremendous amount of material and human resources into the development of product concepts and ideas, including product names").

- **Religious materials.** *Bridge Publ'ns*, 827 F. Supp. at 632-33 (considering a trade secret claim by religious organizations against a religion instructor). The plaintiff organizations claimed that the defendant instructor used plaintiffs' religious materials obtained from plaintiffs under a written confidentiality agreement. *Id.* at 633. The district court held that the plaintiffs satisfied the "independent economic value" element for trade secret protection on the ground that plaintiffs used proceeds from the sale of the materials in question to support the operations of Scientology churches worldwide. *Id.* The court further opined that the religious materials had economic value because the defendant instructor charged students for course packages which included the plaintiffs' materials. *Id.* at 634. The district court held that these facts, as well as the U.S. Supreme Court's recognition that churches have economic need to receive proceeds of this nature to remain a going concern, satisfied the "independent economic value" requirement. *Id.*

The court in *Religious Tech. Ctr. v. Netcom On-Line Commc'n Servs., Inc.*, 923 F. Supp. 1231, 1253 (N.D. Cal. 1995), followed the ruling in *Bridge Publ'ns*, 827 F. Supp. at 632-33, and similarly held that religious materials met the economic value test. The court reasoned that the religious materials at issue significantly impacted the church's donations and provided the majority of funds for its operating expenses. *Id.* at 1253. In so ruling, the court instructed that a trade secret plaintiff need not show that it has any competitors to maintain a trade secret misappropriation claim; the potential for future competition suffices. *Id.*

b. Court Findings That Information Lacked Economic Value

- **Business forms and procedures.** *Scott*, 732 F. Supp. at 1045 (finding that trade secret claimant failed to carry its burden of establishing that forms and procedures derived independent economic value in light of proof that forms and procedures were widely used in the industry and nonexclusive to the trade secret claimant).

- **Customer information.** *Liberty Mut.*, 1994 WL 715613, at *4 (holding that information readily obtainable through public sources such as directories, including the identities of prospective customers, does not derive the independent economic value necessary for a trade secret) (citations omitted).

- **General categories of information.** *Cisco Sys., Inc. v. Chung*, No. 19-CV-07562-PJH, 2020 WL 4505509, *5-6 (N.D. Cal. Aug. 5, 2020) (alleged investment of resources in general categories of information deemed insufficient to show independent economic value (in reference to prototypes, design documentation and source code). "[S]ecrecy ***itself*** does not establish value").

- **Information relating to bankrupt customer.** *Gemini Aluminum*, 95 Cal. App. 4th at 1263-64 (stating that the identity of a customer and die drawings used for that particular customer lacked any actual or potential economic value to the plaintiff when the customer owed the plaintiff $326,219.21 and had filed for bankruptcy). The court held that information regarding a customer who is not likely to provide any economic benefit to the plaintiff cannot form the basis for a trade secret claim. In light of these facts, the court found that the plaintiff's trade secret claim was objectively specious and it affirmed the award of attorneys' fees to the defendant. *Id.* at 1263.

- **Insurance rates and underwriting methods.** *Agency Solutions.com*, 819 F. Supp. 2d at 1022 (finding methods of insurance underwriting to lack independent economic value, noting that "any provider of front-end software has the same basic information; they may just handle it differently").

- **Meeting Minutes.** *Payward, Inc. v. Runyon*, No. 20-CV-02130-MMC, 2020 WL 5642612, *2-3 (N.D. Cal. Sept. 22, 2020) (finding that board meeting minutes were not trade secret under the DTSA or CUTSA because there was no allegation the defendant used the board meeting minutes to gain a competitive advantage).

- **Personnel records.** *Pillsbury, Madison & Sutro v. Schectman*, 55 Cal. App. 4th 1279, 1287 (1997) (finding that, from a trade secret law perspective, law firm's personnel records at issue had no intrinsic value to anyone other than their owner; the case concerned an action to recover documents and not a claim of misappropriation under the CUTSA).

- **Salary information.** *GAB Bus. Servs.*, 83 Cal. App. 4th 409, 428-29, *disapproved of on other grounds*, *Reeves v. Hanlon*, 33 Cal. 4th 1140 (affirming jury verdict that salary information lacked independent economic value).

- **Source code segments.** *Yield Dynamics, Inc. v. TEA Sys. Corp.*, 154 Cal. App. 4th 547, 568 (2007) (affirming bench trial ruling that source code segments did not constitute a trade secret because the segmented source code lacked independent economic value). The court based this decision on plaintiff's failure to provide persuasive testimony from a qualified witness that the particular routines at issue were so distinctly advantageous to a competitor that their secrecy itself had economic value.

- **Vendor product roadmaps**. *Cisco Sys., Inc. v. Chung*, No. 19-CV-07562-PJH, 2020 WL 4505509, *8 (N.D. Cal. Aug. 5, 2020) (denying vendor product roadmaps as deriving independent economic value because having industry status in and of itself is not tied to those products).

3. "Unknown"—When Is Information "Not Generally Known to the Public or to Other Persons Who Can Obtain Economic Value From its Disclosure or Use?"

By definition, trade secret information must not be generally known. The definition recognizes two audiences: (1) the public; and (2) other persons who can obtain economic value from its disclosure or use. Cal. Civ. Code § 3426.1(d). Thus, for information to be deemed not generally known for trade secret purposes, it must not be generally known to either (1) the public; or (2) others who can obtain economic value from disclosure or use of the information.

The CUTSA and the DTSA require that trade secret information have value to others who are unaware of the information and who could put that information, if known, to beneficial use. *ABBA Rubber*, 235 Cal. App. 3d at 19; 18 U.S.C. § 1839(3). "In other words, the core inquiry is the value to the owner in keeping the information secret from persons who could exploit it to the relative disadvantage of the original owner." *Yield Dynamics*, 154 Cal. App. 4th at 568.

a. Court Rulings That Information Is Not Generally Known

- **Customer list information.** *Morlife*, 56 Cal. App. 4th at 1522 (ruling that the customer list information at issue was not generally known based upon proof, including that the customers were only discoverable with great effort, that the customers' patronage was secured through the expenditure of considerable time and money, and that the plaintiff's sales personnel encountered difficulty in getting past the "gatekeepers" and identifying and gaining access to the actual decision makers with the authority to purchase the services).

In *ABBA Rubber*, 235 Cal. App. 3d at 20-21, the court affirmed the trial court's ruling that the plaintiff's customer list information was not generally known. The appellate court found that substantial evidence supported that it was not generally known that the businesses on the customer list were consumers of the product in question. The plaintiff made this showing with proof of the difficulty in determining which companies need the product in question, that customers are not readily recognizable or identifiable, that identifying customers is expensive and time consuming, that the customer list represents a winnowing down from a generalized list of companies that may use the product in question, and that the plaintiff's list could not be duplicated without years of effort and expense. *Id.*

- **Insurance policy renewal dates.** *Liberty Mut.*, 1994 WL 715613, at *5 (holding that renewal dates for insurance policies are not generally known; even if it is well known that all companies need insurance, it remains not generally known when those companies' existing policies come up for renewal).

b. Court Rulings That Information Is Generally Known

- **Course materials, training materials, and instruction techniques.** *Self Directed*, 908 F.2d at 465-66 (affirming the district court's determination that information regarding employment counseling courses that had been given to more than 30,000 students was a matter of common public knowledge).

- **Customer list information.** *Am. Paper & Packaging*, 183 Cal. App. 3d at 1326 (finding that even though the customer list was not generally known to the public, it certainly would be known to others in the relevant business, and affirming the denial of a preliminary injunction); *Hilderman*, 551 F. Supp. 2d at 1201 (stating that if all or almost all businesses in the relevant industry use the type of services or if the number of businesses in the relevant industry is very small, then customer information may not qualify as "not being generally known to the public").

- **Information in trade journals.** *Knudsen Corp. v. Ever-Fresh Foods, Inc.*, 336 F. Supp. 241, 244 (C.D. Cal. 1971) (ruling that proof that the purported trade secret pricing, marketing, sales, and customer information appeared in trade journals showed that information was a matter of general knowledge in the industry).

- **Processes and checklists.** *Hilderman*, 551 F. Supp. 2d at 1198 (granting summary judgment against claimant for failure to demonstrate how processes and checklists for compliance with FAA standards differed from publicly available information).

c. "Readily Ascertainable"—Not Part of the Definition of a Trade Secret in California

California's trade secret definition is noteworthy for the fact that it does not contain the phrase "readily ascertainable." In other jurisdictions, a trade secret must not be generally known or "readily ascertainable." Under California law, information may remain a trade secret, even if it is "readily ascertainable" by reference to trade directories, telephone books, or other resources, provided that others in the industry have not yet ascertained the information. In contrast, the DTSA and the Model Uniform Trade Secrets Act, as proposed by the National Conference of Commissioners on Uniform State Laws, define a trade secret as information that others cannot readily ascertain through proper means.

Thus, California's definition of "trade secret" favors trade secret holders over jurisdictions where the "readily ascertainable" restriction applies. In this manner, California law broadens the scope of information that can qualify as a protectable trade secret as compared to the definition of a trade secret under the Model Uniform Trade Secrets Act. For discussion of the California legislature's decision not to adopt the phrase "readily ascertainable" as part of the definition of a trade secret, *see ABBA Rubber*, 235 Cal. App. 3d at 21-22.

Some practice pointers regarding readily ascertainable are:

- Although "readily ascertainable" is not part of the definition of a trade secret, it still can serve as a defense to misappropriation. *ABBA Rubber*, 235 Cal. App. 3d at 21-22 n.9 ("While ease of ascertainability is irrelevant to the definition of a trade secret, the assertion that a matter is readily ascertainable by proper means remains available as a defense to a claim of misappropriation.") (internal quotation marks and citation omitted). Defendants may prevail by arguing that the information's availability elsewhere shows that the information was not misappropriated from the plaintiff. "That defense, however, will be based upon an absence of misappropriation, rather than the absence of a trade secret." *Id.*

- While California's legislature excluded "readily ascertainable" from the definition of a trade secret, it is nonetheless helpful to recognize the inverse relationship between a competitor's ability to ascertain information and the information's value—readily ascertainable information has little value compared to information that is obscure or expensive to gather. *See Syngenta Crop Prot., Inc. v. Helliker*, 138 Cal. App. 4th 1135, 1172 (2006) ("information that is readily ascertainable by a business competitor derives no independent value from not being generally known").

- Most states, other than California, that adopted some form of the Uniform Trade Secrets Act adopted the phrase "readily ascertainable" in the definition of "trade secret." Thus, any reference to an out-of-state decision must assess whether the statutory language "readily ascertainable" impacts the applicability of the reasoning from that case.

4. "Secret"—When Is Information Secret?

Trade secret protection is the "marathon" of intellectual property protection. Unlike patents and copyrights, trade secret protection lasts however long the protectable information remains secret.

Courts require that trade secret holders take "reasonable" steps to maintain the secrecy of their trade secrets. California law does not require "absolute secrecy." Courts do not require that companies take all measures conceivable to maintain the secrecy. Rather, the measures simply must be reasonable under the circumstances.

In almost every case of trade secret misappropriation, secrecy measures fail at some level. Misappropriation usually only occurs because of a breach of secrecy. Therefore, it is no defense for the defendant to argue that the misappropriation itself shows that secrecy measures were inadequate. It is usually a given that secrecy was compromised. Instead, the relevant inquiry is what efforts the trade secret holder can show it undertook to protect its trade secrets.

Facts that may support a secrecy finding in one case may not support such a finding in another case. As an example, reasonable efforts to keep a customer list secret may not suffice to keep source code secret. Although no single measure of protection will demonstrate that a trade secret has been kept secret, a single knowing or deliberate public disclosure of a trade secret by the trade secret holder itself can cause the loss of trade secret status.

a. Factors Influencing Courts That Information Is Secret

Some of the most obvious secrecy measures include limiting access to the trade secrets, marking documents as confidential, and obtaining signed employment agreements, confidentiality agreements, and nondisclosure agreements that confirm protection for trade secrets. Yet, no single measure controls in any given case. California courts assessing secrecy have found that the following measures supported a finding of reasonable efforts to maintain secrecy under the circumstances of the particular case:

- **Advising employees that trade secret material is company property.** *Paperloop.com, Inc. v. Gow*, No. 322044, 2001 WL 1674804, at *2 (Cal. Super. Ct. Sept. 14, 2001) (reasonable secrecy efforts taken where company advised employees that its confidential source lists belonged to the company, and provided employees with handbook stating that compilations of information constituted company property).

- **Attaching electronic sensors to trade secret documents.** *Religious Tech. v. Netcom*, 923 F. Supp. at 1254.

- **Auditing the files of employees for the unauthorized possession of trade secret documents.** *People v. Serrata*, 62 Cal. App. 3d 9, 23 (1976) (pre-CUTSA criminal action) (continually spot auditing the files of random employees for unauthorized possession of trade secrets).

- **Communicating expectations of secrecy to employees.** *Hall, Mahar & Assocs. Ins. Servs., Inc. v. Sanborn & Churton Ins. Servs., Inc.*, No. G051572, 2016 WL 6872958 (Cal. Ct. App. Nov. 22, 2016) (confidentiality policy in employee handbook demonstrated expectation of protecting customer and company information); *Syntron Bioresearch, Inc. v. Fan*, No. D033894, 2002 WL 660446, at *9 (Cal. Ct. App. Apr. 23, 2002) (emphasis of strictly confidential nature of work contained in personnel manuals); *Gable-Leigh, Inc. v. N. Am. Miss*, No. CV 01-01019 MMM(SHX), 2001 WL 521695, at *16-17 (C.D. Cal. Apr. 13, 2001) (informing employees that information belonged to the company and should be kept confidential); *Bayer Corp. v. Roche Molecular Sys., Inc.*, 72 F. Supp. 2d 1111, 1114 (N.D. Cal. 1999) (notifying employees that the information was confidential and should be treated as such); *Bridge Publ'ns*, 827 F. Supp. at 633 (finding that the confidential nature of the information was known); *In re Providian*, 96 Cal. App. 4th at 306-07 (annually requiring employees to execute corporate policies outlining expectations of confidence; holding that secrecy was destroyed on other grounds); *Courtesy Temp.*, 222 Cal. App. 3d at 1288 ("[E]mployees are told of the confidential and proprietary nature of such information."); *see* Cal. Stat. tit. 5, § 3426.1, Leg. Comm. com.-Senate (1984 addition) at 239.

- **Disclosing trade secrets exclusively to higher level employees.** *Bridge Publ'ns*, 827 F. Supp. at 633 (disclosing trade secrets only to those that attained the requisite level of spiritual training).

- **Disclosing trade secrets only in a confidential setting.** *U.S. Surgical Corp. v. Origin Medsystems*, 27 U.S.P.Q.2d (BNA) 1526, 1530 (N.D. Cal. 1993) (disclosing a trade secret only during negotiations).

- **Educating employees regarding what constitutes a trade secret.** *Gopal*, 171 Cal. App. 3d at 538 (pre-CUTSA criminal action) (annually requiring employees to read section 499c of the California Penal Code, defining trade secrets and theft of a trade secret, and sign that they understand it).

- **Having a written trade secret protection plan and following the plan.** *Vacco Indus.*, 5 Cal. App. 4th at 42 (following a document destruction policy).

- **Keeping hard copies of secret materials in a locked vault, safe, or cabinet.** *Religious Tech. v. Netcom*, 923 F. Supp. at 1254 (storing materials in locked cabinets and safes); *U.S. Surgical*, 27 U.S.P.Q.2d (BNA) at 1530 (storing drawings in a locked filing cabinet and leaving designs with patent counsel); *Vacco Indus.*, 5 Cal. App. 4th at 42 (using locked storage cabinets to store confidential information).

- **Limiting access.** *Cisco Sys., Inc. v. Chung*, No. 19-CV-07562-PJH, 2020 WL 4505509, *5 (N.D. Cal. Aug. 5, 2020) (limiting access to employees' work databases and monitoring employees' network activity for improper information usage); *AAA Blueprint & Digital Reprographics v. Ibarra*, No. G037831, 2007 WL 3105887, at *4 (Cal. Ct. App. Oct. 24, 2007) (single copy of price list kept beneath work orders in a cubbyhole or in a locked drawer to which only employees with billing duties were granted access); *Bayer Corp.*, 72 F. Supp. 2d at 1114 (disbursing confidential information beyond senior management on a "need-to-know" basis); *Morlife*, 56 Cal. App. 4th at 1521 ("Morlife made reasonable efforts to maintain the secrecy of its customers' identity by limiting circulation of its customer lists . . . ."); *Courtesy Temp.*, 222 Cal. App. 3d at 1288 (limiting access to employees on an "as needed basis"); *see* Cal. Stat. tit. 5, § 3426.1, Leg. Comm. com.-Senate (1984 addition) at 239 ("[R]easonable efforts to maintain secrecy have been held to include . . . limiting access to a trade secret on 'need to know basis.'"); *Hall, Mahar & Assocs. Ins. Servs., Inc. v. Sanborn & Churton Ins. Servs., Inc.*, No. G051572, 2016 WL 6872958, *5 (Cal. Ct. App. Nov. 22, 2016) (requiring user names and passwords for customer information, limited access, and restricting employees from taking customer files out of the office supports reasonable efforts to maintain secrecy)

- **Limiting and monitoring the number of copies of a trade secret to the extent necessary to accomplish work projects.** *In re Providian*, 96 Cal. App. 4th at 307 (limiting the number of copies that are produced to the extent necessary for use with ongoing work or projects; holding that secrecy was destroyed on other grounds).

- **Limiting the availability of the trade secret within computer systems.** *Art of Living Found.*, 102 U.S.P.Q.2d at 1838 (keeping trade secret manuals and teaching notes on password-protected computers); *Lighthouse Worldwide Solutions, Inc. v. Giandomencio*, No. H030748, 2008 WL 256974, at *6 (Cal. Ct. App. Jan. 31, 2008) (portions of customer list maintained in separate databases); *Gable-Leigh*, 2001 WL 521695, at *17 (maintaining customer lists on computer at home in order to maintain control over them and protect their secrecy); *Bayer Corp.*, 72 F. Supp. 2d at 1114 (incorporating passwords for access to trade secrets through computers and email).

- **Limiting the information made available to vendors and subcontractors.** *Vacco Indus.*, 5 Cal. App. 4th at 42 (addressing "strict security control measures with respect to documents which necessarily had to be made available to third party vendors or subcontractors," and noting that "engineering notes were never made available to third parties nor were detailed plans or drawings which Vacco used in the manufacturing process").

- **Limiting third parties' access to the whole trade secret.** *San Jose Constr.*, 155 Cal. App. 4th at 1538-39 (reasonable efforts to maintain secrecy of project binders found despite argument that materials included information generated by or disclosed to third parties, because third parties each only had a piece of a project; trade secret owner was the only one with the "completed puzzle"); *MCL Fin. Grp., Inc. v. Bak*, No. G035192, 2006 WL 1320543, at *7 (Cal. Ct. App. May 12, 2006) (disclosure of list of client names in court pleading not enough to destroy secrecy of client list, because trade secret was the aggregate of information in client list database, not merely the names of clients or prospects).

- **Maintaining logs identifying trade secrets.** *Religious Tech. v. Netcom*, 923 F. Supp. at 1254.

- **Marking documents as confidential or trade secret.** *AAA Blueprint*, 2007 WL 3105887, at *4 (while written confidentiality agreements and labeling documents as confidential are not absolute requirements, a court may consider such agreements and labels as factors in deciding whether a proprietor reasonably tried to maintain secrecy); *In re Providian*, 96 Cal. App. 4th at 308 (recognizing the importance of stamping documents confidential, and also considering party's actions in stamping some documents confidential but not stamping other documents confidential as circumstantial evidence that documents not stamped were not treated as secret).

- **Obtaining employment agreements acknowledging employees' obligations to treat information as secret.** *Syntron Bioresearch*, 2002 WL 660446, at *9 (trade secret material stored in employee homes did not destroy secrecy, because employees had signed confidentiality agreements); *Morlife*, 56 Cal. App. 4th at 1521 (stating in the employment agreement and employee handbook that information was considered valuable and confidential); *Am. Paper & Packaging*, 183 Cal. App. 3d at 1325 (designating customer lists confidential in employment agreements a factor but not "decisive"; holding against trade secret protection on other factors). *But see Moss, Adams*, 179 Cal. App. 3d at 126-29 (labeling collection of names and information as trade secrets in the employment agreement did not preclude defendants from using names and addresses known through personal contact).

- **Obtaining orders sealing court records that contain information that discloses the trade secret.** *Masonite v. Mendocino Air Quality*, 42 Cal. App. 4th at 442 (maintaining the trade secret status of documents under a sealing order despite their inadvertent disclosure by government agencies).

- **Omitting the trade secret as an asset in financial statements.** *U.S. Surgical*, 27 U.S.P.Q.2d (BNA) at 1530 (viewing the failure to list a trade secret on financial statements as possible evidence of secrecy—this measure obviously implicates other legal considerations).

- **Protecting against physical access to trade secrets, including the use of security systems and personnel, escorts, and visitor badges.** *Syntron Bioresearch*, 2002 WL 660446, at *9 (permissible to store trade secret material in unlocked tanks given that company limited keys for room housing tanks to top researchers and managers); *Bayer Corp.*, 72 F. Supp. 2d at 1114 (limiting access to its offices, requiring electronic keys to access floor on which trade secrets are kept); *Religious Tech. v. Netcom*, 923 F. Supp. at 1254 (using alarms, photo identifications, and security personnel to protect and restrict physical access); *Plant Indus., Inc. v. Coleman*, 287 F. Supp. 636, 642-43 (C.D. Cal. 1968) (pre-CUTSA) (posting several signs denying admittance on entrances to the plant and properties); *Vacco Indus.*, 5 Cal. App. 4th at 42 (maintaining visitor logs); *see* Cal. Stat. tit. 5, § 3426.1, Leg. Comm. com.-Senate (1984 addition) at 239 ("[R]easonable efforts to maintain secrecy have been held to include . . . controlling plant access.").

- **Removing nonpublic customer list information prior to making public filings or recordings of documents.** *Greenly v. Cooper*, 77 Cal. App. 3d 382, 392 (1978) (pre-CUTSA) (substituting mortgage loan broker's own name for home loan investor customers prior to publicly recording deeds of trust, maintaining secrecy of customers' identities).

- **Requiring a checkout procedure for trade secret information removed from the work area.** *Vacco Indus.*, 5 Cal. App. 4th at 42 (requiring sign-out sheets for proprietary documents).

- **Requiring confidentiality agreements or nondisclosure agreements (NDAs).** *MAI Sys.*, 991 F.2d at 521 (seminal case); *Art of Living Found.*, 102 U.S.P.Q.2d at 1838 (finding that methods for teaching meditation exercises may be protectable trade secrets even though they are observed by students enrolled in the course because the students were required to sign nondisclosure agreements); *Merrill Lynch, Pierce, Fenner & Smith Inc. v. Chung*, No. CV 01-00659 CBM RCX, 2001 WL 283083, at *4 (C.D. Cal. Feb. 2, 2001); *Bayer Corp.*, 72 F. Supp. 2d at 1114; *Religious Tech. v. Netcom*, 923 F. Supp. at 1254; *Bridge Publ'ns*, 827 F. Supp. at 633; *Imi-Tech Corp. v. Gagliani*, 691 F. Supp. 214, 222 (S.D. Cal. 1986); *Am. Credit*, 213 Cal. App. 3d at 630-31; *Whyte*, 101 Cal. App. 4th at 1454. The absence of confidentiality agreements with employees, though, does not automatically destroy trade secret protection. *See Hilderman*, 551 F. Supp. 2d at 1201 ("lack of confidentiality agreements is not dispositive on the issue of secrecy"); *AAA Blueprint*, 2007 WL 3105887, at *4 (written confidentiality agreements and labeling documents as confidential are not absolute requirements under trade secret law; such agreements and labels are merely factors which a court *may* consider in deciding whether a proprietor reasonably tried to maintain secrecy); *Medipro Med. Staffing, LLC v. Certified Nursing Registry, Inc.*, No. B294391, 2021 WL 387879, *9 (Cal. Ct. App. Feb. 4, 2021) (requiring employees to sign confidentiality agreements satisfies the secrecy requirement); *Gable-Leigh*, 2001 WL 521695, at *17 (finding that it was not unreasonable for the trade secret holder to forego confidentiality agreements in light of the small number of employees with access to the information and the longstanding relationship with the employees). Note that failure to sign an NDA is not dispositive. See *Ansett Aircraft Spares & Servs., Inc. v. Cue*, No. B272100, 2018 WL 2425713, *4-5 (Cal. Ct. App. May 30, 2018) (disclosing trade secrets to a long-time business partner's subsidiary without a nondisclosure agreement did not destroy secrecy because there were other security measures as well as negotiations that were implicitly confidential).

- **Requiring photo identification of persons seeking access.** *Religious Tech. v. Netcom*, 923 F. Supp. at 1254.

- **Requiring that the trade secret information be limited to as few physical locations, branches, or office buildings as feasible.** *Religious Tech. v. Netcom*, 923 F. Supp. at 1254 (limiting the availability of trade secret information to only a "handful" of sites worldwide).

- **Requiring the use of passwords for access to soft copy trade secret material.** *Bayer Corp.*, 72 F. Supp. 2d at 1114.

- **Restricting disclosure to company employees.** *Imi-Tech*, 691 F. Supp. at 222; *Whyte*, 101 Cal. App. 4th at 1454 (noting that the company had not publicly disseminated certain trade secret information); *Courtesy Temp.*, 222 Cal. App. 3d at 1288; *Greenly*, 77 Cal. App. 3d at 392 (pre-CUTSA) (prohibiting disclosure to anyone outside the company); *Components for Research*, 241 Cal. App. 2d at 729 (pre-CUTSA).

- **Screening employees exposed to trade secrets to determine whether they present a risk of disclosure.** *In re Providian*, 96 Cal. App. 4th at 307 ("[S]creen[ing] potential employees (including conducting criminal background checks, credit bureau checks, and finger printing) in an effort to identify those who might present a risk to the security of the business"; holding that secrecy was destroyed on other grounds).

• **Separating sensitive departments or processes from the central facility.** *Gable-Leigh*, 2001 WL 521695, at *17 (maintaining customer lists on home computer away from the work facility).

• **Transporting trade secret materials under lock.** *Religious Tech. v. Netcom*, 923 F. Supp. at 1254 (transporting materials in locked briefcases).

• **Using court protective orders to govern the handling of trade secrets in litigation.** *Am. Credit*, 213 Cal. App. 3d at 631.

b. Factors Courts Have Found Show a Failure of Secrecy Efforts

A single knowing disclosure of a trade secret into the public domain can destroy trade secret protection. While no single factor controls the secrecy determination, a finding of one or more of the following disclosures could bar trade secret protection:

• **Disclosing trade secrets in publicly filed complaint.** *Rita Med. Sys., Inc. v. Resect Med., Inc.*, No. C-05-03291 WHA, 2007 WL 161049, at *7 (N.D. Cal. Jan. 17, 2007) (identification of customer name in complaint considered as factor in determination that customer name cannot constitute a trade secret). *But see MCL Fin.*, 2006 WL 1320543, at *7 (disclosure of client names in court pleading not enough to destroy secrecy of client list, because trade secret was the aggregate of information in database rather than the names of clients or prospects).

• **Disclosing trade secrets through marketing and sales efforts.** *VSL Corp. v. Gen. Techs.*, 44 U.S.P.Q.2d (BNA) at 1303 (distributing marketing information which provided drawings, measurements, and samples); *Integral Sys., Inc. v. Peoplesoft, Inc.*, No. C-90-2598-DLJ, 1991 WL 498874, at *15-16 (N.D. Cal. July 19, 1991) (waiving confidentiality of trade secret materials included in a bid and presentations to prospective clients); *In re Providian*, 96 Cal. App. 4th at 304-05 (disclosing proprietary telemarketing scripts to the public through sales calls); *Futurecraft*, 205 Cal. App. 2d at 289-90 (pre-CUTSA).

• **Displaying the trade secret at a trade show.** *VSL Corp. v. Gen. Techs.*, 44 U.S.P.Q.2d (BNA) at 1303.

• **Failing to challenge a request for release of trade secret information by a governmental agency.** *Masonite v. Mendocino Air Quality*, 42 Cal. App. 4th at 452.

• **Failing to designate information as a trade secret in governmental filings.** *Masonite v. Mendocino Air Quality*, 42 Cal. App. 4th at 454 (failing to identify items as trade secret information in some governmental reports, although properly designated in other reports).

• **Failing to investigate or bring suit when suspicious or aware of misappropriation.** *Alamar Biosciences, Inc. v. Difco Labs., Inc.*, No. Civ-S-941856 DFL PAN, 1995 WL 912345 at *3-7 (E.D. Cal. Oct. 13, 1995) (having "concerns" and "suspicions" about misappropriation and knowing or having circumstantial evidence of facts necessary to bring suit triggered the limitation period); *Glue-Fold, Inc. v. Slautterback Corp.*, 82 Cal. App. 4th 1018, 1027 (2000) (failing to bring suit despite notice of misappropriation).

- **Failing to obtain signed nondisclosure agreements or confidentiality agreements.** *Cinebase Software*, 1998 WL 661465, at *10-11 (failing to secure nondisclosure agreements constituted unreasonable efforts to maintain secrecy despite securing the information with passwords, limiting access to a "need-to-know" basis, and marking documents confidential); *Integral Sys.*, 1991 WL 498874, at *15 (failing to require nondisclosure agreements in marketing demonstrations to prospective clients); *Whyte*, 101 Cal. App. 4th at 1455 (disclosing information to a customer without a secrecy agreement).

- **Having domestic or international patent applications published that disclose the trade secret.** *Forcier v. Microsoft Corp.*, 123 F. Supp. 2d 520, 522, 528 (N.D. Cal. 2000). *But see SkinMedica*, 869 F. Supp. 2d at 1195 ("[R]egardless of whether a patent application is accepted or rejected, a plaintiff may certainly have a viable trade secret claim where the implementation details and techniques or other elements of the trade secret go beyond what was disclosed in the patent.") (internal citation and quotation marks omitted).

- **Leaving documents disclosing a trade secret in garbage cans without shredding.** *Ananda Church of Self-Realization v. Mass. Bay Ins. Co.*, 95 Cal. App. 4th 1273, 1282 (2002); *California v. Greenwood*, 486 U.S. 35, 40 (1988) (seminal case).

- **Obtaining issuance of a patent disclosing the trade secret.** *Forcier*, 123 F. Supp. 2d at 528; *Stutz Motor Car*, 909 F. Supp. at 1359-60.

- **Posting trade secret information on the Internet or websites.** *Religious Tech. Ctr. v. Netcom On-Line Commc'n Servs., Inc.*, No. C-95-20091 RMW, 1997 U.S. Dist. LEXIS 23572, at *37-42 (N.D. Cal. Jan. 3, 1997) (order modifying preliminary injunction, stating that "[t]he question of when posting causes the loss of trade secret status requires a review of the circumstances surrounding the posting and consideration of the interests of the trade secret owner, the policies favoring competition and the interests, including first amendment rights, of innocent third parties who acquire information off the Internet."); *Religious Tech. v. Netcom*, 923 F. Supp. at 1256 ("Although a work posted to an Internet newsgroup remains accessible to the public for only a limited amount of time, once that trade secret has been released into the public domain there is no retrieving it . . . . [O]nce posted, the works lost their secrecy."); *DVD Copy Control Ass'n, Inc. v. Bunner*, 116 Cal. App. 4th 241, 251 (2004) ("Widespread, anonymous publication of the information over the Internet may destroy its status as a trade secret"; but also noting whether publication on the Internet destroys trade secret status depends on the facts of any given case); *HiRel Connectors, Inc. v. United States*, No. CV01-11069 DSF-VBKX, 2006 WL 3618011, at *10, *11 (C.D. Cal. Jan. 25, 2006) (recognizing that information loses status as a trade secret upon becoming available to members of the industry who can access the information on website); *DVD Copy Control Ass'n, Inc. v. McLaughlin*, No. CV 786804, 2000 WL 48512, at *3 (Cal. Super. Ct. Jan. 21, 2000) (holding that secrecy was not destroyed by merely posting a trade secret on the Internet). *But see Silicon Image, Inc. v. Analogix Semiconductor, Inc.*, No. C-07-00635 JCS, 2008 WL 166950, at *16 (N.D. Cal. Jan. 17, 2008) (questioning whether register maps posted on Internet revealed enough about the trade secrets to be useful to competitors, and whether postings were generally known to the relevant competitors, and concluding that postings did not destroy secrecy of trade secret information).

- **Publishing professional journal articles, technical literature, or service manuals that disclose a trade secret.** *VSL Corp. v. Gen. Techs.*, 44 U.S.P.Q.2d (BNA) at 1303 (publishing reports on the alleged trade secret).

- **Refusing to agree to redact trade secret information from documents for court filings.** *In re Providian*, 96 Cal. App. 4th at 309 (taking into account the party's refusal to redact trade secret information from documents in dispute over unsealing of court records, and ordering that documents be unsealed in their entirety).

- **Relying on a hidden or undisclosed intention for secrecy.** *VSL Corp. v. Gen. Techs.*, 44 U.S.P.Q.2d (BNA) at 1303 (involving a party who asserted belief of an alleged oral agreement that the information was trade secret, while party freely disclosed, displayed, and published purported trade secrets elsewhere); *Aetna Bldg. Maint.*, 39 Cal. 2d 198 (pre-CUTSA).

- **Selling a product that discloses the trade secret or enables reverse engineering.** *Self Directed*, 908 F.2d at 465 (finding that a training program was not a trade secret where it had been completely disclosed to students taking the course or was already a matter of general knowledge); *Futurecraft*, 205 Cal. App. 2d at 289 (pre-CUTSA) ("[T]he so called trade secrets were embodied in each valve that was sold.").

- **Showing a trade secret to professional colleagues who have not signed NDAs or confidentiality agreements.** *See VSL Corp. v. Gen. Techs.*, 44 U.S.P.Q.2d (BNA) at 1303 (giving samples and other data to consulting engineers without requiring a confidentiality agreement).

No single factor controls the secrecy determination in any given case. In each case, the court considers all of the circumstances surrounding the particular trade secrets to determine whether the secrecy efforts were reasonable. With sufficient planning and effort, trade secret holders such as The Coca-Cola Company can maintain trade secrets for more than a century.

5. "Confidential Information"—Distinct from Trade Secrets

California law distinguishes confidential information and proprietary information from trade secrets. Despite the differences in the phrases "confidential information" and "proprietary information" on the one hand, and "trade secrets" on the other hand, these phrases are at times erroneously used interchangeably. *Oral Vision*, 1995 WL 66790, at *1 ("Plaintiff appears to confuse or intermingle the use of 'trade secrets' with the use of 'confidential information.'").

Distinct differences exist between trade secret information and confidential information:

- **Economic value.** A trade secret must have economic value; confidential information need not necessarily have economic value. *Cisco Sys., Inc. v. Chung*, No. 19-CV-07562-PJH, 2020 WL 4505509, *6 (N.D. Cal. Aug. 5, 2020) ("a lot of information may be proprietary (i.e., owned) but not economically valuable"). In *Religious Tech. v. Wollersheim*, 796 F. 2d at 1090, the

Ninth Circuit dissolved an injunction, finding that spiritual value in confidential scriptural materials failed to convey the commercial advantage required under the CUTSA.

- **Secrecy.** Trade secret owners must undertake reasonable efforts to maintain secrecy. "Confidentiality" is a lesser standard than "secrecy."

- **Claims for relief.** Claims for misuse of confidential information include breach of contract and breach of confidence. *Ent. Research Grp., Inc. v. Genesis Creative Grp., Inc.*, 122 F.3d 1211, 1227 (9th Cir. 1997); *ITT Telecom Prods. Corp. v. Dooley*, 214 Cal. App. 3d 307, 320 (1989); *Faris v. Enberg*, 97 Cal. App. 3d 309, 318-23 (1979). Improper acquisition, disclosure, or use of trade secrets gives rise to a statutory action for misappropriation under section 3426 of the California Civil Code, as well as for breach of contract in some cases. The statutory misappropriation claim allows for award of attorneys' fees, which is not available for misuse of confidential information absent agreement by the parties.

- **Different information.** A claimant asserting breach of confidence need not show the information is a trade secret. *Tele-Count Eng'rs, Inc. v. Pac. Tel. & Tel. Co.*, 168 Cal. App. 3d 455, 462-63 (1985); *see also ITT Telecom*, 214 Cal. App. 3d at 320.

- **Differing procedural requirements for disputes.** Procedural rules such as the protections in section 2019.210 of the California Code of Civil Procedure (requiring that plaintiffs identify trade secrets with reasonable particularity prior to commencing discovery) apply to actions for trade secret misappropriation but not to actions for breach of contract for misuse of confidential information.

Confidential information claims may, in some cases, be preempted by the CUTSA:

- **Breach of confidence.** *Wang v. Palo Alto Networks, Inc.*, 106 U.S.P.Q.2d 1418, 1421-22 (N.D. Cal. 2013) (finding CUTSA preemption because the breach of confidence claim was based on the same nucleus of facts as the trade secret claim).

- **Misappropriation of non-trade secret proprietary information.** *SunPower Corp. v. SolarCity Corp.*, No. 12-CV-00694- LHK, 2012 WL 6160472, at *5-6 (N.D. Cal. Dec. 11, 2012) (concluding that, even if proprietary information did not meet the trade secret standard, it was "sufficiently close" to a trade secret and should be preempted to prevent a party from avoiding CUTSA's preclusive effect by simply failing to allege one of the necessary elements of a trade secret claim).

For more information about CUTSA preemption, *see infra* Chapter 9.

§ 1.04 Criminal Law Definitions of a Trade Secret

In criminal law, both the California Penal Code and the federal Economic Espionage Act define a trade secret.

Section 499c(a)(9) of the California Penal Code defines a trade secret for California criminal law purposes and it conforms to the civil litigation definition in section 3426.1(d) of the California Civil Code:

> "Trade secret" means information, including a formula, pattern, compilation, program, device, method, technique, or process, that:
>
> (A) Derives independent economic value, actual or potential, from not being generally known to the public or to other persons who can obtain economic value from its disclosure or use; and
>
> (B) Is the subject of efforts that are reasonable under the circumstances to maintain its secrecy.

Cal. Penal Code § 499c(a)(9) (2011).

The federal Economic Espionage Act shares its definition of a trade secret with the DTSA definition.

> [T]he term "trade secret" means all forms and types of financial, business, scientific, technical, economic, or engineering information, including patterns, plans, compilations, program devices, formulas, designs, prototypes, methods, techniques, processes, procedures, programs, or codes, whether tangible or intangible, and whether or how stored, compiled, or memorialized physically, electronically, graphically, photographically, or in writing if—
>
> (A) the owner thereof has taken reasonable measures to keep such information secret; and
>
> (B) the information derives independent economic value, actual or potential, from not being generally known to, and not being readily ascertainable through proper means by, another person who can obtain economic value from the disclosure or use of the information.

18 U.S.C. § 1839(3) (2016).

Chapter 2
MISAPPROPRIATION

By: Rebecca ("Bec") Edelson, Esq.
and Seong H. Kim, Esq.

---

§ 2.01 The Definition of Misappropriation

A. Misappropriation

1. CUTSA

The California Uniform Trade Secrets Act (CUTSA) defines "misappropriation" as:

> (1) Acquisition of a trade secret of another by a person who knows or has reason to know that the trade secret was acquired by improper means; or
> (2) Disclosure or use of a trade secret of another without express or implied consent by a person who:
> (A) Used improper means to acquire knowledge of the trade secret; or
> (B) At the time of disclosure or use, knew or had reason to know that his or her knowledge of the trade secret was:
> (i) Derived from or through a person who had utilized improper means to acquire it;
> (ii) Acquired under circumstances giving rise to a duty to maintain its secrecy or limit its use; or
> (iii) Derived from or through a person who owed a duty to the person seeking relief to maintain its secrecy or limit its use; or
> (C) Before a material change of his or her position, knew or had reason to know that it was a trade secret and that knowledge of it had been acquired by accident or mistake.

Cal. Civ. Code § 3426.1(b).

2. DTSA

The Defend Trade Secrets Act of 2016 ("DTSA") defines "misappropriation" similarly as:

> (1) Acquisition of a trade secret of another by a person who knows or has reason to know that the trade secret was acquired by improper means; or
> (2) Disclosure or use of a trade secret of another without express or implied consent by a person who:
> (A) Used improper means to acquire knowledge of the trade secret;
> (B) At the time of disclosure or use, knew or had reason to know that the knowledge of the trade secret was:
> (i) Derived from or through a person who had used improper means to acquire the trade secret;
> (ii) Acquired under circumstances giving rise to a duty to maintain the secrecy of the trade secret or limit the use of the trade secret; or
> (iii) Derived from or through a person who owed a duty to the person seeking relief to maintain the secrecy of the trade secret or limit the use of the trade secret; or

> (C) Before a material change of the position of the person, knew or had reason to know that:
> (i) The trade secret was a trade secret; and
> (ii) The knowledge of the trade secret had been acquired by accident or mistake.

18 U.S.C. § 1839(5).

The DTSA models its definition of misappropriation on the Uniform Trade Secrets Act (UTSA). House of Representatives, Report No. 114-529 (April 26, 2016). As such, federal courts addressing misappropriation under the DTSA may look to decisions involving the state's version of the UTSA for guidance.

B. Trade Secret

The definition of misappropriation uses the term "trade secret," which is itself defined at section 3426.1(d) of the California Civil Code for CUTSA and 18 U.S.C. § 1839(3) for the DTSA. *See supra* Chapter 1.

C. Person

"Person" within the CUTSA's definition of misappropriation is defined at section 3426.1(c) of the California Civil Code. It provides that "person" "means a natural person, corporation, business trust, estate, trust, partnership, limited liability company, association, joint venture, government, governmental subdivision or agency, or any other legal or commercial entity." Cal. Civ. Code § 3426.1(c). The DTSA does not define "person" as used in the definition of misappropriation.

D. Improper Means

1. CUTSA

"Improper means" within the CUTSA's definition of misappropriation is itself defined to "include[] theft, bribery, misrepresentation, breach or inducement of a breach of a duty to maintain secrecy, or espionage through electronic or other means. Reverse engineering or independent derivation alone shall not be considered improper means." Cal. Civ. Code § 3426.1(a).

As the CUTSA's definition of "improper means" indicates by use of the term "includes," its list of improper means is not exhaustive. Cal. Civ. Code § 3426.1(a). Thus, other means not expressly identified in section 3426.1(a) may be improper means.

For examples of cases addressing improper means, *see*:

- *Vacco Indus., Inc. v. Van Den Berg*, 5 Cal. App. 4th 34, 50 (1992) (acknowledging that theft and breach of a duty to maintain secrecy are improper means).

- *K.C. Multimedia, Inc. v. Bank of Am. Tech. & Operations, Inc.*, 171 Cal. App. 4th 939, 960-61 (2009) (acknowledging that helping and encouraging employee's trade secret theft "falls within the statutory definition of 'improper means' of acquiring a trade secret, which 'includes . . . breach or inducement of a breach of duty to maintain secrecy . . . .'") (citation omitted, ellipses in original).

- *Allergan, Inc. v. Merz Pharms., LLC,* No. SACV 11-446 AG, 2012 WL 781705, at *11-12 (C.D. Cal. Mar. 9, 2012) (sending the information to personal email accounts and/or copying it onto personal electronic storage media in breach of defendants' contractual obligations to plaintiff constituted acquisition through improper means).

- *Duncan v. Stuetzle*, 76 F.3d 1480, 1488 (9th Cir. 1996) (the complaint arguably stated a claim for misappropriation where it alleged the defendant obtained the information by pretending to conduct business negotiations).

- *Speech Tech. Assocs. v. Adaptive Commc'n Sys., Inc.*, No. C-88-2392-VRW, 1994 WL 449032, at *9 (N.D. Cal. Aug. 16, 1994) (acknowledging breach of a duty to maintain secrecy constitutes improper means).

The CUTSA's definition of "improper means" provides, however, that certain conduct is exempted. The definition states: "Reverse engineering or independent derivation alone shall not be considered improper means." Cal. Civ. Code § 3426.1(a). In *Aqua Connect, Inc. v. Code Rebel, LLC*, No. CV 11-5764-RSWL, 2012 WL 469737, at *2 (C.D. Cal. Feb. 13, 2012), the court ruled that reverse engineering is not "improper means" even if it is in violation of a license agreement. *See id.* (citing *DVD Copy Control Ass'n, Inc. v. Bunner*, 31 Cal. 4th 864, 901 n.5 (2003) (Moreno, J., concurring)); *cf. S.O.S., Inc. v. Payday, Inc.*, 886 F.2d 1081, 1090 (9th Cir. 1989) (applying California law and suggesting that acquisition of the trade secret by a licensee may constitute misappropriation if the trade secret was obtained in a manner not authorized by the license agreement).

Further, "[even] assuming the information was originally acquired by improper means, it does not necessarily follow that once the information became *publicly* available that everyone else would be liable ... for republishing it simply because they knew about its unethical origins." *DVD Copy Control Ass'n, Inc. v. Bunner*, 116 Cal. App. 4th 241, 253 (2004). *But see infra* Section 2.04, discussing imputed, vicarious, and joint liability for misappropriation.

2. DTSA

The DTSA's definition of "improper means" is similar. Improper means:

> (A) includes theft, bribery, misrepresentation, breach or inducement of a breach of a duty to maintain secrecy, or espionage through electronic or other means; and
> (B) does not include reverse engineering, independent derivation, or any other lawful means of acquisition[.]

18 U.S.C. § 1839(6).

But, some courts have held that not all reverse engineering is immune from forming the basis of a misappropriation claim. *See, e.g.*, *Compulife Software Inc. v. Newman*, 959 F.3d 1288, 1312-1315 (11th Cir. 2020) ("scraping" (*i.e.*, extracting large volumes of data from a website through a computer program) can constitute misappropriation); *NEXT Payment Sols., Inc. v. CLEAResult Consulting, Inc.*, No. 17 C 8829, 2018 WL 3637356, at *14 (N.D. Ill. July 31, 2018) ("[L]awful reverse engineering does not violate the DTSA. Plaintiff, however, alleges more than reverse engineering, and alleges that Defendant allowed dissemination and use of Plaintiff's trade secrets by unauthorized persons in breach of a confidentiality agreement.") (citation omitted).

§ 2.02 Acquisition, Disclosure, and Use

A. CUTSA

Three primary activities can give rise to misappropriation: acquisition, disclosure, and use. Cal. Civ. Code § 3426.1(b). None of these activities is defined by the CUTSA. To date, none of them has been expressly defined through case law either, but in the course of holding that a party cannot be held liable for misappropriation if it did not gain knowledge of the trade secret, the court in *Silvaco Data Systems v. Intel Corp.*, 184 Cal. App. 4th 210, 220, 224 (2010), disapproved of on other grounds by *Kwikset Corp. v. Superior Court,* 51 Cal. 4th 310 (2011), explored the types of conduct that can constitute misappropriation under the CUTSA.

The court held that there was no basis to conclude that the defendant ever "acquired" the trade secrets, because the trade secrets were embodied in source code that the defendant never received. *Id.* at 222-24 (executing or running executable software made from the trade secrets—did not constitute a "use" of the trade secrets under the CUTSA). "'[U]se' … is not present when the conduct consists entirely of possessing, and taking advantage of, *something that was made* using the secret." *Silvaco*, 184 Cal. App. 4th at 224.

A variety of disclosures or uses of trade secrets can give rise to misappropriation. For example:

- *Using* a trade secret in manufacturing, production, research, or development can all potentially constitute misappropriation. *See PMC, Inc. v. Kadisha*, 78 Cal. App. 4th 1368, 1383 (2000); *O2 Micro Int'l Ltd. v. Monolithic Power Sys.*, 399 F. Supp. 2d 1064, 1075 (N.D. Cal. 2005); *Duncan*, 76 F.3d at 1488.

- Disclosure of another's trade secrets in a patent application also can constitute misappropriation. *See, e.g.*, *Altavion, Inc. v. Konica Minolta Sys. Lab., Inc.* 226 Cal. App. 4th 26, 66 (2014).

- An intangible or nonphysical use, or use of the trade secret from memory, can give rise to a misappropriation. *See Morlife, Inc. v. Perry*, 56 Cal. App. 4th 1514, 1522 (1997); *Klamath-Orleans Lumber, Inc. v. Miller*, 87 Cal. App. 3d 458, 462-66 (1978); *MAI Sys. Corp. v. Peak Comput., Inc.*, 991 F.2d 511, 521 (9th Cir. 1993).

A misappropriation can also be based on a disclosure or use of some, but not all, of the trade secret information. *Religious Tech. Ctr. v. NetCom On-Line Commc'n Servs.*, 923 F. Supp. 1231, 1257 n.31 (N.D. Cal. 1995) (applying California law and noting that a partial disclosure of a trade secret is actionable); *SkinMedica, Inc. v. Histogen Inc.*, 869 F. Supp. 2d 1176, 1197 (S.D. Cal. 2012); *Speech Tech. Assocs. v. Adaptive Commc'n Sys., Inc.*, No. C-88-2392-VRW, 1994 WL 449032, at *10 (N.D. Cal. Aug. 16, 1994).

A misappropriation can also be based on the acquisition, disclosure, or use of a trade secret that was previously misappropriated by another (for example, using a trade secret *knowing* it was previously misappropriated by another). *See PMC, Inc.*, 78 Cal. App. 4th at 1383, 1385; *Vacco*, 5 Cal. App. 4th at 49-50; *Religious Tech.* 923 F. Supp. at 1256 (applying California law); *O2 Micro*, 420 F. Supp. 2d at 1091; *Ajaxo Inc. v. E*Trade Group, Inc.*, 135 Cal. App. 4th 21, 66 (2005); *MedioStream, Inc. v. Microsoft Corp.*, 869 F. Supp. 2d 1095, 1114 (N.D. Cal. 2012).

Constructive knowledge is sufficient to impose liability under certain circumstances. Cal. Civ. Code § 3426.1(b); *see also Ralph Andrews Prods., Inc. v. Paramount Pictures Corp.*, 222 Cal. App. 3d 676, 682-83 (1990) ("When a competitor hires a former employee of plaintiff who is likely to disclose trade secrets, '[i]t is a question of fact whether the competitor had constructive notice of the plaintiff's right in the secret . . . .'") (citation omitted).

Joint owners of trade secrets are on equal footing to assert a claim of misappropriation and one joint owner can assert a misappropriation claim against the other according to *Morton v. Rank Am., Inc.*, 812 F. Supp. 1062, 1074-75 (C.D. Cal. 1993).

Certain disclosures and uses do *not* give rise to a misappropriation under the CUTSA. For example, some courts have held that, assuming the trade secret information was properly acquired, merely possessing it without more does not constitute misappropriation. *See Golden State Linen Serv., Inc. v. Vidalin*, 69 Cal. App. 3d 1, 8 (1977); *Pellerin v. Honeywell Int'l, Inc.*, 877 F. Supp. 2d 983, 989 (S.D. Cal. 2012); *Gibson-Homans Co. v. Wall-Tite, Inc.*, No. 92 2750 JGD, 1992 WL 512411, at *4 (C.D. Cal. Oct. 27, 1992).

Also, a "passive consideration" of the trade secret information is not necessarily "use" for purposes of CUTSA. *Masimo Corp. v. Sotera Wireless, Inc.*, 591 B.R. 453, 460, 466 (S.D. Cal. 2018) (one to two minute consideration of the alleged trade secret, accompanied by no further action did not constitute "use").

In addition, a finding that the putative misappropriator independently derived the same information negates that it "used" the alleged trade secret. *Masimo*, 591 B.R. at 460-461; *cf., BladeRoom Grp., Ltd. v. Emerson Elec. Co.*, 331 F. Supp. 3d 977, 986-87 (N.D. Cal. 2018) ("[A]n actor is liable for using the trade secret with independently created improvements or modifications if the result is substantially derived from the trade secret."; ruling the jury could find, based on the evidence, that the defendant used and disclosed the trade secrets in patent applications) (citation omitted).

B. DTSA

For a few examples of cases addressing whether certain conduct qualified as misappropriation under DTSA, see:

- *1-800 Remodel, Inc v. Boder*, 2018 WL 6340759, at *5 (C.D. Cal. Oct. 17, 2018) (forwarding of confidential and proprietary information to personal email address constituted improper acquisition).

- *WeRide Corp. v. Kun Huang,* 379 F.Supp.3d 834, 848 (N.D.Cal. 2019) (copying the confidential files to a personal storage device and deleting files from the computers gave rise to misappropriation).

- *Cutera, Inc. v. Lutronic Aesthetics, Inc.*, 444 F. Supp. 3d 1198, 1207-1208 (E.D. Cal. 2020) (evidence indicating that the employees copies filed at the time of their departure strongly suggests that they intend to use the information in their new employment).

- *Payward, Inc. v. Runyon*, 2021 WL 242903, at *4 (N.D. Cal. Jan. 25, 2021) (misappropriation where defendant gave information to another employee who did not otherwise have access to the document).

- *NEXT Payment Solutions, Inc. v. CLEAResult Consulting, Inc.*, 2018 WL 3637356, at *14 (N.D. Ill. July 31, 2018) (an abuse or misuse of access that had been provided was misappropriation); *Syntel Sterling Best Shores Mauritius Ltd. v. Trizetto Grp., Inc.*, 2016 WL 5338550, at *6 (S.D.N.Y. Sept. 23, 2016) (same).

- *AUA Private Equity Partners, LLC v. Soto*, 1:17-cv-8035-GHW, 2018 WL 1684339, at *5-6 (S.D.N.Y. April 5, 2018) (acquisition of trade secrets in breach of confidentiality agreement constituted improper means; former employee did not improperly acquire trade secrets merely by gaining access to them in her employment; improper acquisition occurred when she uploaded documents to her personal Google drive).

- *In* re *Dealer Mgmt. Sys. Antitrust Litig.*, 362 F. Supp. 3d 558, 566 (N.D. Ill. 2019) (misappropriation where trade secrets were accessed without authorization).

- *Protege Biomedical, LLC v. Z-Medica, LLC*, 394 F.Supp.3d 924, 939-940 (D.Minn. 2019) (misappropriation where competitor incorporated the plaintiff's trade secrets, obtained during acquisition discussions, into its patent applications).

For additional examples in the employment context, *see infra* Section 2.03.

§ 2.03 Disclosures and Uses by Former Employees

A. CUTSA

The propriety of disclosures or uses of trade secrets by former employees is a commonly litigated issue under the CUTSA. *Morlife, Inc. v. Perry*, 56 Cal. App. 4th 1514, 1520, 1525-27 (1997).

Generally, using a former employer's trade secret customer information to solicit those customers constitutes misappropriation. *See Reeves v. Hanlon*, 33 Cal. 4th 1140, 1155 (2004); *PMC, Inc. v. Kadisha*, 78 Cal. App. 4th 1368, 1383 (2000); *Morlife*, 56 Cal. App. 4th at 1524; *MAI Sys. Corp. v. Peak Computer, Inc.*, 991 F.2d 511, 521 (9th Cir. 1993); *Gable-Leigh, Inc. v. North Am. Miss*, No. CV 01-01019 MMM (SHX), 2001 WL 521695, at *15 (C.D. Cal. Apr. 13, 2001); *Merrill Lynch, Pierce, Fenner & Smith Inc. v. Garcia,* 127 F. Supp. 2d 1305, 1306 (C.D. Cal. 2000).

However, some courts have held that a former employee's professional announcement to the customers of his or her former employer of a change in employment is not in and of itself a misappropriation, even if the customer identities and information are trade secrets. *See, e.g.*, *Am. Credit Indem. Co. v. Sacks*, 213 Cal. App. 3d 622, 633-36 (1989) (defendant went beyond a mere professional announcement and instead used the trade secret customer information to solicit the customers). For other cases that recognize the professional announcement exception, *see Hilb, Rogal & Hamilton Ins. Servs. of Orange County, Inc. v. Robb*, 33 Cal. App. 4th 1812, 1821 (1995); *MAI Sys.*, 991 F.2d at 521; *Reeves*, 33 Cal. 4th at 1156; *cf., Moss, Adams & Co. v. Shilling*, 179 Cal. App. 3d 124, 130 (1986) ("former employees cannot use trade secrets to announce a change of employment to the former employer's customers"); *Aetna Building Maintenance v. West*, 39 Cal. 2d 198, 204 (1952) ("even in the absence of solicitation, Aetna is entitled to protection against West's use, or disclosure in competition with it, of trade secrets given to him only for the purpose of carrying on his employer's business.").

Courts have also held that merely accepting business from customers of the former employer does not constitute a misappropriation. *See Hilb*, 33 Cal. App. 4th at 1821-22; *Aetna Bldg.*, 39 Cal. 2d at 204. Merely discussing business with such customers (as long as no trade secret information is used) also does not constitute misappropriation. *See Hilb,* 33 Cal. App. 4th at 1821-22; *Aetna Bldg.*, 39 Cal. 2d at 204.

Likewise, generally competing with a former employer (without the use of any of the former employer's trade secrets) does not constitute misappropriation. *See Hilb,* 33 Cal. App. 4th at 1822; *Am. Credit*, 213 Cal. App. 3d at 633; *Aetna Bldg.*, 39 Cal. 2d at 204.

B. DTSA

DTSA litigation similarly can involve claims by employers against former employees, often in the context of former employees joining competitors.

Several courts have found a former employee's forwarding of company information to a personal email address may support a determination of misappropriation. *See, e.g.*, *Henry Schein, Inc. v. Cook,* 191 F. Supp. 3d 1072, 1077 (N.D. Cal. 2016); *Select Energy Servs., Inc. v. Mammoth Energy Servs., Inc.*, No. CIV 19-28-R, 2019 WL 1434586, at *8 (W.D. Okla. Mar. 29, 2019); *Iacovacci v. Brevet Hldgs., LLC*, 437 F. Supp. 3d 367, 381 (S.D.N.Y. 2020).

However, some courts have said continued possession or knowledge of a former employer's trade secret is insufficient to establish misappropriation because it is not acquisition, disclosure, or use. *See, e.g.*, *McGriff Seibels & Williams, Inc. v. Sparks*, No. 2:19-cv-1196-ACA, 2020

WL 5809971, at *3 (N.D. Ala. Jan. 23, 2020); *Prominence Advisors, Inc. v. Dalton*, No. 17 C 4369, 2017 WL 6988661, at *4-5 (N.D. Ill. Dec. 18, 2017).

The use of a former employer's trade secrets to solicit the former employer's customers can constitute misappropriation. *Philips N. Am. LLC v. Hayes*, 2020 WL 5407796, at *10 (D. Md. Sept. 9, 2020); *Gen. Secur., Inc. v. Commercial Fire & Secur., Inc.*, No. 17-CV-1194 (DRH) (AYS), 2018 WL 3118274, at *5 (E.D.N.Y. June 25, 2018); *Lux Global Label Co., LLC v. Shacklett*, No. 18-5061, 2019 WL 3530424, at *5 (E.D. Pa. July 31, 2019); *Biomin Am., Inc. v. Lesaffre Yeast Corp.*, No. 2:20-cv-02109-HLT, 2020 WL 2395200, at *5 (D. Kan. May 12, 2020).

For additional information regarding misappropriation in the employment context, *see infra* Chapter 4.

§ 2.04 Imputed, Vicarious, or Joint Liability for Misappropriation

A. Individuals' Liability for Corporate Misappropriation

Under the CUTSA, individuals can be held personally liable for misappropriation by a corporation. *PMC, Inc. v. Kadisha*, 78 Cal. App. 4th 1368, 1387-88 (2000); *see also Components for Research, Inc. v. Isolation Prods., Inc.*, 241 Cal. App. 2d 726, 729-30 (1966) (finding directors personally liable for the corporation's misappropriation). "[A]s employees and agents of [a corporate misappropriator], [individuals] are jointly liable for torts committed in the corporate name." *Vacco Indus., Inc. v. Van Den Berg*, 5 Cal. App. 4th 34, 53 n.20 (1992) (citation omitted).

Under the DTSA, an individual employee can be held personally liable for misappropriation undertaken on behalf of their employer. *See, e.g., Select Energy Servs., Inc. v. Mammoth Energy Servs., Inc.*, No. CIV 19-28-R, 2019 WL 1434586, at *7 (W.D. Okla. Mar. 29, 2019); *Corporate Synergies Grp., LLC v. Andrews*, 2019 WL 3780098, at *5-6 (D.N.J. Aug. 12, 2019); *G.W. Henssler & Assocs., Ltd. v. Marietta Wealth Mgmt., LLC*, No. 1:17-cv-2188-TCB, 2017 WL 6996372, at *5 (N.D. Ga. Oct. 23, 2017). *But see WeRide Corp. v. Kun Huang*, 379 F.Supp.3d 834, 850 (N.D.Cal. 2019) (plaintiff was not likely to prove its misappropriation claims against individual defendant Wang where it did not allege that Wang himself improperly took any of the trade secrets and where Wang denied involvement in the corporate defendant's alleged misappropriation conduct).

B. Conspiracy Liability

The court in *Genentech, Inc. v. JHL Biotech, Inc.* announced that "there can be no independent civil conspiracy claim under CUTSA." *Genentech, Inc.*, No. C 18-06582 WHA, 2019 WL 1045911, at *12 (N.D. Cal. Mar. 5, 2019). The same court also stated that there was "no authority suggesting that Section 1836(b) of the DTSA provides for a stand-alone private action for conspiracy to misappropriate trade secrets." *Id.*; *cf., AccuImage Diagnostics Corp. v. Terarecon, Inc.*, 260 F. Supp. 2d 941, 950-52 (N.D. Cal. 2003) (applying CUTSA and denying motion to dismiss conspiracy to commit misappropriation claim against corporate shareholder).

C. Respondeat Superior Liability

Under the CUTSA, employers can be held liable "for the acts of misappropriation committed by their employees and former employees." *Allergan,* 2012 WL 781705, at *12; *Language Line Servs., Inc. v. Language Servs. Assocs., LLC*, No. CV 10-02605 RS, 2013 WL 1891369, at *9 (N.D. Cal. May 6, 2013) (denying corporate defendant's summary judgment motion based on argument that employers cannot be held liable for unauthorized actions of certain "rogue" employees, and holding that respondeat superior doctrine can apply in trade secret cases); *Extreme Reach, Inc. v. Spotgenie Partners, LLC*, No. CV 13-07563-DMG (JCGx), 2013 WL 12081182, at *7 (C.D. Cal. Nov. 22, 2013) ("SpotGenie may be liable for the Sales Managers' misappropriation of trade secrets under the doctrine of respondent superior."); *see also Silvaco Data Sys.,* 184 Cal. App. 4th at 225 n.7 ("Nothing said here should be taken to suggest that a defendant cannot be liable for misappropriation unless he personally possessed knowledge of the trade secret. He can of course acquire such knowledge, and indeed can conduct the entire misappropriation, *vicariously*, *e.g.*, through an agent.").

Some courts have ruled that an employer may be held liable under the DTSA for acts of misappropriation committed by their employees. *See, e.g., Bombardier Inc. v. Mitsubishi Aircraft Corp.*, 383 F. Supp. 3d 1169, 1188 (W.D. Wash. 2019). These courts have found it appropriate to impute liability to employers where the employees' misappropriation was within the scope of their employment, or intended to benefit their employer. *See, e.g., Navigation Holdings, LLC v. Molavi*, No. 19-CV-02644-LHK, 2020 WL 5074307, at *4 (N.D. Cal. Aug. 25, 2020); *Bombardier Inc.*, 383 F. Supp. 3d at 1188; *SolarCity Corp. v. Pure Solar Co.*, No. CV 16-01814-BRO (DTBx), 2016 WL 11019989, at *5 (C.D. Cal. Dec. 27, 2016); *Mallet & Co. Inc. v. Lacayo*, No. 19-1409, 2020 WL 6866386, at *8 (W.D. Pa. Nov. 23, 2020); *cf. WeRide Corp. v. Kun Huang,* 379 F.Supp.3d 834, 849-850 (N.D. Cal. 2019) (plaintiff likely could prove that the corporate defendants knew or had reason to know that individual defendant Huang misappropriated its trade secrets). *But see Biomin Am., Inc. v. Lesaffre Yeast Corp.*, No. 2:20-cv-02109-HLT, 2020 WL 2395200, at *5 (D. Kan. May 12, 2020) ("although… there are some circumstances where an employee's misappropriation can be imputed onto his or her new employer, Biomin fails to plead any facts to support this allegation here.").

However, some courts have declined to decide whether vicarious liability for misappropriation exists under the DTSA. *See, e.g., Freedom Med. Inc. v. Whitman*, 343 F. Supp. 3d 509, 526 (E.D. Pa. 2018).

§ 2.05 Proof of Misappropriation

A. CUTSA

Frequently, it is difficult to offer direct evidence of defendant's misappropriation, such as an admission from the defendant that it used the plaintiff's alleged trade secret in creating its competing product. Often a trade secret holder relies on circumstantial evidence of misappropriation. *See Ajaxo Inc. v. E*Trade Grp., Inc.*, 135 Cal. App. 4th 21, 50 (2005) (the evidence showed that the trading company needed plaintiff developer's technology to stay competitive, the developer did not have comparable technology but developed the same technology in an unusually short time after plaintiff demonstrated it to the trading company, the trading company chose the other developer as its partner when that developer had not shown the requisite technology, and the trading company invested in the other developer); *Sargent Fletcher, Inc. v. Able Corp.*, 110 Cal. App. 4th 1658, 1673 (2003) ("The plaintiff … can demonstrate that defendant had access to its trade secret; that the defendant's design mirrors the plaintiff's design; that the defendant could not have discovered the intricate details of the plaintiff's design independently or through reverse engineering from publicly available material; that the defendant's design configuration is one of many that were possible and matches the plaintiff's design; or that the defendant designed the product in less time than typically required to complete the trial and error process of independent derivation or reverse engineering."); *cf. Hooked Media Group, Inc. v. Apple Inc.,* 55 Cal. App. 5th 323, 332-333 (2020) (affirming summary judgment in favor of defendant; while inferential evidence can be used to prove misappropriation, Hooked's evidence only "suggest[ed] the engineers drew on knowledge and skills they gained from Hooked to develop a product for their new employer" which was permitted by "California's policy favoring free mobility for employees"; "evidence that Apple hired engineers with knowledge of Hooked's trade secrets and that the engineers inevitably would have relied on that knowledge in their work for Apple does not support a claim for improper acquisition of a trade secret.").

For other cases addressing circumstantial evidence of misappropriation, *see BladeRoom Grp., Ltd. v. Emerson Elec. Co.*, 331 F. Supp. 3d 977, 983-984 (N.D. Cal. 2018); *Brocade Commc'ns Sys., Inc. v. A10 Networks, Inc.*, 873 F. Supp. 2d 1192, 1216 (N.D.Cal. 2012); *Allergan, Inc. v. Merz Pharms., LLC,* 2012 WL 781705, *13 (C.D. Cal. Mar. 9, 2012); *O2 Micro Int'l Ltd. v. Monolithic Power Sys.*, 399 F. Supp. 2d 1064, 1072-74 (N.D. Cal. 2005); *Integral Sys., Inc. v. Peoplesoft, Inc.*, No. C-90-2598-DLJ, 1991 WL 498874 (N.D. Cal. July 19, 1991); *Imi-Tech Corp. v. Gagliani*, 691 F. Supp. 214, 230 (S.D. Cal. 1986).

B. DTSA

Litigants in DTSA actions similarly rely on circumstantial evidence of misappropriation. *See, e.g., Power Integrations, Inc. v. De Lara*, 2020 WL 4582675, *12-*13 (S.D.Cal. 2020) (denying motion to dismiss); *UCAR Technology (USA) Inc. v. Yan Li*, 2017 WL 6405620, at *9-11 (N.D. Cal. Dec. 15, 2017) (same); *see also WeRide Corp. v. Kun Huang*, 379 F.Supp.3d 834, 848-50 (N.D.Cal. 2019); *Pawelko v. Hasbro, Inc.*, 2018 WL 6050618, at *5 (D.R.I. Nov. 19, 2018); *Mickey's Linen v. Fischer*, 2017 WL 3970593, at *12 (N.D. Ill. Sept. 8, 2017); *Keystone Transp. Solutions, LLC v. Nw. Hardwoods, Inc.*, 2019 WL 1756293, at *6 (W.D. Va. April 19, 2019); *Capstone Logistics Hldgs., Inc. v. Navarette*, 2020 WL 3429775, at *5 n. 9 (S.D.N.Y. June 23, 2020).

§ 2.06 Burden of Proof on a Misappropriation Claim

A. CUTSA

The party claiming misappropriation bears the burden of proof on its claim, and the defendant bears the burden of proof on any affirmative defenses. *Sargent Fletcher, Inc. v. Able Corp.*, 110 Cal. App. 4th 1658, 1669 (2003) ("It is the plaintiff's burden to show improper use as a part of its prima facie case. Proof that defendant's use resulted from independent derivation or reverse engineering is evidence that there was no improper use on its part. The defendant does not have a 'burden of proof' to make that showing. But it acts at its peril if it fails to present evidence that rebuts the plaintiff's showing."). *See also Brocade Commc'ns*, 873 F. Supp. 2d at 1215. For discussion of potential affirmative defenses, *see* Chapters 8 and 9.

B. DTSA

A plaintiff who seeks relief for misappropriation of trade secrets under the DTSA must prove that the allegedly misappropriated information was trade secret information and that misappropriation occurred. *LigTel Comms., Inc. v. Baicells Techs., Inc.*, 455 F. Supp. 3d 792, 807 (N.D. Ind. April 21, 2020) (denying preliminary injunction). The defendant bears the burden of proof on any affirmative defenses. *Array Techs., Inc. v. Mitchell*, 2020 WL 1976374, at *2 (D.N.M. April 24, 2020).

§ 2.07 Avoiding Misappropriation Claims

While the risk of a misappropriation claim can never be completely eliminated, there may be steps that can be taken to reduce that risk, and the likelihood that any claim will be successful. The steps to be taken are heavily dependent on the particular circumstances. Careful thought should be given to the steps to be implemented, and the steps identified herein should not be blindly applied.

A. Danger Areas

Risk that a misappropriation claim will be asserted is especially acute in various circumstances. In these circumstances, special thought should be given to reducing the possibility that misappropriation claims will be asserted or at least the possibility that they will be successful.

1. New Employees and Departing Employees

There is risk that a misappropriation claim will be made when a new employee arrives to the extent the employee has knowledge of trade secret information of another, such as a former employer. The risk increases if the scope of the new employee's job involves competing with the trade secret holder's business. The fact that California has rejected the doctrine of inevitable disclosure (*see infra* Chapter 12) does not change that; as a practical matter, the risk of a misappropriation claim being asserted increases when the new position implicates the trade secret holder's confidential information.

The following are potential measures to consider that may reduce the risk of a misappropriation claim:

- Due diligence about the potential new employee.

The new employer should conduct due diligence about the potential new employee, including by assessing whether she is trustworthy and does not otherwise have a problematic history.

- Discussions with the potential employee about whether she can do the job without violating any obligations to another and whether she has already violated any such obligations.

A company hiring a new employee may want to proactively explore with the proposed new employee whether she can realistically perform the proposed employment obligations without using the trade secrets of another, such as those of her former employer.

Ask the proposed new employee to think critically about the issue and to view the situation from her former employer's perspective. Ask her what her former employer would say and why. Consider whether what the proposed new employee is asserting makes sense, keeping in mind that she has an incentive to downplay potential problems in order to get the job.

Companies looking to make a new hire should make clear to the proposed new employee that nothing should be construed as asking her to disclose any confidential information of another. The business should require the proposed new employee to agree and to expressly acknowledge that she will not disclose any confidential information of another. Ask the proposed new employee to err on the side of caution as to what is confidential information of another.

Consider whether the proposed new employee should speak with separate counsel so she can discuss the issues freely with the separate counsel who can then appropriately filter what is disclosed to the proposed new employer. The employee needs to understand that the company's counsel is not her counsel and she is not to share the former employer's trade secrets with the company's counsel.

Consider whether the proposed new employee may be better off in a different area of the company (unrelated to her former job) until the former employer's trade secret information becomes stale.

Similarly, consider instructing applicable employees that no one is to communicate with the proposed new employee about projects that relate to her former employer's trade secret information.

During the preliminary discussions before the employee is hired, tell her what she will be expected to agree to and represent to the company if she is hired. This would include agreeing not to bring or use her former employer's trade secrets in her new job. If any of it seems to present problems, stop and think before proceeding as those problems may increase the likelihood of a misappropriation claim being made.

Also consider whether there is already evidence of an intent to misappropriate. Red flags could include the candidate telling the new employer that she will give the new employer the trade secrets of her former employer if the new employer hires her, or an existing employee asked the candidate if she will give the new employer the trade secrets of the former employer upon being hired. While management at the new employer may then make clear that she is prohibited from bringing or using her former employer's secrets, it may be difficult to overcome the negative inference of such communications if there is litigation.

If a candidate were to offer to the new employer a former (or current) employer's trade secrets, the new employer may want to consider whether to report the incident to the former (or current) employer. Such disclosure may instill in the former employer a perception that the new employer is reputable and respects the sanctity of other's trade secret information. Perceptions are not to be ignored in analyzing how to reduce the risk of misappropriation claims. If companies have good working relationships and trust one another to abide by their commitments to avoid misappropriation, they are more likely to attempt to resolve a concern informally before resorting to litigation.

Similarly, such favorable evidence of diligence by the new employer to avoid misappropriation may be useful in the event of litigation.

• Agreements.

If the new employer is satisfied that the employee can do the new job without misappropriating, consider incorporating into the employment agreement a promise by the employee that she will not use or disclose (or cause the employer to use or disclose) any trade secret information of another, such as former employers.

Similarly, the new employer should consider including in the agreement representations that: (1) the employee has no other agreements or relationships that conflict with her responsibilities to the new employer; and (2) the employee has returned all property and tangible embodiments of her former employers' confidential information.

If the employee discloses other agreements or relationships that conflict with her responsibilities to the new employer, careful thought should be given before proceeding. A new employer's knee-jerk reaction may be to walk away from the proposed employment. However, this may give rise to a claim by the employee. *See, e.g.*, Section §4.05.A.2 (discussing *Silguero v. Creteguard, Inc.*, 187 Cal. App. 4th 60 (2010), which held that acquiescing to another's use of an invalid noncompetition agreement may give rise to liability. Note, however, that the unenforceability of a noncompete agreement under California law does not preclude the possibility that it is enforceable in a different jurisdiction and the employer may find itself in litigation in that other jurisdiction.

Similarly, if the employee discloses that she has not returned all property and tangible embodiments of former employers, then the prospective new employer will need to think how it should respond. Possibilities include declining to hire the employee, telling the employee to return all material to the prior employer immediately, etc. If hiring the employee is very important, the company may not simply want to walk away from the employment, especially if the retention of the former employer's property or information was an innocent mistake. On the other hand, alerting the former employer about the issue may open a can of worms, and potentially provoke a misappropriation claim and/or other claims. Advising the employee simply to destroy the retained property or information may also result in undesired consequences. For example, if the employee had a contractual obligation to the former employer to return all property, the instruction to destroy it may be argued to be tortious interference with her contractual obligations. Similarly, whether the employee has an obligation not to spoliate potential evidence (*see* Chapter 23) must also be considered before the company gives any direction to the employee to destroy the retained property. This is especially true if the employee kept her old company's information on purpose and intended to or did use it in her new job.

The employment agreement also should be forward-looking and not simply address issues tied to former employers. If the employee may have access to third party confidential information in her new job, the employment agreement should address the employee's treatment of that confidential information as well. For example, the agreement should include a promise by the employee not to use or disclose (or to cause any others to use or disclose) the company's trade secret information or that of any third party to which the employee had access during the employment, except as authorized.

• Professional announcements and solicitations (*see supra* § 2.03.A).

If it is possible that the former employer will claim its customer, vendor, supplier, etc. lists are trade secrets, the new employer should consider asking the new employee not to make a professional announcement of the new employment to those persons to avoid a misappropriation claim, especially if the announcement has little or no value to the new employer.

If the announcement is of value to the new employer, the employer should consider advising the new employee to make the announcement without disclosing the recipient lists to the new employer. This could be done by instructing the employee not to have the announcement emailed from the new employer's systems, and by requiring that the employee personally make the announcement rather than having the employer do it.

The employer also should consider educating the new employee about what constitutes solicitation. *See supra* § 2.03.A.

If a professional announcement is to be made, careful thought should be given to whether the professional announcement should be oral or in writing. A writing can create an objective record, which can show that there was (or was not) solicitation as part of the announcement. On the other hand, frequently someone who receives such an announcement may call the employee in response to the announcement, creating the potential for the prior employer to argue that the employee solicited the recipient during the telephone call. In such a situation, the new employer should consider whether it makes sense for the employee to keep a contemporaneous record of her conversations with the recipients, so that if the former employer later claims that there was solicitation, the employee can use the record to show that was not the case. Depending on the circumstances, the contemporaneous records may be shared with the employee's separate counsel as privileged communications. Counsel can then advise the employee when the communications with the recipients appear to cross over the solicitation line and what the employee should do to refrain from such conduct going forward.

Whenever records are created to respond to potential misappropriation claims in the future, consideration should be given to how they could backfire under the particular circumstances. For instance, if the employee solicits the recipients of the professional announcement, the contemporaneous records the employee keeps at the new employer's request could be used as evidence of misappropriation.

• Employee's behavior toward the former employer.

The employee should not try to provoke the former (or soon to be former) employer. Such conduct could include misleading the former employer about the employee's plans, terminating the employment with no notice or unreasonably short notice, refusing reasonable requests to assist in the transition of the employee's replacement, destroying or discarding files, not telling the former employer about appointments, deadlines or other information important to the former employer's business, repudiating the employee's obligation to maintain in trust the former employer's trade secret information, and beginning to work for the new employer before the prior employment terminates.

Provocative conduct of this type could raise the former employer's suspicion that the employee cannot be trusted and that its trade secrets are at risk of misappropriation, and increase the likelihood of a misappropriation claim. Such conduct may also be used as evidence of misappropriation or threatened misappropriation if a claim is made.

• Education, policies, practices and corporate culture.

The importance of creating a culture that respects the intellectual property rights of others cannot be emphasized enough as a measure to reduce the possibility of misappropriation claims. This is true whether the employee is new or old. Education, policies, practices, and corporate culture are addressed in Chapters 3 and 5. They are instrumental not only in reducing the risk that employees will misappropriate the company's trade secrets, but also former employers' or third parties' trade secret information.

General policies against misappropriation may not be sufficient to make a particular employee understand what knowledge acquired from prior employment she can and cannot use or disclose in her employment with the company. Education may be needed for the employee to understand what limitations she must be mindful of in her employment and how she may test her assumption that the information is already in the public domain.

Training may be more effective if it is tailored to particular employees' responsibilities. For example, a sales associate may not encounter the same types of situations as a research scientist, and thus may benefit from training hypotheticals that apply to her particular job responsibilities.

An employee who understands what misappropriation of trade secrets is, how it can damage a company, and what its consequences are is presumably less likely to engage in such conduct.

Employees need to understand the importance of dotting all the "i's" and crossing all the "t's" when it comes to trade secrets, including the trade secrets of a third party that the company is obligated to protect. They need to understand that the third party's trade secret information is not to be used or disclosed without (or in excess of) permission even if they think the proposed activity is innocent or makes sense to them.

Similarly, employees need to understand that just because they can access a third party's trade secret information does not mean that they should if the goal is to avoid misappropriation claims. Analogies can often help the employee understand; just because a person leaves her door unlocked does not mean that you are free to walk in and take her television.

Friendships with competitors' employees also should be addressed. Even if an employee's friend at a competitive company is willing to give the employee the competitor's information, that does not mean there will not be a misappropriation claim made by the competitor. The competitor may argue that the employee knew or should have known that asking the competitor's employee for the information would induce the employee to breach her confidentiality agreement to the competitor. Employees should acquire information from public domain sources rather than using shortcuts, such as exploiting relationships at the competitor company. While there may be times that businesses will desire to share information, such arrangements should be handled through proper channels rather than informally among employees.

• Memorializing technical developments.

A company should consider whether it makes sense for a new employee to keep a contemporaneous record of her work, such as how an invention was developed (including negative research), to show inferentially that the former employer's trade secret information was not used and instead the work was the result of independent development.

But again, whenever records are created to avoid potential misappropriation claims in the future, consideration should be given to how they could backfire under the particular circumstances. For example, the former employer may point to such records as demonstrating that the new employer knew of the misappropriation but was simply trying to create bogus records to cover up the misappropriation.

Also consider whether the creation of the records will serve any useful purpose if the misappropriation at issue is unconscious use of trade secrets. These sorts of claims may be more difficult to refute through record-keeping.

• Exit interviews.

An exit interview may be used to reduce the possibility of misappropriation of third-party trade secret information entrusted to the company. The company should consider reminding a departing employee who had access to such information that she has the obligation to protect the confidentiality of third-party trade secret information entrusted to the company as well as the confidentiality of the company's trade secret information. The company should consider addressing with the employee the return of all property containing confidential third-party information. *See* Chapter 5 for a further discussion of exit interviews.

2. Alliances Between Businesses Where Confidential Information is Shared or Developed

Parties often need to share confidential information in the course of negotiating or engaging in a joint business relationship. Relationships such as partnerships, joint ventures, and informal strategic alliances can often give rise to misappropriation claims.

Generally, confidential information should not be shared unless there is an appropriate non-disclosure agreement (NDA) in place. Before executing an NDA, the party to receive confidential information disclosed by the other party should consider:

- Whether the definition of the protected information is proper in scope (e.g., will the definition extend to information that the disclosing party could not legitimately or reasonably claim qualifies as proprietary information).

- Whether the duty to maintain confidentiality should have a time limit.
- Whether any other events or circumstances should trigger expiration of the duty to maintain confidentiality (e.g., the information falls into the public domain through no fault of the receiving party).
- Whether the procedures for designating the information to be protected is sufficient to put the receiving party on notice when it receives information that it must protect under the NDA.
- Whether there should be specific procedures governing the return or destruction of the protected information or document if the contemplated relationship does not go forward or terminates.
- Ownership of information developed in the course of the relationship.
- Whether any proposed or existing non-compete and non-solicitation obligations are enforceable and whether such obligations could cause problems in the future.
- With respect to potential future misappropriation claims, whether any attempts to shift the burden of proof to the receiving party (*e.g.*, "the receiving party shall have the burden to prove that it did not use or disclose the information except as permitted under the agreement") may be too difficult for the receiving party to meet or may give the disclosing party an incentive to assert questionable misappropriation claims.
- Whether provisions like choice-of-law, arbitration or other forum-selection, attorneys' fees, and liquidated damages may give the disclosing party an incentive or disincentive to bring questionable misappropriation claims.

The foregoing is an illustrative but not exhaustive list of issues for consideration in connection with a proposed NDA. There may be additional issues that should be considered before proceeding depending on the particular circumstances. *See* Chapter 4 for a further discussion of NDAs.

The receiving party also should consider whether to segregate from its other operations those employees who receive the disclosing party's confidential information. It also may be advisable for the receiving party's employees working in the disclosing party's market area to keep a contemporaneous record of their work (*e.g.*, how an invention was developed) so that the company will be in a better position in the future to demonstrate that the disclosing party's confidential information was not used.

3. Reverse Engineering

Reverse engineering is generally understood as the process of using a product to work backward to divine information from the product (*e.g.*, regarding the product's design, formulation or manufacture). Ordinarily, acquiring information through reverse engineering does not constitute misappropriation of trade secrets. *See, supra,* Section 2.01.D. However, under various circumstances, reverse engineering may be considered improper and, thus, give rise to a misappropriation claim.

For example, a misappropriation claim may arise from reverse engineering if:

- an applicable contract prohibits the proposed reverse engineering conduct (*e.g.*, the thing to be reverse engineered was acquired pursuant to a contract that restricts its use for a particular limited purpose);
- the thing to be reverse engineered was wrongfully acquired (*e.g.*, in breach of a duty, through dishonesty); or
- the reverse engineering conduct was improperly facilitated or expedited by information provided in breach of a duty (*e.g.*, to a former employer or under an NDA).

Some potential best practices to reduce the risk of a misappropriation claim based on reverse engineering conduct may include:

- educating those working on potential reverse engineering projects to understand that not all reverse engineering is permissible;
- excluding from working on reverse engineering projects persons who have had restricted access to information that may facilitate or expedite the reverse engineering activity; and
- proactively confirming that the proposed reverse engineering activity does not breach any existing obligations and that possession of the thing to be reverse engineered is proper.

4. Discovery Of Potential Misappropriation By An Employee

If a company discovers that, notwithstanding its directives that there be no misappropriation, one its employees misappropriated a former employer's trade secrets (or what the former employer may claim are its trade secrets), the company should carefully consider with the assistance of qualified counsel -- its potential response since the response (or lack thereof) may affect the level of risk for the company. Although a strategic response can potentially improve the situation for the company, a poorly designed response can make matters worse for the company.

Although the response by the company will depend on the circumstances and various factors, the following are a few potential measures that a company may wish to consider as part of a potential response to the discovery:

- Extract from the company's systems any perceived misappropriated documents or those perceived as derived from misappropriated information. Use an outside forensic consultant to preserve a copy of what is extracted from the company's systems so that the company can reduce the risk of a spoliation claim (*see* Chapter 23) if there is litigation.
- Direct employees not to use information received from the subject employee unless the information is in the public domain or from a third party source (which is not the subject employee's former employer).

- Direct employees that, if they have already used information received from the subject employee, then the work is to be repeated by personnel who were not privy to the information received from the subject employee.
- Suspend the subject employee during the company's investigation of the subject employee's conduct and then terminate of the employment if warranted based on the investigation.
- Disclose to the former employer the subject employee's potential misconduct (hereafter, "Disclosure"). Some potential benefits of a Disclosure may include: 1) heightened credibility for the company if there is litigation; 2) persuading the former employer that the company is trustworthy and conducting itself in good faith, thereby increasing the chance that the situation can be resolved without litigation; and 3) negating the possibility that the former employer will discover the situation on its own and then will assume that company was complicit since the company did not voluntarily disclose the situation. On the other hand, a significant possible negative ramification of a Disclosure is that the former employer will file unwanted litigation against the company.

B. Miscellaneous

1. Responding to Demand Letter

A company that receives a demand letter alleging misappropriation and threatening suit has many issues to consider. For example, it should consider whether such a letter is an empty threat, whether ignoring the letter could provoke or expedite litigation, and what the optics of the response would be in litigation. Similarly, a recipient should assess whether an aggressive or more moderate response would be most effective in furthering the recipient's goals.

It is important to investigate and evaluate relevant facts and vulnerabilities (both the recipient's and those of the sender) prior to responding. In forming a strategy, the recipient should consider substantive claim-based facts (*e.g.*, whether there has been actual misappropriation, whether there is a threat of misappropriation, whether the information at issue qualifies as trade secret). But, it also should consider material practical facts unrelated to the merits of the claims (*e.g.,* whether the sender of the letter is a small company that is unlikely to be able to afford litigation; whether there is already such animus between the sender and recipient that there is little chance of avoiding litigation no matter what the recipient does).

The recipient of the letter also should consider whether the sender of the letter is trawling for information or evidence to support litigation. Generally, when crafting a response to the demand letter, the recipient should avoid language that could be characterized as a threat of misappropriation, and avoid including in its response information that could be used against it.

In addition, the recipient of the demand letter should consider whether it can offer accommodations or information that may satisfy the sender. For example, it may be possible for the recipient, with little interference to its operation, to place the new employee for some time period in a different area that does not impact the sender's trade secret information. Alternatively, the sender may be under a misapprehension that the new employee is going to be working in an area that impacts the sender's trade secret information, when in fact she is not. But again, the recipient should give careful thought before providing any accommodations or substantive information to the sender.

The recipient also will want to consider whether its response should be an inadmissible settlement communication, or whether it wants the response to be available at trial. While the recipient will not want any concessions it offers to be used against it, it also may want to create evidence that it addressed the sender's concerns appropriately and that it did not engage in willful misappropriation.

At bottom, how to respond to a demand letter depends on the particular circumstances and ordinarily requires careful thought about various practical, factual, and legal issues.

2. Raiding of Employees

Hiring a significant number of employees from a company to disrupt its operations is sometimes known as "employee raiding." Regardless of whether raiding is tortious (it varies across jurisdictions), raiding can inflame the raided company to assert misappropriation claims against the new employer. Raiding can be perceived by the raided company as a threat that the new employer will use the raided employees as a means to access trade secret information. This potential risk should be considered before hiring a significant number of employees from a company with trade secret information that could be useful to the hiring company's operations.

Chapter 3
TRADE SECRET PROTECTION PROGRAMS; PRACTICAL TIPS ON PROTECTING TRADE SECRETS WITHIN A COMPANY

By: Robert B. Milligan, Esq., Elizabeth McBride, Esq., Mark Leonard, Esq., D. Joshua Salinas, Esq., and Gabrielle Walker, Esq.

---

§ 3.01 Introduction

A. Overview

Trade secret information is defined as any information that:

- is not generally known to others;
- confers an economic advantage on a company; and
- is the subject of reasonable efforts to maintain secrecy. *See* Cal. Civ. Code § 3426.1 and *supra* Chapter 1.

By definition, trade secrets need not be kept absolutely confidential, but need only be the subject of reasonable efforts to maintain secrecy.

It is by virtue of its relative confidentiality that a company gains an economic advantage over its competitors. It is imperative that a company be vigilant in how it treats its confidential information in order to protect such information.

In addition, a company must be careful in its treatment of the confidential information of third parties to avoid (intentionally or unintentionally) misappropriating the trade secrets of others. Although the exchange of third party confidential information may be a common and even necessary occurrence in a business relationship, it is important that the company not become polluted by unwanted third party information.

You can provide valuable assistance to your clients by helping them develop and implement security procedures that will (i) reduce the risk that their trade secrets will be improperly disclosed; and (ii) provide evidentiary support should the need for obtaining legal relief for trade secret theft become necessary. In addition, you can provide guidance to your clients to reduce the risk of your clients being sued for trade secret misappropriation.

B. Secrecy Is Key

Since an owner of a trade secret must take reasonable steps to maintain its secrecy, by definition, the trade secret will be lost if the owner fails to take such steps. If proprietary information is disclosed without a confidentiality agreement or it otherwise becomes generally known to others, trade secret protection may be lost, even if the company has been vigilant prior to that point in maintaining confidentiality.

The good news is that "reasonable efforts" means just that. Absolute secrecy and heroic measures are not required. There must be a substantial element of secrecy, however, so that a third person would have difficulty acquiring the trade secret information without resorting to improper means. The company's efforts to maintain confidentiality of its trade secrets need to be reasonable under the circumstances, depending on the value and type of the information and the risk of loss of the information. From a practical standpoint, efforts to maintain such protection should be directly proportional to the value of the particular trade secret. A company will find it difficult to obtain legal relief for misappropriation of its trade secrets if the company does not treat such information as a trade secret. For example, it is pointless to stamp or otherwise mark highly sensitive information as "confidential" if such information is easily accessible to external parties or even to unauthorized personnel. To ensure such information remains a trade secret, the company must take affirmative steps to keep it secure (for example, keep it in a limited access area and make it available only to authorized personnel).

Reasonable efforts often represent a combination of measures that together safeguard against the risk of loss. Examples of such company efforts include policies, contracts, technical controls, monitoring and data loss prevention technology, physical security, document labeling, and training.

C. Standard of Care

Whether reasonable measures were taken by the trade secret owner is a question of fact, and the burden of proof is on the plaintiff. Consequently, a showing of reasonable efforts to maintain the secrecy of a trade secret is an important part of the company's affirmative case in trade secret misappropriation litigation. The standard applied to your client by a court in determining whether your client has expended sufficient efforts to maintain the confidentiality of a trade secret is likely to be what a company of your client's size and sophistication would reasonably do under the circumstances in view of the importance and value of the information being protected. This means that as your client grows in size and sophistication, the measures taken by your client to protect its trade secrets should be reviewed and adjusted accordingly on an ongoing basis.

Your clients should also keep in mind that if they have trade secret protection policies and procedures in place, to the extent they are not applied to a particular category of information, they may have difficulty establishing that such information is a trade secret. In this chapter, we suggest various means by which a trade secret holder may protect its trade secrets, without implying that any of them constitute measures necessary to a finding of "reasonable efforts to maintain secrecy." Again, reasonableness depends on the circumstances of each particular case.

D. Benefits of a Trade Secrets Program

There are several significant benefits to a company in adopting a trade secrets program including, but not limited to:

- Protecting the company's valuable trade secrets and preventing unnecessary loss;
- Maintaining the company's competitive edge in the marketplace;
- Managing and extracting the value of innovations;
- Notifying employees and third parties of the company's interest in protecting proprietary information;
- Educating employees on what constitutes the company's confidential information, how to protect it, and the consequences of failing to do so;
- Maintaining centralized policies and procedures for handling company proprietary information;
- Creating evidentiary support that the company has made reasonable efforts to maintain the secrecy of its trade secrets in the event of trade secret litigation;
- Discouraging misappropriation of the company's trade secrets;

- Discouraging misappropriation of third party trade secrets; and
- Avoiding unnecessary and costly litigation.

§ 3.02 Identifying and Classifying Trade Secrets

The first step to protecting a trade secret is identification of the information the company considers to be a trade secret (*i.e.*, confidential information that provides the company with a business advantage). You can assist your client in determining what information is confidential and what can be released to the public. More complex decisions during the innovation process involve differentiating what inventions should be patented and what should be instead protected as trade secret. You can also assist your client in determining the criteria to be used in classifying trade secrets. In assessing what information is to be protected as their trade secrets, employers should be mindful not to sweep in information that is not their trade secrets, including the information that is generally known or is part of the general skill, knowledge, and experience of their employees, or information obtained from third parties and subject to confidentiality obligations. Once these determinations have been made, they should be made known to company employees for consistent implementation, with particularized training for employees in critical engineering, customer-facing, and supply chain roles. To be clear, the exercise of identifying and classifying trade secrets for the purpose of company management and protection of its trade secrets is different than in the litigation context, where the purpose is to identify with particularity what trade secrets are alleged to have been stolen. You can assist your client in understanding the appropriate identification and classification schemes in this context.

Confidential information is more likely to be disclosed in an unauthorized manner if the party disclosing or receiving the information is not put on notice that the information is to be kept confidential. Although most employees generally are aware that they should not disclose confidential information, they need guidelines for making the determination in a consistent way, or technical controls that limit their individual discretion regarding certain trade secret information. The risk for the company with respect to a given piece of valuable information is that one or more employees may be disclosing it based on their individual assessment and discretion. Since it is the company's burden to take "reasonable" steps to protect trade secrets, such inconsistent treatment may destroy all trade secret protection for the particular information. Once standard criteria have been established to determine trade secret status and formal consensus procedures have been implemented, the trade secrets that have been identified should be updated and supplemented periodically by discussion with inventors and meetings with supervisors along with more strategic discussions with the legal department and executive staff.

Employers and employees alike should be aware of the fact that there may be a "lag" in identifying new trade secret information that is being developed. A company's trade secrets are typically not frozen in time. The fact that information developed five years into an employee's career with an organization is not identified as a trade secret in the initial onboarding materials does not mean that the employer cannot subsequently identify this information as a trade secret through training, processes, and exit proceedings. In turn, the fact that the employer properly identified information as a trade secret five years before does not mean that the information remains a trade secret now.

A. Determining What Information Is Confidential

In order to determine what company information is confidential and should be protected, the company may rely on an audit for the purposes of (i) identifying all company intellectual property and any other information that the company considers to be proprietary; and (ii) assigning a value to each class of assets. The audit should be conducted by the company's management and other individuals who are knowledgeable about the company and its products, technology, and services. It should be communicated by counsel, and the responses should be sent to counsel to attempt to protect it from discovery under the attorney-client privilege in future litigation regarding the company's trade secrets.

While the type of information that will qualify as a trade secret will vary from company to company, as a general rule, if the information is not generally known and would be considered valuable to a competitor, then it probably affords the company a competitive advantage and should be treated as a trade secret. When identifying trade secrets, the company should be careful not to be constrained by the form of such information or material. Trade secret information and material can take almost any form, tangible or intangible including, but not limited to, the following:

1. Technical Information

- Computer code (including object and source code) of the company's software products;
- Program logic, file structure and algorithms used in the company's software products;
- Product specifications;
- Strategic and roadmap information concerning the company's products;
- System documentation, user and design manuals, and training instructions;
- Data structures—input or output formats;
- Engineering drawings and designs, schematics, and performance data;
- Systems design and architecture;
- Software development tools, drawings, and product sketches;
- Photographs, negatives, films, microforms, magnetic tapes and disks;
- Manufacturing plans and strategies; and
- Other technical information and know-how relating to unannounced company products.

2. Financial Information

- Sales data;
- Customer data, including purchasing history;
- Cost and pricing information;
- Quarterly financial results before they are announced;
- Profit and loss information below the revenue line; and
- Royalty information from customers, including the number of units shipped by each customer.

3. Marketing Information

- Customer and prospect lists;
- Mailing lists for company newsletters;
- Product plans;
- Product acquisition candidates;
- Unannounced ship dates of new products;
- Unannounced relationships with other companies;
- Marketing and product positioning strategies;
- Dealer lists;
- Dealer and distributor sales reports; and
- Information provided to reproduction facilities regarding product build rates.

4. Other Information

- Nonpublic information regarding employee ownership in the company;
- Organization charts; and
- Other information identified by the company as "Confidential."

Remember, once the company's trade secrets have been identified, the list should be reviewed and updated on a regular basis and the classification of the company's confidential information should be communicated to all employees and contingent workers who will have access to such confidential information. You can assist your clients in this endeavor by checking in with them periodically and offering to review their existing trade secrets, along with their identification and classification frameworks and then helping to update or supplement their process, controls, and corpus of trade secrets as appropriate.

B. Determining the Criteria To Be Used in Classifying Trade Secrets

Once your client's proprietary information has been inventoried in some fashion, it should be classified according to its value. Not all trade secrets require the same treatment. What is appropriate for one type of information may not be appropriate for another. Your client should classify its confidential information and allocate resources for the protection of its trade secrets in proportion to the nature and value of the confidential information or trade secret to the client. The goal is to create a consensus as to the standard of care and the procedures to be applied with respect to each of the company's trade secrets. This will help your clients maintain consistency and a reasonable level of protection for their trade secrets. It will also help your client centralize and standardize their policies, program, and compliance efforts.

For example, some companies have adopted the following two-tier classification system for labeling proprietary information:

Tier 1: "Company Secret"—Need to Know Only

This classification is for important confidential information of the highest sensitivity. Information categorized as "Company Secret" information consists of information that if disclosed to a competitor or the public would seriously undermine the company's competitive advantage in the market. This information should be made available only to company employees on a need-to-know basis (and possibly certain limited authorized third parties who have a need to use such information and who are under the terms of a specially negotiated confidentiality agreement).

Company employees who receive "Company Secret" information are required to take special measures to protect it including, without limitation, (i) labeling the tangible copies with an appropriate legend, and following up oral disclosures with a writing confirming that the information is a company trade secret; and (ii) complying with additional security measures designated by the company for the protection of "Company Secret" information. It can be challenging to drive strict compliance across a company's workforce, and frequent training is critical to ensuring consistent adherence to these requirements.

Tier 2: "Company Confidential"—Internal Use Only

This classification is for less sensitive information that is not available to the public and intended for use by employees within the company in carrying out the company's business. Such information is available without restriction within the company. Information categorized as "Company Confidential" information consists of information which may be necessary for the company to share with certain third parties (such as customers or strategic or channel partners) but which, if disclosed to a competitor or the public, could damage the company's competitive advantage in the market.

"Company Confidential" information may be made available to contingent workers and other third parties only on a need-to-know basis under the terms of a confidentiality agreement (or another agreement containing comparable confidentiality provisions). Generally, the company intends for "Company Confidential" information to remain confidential forever. However, from time to time company management may determine that certain information categorized as "Company Confidential" may be downgraded for external use and thus made public, for example, certain prelaunch product or services information or certain financial information. The decision to make any "Company Confidential" information public should be made only by company management.

Company employees who receive "Company Confidential" information should be required to take all reasonable and appropriate measures to protect such information including, without limitation (i) marking tangible copies with appropriate legends and, in oral disclosures, identifying the information as confidential; and (ii) complying with the security measures designated by the company for the protection of "Company Confidential" information.

Whatever classification method your client elects to use, to be effective, designation of an item as a trade secret must be a selective process. Random use of a confidentiality notice will dilute a company's claim that it has taken reasonable steps to keep the trade secret information secret. As a result, many companies embed document labels within their data repositories and document management systems. A confidentiality label, to be effective, should be applied only to information or documents that the company wishes to keep confidential.

C. One Size Does Not Fit All

It is important to remember that there is no single method for classifying and protecting trade secrets. The key to success is creating a consensus as to the standard of care and procedures to be applied with respect to various trade secret materials, to ensure that treatment of such materials is both adequate and consistent, and to drive adoption and compliance across the company's workforce. Whatever methods are adopted by the company must:

- Reasonably maintain secrecy of the information;
- Be communicated to employees;
- Be periodically reviewed and updated; and
- Be consistently and continually enforced.

Your client's efforts to establish security measures will be futile unless they are reasonable and enforced. Many companies have lost valuable trade secrets by either failing to implement adequate security procedures or by ignoring security procedures once they have been put in place.

Once your client surveys and classifies its proprietary information, the next step is to implement adequate safety procedures, such as those described in the following section.

§ 3.03 Implementing Procedures to Protect Trade Secrets—The Trade Secrets Program

A. Proprietary Rights Team

The optimal approach for implementing a trade secret program at a company is through formation of a team who will be in charge of identifying the company's trade secrets and implementing a trade secrets program (the "Proprietary Rights Team"). The Proprietary Rights Team should be composed of participants from several key areas in the company, such as human resources, information technology (including information security), physical security, contract administration, marketing, sales, representative product or services groups, and legal personnel. The function of the group is to coordinate the implementation and operation of the trade secret program.

The first action for the Proprietary Rights Team is to identify (for each department of the company) the trade secrets and confidential information in its domain and categorize the relative value of the proprietary asset. In the course of such evaluation, special care should be taken to identify "less obvious," though valuable, assets (for example, hardware schematics, repair manuals, and utility programs intended for internal use) since the tendency may otherwise be to focus exclusively on development results and not the tools used.

Once the company's trade secrets have been identified, the Proprietary Rights Team should take action according to the value and type of proprietary asset. The resources allocated for protecting a proprietary asset should be proportional to the value of the asset to the company. Company polices should be established as to the manner of protection to be used for various categories of proprietary assets. Some minimal level of appropriate protection should be afforded to all trade secrets of any value.

The Proprietary Rights Team may operate formally, meeting quarterly to review new trade secrets and emerging risks, and convening ad hoc where an important project or risk requires immediate attention. On the other hand, the role of the Proprietary Rights Team may be to set standards and to delegate trade secret identification to appropriate managers. The Proprietary Rights Team may also consider trade secret strategy and administration issues and review status reports and program progress.

You can provide a valuable service to your client by offering to help the Proprietary Rights Team identify potential trade secrets, either through participation in the formal quarterly meetings or through assistance in drafting identification standards for use by managers.

B. Employee Education

Employee education and training is an effective way to implement and maintain a culture of confidentiality. The proprietary protection policies for the various trade secrets should be communicated to employees. Each employee's responsibility with respect to proprietary protection should be made clear, and in some cases particularized role-based training may be warranted. Certain employees will have more responsibility for initiating and maintaining protection for proprietary assets but, from a maintenance standpoint, almost all employees will have some role to play in a proprietary rights protection program. Each employee must be made aware of what is considered a trade secret or confidential information of the company. Each employee must be instructed on how to protect such information and the consequences for not doing so. Without consistent employee participation in the company's protection strategy, its trade secrets and confidential information cannot be protected adequately.

Continuing education for employees is a critical component in any strategy for protecting the company's proprietary assets. Some company employees may have come from large corporations before joining the company. Such large corporations may have had formal proprietary rights training programs. Such employees may, therefore, have some sensitivity to trade secret protection, although the approach will vary depending upon the former employer. For many employees however, this will be their first job and they will have no former training to fall back on. Without a formal education program, the company's employees may either fail to implement appropriate protections or may implement protections in different and perhaps inconsistent manners.

As part of the company's implementation of the trade secret program, the proprietary rights policies and procedures ideally should be made available to employees in handbook form for quick reference. This information can be included in the employee manual or distributed separately and made available and readily accessible online and through company mobile apps.

Quarterly presentations via virtual platforms (e.g. Zoom) and e-learning modules are a cost effective way to educate employees about obligations with respect to proprietary information in an effort to prevent accidental disposition of valuable company assets. All employees should be educated about the company's trade secrets and sensitized and reminded of issues of confidentiality and ownership. Specialized training for your client's managers is particularly important, since they will be relied upon to provide job specific guidance to employees in their areas. With proper training, managers can also play a role in appropriate oversight of employees along with independent contractor agreements, exit interviews for employees (and independent contractors), and monitoring the disposition of your client's intellectual property.

In addition, all new employees should be provided with an appropriate level of proprietary rights protection training, tailored for their position, when they first join the company. A portion of this training could be in the form of a short video presentation on the employee's role in protecting your client's proprietary assets and trade secrets. This should be shown to all new employees as part of their orientation. The training video should (i) provide a sufficiently detailed overview of the categories of information that the employer considers to be its trade secrets, including third-party information with which the employer and employee deal; (ii) emphasize the company's commitment to protecting its proprietary assets; (iii) briefly describe the forms of protection relied upon by the company; and (iv) describe the written materials and other company resources available to provide further guidance to the employee. It should also provide case studies to illustrate the policies in practice and clarify expectations of each and every employee.

Training should focus on both sides of the trade secret continuum: safeguarding the employer's trade secrets and guarding against the improper receipt, use, or disclosure of the trade secrets of others, such as former employers. Practical training that provides tips on how to manage real-life situations can be particularly effective. For example, training on preventing use of former-employer information can include practical guidance on searching the public domain and documenting public sources of information when an employee is wondering whether he or she is able to use an item of information. Another practical training exercise could involve how to speak up when coworkers, customers, vendors and others may be inappropriately sharing information that might appear to be the trade secrets of others. Training exercises that focus on information sharing with customers and suppliers is also important, providing examples on what should and should not be shared along with the most safe and secure methods to use when sharing information.

Employees should also understand that just because they can access another company's trade secret information does not mean that they should. Analogies can often help the employee understand: just because a person leaves the door to the house unlocked does not mean that you are free to walk in and take the television. Extending the analogy, just because someone else walked in and took the television and is offering to sell it does not mean employees can now legally help themselves to it.

Similarly, employees should understand that they have proper internal recourse if they are concerned that coworkers, consultants, vendors, or business partners may be engaged in conduct that has given, or could give, rise to misappropriation. To that end, employees should be aware of 1) their primary point of contact for reporting purposes; 2) what steps to take to document or memorialize the conduct in question; and 3) the protection the company will afford them for identifying and reporting on such conduct.

After the initial training, such policies and procedures should be reinforced by email reminders on a periodic basis. Additionally, employees should be briefed from time to time as to what items the company considers to be confidential, the level of confidentiality for each item, and how the company expects the confidential information to be handled.

C. Use of Agreements to Protect Confidential Information

All persons (employees, vendors, consultants, contingent workers, and the like) coming into contact with the company's trade secret information ideally should be bound by an appropriate written confidentiality agreement. The company should avoid relying on verbal arrangements to protect its trade secrets. Reliance on "verbal understandings" or a "code of conduct" could be deemed insufficient to protect trade secrets. Generally speaking, different forms of confidentiality agreements should be used for employees, vendors and independent contractors (such as consultants) as described below:

1. Employees

As mentioned above, the company's employee handbook should address the company's confidentiality policy and the employees' obligations with respect to the company's proprietary assets. The handbook should be distributed to all employees and each employee should be required to sign a confidentiality and inventions assignment agreement (to the extent appropriate).

Some employees tend to believe that what they have used and developed over time is their own. Each new employee should be counseled at the outset that information and materials used and developed in the course of their employment with the company belong to the company.

2. Contingent Workers (Independent Contractors, Consultants)

Companies must consider what and whether to provide access to trade secrets to their contingent workforce. This is a necessary consideration of any trade secret protection program. If practical, the company should have standardized forms of independent contractor agreements which are tailored to the types of independent contractors used by the company. Responsible company employees (such as managers) need to understand which (if any) form of agreement is appropriate to use. They also need to understand what obligations are imposed under the various agreements. Ideally, only a limited number of company employees should be authorized to enter into agreements with independent contractors.

3. Vendors

Vendors should be asked to sign confidentiality agreements when company confidential information may be disclosed.

It is not uncommon for a company to incorrectly assume that it owns valuable intellectual property (for example, website, logo design, software or other technology) that has been developed or created by third parties at the company's request and at the company's expense. The assumption is "I paid for it, so I own it." While in most cases, works created by employees will belong to the employer, works created by independent contractors and third parties are owned by such parties unless such party *assigns* the ownership rights in the technology to the company *in writing*. Failure to do so can be devastating to a company. Consequently, one of the most important ways that you can effectively serve your clients is by drafting confidentiality agreements for use by the company that not only impose appropriate duties of confidentiality but also appropriately assign ownership and use rights to the company.

D. DTSA Whistleblower Language

The Defend Trade Secrets Act (DTSA) allows trade secret owners to bring a federal, civil, private cause of action for trade secret misappropriation. The DTSA provides that employers "shall" include a notice of whistleblower immunity in any contracts with employees, contractors, or consultants that include provisions restricting the use or disclosure of trade secrets. Absent providing such notice, employers cannot recover attorneys' fees or enhanced exemplary damages. The notice must inform employees that they are permitted to disclose a trade secret in confidence to a federal, state, or local government official, or to an attorney, when such disclosure is made to investigate or report a suspected violation of law, or in a complaint or other document filed in a lawsuit or other proceeding, if such filing is made under seal. Additionally, the notice, which can be expressed in general, easy-to-understand terms, should advise that individuals suing their employers for retaliation based on the reporting of a suspected violation of law may disclose a trade secret to their attorneys and use the trade secret information in the court proceeding, so long as any document containing the trade secret is filed under seal and the individual does not disclose the trade secret except pursuant to court order. The required disclosures can, in the alternative, be contained in a nondisclosure agreement or other appropriate company policy or handbook, including cross-referencing the immunity language in the company's general whistleblower procedures.

E. Security Measures

The security measures taken by each company will vary, depending on the size and type of company and the value of the company's trade secrets. The technology landscape is changing rapidly, and you should advise your client of the latest updates and how that may impact the adequacy of the company's trade secret protection program. There are a number of security measures that your clients should consider, including, but not limited to, the following:

1. Marking Confidential Information

As a matter of internal practice, all confidential information should be marked with an appropriate legend, such as "[Company Name] Confidential." A "Confidential" notice should be applied only to information that the company truly deems to be a trade secret and wishes to keep confidential. In some companies, employees stamp almost everything confidential (or use automatic "confidential" footers) in place of making a considered determination of whether or not the item was confidential. Remember, excessive use of the word "Confidential" on unimportant materials runs the risk of devaluing the protection given by such designation.

2. Limiting Access to Confidential Information

One of the best ways to keep trade secrets confidential is to limit access to them. The company should strongly discourage the making of unnecessary copies of confidential information and should limit the people who have access to it to those with a "need to know." The company should shred, rather than simply discard, sensitive materials. No confidential materials should leave the company's facilities unless necessary and appropriate precautions are taken, and access to copies and facsimile equipment should be limited. All requests for information from the press, other media or analysts should be referred to a specific person or public relations department with an adequate understanding of what information the company considers to be confidential. The company should similarly review all speeches and publications in advance to avoid unnecessary disclosure of trade secrets.

3. Keeping Electronic Information Secure

In this digital age, companies most often store their most important information electronically. A trade secret protection program must collaborate closely with information security teams and devote substantial attention to the control of electronic information.

a. Locations of Electronically Stored Information

Companies should be aware of the various locations Electronically Stored Information ("ESI") may be stored. Not only can confidential information be stored on computer systems/harddrives, but it may also be stored in emails, text messages, the cloud, removable devices (such as USB drives), backup repositories, and more. Therefore, companies should have policies in place for tracking where and how confidential data may be stored and managed.

b. Computer Systems

The company should consider using firewalls, passwords and file locks to prevent unauthorized access to trade secret and confidential data maintained in its computers. The company should consider embedding a confidential notice in each file containing trade secret information. The company also should consider taking appropriate precautions to protect stored information when a computer or other electronic device is sent out of the building.

c. Passwords/Restricted Use

The company should consider requiring passwords to access its computer system. These passwords should be *at least* eight (8) alpha-numeric characters, and should be changed regularly. The company should consider multi factor authorization before employees are permitted to access company systems. The company may also require all users to log off computers and other electronic devices when they are not in use. As an alternative (or companion) to password-protected data, the company may choose to encrypt its data.

d. Email

As most all companies rely extensively on email to communicate both inside the company and with the company's remote sites, the following considerations should be reviewed by the company:

(1) Security of the System

The company should review the email and network system to ensure it is secure from unauthorized entry. The company should formulate a policy regarding the type of information that is appropriate to be sent by email in light of the security level of the system. Consider that even if the computer system requires a password for entry, employees may log on to their machines and at the end of a session leave the machines on while away from the desk or overnight. Computers that are left on and unattended may be subject to unauthorized entry and printing out of information by anyone seated at the terminal. The company should take steps to reduce this possibility, such as having a mechanism that unattended computers lock after a period of nonuse so that a password must be entered to continue using that computer.

(2) Encryption and Digital Signatures

For emails that contain trade secret or other highly sensitive information, the company should consider using software that allows for encryption of the email message contents and attachments. In addition, the company should consider using software that requires an authorized digital signature in order for the recipient to view an email's content or attachments. This is particularly useful in preventing unauthorized persons from viewing a sensitive or classified email, which has been forwarded or sent to individuals who are not authorized to view the email contents or attachment.

(3) User Training

The company should consider email user training which will set standards for transmission of confidential information.

(4) Use of Email and Prohibiting Use of Email for Trade Secrets

Companies may want to consider prohibiting use of email for some trade secret information. If feasible, some trade secrets can be memorialized only by handwriting and other non-electronic communications. In some situations this could reduce the likelihood of accidental dissemination of the information. Companies should notify their workforce of any trade secret information that is off limits from the email system. If companies find it necessary to use email for trade secret information, any emails external to the company should be sent through a secure tunnel, a firewall, or other encrypted transmission. Another technique for limiting risk while sending trade secret information via email is to send the information in multiple emails, so that no single email discloses the whole trade secret.

(5) Email Retention

The company should review and evaluate its practices relating to email dissemination, retention and access to the email system. If it does not already have one, the company should implement an email records retention policy, and stored emails should be destroyed on a schedule consistent with such policy (unless, of course, there are countervailing reasons to retain them such as a litigation hold). In addition, employees should be counseled on the use of email to avoid inadvertent disclosures of sensitive materials in an email communication.

e. Databases

Electronic databases often contain company trade secrets. Companies should see that databases are accessible on a "need-to-know" basis within the company. For example, there is no reason for all employees to have access to payroll information containing trade secret compensation information. Nor should all employees have access to trade secret company customer lists, cost information, manufacturing information or pricing. Database access can be limited by password or computer systems can make databases unavailable to anyone who does not have permission to access them.

f. Data Loss Prevention and Threat Monitoring

The company may consider deploying technology designed to monitor and detect information security threats. This includes platforms that monitor unusual user activity on the network and systems, such as suspicious user activity regarding file access and transfers, email activity, cloud storage activity, and external drive activity. Companies can use this technology to detect potential trade secret theft in real-time and also use such reports during the employee exit process.

4. Keeping Facilities Secure

Several security features that can be implemented at the company's facilities include visitor sign-in procedures, visitor name-tags and off-site storage. Visitors should enter only through main lobbies. The company may also want to consider camera surveillance, video recording and card readers (that record who, when and where) on external doors.

Other specific security measures the company may want to consider for use at its facilities now, or at an appropriate time in the company's future, include:

a. Open Areas

If open workspace is used, employees need to be sensitized to the need to protect the confidentiality of the company's information. They should be encouraged to use conference rooms for meetings with non-company individuals. This will prevent company business that is being conducted in the next workspace from being overheard. Employees should also be counseled not to discuss confidential information in non-secure locations, such as elevators, restrooms, and restaurants. In addition, employees should be cautioned against discussing the company's private business on cell phones or other devices where it can be overheard. Additionally, to the extent visitors can view work areas, consideration needs to be given to the type of written materials that are hung on cubicle interiors, walls and other workspace areas.

b. Clean Desk Policy

A clean desk policy may be appropriate and practical in certain areas of the company.

c. Locked Desks and File Cabinets

Adequate locked storage space should be made conveniently available to employees who have a legitimate need for it. This is one of the least expensive security methods, but it is very effective when used.

d. Reception Desk/Area

The company should have a receptionist to greet and check in all visitors to the company. The reception desk should be staffed at all times during the company's business hours and during any after-hours company events.

e. Photocopier Use and Placement

Photocopiers in the facility should have an audit trail that requires the user to input an identification number to use the copiers, and the copiers should be placed away from areas where important confidential materials are kept.

f. Destroying/Shredding Documents

All documents marked confidential should be placed in shredding bins, and not in the regular trash. Shredding bins should be locked and strategically located (such as by the printers) and their contents disposed of in a secure manner. All disks which have ever contained confidential information should be destroyed and not re-used.

g. Whiteboards

Employees need to be trained to erase the whiteboards in conference rooms after the conclusion of a meeting to avoid inadvertent disclosure. In addition, reminders can be posted adjacent to whiteboards advising employees to erase all written information.

h. Visitors

Company visitors should not be permitted to travel on site without an escort. Companies should consider using NDAs with visitors that obtain access to sensitive facility locations. As the company grows and the number of employees increases, it will become necessary to issue visitor tags to identify any unescorted visitors. Employees should be advised to stop such visitors and assist them in returning to the appropriate area.

i. Self-Help Protections

Where feasible, copy protections and footprinting (*i.e.*, embedding nonsense code into software for proof purposes or planting a relatively unknown employee's contact information in a customer list shared with a third party to track whether the third party is misusing your list for its own purposes) should be used.

j. Track Disclosure of Company Confidential Information

The company should examine the current procedures for releasing its proprietary information to third parties, and, depending on the value of the item, implement procedures to audit and track such releases to third parties as appropriate. It is important for the company to be aware of: (i) who has company confidential information; (ii) what information has been delivered or shared with each third party; (iii) what restrictions have been imposed on such third parties; (iv) when such third party's right to access or use such confidential information expires; and (v) the means by which such information must be returned or destroyed by such third party.

k. Track Disclosure of Third Party Confidential Information

The company should also examine the current procedures for managing the secrecy of third party information that the company has agreed to protect. It is important that the company adhere to the restrictions imposed by third parties. Most agreements involving technology include confidentiality provisions with specific restrictions on use and obligations with respect to the destruction or return of third party confidential information.

Forms that memorialize the release of confidential information should be used in conjunction with any confidentiality agreement under which the company will be making any disclosure. Using these types of forms serves as a tracking system for determining precisely what information was given to whom. For example, at the termination of a confidential relationship, most contracts require the return or destruction of all disclosed materials. This tracking system can help track the accomplishment of that obligation. In addition, such a system can be useful in future infringement scenarios.

5. Remote Work Considerations

As a result of COVID-19, many companies allowed their employees to work remotely. But now, as many companies have allowed their employees to return to office, companies may no longer require employees to come to the office five days a week. Therefore, even after the pandemic is over, companies will need to consider how to maintain the security of their information while their employees and contingent workers are working from home. The following are steps employers can take to protect the secrecy of their trade secrets:

- Clearly identify for employees what information the company considers trade secret. Employees should be periodically reminded that the protection of trade secrets is a corporate priority. When an employee opens trade secret information via an electronic device, pop-ups can remind the employee of the confidential nature of such material.

- Require employees with access to the trade secret material to sign confidentiality or non-disclosure agreements.

- Restrict access to trade secrets on a "need to know basis" and encrypt or password-protect such confidential information.

- Consider prohibiting the transfer of trade secret information onto employees' personal computers, storage devices, or virtual repositories.

- Limit, or even prohibit, physical printing of trade secret documents. If printing is allowed, ensure that the physical documents contain a "trade secret" designation and that there is a protocol for their secure destruction.

- Consider investing in data loss prevention and other monitoring technology that provides visibility into access and transfer activity related to trade secret data and repositories where trade secret information is stored.

- Stay up to date with hacking and virus protection software, including using firewalls.

- Prepare a plan to secure company devices and materials in the event the employee is terminated.

- Remind employees to ensure that family or friends living with or visiting them cannot access the confidential information.

- Take immediate action if unauthorized acquisition, use, or disclosure is suspected.

6. Avoid Misappropriation of Trade Secrets in Hiring and Onboarding

There are several simple and practical steps companies should consider following during the hiring process to reduce the possibility of a new employee retaining or using any proprietary information of his or her former employer and to reduce the chances of a misappropriation of trade secrets claim by the former employer:

(a) Consider the similarities between the work the recruit did for his or her former employer and the work the recruit would be doing for your company. Identify areas where the former employer's trade secrets may inadvertently be disclosed.

(b) Do not ask the recruit about a competitor's confidential information. This includes during the interview process, during which employers should not ask candidates specific questions about their prior employment that may reveal trade secrets and should caution candidates that they should not reveal trade secrets in the course of the interview.

(c) Before hiring a prospective employee, consider asking for and reviewing any non-confidential contracts between the prospective employee and his or her current employer so the company can refrain from interfering with those contracts.

(d) Before extending an offer letter, companies should take into consideration the specific responsibilities of the position so that potential violations are avoided before employment starts. As the interviewing process proceeds, any restrictions the new employer concludes are advisable should, where possible, be communicated to the employee before acceptance of the offer.

(e) Ask the recruit to sign a statement that no confidential information of a previous employer will be brought over or revealed to the company.

(f) Use extreme caution in hiring an employee based on a claim that he or she "owns" certain technology—the employee may not fully understand the ownership issues.

(g) Do not knowingly use another company's confidential information to solicit employees from that company or otherwise compete with the company.

(h) Do not allow a prospective employee to do any work until after he or she has left the prior employer.

(i) Instruct a new employee that he or she is not to use any trade secrets or confidential information of his or her former employer during his or her work for the company, and get a written acknowledgement of this from the new employee.

(j) Consider the potential for a claim of threatened misappropriation of trade secrets by the new employee's former employer(s).

(k) Consider obtaining a written representation from the new employee that he or she can fulfill his or her responsibilities without using any trade secrets or confidential information of any former employers, perhaps even including it in his or her offer letter or employee agreement.

(l) When using external recruiters, employers should require the recruiters to ask candidates to identify any limitations on their ability to take on employment and any obligations to former (or soon to be former) employers that survive termination of employment, including but not limited to restrictive covenant agreements, and to confirm that, if hired, they are able to take the position and perform the related responsibilities without violating any obligations to others. See also Chapter 2, which also addresses how to avoid misappropriation claims.

7. Exit Procedures for Employees

Companies should consider establishing exit procedures for use with all departing employees. Exit procedures are addressed in detail *infra* in Chapter 5.

8. Protections While Negotiating with Third Parties

Prior to disclosing trade secrets to any prospective business partner, a company should assess the desirability of a nondisclosure agreement (NDA). An NDA can address issues including existence of trade secrets, confidentiality and secrecy, disclosures, limits on access and use, time limits on duties, and ownership. Standard operating procedure often involves obtaining a signed NDA prior to any disclosure of confidential or trade secret information. In fact, failure to obtain an NDA prior to disclosure could result in loss of trade secret rights. *See supra* Chapter 1. Even with a signed NDA, however, the company still bears the risk that the third party may not abide by the agreement. Therefore, companies providing information pursuant to an NDA should explore arrangements such as using a third party intellectual property escrow company to store the trade secrets that the prospective business partner accesses. In this arrangement, the prospective business partner does not gain actual possession of the information and the escrow company maintains proof of the information disclosed under the arrangement. The company may also consider appropriate arrangements upfront by contemplating the dissolution of the relationship and what clawback or other requirements would be expected.

9. Monitoring Contractual Obligations

Confidentiality obligations imposed by third parties via contract should be taken seriously by the company and enforced in accordance with the specific contractual terms. When the company enters into a contract which imposes obligations, affected employees should be informed of such obligations so that they can act accordingly. You can advise your client on how to implement a contract compliance program to ensure that such obligations are understood by the company and compliance is both operationalized in business workflows and documented in the event of a later audit or dispute.

F. Social Media Policies

The increased popularity and wide use of social networking sites such as Facebook, Instagram, Twitter, Pinterest, and LinkedIn provide a good reason for companies to review and update their trade secret protection programs to include a social media policy and train employees on the use of social media—particularly as it relates to the company and its business. Without a social media policy and employee training, it will be difficult for the company to combat the increased risk social media poses to the protection of the company's trade secrets.

If your company does not yet have a social media policy, it may be time to put one in place and attempt to ensure that all employees are trained on the use of social networking sites—particularly as it relates to sharing or posting information about the company or its business, including the company's customers and vendors. When drafting the policy, set clear guidelines for employees as to what information can be shared, if any, about the company and its business on social networking sites, whether in the form of blogs, online comments, general postings or tweets, YouTube videos, and the like.

The policy guidelines may vary from company to company and determining where to draw the boundaries is not always clear. On one hand, social media networks can be a very useful and effective tool for connecting people, reaching out to customers, and disseminating information about the company or its products or services, so banning the use of such social media may not be practical or in the best interests of the company. On the other hand, given the casual nature of such networks and the desire to share topical information, without proper guidance, employees could easily share information that is not meant for public dissemination or make statements that could be misconstrued or otherwise be harmful to the company.

While the rules may differ significantly depending on the nature and business of the company, the following considerations are generally applicable to most companies:

- Consider how social media will be used within the company (*e.g.*, by the marketing department and by employees) and how social media will be used outside of the company by employees—both professionally and personally.
- Understand the publicity settings (*e.g.*, private, public, friends only, etc.) and train employees on the proper settings for any approved work-related postings.
- Remind employees that they are ambassadors of the company and that their behavior (good and bad) reflects on the company.
- Remind employees that information posted in social networking sites is not protected by confidentiality just because their settings are on "private" or meant to be shared with "friends only." Friends and others with access to the site may share the information with their "friends" or others, some of whom could work for the company's competitors. Social media networks are public sites and not a place to post or share the company's confidential information.
- Remind employees of the company's policy regarding the handling of confidential information and make it clear that social media is not an exception to such policy.
- Review and understand the terms of use of social media sites to ensure that ownership of the company's information is not transferred as a result of a post to the site.
- Consider that different guidelines may apply depending on the activity involved (*e.g.*, blog contributions, online comments or postings, message boards, online conversations or chats, and making online "connections" and "friends").
- Consider what, if any, social media activity should be banned entirely.
- Strongly discourage or prohibit employees from making any disparaging remarks about the company, its customers, vendors, or other third party to avoid exposing the company (and potentially the employee) to third party claims, except where prohibited by applicable labor laws.
- Use search engines or other services to monitor how the company is being referenced and/or discussed on the Internet, and consider letting employees know about the monitoring to discourage inappropriate activity.
- Consider establishing an internal process for the review and approval of all information about the company on blogs, in videos, etc., prior to posting by employees.
- Consider to what extent employees can make connections with customers and vendors. For example, if your sales reps are "connected" to all or most of your customers on LinkedIn, consider to what extent that will lead to the disclosure of your customer list to competitors and others.
- Consult an employment attorney to advise whether the proposed social media policies comply with applicable labor laws.

Once you have drafted the company's social media policy, train all company employees on the company's policy so that they understand the company's expectations regarding the use of social media. Left on their own to decide, employees may inadvertently post information that the company is not ready to share publicly, which could be harmful to the company if such information is in the form of trade secrets or confidential information.

G. BYOD Policies

Many companies have adopted, formally or informally, Bring Your Own Device ("BYOD") programs and the trend is likely to continue to grow. Under such programs, employees are allowed to use their own personal computing devices (*e.g.*, smartphones, tablets, laptops, etc.) for both personal and company purposes and often employees can access the company's network when using such devices.

If your company has adopted or is considering implementing a BYOD program, the company should update its trade secret program to include a formal BYOD policy and to ensure that all employees are trained on the use of the company's proprietary information contained on such devices.

While BYOD policies can be very useful in improving efficiency, reducing costs and enabling mobility for employees, they also increase the risk that sensitive company confidential information could be compromised, particularly if such devices are lost or stolen or shared with others without appropriate protections in place. Confidential information may also be compromised if an employee departs from the company while retaining access to the company's confidential information on his or her personal devices or online accounts.

For company-issued devices, companies should also retain control of the device's access credentials. There have been far too many instances where an employee has departed and the company is left with a device that it cannot unlock. If the company does not wish to retain direct control of the passwords, it should at least be able to reset the passwords through a mobile device management system.

Each BYOD policy should be tailored to the specific needs of the company, but the following issues should be carefully considered when adopting a BYOD policy:

- Work with IT and security teams to determine which (all or some) employees and devices will be included in the BYOD program.

- Isolate the company information on the device so that it can easily be identified and wiped from the device if necessary.

- If the device will be used to access the company's network, require that such devices include encryption and password protection.

- Remind employees of the risk to the company's confidential information if their device is lost or stolen and reiterate that company confidential information must not be accessible by others using the device.

- Include in your policy the right to remotely wipe/delete any sensitive company data from the device in the event of loss or theft of the device or upon the employee's suspension or departure from the company.

- Require employees to notify the company immediately in the event of loss or theft of the device or if they believe that the company's confidential information has been accessed by unauthorized persons.

- Include the right for the company to locate the device at any time if it is used to access the company network.

- Include the right for the company to take possession of the device if needed in connection with litigation or discovery.

- Remind employees that their Internet activity may be monitored and logged while they are connected to the company network using their device.

- Train employees on the BYOD policy and have each employee provide written acknowledgement of the terms of the policy.

- For company-issued devices, retain the ability to control the device's access credentials.

Because BYOD devices are used for both personal and company purposes, they raise a number of issues that should be considered by the company, including employment, technical, financial, legal and security issues. As such, when adopting a BYOD program, it is recommended that you consult with members of the company's HR, legal, IT, security and finance teams.

H. Incidental Personal Use of Corporate Issued Devices

For those companies that do not implement a BYOD policy, many permit incidental personal use of corporate issued laptops, tablets and mobile phones. It is important to create policies and training for employees to understand that they should not have an expectation of privacy for any personal content they decide to commingle with business content on their corporate devices. Further, employees should understand that their company devices may be collected and forensically examined at any time in connection with the protection of the company's trade secrets.

I. Cloud Considerations

The digital age has significantly changed how companies store their data. Whereas, the practice used to be that companies maintained "hard copies" (*e.g.*, actual paper documents), the practice now for most companies is to maintain records in digital form. As a result, many companies store their information, including proprietary trade secrets and other confidential information, in electronic form using a digital network or "Cloud".

A Cloud can be a private network housed on servers behind the company's firewall, or it can be a Cloud hosted and maintained by a third party. In either case, use of the Cloud by companies to store their sensitive data, raises new security issues for companies regarding the protection of trade secrets.

There is still some uncertainty around whether using a Cloud to store trade secrets constitutes "reasonable measures" to maintain the secrecy of trade secrets; however, given the broad use by companies of the Cloud to store sensitive data, and the likelihood that companies will continue to do so, the following issues should be considered when determining whether to store trade secrets and other sensitive information in the Cloud. This is not an exhaustive list, and the courts will continue to review the specific circumstances involved to determine whether reasonable measures were taken to protect the company's trade secrets in the Cloud:

- Employees may erroneously think that the Cloud—like the Internet or the company's public website—is publicly available to everyone. Be sure to let them know that all company information maintained in the Cloud should be treated as the company's confidential information.
- Include specific training for employees on the types of company sensitive information contained in the Cloud and remind them of their responsibility to protect the company's trade secrets—whether such information is available in the Cloud or otherwise.
- Encrypt the data when it is stored in the Cloud and include electronic tagging to identify the data as the company's confidential information.
- Require secure log-in and passwords to the Cloud and consider the requirement to change passwords to the Cloud on a periodic basis.
- Consider segregating information in the Cloud based on its sensitivity and limiting access to highly sensitive information by groups or individuals on a strict "need to know" basis.
- Not all hosted Clouds are the same. Before using a third party hosted Cloud, carefully review the terms of service and negotiate them as needed to provide the company with the terms it needs to protect any sensitive company information contained in the hosted Cloud, including security, confidentiality, limitations of liability, etc. Confirm that the third party host is reputable and reliable.
- If the third party has limited confidentiality terms or has limited its liability against breach or data loss to an amount so low that a court may determine it is unreasonable for the company to have placed trade secrets in the hosted Cloud, then consider storing such information (especially the company's trade secrets), elsewhere—such as the company's private, secure network—to protect such information.
- Work with your IT team to ensure that sufficient security safeguards are in place to protect the company's trade secrets while they are in the Cloud. You will want to ensure that you have appropriate audit rights to track Cloud activities.
- Consider monitoring and/or disabling the ability to download, copy or email sensitive information from the Cloud by employees or others with authorized access to the Cloud.
- Immediately terminate access to the Cloud when an employee is suspended or leaves the company. Do not permit employees to store company confidential information

in their own clouds. The company should control all clouds used to store company confidential information.

- Work with your security, HR, legal and management teams, in advance, to develop a plan to immediately deal with a breach of security or loss of information caused by hackers, employees or third party's hosting the Cloud.

Technological advances, such as using the Cloud to store large amounts of data, provide many benefits to companies; however, they also increase the risk that, if sufficient precautionary measures are not taken, valuable trade secrets can be lost or stolen, potentially resulting is huge losses and unwanted exposure for companies that have not carefully considered and prepared for such consequences.

§ 3.04 Practical Tips—Dos and Don'ts

The following dos and don'ts will generally apply to any company that has trade secrets worth protecting:

A. Do

- Identify and classify the company's proprietary information.
- Act vigilantly in protecting the company's confidential information.
- Notify employees and third parties of the confidential nature of the information, their role in protecting it, and the consequences for not doing so.
- Conduct due diligence before disclosing confidential information.
- Limit access to confidential information to those who "need to know."
- Implement contractual protections with employees, contractors, and vendors.
- Implement and enforce reasonable security measures to maintain secrecy.
- Create a written trade secrets policy for distribution to employees.
- Track disclosure of the company's confidential information.
- Update the company's trade secret protection program on a regular basis.
- Use copy protection and footprinting to protect assets.
- Conduct exit interviews with all employees who have had access to trade secrets.
- Include training on social media, BYOD and the protection of trade secrets in the Cloud in new employee orientations and in all employee exit interviews.

B. Don't

- Allow unrestricted access to the company's facilities or computer system.
- Allow visitors or service providers to roam the premises unattended.
- Leave sensitive information out in the open or on whiteboards.
- Allow photographs to be taken of the company's operations.
- Designate or mark non-confidential documents as "confidential."
- Assume that your employees know how to identify the company's trade secrets.
- Assume that your employees know how to treat confidential information.

- Allow employees to individually value the company's trade secrets.
- Allow inconsistent treatment of company trade secrets.
- Give employees access to confidential company information unnecessarily.
- Allow service providers access to premises without verifying credentials.
- Ignore security measures once they have been established.
- Reveal confidential information to anyone who is not contractually bound to obligations of confidentiality.
- Assume that your employees will use social media or personal devices appropriately regarding company information.
- Assume that third party hosted Clouds will provide adequate protections for your company.
- Assume employees will not set up their own clouds to store company confidential information.

§ 3.05 Conclusion

A company's success depends on its ability to keep its competitive edge. As such, it is imperative that the company protect the trade secrets that set its business apart from its competitors. It is equally important that your client avoid unnecessarily exposing itself to costly and potentially damaging trade secret litigation. You can play a vital role in assisting your clients in this endeavor by providing the following services:

- Educate your clients on the importance of protecting their trade secrets.
- Help your clients identify their trade secrets.
- Assist your clients in inventorying and classifying their trade secrets and proprietary information.
- Help your clients develop and implement reasonable measures for protecting their trade secrets.
- Assist your clients in educating and training their employees and in preparing an employee handbook.
- Instruct your clients on the proper use of confidentiality agreements.
- Prepare appropriate forms of employment and confidentiality agreements for your clients.
- Work with your clients periodically to review and update, as necessary, their trade secrets programs.
- Work with your clients to prepare and educate their employees on the company's social media, BYOD policies and the Cloud.

Chapter 4
EMPLOYMENT LAW AND CONTRACT ISSUES
By: Rebecca ("Bec") Edelson, Esq. and Travis J. Anderson, Esq.

---

5. **Assignment of Inventions Agreements**
6. **"Interpreting" Noncompete Agreements versus "Re-Writing" Them**

B. Additional Considerations When Drafting Noncompetition Provisions

§ 4.01 Protection of Trade Secrets Within the Employment Relationship

A. Common Law Duties

There are common law duties to maintain the secrecy of certain kinds of information. *See Hollywood Motion Picture Equip. Co. v. Furer*, 16 Cal. 2d 184, 187 (1940); *Am. Loan Corp. v. Cal. Commercial Corp.*, 211 Cal. App. 2d 515, 522 (1963). For a federal case recognizing a California employee's common law duty of loyalty to the employer, see *Fields v. QSP, Inc.*, No. CV 10-5772 CAS (SSx), 2011 WL 1375286, at *3 (C.D. Cal. Apr. 8, 2011); *E.D.C. Techs., Inc. v. Seidel*, 216 F. Supp. 3d 1012, 1016 (N.D. Cal. 2016). *Cf. Mattel, Inc. v. MGA Entm't, Inc.*, 782 F. Supp. 2d 911, 984-87 (C.D. Cal. 2011) (breach of duty of loyalty claim preempted to the extent it is based on misappropriation of Mattel's information).

Officers and directors and management employees also have fiduciary duties not to use or reveal the corporation's trade secrets, even in the absence of a written nondisclosure agreement. *GAB Bus. Servs., Inc. v. Lindsey & Newsom Claim Servs., Inc.*, 83 Cal. App. 4th 409, 419-21 (2000), *disapproved of on other grounds*, *Reeves v. Hanlon*, 33 Cal. 4th 1140 (2004); *Components for Research Inc. v. Isolation Prods., Inc.*, 241 Cal. App. 2d 726, 729 (1966); *Bancroft-Whitney Co. v. Glen*, 64 Cal. 2d 327, 351 (1966); *Diodes, Inc. v. Franzen*, 260 Cal. App. 2d 244, 249-51 (1968); *Imi-Tech Corp. v. Gagliani*, 691 F. Supp. 214, 230 (S.D. Cal. 1986); *WeRide Corp. v. Kun Huang*, 379 F. Supp. 3d 834, 852 (N.D. Cal. 2019); *Hill Phoenix, Inc. v. Classic Refrigeration SoCal, Inc.*, No. SA CV 19-0695-DOC (JDEx), 2019 WL 7172977, at *7 (C.D. Cal. Sept. 6, 2019).

B. The Employee's Duty to Maintain Secrecy

An employee owes the employer an implied-in-law duty to protect the employer's confidential information, even after the employment is terminated. *Plant Indus., Inc. v. Coleman*, 287 F. Supp. 636, 644-45 (C.D. Cal. 1968); *Ungar Elec. Tools, Inc. v. Sid Ungar Co.*, 192 Cal. App. 2d 398, 403 (1961); *Houston v. Imperial Credit Commercial Mortg. Inv. Corp.*, 179 F. Supp. 2d 1157, 1177 n.19 (C.D. Cal. 2001) ("[O]fficers are also charged with a continuing duty to protect privileged and confidential information, which continues even after they leave the company."). Yet, the better practice is to obtain written nondisclosure agreements and to include provisions allowing for the continued enforcement of the nondisclosure agreements after termination, to ensure that employees are aware of these duties and to show that reasonable efforts have been taken to maintain confidentiality. *See infra* § 4.04.

C. Trade Secrets Developed in the Course of Employment Belong to the Employer

The law protects the employer's trade secrets from misappropriation by an employee, not only where the employer discloses pre-existing trade secrets to an employee, but also arguably where the employee participates in the development of trade secret or confidential information. *Morlife, Inc. v. Perry*, 56 Cal. App. 4th 1514, 1526 (1997); *see also Chartwell Staffing Servs. Inc. v. Atl. Sols. Grp. Inc.*, No. 8:19-cv-00642-JLS-JDE, 2019 WL 2177262, at *7 (C.D. Cal. May 20, 2019) ("[T]hat some Defendants developed relationships with some of Chartwell's customers *while working for Chartwell* does not make those customers' information ineligible for trade secret protection.") (emphasis in original).

An employee may be obligated to disclose to the employer all trade secrets which the employee has developed on behalf of the employer. *See* CAL. LAB. CODE § 2860; *see also Diodes*, 260 Cal. App. 2d at 252-53 (recognizing officers and directors who failed to advise board of directors of their development of a trade secret process may be liable to the company); *General Elec. Co. v. Wilkins*, No. 1:10-cv-00674-OWW-JLT, 2011 WL 902036, at *5 (E.D. Cal. Mar. 15, 2011) ("... section 2860 embodies the universally accepted principal that work product created by an employee belongs to the employer where the employee was hired to create such work product."). *But see Premier Displays & Exhibits v. Cogswell*, No. SACV 09-354 JVS (ANx), 2009 WL 8623588, at *6 (C.D. Cal. Dec. 23, 2009) (finding that section 2860 did not apply to sketches created—not acquired—by the employee during the employment) (citing *Williams v. Weisser* (1969) 273 Cal. App. 2d 726, 733 (rejecting that UCLA owned certain notes created by one of its professors)).

§ 4.02 Protection of Trade Secrets Within the Independent Contractor Relationship

Even in the absence of a written nondisclosure agreement, an independent contractor may have a common law duty of confidence to the business to which it is providing services. *Hollywood Motion Picture Equip. Co. v. Furer*, 16 Cal. 2d 184, 188 (1940). However, the safer practice is to use a written nondisclosure agreement.

It is also prudent to consider whether the independent contractor's employees or subcontractors should be required to have similar nondisclosure obligations.

The use of outside contractors poses the risk that the company's pre-existing trade secrets will be lost inadvertently. The parties' rights or nonrights in these pre-existing intellectual property should be clearly defined and articulated. It may be necessary to conduct pre-contract due diligence (under an appropriate nondisclosure agreement) to establish the nature and extent of any such pre-existing matter. This would include determining whether the contractor possesses any information that is substantially similar to the company's own trade secrets or necessary for completion of the project.

In addition, because outside contractors will move from company to company, and may on occasion provide the same or similar services to competitors, it is particularly important to take all reasonable steps to ensure against potential "cross-fertilization" of trade secrets. To that end, carefully limit the kind and amount of information to be used or disclosed to the contractor. This may involve following a strict "need to know" policy which will limit the information exchange.

Similarly, internal security procedures need to address the presence of such persons on the work site. Additional security measures may be required to limit access and availability of trade secret material.

It is also advisable to require prior notification before any contractor enters into a contract with the company's major competitors. Such notification will alert the company to watch for potential evidence of misappropriation.

§ 4.03 Protecting Trade Secrets Through Employment Agreements

Written employment agreements notify employees of the existence and nature of trade secrets that exist or may be developed during the course of employment and to establish other terms that can strengthen an employer's ability to protect its trade secrets.

A. The Scope of the Protection

It remains an unresolved question of law as to whether a purely contractual duty of confidentiality will be enforced beyond that allowed under CUTSA. Some courts suggest that a contract may impose broader protections than CUTSA. *See, e.g.*, *Albert's Organics, Inc. v. Holzman*, 445 F. Supp. 3d 463, 476 (N.D. Cal. 2020) ("a defendant may breach a contract for disclosing confidential information that does not constitute a trade secret."); *Scott v. Snelling & Snelling, Inc.*, 732 F. Supp. 1034, 1043 (N.D. Cal. 1990); *see also Farmers Ins. Exch. v. Steele Ins. Agency, Inc.*, No. 2:13-cv-00784-MCE-DAD, 2013 WL 3872950, at *8 (E.D. Cal. July 23, 2013); *Balboa Ins. Co. v. Trans Global Equities*, 218 Cal. App. 3d 1327, 1345 n.20 (1990); *ITT Telecom Prods. Corp. v. Dooley*, 214 Cal. App. 3d 307, 320 (1989) ("the disclosure of confidential information not amounting to trade secrets is arguably a breach of Dooley's express contract."). However, other courts have questioned the enforceability of use restrictions on agreed-upon "confidential" matter not rising to the level of trade secret. *HighMark Digital, Inc. v. Casablanca Design Centers, Inc.*, 2020 WL 2114940, at *22 (C.D. Cal. Mar. 26, 2020) ("the Court holds that the CUTSA preempts all claims based on misappropriation of confidential information, even if the information does not constitute a trade secret."); *Am. Paper & Packaging Prods., Inc. v. Kirgan*, 183 Cal. App. 3d 1318, 1325 (1986); *Hollingsworth Solderless Terminal Co. v. Turley*, 622 F.2d 1324, 1331-32 (9th Cir. 1980); *Morlife, Inc. v. Perry*, 56 Cal. App. 4th 1514, 1522 (1997); *Ingrassia v. Bailey*, 172 Cal. App. 2d 117, 123-24 (1959).

B. Legal Limitations on Employment Agreements

1. The Prohibition Against Illegal Terms or Conditions as a Condition of Employment

Under California law, employers cannot require employees to consent to an illegal term or condition as a condition of employment or application for employment. Cal. Lab. Code §§ 432.5, 2871.

2. The Prohibition Against Retaliation for Whistleblowing

Employers cannot prohibit employees from reporting suspected violations of the law or participating in a government investigation. Cal. Lab. Code § 1102.5; *Green v. Ralee Engineering Co*, 19 Cal. 4th 66, 77 (1998) (statute "reflects the broad public policy interest in encouraging workplace whistle blowers to report unlawful acts without fearing retaliation."); *Erhart v. BofI Holding, Inc.*, 2017 WL 588390, *10 (S.D. Cal. Feb. 14, 2017) (confidentiality agreement deemed unenforceable to the extent it prohibited plaintiff from reporting suspected unlawful activities by employer). See also Chapters 6 and 13. (DTSA expressly conditions its remedies on an employer providing a prescribed notice to employees that they are immune from civil or criminal liability if they disclose a trade secret in confidence to the government or an attorney, solely for the purpose of reporting a suspected violation of the law).

3. The Partial Prohibition Against Foreign Choice-of-Law and Forum Selection Provisions

California restricts an employer's ability to require California employees to agree as a condition of employment to either: (1) a forum selection clause that would require the employee to "adjudicate outside of California a claim arising in California" or (2) a choice of law provision that would deprive the employee of "the substantive protection of California law with respect to a controversy arising in California." Cal. Lab. Code § 925(a). However, this protection does not apply "to a contract with an employee who is in fact individually represented by legal counsel in negotiating the terms of an agreement to designate either the venue or forum" of a controversy under the agreement "or the choice of law to be applied." Cal. Lab. Code § 925(e).

4. Assignment of Inventions Made by an Employee

In order to buttress the ability to enforce employers' trade secret rights in material developed by employees, it is a common practice to include an assignment of rights provision in the employment agreement.

An employer can require the employee to assign inventions that "[r]elate at the time of conception or reduction to practice of the invention to the employer's business, or actual or demonstrably anticipated research or development of the employer." Cal. Lab. Code § 2870(a)(1). Sections 2870 through 2872 of the California Labor Code, however, prohibit an employer from requiring an employee to assign an invention that the employee developed entirely on his or her own time without using the employer's equipment, supplies, facilities, or trade secret information. Cal. Lab. Code §§ 2870-2872. An employer has no right to claim ownership over trade secret information that employees acquired *prior to* the employment. *Rigging Int'l Maint. Co. v. Gwin*, 128 Cal. App. 3d 594, 613-14 (1982).

Any employment agreement which includes an employee's assignment of inventions must contain written notification to the employee that the agreement does not apply to an invention which "qualifies fully under section 2870[,]" meaning an invention that section 2870 provides that the employee may not be required to assign.

In determining the degree to which employers can require employees to assign rights in ***post***-employment development, such hold-over clauses have been strictly construed and held unenforceable at times. In *Whitewater West Industries, Ltd. v. Alleshouse*, 981 F.3d 1045, 1057-58 (9th Cir. 2020), the Ninth Circuit invalidated a post-employment invention assignment agreement, concluding "it is at least a fair reading of [section] 2870(a)—and given the duty to harmonize it with [section] 16600 it is ultimately a necessary reading—that it simply does not apply to post-employment inventions." *See also Armorlite Lens Co. v. Campbell*, 340 F. Supp. 273, 275 (S.D. Cal. 1972) (deeming a one-year hold-over clause void as an unreasonable restraint on trade). However, where the post-employment rights build upon trade secrets of the prior employer, courts have limited the employee's use of such properties. *See, e.g.*, *GCA Corp. v. Chance*, 217 U.S.P.Q. (BNA) 718, 721

(N.D. Cal. 1982) (finding nondisclosure agreements signed by employees to protect trade secrets to be beyond the reach of section 2870 of the California Labor Code).

5. Provisions Affecting the Right to Injunctive Relief

Employment agreements sometimes include language requiring the employee to agree that in the event of a breach, irreparable harm will occur and/or the employer is entitled to injunctive relief. However, individual judges may ignore the contract and require proof of what is ordinarily required by law. See Chapter 12.

§ 4.04 Protecting Trade Secrets Through Nondisclosure Agreements (NDAs)

A. Applicable to Employees and Others Who Have a Need to Know Trade Secrets

Express written promises not to use or disclose trade secrets (except as authorized) are often included in employment agreements, independent contractor agreements, and other legal documents produced in the course of creating relationships in which trade secrets may be disclosed, used or developed. NDA provisions may also be included in personnel policies and employee handbooks, which may be deemed contractually binding. *See Guz v. Bechtel Nat'l, Inc.*, 24 Cal.4th 317, 344–45 (2000).

B. Advantages of Written NDAs

While the existence or nonexistence of an NDA is not necessarily determinative, it may be relevant to the right to relief from perceived misappropriation. *Hollingsworth Solderless Terminal Co. v. Turley*, 622 F.2d 1324, 1334 n.7 (9th Cir. 1980); *Bayline Partners L.P. v. Weyerhaeuser Co.*, 31 U.S.P.Q.2d (BNA) 1051, 1055 (N.D. Cal. 1994).

C. Risk of Failing to Update NDAs

The failure to update an NDA may result in loss of later acquired properties. Thus, the terms describing the protected matter must not only be carefully drafted so that all matters claimed to be trade secrets are included, but also the agreements themselves should be reviewed and revised periodically, as appropriate.

D. Risk of Overbroad NDAs

An NDA that, on its face, extends to non-confidential information may be deemed an invalid restraint on employee mobility. *See, e.g., Brown v. TGS Mgmt. Co., LLC*, 57 Cal. App. 5th 303, 317–318 (2020). An employer should take care to consider whether the scope of the information governed by the NDA it intends to require will, as a practical matter, deprive the employee from engaging in his or her profession post-employment.

If applicable, employers may consider asserting National Labor Relations Act (NLRA) preemption as a defense to a state law claims challenging an overbroad NDA. However, in *Doe v. Google, Inc.*, 54 Cal. App. 5th 948, 961 (2020), the appellate court ruled that NLRA did not preempt state law claims that a confidentiality provision was overbroad in violation of Business and Professions

Code section 16600. The court reasoned that the plaintiffs' challenge related to California's "traditional local concern" of protecting worker mobility, and "may reasonably be seen as peripheral to the NLRA," which instead focuses on the rights to join unions and engage in collective bargaining. *Id.* at 961-62.

E. Risk of Interference with NLRA Rights

An NDA may be challenged on the ground that it interferes with rights afforded to employees under the National Labor Relations Act (NLRA), such as the right to join unions or engage in collective bargaining. For example, in *Legacy Charter, LLC d/b/a Legacy Traditional School*, 2018 WL 3955527 (N.L.R.B. Div. of Judges 2018), a teacher challenged a confidentiality provision as violating the NLRA on the grounds of overbreadth. The judge disagreed, finding the provision to be "clearly directed at preventing disclosure of business information that is both confidential and proprietary" and that it "would not potentially prohibit disclosure of" terms and conditions of employment or to interfere with an employees' rights under the NLRA. *Legacy Charter*, 2018 WL 3955527. Nevertheless, employers may want to consider expressly carving out from the employee NDA activities protected by the NLRA.

F. Strategic Considerations When Drafting NDAs

The following is a checklist of items to be considered when drafting an NDA:

- Define the parties bound by the agreement. Make sure they *each* sign the agreement that purports to bind them.
- Define carefully the trade secrets or the protected confidential information.

  (1) Include the categories of information to be protected.

  (2) How specific or general the categories are identified in the NDA depends on the circumstances, but avoid inadvertent disclosure of the substance of the trade secrets through overly detailed description of the matters to be protected.

  (3) Avoid including matters not reasonably or properly protectable (such as the employee's general knowledge or information in the public domain).

- Define express exclusions carefully.

  (1) Avoid over-inclusion, which may serve to defeat a later claim for protection.

  (2) Consider excluding information created or discovered by the receiving party prior to or independent of the relationship.

  (3) Consider excluding information that is generally known.

(4) Consider excluding information that is readily available to the public or to those in the employer's industry.

(5) Consider excluding information or disclosures that must be excluded by law (such as the employee's wage information, or subpoenaed information).

- Define the obligations of the receiving party.

    (1) Include affirmative promises not to use or disclose the protected matter outside the limitations set by the agreement.

    (2) Include affirmative promises not to induce others to use or disclose protected matter outside the limitations set by the agreement.

- Considering specifying a time frame for protection, including throughout the employment period.

- Include an affirmative obligation to continue to protect the information even after the relationship is terminated.

- Define the mechanism for identifying protected matter.

Some NDAs include provisions stating that all matters to be protected will be labeled clearly. Note, however, that labeling requirements can be cumbersome to enforce and there is a danger that something will fall through the cracks. In addition, information may be exchanged orally. Alternatively, include a provision that all information will be presumed confidential unless otherwise agreed upon in writing. The danger is that such all-inclusive provisions may later be challenged as overly broad and not constituting reasonable measures to maintain secrecy.

- Define the security measures for maintenance of confidentiality.

    (1) The receiving party should affirmatively promise to use security measures which are at least as good as the methods it uses to protect its own information.

    (2) In addition, specify the exact security measure expected to be maintained.

- Define procedures for treatment of protected information upon termination of the relationship.

    (1) E.g., upon termination, all information should be returned to the disclosing party and all copies destroyed. Address the disposition of work product created using the other party's confidential information and of work product created using both parties' confidential information.

(2) Define procedures for returning information and destroying copies, and specify who is to receive the information and where it is to be shipped.

(3) Consider addressing in the agreement the disposition of the confidential information where one party breaches. Depending on the circumstances, the non-breaching party may or may not be entitled to continue using the breaching party's confidential information.

- Consider addressing the ownership of information (e.g., which party will own jointly developed information).

- Consider forum-selection provisions (e.g., is private arbitration a more favorable forum to maintain the confidentiality of the information or to obtain a faster resolution, or are there disadvantages of arbitration that outweigh the perceived benefits).

- Consider including an attorneys' fees and costs provision.

- Consider including a provision that the agreement is specifically enforceable and breaches may be enjoined to prevent irreparable injury.

- Establish procedures to handle potential audit and compliance issues.

(1) Include provisions allowing for inspection rights at any facility where the receiving party may house the trade secrets. Other auditing methods may also be necessary.

(2) Include provisions to account for the receipt of trade secrets and protection thereof by employees and independent contractors of the recipient.

It is important that form or sample agreements (or our suggestions for consideration herein) not be blindly followed and any NDA be tailored specifically to the particular situation at hand.

§ 4.05 Protecting Trade Secrets Through Noncompetition Agreements

Noncompetition agreements are used in various situations and are not specifically limited to the protection of trade secrets. However, noncompetition agreements have particular significance for trade secret owners because they afford a mechanism to reduce the threat of misappropriation.

A. Public Policy Embodied by Section 16600 of the California Business and Professions Code

"During the term of employment, an employer is entitled to its employees' 'undivided loyalty.'" *Fowler v. Varian Assocs.*, 196 Cal. App. 3d 34, 41 (1987) (quoting *Sequoia Vacuum Sys. v.*

Stransky, 229 Cal. App. 2d 281, 287 (1964)). *See also Angelica Textile Services, Inc. v. Park*, 220 Cal. App. 4th 495, 509 (2013); *Stokes v. Dole Nut Co.*, 41 Cal. App. 4th 285, 296 (1995).

However, California has a strong public policy disfavoring post-employment covenants not to compete embodied in section 16600 of the California Business and Professions Code, which provides "Except as provided in this chapter, every contract by which anyone is restrained from engaging in a lawful profession, trade, or business of any kind is to that extent void." *See also Edwards v. Arthur Andersen LLP*, 44 Cal. 4th 937, 945-46 (2008); *Cont'l Car-Na-Var Corp. v. Moseley*, 24 Cal. 2d 104, 110 (1944).

1. Construing Section 16600 of the California Business and Professions Code

Post-termination noncompete provisions. Under California law, post-termination covenants not to compete are enforceable under limited circumstances. *See, e.g.,* Cal. Bus. & Prof. Code § 16601 (sale of business exception to Section 16600's prohibition against covenants not to compete); Cal. Bus. & Prof. Code § 16602 (dissolution of partnership exception to section 16600's prohibition against covenants not to compete).

In *Edwards*, in holding that the former employee's agreement not to solicit the employer's customers was invalid under section 16600, the California Supreme Court rejected a line of cases that had embraced a "narrow restraint" doctrine as an exception to section 16600. Under the "narrow restraint" doctrine, some courts had allowed a noncompetition agreement if the agreement only restrained a portion of a profession, trade or business. *Edwards*, 44 Cal. 4th at 950.

After *Edwards,* whether there is a common law "trade secret exception" (i.e., noncompete agreements are permitted if to protect trade secrets) to section 16600's prohibition remains unsettled but the viability of the trade secret exception is in doubt. *See Dowell v. Biosense Webster, Inc.*, 179 Cal. App. 4th 564, 577 (2009) *Ret. Grp. v. Galante*, 176 Cal. App. 4th 1226, 1238 (2009); *Depuy Synthes Sales, Inc. v. Stryker Corp.*, 2020 U.S. Dist. LEXIS 199271, at *28 (C.D. Cal. Sep. 29, 2020); *PSC Indus. Outsourcing, LP v. Kodysz*, No. 1:13–cv–0964, 2013 WL 3354452, at *3 (E.D. Cal. July 3, 2013); *Artec Group, Inc. v. Klimov*, 2016 U.S. Dist. LEXIS 170194, at *8 (N.D. Cal. Dec. 8, 2016); *Green Payment Solutions, LLC v. First Data Merch. Servs. Corp.*, 2019 U.S. Dist. LEXIS 165652, at *14 (C.D. Cal. Aug. 5, 2019). However, there are other courts that appear to think that the trade secret exception may still exist (although they do not necessarily find it applicable to the noncompete agreements before them). *See, e.g., Power Integrations, Inc. v. De Lara*, No. 20-cv-410-MMA (MSB), 2020 U.S. Dist. LEXIS 52724, at *38-39 (S.D. Cal. March 26, 2020); *Conversion Logic, Inc. v. Measured, Inc.*, 2019 U.S. Dist. LEXIS 215195, at *15 (C.D. Cal. Dec. 13, 2019); *West Air Charter, Inc. v. Schembari*, 2017 U.S. Dist. LEXIS 217520, *14 (C.D. Cal. Dec. 14, 2017); *Gatan, Inc. v. Nion Co.*, 2016 U.S. Dist. LEXIS 42764, at *7 (N.D. Cal. Mar. 30, 2016); *Henry Schein, Inc. v. Cook*, 2016 U.S. Dist. LEXIS 81369, at *19 (N.D. Cal. Jun. 22, 2016).

In-term noncompete provisions. Although a section 16600 challenge is most often made in the context of a post-termination noncompetition agreement (*e.g.*, contractual restrictions on activities after the relationship ends), in-term noncompetition agreements (*e.g.*, contractual restrictions on activities during the relationship) have been challenged under section 16600.

Currently, although the California Supreme Court has not addressed the issue squarely, the general view among Court of Appeals in California is that an *in-term* contractual prohibition against employee competition with the employer does not violate section 16600. *Angelica Textile Services, Inc. v. Park,* 220 Cal. App. 4th 495, 509 (2013); *Techno Lite, Inc. v. Emcod, LLC*, 44 Cal.App.5th 462, 471-472 (2020).

2. Ramifications of An Invalid Noncompete Agreement

Use of an employee noncompetition agreement that is invalid under section 16600 may give rise to liability to the employer. *See Couch v. Morgan Stanley & Co., Inc.*, 2015 WL 4716297, at *21 (E.D. Cal. Aug. 7, 2015); *D'sa v. Playhut, Inc.,* 85 Cal. App. 4th 927, 932 (2000); *Application Grp., Inc. v. Hunter Grp., Inc.*, 61 Cal. App. 4th 881, 906-07 (1998).

Acquiescence to another's use of an invalid noncompetition agreement also may give rise to liability. *See Silguero v. Creteguard, Inc.*, 187 Cal. App. 4th 60 (2010). In that case, the court held that, given California's "settled legislative policy in favor of open competition and employee mobility[,]" an employee has a claim for wrongful termination in violation of public policy against a subsequent employer that terminates her due to her noncompete agreement with a former employer. *Silguero*, 187 Cal. App. 4th at 63, 67-68.

Occasionally, a party will argue that if an agreement contains a provision that is void under section 16600, the entire agreement is unenforceable. *See, e.g., Thomas Weisel Partners LLC v. BNP Paribas*, No. C 07-6198 MHP, 2010 WL 546497, at *7 (N.D. Cal. Feb. 10, 2010) (ruling that "[t]his harsh remedy [was] inappropriate …" there.); *Roadrunner Intermodal Services, LLC v. T.G.S. Trans., Inc.*, 2019 WL 1400093, at *10 (E.D. Cal. Mar. 28, 2019) (reforming an otherwise overbroad non-compete provision and explaining: "While the undersigned recognizes that courts should generally be hesitant to reform the parties' contract, the narrowing of the geographical scope of the non-competition provision is appropriate in this case" and enforcing the non-competition provision "to prevent Cox from competing with Roadrunner only in areas where Central Cal [which had previously been acquired by Roadrunner] carried on business and had established goodwill."). *Cf. Arthur J. Gallagher & Co. v. Tarantino*, 2020 WL 6415272, at *9 (N.D. Cal. Nov. 2, 2020) (invalidating the non-compete provisions in two former employees' employment agreements and refusing to "blue pencil" or alter the problematic timing and activity restrictions in those provisions); *Applied Materials, Inc. v. Advanced Micro-Fabrication Equip. (Shanghai) Co.*, 630 F. Supp. 2d 1084, 1091 (N.D. Cal. 2009) (court ruling that it was not permitted to limit the application of the assignment clause, which was invalid under section 16600).

3. Employee Non-Solicitation Provisions

Although there is no definitive California Supreme Court case invalidating post-term employee agreements that prohibit solicitation of the employer's personnel, the majority of courts appear to treat them like other post-term noncompete agreements (*e.g.*, prohibitions against soliciting customers or working in the employer's market). *See, e.g., AMN Healthcare Inc. v. Aya Healthcare Servs., Inc.*, 28 Cal.App.5th 923, 936, 938-39 (2018) (invalidating the nonsolicitation provision in the context of a recruiter context); *Barker v. Insight Global*, 16-cv-07186, 2019 WL 176260, at *3 (N.D. Cal Jan. 11, 2019) (invalidating an employee nonsolicitation provision outside of the recruiter context); *WeRide Corp. v. Kun Huang*, 379 F.Supp. 3d 834, 851 (N.D. Cal. Apr. 1, 2019) (same); *see also Depuy Synthes Sales, Inc. v. Stryker Corp.*, 2020 U.S. Dist. LEXIS 199271, *29-30 (C.D. Cal. Sept. 29, 2020); *Green Payment Solutions, LLC v. First Data Merch. Servs. Corp.*, 2019 U.S. Dist. LEXIS 165652, *13-14 (C.D. Cal. Aug. 5, 2019); *Sricom, Inc. v. Ebislogic, Inc.*, No. 12-cv-00904-LHK, 2012 WL 4051222, at *4-5 (N.D. Cal. Sept. 13, 2012); *Thomas Weisel Partners*, 2010 WL 546497, at *6. *But see Hamilton v. Juul Labs Inc.* 20-cv-03710-EMC, 2020 WL 5500377, *7 (N.D. Cal. Sept. 11, 2020) (employee non-solicitation provision potentially enforceable where the plaintiff did "not allege that the [covenant] prevents her from engaging in her profession like the plaintiffs in *AMN* who were recruiters"); *Solutionz Videoconferencing Inc. v. Davidson* SACV 19-01132 AG (DFMx), 2019 WL 6872904, *2 (C.D. Cal. Aug. 22, 2019) (denying motion to dismiss employer breach of non-solicitation provision, on the ground that the facts in *AMN* were "unique," and "the present law in the California is not as clear as defendant claims.").

4. Business to Business Non-Competes

In contrast to employee non-compete agreements, non-competition agreements *between businesses* are enforceable so long as they are reasonable. *Ixchel Pharma, LLC v. Biogen, Inc.*, 9 Cal.5th 1130, 1150 (2020) ("section 16600 is best read not to render void per se all contractual restraints on business dealings, but rather to subject such restraints to a rule of reason.").

5. Assignment of Inventions Agreements

Assignment of inventions agreements may also be attacked under section 16600 of the California Business and Professions Code. *See Applied Materials, Inc.*, 630 F. Supp. 2d 1084, at 1086, 1088-89, 1090-91 (ruling that the assignment clause was a post-employment penalty that violates the public policy codified in section 16600 because the assignment provision was overly broad with respect to both subject matter and temporal scope; "[it] touche[d] post-employment inventions, regardless of when they were conceived or whether they were based on Applied's confidential information, [and therefore] the Clause necessarily operate[d] as a restriction on employee mobility.").

6. "Interpreting" Noncompete Agreements versus "Re-Writing" Them

Under California law, when interpreting a noncompete provision subject to section 16600, a court '"must . . . construe [it] to be lawful if possible."' *Jones v. Humanscale Corp.*, 130 Cal. App. 4th 401, 411 (2005) (citing Cal. Civ. Code §§ 1643, 3541 and *Loral Corp.*, 174 Cal. App. 3d at 278-79); *State Farm Mut. Auto. Ins. v. Dempster*, 174 Cal. App. 2d 418, 427 (1959) (holding the trial court properly limited the enforcement of the noncompete agreement to the trade secrets at issue, "following the rule that a construction of a noncompetitive covenant to render it lawful is preferable to an interpretation causing the opposite result") (citations omitted). *But see Brown v. TGS Mgmt. Co., LLC*, 57 Cal. App. 5th 303, 317–318 (2020) (invalidating an overbroad NDA).

However, according to other case law, in construing a noncompete agreement, a court may not re-write the basic subject matter of the noncompete agreement. *See, e.g., Strategix, Ltd. v. Infocrossing West, Inc.*, 142 Cal. App. 4th 1068, 1074 (2006) (declining to rewrite an overbroad covenant not to solicit buyer's employees and customers); *Kolani v. Gluska*, 64 Cal. App. 4th 402, 408 (1998) (trial court properly declined to rewrite the broad covenant not to compete into a narrow bar on theft of confidential information). *Cf. Comedy Club II, Inc. v. Improv W. Assocs.*, 553 F.3d 1277, 1293 (9th Cir. 2009) (district court should enforce the arbitrator's injunctive relief only as to those counties where the plaintiff operates Improv clubs) citing *Armendariz v. Found. Health Psychare Servs. Inc.*, 24 Cal. 4th 83, 123 (2000) ("overbroad covenants not to compete may be restricted temporally and geographically") (citation omitted).

It is, thus, difficult to predict how a judge will draw the line between permissible interpreting and impermissible re-writing of a noncompete agreement.

B. Additional Considerations When Drafting Noncompetition Provisions

- **Statute of Frauds**

A covenant not to compete must be in writing so as to comply with the statute of frauds. *Summerhays v. Scheu*, 10 Cal. App. 2d 574, 576-77 (1935).

- **Choice of Law**

California courts do not necessarily feel bound by out-of-state noncompete provisions. *Application Group*, 61 Cal. App. 4th at 892, 895 96, 902. *See also Arkley v. Aon Risk Servs. Cos., Inc.*, No. CV 12–1966 DSF (RZx), 2012 WL 2674980, at *3 (C.D. Cal. June 13, 2012) (ruling that California law applied because application of Illinois law—which permits covenants not to compete—"creates a conflict with a fundamental policy of California law", namely, that "[s]uch covenants are specifically unenforceable under California Business and Professions Code § 16600").

However, a business may be able to enforce outside of California a covenant not to compete to be performed by a party in California. *See Advanced Bionics Corp. v. Medtronic, Inc.*, 29 Cal. 4th 697, 706-07 (2002) ("[although] California has a strong interest in protecting its employees from noncompetition agreements under section 16600," the existence of the policy does not authorize enjoining out-of-state legal proceedings to enforce a covenant not to compete); *Biosense Webster, Inc. v. Superior Court*, 135 Cal. App. 4th 827, 836-37 (2006) (applying the same rule to enjoining prospective litigation to enforce a noncompetition agreement). *But see* Cal. Lab. Code § 925 (prohibiting foreign choice-of-law provisions in employment agreements unless employee represented by counsel) (see, *supra*, Section 4.03.B.3).

- **Forum Selection**

Even if a court sitting in California is unwilling to enforce a choice-of-foreign law provision in light of section 16600, it still may be willing to enforce a choice-of-foreign forum provision. *See, e.g., Hartstein v. Rembrandt IP Solutions, LLC*, No. 12–2270 SC, 2012 WL 3075084, at *6 (N.D. Cal. July 30, 2012); *see also Universal Operations Risk Mgmt., LLC v. Global Rescue, LLC*, No. C 11–5969 SBA, 2012 WL 2792444 (N.D. Cal. July 9, 2012); *Loughlin v. Ventraq, Inc.*, No. 10–CV–2624–IEG BGS, 2011 WL 1303641, at *7 (S.D. Cal. Apr. 5, 2011); *Besag v. Custom Decorators, Inc.*, No. CV08–05463 JSW, 2009 WL 330934, at *4 (N.D. Cal. Feb. 10, 2009); *Mahoney v. Depuy Orthopaedics, Inc.*, CIVF 07–1321 AWI SMS, 2007 WL 3341389, at *8 (E.D. Cal. Nov. 8, 2007); *Swenson v. T-Mobile USA, Inc.*, 415 F. Supp. 2d 1101, 1104 (S.D. Cal. 2006). *But see* Cal. Lab.

Code § 925 (prohibiting foreign forum selection provisions in employment agreement unless employee represented by counsel) (*see, supra*, Section 4.03.B.3).

- **Arbitration Provision**

Courts reviewing an arbitrator's enforcement of a noncompete agreement apply varying standards of review. *See Jones*, 130 Cal. App. 4th at 411 (holding that the arbitrator's findings and decision on the enforceability of the covenant not to compete were not palpably erroneous under California law; consequently, the trial court erred in vacating the award because it disagreed with the arbitrator's findings on the applicable law and the enforceability of the noncompetition clause); *Brown v. TGS Mgmt. Co., LLC*, 57 Cal. App. 5th 303, 318-19 (2020) (refusing to enforce arbitration award because the employee confidentiality agreement at issue constituted a de facto noncompete which was unlawful under section 16600); *Comedy Club II*, 553 F.3d at 1293 (holding the arbitrator's ruling upholding the covenant not to compete ignored section 16600 and thus was a manifest disregard of the law)

Chapter 5
ADVISING THE CORPORATE CLIENT WHEN AN EMPLOYEE DEPARTS FOR A COMPETITOR

By: Janet Craycroft, Esq.[1]

---

[1] The views expressed in this chapter are those of the author and not Intel Corporation.

§ 5.01 Introduction

In 2020 corporations around the globe were caught off guard when a virus was unleashed on the world. The ensuing government-ordered lockdowns resulted in millions of employees being barred from going to their places of work. As corporations around the globe shuttered their doors, employees who were able to work remotely transformed their homes into remote offices.

Working remotely has been an option for many employees prior to COVID-19. Thus, many companies have experience processing the departure of remote employees departing for a competitor. With the pandemic, however, the numbers of employees working remotely at locations other than their employer's facilities exploded as this was the only option available to keep businesses running. Now after over a year, it has become evident to corporate employers that many employees working remotely can maintain productivity without having to be co-located in an office. As a result, corporations of all sizes and in different industries are considering how to support employees who now want the flexibility of working remotely. Many are considering models where employees are permitted to work part-time from locations other than their employers' facilities also known as "telework." The debate, adoption, and success of telework is in its early stages. It remains to be seen what telework models will work and for whom. However, it appears fairly certain that many corporate employers will end up allowing employees the flexibility of teleworking. The acceptance of telework as an option for employees means corporations will need to include in their termination process considerations presented by departing teleworking employees.

This chapter covers the fundamentals for protecting trade secrets when an employee departs for a competitor. These fundamentals have not changed. It also includes key learnings from the pandemic to help corporations in reviewing their current practices to address the added risks presented by departing employees who have been working remotely. It is important to note that corporations are grappling with how to safeguard corporate trade secrets in this new world order. This chapter does not cover the myriad of challenges organizations face on a daily basis as a result of telework.[2] It does, however, focus on the specific issues related to employees who leave for a competitor and how to protect a corporate client's trade secrets in such a scenario.

A. Background

In February 2013, Symantec Corporation and the Ponemon Institute released the results of a survey of employees working in six different countries: the United States, Brazil, China, France, Korea, and the United Kingdom. "What's Yours is Mine: How Employees are Putting Your

[2] For an overview of the numerous issues presented by a teleworkforce, the October 2020 Ponemon Institute LLC's report entitled, "Cybersecurity in the Remote Work Era: A Global Risk Report," is a good start. This report, sponsored by Keeper Security, Inc., shares the results and analysis of Ponemon's survey of 2,215 IT and IT security personnel in the United States, United Kingdom, DACH, Benelux, Scandinavia, Australia and New Zealand. *See October 2020 Ponemon Institute LLC Report sponsored by Keeper Security, Inc.; see also "The Impact Of Covid-19 Is Forcing Companies To Adopt New Technology, October 30, 2020*" (https://www.forbes.com/sites/kevinanderton/2020/11/30/the-impact-of-covid-19-is-forcing-companies-to-adopt-new-technology-infographic/?sh=613d2b696089); "*How the Covid-19 Pandemic is Impacting Cyber Security Worldwide*," (https://innovationatwork.ieee.org/how-the-covid-19-pandemic-is-impacting-cyber-security-worldwide/).

Intellectual Property at Risk," (February 2013).[3] The results from the 3,317 respondents reflect a disturbing portrait of what corporate employees may really think about corporate trade secrets:

- 50% of employees who left/lost a job admitted to taking their employer's confidential information.
- 40% plan to use the confidential information in their new jobs.

The fact that 50% of departing employees—even in this limited sample—admitted to stealing their employer's confidential information and 40% of them planned to use the confidential information in their new jobs is shocking. However, consider the following data also from the same survey:

- Only 38% say their manager views data protection as a business priority.
- 47% say their organization takes no action when employees take sensitive information.
- 51% think it is acceptable to take corporate data because their company does not strictly enforce policies.

These data demonstrate that corporations have not done enough to educate their workforce and enforce their own policies. If companies wish to prevent departing employees from taking trade secret information to another employer with the intent to use it in their new jobs, they need be more effective in mitigating the risks posed by their own departing employees.

As discussed in this chapter, protecting a company's trade secrets when an employee departs the company should begin the moment an employee is hired. Starting with the importance of establishing a culture of information security through policies, procedures, and education, this chapter sets forth practical steps companies should consider adopting to guard against the theft of trade secrets by departing employees. This chapter then discusses the actions companies may take when a departing employee is suspected of taking sensitive information. With a prioritized and comprehensive approach to trade secret protection targeted at employees, companies should be able to avoid mirroring the types of statistics reflected by the Symantec/Ponemon survey.

---

[3] This survey is no longer available online. The data, however, are referenced in other resources that are available. *See, e.g.,* "Trade Secret Protection Best Practices Hiring Competitors' Employees and Protecting the Company When Competitors Hire Your," Robert Milligan et al.
(https://www.tradesecretslaw.com/wp-content/uploads/sites/232/2015/10/Trade-Secret-Protection-Best-Practices.pdf);
"What's Yours is Mine: How Employees are Putting Your Intellectual Property at Risk,"
(https://www.ciosummits.com/media/solution_spotlight/OnlineAssett_Symantec_WhatsYoursIsMine.pdf);
"Is Stolen IP Walking in the Door with New Employees,"
(https://www.cio.com/article/2388472/is-stolen-ip-walking-in-the-door-with-new-employees-.html.);
"Symantec Study Shows Employees Steal Corporate Data And Don't Believe It's Wrong," February 6, 2013 (https://investor.nortonlifelock.com/About/Investors/press-releases/press-release-details/2013/Symantec-Study-Shows-Employees-Steal-Corporate-Data-And-Dont-Believe-Its-Wrong/default.aspx);
"Workers Stealing Company Data," The results of the 2013 study are consistent with an earlier 2009 study "More Than Half Of Ex-Employees Admit To Stealing Company Data According To New Study, Ponemon Institute and Symantec Corporation (Feb. 23, 2009), available at
https://investor.nortonlifelock.com/About/Investors/press-releases/press-release-details/2009/MoreThan-Half-Of-Ex-Employees-Admit-To-Stealing-Company-Data-According-To-NewStudy/default.aspx.

§ 5.02 Proactive Steps to Deter Theft of Trade Secrets by Departing Employees Should Begin When They are Hired

A recent report estimated the cost of trade secret theft had reached up to $1.7 trillion annually.[4] In another survey, 90% of cybersecurity professionals who responded to the survey felt vulnerable to threats coming from trusted and authorized users inside the company, i.e., employees.[5] Yet, in order to create the intellectual property that drives a company's success, employees necessarily must have access to such intellectual property. In fact, it is often the employees who are creating the intellectual property.

Companies cannot rely on employee loyalty to safeguard their trade secrets when they leave the company. In a 2018 survey of 2,000 full-time, U.S. employees, WestMonroe found that while 82% felt a high degree of loyalty to their employer, 59% of them would readily leave for a job with a better offer.[6] Perhaps of more interest – though probably not surprising - for corporate employers the problem is generational. Millennials – those between the ages of 25 and 28 – do not see themselves remaining with the same employer beyond 5 years. This translates to more frequent turnover requiring corporations to process more departing employees than before as employees are more apt to leave for other opportunities[7]

Given this state of affairs, it is essential for companies to take action well before an employee leaves the company to protect their trade secrets. By putting in place certain measures from the time an employee is hired, a company can help assure that when an employee leaves, the employee will understand his obligations. In addition, proactive measures may not only help deter potential misappropriation, they may enable a company to detect it when it occurs so that immediate action can be taken. So, if a departing employee chooses to take trade secret information with him when he leaves, the company will be better able to take action to protect its trade secrets.

A. Establishing A Corporate Culture that Respects Intellectual Property Rights & Obligations

A fundamental first step for a company to protect its trade secrets is to establish a corporate culture that respects intellectual property because it helps employees understand their obligations. Such a "culture of information security" also promotes protection of a company's trade secret assets because employees will be empowered to proactively safeguard those trade secrets and be vigilant about any activity they perceive as inconsistent with protecting the company's trade secrets.

---

[4] "45% of execs failing on trade secret basis: report," World Intellectual Property Review, June 9, 2021 (https://www.worldipreview.com/news/45-of-execs-failing-on-trade-secrets-basics-report-21429).

[5] A 2018 survey of 472 cybersecurity professionals (http://haystax.com/wp-content/uploads/2018/02/Insider-Threat-Report_Haystax-2018.pdf)

[6] "Keeping Employees Loyal in a Tight Labor Market," September 2018 (https://www.westmonroe.com/perspectives/report/keeping-employees-loyal-in-a-tight-labor-market)

[7] Id.

1. Agreements and Policies for Employees

a. The Standard Employee Agreement

Establishing a corporate culture that respects intellectual property rights starts the moment an employee is hired. Every incoming employee should sign an employee agreement that recites the obligation to protect intellectual property. Covenants such as the following are something that employees, particularly in Silicon Valley, are familiar with and routinely execute:

Sample #1:

I will hold in confidence and will not disclose, both during and after my employment with the company, any proprietary information or trade secret of my employer or of any third party to which I gain access pursuant to my employment ("Confidential Information"). I will use the Confidential Information only for the benefit of and at the direction of my employer. I will disclose the Confidential Information to others only with written authorization from my employer, except to the extent I am authorized to do so in the course of my duties.

I will hold the Confidential Information in confidence until such information becomes public and rightfully known, or for the maximum period of time for maintaining trade secrets as permitted by law in the jurisdiction in which I am employed, if such time period is shorter.

I agree to not make unauthorized copies of such Confidential Information. I agree to return to my employer immediately upon termination of employment, or upon request by my employer, all tangible forms of such Confidential Information.

Another version of this covenant provides:

Sample #2:

This Agreement concerns trade secrets, confidential business and technical information, and know-how not generally known to the pubic ("Confidential Information") which is acquired or produced by me in connection with my employment. Confidential Information may include, without limitation, information on the company's organizations, staffing, finance, structure, information or employee performance, compensation of others, research and development, manufacturing and marketing, files, keys, certificates, passwords, and other computer information, as well as information that the company receives from others under an obligation of confidentiality. I agree: (a) to use such information only in the performance of my duties; (b) to hold such information in confidence and trust; and (c) to use all reasonable precautions to assure that such information is not disclosed to unauthorized persons or used in an unauthorized manner, both during and after my employment.

Employment Agreements with provisions like these are important, but only the first step in a strategy for establishing a culture that respects intellectual property rights.

b. A Policy on Information Security

Incoming employees should acknowledge in writing a policy that defines the employee's responsibility with respect to securing the company's intellectual property. These types of policies are often referred to as "Information Security" policies. A key component of such a policy is that it should explicitly provide that each employee is "personally responsible" for safeguarding corporate trade secrets and intellectual property. While the Employee Agreement is a contractual obligation agreed to by the employee, this is the employer's opportunity to provide details about this obligation. For example, language such as the following may be useful:

As an employee you are required to:

1. Protect the confidentiality of the company's trade secrets from unauthorized use or disclosure.

2. Hold in confidence and not use the company's confidential information and trade secrets except for the benefit of the company.

3. Be personally responsible for protecting the company's trade secrets.

4. Report any unauthorized access, use or disclosure of the company's trade secret information to your manager or the legal department.

5. Not seek access to confidential information without appropriate need-to-know and authorization from your manager or the legal department.

While the Employee Agreement focuses on the employee's personal obligations regarding his or her own conduct, this policy makes it clear that the employee has an affirmative obligation to report potential misconduct by others which is essential to a comprehensive strategy for protecting against employee theft of trade secrets.[8]

c. Policies on Authorized Devices and Limited Personal Use

With the emergence of telework, the need to be both proactive and vigilant is heightened. A recently released survey of 314 senior corporate executives located in China, France, Germany, Singapore, the UK and the US across sectors (consumer goods and retail; finance; energy and natural resources) found that 36% planned to increase monitoring of employees' electronic activity over the next two years.[9]

---

[8] *See, e.g.,* "How to Confront Intellectual Property Theft by Employees," July 12, 2020 (https://www.shrm.org/ResourcesAndTools/hr-topics/risk-management/Pages/How-to-Confront-Intellectual-Property-Theft-by-Employees.aspx).

[9] *See* "45% of execs failing on trade secret basis: report," World Intellectual Property Review, June 9, 2021 (https://www.worldipreview.com/news/45-of-execs-failing-on-trade-secrets-basics-report-21429); Cybersecurity Insiders in partnership with the Information Security Community on LinkedIn worked with Crowd Research Partners to identify the latest trends and challenges regarding insider threats as well as solutions to prevent or mitigate insider attacks. Their 2018 survey showed that monitoring is accelerating with 94% of organizations deploying some method of monitoring

To facilitate monitoring, companies should have in place two policies. First, there should be a policy that permits only company-provided and company-managed devices to be used for work (e.g., laptops and mobile devices). Employees should not be permitted to use personal devices which the company cannot properly secure or track.

Second, companies should consider a "limited personal use" policy for the corporate systems and devices employees use to conduct business. In particular, a company should be clear that its assets and equipment are not intended as storage mechanisms for an employee's private information. And employees should be told they have no expectation of privacy when using a company's assets beyond any expectation specifically provided by applicable law. Employees should also understand that the company may monitor its network traffic, all devices that connect to its network, and if applicable, employee electronic activity.

d. A Policy on Discipline and Discharge

In addition to what may be regarded as a standard covenant in an Employee Agreement and Information Security policy, companies should consider having new employees execute a document that details the consequences for failure to comply with their obligations to protect the company's trade secrets. A document like this helps put incoming employees on notice of the consequences of misconduct. An example of such a document is as follows:

> Policy on Discipline and Discharge: The purpose of this policy is to describe the rules for disciplining and discharging employees. Disciplinary actions are taken to reinforce the expectations, rules, regulations, policies, procedures, etc., required to be followed by employees.

To that end, the purpose of disciplinary actions not only serves to put employees on notice that they have failed to meet the company's expectations in these areas, but also to give employees an opportunity to meet these expectations.

Examples of conduct that may lead to immediate termination:

1. Disclosing or using the company's trade secrets or confidential information without proper authorization.

2. Disclosing or using trade secrets or confidential information belonging to a former employer.

3. Failing to follow the company's security procedures to safeguard the company's trade secret or confidential information from unauthorized publication, disclosure, or use.

---

users and 93% monitoring access to sensitive data. With the increase in the number of employees teleworking, monitoring is potentially a corporation's best defense against theft of trade secrets. (http://haystax.com/wp-content/uploads/2018/02/Insider-Threat-Report_Haystax-2018.pdf)

4. Failing to report the theft of company trade secrets or other property by other employees.

5. Removing any company property without proper authorization.

6. Stealing or being involved in stealing the company's property.

7. Violating federal or state law.

The above policy is intended to give notice to employees that, at a minimum, they may expect to lose their jobs if they fail to safeguard the company's trade secrets. Moreover, it sets the tone for how seriously the company views the protection of its intellectual property by its employees.

e. A Code of Conduct

In addition to the foregoing, many companies have adopted a code of conduct. At Intel Corporation, for example, employees must acknowledge Intel's Code of Conduct.[10] This code of conduct—which is published on Intel's public web site—provides as follows:

> Intellectual property rights are crucial to protecting the investments that companies and individuals make in developing new products and ideas. We protect our intellectual property and respect the intellectual property rights of others.
>
> We may not copy, reproduce, or transmit protected material, such as writing, artwork, music, video, photographs, movie clips and software unless we have authorization or license.
>
> We must use the confidential information of Intel or others only for business purposes and disclose it only to those who are authorized and have a need to know. Even after we leave Intel employment, we must continue to protect confidential information (whether Intel's or another party's) and not use or disclose it without authorization.
>
> Furthermore, we must not request or encourage anyone to use or disclose privileged or confidential information unless they are authorized to do so by the owner of that information.

There are numerous types of agreements and variations on policies that employers can and should adopt as part of their strategy to deter trade secret theft by employees. The key is that employers should evaluate their needs and ensure that their policies are clearly communicated to their employees. From the moment an employee commences employment, the employee should understand that the company expects its employees to protect its intellectual property.

Having employees acknowledge and agree to these policies in writing is important for at least three reasons. First, these documents help inform employees about their obligations. Second, such documents may provide evidence that a company has taken reasonable steps to protect its trade secrets. Third, an employee's acknowledgement of these documents can help defeat a claim by the

---

[10] *See* Intel Corporation, "Intel Code of Conduct," January 2021, p. 11, available at https://www.intel.com/content/dam/www/public/us/en/documents/corporate-information/code-of-conduct-eng.pdf.

employee that he did not understand his obligations or know what conduct was permitted by the employer.

2. Internal Messaging

Setting the tone with an employment agreement and assorted policies is a good start. It is, however, not the end of an employer's strategy to deter employee theft of trade secrets. It is important that employees' obligations to protect the company's intellectual property be messaged consistently, regularly, and from the top of the company on down. This messaging helps reinforce to managers and employees that trade secret protection is a business priority.

The methodologies that can be used to remind employees about the importance of intellectual property and their obligations are limited only by the creativity of the company.[11]

Regular messaging via a company's internal web site can also be an efficient vehicle to remind employees about their obligations to protect the company's trade secrets and other intellectual property. Having senior leaders discuss protecting the company's trade secrets helps everyone be mindful of the importance of protecting the company's trade secrets to the company's business and employees' jobs.

B. Training and Education

While messaging is important, training and education are also essential. The concept of what constitutes a trade secret is not always obvious to employees. Accordingly, employers need to devote resources to educating employees about the basics of intellectual property protection. Indeed, training and education go hand-in-hand with the company's policies. Training should be structured, and it should reinforce the company's policies and internal messaging.

Here are sample course topics that might be part of a comprehensive education program:

1. Understanding the different types of intellectual property (i.e., trade secrets, patents, copyrights, and trademarks).

2. Understanding the company's information security policies, processes for data classification and handling, authorized devices, where to get answers to questions, etc.

3. Understanding the potentially dire consequences to the company of not properly safeguarding a company's intellectual property (e.g., loss of competitive advantage,

---

[11] *See, e.g.,* Fair Competition Law has created a 10-minute training video entitled, "*Protecting Trade Secrets – Working at Home,* "for companies to distribute to their employees to help minimize the risks posed to trade secrets as a result of so much of the workforce working from home. This site has many other helpful resources for in-house counsel. *See* https://faircompetitionlaw.com/2020/06/14/psa-employee-training-video-now-available/; the U.S. Patent & Trademark Office has produced this 3-minute video provides a brief introduction to trade secrets, why they are important to a business's bottom line. *See* https://www.youtube.com/watch?v=1dXA5A4l0Rg.

export controls violations, disciplinary action, termination of employment, criminal prosecution, civil liability, etc.).

4. Understanding the importance of reporting any activity which is inconsistent with protection of the company's trade secrets and other intellectual property.

5. Understanding the company's procedures for protecting its intellectual property when employees leave the company.

6. Managers' obligations with respect to protecting the company's trade secrets and other intellectual property.

7. Understanding the company's BYOD (bring your own device) policy, if applicable.

8. Sharing case studies about trade secret actions involving former employees can make a course come alive and inspire good discussions that support educational objectives. And it is quite easy to cull stories about companies commencing legal action against former employees with a quick Internet search.[12]

9. Understanding how inadvertent or unintentional disclosure of trade secret information can occur and how to avoid pitfalls. For example, employees should be cautioned about inadvertently disclosing trade secret information or other confidential information in their LinkedIn profile or other social media by oversharing information.

At the end of these courses, employees should be able to answer the following questions:

1. How do I mark and store sensitive documents?

2. With whom is it appropriate to share trade secret information?

3. Why is it not appropriate for me to use my home computer for sensitive work?

4. Why is it not appropriate for me to send sensitive documents over the Internet?

5. What company resources are available to store and manage sensitive documents?

6. What is the role of the legal department in protecting intellectual property?

7. Who can I call if I have questions about my obligations?

---

[12] Here are some recent trade secret cases involving former employees: "Tesla settles lawsuit against former employee accused of stealing autopilot trade secrets," April 16, 2021 (https://www.businessinsider.com/tesla-settles-autopilot-trade-secrets-lawsuit-2021-4); "Former Uber Exec Accused Of Stealing Trade Secrets For Bezos-Backed Startup," October 28, 2020 (https://www.forbes.com/sites/rachelsandler/2020/10/28/former-uber-exec-accused-of-stealing-trade-secrets-for-bezos-backed-startup/?sh=2ca31ab92303); "*Star Technologist Who Crossed Google Sentenced to 18 Months in Prison,*" August 4, 2020 (https://www.nytimes.com/2020/08/04/technology/levandowski-google-uber-sentencing-trade-secrets.html).

8. What should I do if I am concerned that another employee may have violated his or her obligations?

9. What are the consequences to me if I have not adhered to the company's policies for protecting trade secret information?

10. What are the consequences to the company if I do not properly safeguard a company's intellectual property (e.g., loss of competitive advantage that results in poor quarter or lost jobs)?

11. What is the intellectual property that I have access to and/or am exposed to and how am I expected to safeguard it from unauthorized use or disclosure?

12. What are a manager's responsibilities to assure trade secrets are protected when an employee leaves the company, whether voluntarily or involuntarily.

The above lists are not exhaustive and should be tailored for each company.[13]

§ 5.03 When a Departing Employee is Suspected of Misappropriation

Now that we have discussed creating a culture of information security to help employees understand the importance of protecting trade secrets as well as their obligations, we turn to the steps companies should be prepared to take when an employee leaves the company and is suspect of taking trade secrets. Remember that the failure of companies to enforce their trade secret policies was cited by the Symantec/Ponemon study as a reason employees thought it was acceptable to steal trade secret information from their employer. Thus, it is essential that a company take action where there is concern that a departing employee has or will misappropriate trade secrets. With the advent of telework, the importance of being able to conduct swift analyses and even swifter action to protect trade secrets becomes vital.

A. The Role of Managers

At the outset it is essential to highlight that managers play a critical role in protecting a corporation's trade secrets. If they observe behavior by a departing employee that is unusual or concerning, they are the corporate representatives who are best positioned to alert the company's legal department as well as Information Security or the IT group.

Indeed, if a manager has sufficient concern, he or she should trigger the termination process immediately. The termination process should include prompt notification to Information Security or equivalent group and the company's legal department. By taking prompt action even before

[13] For corporations that are looking to streamline their investments in developing education for employees, there are a variety of public resources to support education initiatives focused on trade secrets. The USPTO, for example, has published a guide entitled "7 Steps to Protecting Your Trade Secrets." https://www.uspto.gov/sites/default/files/documents/CRS-LA-OBrien-trade-secrets.pdf.

the employee has left the company, the company can determine whether any theft or potential theft has occurred by looking for the following types of activity:

- Unusual log-in activity, e.g., during non-work hours, when the employee is allegedly on vacation, etc.
- Accessing document repositories where there is no business need or close proximity to the employee's departure
- Forwarding files to non-work email accounts
- Excessive downloading
- Deletion of files or other data
- Wiping of devices
- Use of storage devices (e.g., USB drives)

Needless to say, conducting this type of analysis cannot be done for every departing employee and should not need to be performed for every employee. That is again why the manager plays such an important role in assessing whether there is a potential risk of misappropriation so that these processes could be triggered if warranted.

B. Interviewing the Client

When there is a concern that a departing employee has or will misappropriate trade secrets, it is important to gather the facts as quickly as possible. A first step for company counsel may be to interview the employee's manager. As a general rule, it is best to do this in person if at all possible. When interviewing the client, the types of information you should try to glean include the following:

1. Background

- What is the employee's position with the company?
- How long has the employee been with the company?
- What has been the employee's performance record?
- Does the employee manage other employees? Could raiding be a concern?
- What is the employee's field of expertise and knowledge?
- Has the employee received training about trade secrets and his or her obligations not to use or disclose them without the company's authorization?

- What agreements does the employee have with the company? Were they ever modified? In writing? Orally?

- What are the reasons for concern about the loss of trade secrets?

2. Identify Trade Secrets at Issue

- What trade secrets and other confidential information does the employee know? What projects has the employee worked on? What documents has the employee prepared or received?

- What trade secrets and other confidential information has the employee had access to?

- Does the employee have any invention disclosures or pending patent applications in process?

- Try to determine what specific trade secrets are generating the concern based on the employee's new position with a future employer. If the case proceeds to litigation, the plaintiff company will be required to provide a list of the trade secrets at issue pursuant to section 2019.210 of the California Code of Civil Procedure before commencing discovery. *See infra* Chapter 11.

3. Circumstances Surrounding Departure

- Has the employee given a reason for leaving?

- Is it because of conflict with the manager?

- If the employee is leaving to join a competitor, is it because the competitor is promising extraordinary compensation and a lofty new title?

- Has the employee had any performance issues?

- An individual facing performance issues could be a red flag that the employee is not only leaving but is disgruntled enough to consider taking trade secret information with him. In fact, managers should be educated to be vigilant in such circumstances.

- Unusual behavior – has the individual exhibited any unusual behavior (e.g., working on vacation, coming into the office on the weekend, trying to attend sensitive meetings which he should now avoid, etc.).

- If possible, it is useful to try to determine how the employee learned about his or her new job.

- If the employee was contacted by a recruiter, for example, this information can be useful if other employees start to leave for the same company and identify the same recruiter. A pattern may develop that could suggest the need to investigate possible raiding.

- Or is the employee declining to disclose any information about his future employer? This could also be a red flag that the employee is heading to a competitor.

C. Marshalling Evidence

In addition to interviewing the client, it is important to gather and preserve relevant evidence immediately. Evidence can be lost if you do not act quickly.[14]

Sources of key evidence include the departing employee's business email files. If consistent with company policies on computer usage and privacy, you may want to review the former employee's emails. Items of interest would include emails discussing the employee's departure from the company or emails used to transmit company information to the departing employee's home email address or even to the new employer.

Care should be taken to preserve the hard drive from the departing employee's company-issued computer. The hard drive could contain evidence of wrongdoing. Company management or counsel should take care to record chain of custody of the departing employee's hard drive and store it in a safe place pending any litigation.

The types of documents and other information you should collect—both hard copy and soft copy—include the following:

1. Employment Records

- Agreements in which the employee has agreed not to use or disclose the company's trade secrets and to protect the company's intellectual property. This can include contracts referencing inventions and company property, ethics agreements, and any other employment-related agreements.

- Documents reflecting the employee's performance history. It is useful, for example, to know if the departing employee has had performance or disciplinary problems in the past, particularly if they relate to a disregard for protecting the company's intellectual property.

[14] "Intel accuses ex-employee of stealing trade secrets linked with Xeon cloud chips," February 8, 2021 (https://www.techradar.com/news/intel-accuses-ex-employee-of-stealing-trade-secrets-linked-with-xeon-cloud-chips)

2. Employee Communications

To the extent permitted by law and to the extent that it is practical, you should gather, take custody of, and analyze the employee's recent work product and communications.

3. Organizational Charts

In addition to asking your client for the names of other individuals with whom you should speak to gather the facts, organizational charts can also help. An overview of the organization may help identify people with relevant information. In some instances, talking to a departing employee's colleagues may give them the opportunity to report inappropriate activity that they otherwise might have been hesitant to mention. However, when interviewing other employees, you should be sensitive to the fact that these people may regard the departing or departed employee as a friend.

4. Forensic Analysis of Employee's Electronic Activity

As noted previously, a study by Cybersecurity Insiders showed that monitoring employee electronic activity was accelerated even before the pandemic. With the seismic shift of employees to telework, this trend will no doubt not only continue, it will probably expand. That said, the success of analyzing forensic evidence collected through monitoring is highly dependent on how quickly such evidence can be gathered and preserved. This dependency makes the role of the manager of a departing employee, or any other corporate representative familiar with the departing employee, very important. If a manager observes unusual behavior or has concerns, the manager can alert the legal department and Information Security group (or equivalent) so that forensic data can be gathered and preserved. Thus, it is prudent for the legal group to work with Information Security, IT, or other group to ensure that there is a process in place so that a manager who believes there is a reason to believe trade secrets are at risk, can alert them so prompt action can be taken to collect this information.

D. Conducting an Exit Interview

It is important to conduct an exit interview with the employee before he or she leaves, if possible. One purpose of the interview is to remind the employee of his or her obligations to the company and to assist the employee in complying with those obligations. It is also an opportunity to assess from the employee's behavior whether he or she intends to honor the obligations not to use or disclose the company's trade secrets.

1. Who Should Conduct the Exit Interview

Not surprisingly, companies approach exit interviews in a variety of ways. Some have in-house attorneys conduct the interviews. Some have the employee's manager conduct the interview. Others rely on human resources or a combination of the attorneys, managers and human resources representatives. Generally though, the best person to conduct an exit interview where trade secrets are to be discussed may be the company attorney. It is also useful to have the departing employee's manager present. In many cases having the employee's manager present will make the employee more comfortable when meeting with a company attorney. In addition, the manager can help the attorney and employee identify trade secrets that should be discussed.

2. Tone of Exit Interview

An exit interview is an opportunity for a candid conversation about the company's expectations of the departing employee. The meeting should be professional and cordial. A properly conducted exit interview, coupled with cooperation by a departing employee, can defuse concerns and avoid further escalation. Similarly, if an employee demonstrates a cavalier attitude toward your client's trade secrets or is overtly hostile, these are indicators that signal that the company's trade secrets are in fact at risk.

3. Exit Interview Certification or Trade Secret Acknowledgement

A useful tool for the exit interview is a form on which the employee will acknowledge or certify his or her understanding of his or her obligations. The form offers an opportunity to identify the trade secrets of concern and to remind the employee of his or her obligations not to use or disclose trade secrets.

A prerequisite to an exit interview certification form is a confidentiality or proprietary information agreement. Generally speaking, every company should have an agreement with each of its employees that sets forth the terms of employment. The agreement should contain a provision in which the employee agrees not to use or disclose the company's trade secrets without the authorization of the company. This agreement should be a condition of employment and should be executed by each employee when they are hired. *See also*, Section 5.02.A.1.a above regarding confidentiality agreements.

4. Agenda for Exit Interview

An exit interview can cover various topics. Generally speaking, the following should be covered when interviewing a departing employee:

- Explain the purpose of the interview.
- Explain any continuing contractual and/or legal obligations the employee may have with the company.
- Provide the employee with the termination certification or acknowledgment form.

By having an employee acknowledge his or her obligations, you remind the employee about the obligations he or she already agreed to undertake. Moreover, by providing the employee with a general idea of what trade secrets he or she has been exposed to, you give the employee an opportunity to understand what trade secrets should not be used or disclosed. To the extent the employee repudiates any of these obligations, the repudiation may constitute valuable evidence that there is an actual threat to the company's trade secrets.

- Confirm the return of all company property.

In some cases, employees mistakenly forget that they have sensitive documents in their possession. It is important to ask the employee if he or she has any documents or other company property in such places as at home, in his or her car, or on a personal or home computer. If the employee has documents in his or her possession, custody or control, make specific arrangements to have the documents returned by an agreed upon deadline. Asking for the return of documents may be particularly useful if it turns out the employee did not return all documents in his or her possession. In litigation, for example, the employee may be required to explain such conduct under oath and a reasonable explanation may not be possible.

- Ask the employee why he or she is leaving.

The answer to this question can be helpful in a pre-litigation investigation. If the employee has, for example, a serious conflict with his or her manager, this could be useful insight into the manager's alleged concern about trade secret misappropriation. Perhaps the concern is the outgrowth of unrelated issues; perhaps it is not. Either way, having an understanding of why the employee is leaving is further information to help you formulate a recommendation to the client.

- Ask the employee what his or her new position will be.

You want to try to determine whether the scope of the new responsibilities is in conflict with guarding the company's trade secrets. Probe how the employee can fulfill his or her new responsibilities without breaching the obligation to guard the company's trade secrets. The employee's responses may provide valuable evidence that there is an actual threat to the company's trade secrets.

- Give the employee an opportunity to ask questions.

An employee may have questions about his or her obligations not to use the company's trade secrets. It may be both useful and appropriate to respond to such questions. However, to avoid potential confusion the employee may have about your role, it is important to ensure that the employee understands you represent the company. This is a means to avoid a situation where the employee tries to claim he or she thought you were giving him legal advice and acting as his or her attorney. Of course, depending on the questions, you may be unable to provide any response and you will need to tell the employee that he or she should seek the counsel of his or her own attorney.[15]

§ 5.04 Determining the Client's Objective

Virtually all clients will tell you they want to protect their company's trade secrets. However, clients need to understand that protecting their trade secrets may require that they invest substantial management time, as well as company money, depending on what goal they want to

[15] "Trade Secret Protection Best Practices," 2021 (https://www.seyfarth.com/dir_docs/publications/TradeSecretBreakfastBriefingHandoutWebinarVersion.pdf); "When Employees Leave With Your Secrets," January 28, 2017 (https://pooley.com/when-employees-leave-with-your-secrets/).

achieve. For example, if a client is faced with a threat of misappropriation but is not willing or capable of allocating the funds to support litigation, it is essential that you know this at the outset in order to prepare the appropriate strategy.

Furthermore, clients need to be educated about the realistic remedies they may be able to obtain. Clients who have read newspaper stories about the *Cadence Design Sys., Inc. v. Avant! Corp.* trade secret saga, *reported at* 125 F.3d 824 (9th Cir. 1997) and 29 Cal. 4th 215 (2002), for example, may incorrectly assume that if they pursue a trade secret case against a competitor, they too will see executives sent to jail and a competitor forced to pay hundreds of millions of dollars. This, however, is an exceptional case.

Accordingly, in order to identify the objective the client is prepared to pursue, it is advisable to review the client's stated objective as compared to the potential costs to achieve that objective. Once the client understands the costs and benefits, the client can make an informed decision about how far it is willing to go to protect its trade secrets.

A. The Client's Objective

Assuming that the pre-litigation investigation uncovers evidence of actual or threatened misappropriation, your client will need to determine what it wants to do. Does it want an injunction to stop further misappropriation? Does it want damages to compensate for the misappropriation? If the client wants damages or an injunction, is it prepared to incur the burden and expense of litigation? If the client is unwilling to commence litigation, will the client accept assurances from the employee that he or she will not misappropriate any trade secrets in the future? Will those assurances be meaningful in light of the scope of the employee's new position? The gamut of options runs from doing nothing to litigation. Since litigation is the costliest option, it is wise to determine if your client is prepared to incur this burden and understands what remedies it can pursue.

B. Litigation Costs

There are a number of monetary and nonmonetary costs a client should be prepared to incur before making the decision that it is committed to protecting the company's trade secrets even if it means litigation. These costs include the following:

1. Attorneys' Fees and Litigation Costs

The cost of litigating a trade secret case can be significant. Simply filing a case, conducting discovery, and litigating through the preliminary injunction phase can cost over $1 million in some cases. If your client's objective is to protect its trade secrets even if it means commencing litigation, you need to ensure that the client understands that the company's costs could be substantial. In addition to attorneys' fees, litigation costs can include the following:

a. Expert Fees

Experts on the technology involved may need to be retained. If you bring a trade secret case, you will necessarily have to review and analyze the defendant company's trade secrets. The court may not permit one of your client's employees to look at documents containing the competitor's intellectual property. In addition, you may not want your client contaminated with trade secrets that he or she must not use or disclose. Therefore, you may need an independent expert. Independent experts, particularly those in technology fields, can be expensive.

b. Jury Consultant Fees

If the case is likely to go to trial, it may be prudent to have a jury consultant on the team. Jury consultants can assist by evaluating themes and assessing the strengths and weaknesses of issues and evidence in a case. Jury consultants also assist by probing into preconceived biases that prospective jurors may have regarding the issues in a case. Jury consultants can conduct focus groups where mock jurors hear presentations about both sides of a case before participating in mock jury deliberations. Following the focus group exercise, jury consultants can advise counsel and clients on case themes and strategies for enhancing one's position in court during jury selection and case presentation. Jury consultant fees vary depending on the services chosen for a given case. Fees can exceed $100,000 in cases involving focus groups, jury research and assistance during jury selection.

c. Graphics Consultant Fees

A graphics consultant may be necessary to help communicate complicated technology to the judge or jury. These costs vary. Some law firms are beginning to do this work in-house. Whether the firm prepares the necessary graphics or whether a specialist prepares the graphics, the costs can be significant.

d. Special Master Fees

Many courts are finding it difficult to handle the seemingly endless discovery disputes that arise with complex trade secret litigation. Accordingly, they often suggest a private special master. Using a private special master has many advantages because you have quick access to a professional who can hear and decide a discovery dispute. However, unlike the court, they are paid for their time. Special masters' fees are usually billed on an hourly basis, similar to attorneys, with fees that can run $500 or more per hour.

e. Mediation Fees

Lastly, many trade secret cases eventually settle. Often, this is with the help of a mediator. Capable mediators can be worth their weight in gold, and the good ones charge about that much (i.e., $10,000 or more per side for a complex multi-day mediation).

2. Management Time and Burden

A trade secret case is one that usually requires the attention of upper management. Management will be called upon to make decisions about the case and will need to spend time understanding the issues. Moreover, senior executives may be called as witnesses, thereby increasing the demands on their time and the burden on the business by having their attention diverted to litigation. Clients need to understand that if they elect to pursue a strategy that may lead to litigation, they will be called upon to spend precious time on the case.

3. Impact on Employees

Employees involved with the technology or trade secrets at issue are likely to become witnesses in the case. Their documents will be collected, they will need to meet with counsel, and they may be deposed and called upon to testify. The burden should not be underestimated. Each hour that these employees spend with attorneys is an hour that these employees are not developing a product or contributing to the company's bottom line.

Moreover, the impact on morale is one that is hard to measure but cannot be overlooked. At a minimum, it can be distracting and unnerving to employees if they learn their employer is pursuing litigation against a former colleague.

4. Potential Adverse Publicity

A trade secret dispute, particularly the filing of a trade secret lawsuit, may result in unwanted media attention. Some clients and cases are more likely to receive coverage than others. Some clients like publicity, some are indifferent, and some want to avoid it. In all cases, clients should understand that publicity is something that they will have little, if any, control over.

5. Potential Exposure of Highly Sensitive Information at Trial

The value of a trade secret lies in the fact that it is a "secret." Trials, however, are intended to be public. One cause for tension and a risk that a client needs to understand is the theoretical possibility that a judge could decide that the trade secret trial will be open to the public. Most courts are sensitive to the need to seal the courtroom and protect the trade secrets. Nevertheless, there is no guarantee that the court will do this. *See also infra* Chapter 10.

6. Interference with Customer Relationships

Customers who are called upon to produce documents or witnesses in a trade secret dispute will not be happy. The effect on such relationships is another factor to consider.

C. Litigation Remedies

Clients should be advised that even if they commence litigation, the remedies they ultimately may receive from the court may not be hundreds of millions of dollars such as in the highly publicized *Cadence Design* case. *Cadence Design*, 125 F.3d 824 and 29 Cal. 4th 215. Moreover, unlike the *Cadence Design* case, it is not likely that your client will see its competitor's executives get sentenced to spend time in jail. Even with the proverbial smoking gun, the possible remedies that a client may be awarded may fall far short of their expectations, even if the outcome is successful and the award a good one. It is, therefore, prudent to explain the possible remedies to your client and, if possible, determine whether the client will consider such remedies worthwhile. *See infra* Chapters 12 and 13.

§ 5.05 Determining Strategy

Once your client understands the costs to protect its trade secrets and is willing to proceed, you need to determine the strategy. Needless to say, strategy is contingent upon what your pre-litigation investigation has uncovered. Based on whether your pre-litigation investigation has uncovered evidence of actual or threatened misappropriation, the following are options to consider:

A. The Pre-litigation Investigation Shows No Evidence of Misappropriation

If your pre-litigation investigation has not produced any evidence of misappropriation, the course of action is fairly narrow. Some of the possible options are as follows:

1. Take No Action

This is the one option that few, if any, clients with concerns about the potential loss of trade secrets want to hear from their attorney. Assuming that this is the case, it is worthwhile to be prepared to explain to the client that pursuing this matter further in the absence of probable cause could subject the company to a declaratory judgment action, a malicious prosecution action, or an embarrassing settlement. One need only recall the *Informix Software, Inc. v. Oracle Corp.*, 927 F. Supp. 1283 (N.D. Cal. 1996) dispute in which Informix ended up issuing a very public apology for pursuing a trade secret claim that it was unable to substantiate.

2. Contact the Former Employee

Send a letter to the employee reminding him or her of obligations not to use or disclose your client's trade secrets. The letter can be a cordial follow-up to an exit interview.

3. Contact the Prospective Employer

Contacting the prospective employer is another option. This can be limited to a letter advising the employer that your client has concerns and that the employee has obligations not to use or disclose your client's trade secrets.

B. The Pre-litigation Investigation Has Uncovered Evidence of Misappropriation

Perhaps the most interesting case from the attorney's perspective is one where your pre-litigation investigation has uncovered evidence that misappropriation has occurred or will occur. In this instance, you and your client have several options. The option your client selects will depend on many factors, including the client's willingness and ability to commence litigation.

1. Confront the Employee

Depending on the circumstances, your client may wish to talk to the departing employee directly. This gives the departing employee the opportunity to explain his or her actions. If no explanation is forthcoming, then your client may wish to take further action.

2. Confront the Prospective Employer

If the employee has already departed, it is more difficult to deal with him or her directly. Some employees would be receptive to a meeting, but this is probably the exception. Once they become the employee of the competitor, it may be better to work with the new employer. Indeed, the new employer is likely to respond to any attempt to contact the former employee since it has a vested interest in responding to allegations of misappropriation.

How to approach the employee's new employer may be determined by your client's history with that company. If the company is one that is reputable and has demonstrated that it respects the intellectual property rights of your client and others, it may be possible to work with them to investigate any misappropriation. This, of course, depends on whether the evidence suggests that they were complicit or not. If they were complicit, or if the company has a reputation for disregarding the rights of your client or others, the approach will necessarily be different. In such instances, it is not uncommon for a letter to be sent demanding cooperation and assurances by a certain date.

3. Refer the Matter to a State or Federal Prosecutor

Calling a district attorney or federal prosecutor is an option if you have concrete evidence of misappropriation. However, calling the prosecutor and getting them interested in pursuing a case are two different things. It is important to know that once an action becomes criminal, any civil proceeding you might want to initiate may be stayed pending outcome of the criminal case. Moreover, once a matter becomes a criminal case, your client will lose a significant amount of control over the litigation.

4. Commence Civil Litigation

Litigation may be a last resort. It is expensive and the results are never guaranteed. Nonetheless, if you and your client are ready to litigate, you may wish to consider the following:

a. Prepare a List of Trade Secrets

As a plaintiff in California state court, you will be required to provide a list of trade secrets at issue, identified with "reasonable particularity," before commencing discovery relating to the trade secrets. *See* Cal. Civ. Proc. Code § 2019.210. Preparing this list in advance of filing the lawsuit will help you draft the complaint to address the trade secrets at issue.

b. Retain an Expert

Where technology is involved, you will likely need an independent source to analyze whether trade secrets have been misappropriated. The importance of experts, particularly in cases involving technology, cannot be overstated. Retaining the expert before you commence litigation may ensure that you get your first choice.

c. Determine Where to Commence Litigation

Trade secret law varies by state. In California, for example, the doctrine of inevitable disclosure has been rejected by an appellate court. *See infra* Chapter 12. So, if your case relies on the theory of inevitable disclosure of trade secrets, you will need to assess whether you can bring such an action in a forum where this doctrine is still viable.

d. Determine Who to Name as Defendants

You will need to determine whether to sue the individual employee. This is a decision that can have negative repercussions for the employees who remain at the company. On the other hand, if the employees feel victimized by the misappropriation, naming their former colleague may be something they both expect and want.

Needless to say, there are a number of other considerations that will go into preparing an actual complaint. *See infra* Chapter 8.

§ 5.06 Conclusion

As a new generation enters the workforce, one that is less likely to stay at any employer beyond five years, employee turnover is likely to increase. In addition, the adoption of teleworking will need to be considered by corporations as they weigh how to protect their trade secrets when employees leave. Even today, there are predictions that expanding workforce mobility will drive an increase in trade secret litigation.[16] That said, companies can mitigate the risks of misappropriation of trade secrets presented by departing employees by educating their employees and showing that they will enforce their policies and take actions against employees who steal trade secret information.[17]

---

[16] "Trends in Trade Secret Litigation Report 2020," at p. 6 ("Expanding workforce mobility, as well as technological advances and the digitization of information, are expected to continue to drive the increased trade secret-related litigation associated with labor and employment matters.") (https://www.winston.com/images/content/2/0/v2/203824/trends-in-trade-secret-litigation-report-2020.pdf).

[17] For an authoritative publication on trade secret law for corporations, see "Trade Secret Law and Corporate Strategy," authored by Darin Snyder & David Almeling (2014) LEXISNEXIS (December 19, 2014).

Chapter 6
WHISTLEBLOWER IMMUNITY

**By: Robert B. Milligan, Esq.
and D. Joshua Salinas, Esq.**

---

§ 6.01 Introduction

The DTSA protects individuals from criminal or civil liability for disclosing a trade secret if the disclosure is made (a) in confidence to a government official, directly or indirectly, or to an attorney, and (b) for the purpose of reporting a violation of law. *See* 18 U.S.C. § 1833(b)(1)(A).

Notably, the DTSA also requires employers to provide employees notice of this whistleblower immunity provision in "any contract or agreement with an employee that governs the use of a trade secret or other confidential information." *See* 18 U.S.C. § 1833(b)(3). The notice requirement is met if the employer provides in the contract or agreement a "cross-reference" to a policy given to the relevant employees that lays out the reporting policy for suspected violations of law. *See* 18 U.S.C. § 1833(b)(3)(B).

If an employer does not comply with the notice requirement, the employer may *not* recover exemplary damages or attorney fees in an action against an employee to whom notice was not provided. *See* 18 U.S.C. § 1833(b)(3)(C); *see also Xoran Holdings LLC v. Luick*, No. 16-13703, 2017 WL 4039178, at *7 (E.D. Mich. Sept. 13, 2017) ("Xoran did not provide notice of employee whistleblower immunity provisions in the Employment Agreement (or elsewhere)…For that reason, Plaintiffs also cannot, as a matter of law, recover attorneys fees or exemplary damages on their DTSA claim.")

Employers should be aware that the DTSA's whistleblower notice requirement is not retroactive and applies only to contracts and agreements entered into or updated after May 11, 2016. Accordingly, the DTSA does not require employers to revise and update all such contracts entered into or updated before May 11, 2016.

The definition of "employee" under the DTSA's whistleblower immunity provision is drafted broadly to include individuals who have done contractor and consultant work for an employer. *See* 18 U.S.C. § 1833(b)(4).

The DTSA's whistleblower immunity provision is consistent with California public policy on whistleblower protections. For example, the California Legislature in January 2014 expanded the general whistleblowing statute, California Labor Code section 1102.5, to prevent employers from taking retaliatory action on a belief that "the employee disclosed or may disclose" relevant information. In *Diego v. Pilgrim United Church of Christ*, 231 Cal. App. 4th 913 (2014), the California Court of Appeal clarified that section 1102.5, even in its pre-amended version, forbids employers to terminate "perceived whistleblowers," even if the employer's belief is mistaken.

§ 6.02 Statutory Language

The DTSA's whistleblower immunity provision provides:

> **(b) Immunity from liability for confidential disclosure of a trade secret to the Government or in a court filing.**
>
> **(1) Immunity.** An individual shall not be held criminally or civilly liable under any Federal or State trade secret law for the disclosure of a trade secret that

(A) is made

(i) in confidence to a Federal, State, or local government official, either directly or indirectly, or to an attorney; and

(ii) solely for the purpose of reporting or investigating a suspected violation of law; or

(B) is made in a complaint or other document filed in a lawsuit or other proceeding, if such filing is made under seal.

(2) Use of trade secret information in anti-retaliation lawsuit. An individual who files a lawsuit for retaliation by an employer for reporting a suspected violation of law may disclose the trade secret to the attorney of the individual and use the trade secret information in the court proceeding, if the individual

(A) files any document containing the trade secret under seal; and

(B) does not disclose the trade secret, except pursuant to court order.

(3) Notice.

(A) In general. An employer shall provide notice of the immunity set forth in this subsection in any contract or agreement with an employee that governs the use of a trade secret or other confidential information.

(B) Policy document. An employer shall be considered to be in compliance with the notice requirement in subparagraph (A) if the employer provides a cross-reference to a policy document provided to the employee that sets forth the employer's reporting policy for a suspected violation of law.

(C) Non-compliance. If an employer does not comply with the notice requirement in subparagraph (A), the employer may not be awarded exemplary damages or attorney fees under subparagraph (C) or (D) of section 1836(b)(3) in an action against an employee to whom notice was not provided.

(D) Applicability. This paragraph shall apply to contracts and agreements that are entered into or updated after the date of enactment of this subsection.

(4) Employee defined. For purposes of this subsection, the term "employee" includes any individual performing work as a contractor or consultant for an employer.

(5) Rule of construction. Except as expressly provided for under this subsection, nothing in this subsection shall be construed to authorize, or limit liability for, an act that is otherwise prohibited by law, such as the unlawful access of material by unauthorized means.

18 U.S.C. § 1833(b).

§ 6.03 Early Case Law

At least one federal district court has characterized whistleblower immunity as an affirmative defense and declined to rule on the merits of the defense at least at the pleading stage before discovery and the presentation of evidence. In *Unum Group v. Loftus*, No. 4:16-CV-40154-TSH, 2016 WL 7115967 (D. Mass. Dec. 6, 2016), the federal district court for the district of Massachusetts denied a defendant employee's motion to dismiss and held that a defendant must present evidence to justify the whistleblower immunity.

The defendant in *Unum* was employed by Unum Group as the Director of Individual Disability Insurance Benefits, during which he was exposed to a significant amount of confidential information, including Unum's trade secrets. *Id.* at *1. In September 2016, the defendant was captured on video leaving Unum's office building with two boxes and a briefcase. *Id.* Two days later, the defendant was again captured on video exiting the office building with a shopping bag full of documents. *Id.* at *2. When Unum investigated the defendant's removal of documents, he refused to cooperate, and was subsequently seen leaving the office with his company laptop and a bag full of documents. *Id.*

After Unum received only the laptop from the defendant despite numerous requests for both the laptop and the documents, the company filed suit in federal court under the DTSA and the Massachusetts Trade Secrets Act, and for conversion. *Id.* Unum sought a preliminary injunction to enjoin the defendant from copying the documents, and to compel him to return all of the documents and make a mirror-image copy of the laptop as they had previously agreed. *Id.* at *1. Unum claimed that it was highly likely that the documents that the defendant took contained confidential customer and employee information and/or trade secrets, including protected health insurance information. *Id.* at *2.

The defendant moved to dismiss Unum's federal and state law claims for trade secret misappropriation on the grounds that he had turned over the documents that he removed from Unum to his attorney to report and investigate a violation of law, invoking the whistleblower immunity provision of the DTSA, 18 U.S.C. § 1833(b). *Id.*

The district court deemed the defendant's DTSA immunity defense an affirmative defense and stated that, as a general rule, a properly raised affirmative defense can only be decided at the motion to dismiss stage if "the facts establishing the defense are definitively ascertainable from the complaint and the other allowable sources of information," such as public records that the court can take judicial notice of and "those facts suffice to establish the affirmative defense with certitude." *Id.* at *2. Upon examining the complaint, the court denied the defendant's motion to dismiss, holding that "the record lacks facts to support or reject his affirmative defense at this stage of litigation." *Id.* The court continued, "There has been no discovery to determine the significance of the documents taken or their contents and [defendant] has not filed any potential lawsuit that could be supported by information in those documents" of which the court could take judicial notice. *Id.* The court further stated that "it is not ascertainable from the complaint whether [defendant] turned over all of Unum's documents to his attorney, which documents he took and what information they contained, or whether he used, is using, or plans to use, those documents for any purpose other than investigating a potential violation of law." *Id.* Accordingly, the court found that the complaint stated a plausible claim for trade secret misappropriation.

One of the concerns with the DTSA's whistleblower immunity provision is that employees who have wrongfully misappropriated trade secrets and other confidential information may use it as an after-the-fact defense. For example, an employee accused of trade secret misappropriation may later attempt to disclose the trade secret information to an attorney or government official solely to invoke the DTSA's whistleblower protections and not for true whistleblowing. The *Unum* decision suggests that defendants asserting the defense may be required to provide evidence substantiating that their misappropriation activity was actually in furtherance of whistleblowing.

§ 6.03.5 Subsequent Case Law

The few cases that have issued public opinions after *Unum* have generally followed its ruling and refused to dismiss DTSA claims based on the whistleblower immunity affirmative defense at the pleading stage. *See Garcia v. Vertical Screen, Inc.*, No. CV 19-3184, 2020 WL 2615624, at *5 (E.D. Pa. May 22, 2020); *Argos USA LLC v. Young*, No. 1:18-CV-02797-ELR, 2019 WL 4125968, at *6 (N.D. Ga. June 28, 2019); *1-800 Remodel v. Bodor*, No. CV 18-472-DMG (EX), 2018 WL 6340759 (C.D. Cal. Oct. 17, 2018).

At least one decision from the federal district court for the Eastern District of Pennsylvania dismissed DTSA claims at the pleading stage based on whistleblower immunity. *See Christian v. Lannett Co., Inc.*, 2018 WL 1532849, at *4 (E.D. Pa. Mar. 29, 2018). The court in *Christian* found an employee's disclosures of employer's confidential information (concerning alleged violations of Title VII, the Americans with Disabilities Act, and the Family and Medical Leave Act) to employee's counsel under a discovery order were entitled to immunity under the DTSA. *See Christian v. Lannett Co., Inc.*, 2018 WL 1532849, at *4 (E.D. Pa. Mar. 29, 2018). That court distinguished the facts in *Christian* from *Unum*:

> "In *Unum Grp. v. Loftus*, the misappropriation at issue was a disclosure made by the defendant to his attorney. 220 F.Supp.3d 143, 146 (Dist. Mass. 2016). However, the defendant had only "indicated that he [was] contemplating [an action]" when he made the disclosure. *Id.* The court noted that it was "unclear" what "suspected violation of law," was under investigation by the disclosing party. *Id.* In the case at bar, it is clear the disclosure occurred pursuant to the initial discovery Order entered by this Court in relation to Plaintiff's underlying discrimination suit involving violations of federal law."

Id. Curiously, the court's subsequent decision referenced above in *Garcia* did not address *Christian.*

Additionally, the whistleblower immunity can be used to dismiss DTSA claims at the pleading stage in "the unusual circumstance where Plaintiffs' own pleadings demonstrate the applicability of the immunity defense...." *See FirstEnergy Corp. v. Pircio*, No. 1:20-CV-1966, 2021 WL 857107, at *4-5 (N.D. Ohio Mar. 8, 2021). The federal district court for the Northern District of Ohio in *FirstEnergy* granted a motion to dismiss plaintiff's DTSA claim because the "pleadings alleged that former employee took no actions other than to acquire client's electronic files and provide them to his counsel who provided them to government officials for investigation." *Id.* In other words, the court noted that the plaintiff had failed to provide any plausible, non-speculative allegations that the defendant engaged in any wrongful conduct outside the ambit of the whistleblower immunity provision. *Id.*

§ 6.04 Potential Notice Language

The DTSA precludes employers from recovering exemplary damages or attorneys' fees for DTSA claims against employees to whom the whistleblower immunity notice was not provided. *See* 18 U.S.C § 1833(b)(3). There is no case law, however, addressing the application or construction of this provision.

Below is potential language that can be used in employee agreements or company policies to comply with the DTSA's whistleblower immunity notice provision. Importantly, employers should consult with appropriate legal counsel before utilizing or revising any whistleblower immunity notices:

> You are hereby notified in accordance with the Defend Trade Secrets Act of 2016 that you will not be held criminally or civilly liable under any federal or state trade secret law for disclosure of a trade secret that: (a) is made (i) in confidence to a federal, state, or local government official, either directly or indirectly, or to an attorney; and (ii) solely for the purpose of reporting or investigating a suspected violation of law; or (b) is made in a complaint or other document that is filed under seal in a lawsuit or other proceeding.
>
> You are further notified that if you file a lawsuit for retaliation by an employer for reporting a suspected violation of law, you may disclose the employer's trade secrets to your attorney and use the trade secret information in the court proceeding if you: (a) file under seal any document containing the trade secret; and (b) do not disclose the trade secret, except pursuant to court order.

Chapter 7
EXTRATERRITORIALITY OF THE DTSA
By: Randall E. Kay, Esq.

---

§ 7.01 Extraterritoriality

This chapter addresses extraterritorial reach of the Defend Trade Secrets Act ("the DTSA") under 18 U.S.C. § 1837. That is, will a federal district court hear a DTSA lawsuit based on misappropriation alleged to have occurred exclusively outside the United States? Section 1837—titled "Applicability to conduct outside the United States" and originally enacted as part of the Economic Espionage Act in 1996—provides for extraterritorial jurisdiction. This statute governs misconduct occurring outside the United States in two situations: "(1) the offender is a natural person who is a citizen or permanent resident alien of the United States, or an organization organized under the laws of the United States or a State or political subdivision thereof; or (2) an act in furtherance of the offense was committed in the United States." 18 U.S.C. § 1837 (1996).

Questions arose upon passage of the DTSA whether Section 1837 applied to civil DTSA claims. Opponents pointed to the terms "offender" and "offense" in the statute to argue that Section 1837 only applied to criminal lawsuits under the Economic Espionage Act. The courts, however, have ruled uniformly that the DTSA may apply extraterritorially in cases satisfying either of the requirements of Section 1837. In *Motorola Sols., Inc. v. Hytera Commc'ns Corp.*, 436 F. Supp. 3d 1150, 1157–63 (N.D. Ill. 2020), the court reasoned that Congress clearly indicated its intention to extend the extraterritorial provisions of Section 1837 to DTSA claims. The *Motorola* court referenced the "sense of Congress" statements that "trade secret theft occurs in the United States and around the world" as well as "trade secret theft, wherever it occurs, harms the companies that own the trade secrets and the employees of the companies". *Id.* at 1160. *See also*, *Luminati Networks, Ltd. v. BIScience, Inc.*, No. 2:18-cv-00483, 2019 WL 2084426, at *10 (E.D. Tex. May 13, 2019).

Disputes over extraterritoriality in claims under the DTSA have centered on the meaning of the undefined phrase "act in furtherance of the offense" in the United States under Section 1837(2). While the DTSA does not define the governing phrase "act in furtherance," case law informs the meaning of an "act in furtherance of the offense" occurring in the United States. More than a dozen court decisions have evaluated whether a requisite "act in furtherance" was committed in the United States. Courts interpreting "in furtherance of the offense" under Section 1837(2) have looked to the common law meaning as it is regularly used in federal conspiracy law. *See Luminati*, 2019 WL 2084426, at *10; *Motorola*, 436 F. Supp. 3d 1150 at 1165. Using this analogy, courts recognize that an "act in furtherance" (i) need not be the offense itself or any element of the offense; (ii) must simply manifest that the offense is "at work;" and (iii) the act itself need not even be committed by the defendant. *See Luminati*, 2019 WL 2084426, at *10; *vPersonalize, Inc. v. Magnetize Consultants Ltd.*, 437 F. Supp. 3d 860, 878 (W.D. Wash. 2020).

§ 7.02 What is an "Act in Furtherance"?

A. Meeting the Standard for an Act in Furtherance

Cases establishing an "act in furtherance" often fall into one of four categories:

i. <u>Accessing U.S. servers</u>. Downloading trade secrets from the owner's U.S. servers or storing the stolen trade secrets on U.S. servers can meet the test. *Micron Tech., Inc. v.*

United Microelectronics Corp., No. 17-CV-06932-MMC, 2019 WL 1959487, at *3 (N.D. Cal. May 2, 2019); *MedImpact Healthcare Sys., Inc. v. IQVIA Inc.*, No. 19CV1865-GPC(LL), 2020 WL 5064253, at *15 (S.D. Cal. Aug. 27, 2020); *Dmarcian, Inc. v. Dmarcian Europe BV*, No. 1:21-cv-00067-MR, 2021 WL 2144915, at *22 (W.D. N.C. May 26, 2021).

ii. In person contacts. Visits by the wrongdoer to the United States in connection with the overall theft—such as meeting with recruits, vendors, suppliers, or partners in the United States—can constitute an act in furtherance. *Micron Tech. Inc.,* 2019 WL 1959487, at *3-4; *Philips Medical Systems (Cleveland), Inc. v. Buan*, No. 19-cv-02648, 2021 WL 3187709, at *10 (N.D. Ill. July 28, 2021); *Medcenter Holdings Inc. v. WebMD Health Corp.*, No. 1:20-cv-00053, 2021 WL 1178129, at *6 (S.D.N.Y. Mar. 29, 2021).

iii. U.S. commerce. Selling or marketing products or services derived from or embodying the trade secrets in the United States can serve as an act in furtherance. *See Luminati,* 2019 WL 2084426, at *10 (finding the plaintiff stated a claim under the DTSA based on a "reasonable inference" that the defendant used the plaintiff's trade secrets in the United States when selling a service using the plaintiff's trade secrets); *vPersonalize Inc.,* 2020 WL 534505, at *13 (refusing to dismiss the plaintiff's DTSA claim because the plaintiff alleged the defendant used that trade secret by offering its products and services throughout the United States); *Motorola Solutions,* 436 F. Supp. 3d at 1165 (finding an act in furtherance of trade secret misappropriation where the defendant "advertised, promoted, and marketed products embodying the allegedly stolen trade secrets domestically at numerous trade shows"); *Dmarcian, Inc.,* 2021 WL 2144915, at *22; *Inventus Power, Inc. v. Shenzhen Ace Battery Co., Ltd.*, No. 20-cv-3375, 2020 WL 3960451, at *7 (N.D. Ill. July 13, 2020); *MACOM Tech. Solutions Inc. v. Litrinium, Inc.*, No. SACV 19-220 JVS (JDEx), 2019 WL 4282906, at *4–5 (C.D. Cal. June 3, 2019).

iv. Patent filings. Filing for U.S. patent protection on the stolen trade secrets using U.S. patent agents can qualify as an act in furtherance. *Micron Tech., Inc.,* 2019 WL 1959487, at *4-5.

The case law provides additional guidance for establishing the requisite "act in furtherance":

- A single act can suffice ("*an act* in furtherance").

- The act need not be the offense itself or any element of the offense. *Luminati Networks, Ltd.,*2019 WL 2084426, at *10 (citing *Yates v. United States*, 354 U.S. 298, 334 (1957)).

- The act simply must manifest that the offense is "at work". *Id.*

- The act itself need not be committed by the defendant—it can be performed by a vendor, a supplier, a partner, a co-defendant or another player in the stream of commerce. *vPersonalize Inc.*, 437 F. Supp. 3d at 878; *Philips Medical Systems (Cleveland), Inc.*, 2021 WL 3187709, at *10.

- Foreign defendants' virtual contacts with the United States may meet the requirement. *MedImpact Healthcare Sys., Inc.*, 2020 WL 5064253, at *14–15 (foreign defendants' communications to the United States through virtual meetings, phone calls and correspondence supported finding that misappropriation was "at work" and acts in furtherance were committed in the United States).

B. Opposing the Act in Furtherance Determination

Courts finding an inadequate showing of an "act in furtherance" do so for numerous reasons:

- No act in the United States. In many cases, plaintiffs fail to allege any act in furtherance occurring in the United States or plaintiffs fail to show that a given activity, such as accessing servers, actually occurred in the United States to satisfy 18 U.S.C. § 1837(2).

- Timing matters. Courts will reject acts taking place before the operation is underway or after the operation is fully completed. *MedImpact Healthcare Sys., Inc.*, 2020 WL 5064253, at *15.

- Insufficiently related acts. Some plaintiffs fail to plead sufficient connection between the alleged U.S. act and the foreign misappropriation. *ProV Int'l Inc. v. Lucca*, No. 8:19-cv-978-T-23AAS, 2019 WL 5578880, at *3 (M.D. Fla. Oct. 29, 2019) (concluding former employee's trip to a trade show in Nevada and to tender his resignation to the plaintiff were unconnected to the alleged misappropriation of trade secrets).

- Damages. Courts have rejected arguments that damages in the United States constitute part of the offense; rather, damages result from a fully completed operation. *Id.*

A number of defendants have argued without success at the trial court level that 18 U.S.C. § 1837's "act in furtherance of the offense" should not apply to civil DTSA cases. *See, e.g.*, *Motorola*, 436 F. Supp. 3d 1150 at 1157-63. While the trial courts have ruled against this argument, it remains untested in the appellate courts. Appellate courts have neither embraced nor rejected the concept.

§ 7.03 Extraterritoriality Based on United States Citizenship or Other Recognized Affiliation

Of significantly less debate is the extraterritorial reach under 18 U.S.C. § 1837(1) for DTSA claims against "a natural person who is a citizen or permanent resident alien of the United States, or an organization organized under the laws of the United States or a State or political subdivision thereof". The court in *T&S Brass & Bronze Works, Inc. v. Slanina*, No. 6:16-03687-MGL, 2017 WL 1734362, at *12 (D.S.C. May 4, 2017) stated that the defendants in that case met the standard in 18 U.S.C. § 1837(1)).

Chapter 8
INITIAL PLEADINGS
By: Michael E. Pappas, Esq.

---

§ 8.01 The Misappropriation of Trade Secrets Complaint

A. Pleading Requirements for Plaintiffs

To establish a claim under the California Uniform Trade Secrets Act ("CUTSA"), a plaintiff must prove:

1. That the plaintiff owned or was a licensee of a trade secret;

2. That the information was a trade secret at the time of the misappropriation;

3. That the defendant improperly acquired, used, or disclosed the trade secret (or in the case of an injunction, threatens to use or disclose);

4. That the plaintiff was harmed or the defendant was unjustly enriched (or in the case of an injunction, threat of irreparable harm); and

5. That the defendant's acquisition, use, or disclosure was a substantial factor in causing the plaintiff to be harmed or the defendant to be unjustly enriched.

See California Civil Jury Instructions (CACI), Trade Secret Series, CACI 4401 (Judicial Council of California, 2021) (citing authorities) (reproduced *infra* at Appendix A); *see also Cent. Valley Gen. Hosp. v. Smith*, 162 Cal. App. 4th 501, 528 (2008) (listing four possible variations for establishing a claim of threatened misappropriation). The Court of Appeal in *Silvaco Data Systems v. Intel Corp.*, 184 Cal. App. 4th 210, 220 (2010), *disapproved of on other grounds by Kwikset Corp. v. Superior Court*, 51 Cal. 4th 310 (2011), characterized a CUTSA claim as consisting of three basic elements: "(1) possession by the plaintiff of a trade secret; (2) the defendant's misappropriation of the trade secret, meaning its wrongful acquisition, disclosure, or use; and (3) resulting or threatened injury to the plaintiff." The court concluded that "[t]he first of these elements is typically the most important, in the sense that until the content and nature of the claimed secret is ascertained, it will likely be impossible to intelligibly analyze the remaining issues." *Silvaco*, 184 Cal. App. 4th at 220. A trade secret plaintiff must plead facts sufficient to establish each of these elements in its complaint. *See, e.g., Brocade Commc'ns. Sys. Inc. v. A10 Networks, Inc.*, No. 10-CV-03428-LHK, 2011 WL 1044899, at *5, *18 (N.D. Cal. Mar. 23, 2011) (discussing the *Bell Atlantic Corp. v. Twombly*, 550 U.S. at 555 (2007) standard and its application to CUTSA allegations).

A trade secret complaint under the federal Defend Trade Secrets Act ("DTSA") must plead the same basic elements as a complaint under the CUTSA in state court: 1) the plaintiff owned a trade secret; (2) the defendant misappropriated the trade secret; and (3) the defendant's actions damaged the plaintiff. *See Alta Devices, Inc. v. LG Elecs., Inc.*, 343 F. Supp. 3d 868, 877 (N.D. Cal. 2018). But unlike a claim in state court, the DTSA complaint will be judged under the federal pleading standards set forth in *Ashcroft v. Iqbal*, 556 U.S. 662, 678 (2009) and *Bell Atlantic Corp. v. Twombly*, 550 U.S. 544, 570 (2007). That is, the complaint must contain sufficient factual matter that, if accepted as true, states a claim for relief that is plausible on its face. *Id.*

1. Identification of the Trade Secret

(a) CUTSA Standards

One issue that each plaintiff must face is the extent to which it must identify its trade secrets in the complaint. The CUTSA defines a trade secret as:

> [I]nformation, including a formula, pattern, compilation, program, device, method, technique, or process, that: (1) [d]erives independent economic value, actual or potential, from not being generally known to the public or to other persons who can obtain economic value from its disclosure or use; and (2) [i]s the subject of efforts that are reasonable under the circumstances to maintain its secrecy.

Cal. Civ. Code § 3426.1(d). *See supra* Chapter 1.

In a case that predates the CUTSA, the court held that a plaintiff must do more than plead the bare existence of a trade secret in order to survive a demurrer.

> One who seeks to protect his trade secrets from wrongful use or disclosure does not have to spell out the details of the trade secret to avoid a demurrer to a complaint. To do so would require that the complainant would have to destroy the very thing for which he sought protection by making public the secret itself.
>
> The plaintiff must nevertheless allege the ultimate facts showing the existence of a trade secret or other confidential data to state such a cause of action. An averment simply that the plaintiff has a "secret process" is a bare legal conclusion.
>
> Before a defendant is compelled to respond to a complaint based upon claimed misappropriation or misuse of a trade secret and to embark on discovery which may be both prolonged and expensive, the complainant should describe the subject matter of the trade secret with sufficient particularity to separate it from matters of general knowledge in the trade or of special knowledge of those persons who are skilled in the trade, and to permit the defendant to ascertain at least the boundaries within which the secret lies. If the subject matter of the claimed trade secret is a manufacturing process, the plaintiff must not only identify the end product manufactured, but also supply sufficient data concerning the process, without revealing the details of it, to give both the court and the defendant reasonable notice of the issues which must be met at the time of trial and to provide reasonable guidance in ascertaining the scope of appropriate discovery. No more comprehensive rules for pleading can be generally enunciated because no inclusive definition of trade secrets is possible.

Diodes, Inc. v. Franzen, 260 Cal. App. 2d 244, 252-53 (1968) (citations omitted).

Recent California decisions have not discussed whether the *Diodes* rule remains a pleading requirement, or is now a discovery rule. Since *Diodes* was decided, the California legislature enacted section 2019.210, which provides that a plaintiff must identify its trade secrets with reasonable particularity before commencing discovery relating to the trade secret. Cal. Civ. Proc. Code § 2019.210; *see infra* Chapter 11. A number of courts have cited *Diodes* in interpreting section 2019.210. *See, e.g.*, *Advanced Modular Sputtering, Inc. v. Superior Court*, 132 Cal. App. 4th 826, 835 (2005); *Pixion, Inc. v. PlaceWare, Inc.*, 421 F. Supp. 2d 1233, 1241 (N.D. Cal. 2005). In *Advanced Modular*, the court observed that the trade secret designation mandated by section 2019.210 "is not itself a pleading but it functions like one in a trade secret case because it limits the scope of discovery in much the same way as the allegations of a complaint limit discovery in other types of civil actions." *Advanced Modular*, 132 Cal. App. 4th at 835.

Notwithstanding the Court of Appeal's statement in *Silvaco* of the importance of ascertaining the content and nature of the claimed secret, the court stopped short of holding that the trade secrets must be identified with particularity *in the pleadings.* While noting that "[i]t is critical to any CUTSA cause of action—and any defense—that the information claimed to have been misappropriated be clearly identified," the *Silvaco* decision does not address whether the particularity rule continues to be a pleading rule, or is only a discovery rule pertinent to California Civil Code section 2019.210. Federal courts that have considered this issue have found that section 2019.210 is a discovery rule that does not affect a plaintiff's pleading requirements. *See, e.g.*, *Resonance Tech., Inc. v. Koninklijke Philips Elecs.*, N.V., No. CV 08-2580 PSG(PLAX), 2008 WL 4330288, at *4 (C.D. Cal. Sept. 17, 2008) (finding that motion for a more definite statement of trade secrets was premature at pleading stage because section 2019.210 requirement is related to discovery, not pleading); *Computer Econ., Inc. v. Gartner Group, Inc.*, 50 F.Supp.2d 980, 990 n.11 (S.D.Cal.1999) (noting that section 2019.210 is a discovery rule that "does not affect plaintiff's pleading requirements").

Nevertheless, federal district court decisions have applied the *Diodes* rule in the context of Rule 12(b)(6) motions to dismiss under the standards set forth in *Twombly,* 550 U.S. at 555. In *Farhang v. Indian Institute of Technology, Kharagpur*, No. C-08-02658 RMW, 2010 WL 2228936, at *14 (N.D. Cal. June 1, 2010), the district court held that plaintiff's allegation that its confidential "business models and implementations" were trade secrets was a "vague description" lacking particularity under the *Diodes* rule. *Id.* at *14. Plaintiff's allegation of a separate trade secret—its core technology described as "enabling fluid mobile access to data on handheld devices, including dynamic real-time access and parsing of data that is not dependent upon continuous wireless data connection"—would have been an insufficiently precise allegation, standing alone, but was held to be adequate because the complaint also identified the patent application for this core technology. *Id.* at *13. Similarly, the district court in *Southern California Institute of Law v. TCS Education System,* No. CV 10-8026 PSG (AJWx), 2011 WL 1296602, at *7 (C.D. Cal. Apr. 5, 2011), held that plaintiff's trade secret allegations were insufficiently specific because the complaint only listed a series of documents without identifying what information in the documents was trade secret. *Accord Pellerin v. Honeywell*, 877 F. Supp. 2d 983, 988-89 (S.D. Cal. 2012) (failure to describe manufacturing process in complaint with sufficient particularity to give notice of what the trade secret was merited motion to dismiss); *Invisible Dot, Inc. v. DeDecker*, No. 218CV08168RGKRAO, 2019 WL 1718621, at *5 (C.D. Cal. Feb. 6, 2019) (laundry list of items which included "information related to 'research, business plans, product plans, products, services, customer lists and customers ... market research, works of original authorship, intellectual property ... photographs, negatives digital images, software, computer programs, ideas, developments, inventions ...'" did not meaningfully define the trade secrets at issue).

Other recent district court decisions, also following *Twombly*, applied the pleading with particularity rule in *Diodes*, but accepted much broader allegations as sufficient to withstand a motion to dismiss. *See Ikon Office Solutions, Inc. v. Rezente*, No. 2:10-1704 WBS KJM, 2010 WL 5129293, at *2 (E.D. Cal. Dec. 8, 2010); *TMX Funding, Inc. v. Impero Techs., Inc.*, No. C 10-00202 JF (PVT), 2010 WL 2509979, at *3-4 (N.D. Cal. June 17, 2010); *TMC Aerospace, Inc. v. Elbit Sys. of Am. LLC,* No. CV 15-07595-AB (EX), 2016 WL 3475322, at *5 (C.D. Cal. Jan. 29, 2016) (plaintiff's identification of trade secrets as its "proprietary design drawings, manufacturing techniques, and manufacturing equipment including moulds and jigs" developed to manufacture its patented de-icing system was sufficient to withstand a motion to dismiss).

If plaintiff's counsel fears that the level of specificity in the complaint will destroy the secret nature of the information, counsel could limit the details in the publicly filed complaint and approach defense counsel with a proposed stipulated protective order and a more detailed identification of trade secrets pursuant to section 2019.210. Alternatively, plaintiff's counsel could consider seeking court approval to file the complaint under seal pursuant to Rules 2.550 - 2.551 of the California Rules of Court and section 3426.5 of the California Civil Code. *See infra* Chapter 10.

(b) DTSA Standards

Courts generally agree on the pleading standard for identifying the trade secret under the DTSA— that the plaintiff must "describe the subject matter of the trade secret with sufficient particularity to separate it from matters of general knowledge in the trade or of special persons who are skilled in the trade, and to permit the defendant to ascertain at least the boundaries within which the secret lies." *See, e.g., Alta Devices, Inc.*, 343 F. Supp. 3d at 881; *Vendavo, Inc. v. Price f(x) AG*, 2018 WL 1456697, 4 (N.D. Cal. Mar. 23, 2018); *Space Data Corp. v. X*, 2017 WL 5013363, *2 (N.D. Cal. Feb. 16, 2017). But the way the standard is applied varies. Some courts have required the trade secret plaintiff to identify the trade secret in detail and how it was misappropriated. *See, e.g., Cisco Sys., Inc. v. Chung*, 462 F. Supp. 3d 1024 (N.D. Cal. 2020); *AlterG, Inc. v. Boost Treadmills LLC*, 388 F. Supp. 3d 1133, 1145–46 (N.D. Cal. 2019); *Vendavo, Inc.*, 2018 WL 1456697 at *4; *Space Data Corp.*, 2017 WL 5013363 at *2. Other courts have been more lenient, requiring less detail and allowing certain trade secrets to be described more categorically. *See, e.g., Alta Devices, Inc.*, 343 F. Supp. 3d. at 881; *Navigation Holdings, LLC v. Molavi,* 445 F. Supp. 3d 69 (N.D. Cal. 2020); *Five Star Gourmet Foods, Inc. v. Fresh Express, Inc.*, 2020 WL 513287, *7 (N.D. Cal. Jan. 31, 2020); *Glam & Glits Nail Design, Inc. v. #NotPolish, Inc.*, 2021 WL 2317410, *5 (S.D. Cal. June 7, 2021).

As of the time of writing, the one federal circuit court to address DTSA pleading requirements took a more lenient approach. In *Oakwood Laboratories, LLC v. Thanoo*, 999 F3d. 892 (3d Cir. 2021) a pharmaceutical company sued Dr. Thanoo, its former vice president of product development and Aurobindo Pharma, USA, the pharmaceutical company that hired Dr. Thanoo, for trade secret misappropriation under the DTSA. The trial court dismissed the plaintiff's third amended complaint for failure to identify trade secrets sufficiently. The Third Circuit reversed and found that the plaintiff sufficiently identified the trade secrets at issue, sufficiently alleged that the defendants had "used" trade secrets, and sufficiently alleged harm simply by alleging the misappropriation of trade secrets.

Oakwood was a specialty pharmaceutical company "focused on hard-to-develop generic and quasi-generic, sustained-release, and small molecule injectable drugs" which used a trade secret "microsphere process technology." Dr. Thanoo was its senior scientist "principally responsible for the development of the Oakwood Products" and directly involved in designing Oakwood's microsphere process technology. Oakwood and Aurobindo began discussions pursuant to a confidentiality agreement to collaborate on the development of the microsphere technology. Oakwood provided information on its technology, but those talks ended without agreement being reached. A short time later, Dr. Thanoo joined Aurobindo and Aurobindo began developing competing products based on microsphere technology.

Oakwood alleged that "the 'Defendants could not [have] develop[ed] [its] product within the rapid timeframe set forth above without Dr. Thanoo's assistance and his use of Oakwood's ... trade secret information related to the Microsphere Project." Nor could they have done so "without Oakwood's trade secret information contained in the Leuprolide Memo that Oakwood sent to Aurobindo and AuroMedics" for the limited purpose of discussing a "potential business venture[.]" *Id.* at 899. The initial complaint and subsequent versions contained details regarding the categories of trade secrets and specific items that Oakwood claimed were misappropriated.

In dismissing the third amended complaint without leave to amend, the district court found that Oakwood had sufficiently identified trade secrets, but it had failed to identify which of the specific trade secrets was misappropriated and how it was used by the defendants. The Third Circuit rejected the exacting standard imposed by the district court:

> Given the allegations of the Complaint, a reasonable inference – one might say the only reasonable inference – is that the trade secrets identified in the Complaint are the ones Oakwood is claiming were misappropriated. The District Court's demand for further precision in the pleading is thus misplaced and ignores the challenges a trade secret plaintiff commonly faces when only discovery will reveal exactly what the defendants are up to. . . . "If the list is too general, it will encompass material that the defendant will be able to show cannot be trade secret. If instead it is too specific, it may miss what the defendant is doing." [Citing *DeRubeis v. Witten Techs., Inc.*, 244 F.R.D. 676, 680 (N.D. Ga. 2007).]
>
> While we agree with the District Court that care must be taken to not allow a plaintiff in a trade secret misappropriation case to make generalized claims that leave a defendant wondering what the secrets at issue might be, there was no risk of that here, given the specificity of the allegations in the Third Amended Complaint.

Oakwood Laboratories, LLC, 999 F3d. 892 at 907.

The Ninth Circuit in *InteliClear, LLC v. ETC Glob. Holdings, Inc.*, 978 F.3d 653 (9th Cir. 2020), reviewed the grant of a summary judgment motion and similarly found that the district court applied too stringent a requirement on the plaintiff to identify its trade secrets. In that case, a software company sued a competitor, alleging misappropriation of its trade secrets in its securities tracking database in violation of the DTSA. The trial court granted summary judgment to the defendant on the grounds that the plaintiff failed to identify its trade secrets sufficiently. The Ninth Circuit reversed holding that fact issues existed as to whether the plaintiff had identified a trade secret with sufficient particularity and as to whether the plaintiff had taken reasonable measures to keep information secret. The purported trade secrets were described broadly as "the InteliClear System's unique design and concepts and the unique software, formulas, processes, programs, tools, techniques, tables, fields, functionality, and logic by which its components interrelate and process data," which the plaintiff claimed were improperly used and incorporated in a similar securities tracking database the defendant had created. The plaintiff introduced two declarations under seal that further described what was meant by the various categories. The defendant claimed that the purported trade secrets were too broadly defined and, among other things, insufficiently separated from matters known in the industry.

The Court of Appeals held that whether certain matters were trade secrets was an issue of fact and discovery should have proceeded to allow the plaintiff to refine its identification of trade secrets: "A reasonable jury could conclude that the uniquely designed tables, columns, account number structures, methods of populating table data, and combination or interrelation thereof, are protectable trade secrets." *Id.* at 659. Although this case involved review of a grant of summary judgment, it is instructive as to pleading requirements in that it acknowledges that, at the pleading stage and before discovery is undertaken, a plaintiff should be allowed some leeway in having a broader and less specific identification of the trade secrets at issue. Also, whether particular information is a trade secret can be an issue of fact and, therefore, inappropriate for determination at the pleading stage.

Examples of DTSA cases where trade secret allegations were found sufficient:

In *Alta Devices, Inc. v. LG Elecs., Inc.*, 343 F. Supp. 3d 868 (N.D. Cal. 2018), the plaintiff manufacturer of thin-film solar technology brought action against electronics manufacturer LG alleging that LG breached its duties under a non-disclosure agreement (NDA) and used information provided by Alta to create a competing product. The complaint alleged the exact technology in question: thin-film GaAs solar technology. It also alleged the type of information at issue: "Alta's Methods of: high throughput thin-film deposition; epitaxial lift-off of the thin-film; and GaAs substrate maintenance and re-use. It includes confidential cost analysis; proofs and tests of manufacturing concepts and techniques; tool roadmaps; manufacturing process flows; and identification of equipment and equipment vendors; and information related to the foregoing." Alta also referenced an attachment to the NDA that described the type of confidential information the parties contemplated sharing under the agreement. *Id.* at 881. Consequently, the court rejected LG's contention that it could not "ascertain the boundaries within which the secret lies."

The court in *Navigation Holdings, LLC v. Molavi,* 445 F. Supp. 3d 69 (N.D. Cal. 2020), determined that the plaintiff's customer information was a trade secret based on the following allegations:

> Plaintiffs' clientele includes key players in the metal alloy industry, including specialized mills, decision makers at various aerospace, medical and automobile companies, and specialized distributors of refined metals, as well as hundreds of engineers and industrial designers who use services to procure specialized aluminum alloys. Plaintiffs maintain confidential information about their clients in

> their files and databases. This information is not only a list of potential clients, but a compilation of price information about proven clients that often includes each client's name, address, telephone number, contact person and private email address. Plaintiffs' database contains client information that Plaintiffs have gathered over the entire history of their operations, which span not only many years but hundreds of thousands of hours of research, including prior order/pricing information. Many of the clients are regular and frequent consumers of Plaintiffs' services and have been so for years.

Id. at 77.

In *Five Star Gourmet Foods, Inc. v. Fresh Express, Inc.*, 2020 WL 513287, *7 (N.D. Cal. Jan. 31, 2020), the court found that although some information regarding the plaintiff's packaged salads was public and not trade secret, allegations that the plaintiff showed the defendants a protected tool set and "how it staffs its production lines, the equipment and equipment vendors it uses," and the order of operations, machinery, and live-personnel it uses on its assembly lines were sufficient to allow the defendants to "ascertain at least the boundaries within which the secrets lie and the scope of appropriate discovery." *Id.* As to misappropriation, the court found that touring the plaintiff's production facilities and gathering information under a non-disclosure agreement sufficiently alleged access to the trade secrets and the allegations that the defendant copied its business operations down to using the same tool set to create its packaging was sufficient to allege misappropriation. *Id.* at *8.

In *Glam & Glits Nail Design, Inc. v. #NotPolish, Inc.*, 2021 WL 2317410, at *5 (S.D. Cal. June 7, 2021), the plaintiff was a nail care products manufacturer and vendor focusing in part on nail salons owned and operated by Vietnamese Americans, and sued its former employee and her new employer alleging misappropriation of confidential customer information. The court found that the information could qualify as trade secret. According to the court: "the Information is more than just a 'client list.' It includes non-public personal cellphone numbers of the owners and operators of G&G's customers and distributors who prefer conducting business in Vietnamese, the customers' and distributors' account purchasing histories, their corresponding pricing tiers, and their product and billing preferences …. [T]he CEO of G&G himself compiled them over many years and took various measures to keep the Information exposed as little as possible …. And it is easy to see how knowing private cellphone numbers of the owners/operators and their preferences to the most intricate detail would provide a competitive edge." *Id.* at *5 Allegations that, among other things, the defendants began contacting the plaintiff's Vietnamese speaking customers to solicit their business using their private cell phone numbers were sufficient to allege misappropriation. *Id.*

Examples of DTSA cases where trade secret allegations were found insufficient:

In *Cisco Sys., Inc. v. Chung*, 462 F. Supp. 3d 1024 (N.D. Cal. 2020), Cisco sued a competitor and four former employees alleging that they schemed to improperly reveal a range of Cisco's trade secrets relating to Cisco's collaboration platform. The court found that Cisco's allegations of trade secrets consisting of, among other things, "source code, schematics, design details and specifications, user feedback, design documentation, and features relating to Cisco's existing and future products, as well as Cisco business information such as marketing strategy, cost and pricing information, and payment information," and "design and architectural documents, hardware diagrams, schematics, source code stacks, and engineering specifications relating to existing and future Cisco products, and non-public financial information" were sufficient when combined with more specific allegations that one of the defendants took technical information "relating to architectural design documents for an unreleased Cisco headset concept, a hardware diagram for a Cisco headset prototype, design and configuration documents for Cisco's headset prototypes, a schematic for an unreleased IP telephone project, and a full engineering specification for a next-generation conference room collaboration device." However, the court granted certain of the defendants' motions to dismiss because Cisco made only conclusory allegations that any such specific information had independent economic value:

> The above allegations only generally relate to plaintiff's collaboration platform. They say nothing about the economic value of the categories of information purportedly misappropriated by Chung or He that concern the handful of subject matter that plaintiff alleged with sufficient particularity. While that subject matter may serve as constituent parts falling under the umbrella of plaintiff's "collaboration platform," that relationship does not compel a reasonable inference that any information about such particular subject matter is itself economically valuable.

Id. at 1053.

The court in *Vendavo, Inc. v. Price f(x) AG*, 2018 WL 1456697, *3-*4 (N.D. Cal. Mar. 23, 2018), determined that the plaintiff failed to allege its trade secret claim with sufficient particularity where the plaintiff claimed that the defendant had misappropriated trade secrets including "source code, customer lists and customer related information, pricing information, vendor lists and related information, marketing plans and strategic business development initiatives, 'negative knowhow' learned through the course of research and development, and other information related to the development of its price-optimization software, including ideas and plans for product enhancement."

In *Space Data Corp. v. X*, 2017 WL 5013363, *2 (N.D. Cal. Feb. 16, 2017), the district court found that general allegations of trade secrets consisting of "data on the environment in the stratosphere" and "data on the propagation of radio signals from stratospheric balloon-based transceivers" were insufficient to identify trade secrets. In addition, the plaintiff's misappropriation allegations were insufficient when the plaintiff alleged only that the "[d]efendants have engaged in other business activity based on Space Data's confidential trade secret information, which conflict with their legal obligations to Space Data." The "conclusory allegations" were not supported with adequate "factual allegations." *Id.* at *2.

In *AlterG, Inc. v. Boost Treadmills LLC*, 388 F. Supp. 3d 1133, 1145–46 (N.D. Cal. 2019), the court determined that the plaintiff failed to allege trade secrets with sufficient particularity where the plaintiff alleged that the defendants misappropriated "[n]umerous learnings from [the plaintiff's] Low-Cost Platform Project," which included "positive and negative learnings of low cost mechanical unweighted systems, air pressure systems," trade secrets related to its "development of anti-gravity rehabilitation products" and "mechanical unweighting mainframes," including "technology and negative information and learnings," and "trade secret information related to design and development of anti-gravity rehabilitation and training units . . . marketing and product strategy, cost strategies, customer needs, material selection and fabrication techniques, engineering and structural technology, selection and qualification of components, knowledge of vendors with appropriate, specialized skills, and technology innovation." *Id.* The court explained that such broad categories of information were too vague. Although the plaintiff alleged that the trade secrets at issue were covered by confidentiality agreements, the court noted that the plaintiff only summarized broadly the categories of information protected by the agreements, which was not sufficient to identify the trade secrets at issue. *Id.*

2. Alleging Ownership

A plaintiff must be able to allege ownership rights in the trade secret. *See Jasmine Networks, Inc. v. Superior Court*, 180 Cal. App. 4th 980, 996, 999 (2009); *see also Cal. Police Activities League v. Cal. Police Youth Charities*, No. C 08-1991 PJH, 2009 WL 537091, at *4 (N.D. Cal. Mar. 3, 2009) (holding plaintiff failed to allege any factual basis for ownership of the alleged trade secrets); *see also Farhang*, 2010 WL 2228936, at *12-*13 (holding plaintiffs' inconsistent allegations of ownership of some of the alleged trade secrets, though "troubling," were not a basis for dismissal of the complaint). There is no requirement that plaintiff must be the current owner of the trade secrets, but a former owner must be able to allege ownership at the time of the misappropriation and/or injury resulting from the misappropriation. *Jasmine Networks*, 180 Cal. App. 4th at 986, 996, 999.

3. Alleging Independent Economic Value of the Trade Secret

A plaintiff is required to allege that the information has independent economic value that is derived from not being generally known to the public or other persons who can obtain economic value from its disclosure or use. Cal. Civ. Code section 3426.1(d)(1). The focus of the inquiry is "on whether the information is generally known to or readily ascertainable by business competitors or others to whom the information would have some economic value." *Altavion, Inc. v. Konica Minolta Sys. Lab'y, Inc.*, 226 Cal. App. 4th 26, 62 (2014) (citing *Syngenta Crop Protection, Inc. v. Helliker* 138 Cal.App.4th 1135, 1172 (2006)).

An allegation of "significant competition in the mobile space to achieve similar objectives and the known demand for solutions to known needs and problems in the mobile platform space" adequately alleged the independent economic value element of a CUTSA claim. *See Farhang*, 2010 WL 2228936, at *14; *see also TMX Funding*, 2010 WL 2509979, at *4 (holding this element is satisfied with respect to passwords as the information's only economic value derives from not being generally known to others); California Civil Jury Instructions (CACI), Trade Secret Series, CACI 4412 (Judicial Council of California, 2021) (detailing factors for jury to consider when determining whether trade secret has actual or potential independent economic value). Even if component parts of the alleged trade secret are readily ascertainable (*i.e.*, doll names Bratz and Jade could readily be found in a dictionary), they still may be entitled to trade secret protection if their use for a product in development is secret and that secrecy provides the idea value. *See Mattel, Inc.*, 782 F. Supp. 2d at 962-63, 964 ("Not all product plans derive independent economic value from not being generally known to the public, but some may."). Likewise, allegations of the amount of resources invested by the plaintiff in the production of the information, the precautions taken by the plaintiff to protect the secrecy of the information, and the willingness of others to pay for access to the information, may also support this element. *Altavion, Inc.*, 226 Cal. App. 4th at 62.

4. Alleging Reasonable Efforts to Maintain Secrecy

Allegations that hospital required employees to sign nondisclosure agreements, password protected computer files, limited access to sensitive materials to a need-to-know basis, locked office doors and file cabinets, and required employees to acknowledge employee handbook which outlined confidentiality duties were sufficient allegations of reasonable efforts to maintain secrecy. *Coast Hematology-Oncology Assocs. Med. Grp., Inc. v. Long Beach Mem'l Med. Ctr.*, 58 Cal. App. 5th 748, 764 (2020); *accord TMX Funding*, 2010 WL 2509979, at *4 (allegations that a company required employees to sign agreements to protect the confidentiality of the trade secrets and that the company employed computer login procedures and password protection to protect the information are sufficient to support the element of making reasonable efforts to maintain secrecy); *see also* California Civil Jury Instructions (CACI), Trade Secret Series, CACI 4404 (Judicial Council of California, 2021) (detailing factors jury should consider when deciding whether reasonable efforts were used to protect secrecy of the trade secret). Generally speaking, allegations that a trade secret was disclosed in a publicly filed patent or copyright application will defeat this required element of a CUTSA claim. *See Aqua-Lung Am., Inc. v. Am. Underwater Products, Inc.*, 709 F. Supp. 2d 773, 788 (N.D. Cal. 2010) (holding that issuance of patent extinguishes trade secret, but reserving for jury whether the defendant misappropriated the trade secret during the window of time before the patent was published); *Spring Design, Inc. v. Barnesandnoble.com, LLC*, No. C 09-05185 JW, 2010 WL 5422556, at *4-*5 (N.D. Cal. Dec. 27, 2010) (trade secret extinguished upon patent publication); *Kema, Inc. v. Koperwhats*, No. C-09-1587 MMC, 2010 WL 726640, at *3-*4 & n.3 (N.D. Cal. Mar. 1, 2010) (allegations of submission of source code to Copyright Office contradicts allegation that reasonable efforts were made to maintain the secrecy of the source code). *But see Farhang*, 2010 WL 2228936, at *14 (allegation that plaintiff included trade secret core technology in patent application did not defeat CUTSA secrecy element because plaintiff alleged that it filed the patent application with a "non-published status"). Thus, allegations regarding materials submitted to the Patent or Copyright Offices must be carefully tailored to avoid inconsistency with allegations that the same or similar materials are trade secrets.

5. Alleging Misappropriation

Plaintiff must plead facts alleging that the defendant improperly acquired, used, or disclosed the trade secret. Mere possession of the trade secret is not enough. If the misappropriation theory is based on improper acquisition of a trade secret, there need to be facts alleged from which it can be concluded that the defendant is in wrongful possession, even if the defendant was originally entitled to possess the trade secret. California Civil Jury Instructions (CACI), Trade Secret Series, CACI 4401 (Judicial Council of California, 2021). "The owner of the trade secret is protected only against the appropriation of the secret by improper means and the subsequent use or disclosure of the improperly acquired secret. There are various legitimate means, such as reverse engineering, by which a trade secret can be acquired and used." *Cadence Design Sys., Inc. v. Avant! Corp.*, 29 Cal. 4th 215, 222 (2002). Defendants' breach of confidence, copying materials and taking designs and plans and similar allegations are sufficient to allege improper acquisition. *See, e.g., Vacco Indus., Inc. v. Van Den Berg*, 5 Cal. App. 4th 34, 50 (1992), modified (Apr. 14, 1992). If plaintiff's misappropriation theory is grounded on improper use or disclosure of the trade secret, plaintiff must allege sufficient facts to indicate such improper use or disclosure has occurred. *Compare Farhang*, 2010 WL 2228936, at *7 (plaintiff did not allege misappropriation of trade secret in violation of terms of a non-disclosure agreement where a joint venture agreement's terms superseded the NDA and plaintiff otherwise did not allege sufficient facts indicating that third parties had access to and used the trade secrets) *with TMX Funding*, 2010 WL 2509979, at *4 (allegation on information and belief that defendants used trade secret passwords and login information to access plaintiff's servers and computer network in order to misappropriate and destroy plaintiff's trade secret information on those systems was adequate to allege misappropriation). *But see JustMed, Inc. v. Byce*, 600 F.3d 1118, 1131 (9th Cir. 2010) (holding under Idaho's version of the Uniform Trade Secrets Act ("UTSA") that defendant's acts to delete and withhold source code from employer to gain leverage in pending dispute with employer did not constitute misappropriation because his actions did not diminish the value or secrecy of the code). Misappropriation of a trade secret customer list was adequately alleged where the complaint stated defendant accessed plaintiff's customer information hours before his resignation, taking massive amounts of records with him, and further alleged defendant later made sales to certain of those customers. *Ikon Office Solutions*, 2010 WL 5129293, at *3; *see also DocMagic, Inc. v. Ellie Mae, Inc.*, 745 F. Supp. 2d 1119, 1145 (N.D. Cal. 2010) (holding factual allegations regarding difficulty and expense in compiling customer list, defendant's misuse of the list and solicitation of plaintiff's customers support plausible inference of misappropriation).

In order to use or disclose a trade secret, a defendant need not comprehend how the trade secret works. *Silvaco*, 184 Cal. App. 4th at 229. However, in order to use the trade secret, one must have knowledge of the trade secret. *Id.* at 225-26. The defendant does not, however, have to have knowledge of the original means of acquisition of a trade secret by the third party from whom the defendant acquired the trade secret—just knowledge sufficient to allow a reasonable person to infer that he or she was in wrongful possession of another's trade secret. *See Monex Deposit Co. v. Gilliam*, 680 F. Supp. 2d 1148, 1165-66 (C.D. Cal. 2010); *Silvaco*, 184 Cal. App. 4th at 226, 229 (discussing knowledge requirement under CUTSA "use" provision; separately discussing that "liability presupposes the defendant's 'possession' of misappropriated information"); *PMC, Inc. v. Kadisha*, 78 Cal. App. 4th 1368, 1385 (2000), *as modified on denial of reh'g (Apr. 7, 2000)* (the fact that company improperly acquired trade secret before defendants invested in company did not insulate defendants from liability).

While possession of the trade secret is a necessary predicate to misappropriation, possession alone without allegations of use or disclosure of the trade secrets will not give rise to a valid claim under the CUTSA. *See Silvaco*, 184 Cal. App. 4th at 223, 226 and 229 ("one who passively receives a trade secret, but neither discloses or uses it, would not be guilty of misappropriation"); *Aqua-Lung*, 709 F. Supp. 2d 773 at 788. Where a company acquires a competitor's employees who possess trade secrets, the business decision not to segregate those employees may not in itself be enough to demonstrate an affirmative threat to use or disclose trade secrets. *Edifecs Inc. v. TIBCO Software Inc.*, 756 F. Supp. 2d 1313, 1319-20 (W.D. Wash. 2010). "The only 'threat' that TIBCO has made with respect to Plaintiff's trade secret is the 'threat' of opting not to segregate its employees following a lawful acquisition of another company. The Court declines to interpret TIBCO's business decision with respect to how to comply with its confidentiality obligations as commensurate to an affirmative threat to disclose Edifecs' trade secret. Because plaintiff has not alleged that TIBCO has made any threat, manifested by words or conduct, that would indicate imminent misuse, Plaintiff has failed to state a claim upon which relief can be granted." *Id.* Moreover, it must be clear that it is the trade secret itself that the defendant has used, and not simply "something that was made using the secret" such as use of machine-readable code for a computer program rather than the trade secret source code. *Silvaco*, 184 Cal. App 4th at 224. Similarly, lawful possession of trade secrets with only allegations that plaintiff believes the defendant "intends to disclose" the trade secrets without any plausible factual allegations indicating imminent misuse falls short of a valid CUTSA claim. *So. Cal. Inst. of Law v. TCS Educ. Sys.*, No. CV 10–8026 PSG (AJWx), 2011 WL 1296602, at *8 (C.D. Cal. Apr. 5, 2011).

In *Oakwood Laboratories, LLC v. Thanoo*, the court rejected the district court's conclusion under the DTSA that the plaintiff had failed to allege adequately how the defendants misappropriated the plaintiff's trade secrets. The district court determined that allegations of access or that products or processes were similar were insufficient and that Oakwood's allegations needed to show that use of Oakwood's trade secrets was the only way Aurobindo could have developed its new products.

The Third Circuit found that the district court's understanding of "use" was unduly restrictive and that circumstantial evidence could be used to imply use. In the context of the DTSA, "the 'use' of a trade secret encompasses all the ways one can take advantage of trade secret information to obtain an economic benefit, competitive advantage, or other commercial value, or to accomplish a similar exploitative purpose, such as 'assist[ing] or accelerat[ing] research or development.'" *Id.* at *12. The Third Circuit explained:

> Because the term "use" is incorporated into substantively identical definitions of "misappropriation" under the DTSA and UTSA, and because courts have consistently interpreted the term "use" in a broad manner under the UTSA – which also aligns with its ordinary meaning – there is every reason to continue giving "use" that expansive interpretation. [Citations omitted.] Avoiding a cramped definition of "use" is also consistent with giving trade secret owners a fair opportunity to prove misappropriation. The implication of use, especially at the pleading stage, can flow from circumstantial evidence alone. [Citations omitted.]

Id. at *11–12.

The Court found that the allegations of access, similarities of products, timing and other facts were certainly sufficient to raise an inference of use and the plausibility of trade secret misappropriation. The court specifically rejected a heightened pleading standard of probability rather than plausibility. *Id.* at *15.

In *Alta Devices, Inc. v. LG Elecs., Inc.*, 343 F. Supp. 3d 868 (N.D. Cal. 2018), the plaintiff manufacturer of thin-film solar technology brought action against electronics manufacturer LG alleging that LG breached its duties under a non-disclosure agreement (NDA) and used information provided by the plaintiff (Alta) to create a competing product. The court examined LG's contention that Alta had failed to plead facts that sufficiently alleged that LG had used Alta's trade secrets. LG argued that it properly received Alta's confidential information through the NDA and the fact that its products were similar to Alta's was not sufficient to show that it had used Alta's trade secrets. The court noted that Alta's allegations describing specific types of information it shared along with features of LG's products provided support for Alta's claims of misappropriation. Moreover, the court agreed with prior case law that under the DTSA there is no requirement that a plaintiff plead exactly how a defendant improperly obtained or used an alleged trade secret, and that in the absence of discovery it would be unreasonable to require a plaintiff to demonstrate the precise ways a defendant may have used its trade secrets. *Id.* at 883 (citing *Autodesk, Inc. v. ZWCAD Software Co.*, 2015 WL 2265479, at *6 (N.D. Cal. May 13, 2015)).

In *Five Star Gourmet Foods, Inc. v. Fresh Express, Inc.*, 2020 WL 513287, at *7 (N.D. Cal. Jan. 31, 2020), where the defendant was accused of misappropriating the plaintiff's trade secrets and using them to replicate the plaintiff's salad production facility, the court found that touring the plaintiff's production facilities and gathering information under a non-disclosure agreement sufficiently alleged access to the trade secrets. Those allegations along with allegations that defendant copied the plaintiff's business operations down to using the same tool set to create its packaging was sufficient to allege misappropriation under the DTSA. *Id.* at *8.

In *Navigation Holdings, LLC v. Molavi,* 445 F. Supp. 3d 69 (N.D. Cal. 2020), the court found allegations sufficient that former employee (Molavi) had misappropriated trade secrets, but allegations of indirect misappropriation against others acting in concert with him were insufficient. To state a claim for indirect trade secret misappropriation, a plaintiff must allege facts showing that a defendant:

> (a) knew or had reason to know before the use or disclosure that the information was a trade secret and knew or had reason to know that the disclosing party had acquired it through improper means or was breaching a duty of confidentiality by disclosing it; or (b) knew or had reason to know it was a trade secret and that the disclosure was a mistake.

Id. at 78–79.

The court found that the complaint made only a conclusory assertion that defendants other than Molavi "had reason to know that the confidential information and trade secrets were acquired under circumstances giving rise to the duty to maintain their secrecy or limit their use." Such a bare assertion was held inadequate under federal law as it was "devoid of any factual substantiation of Defendants' knowledge." *Id.*

In *Glam & Glits Nail Design, Inc. v. #NotPolish, Inc.*, 2021 WL 2317410, *5 (S.D. Cal. June 7, 2021), the plaintiff was a nail care products manufacturer and vendor focusing in part on nail salons owned and operated by Vietnamese Americans and sued its former employee and her new employer alleging misappropriation of confidential customer information. Allegations that, among other things, the defendants began contacting the plaintiff's Vietnamese speaking customers to solicit their business using their private cell phone numbers were sufficient to allege misappropriation under the DTSA.

6. Alleging Damages

A plaintiff must plead facts showing that misappropriation caused damage to the plaintiff. *E. & J. Gallo Winery v. Instituut Voor Landbouw-En Visserijonderzoek*, No. 117CV00808DADEPG, 2018 WL 2463869, at *7 (E.D. Cal. June 1, 2018). A general statement that plaintiff has as a "'direct and proximate result' of defendant's violation, 'sustained special and general damages'" can be a sufficient allegation to withstand a Rule 12(b)(6) motion and a more detailed statement of damages is not required, provided other allegations in the complaint support the misappropriation claim. *See, e.g., VasoNova, Inc. v. Grunwald*, No. C 12-02422 WHA, 2012 WL 6161041, at *4 (N.D. Cal. Dec. 11, 2012).

But where a plaintiff sells its trade secrets and retains the right to sue for misappropriation occurring prior to the sale, it may lose its damages claim, unless it can allege that the sale price was adversely affected. *Jasmine Networks, Inc. v. Superior Court*, 180 Cal. App. 4th 980, 996 (2009) (noting in a trade secret case that "if [plaintiff] sold the property for the same value it would have had in the absence of the defendant's conduct, and if he himself has not been sued by the purchaser, he is unlikely to establish any compensable harm"). *See also E. & J. Gallo Winery* at *8 (Where a plaintiff sold its business, it could not plausibly allege that it suffered any damages as a result of defendants' alleged trade secret misappropriation. "Plaintiff MCD divested itself of all interest in the RW dryer business well before defendants allegedly took any action with respect to plaintiffs' trade secrets. Even if defendants are currently using the alleged trade secrets to sell a rival RW dryer, the resulting harm would accrue only to plaintiffs Gallo and G3, the respective owner and licensee of the RW dryer business.")

In *Oakwood Lab'ys LLC v. Thanoo*, 999 F3d. 892, 2021 WL 2325127 (3d Cir. June 8, 2021), the Third Circuit held that by pleading misappropriation of a trade secret, the plaintiff sufficiently pleads damages under the DTSA. "By statutory definition, trade secret misappropriation *is* harm." *Id.* at 913 (emphasis in original). "The trade secret's economic value depreciates or is eliminated altogether upon its loss of secrecy when a competitor obtains and uses that information without the owner's consent. Thus, cognizable harm is pled when a plaintiff adequately alleges the existence of a trade secret and its misappropriation." *Id.* As explained by the Court of Appeals, there is no need to allege that a defendant has launched a competing product or otherwise employed the information for profit. *Id.* at 914.

> There are other, if not yet fully realized, injuries. Aurobindo's rapid market entry into a sector of the pharmaceutical industry with few competitors may well deprive Oakwood of market share. Utilizing Oakwood's trade secrets provides Aurobindo a jumpstart in an industry it would otherwise not have competitively joined for another decade. Aurobindo will avoid substantial research and development costs that Oakwood has already invested in its own product development. Those are competitive harms recognized in the DTSA, 18 U.S.C. § 1836(b)(3)(B), and they represent a sample of the several approaches by which the amount of harm—not simply the fact of harm (which inheres in the unlawful use itself)—may be measured.

Id.

B. Practice Tips

Draft pleadings carefully by:

- Being mindful not to disclose the actual substance of trade secrets in publicly filed documents;

- Providing reasonable notice of the issues;
- Giving reasonable guidance so the defendant can initiate and respond to discovery;
- Considering whether the allegations may invite an anti-SLAPP special motion to strike, *see infra* Chapter 9;
- Avoiding copyright or patent preemption, *see infra* Chapter 9; and
- Avoiding CUTSA preemption of concurrent common law and statutory causes of action, *see infra* Chapter 9.

C. Sample Trade Secret Allegations

The following paragraphs contain representative allegations for a trade secret complaint. These allegations should follow the jurisdictional, venue, capacity of parties, and other introductory allegations.

In the course of its business, [Plaintiff] has invested ____________ in the development of confidential and trade secret information. This trade secret information includes, but is not limited to, the following category [or categories] of information: _________. Plaintiff is and at all relevant times has been the owner of the trade secret information.

The trade secret information derives independent economic value from ____________ [specify why it has independent economic value]. The trade secret information is not generally known to the public or to persons who can obtain economic value from its disclosure or use, and it gives [Plaintiff] a competitive advantage in its ability to __________.

[Plaintiff] has used and uses a variety of reasonable means to protect the secrecy of the information, including _______________.

On or about _____ [and continuing to the present], [Defendant] misappropriated the trade secret[s] by ____________. [Or on or about _____ [and continuing to the present], [Defendant] has threatened imminently to misappropriate the trade secret[s] by ____________.]

As a result of the ______, [Plaintiff] has been harmed and [Defendant] has been unjustly enriched in an amount to be determined according to proof at trial, but in no event less than $______.

To the extent [Defendant] is permitted to continue to misappropriate ______, [Plaintiff] will be irreparably harmed and the economic damages to [Plaintiff] will be difficult to quantify. Moreover, [Defendant] will not be able to compensate [Plaintiff] for the loss of its _____________. [Explain].

[Plaintiff] has no adequate remedy at law.

[Plaintiff] is informed and believes and based thereon alleges that [Defendant's] acts alleged above were done willfully, with malice toward [Plaintiff], and such that [Plaintiff] is therefore entitled to an award of exemplary damages against [Defendant] in an amount according to proof.

§ 8.02 Defenses to the Misappropriation of Trade Secrets Complaint

There are a number of ways in which a litigant can defend against a claim of trade secret misappropriation, including attacking the elements of the trade secret claim and asserting a variety of affirmative defenses. In federal court, allegations of affirmative defenses to a trade secret action must satisfy the same pleading requirements as the complaint; they must meet the *Iqbal/Twombly* standard. A trade secret defendant must, therefore, be prepared to do more than simply state the applicability of a defense, and may be challenged by plaintiff if he fails to allege facts in support of those defenses in the answer. *See Nextdoor.com, Inc. v. Abhyanker*, No. C-12-5667 EMC, 2013 WL 3802526, at *9-*10 (N.D. Cal. July 19, 2013).

A. Attacking the Elements of the Claim

The most common defense to a trade secret claim is to attack the basic elements of the claim. Challenges of this type do not need to be made with affirmative defenses, as the trade secret owner bears the burden of proving the elements of the claim. *Sargent Fletcher, Inc. v. Able Corp.*, 110 Cal. App. 4th 1658, 1668-70 (2003).

1. Ownership Element / Standing

Counsel opposing a misappropriation claim may attack a plaintiff's standing to assert the claim if there is any doubt that the plaintiff owns the trade secret information. *See, e.g.*, *Computer Sciences Corp. v. Computer Assocs. Int'l*, Nos. CV 98-1374-WMB SHX, CV 98-1440-WMB SHX, 1999 WL 675446, at *6 (C.D. Cal. Aug. 12, 1999) ("In the present case, ownership of the alleged trade secrets is synonymous with standing."); *Voith Hydro, Inc. v. Hydro West Group, Inc.*, No. C-96-1170 SC, 1997 WL 154400, at *7 (N.D. Cal. Mar. 26, 1997) ("[P]laintiff has not met the requirement [of proving] that it ever owned a trade secret in the potential flow turbine and therefore has failed to establish the misappropriation of a trade secret.").

The issue of whether a former trade secret owner continues to have standing to bring a claim for violation of the CUTSA may be closely tied to the terms of plaintiff's agreements to sell its trade secrets, including whether plaintiff reserved the right to bring claims for past infringement or sold that right along with the trade secrets. *See Jasmine Networks*, 180 Cal. App. 4th at 1010. Another issue is whether plaintiff's sale of the trade secrets destroys his standing because it eliminates any claim for damages. *See id.* at 996-97 ("[T]he viability of his claim may hinge on his ability to prove damages; if he sold the property for the same value it would have had in the absence of defendant's conduct, and if he himself has not been sued by the purchaser, he is unlikely to establish any compensable harm.").

2. Secrecy Element

Counsel may focus on proving that the alleged secrets do not qualify for trade secret protection or that they have lost that protection through voluntary disclosure. Whether the plaintiff consistently applied procedures for maintaining the secrecy of alleged trade secrets is a possible argument to undermine a CUTSA claim. *Mattel, Inc. v. MGA Entm't, Inc.*, 782 F. Supp. 2d 911, 959-60, 965 (C.D. Cal. 2011) (noting mixed evidence regarding Mattel's procedures for maintaining secrecy, including vague direction to employees and failure to mark all documents as confidential).

3. Misappropriation Element

Counsel may also focus on denying the element of misappropriation. Two common ways of doing so are to contend that the defendant independently developed the information or reverse engineered the information. In practice, defendants present their proof of independent development or reverse engineering as evidence to rebut any showing of misappropriation made by plaintiffs. In addition, to the extent that the alleged trade secret is easily subject to discovery by reverse engineering, it probably negates that it is a true trade secret, which is another element of the plaintiff's prima facie case. *See supra* Chapter 1.

Counsel also may wish to focus on whether plaintiff can prove defendant's improper acquisition, use or disclosure of the alleged trade secrets. *See, e.g., JustMed, Inc. v. Byce*, 600 F.3d at 1131 (holding under analogous Idaho UTSA provision, there was no "use" of trade secret because there was no diminution in the value or secrecy of the trade secret); *Aqua-Lung,* 709 F. Supp. 2d at 788 (holding disputed issues of fact existed concerning whether defendant gained any competitive advantage as a result of having possession of trade secret information that was subsequently patented and made public); *Edifecs Inc. v. TIBCO Software Inc.*, 756 F. Supp. 2d 1313, 1319–20 (W.D. Wash. 2010) (mere possession of trade secret does not constitute misappropriation without threat to use).

A defendant's compliance with a court order to return trade secret information is *not* a defense to a misappropriation claim. *See Monex Deposit Co. v. Gilliam*, 680 F. Supp. 2d 1148, 1166 (C.D. Cal. 2010). Likewise, the mere fact that a defendant did not actively "steal" the document containing the trade secret information and was never an employee or partner of the plaintiff and had never signed a non-disclosure agreement, are unavailable defenses to a CUTSA claim where the defendant had reason to know that the trade secret was acquired through improper means by the third party who provided the trade secret to defendant. *See id.*

In cases alleging the misappropriation of a customer list, defendants may deny the element of misappropriation by raising the so-called "professional announcement" argument. *See supra* Chapter 2.

4. Remedies

Though challenging plaintiff's ability to prove his damages is not an affirmative defense, defendant should consider challenging whether plaintiff can support a causal relationship between the misappropriation and claimed damages, whether plaintiff can prove actual loss, unjust enrichment or entitlement to a reasonable royalty, and whether plaintiff can prove the requisite intent for exemplary damages. *See, e.g.*, Cal. Civ. Code § 3426.3; *Ajaxo Inc. v. E*Trade Fin. Corp.*, 187 Cal. App. 4th 1295, 1305 (2010); *E. & J. Gallo Winery,* 2018 WL 2463869, at *8; California Civil Jury Instructions (CACI), Trade Secret Series, CACI 4409, 4411 (Judicial Council of California, 2021); *see also infra* Chapter 13.

B. Readily Ascertainable By Proper Means

A defendant may defend against a claim of misappropriation by arguing that the information was readily ascertainable by proper means. In California, this contention is an affirmative defense on which the defendant bears the burden of proof. *See* California Civil Jury Instructions (CACI), Trade Secret Series, CACI 4420 (Judicial Council of California, 2021) (instruction for readily ascertainable by proper means) and CACI 4408 (Judicial Council of California, 2021) (detailing means through which it is *not* improper to acquire a trade secret); *DVD Copy Control Ass'n v. Bunner*, 31 Cal. 4th 864, 899 (2003) (Moreno, J., concurring) ("[T]he assertion that a matter is readily ascertainable by proper means remains available as a defense to a claim of misappropriation. Information is readily ascertainable if it is available in trade journals, reference books, or published materials.") (citation and internal quotation marks omitted); *ABBA Rubber Co. v. Seaquist*, 235 Cal. App. 3d 1, 21-22 n.9 (1991) (listing elements a defendant must establish to prove the defense).

C. Equitable Defenses

Traditional equitable defenses, including laches, unclean hands, estoppel, judicial estoppel, and waiver, may apply in trade secrets cases. *See Vacco Indus. v. Van Den Berg*, 5 Cal. App. 4th 34, 52-53 (1992); *Whitted v. Williams*, 226 Cal. App. 2d 52, 58 (1964); *Ingrassia v. Bailey*, 172 Cal. App. 2d 117, 125 (1959); *Ajaxo Inc.*, 187 Cal. App. 4th at 1295.

D. Contract Defenses

When the action is based on an employment contract or other agreement, counsel should consider and plead appropriate contractual defenses.

E. Federal Preemption

Federal patent and copyright law may preempt CUTSA or DTSA claims under certain circumstances. *See infra* Chapter 9. Defendants should plead federal preemption as an affirmative defense in appropriate cases.

F. Litigation Privilege

The litigation privilege under section 47 of the California Civil Code may provide a defense if the alleged improper disclosure was made in a legislative proceeding, judicial proceeding, or other protected setting, and the other requirements of section 47 are satisfied. *See* Cal. Civ. Code § 47(b). *But see ITT Telecom Prods. v. Dooley*, 214 Cal. App. 3d 307, 319-20 (1989) (holding that section 47 of the California Civil Code litigation privilege does not trump employee's nondisclosure agreement in which he agreed to protect employer's trade secrets, noting factual situation before the court did not involve judicially compelled disclosure of trade secrets).

G. Preemption

Though not an affirmative defense to a misappropriation claim, defendants should consider asserting a trade secrets preemption defense to common law and statutory causes of action alleged alongside the trade secrets claim. To the extent these claims arise from similar facts as the trade secrets claim, they may be preempted. *See* Cal. Civ. Code § 3426.7; *see also infra* Chapter 9.

H. Statute of Limitations

The three-year statute of limitations is an affirmative defense under both the CUTSA and the DTSA for which defendant has the burden of proof. This defense should be alleged if there is a possibility plaintiff's claim is untimely. *See* CACI 4421 (Judicial Council of California, 2021); 18 U.S.C. § 1836(d). For a more detailed discussion of this defense, *see infra* Chapter 9.

Chapter 9
OTHER PROCEDURAL ASPECTS
By: James D. McNairy, Esq.

---

§ 9.01 Statute of Limitations

A. Three Years

Claims for misappropriation of trade secrets under both the California Uniform Trade Secrets Act ("CUTSA") and the Defend Trade Secrets Act ("DTSA") are subject to three-year statutes of limitations. 18 U.S.C. § 1836(d); Cal. Civ. Code § 3426.6.

The Judicial Council of California introduced a new jury instruction in 2009 directed to the CUTSA statute of limitations. *See* California Civil Jury Instructions (CACI), Trade Secret Series, CACI 4421 (2011). The instruction makes clear that, while it is the defendant's burden to prove that the misappropriation occurred more than three years before the lawsuit was filed in order to prevail on the statute of limitations defense, it is the plaintiff's burden to prove (to overcome the defense if the defendant meets its burden) that the statute should be tolled because plaintiff did not and could not have discovered the trade secret misappropriation any earlier. *Id.*; *see also Glue-Fold, Inc. v. Slautterback Corp.*, 82 Cal. App. 4th 1018, 1024, 1026 (2000).

A defendant who contends in a motion to dismiss that a CUTSA or DTSA claim is time-barred must be able to establish that it is clear from the face of the complaint that the statute has run and no tolling is possible. *See Mediostream, Inc. v. Microsoft Corp.*, 869 F. Supp. 2d 1095, 1110 (N.D. Cal. 2012); *Brocade Commc'ns Sys. v. A10 Networks, Inc.*, No. 10-CV-03428-LHK, 2011 WL 1044899, at *3 (N.D. Cal. Mar. 23, 2011); *Zirvi v. Flatley*, 433 F. Supp. 3d 448, 459-460 (S.D.N.Y. 2020), *aff'd 838 Fed. Appx. 582 (2d Cir. 2020)* (granting 12(b)(6) on ground that action was time barred under the DTSA). A plaintiff who opposes a motion to dismiss by contending that the statute should be tolled because it could not have discovered the misappropriation any earlier cannot contradict facts alleged in its complaint. *See Creative Compounds, LLC v. Boldt*, No. 10-CV-1411-WQH, 2011 WL 108550, at *2 (S.D. Cal. Jan. 12, 2011). A plaintiff can also take the offensive at the pleading stage by moving to strike an inadequately pled statute of limitations defense, provided the complaint alleges that any acts of misappropriation occurred within three years of the filing of the action. *Cisco Systems, Inc. v. Chung*, No. 19-CV-07562-PJH, 2021 WL 427293, at *7 (N.D. Cal. Feb. 8, 2021) (granting motion to strike the defense under both the CUTSA and DTSA).

Where reference to evidence outside the pleadings is necessary to demonstrate that a CUTSA or DTSA claim is time-barred, a summary judgment motion is the appropriate vehicle. *See Brocade Commc'ns Sys.*, 2011 WL 1044899, at *4. However, a defendant who moves for summary judgment must (1) conclusively prove when the cause of action accrued, and (2) negate the discovery rule, if it has been raised, by proving as a matter of law that there is no genuine issue of material fact about when the plaintiff discovered, or should have discovered, the misappropriation. *Raytheon Co. v. Indigo Sys. Corp.*, 688 F.3d 1311, 1318 (Fed. Cir. 2012) (applying California and Texas law). Whether or not a plaintiff "should have known" under the discovery rule is ordinarily a question of fact. *Id.* at 1316; *see also Delphix Corp. v. Actifio, Inc.*, No. 13-CV-04613-BLF, 2014 WL 4792232, at *2 (N.D. Cal. Sept. 24, 2014) (citing to *Raytheon*).

B. No Tolling for Continuing Misappropriation

A common practice flaw is the view that a continuing act of misappropriation tolls the statute of limitations. However, section 3426.6 of the California Civil Code provides: "An action for misappropriation must be brought within three years after the misappropriation is discovered or by the exercise of reasonable diligence should have been discovered. For the purposes of this section, a continuing misappropriation constitutes a single claim." Cal. Civ. Code § 3426.6. The counterpart subsection of the DTSA is substantially the same, providing that a claim "may not be commenced later than 3 years after the date on which the misappropriation with respect to which the action would relate is discovered or by the exercise of reasonable diligence should have been discovered. For purposes of this subsection, a continuing misappropriation constitutes a single claim of misappropriation." 18 U.S.C. § 1836(d).

The California Supreme Court held in *Cadence Design Systems, Inc. v. Avant! Corp.*, 29 Cal. 4th 215 (2002), that "a *claim* for misappropriation of a trade secret arises for a given plaintiff against a given defendant only once, at the time of the initial misappropriation, subject to the discovery rule provided in section 3426.6." *Id.* at 222 (emphasis in original); *see also Whittaker Corp. v. Execuair Corp.*, 736 F.2d 1341, 1345 (9th Cir. 1984); *Monolith Portland Midwest Co. v. Kaiser Aluminum & Chem. Corp.*, 407 F.2d 288, 292-93 (9th Cir. 1969); *Sec. People, Inc. v. Medeco Sec. Locks, Inc.*, 59 F. Supp. 2d 1040, 1044 (N.D. Cal. 1999), *aff'd mem.*, 243 F.3d 555 (Fed. Cir. 2000) (same); *Intermedics, Inc. v. Ventritex, Inc.*, 822 F. Supp. 634, 646 (N.D. Cal. 1993). Therefore, under both the CUTSA and the discovery rule, a continuing misappropriation constitutes a single claim, and suspicion of the first act of alleged misappropriation triggers the statute of limitations for the entire claim, even as to later acts of misappropriation. *Gabriel Techs. Corp. v. Qualcomm Inc.*, 857 F. Supp. 2d 997, 1003 (S.D. Cal. 2012). In the face of this authority, even the artful pleader cannot avoid the three-year limitations period by claiming that the defendant continues to misappropriate the trade secrets at issue. This holds true for claims under the DTSA as well. *See Profil Institut fur Stoffwechselforschung GmbH v. ProSciento, Inc.*, No. 16CV1549-LAB (BLM), 2017 WL 1198992, at *3 (S.D. Cal. Mar. 31, 2017).

Although a continuing misappropriation does not give rise to multiple statutes of limitations dates under section 3426.6, there may be more than one statute of limitations date in cases involving more than one defendant. "[A] plaintiff may have more than one claim for misappropriation, each with its own statute of limitations, when more than one defendant is involved." *Cypress Semiconductor Corp. v. Superior Court*, 163 Cal. App. 4th 575, 583 (2008). In that case, the court found that the plaintiff's derivative misappropriation claim against a third-party customer of the original misappropriator was subject to its own separate statute of limitations analysis. *Id.*

Federal courts have also concluded that separate acts of misappropriation by co-defendants are not necessarily continuing misappropriation under Cal. Civ. Code § 3426.6, and thus separate statutes of limitations can apply to multiple defendants. *See Cadence Design Systems,* 29 Cal. 4th at 225 (rule that separate claims of misappropriation among different defendants may exist does not conflict with court's conclusion that "there is only a single [C]UTSA claim against a single defendant misappropriating a single plaintiff's trade secret"); *Mattel, Inc. v. MGA Entm't, Inc.*, 782 F. Supp. 2d 911, 1000-1001, 1003 (C.D. Cal. 2011) ("'continuing misappropriation' refers to multiple acts by *one* individual and not, as here, many other employees"). *But see Mediostream, Inc.,* 869 F.

Supp. 2d at 1111 (separate claims for trade secret misappropriation against multiple defendants all barred based on earlier litigation of trade secret claim involving one of the defendants where same nucleus of facts involved in both cases).

Unlike the CUTSA, the DTSA applies where at least some misappropriation occurred after the date of its enactment. *See* 18 U.S.C. § 1839(5). Thus, provided some act of acquisition, disclosure, or use of a trade secret occurred after May 11, 2016, a party can sue under the DTSA for protection of a trade secret that was initially disclosed before that date. *AlterG, Inc. v. Boost Treadmills LLC*, 388 F.Supp.3d 1133, 1146 (N.D. Cal. 2019) (noting that "courts have generally held that the continued use of a trade secret after the effective date of the DTSA is actionable, even if the secret was initially disclosed prior to May 11, 2016").

C. No Tolling for Lack of Activity

Another common limitations-related mistake is the view that if the misappropriator stops his misuse of the trade secret information, the statute of limitations also stops running. Trade secret owners should not be lulled to sleep by a misappropriator's apparent decision to cease using their trade secrets. Under both the CUTSA and the DTSA, the first act of disclosure, acquisition, or use of a trade secret triggers the running of the statute of limitations, and subsequent inactivity or cooperation by the defendant does not toll the limitations period. *Glue-Fold*, 82 Cal. App. 4th at 1024, 1026 ("'If objectively reasonable notice of misappropriation exists, three years is sufficient time to vindicate one's legal rights.' . . . [I]t is the first discovered (or discoverable) misappropriation of a trade secret which commences the limitation period.") (citation omitted); *see also B&P Littleford, LLC v. Prescott Machinery, LLC*, 417 F.Supp.3d 844, 851 (E.D. Mich. 2019) (citing to the same quoted language in interpreting the DTSA). Because a three-year period of inactivity followed by renewed misappropriation will relate back to the original act of misappropriation, a claim for renewed use after three years of inactivity will likely be barred.

D. Accrual

"The general rule is that a statute of limitations begins to run when the cause of action accrues. A cause of action accrues when, under the substantive law, the wrongful act is done, or the wrongful result occurs, and the consequent liability arises." *Cypress Semiconductor*, 163 Cal. App. 4th at 585 (citations and internal quotation marks omitted). "Developed to mitigate the harsh results produced by strict definitions of accrual, the common law discovery rule postpones accrual until a plaintiff discovers or has reason to discover the cause of action." *Glue-Fold*, 82 Cal. App. 4th at 1029. The DTSA and the CUTSA codify the common law discovery rule. Cal. Civ. Code § 3426.6 ("An action for misappropriation must be brought within three years after the misappropriation *is discovered or by the exercise of reasonable diligence should have been discovered.*") (emphasis added); 18 U.S.C. § 1836(d) ("A civil action under subsection (b) may not be commenced later than 3 years after the date on which the misappropriation with respect to which the action would relate *is discovered or by the exercise of reasonable diligence should have been discovered.*") (emphasis added).

Courts have articulated the moment at which a trade secret cause of action accrues, and the limitations period begins to run, in different ways:

- When the plaintiff has "suffered appreciable harm from [the defendant's] wrong." *Glue-Fold*, 82 Cal. App. 4th at 1027.

- When the plaintiff has "a *suspicion* of wrongdoing, coupled with a knowledge of the harm and its cause." *Snapp & Assocs. Ins. Servs. v. Robertson*, 96 Cal. App. 4th 884, 891 (2002), *disapproved on other grounds by Aryeh v. Canon Bus. Solutions, Inc.*, 55 Cal. 4th 1185, 1196-97 (2013) (emphasis in original); *see also Gabriel Techs. Corp. v. Qualcomm Inc.*, 857 F. Supp. 2d 997, 1003 (S.D. Cal. Mar. 13, 2012) (granting summary judgment and holding misappropriation claim barred on statute-of-limitations grounds because plaintiffs had reason to suspect wrongdoing, notwithstanding failure to follow up on those suspicions); *Mattel, Inc.*, 782 F. Supp. 2d at 1000-1001 (citing *Snapp*); *Teradata Corporation v. SAP SE*, No. 18-CV-03670-WHO, 2018 WL 6528009, at *8 (N.D. Cal. Dec. 12, 2018) (concluding that the plaintiff pled lack of any "*reasonable suspicion* of misappropriation" until a date within the statute of limitations under both the DTSA and the CUTSA) (emphasis added).

- When there is a *threat* of misappropriation (even if all the elements of *actual* misappropriation have not yet been satisfied). Cal. Civ. Code § 3426.2(a); *see also Intermedics*, 822 F. Supp. at 642 & n.7. While no decision has addressed this argument under the DTSA, the DTSA does have a provision parallel to § 3426.2(a) that would permit the same argument. *See* 18 U.S.C. § 1836(b)(3)(A)(i) (permitting injunctions "to prevent any actual or threatened misappropriation"); *see also Alta Devices, Inc. v. LG Electronics, Inc.*, No. 18-CV-00404-LHK, 2019 WL 1924992, at *14 (N.D. Cal. Apr. 30, 2019) (citing to *Intermedics*).

The CUTSA and DTSA impose a duty of reasonable diligence on the plaintiff to act when it is aware of facts that could lead it to suspect misappropriation. *Snapp*, 96 Cal. App. 4th at 891; *Intermedics*, 822 F. Supp. at 653-54 (applying the CUTSA) (analyzing statutory purposes and framework and concluding that "[a] law based on these concerns would impose on plaintiffs a responsibility to take prompt and assertive corrective action with respect to all of plaintiffs' interests whenever plaintiffs detect a fracture in a once confidential relationship"); *HiRel Connectors, Inc. v. United States*, 465 F. Supp. 2d 984, 992 (C.D. Cal. 2005) (statute of limitations begins to run when one using reasonable diligence to discover the misappropriation should have learned of it, rather than upon actual notice of misappropriation); *Mediostream, Inc.*, 869 F. Supp. 2d at 1111 (plaintiff's misappropriation claims against individual and corporate defendant time-barred; plaintiff had notice of their relationship with alleged misappropriator through previously filed lawsuit and reasonable investigation would have revealed alleged complicity in misappropriation); *Medcenter Holdings Inc. v. WebMD Health Corp.*, No. 1:20-CV-00053 (ALC), 2021 WL 1178129, at *5 (S.D.N.Y. Mar. 29, 2021 (applying the reasonable diligence standard to trade secret claims under the DTSA and under New York law). The test for awareness under the statute-of-limitations analysis is not when "'plaintiff is in a position to present evidence which will (regardless of what evidence the defense musters) establish facts which make liability a legal certainty.'" *Cypress Semiconductor*, 163 Cal. App. 4th at 585 (citing *Intermedics*, 822 F. Supp. at 641).

Several federal district court decisions have applied the "suspicion of wrongdoing" accrual standard set forth in *Snapp*. *See Gabriel Techs. Corp. v. Qualcomm Inc.*, No. 08 CV 1992 MMA (POR), 2010 WL 3718848, at *8-*9 (S.D. Cal. Sept. 20, 2010) (holding claim is time-barred because plaintiff had reason to suspect wrongdoing given inquiry into defendant's patent disclosures); *Mattel, Inc.*, 782 F. Supp. 2d at 1000-1001 (citing *Snapp*); *Raifman v. Wells Fargo Advisors, LLC*, No. C 11-02885 SBA, 2014 WL 12013436, at *12 (N.D. Cal. Mar. 31, 2014), *aff'd sub nom. Raifman v. Wachovia Securities, LLC (9th Cir. 2016) 649 Fed.Appx. 611*. Without citing to *Snapp*, one recent decision from the Northern District of California applies essentially the same standard for accrual—of "reasonable suspicion"—to claims arising under both the CUTSA and DTSA *Teradata Corporation v. SAP SE*, No. 18-CV-03670-WHO, 2018 WL 6528009, at *8 (N.D. Cal. Dec. 12, 2018).

The statute of limitations may be tolled by invoking the doctrine of fraudulent concealment. To invoke this doctrine, a plaintiff must "plead with particularity the circumstances surrounding the concealment and state facts showing his due diligence in trying to uncover the facts." *MedioStream*, 869 F. Supp. 2d at 1112 (internal citation omitted); *Zirvi*, 433 F. Supp. 3d at 461 (applying the doctrine to a claim under the DTSA). Plaintiff may not rely on conclusory allegations of concealment.

When a plaintiff-assignee invokes the discovery rule, he bears the burden of proving that all assignors lacked knowledge of the misappropriation and that they diligently pursued their claims when put on notice of their injury. *Bierman v. IBM*, No. C 10-4199 PJH, 2012 WL 506562, at *7-*8 (N.D. Cal. Feb. 15, 2012).

E. No Distinction for Third Parties

The accrual rule is the same whether or not the plaintiff had a previous relationship with the alleged misappropriator. In *Whittaker*, the court emphasized that there is no reason to distinguish between wrongful acquisition of a trade secret by a third party who does not have a confidential relationship with the trade secret holder and wrongful disclosure of a trade secret by a party who stands in a confidential relationship with the trade secret holder: "Whittaker's misappropriation claims in the instant case accrued when Whittaker became aware that [the third party] acquired the drawings alleged to be trade secrets." *Whittaker*, 736 F.2d at 1345.

Some decisions have held that a plaintiff's cause of action against the third party accrues at the time of the breach of the original confidential relationship, *i.e.*, at the time of the original misappropriation. *Ashton-Tate Corp. v. Ross*, 916 F.2d 516, 523 (9th Cir. 1990); *Forcier v. Microsoft Corp.*, 123 F. Supp. 2d 520, 525-26 (N.D. Cal. 2000); *Intermedics*, 822 F. Supp. at 653-54. *But see Cypress Semiconductor*, 163 Cal. App. 4th at 583 ("To the extent *Forcier* holds that the statute of limitations on the third party's misappropriation begins with the initial misappropriation, we reject it.").

In *Cypress Semiconductor*, the court held that "the statute is triggered when the plaintiff knows or has reason to know the third party has knowingly acquired, used, or disclosed its trade secrets." *Id.* at 585 (capitalization omitted). The *Cypress Semiconductor* decision makes clear that a trade secret holder cannot wait until it has certain or direct evidence of misappropriation by a third party (*e.g.*, a customer of an initial misappropriator) to bring its claim against the third party.

§ 9.02 Jurisdiction

A. No Special Rules

There are no special jurisdiction rules for trade secret cases. Jurisdiction for misappropriation claims and other state law claims is properly vested in the superior court. Cal. Const. art. VI, § 4. Absent a specific basis for federal jurisdiction, *see infra* § 9.02(C), a CUTSA trade secrets claim cannot be litigated in federal court. *Duncan v. Stuetzle*, 76 F.3d 1480, 1490-91 (9th Cir. 1996).

B. Trade Secrets Make for Interesting Personal Jurisdiction Questions

While the superior court has general subject-matter jurisdiction over misappropriation claims, the court must also have personal jurisdiction over the defendant in order to adjudicate the case. This treatise does not discuss all of the nuances of achieving personal jurisdiction over a defendant, but it is worth noting that trade secret theories have made for interesting and unique personal jurisdiction questions.

For example, the California Supreme Court has held that the mere posting of trade secret information to a passive website with no interactivity or proven access by California residents, or any demonstration that the infringer knew that posting the trade secret information would harm the trade secret holder in California, was insufficient to establish personal jurisdiction. *Pavlovich v. Superior Court*, 29 Cal. 4th 262, 274-75 (2002). By contrast, the California Court of Appeal held that a foreign national with otherwise insufficient ties to California could be subject to personal jurisdiction in California on the basis that his alleged misappropriation of trade secrets harmed his former employer's customers and business revenues in California. *Integral Dev. Corp. v. Weissenbach*, 99 Cal. App. 4th 576, 587 (2002).

A federal district court held that out-of-state defendants directed their conduct to California in part because many of the customers who were included on the misappropriated trade secret customer list and whom defendants allegedly solicited were located in California. *Language Line Services, Inc. v. Language Services Assoc.*, No. C 10-02605 JW, 2010 WL 5115671, at *3 (N.D. Cal. Dec. 9, 2010). Another district court asserted personal jurisdiction over an entity headquartered in Mexico because its employees directed their conduct towards a California-based plaintiff and because the non-U.S. defendant solicited plaintiff's California-based employees to misappropriate trade secrets. *Bryant v. Mattel, Inc.*, No. CV 04-9049 DOC (RBNx), 2010 WL 3705668, at *18 (C.D. Cal. Aug. 2, 2010). District courts have also found personal jurisdiction in the trade secret misappropriation context when out-of-state defendants made false and misleading statements to the plaintiffs, with the awareness that the plaintiffs were based in California. *MedImpact Healthcare Systems, Inc. v. IQVIA Inc.*, No. 19cv1865-GPC(LL), 2020 WL 5064253, at *9 (S.D. Cal. Aug. 27, 2020); *Cisco Systems Inc v. STMicroelectronics Inc*, No. 5:14-cv-03236-RMW, 2015 WL 5138556, at p. *4 (N.D. Cal. Sept. 1, 2015).

When the complaint does not present a prima facie case showing that it is plausible the defendant misappropriated trade secrets in the jurisdiction, the court may, in its discretion, allow limited discovery to determine the threshold issue of personal jurisdiction. *Heller v. Cepia, L.L.C.*, No. C 11-01146 JSW, 2012 WL 13572, at *13 (N.D. Cal. Jan. 4, 2012).

C. Trade Secret Cases May Be Brought in Federal Court

Although most trade secret cases have historically been litigated in state court, the number of cases brought in federal court has increased since 2016 due to the first of the four following circumstances where cases may be litigated in federal court:

- First, the case may be filed in or removed to federal court on the basis of federal question jurisdiction when a claim arises under the DTSA. 28 U.S.C. §§ 1331, 1441; 18 U.S.C. § 1836(c) (2018). This requires that the trade secret at issue be "related to a product or service used in, or intended for use in, interstate or foreign commerce." 18 U.S.C. § 1836(b); see § 32.02(A) of the Defend Trade Secrets Act Supplement to this treatise (2017).

- Second, the case may be filed in or removed to federal court on the basis of diversity jurisdiction. 28 U.S.C. §§ 1332, 1441 (2018).

- Third, the complaint may require determination of other causes of action that arise under federal law (for example, Lanham Act claims) and the federal court therefore would have jurisdiction of the state claim under its supplemental jurisdiction. 28 U.S.C. § 1367(a) (2018); *Curry v. Del Priore*, 941 F.2d 730 (9th Cir. 1991).

- Fourth, where a case was properly filed in federal court but the federal law causes of action are dismissed or resolved, the court may still exercise its supplemental jurisdiction and resolve the state law claim. 28 U.S.C. § 1367(c)(3) (2018).

Jurisdictional discovery may be permitted to determine a party's domicile when a party relied on the court's diversity jurisdiction in filing its trade secret misappropriation action in federal district court. *Integrated Practice Solutions, Inc. v. Wilson*, No. 13cv00088 BTM (WMC), 2013 WL 3946061, at *4 (S.D. Cal. July 31, 2013). Indeed, the district court abuses its discretion if it denies jurisdictional discovery when that might well demonstrate facts sufficient to constitute jurisdictional basis. *Harris Rutsky & Co. Ins. Services, Inc. v. Bell & Clements Ltd.*, 328 F.3d 1122, 1135 (9th. Cir. 2003).

§ 9.03 Venue

Ordinary rules of venue apply to trade secret claims. *See generally Pac. Coast Title Ins. Co. v. Land Title Ins. Co.*, 97 Cal. App. 2d 829 (1950). *See, e.g., CYBERsitter, LLC v. People's Republic of China*, No. CV 10-38-JST (SHx), 2010 WL 4909958, at *5-*9 (C.D. Cal. 2010) (denying Sony's motion to transfer the CUTSA and copyright action to China on the basis of *forum non conveniens*); *see also Allstate Insurance Company v. Ameriprise Financial Services, Inc.*, 317 F. Supp. 3d 1006, 1011 (N.D. Ill. 2018) (denying defendant's motion to transfer venue where defendant allegedly recruited employees in violation of the DTSA in the judicial district of the ruling court).

Venue is proper for a CUTSA action when the initial misappropriation is alleged to have taken place in the judicial district of the court. *Integrated Practice Solutions, Inc.*, 2013 WL 3946061, at *4.

§ 9.04 Preemption

A. Copyright Preemption

1. Trade Secret Claims Under CUTSA May Be Preempted by the Copyright Act

There is no preemption of claims under the DTSA because these claims arise under federal law. There may be preemption, however, of the CUTSA claims.

There are two elements to consider in determining whether the Copyright Act preempts a state law claim. Preemption occurs when: (1) the work at issue comes within the subject matter of copyright; and (2) the rights granted under state law are equivalent to those protected by the Copyright Act. 17 U.S.C. § 301(a) (2018); *Kodadek v. MTV Networks, Inc.*, 152 F.3d 1209, 1212-13 (9th Cir. 1998); *Valente-Kritzer Video v. Pinckney*, 881 F.2d 772, 776 (9th Cir. 1989); *Del Madera Props. v. Rhodes & Gardner, Inc.*, 820 F.2d 973, 976 (9th Cir. 1987), *overruled on other grounds by Fogerty v. Fantasy, Inc.*, 510 U.S. 517 (1994); *Idema v. Dreamworks, Inc.*, 162 F. Supp. 2d 1129, 1189 (C.D. Cal. 2001); *Balboa Ins. Co. v. Trans Global Equities*, 218 Cal. App. 3d 1327, 1339 (1990).

Is your trade secret claim under the CUTSA preempted?

- Does the subject matter of your trade secret come within the subject matter of copyright?
    - Is your claim based on a:
        - literary work?
        - musical work?
        - dramatic work?
        - pantomime or choreographic work?
        - pictorial, graphic or sculptural work?
        - motion pictures or other audiovisual work?
        - sound recording?
        - architectural work?
        - computer program?
- If so, your claim may be preempted if it seeks rights equivalent to those under copyright law unless:
    - You have alleged an extra element in addition to elements of copyright law:
        - secrecy?
        - disclosure?

2. Do the Works Come Within the Subject Matter of Copyright?

The first prong is met when the works at issue come within the "subject matter of copyright," even where those works may not actually be protected (or even protectable) under the Copyright Act. *Kodadek*, 152 F.2d at 1211-13 (uncopyrighted drawings); *Idema*, 162 F. Supp. 2d at 1189; *Entous v. Viacom Int'l, Inc.*, 151 F. Supp. 2d 1150, 1159 (C.D. Cal. 2001). Works that come within the subject matter of copyright include "original works of authorship fixed in any tangible medium of expression." 17 U.S.C. § 102(a) (2018). "Works of authorship" include (1) literary works; (2) musical works; (3) dramatic works; (4) pantomimes and choreographic works; (5) pictorial, graphic, and sculptural works; (6) motion pictures and other audiovisual works; (7) sound recordings; and (8) architectural works. *Id.* "Compilations and derivative works" are also a subject matter of copyright. 17 U.S.C. § 103(a) (2018). Computer programs are also proper subject matter for copyright protection. *Sega Enters. v. Accolade, Inc.*, 977 F.2d 1510, 1520 (9th Cir. 1992); *Firoozye v. Earthlink Network*, 153 F. Supp. 2d 1115, 1124-25 (N.D. Cal. 2001).

The scope of preemption is broader than the eight categories identified in §§ 102 and 103. "[T]he shadow actually cast by the Act's preemption is notably broader than the wing of its protection." *Endemol Entm't B.V. v. Twentieth Television, Inc.*, 48 U.S.P.Q.2d (BNA) 1524, 1526 (C.D. Cal. 1998) (quoting *United States ex rel. Berge v. Bd. of Trs.*, 104 F.3d 1453, 1463 (4th Cir. 1997)). The works "need only be within the 'subject matter' of copyright," *Idema*, 162 F. Supp. 2d at 1189, regardless of whether they are actually protected under copyright law. Indeed, actual protection is irrelevant to the preemption analysis. *Id.*; *see also Kinsley v. Udemy, Inc.*, No. 19-CV-04334-JSC, 2021 WL 1222489, at *6 (N.D. Cal. Mar. 31, 2021).

3. Are the Rights Protected by Your Trade Secrets Claim Equivalent to Those Protected by the Copyright Act?

The second prong is met "when the rights protected by trade secret law are 'equivalent' to those protected by the Copyright Act." *Idema*, 162 F. Supp. 2d at 1190. To avoid preemption "the state cause of action must protect rights which are qualitatively different from the copyright rights." *Del Madera Props.*, 820 F.2d at 977. Put another way, "[t]he state claim must have an 'extra element' which changes the nature of the action." *Id.*; *see also Kinsley v. Udemy, Inc.*, No. 19-CV-04334-JSC, 2021 WL 1222489, at *6 (N.D. Cal. Mar. 31, 2021) (citing to *Idema*).

This determination is driven by the pleadings. "[T]he court should engage in a fact-specific inquiry into the actual allegations underlying the claims at issue in the case, so as to determine whether the 'gravamen' of the state law claim asserted is the same as the rights protected by the Copyright Act." *Idema*, 162 F. Supp. 2d at 1190 (emphasis omitted).

Consequently, the careful plaintiff should allege extra elements above and beyond the Copyright Act. A passage from *Idema* is instructive:

> [T]o the extent that Plaintiffs' so-called "trade secrets" are merely those same ideas and expressions contained in the above-described materials [which] are within the 'subject matter' of copyright, Plaintiffs' Trade Secrets Act claim is merely a "misappropriation" claim which is preempted by the Copyright Act. There is no

> allegation that the information in the materials was a "trade secret" in the sense that its mere *disclosure* would undermine its value; regardless, there is no allegation that any Defendant *made* such a "disclosure." Rather, the SAC alleges that the Defendants violated the Trade Secrets Act by "using" the information in Plaintiffs' materials. These allegations lack the "element" of "secrecy" that is required to escape preemption under copyright. In other words, Plaintiffs cannot claim that the "use" of their alleged information was a Trade Secrets Act violation without treading on the exclusive domain of copyright; such a claim lacks the "extra element" of "disclosure" of a secret in contravention of a specific duty to keep that information confidential.

Idema, 162 F. Supp. 2d at 1194-95 (citations omitted).

At times, this fact-specific inquiry can lead to different results. *Compare Berkla v. Corel Corp.*, 66 F. Supp. 2d 1129, 1151 (E.D. Cal. 1999) (finding breach of confidence/fiduciary duty claim has extra element of confidential relationship) *and Metrano v. Fox Broad. Co.*, No. CV-00-02279 CAS JWJX, 2000 WL 979664, at *6 (C.D. Cal. Apr. 24, 2000) (same), *with Idema*, 162 F. Supp. 2d at 1191 (finding breach of confidence element not qualitatively different from a copyright claim); *see also Balboa Ins.*, 218 Cal. App. 3d at 1353 (finding that common law trade secret misappropriation and unfair competition claims add "no extra element such as breach of fiduciary duty, breach of confidentiality or improper revelation of a trade secret" and are thus preempted by copyright).

B. Patent Act Preemption

As a general matter, state trade secret law is not preempted by federal patent law. *Kewanee Oil Co. v. Bicron Corp.*, 416 U.S. 470, 484 (1974); *Synopsis, Inc. v. Magma Design Automation, Inc.*, No. C-04-3923 MMC, 2005 WL 8177801, at *8, n. 5 (N.D. Cal. Jan. 20, 2005)

However, "state law cannot operate contrary to the aims of federal patent policy." *Caldera Pharmaceuticals, Inc. v. Regents of University of California*, 205 Cal. App. 4th 338, 352 (2012). Accordingly, patent law does preempt claims in which the plaintiff contends that the defendant misappropriated products or information that are commercially available or in the public domain. *Bonito Boats, Inc. v. Thunder Craft Boats, Inc.*, 489 U.S. 141, 157-60 (1989) (voiding state statute that prohibited use of unpatented, public technology information under the Supremacy Clause) (reconciling *Kewanee*, *Sears, Roebuck & Co. v. Stiffel Co.*, 376 U.S. 225 (1964), and *Compco Corp. v. Day-Brite Lighting, Inc.*, 376 U.S. 234, 237 (1964)); *Sammons & Sons v. Ladd-Fab, Inc.*, 138 Cal. App. 3d 306, 312-13 (1982) (relying on U.S. Supreme Court and other decisions to hold that an unfair competition claim based on defendant's copying of nonsecret product designs was preempted by federal law). To the extent that technology-based state tort claims are premised on the copying, use, or disclosure of nonsecret information, the claims may be preempted by the Patent Act.

As with copyright preemption, avoiding preemption by federal patent law requires that tort claims under state law "include additional elements not found in federal patent law claims." *In re Netflix Antitrust Litigation*, 506 F.Supp. 2d 308, 319 (N.D. Cal. 2007).

C. CUTSA Preemption

Until 2009, California state courts had not addressed one of the most important unresolved questions of California trade secret law: the degree to which the CUTSA preempts common law tort claims. Between the first reported trade secret case in 1913 and the enactment of the CUTSA on January 1, 1985, California courts employed a number of different labels for civil trade secret tort claims, including "trade secret misappropriation," "unfair competition," and "breach of trust."

A foundational question of California trade secret law is whether the CUTSA displaces alternative formulations of civil trade secret claims. Since 1985, the CUTSA has defined secrecy, validated defenses such as reverse engineering, provided for specific remedies, limited exemplary damages, and required pre-discovery identification of trade secrets. Should a plaintiff be permitted to plead alternative tort claims and thus seek different remedies under different procedures? Should the courts recognize two tiers of protected information, one for trade secrets and another for information that is deemed to be somewhere between secret and nonsecret?

In *K.C. Multimedia, Inc. v. Bank of America Tech. & Operations, Inc.*, 171 Cal. App. 4th 939 (2009) , the court of appeal held that the CUTSA preempts other common law tort claims, even if the CUTSA claim itself ultimately proves not to be meritorious. Subsequent decisions have expanded the preemptive or "supersessive" scope of the CUTSA, including where no trade secret claim is pleaded within the complaint—even where no trade secret claim is pleaded, tort claims based on the alleged misuse of confidential information may be preempted.

1. The Statute

California's CUTSA contains a multi-part preemption clause in section 3426.7 of the California Civil Code:

> (a) Except as otherwise expressly provided, this title does not supersede any statute relating to misappropriation of a trade secret, or any statute otherwise regulating trade secrets.
>
> (b) This title does not affect (1) contractual remedies, whether or not based upon misappropriation of a trade secret, (2) other civil remedies that are not based upon misappropriation of a trade secret, or (3) criminal remedies, whether or not based upon misappropriation of a trade secret.

Cal. Civ. Code § 3426.7.

Thus:

- Under section 3426.7(b)(3), the CUTSA does not preempt criminal actions, i.e., those regulated by section 499c of the California Penal Code.
- Under section 3426.7(b)(1), the CUTSA does not preempt claims for breach of a confidentiality contract.

- Under section 3426.7(a), the CUTSA does not preempt statutes that regulate trade secrets or relate to trade secret misappropriation. At the time the CUTSA was enacted, California had a number of statutes on the books that explicitly related to trade secrets—such as section 1060 of the California Evidence Code, which addresses discovery of trade secrets, and various administrative statutes on the handling of trade secrets by government agencies. See, e.g., Cal. Gov't Code § 6254.7(d) (California Public Records Act definition of "trade secrets"). See also, e.g., Cal. Health & Safety Code § 25173; Cal. Lab. Code §§ 6322, 6396. An Assembly Committee digest from the CUTSA's legislative history indicates that this portion of section 3426.7 was intended to clarify that the CUTSA "is generally not intended to affect" such "existing provisions." Assembly Committee Digest for Assem. B. 501 at 2 (Apr. 25, 1983).

The fourth part of the statute, section 3426.7(b)(2), is susceptible of multiple interpretations. The language is based on language from the Model CUTSA stating that the act "displaces conflicting tort, restitutionary, and other law of this State providing civil remedies for misappropriation of a trade secret." Model Uniform Trade Secrets Act § 7(a). The California Legislature altered the proposed Uniform Act language, providing a statement phrased in the negative. The double negative—a statement that the CUTSA does *not* affect other civil remedies that are *not* based on a trade secret—could be interpreted to mean that civil remedies that are based on a trade secret are preempted. However, the statute does not contain a list of tort claims or labels to be preempted. The statute's legislative history indicates that the statute was intended as "substitution of unitary definitions of trade secret and trade secret misappropriation, and a single statute of limitations for the various property, quasi-contractual, and violation of fiduciary relationship theories of noncontractual liability utilized at common law." Letter of Elihu M. Harris to Gov. George Deukmejian presenting Assem. B. 501 for signature, Sept. 14, 1984.

2. California Has Adopted the Majority View That Non-CUTSA Claims Based on Alleged Trade Secret Misappropriation Are Preempted

Shortly after the enactment of the CUTSA in California, some state courts referred generally to the CUTSA's effect on prior law. In *Am. Paper & Packaging Prods. v. Kirgan*, 183 Cal. App. 3d 1318, 1324 (1986), for example, the court of appeal explained:

> The legislative intent was to codify the results of the better-reasoned cases concerning the remedies for trade secret misappropriation and thus provide for a more uniform application in the area of misappropriation through improper means of trade secrets. (CUTSA, 14 U. Laws Ann. 537, 538.)
>
> . . .
>
> Prior to the adoption of the [C]UTSA, decisions in the area of customer lists as trade secrets were founded on equitable principles of common law. To a large extent, those principles have been engrossed by the [C]UTSA. However, to the extent that the [*Aetna Bldg. Maintenance Co. v. West* (1952) 39 Cal. 2d 198] case and its progeny . . . set forth rules in conflict with the dictates of the [C]UTSA, they no longer control.

Am. Paper, 183 Cal. App. 3d at 1324. *See also Cadence Design Sys. v. Avant! Corp.*, 29 Cal. 4th 215 (2002) (indicating, in discussion of the statute of limitations, that conduct taking place before and after the CUTSA's enactment date would be governed by different law); *Vacco Indus. v. Van Den Berg*, 5 Cal. App. 4th 34, 51 n.17 (1992) (holding that if there were a conflict between the common law regarding trade secrets and the CUTSA, the statute would control).

A 1990 California case, *Courtesy Temp. Serv. v. Camacho*, 222 Cal. App. 3d 1278, 1291 (1990), issued a cursory ruling under section 3426.7(a), stating that even if a customer list did not qualify as trade secret, section 17200 of the California Business & Professions Code was still available to bar the defendant's use of the list. It may be argued that the *Courtesy Temp.* decision provides questionable guidance on the scope of the CUTSA preemption for several reasons. First, the *Courtesy Temp.* court seemed to assume without analysis that section 17200 of the California Business & Professions Code was one of the statutes regulating trade secrets that the legislature intended to exempt from the CUTSA preemption through section 3426.7(a) of the California Civil Code. But section 3426.7(a) seems directed to statutes that expressly and directly regulate trade secrets, such as section 1060 of the California Evidence Code. *See supra.* There is no reported California decision in the pre-CUTSA period in which section 17200 was used to regulate trade secret claims. Second, the *Courtesy Temp.* court did not discuss the scope or effect of section 3426.7(b), the statute that most courts consider in deciding the CUTSA preemption. Third, *Courtesy Temp.* did not address general California case law on statutory preemption. Thus, it is not surprising that the brief, conclusory decision in *Courtesy Temp.* was not the final word on the scope of the CUTSA preemption in California.

The scope of the CUTSA preemption under California law was addressed in *K.C. Multimedia*, the first published California state court decision to address the CUTSA preemption in any detail. In that case, the court held that section 17200 claims, like all other non-contractual civil claims, are preempted by the CUTSA if they are based upon the same allegations as the trade secret claim.

The court began its analysis by reference to general principles of statutory interpretation: "[G]eneral and comprehensive legislation, where course of conduct, parties, things affected, limitations and exceptions are minutely described, indicates a legislative intent that the statute should totally supersede and replace the common law dealing with the subject matter." *K.C. Multimedia*, 171 Cal. App. 4th at 953 (quoting *I.E. Assocs. v. Safeco Title Ins. Co.*, 39 Cal. 3d 281, 285 (1985)). The court found that the California CUTSA, with its eleven provisions codified in sections 3426 through 3426.11 of the California Civil Code, is such "general and comprehensive legislation." *Id.* "That breadth suggests a legislative intent to preempt the common law." *Id.*

The court then turned to the language of the statute. Noting that section 3426.7 is a "specific provision concerning preemption," the court adopted the majority view nationwide in holding that section 3426.7(b)(2) "implicitly preempts alternative civil remedies based on trade secret misappropriation." *Id.* (citation omitted). "[W]e agree with the federal cases applying California law, which hold that section 3426.7, subdivision (b), preempts common law claims that are 'based on the same nucleus of facts as the misappropriation of trade secrets claim for relief.' " *Id.* at 958. The court observed that "the determination of whether a claim is based on trade secret misappropriation is largely factual," and "[d]epend[s] on the particular facts pleaded." *Id.* at 954, 958.

Citing the California CUTSA's legislative history, the court stated, "[w]e share the broad view that CUTSA's 'comprehensive structure and breadth' suggests a legislative intent to occupy the field." *Id.* at 957. The court rejected a "narrow view of preemption" pursuant to which preemption would not apply to an alternatively pleaded non-CUTSA claim "so long as it alleges new facts, different injuries and damages, or a different theory of liability." *Id.* at n.7. The court observed that many of the cases applying a narrow view of preemption have different CUTSA preemption statutes than California, and require that the non-CUTSA claim conflict with the CUTSA claim to be preempted. *Id.* at 957. By contrast, non-CUTSA claims are preempted under California law even if they do not conflict with the CUTSA claim. "[T]he CUTSA cases from other jurisdictions that employ a 'something more' test are based on a displacement theory that California did not adopt." *Id.* at 958.

The court rejected the argument that deciding preemption before the ultimate disposition of the CUTSA claims was premature. *Id.* at 952-53. Otherwise, preemption could never be decided until after final judgment. The court held that the preemption analysis should focus on the "facts pleaded," and on "the actual gravamen of [the] complaint." *Id.* at 959. Although the trial court in that case made the preemption decision on a motion *in limine*, the court of appeal found that this was the "functional equivalent" of a demurrer. *Id.* at 952 (citation omitted). In its own application of the preemption doctrine to the facts of the case, the appellate court reviewed the allegations of the complaint and concluded that the plaintiff's claims for breach of confidence, interference with contract, and statutory preemption under section 17200 of the California Business and Professions Code were all based on the same factual underpinnings as the CUTSA claim. *Id.* at 960-96. *But see Courtesy Temp.*, 222 Cal. App. 3d at 1291 (allowing section 17200 claim under section 3426.7(a)).

These claims were preempted and properly dismissed by the trial court even though the CUTSA claim itself ultimately proved unsuccessful. *See K.C. Multimedia*, 171 Cal. App. 4th at 944 (noting that the plaintiff failed to prove its trade secret claim).

The California Court of Appeal followed *K.C. Multimedia* with another important CUTSA preemption decision in *Silvaco Data Systems v. Intel Corp.*, 184 Cal. App. 4th 210 (2010), *disapproved on other grounds by Kwikset Corp. v. Superior Court*, 51 Cal. 4th 310, 337 (2011). In *Silvaco*, the plaintiff Silvaco Data Systems was a computer software vendor that had previously sued its competitor, third party Circuit Semantics, Inc. ("CSI"), for trade secret misappropriation. *Silvaco*, 184 Cal. App. 4th at 216. Silvaco alleged that CSI and two former Silvaco employees misappropriated Silvaco's source code for a software program called "SmartSpice," and used it to develop a competing CSI product called "DynaSpice." *Id.* After obtaining a judgment against CSI, Silvaco sued CSI's customers, including Intel. Silvaco alleged that by using CSI's software, Intel misappropriated the Silvaco trade secrets incorporated into that software. *Id.*

Silvaco asserted a claim for misappropriation of trade secrets under the CUTSA, as well as non-trade secret claims for conversion, common count, common law unfair business practices, statutory unfair business practices under California Business and Professions Code section 17200, and intentional and negligent misrepresentation. *Id.* at 236. The trial court dismissed the non-trade secret claims on the pleadings, sustaining Intel's demurrer on the grounds that those claims were based on the same facts as the trade secret claim, and thus were preempted under California Civil Code section 3426.7(b). *Id.* at 232.

The Court of Appeal affirmed. The court began by conducting a thorough statutory analysis of the CUTSA preemption provision and its legislative history and found that the statutory language and context "manifest a legislative intent to occupy the field of trade secret liability to the exclusion of other remedies." *Id.* at 234. Among other things, the court confirmed that the savings clause of section 3426.7(a) is directed to statutes that expressly and directly regulate trade secrets, such as California Government Code section 6254.7(d). *Id.* at 234-36. "The saving language of section 3426.7, subdivision (a), is readily understood as seeking to preserve the operation of these statutes, and thus to protect confidential, commercially valuable information from disclosure by or through government action—not to preserve preexisting civil remedies for misappropriation of trade secrets." *Id.* at 236.

The *Silvaco* court concluded that the Legislature intended the CUTSA preemption statute to supersede any civil [non-breach-of-contract] remedies "based upon misappropriation of a trade secret," and found based on its review of the complaint's allegations that most of Silvaco's claims were preempted. *Id.* at 236. The claims for conversion and common count were based on Intel's obtaining Silvaco "property"—but the only "property" described in the complaint were Silvaco trade secrets. *Id.* The common law unfair business practices claim was based on "Intel's conduct" as previously alleged, *i.e.* its use of CSI software, and the misrepresentation claims alleged that Intel lied about using CSI software to try to cover up its alleged misappropriation. *Id.* The court observed that "[n]o interest in 'property' was identified other than one arising under trade secrets law . . . . [n]or was any 'conduct' identified that did not depend for its supposed wrongfulness on the use of trade secrets." *Id.* The court did find, however, that the section 17200 claim was not preempted because that claim was based on the contention that Intel aided and abetted CSI in violating a judgment and thus did not relate to the alleged misappropriation of a trade secret. *Id.* at 241-42.

3. Preemption of Non-Trade Secret Information, and Deciding Preemption on a Motion to Dismiss

In affirming the trial court's preemption ruling, the *Silvaco* court rejected certain of Silvaco's arguments that had gained traction in federal courts in California and elsewhere as a basis to deny the preemptive effect of the CUTSA. Silvaco made three related arguments. First, Silvaco argued that preemption is inconsistent with the defense that the information does not constitute "trade secrets" or was not misappropriated, on the theory that only claims that are based upon misappropriation of a "trade secret" are preempted. *Silvaco*, 184 Cal. App. 4th at 231-232, 237. Second, Silvaco argued that it is premature to decide preemption on the pleadings because, at that early stage of the proceedings, there has been no determination whether the information at issue qualifies as a trade secret or was misappropriated. *Id.* at 237. Third, Silvaco contended that it had the right to "plead in the alternative"; that is, if the information over which it claimed trade secret protection ultimately turned out not to be a trade secret, or if it failed to prove the elements of misappropriation, Silvaco had the right to assert alternative causes of action such as conversion and common law unfair competition. *Id.* at 238-40.

The *Silvaco* court "emphatically rejected" these arguments, finding that they would circumvent the statute's purpose of providing a unitary definition of the disparate common law claims relating to the unlawful taking of property:

> [I]nformation is not property unless some law makes it so. If the plaintiff identifies no property right outside of trade secrets law, then he has no remedy outside that law, and there is nothing unsound or unjust about holding other theories superseded.
>
> We emphatically reject the *Cenveo* court's suggestion that the uniform act was not intended to preempt "common law conversion claims based on the taking of information that, though not a trade secret, was nonetheless of value to the claimant." (*Cenveo* [*v. Slater*, 2007 WL 527720 (E.D. Pa. 2007)] at p. *4). On the contrary, a prime purpose of the law was to sweep away the adopting states' bewildering web of rules and rationales and replace it with a uniform set of principles for determining when one is—and is not—liable for acquiring, disclosing, or using "information … of value." (*See* § 3426.8) Central to the effort was the act's definition of a trade secret. (*See* § 3426.1, subd. (d).). Information that does not fit this definition, and is not otherwise made property by some provision of positive law, belongs to no one, and cannot be converted or stolen. By permitting the conversion claim to proceed on a contrary rationale, the *Cenveo* court impliedly created a new category of intellectual property far beyond the contemplation of the act, subsuming its definition of "trade secret" and effectively obliterating the uniform system it seeks to generate.

Silvaco, 184 Cal. App. 4th at 239 & n.22.

The *Silvaco* court also affirmed the trial court's decision to dismiss the preempted claims on a demurrer, holding that the purpose of preemption would be defeated if a court did not dismiss preempted claims on the pleadings. The court referred to other statutes with preemption clauses, such as the workers' compensation act that declares itself the "exclusive remedy" for work-related injuries, and explained that one does not need to analyze whether the claim has merit to determine that preemption applies to bar other claims. *Id.* at 237-38.

The majority of federal district courts that have considered *Silvaco* have followed it in holding that the CUTSA supersedes claims based on the misappropriation of information, even though the information may not satisfy the definition of a "trade secret" under the CUTSA. *SunPower Corp. v. SolarCity Corp.*, No. 12-CV-00694 LHK, 2012 WL 6160472, at *4-*6 (N.D. Cal. Dec. 11, 2012); *see, e.g., Mattel, Inc.,* 782 F. Supp. 2d at 987 (CUTSA "preempts all claims based upon the misappropriation of confidential information, whether or not that information rises to the level of a trade secret"); *Heller,* 2012 WL 13572, at *7 (holding the CUTSA preempts common law claims of wrongful taking and use of confidential information, regardless of whether the information constituted a trade secret); *FormFactor, Inc. v. Micro-Probe, Inc.*, No. C 10-3095 PJH, 2012 WL 2061520, at *14-*15 (N.D. Cal. June 7, 2012) (CUTSA preempts common law claims for breach of confidence and unfair competition regardless of whether the information ultimately meets the statutory definition of a trade secret), *vacated by stipulation,* 2012 WL 6554220, at *1 (N.D. Cal. Nov. 21, 2012); *Valvoline Instant Oil Change Franchising, Inc. v. RFG, Inc.*, No. 12-cv-2079-GPC-KSC, 2013 WL 4027858, at *7-*8 (S.D. Cal. Aug. 5, 2013) (The CUTSA preempts breach of confidence claim because additional factual allegations for claim are based on same nucleus of facts as claim for misappropriation of trade secrets); *Avago Technologies U.S. Inc. v. Nanoprecision Products, Inc.*, No. 16-CV-03737-JCS, 2017 WL 412524, at *6 (N.D. Cal. Jan. 31, 2017) (citing to *SunPower Corp.* and noting that the CUTSA will preempt claims based on misappropriation regardless of whether that information qualifies as a trade secret).

In *SunPower Corp.*, the court followed *Silvaco* and held that claims based on non-trade secret proprietary information are superseded by the CUTSA unless one of the following conditions is met: (1) the plaintiff can allege facts that show that the non-trade secret proprietary information was made property by some provision of positive law on grounds that are qualitatively different from the grounds upon which trade secrets are considered property, or (2) it can otherwise be concluded that the plaintiff's non-trade secret claims allege wrongdoing that is materially distinct from the wrongdoing alleged in a trade secret misappropriation claim. *Id.* at *9 (internal citations omitted). *But see Amron Intern, Diving Supply, Inc. v. Hydrolinx Diving Communication, Inc.,* No. 11-CV-1890-H (JMA), 2011 WL 5025178, at *10 (S.D. Cal. Oct. 21, 2011) (preemption cannot be addressed at the pleading stage "prior to determining whether the allegedly misappropriated information constitutes a trade secret"); *Leatt Corp. v. Innovative Safety Tech., LLC*, No. 09-CV-1301-IEG (POR), 2010 WL 2803947, at *6 (S.D. Cal. July 15, 2010) ("To the extent these claims are based upon non-trade secret information, the Court agrees that they should be allowed to go forward at this stage."); *Navigation Holdings, LLC v. Molavi*, 445 F. Supp. 3d 69, 81-82 (N.D. Cal. 2020) (quoting *SunPower Corp.* and holding that the plaintiffs' tortious interference claims were superseded by the CUTSA because these claims were not "distinct from any trade secret misappropriation").

California courts have also generally followed *Silvaco* in finding that the CUTSA preemption may be decided on the pleadings, *i.e.*, on a demurrer or motion to dismiss. *See RSPE Audio Solutions, Inc. v. Vintage King Audio, Inc.*, No. CV 12-06863 DDP (PJWx), 2013 WL 1120664, at *4 (C.D. Cal. March 18, 2013); *SunPower Corp.*, 2012 WL 6160472, at *14; *see also Heller*, 2012 WL 13572, at *7 (granting motion to dismiss where plaintiff failed to identify any law that confers property rights on his non-trade secret information); *MedioStream, Inc.*, 869 F. Supp. 2d at 1115 (granting motion to dismiss conversion and unfair competition claim on the pleadings); *Farmers Ins. Exch. v. Steele Ins. Agency, Inc.*, No. 2:13-cv-00784-MCE-DAD, 2013 WL 3872950, at *8-*10 (E.D. Cal. July 25, 2013) (dismissing common law claims that are based on the same wrongdoings that are alleged in a CUTSA claim); *Waymo, LLC v. Uber Technologies, Inc.*, 256 F.Supp.3d 1059, 1064 (N.D. Cal. 2017) (Cal. Bus. & Prof. Code § 17200 preempted by the CUTSA); *VibrantCare Rehabilitation, Inc. v. Deol*, No. 2:20-CV-00791-MCE-AC, 2021 WL 1614692, at *4 (E.D. Cal. Apr. 26, 2021) (dismissing claims and portions of claims as preempted on a motion to dismiss).

The court in *Total Recall Technologies v. Palmer Luckey and Oculus VR, LLC*, No. 15-CV-02281 WHA, 2016 WL 199796 (N.D. Cal. January 16, 2016), provided one of the clearest statements of the supersessive scope of the CUTSA:

> Every district court in our circuit to consider this aspect of *Silvaco* has held that CUTSA supersedes claims based on the misappropriation of non-trade secret information, except where there is some other provision of positive law granting a property right in that information [Citations omitted.].
>
> Based on 25 years of practice in California and 16 years on the bench in California, the undersigned judge finds the preemptive sweep of *Silvaco* extraordinarily surprising as a development in California law. Nevertheless, it must be respected and applied.

Total Recall Technologies, 2016 WL 199796, at *7-9 (dismissing as preempted claims for conversion, constructive fraud, and fraud where no trade secrets claim was pleaded).

When claims are not based on the misappropriation of a trade secret, they are not preempted by the CUTSA. *Angelica Textile Servs., Inc. v. Park*, 220 Cal. App. 4th 495, 508 (2013) (breach of fiduciary duty, unfair competition, interference with business relations, and conversion claims survive summary adjudication because theory of liability on these claims was independent of trade secret claim); *Theranos, Inc. v. Fuisz Pharma LLC*, 876 F. Supp. 2d 1123, 1138 (N.D. Cal. 2012) (refusing to find CUTSA preemption where a trade secret claim was not pleaded); *Avago Technologies U.S. Inc. v. Nanoprecision Products, Inc.*, No. 16-CV-03737-JCS, 2017 WL 412524, at *7 (N.D. Cal. Jan. 31, 2017) (distinguishing *Angelica Textile Servs.* and dismissing conversion claim on preemption ground because the value of the property hinged on its confidentiality).

Open questions remain as to whether the CUTSA preempts certain statutory claims expressly predicated upon the misappropriation of data, but federal cases suggest that such claims are not preempted. *See, e.g.*, *Synopsys, Inc. v. Ubiquiti Networks, Inc. et al.*, 313 F.Supp.3d 1056, 1074-1075 (N.D. Cal. 2018) (declining to find preempted a claim for violation of California Penal Code Section 502); *JEB Group, Inc. v. San Jose, et al.*, No. 19-CV-04230-CJC, 2020 WL 2790012, at *4 (C.D. Cal. 2020) (same).

4. Preemption and the DTSA

The DTSA expressly provides that it shall not "preempt or displace any other remedies, whether civil or criminal, provided by United States Federal, State, commonwealth, possession, or territory law for the misappropriation of a trade secret," except that employers must still comply with the whistleblower notice provisions of 18 U.S.C. §§ 1833(b) and 1838. *See infra* Chapter 6; *see also PNR Marketing Solutions LLC. v. Fun Flicks of Southern California*, No. SACV1801600AGKESX, 2018 WL 11263970, at *4 (C.D. Cal., Dec. 3, 2018); *Heska Corporation v. Qorvo US, Inc.*, No. 1:19CV1108, 2020 WL 5821078, at *4 (M.D.N.C. Sept. 30, 2020). In other words, CUTSA claims will still be available to aggrieved parties.

Unlike the CUTSA, the DTSA does not contain language preempting other causes of action that may arise under the same common nucleus of facts of a trade secret claim. The ramifications of this as well as the DTSA's non-preemption provision currently are open questions (e.g., whether a plaintiff can now assert in a DTSA action related state law claims that would be preempted under the CUTSA). *See, e.g., Study Logic LLC v. 7-Eleven, Inc.*, No. 18-CV-5499 (RJD) (LB), 2019 WL 9047030, at *1 (E.D.N.Y. July 25, 2019) (noting without substantial discussion that, after it became clear his state law claims were preempted by his state trade secret cause of action, the plaintiff amended his complaint to substitute out the state trade secret claim for a DTSA claim).

§ 9.05 Strategic Lawsuit Against Public Participation ("SLAPP") Motions

Like other types of claims, trade secret claims may be subject to dismissal pursuant to California's anti-SLAPP statute. *See* Cal. Code Civ. Proc. § 425.16. If the plaintiff's cause of action "arises from an act by the defendant 'in furtherance of the [defendant's] right of petition or free speech . . . in connection with a public issue,'" then it will be stricken on the pleadings unless the plaintiff can show "a probability of prevailing on the claim." *Simpson Strong-Tie Co. v. Gore*, 49 Cal. 4th 12, 21 (2010).

In *Art of Living Foundation v. DOES*, No. 5:10–cv–05022–LHK, 2012 WL 1565281 (N.D. Cal. May 1, 2012), the plaintiff was a quasi-religious, spiritual wellness organization. Two of its former members started blogs that criticized the organization. The organization sued them for copyright infringement and trade secret misappropriation, in part on the basis that certain manuals and teaching notes disclosed on the blogs were its trade secrets. After finding that the blogging activity constituted protected speech, the court found that the plaintiff presented evidence sufficient to show misappropriation of trade secrets only as to one defendant. As a result, the court denied that defendant's anti-SLAPP motion, while granting the motion put forth by the defendant that was not shown to have misappropriated any of the allegedly secret information. *Id.* at *23.

Like federal courts, California state courts treat anti-SLAPP motions in the trade secret context the same as other contexts. *See Neville v. Chudacoff*, 160 Cal. App. 4th 1255, 1267-70 (2008) (in employer's suit against former employee for breach of contract and misappropriation of trade secrets, granting employer's motion to strike former employee's defamation cross-complaint because the letter sent by employer to former employee's customers was protected by anti-SLAPP statute); *World Financial Group, Inc. v. HBW Ins. & Financial Services, Inc.*, 172 Cal. App. 4th 1561, 1567-68 (2009) (denying defendants' anti-SLAPP motion to strike former employer-corporation's suit for misappropriation of trade secrets because corporation's claim did not arise from constitutionally protected activity).

Chapter 10
HANDLING TRADE SECRETS DURING THE LITIGATION PROCESS
By: Benjamin D. Scheibe, Esq.
and Catherine ("Cathy") Lui, Esq.

---

§ 10.01 Introduction

The trade secret practitioner is faced with a dilemma not faced by attorneys specializing in other types of litigation: how to keep a secret secret. The litigation process is, by law, ordinarily a public one. Yet, the continued vitality and value of trade secret information depends upon its remaining unknown to those who could derive economic value from learning and using that information. Therefore, the practitioner must take care not to destroy by disclosure during the litigation process the very thing his or her client seeks by that litigation to preserve.

Fortunately, California's Uniform Trade Secrets Act (CUTSA), Cal. Civ. Code §3426.1, *et seq.* and the federal Defend Trade Secrets Act (DTSA), 18 U.S.C. § 1836, *et seq.* provide procedural safeguards that allow the careful practitioner to preserve the confidentiality of the claimed trade secret while pursuing an action for its misappropriation. The following sections describe some of these procedural safeguards, as well as the practical precautions that should be used to avoid compromising the confidentiality of the client's trade secrets during the litigation process.

A. The Complaint

Litigation, of course, starts with the filing of a complaint. The complaint is ordinarily a public record document, available to the press, the public at large, and the client's competitors. It, therefore, would be a serious mistake for the practitioner to lay out in detail the client's claimed trade secrets in this public document.

Theoretically, it may be possible to seek some form of pre-filing ex parte order allowing a complaint containing a detailed description of the client's trade secrets to be filed under seal. As a practical matter, however, this is neither necessary nor advisable. The requirements for California pleadings are only that the plaintiff allege basic facts in sufficient detail to give "defendant[s] reasonable notice of the issues which must be met at the time of trial . . . ." *Diodes, Inc. v. Franzen*, 260 Cal. App. 2d 244, 253 (1968) (a pre-CUTSA case); *see also Keyssa, Inc. v. Essential Prods*., No. 17-cv-05908-HSG, 2019 WL 176790, at *2 (N.D. Cal. Jan. 11, 2019) (in analyzing trade secret allegations pleaded under the CUTSA and the DTSA, the language should be "sufficiently particular to place Defendant on notice of what information is at issue in this case at the pleading stage"). Therefore, counsel representing the trade secret owner ordinarily should plead the nature and existence of the trade secret in general terms only. In order to be sufficient to withstand demurrer or a motion to dismiss, the complaint should include the following: (1) a basic description of the nature of the business and the nature of the trade secret in question; (2) allegations that the information is not known to the client's competitors or to others who could derive value from the information; and (3) has been the subject of reasonable efforts to preserve its secrecy. *Diodes,* 260 Cal. App. 2d . at 252 (explaining that plaintiff need not "spell out the details of the trade secret" but must "allege the ultimate facts showing the existence of a trade secret").

Examples of the type of general descriptions of a trade secret or secrets that should ordinarily satisfy pleading requirements are:

- Plaintiff's confidential customer information, including the identities, specific needs, preferences and requirements of, and contact persons at, plaintiff's customers.
- Plaintiff's price levels, profit margins, and production costs.
- Proprietary and confidential information concerning plaintiff's manufacturing capabilities and processes, including proprietary equipment designs and manufacturing processes developed by plaintiff.

Any further description of the nature and specifics of plaintiff's claimed trade secrets in the pleading ordinarily is unnecessary and dangerous. *See Keyssa*, 2019 WL 176790 at *2 ("Requiring Plaintiff to go into more detail risks compelling public disclosure of the same trade secrets Plaintiff seeks to protect.").

Keep in mind, however, to the extent that plaintiff's business is complex or has multiple divisions or products, additional specificity may be needed (for example, so the defendant can know *which* customers, products, prices, profit margins, costs, and such are at issue). The level of specificity ultimately depends on the facts of the case.

B. The 2019.210 Designation

Although not found in the CUTSA proper, the trade secret practitioner must be keenly aware of section 2019.210 of the California Code of Civil Procedure. This provision, known as section 2019(d) of the California Code of Civil Procedure prior to July 1, 2005, places a hold on certain discovery at the outset of a trade secret case. Plaintiff may not conduct any discovery concerning the trade secret or secrets at issue until it identifies those trade secrets with particularity by serving (but not filing) a section 2019.210 designation. The identification of trade secrets required under section 2019.210 of the California Code of Civil Procedure is discussed in detail *infra* in Chapter 11. There is no DTSA requirement for a section 2019.210 designation and the Ninth Circuit has yet to require it for federal cases, but certain courts have required the plaintiff to identify the trade secrets with reasonable particularity before discovery may commence. *See, e.g.*, *Openwave Messaging, Inc. v. Open-Xchange, Inc.*, No. 16-CV-00253-WHO, 2018 WL 2117424, at *4 (N.D. Cal. May 8, 2018) (requiring section 2019.210 identification of trade secrets for misappropriation claim alleged under both the CUTSA and the DTSA).

C. Protective Orders

1. Authority for Protective Order

Perhaps the single most important procedural safeguard provided by the CUTSA is its explicit recognition that courts must be empowered to issue protective orders to ensure the confidentiality of the claimed trade secret. Section 3426.5 of the California Civil Code requires that the court take steps to preserve the secrecy of an alleged trade secret:

> "In an action under this title, a court shall preserve the secrecy of an alleged trade secret by reasonable means, which may include granting protective orders in connection with

discovery proceedings, holding in-camera hearings, sealing the records of the action, and ordering any person involved in the litigation not to disclose an alleged trade secret without prior court approval." Cal. Civ. Code § 3426.5.

The CUTSA thus provides a welcome but necessary exception to the increasing reluctance of courts to shield litigants from the public disclosure that results from most litigation. Note that some courts even have local rules specifically stating that protective orders are "disfavored" *except* in cases where trade secrets are at issue. *See, e.g.*, S.D. Sup. Ct. R. 2.5.5.

While the DTSA does not have explicit statutory provisions regarding protective orders to protect trade secrets such as those found in the CUTSA, Rule 26(c) of the Federal Rules of Civil Procedure authorizes federal courts to issue protective orders. The existence of trade secrets has been recognized as a proper basis for issuing a protective order and sealing documents. *See, e.g.*, *Apple Inc. v. Samsung Electronics Co., Ltd.*, 727 F.3d 1214, 1221-1222 (Fed. Cir. 2013); *Brown Bag Software v. Symantec Corp.*, 960 F.2d 1465, 1470 (9th Cir. 1992), *cert denied*, 513 U.S. 1044 (1994).

A protective order should be sought at the outset of the litigation and at the earliest practicable opportunity. Issuance of a protective order can often be accomplished by stipulation because defendants accused of trade secret misappropriation generally know that their own confidential business information will be revealed through the discovery process. In the event that a stipulated protective order cannot be obtained, or there is a dispute over the terms of such an order, the parties should bring the dispute to the attention of the court as soon as possible by filing a motion for a protective order. Of course, any such motion will need to satisfy the ordinary requirements for a motion for protective order. *See, e.g.*, Cal. Civ. Proc. Code § 2017.020.

2. Form of Protective Order

There can be no "standard," one-size-fits-all form of protective order, and any order should be tailored to the specific allegations and information involved in the lawsuit. Nevertheless, a number of courts now post sample orders that can be used as starting points.

See, for example, the U.S. District Court for the Northern District of California, at https://www.cand.uscourts.gov/wp-content/uploads/forms/model-protective-orders/ND_Cal_Patent_Highly_Sensitive_Model_Prot_Ord_Revised.docx,

or the Los Angeles Superior Court, at

http://www.lacourt.org/division/civil/pdf/FormProtectiveOrder1Confidential_1.docx.

Litigants should therefore begin by checking to see if the forum court has posted a suggested form of order and adapt such forms where offered. While it is not recommended that these forms be used slavishly, the fewer the parties deviate from a court's suggested language, the more likely it is that their proposed order will be adopted.

There are certain basic provisions that invariably should be included in any protective order:

First, the protective order should identify generally what types of information will be subject to its coverage. Absent some specification, a court may be reluctant to sign off on a blanket order, especially in light of the increasing reluctance of courts to give litigants and their counsel "carte blanche" in terms of determining what information will be withheld from public scrutiny.

Second, the protective order should provide that the information to be covered thereunder should be identified as such; for example, by being stamped with the designation "Confidential" or "Confidential—Subject to Protective Order." This is important both for practical reasons and to assist in enforcing the order. Without an identifying legend, it may prove difficult to keep track of which documents are covered by the protective order and which are not. This is especially true in cases that involve multiple document productions or that stretch on for months or years. Moreover, should confidential information be misused, proving contempt requires a showing of *willful* disobedience of the protective order. It is more difficult for the alleged wrongdoer to claim that the violation was merely negligent or inadvertent if the information in question is clearly marked as "Confidential" or "Subject to Protective Order." Whatever legend is chosen then should be affixed to all documents containing confidential information, to all discovery responses that discuss or reveal confidential information, to all deposition transcripts that discuss confidential topics or to which confidential documents are attached, and to all motion papers that discuss or synthesize information that has been designated confidential.

Third, the protective order should explicitly prohibit use or disclosure of the information for any purpose other than to prosecute, defend, or settle the lawsuit. Use for business purposes and disclosure to nonparticipants in the litigation process should be prohibited.

Fourth, the protective order should identify by category those persons to whom dissemination and review of the documents will be limited, for example, to counsel and counsel's staff, the clients (if appropriate—see discussion below), experts and consultants (see discussion below), the court, and other persons whose presence is necessary to the litigation (for example, court reporters, videographers, and the like).

Fifth, the protective order should state that any materials subject to the protective order that are to be filed with the court should be filed under seal, following the court's procedures for under seal filings. *See infra* § 10.01(F).

Sixth, the protective order should provide that all persons (besides counsel and the court) who are given access to confidential information be provided with a copy of the order and should be required to sign an acknowledgement that they have read the protective order and agree to be bound by its terms.

Once those general provisions are included, counsel and the client should consider what other provisions to include. Some of the issues that arise are:

- Should the opposing party have access or should dissemination be limited to counsel of record? The client may want certain, super sensitive categories of information withheld from the opposing party and reviewed only by the opposing party's counsel. The parties may want to clarify further that access be limited to a party's outside counsel. *Upjohn Co. v. Hygieia Biological Labs.*, 151 F.R.D. 355, 359 (E.D. Cal. 1993); *Brown Bag Software*, 960 F.2d at 1470. This heightened level of protection should be limited to only very sensitive types of information and information that is understandable to the attorney without assistance from the client or from costly experts.

- Should there be a numerical limitation on access? In those cases where business entity parties are allowed access to confidential information, counsel should consider a numerical limitation on the number of representatives that can review the information. It usually is not necessary for dozens or hundreds of corporate employees to have access to confidential information, and it often is appropriate to limit access to two or three corporate representatives.

- What about experts? Experts are generally given access to information designated confidential and often must see this information in order to form their opinions. Counsel therefore may wish to require that confidential information be provided only to third party experts who do not otherwise have a business affiliation with the client (for example, are neither employees nor business consultants for the client). *See, e.g.*, *Upjohn*, 151 F.R.D. at 361-62. Counsel should consider a provision requiring that all potential experts and consultants be identified in advance so that the producing party can object to having confidential materials shown to a proposed expert or consultant who could pose a competitive threat, though there is likely to be objection that such a requirement improperly compels the premature disclosure of expert identities.

- Should confidential or "Attorneys' Eyes Only" information be shown to mock jurors? Sophisticated parties often test their cases with the aid of jury consultants before a trial. Consider whether this is to the benefit of your client to permit mock jurors access to such information. Usually, jury consultants require the mock jurors to sign confidentiality agreements after they finish the mock jury, but consider whether the protective order should permit mock jurors to review the sensitive materials whatsoever.

- Where should the information be viewed? Although more cumbersome, counsel and the client may wish to require that confidential information (or certain types of confidential information) be reviewed only at the offices of counsel of record and that copies not be distributed to clients or experts. *See, e.g.*, *GT, Inc. v. Superior Court*, 151 Cal. App. 3d 748, 755-56 (1984).

- What about inadvertent disclosure? Particularly in this era of electronic production of large quantities of documents, materials not intended for disclosure (*e.g.*, attorney-client communications) sometimes are inadvertently produced to the opponent. Consider including a "clawback" provision that specifies the procedure to be utilized in the case of such inadvertent production and the manner in which the issue is to be presented to the court if the parties cannot reach agreement on the return of such materials.

- How should confidential materials be handled at the conclusion of the litigation? Alternative ways of proceeding are to require the return of all confidential material (something that can be quite cumbersome and difficult, especially once confidential information is synthesized and discussed in court filings), reciprocal certifications that all confidential materials have been destroyed, or an agreement that confidential materials may remain in the files of litigation counsel but that copies in the possession of opposing clients and experts be returned or destroyed.

- Depositions. Sometimes, it is necessary to show deposition witnesses information that has been designated confidential by one side or the other. This should be done only where necessary to the prosecution of the litigation; otherwise liability may attach. The protective order should anticipate this possibility and require that the court reporter (and videographer if the depositions are videotaped) acknowledge the existence of the protective order and agree to be bound thereby. These support personnel routinely do this. It is significantly more difficult, however, to obtain the consent of an independent third party to agree to be bound by a protective order.

- Dispute resolution mechanism. Once a protective order is in place, a common problem is the "over designation" of materials as confidential. One side or the other may stamp everything confidential, even public record information obviously not deserving of such protection. In those cases where limited categories of information may be designated "Attorney's Eyes Only," disputes often arise over whether this designation is being abused. The protective order should specify the means for resolving these disputes if the parties are unable to agree on a request to remove a "Confidential" or "Attorney's Eyes Only" designation from a certain document or item of information. The burden can be placed on either side to obtain a ruling from the court. The protective order, however, should state that until that ruling is made or the designating party fails to seek a ruling from the court within the allotted time, if it has that burden, the parties shall continue to treat the document in accordance with the designation.

- The jury. The defendant may want a provision in the protective order stating that any physical designations (for example, "Confidential") shall be removed before the document bearing the designations are shown to the jury. In a trade secret misappropriation action, such designations may improperly influence the jury's determination of that claim. For example, the jury may be conditioned to consider the documents truly confidential or sensitive, or may believe the plaintiff took reasonable efforts to protect the alleged trade secret in light of the "Confidential" stamp. The parties may also want to include in the protective order other provisions addressing the use at trial of designated material (and objections thereto). Otherwise, such handling of confidential documents may be addressed with a motion in limine to be decided by the trial judge.

- The courtroom. The protective order may also include a provision, which states that either party whose confidential documents are to be used as exhibits during any hearing or trial should request that the courtroom be closed either throughout the presentation of evidence or at designated times.

3. Checklist of Potential Protective Order Provisions

Again, it should be remembered that every protective order should be tailor-made to the specific case in which it is to be entered. While there is no need to "reinvent the wheel" each time, pre-existing forms and "canned" provisions should be used only after independent thought has been given as to whether each provision is appropriate in the context of the particular case and whether any modification of those provisions is needed.

The following checklist is intended as a guide to the practitioner in determining the issues to be addressed by the protective order:

- What types of information should be protected?
- What levels of protection are required—should there be an "Attorney's Eyes Only" provision?
- How and when should protected information (documents, discovery responses, depositions, and the like) be so designated?
- Which uses and disclosures of confidential information are to be permitted and which are to be prohibited?
- What procedure should be followed if sensitive material is mistakenly delivered without the appropriate designation?
- Who should have access to the information? What about in-house counsel? Is there information that only outside counsel should review? What types of experts should be allowed access and how should that access be handled?
- What security precautions should be required of those who have access to confidential information?
- What obligations should a recipient of confidential information be required to acknowledge?
- How are disputes over the proper classification of materials to be handled?
- How should the use of confidential information at third-party depositions be handled?
- How should the filing of confidential materials with the court be handled?

- What about hearings where confidential information may be referenced?
- What happens if confidential information delivered to the adversary is subpoenaed in another case?
- How should confidential materials remain protected through the trial?
- What should be done with confidential materials upon the conclusion of the litigation? Consider requiring destruction of the confidential materials and a certification within a limited time period after the conclusion of the litigation.

D. Disclosure Through the Discovery Process

Notwithstanding the availability of protections such as protective orders, the party claiming a trade secret nevertheless exposes itself to the possibility that the adverse party might, maliciously or otherwise, destroy the confidentiality of the claimed trade secret. For example, a trade secret defendant might take depositions of plaintiff's other competitors, ostensibly to show that the information plaintiff asserts is a trade secret is generally known. In such cases, the questioning attorney might divulge the trade secrets, deliberately or through the careless framing of the deposition questions. While such disclosure might or might not be considered a violation of whatever protective order is in place, the remedy of contempt is rather hollow in the case of a plaintiff that has just lost its "crown jewels" to a competitor.

1. Section 2025.420 of the California Code of Civil Procedure—A Proactive Means of Avoiding Disclosure

Counsel concerned about the possibility of disclosure by deposition would be well-advised to raise the issue in advance. If the depositions of competitors are noticed, a letter to the noticing party's counsel may be warranted. Counsel can be warned that the trade secret owner will not tolerate any questioning which reveals or even hints at the trade secret process sought to be protected. If counsel for the noticing party does not respond in satisfactory fashion, an application to the court for a protective order under section 2025.420 of the California Code of Civil Procedure or FED. R. CIV. PRO. 26(c)(1)(G) may be sought in advance. Cal. Civ. Proc. Code § 2025.420; FED. R. CIV. PRO. 26(c)(1)(G). Alternatively, once the deposition begins, counsel should be prepared to adjourn the deposition under section 2025.420 or FED. R. CIV. PRO. 26(c)(1)(G) and seek relief from the court if the questioning veers into sensitive areas and risks cluing the competitor or witness in to the client's trade secrets.

2. Non-applicability of Section 47 of the California Civil Code "Litigation Privilege"

Counsel for the party defending the trade secret claim should be aware that the normal protections afforded by the litigation privilege in section 47 of the California Civil Code do not apply in a trade secrets case. Anticipating the problem posed by the deliberate disclosure of a trade secret through the litigation, and in order to guard against such loss of secrecy, the California Legislature in

1992 amended California's version of the CUTSA by adding section 3426.11 to the California Civil Code.

California's litigation privilege, codified in section 47 of the California Civil Code, provides that communications or statements made as part of an official proceeding, such as a lawsuit, are privileged. Cal. Civ. Code § 47. A party cannot be held liable for harm resulting from such a communication though the very same communication might be actionable if it occurred outside of the litigation context. Section 3426.11 of the California Civil Code withdraws the section 47 privilege from certain communications made in a trade secret lawsuit. Specifically, section 3426.11 provides that, notwithstanding section 47, "the voluntary, intentional disclosure of trade secret information, unauthorized by its owner, to a competitor or potential competitor of the owner of the trade secret information or the agent or representative of such a competitor or potential competitor is not privileged and is not a privileged communication" even if done within the context of a lawsuit. Cal. Civ. Code § 3426.11.

As a result, a party or its counsel who intentionally discloses a trade secret to outsiders through the litigation process not only risks exposure to a contempt proceeding based on violation of a protective order but also to civil liability for actual and compensatory damages resulting from the improper disclosure—"misappropriation"—of the trade secret through the litigation process. To date, there are no reported decisions construing section 3426.11.

3. Whistleblower Protection Under the DTSA

Note, however, that the DTSA (in 18 USC §1833(b)(1)(A)), immunizes whistleblowers from civil liability for disclosing trade secrets to a government official or to an attorney if the disclosure is "solely for the purpose of reporting or investigating a suspected violation of law." The District Court in *Christian v. Lannett Co.*, No. CV 16-963, 2018 WL 1532849, *4 (E.D. Pa., March 29, 2018), applied this immunity to a party's transmission, to her own attorney, of documents allegedly containing trade secrets in response to the court's issuance of a discovery order in a case alleging violation of the DTSA. See also Chapter 6.

E. California Evidence Code sections 1060 and 1061

California Evidence Code section 1060 confers upon the owner of a trade secret an evidentiary privilege to refuse to disclose the trade secret and to prevent others from disclosing it, if allowance of the privilege will not tend to conceal fraud or otherwise work injustice. The term "trade secret" is defined in section 1061 by reference to both the CUTSA definition and section 499c. *See also Amgen Inc. v. Health Care Servs.*, 47 Cal. App. 5th 716, 733–34 (2020) (applying the CUTSA definition). Section 1061 sets forth the procedure and evidentiary requirements for asserting the privilege, and the process is discussed in detail in *Stadish v. Superior Court*, 71 Cal. App. 4th 1130, 1144 (1999). There are no parallel evidentiary privileges regarding trade secrets in the Federal Rules of Evidence. *See also* Chapter 16.

F. Court Proceedings and Filing Documents Under Seal

The preceding section dealt with maintaining the confidentiality of claimed trade secrets during the discovery process. Eventually, however, it usually becomes necessary to submit to the court documents containing information claimed by one side or the other to be confidential. This may occur in the context of a discovery dispute (for example, a motion to compel more complete answers to interrogatories requesting a detailed description of the claimed trade secrets), a motion for summary judgment (for example, to seek an adjudication that the information does not qualify for trade secret protection or was not the subject of reasonable efforts to ensure its confidentiality), and, of course, at trial. The following sections discuss the means by which the practitioner may protect the confidentiality of trade secrets when those secrets must be brought before the court at various stages of the litigation.

1. Pretrial Filings—Rules 2.550 and 2.551 of the California Rules of Court

Again, section 3426.5 of the California Civil Code explicitly provides that the court shall preserve the secrecy of an alleged trade secret by reasonable means, which are defined to include "sealing the records of the action." In the past, it was not uncommon for courts handling trade secret claims to simply enter blanket orders sealing the entire file, often at the outset of the case. It may still be possible to induce some courts to do so based on an argument that Rules 2.550 and 2.551 of the California Rules of Court do not apply to trade secret cases. It can be argued that section 3426.5 places documents generated in a trade secrets case within Rule 2.550(a)(2)'s exception: "These rules do not apply to records that are required to be kept confidential by law."

Some implicit support for this argument can be found in *In re Providian Credit Card Cases*, 96 Cal. App. 4th 292 (2002), a non-CUTSA case in which a party sought to have sealed documents that it claimed contained its trade secrets. The court of appeal noted that merely asserting the trade secret privilege in a non-CUTSA context does not bring the mandatory language of section 3426.5 into play, and that Rules 2.550 and 2.551 (then 243.1 and 243.2) therefore govern in non-CUTSA cases involving claims of trade secret. The obvious implication is that, in a CUTSA case, the mandatory language of section 3426.5 should trump Rules 2.550 and 2.551. Given the increasing disfavor with which protective orders and sealed public records are viewed, however, it nevertheless is likely that counsel, even in a CUTSA case, will have to obtain permission to file papers under seal on a motion-by-motion basis under Rule 2.551.[18]

In so doing, counsel should carefully follow the procedures outlined in Rules 2.550 and 2.551, which, in essence, codify the California Supreme Court's decision in *NBC Subsidiary (KNBC-TV) v. Superior Court*, 20 Cal. 4th 1178 (1999). This rather cumbersome procedure requires that the party who wishes to file a document under seal file a noticed motion, "accompanied by a memorandum of points and authorities and a declaration containing facts sufficient to justify the sealing" of the documents in question. Cal. Ct. R. 2.551(b)(1). The motion generally must be accompanied by a copy of the document for which protection is sought, which is only to be lodged with the court. Cal. Ct. R. 2.551(b)(2). Where confidential information is incorporated into a motion

[18] *McGuan v. Endovascular Technologies, Inc.*, 182 Cal. App. 4th 974, 988 (2010), *cert. denied*, 131 S. Ct. 822 (2010), is another non-CUTSA case (a product liability and personal injury action) in which Rule 2.550 was invoked to seal records that contained defendants' trade secrets.

or other document that is to be filed with the court, the party seeking protection should file a redacted version of that motion, omitting all reference to the confidential information (both in the text of the motion and in any attachments) and simultaneously should lodge a complete version of the motion under seal. In this manner, the claimed confidential documents can be returned, unopened, to the party seeking protection in the event that the motion for an order sealing the record is denied. Rule 2.551(d) of the California Rules of Court sets forth the procedure for lodging the confidential information under seal pending a ruling on the request to have the documents filed under seal.

Under the federal rules, a litigant will need to obtain a sealing order to protect its trade secrets and confidential information. Each federal court has local rules regarding how to appropriately seal confidential information. Make sure to check the local rules and the judge's standing orders to comply with the sealing requirements. There is a presumption of public access to court records; therefore, a party seeking to seal court records must show "compelling reasons supported by specific factual findings … outweigh … the public policies favoring disclosure." *Pintos v. Pac. Creditors Ass'n*, 605 F.3d 665, 677-78 (9th Circuit 2010). Compelling reasons include "infringement upon trade secrets." *Id.* at 679, n. 6. The burden is on the party seeking the sealing order to show good cause and a stipulation regarding sealing is often not sufficient. *See Oliner v. Kontrabecki*, 745 F.3d 1024, 1025 (9th Cir. 2014) (despite a joint request to seal the proceedings, sealing was denied as it was still subject to "compelling reasons" standard, which parties did not meet).

The consequences of failing to abide by the procedures specified in Rules 2.550 and 2.551 can be severe. In *Savaglio v. Wal-Mart Stores, Inc.*, 149 Cal. App. 4th 588 (2007), the parties stipulated to a confidentiality order that required any documents designated as "confidential" would be lodged under seal, with a formal motion to follow. Defendant then lodged numerous documents under seal, but did not bring the motions required by Rules 2.550 and 2.551 (and by the stipulated confidentiality order). Some of the "confidential" documents later were lodged with the court of appeal in connection with petitions for writs of mandate challenging the trial court's substantive rulings. By filing with the court of appeal documents for which it had never sought a proper sealing order, the defendant was found to have waived the right to later ask the trial court to seal those records. *Id.* at 598-601.

On the other hand, where confidential materials are mistakenly placed in the public record as a result of a failure to comply with procedures for filing under seal, this will not necessarily result in the loss of trade secret protection. In such a case, the opposing parties and their counsel remain bound to treat such materials in the manner specified by the protective order. *See Wallis v. PHL Assocs.*, 168 Cal. App. 4th 882, 312 (2008). The court in *Wallis* ruled that "substantial compliance" warranted ongoing protection under a protective order. *Id.* at 308-09. Nevertheless, to guard against loss of protection, counsel should take care to adhere to the requirements of Rules 2.550 and 2.551 and any governing protective orders in handling confidential information.

An order sealing or unsealing documents may be directly appealable as a collateral order if it is self-executing. *In re Marriage of Nicholas*, 186 Cal. App. 4th 1566, 1573 n.3 (2010); *H.B. Fuller Co. v. Doe*, 151 Cal. App. 4th 879, 885–886 (2007). Alternatively, review by writ petition may be sought. *In re Marriage of Nicholas*, 186 Cal. App. 4th at 1573 n.3.

2. Discovery Motions

Note that Rules 2.550 and 2.551, by their terms, do not apply to discovery motions or records filed or lodged in connection with discovery motions or proceedings. Cal. Ct. R. 2.550(a)(3). This omission suggests that court approval might not be necessary in order to file under seal a discovery motion containing confidential information. Court clerks, however, may be unschooled in these fine distinctions and may refuse to accept discovery motions that are sought to be filed under seal. Counsel should seek guidance from the court or court personnel in advance, and must be ready to obtain judicial permission to have such motions filed under seal. Usually, it is best to anticipate the need for such filings under seal in a protective order that authorizes filings under seal. *See supra* §10.C.

If documents have been filed under seal with respect to a discovery motion, counsel should further ensure that the courtroom is closed during the hearing on that motion, so as to avoid disclosure to third-party observers. If documents have been marked "attorney's eyes only," it may also be necessary to have the non-disclosing party leave the courtroom during the hearing.

3. Trial

Assuming that counsel and the client have successfully navigated the pretrial process, they will arrive at trial with their claimed trade secrets intact and shielded from the view of competitors and the public. The next step is to ask the trial judge to close the courtroom during those phases of the trial that will involve discussion of the trade secrets. This obviously includes opening statements, testimony, and closing argument but can also include such proceedings as argument on pretrial motions in limine, motions for nonsuit, and post-trial motions for new trial or for judgment notwithstanding the verdict.

Section 3426.5 of the California Civil Code quite clearly authorizes an order closing the courtroom. Although there is no time specified for requesting such an order, it is recommended that counsel raise the issue by motion and do so at the time that other pretrial motions (for example, motions in limine or to bifurcate) are heard. In the Los Angeles Superior Court, for example, this would be at the final status conference and counsel should follow Rule 3.25(f)(2) of the Los Angeles Superior Court Rules, which provides that "trial preparation" motions shall be heard at the final status conference and filed and served sixteen court days in advance of that conference. As part of the motion to close the courtroom, counsel may wish to ask that the reporter be admonished not to provide copies of the transcript to nonparties and that the reporter's transcript bear a legend that it is subject to protective order, and that the clerk not allow nonparties to inspect or obtain copies of trial exhibits that contain or discuss the alleged trade secrets.

In federal courtrooms, there are often local rules or judge's standing orders that govern how the venue will handle confidential exhibits and witnesses testifying about the same at trial. If the local rules or standing rules are not clear, raise these issues at the pre-trial conference with the court so that the parties can plan appropriately for trial.

Section 1062 of the California Evidence Code also sets forth a procedure for excluding the public from criminal proceedings where the owner of a trade secret can demonstrate "a substantial probability that the trade secret would otherwise be disclosed to the public during that proceeding and a substantial probability that the disclosure would cause serious harm to the owner of the secret." Exclusion is appropriate based on such a showing if "the court finds that there is no overriding public interest in an open proceeding."

Finally, counsel should remember that the jury will learn the details of the alleged trade secrets. Voir dire of course should identify any persons who work in competition with any of the parties, and presumably these prospective jurors will be excused. In addition, all jurors are routinely admonished during trial not to discuss what they hear with people outside the courtroom. But jurors are normally freed of this restriction at the time that they are discharged. Therefore, counsel who has successfully prosecuted a misappropriation of trade secrets case should ask the trial judge to admonish the jurors at the conclusion of the case that the information they have learned is confidential and should not be disclosed to others. Counsel may also wish to ask the court to have the jurors sign an acknowledgement that they understand the confidential nature of the information to which they have been exposed if the information is of a type that can be easily understood by a layman, though courts may balk at imposing this additional burden on those who have faithfully discharged their civic duty.

4. The Appellate Record

Rules 2.550 and 2.551 of the California Rules of Court pertain to proceedings in the trial court. Counsel, however, must protect against disclosure of the trade secret during the appellate process as trade secrets will likely be discussed in the parties' briefs, especially if there is any issue on appeal as to whether the information qualifies for trade secret protection or as to the propriety or scope of the injunctive relief issued by the court. Moreover, the reporter's transcript will invariably contain detailed testimony concerning the trade secrets, and it is likely that the trade secrets or other confidential information will be described in various pre- and post-trial filings that are included in the clerk's transcript or the joint appendix or separate appendices. Rule 8.46 of the California Rules of Court governs the sealing of documents filed or lodged with the court of appeal.

In the Ninth Circuit, Circuit Rule 27-13 governs sealed documents. "The Court has a strong presumption in favor of public access to documents." Cir. Rule 27-13(a). Therefore, the Ninth Circuit will permit a filing under seal only if the litigant justifies a motion to seal the document from public view. *Id.* There are certain statutory requirements that permit sealing, see Cir. Rule 27-13(d), but absent a statutory requirement, a party must file a motion to seal, which explains "the specific reasons for the relief and describe the potential for irreparable injury in the absence of such relief." Cir. Rule 27-13(e).

Rule 8.46(c) governs records that previously were sealed in the trial court and that will become part of the appellate record. Such records must be filed under seal and will remain sealed subject only to possible unsealing on motion pursuant to Rule 8.46(f). The parties must include, as part of the appellate record, the trial court's sealing order and all papers filed in the trial court in support of or in opposition to the application or motion that resulted in the trial court order sealing such records. Cal. Ct. R. 8.46(c)(2).

In the Ninth Circuit, if there is no accompanying motion to seal, the district court's sealing order may be lifted and subject to the public record. Cir. Rule 27-13(g). If the filing party does not intend to ask that the district court's sealing order be continued, "the party shall file the documents provisionally under seal, along with a notice of intent to file publicly, in order to allow any other party an opportunity to move for appropriate relief within 21 days of the notice." Cir. Rule 27-13(f). If the other party does not file a motion to continue the seal, then the provisional seal will be lifted without notice and the documents made available to the public. *Id.*

In considering a motion to unseal under Rule 8.46(f), the court of appeal applies (*i.e.*, reapplies) the standards articulated by Rule 2.550(c)-(e). Cal. Ct. R. 8.46(e)(6). The fact that the trial court sealed the record in question is not dispositive; however, the appellate court may order a previously sealed record unsealed. *E.g.*, *H.B. Fuller Co. v. Doe*, 151 Cal. App. 4th 879, 895-98 (2007) (on motion to unseal records sealed by trial court in nontrade secret case, plaintiff failed to carry burden of presenting facts justifying sealing; appellate court therefore ordered records unsealed). If the appellate court orders the records unsealed, it may (but is not required to) order that the records in question be returned, unfiled, to the party seeking to maintain them under seal (a procedure similar to that specified by Rule 8.46(d)). *See Huffy Corp. v. Superior Court*, 112 Cal. App. 4th 97, 109-10 (2003).

Rule 8.46(d) prohibits the sealing of any records that were filed or lodged publicly in the trial court.

Rule 8.46(e) governs the sealing of records that were not filed in the trial court. A party may ask the court of appeal to seal such a record by filing a motion or application similar to that required by Rule 2.551, and by lodging the record that it desires to have sealed in an envelope that "labels the contents as 'CONDITIONALLY UNDER SEAL.' " If the motion or application is denied, the clerk must return the conditionally sealed record(s) to the moving party, unless that party notifies the clerk within 10 days that the record is to be filed notwithstanding the denial of its sealing request.

G. Judgment

The practitioner who successfully prosecutes a claim for trade secret misappropriation has one more task. The judgment in a successful trade secret action will routinely contain a permanent injunction barring the defendants from using, for at least some period of time, the specific information found to be a trade secret. *See infra* Chapter 12. In order to give the enjoined party sufficient notice of that which he or she is to refrain from doing (a due process requirement), such permanent injunctions may be quite specific and contain detailed descriptions of the trade secrets in question.

Because the permanent injunction is made a part of the final judgment, the final judgment must be protected from public view. One way of dealing with this problem is to provide in the judgment that the original judgment be maintained under seal but that a redacted version, omitting only the detailed description of the trade secrets, be made available to the public and to counsel for use in enforcing the monetary provisions of the judgment.

H. Conclusion

Litigating a trade secrets case requires that the practitioner pay close attention to protecting the client's trade secrets. More than one trade secret has been lost by unprotected disclosure during the litigation process. Fortunately, California and federal law provide the practitioner with all the protections needed to prevent such a calamity. The practitioner who plans ahead, and arms himself or herself with a working knowledge of the available procedural mechanisms, should have no problem keeping the secret secret.

Chapter 11
IDENTIFYING TRADE SECRETS IN LITIGATION
By: Randall E. Kay, Esq.

---

§ 11.01 Introduction

In trade secret disputes, California law and Ninth Circuit precedent require that the trade secret holder identify its trade secrets. That identification serves multiple purposes including: (a) enabling the defendant to prepare its defense; (b) equipping the court to rule on pretrial motions; and (c) allowing the trier of fact to determine whether misappropriation occurred. The requirement that trade secret holders identify their trade secrets with "reasonable" or "sufficient" particularity also aids plaintiffs in evaluating the strengths and weaknesses of their own claims early in the life of their lawsuit. California courts require that the plaintiff identify trade secrets before discovery relating to the claimed trade secrets can begin. Federal courts vary in the way they handle pre-discovery disclosure of trade secret identification.

§ 11.02 Ethical Requirements

Ethical rules (*i.e.*, section 128.7 of the California Code of Civil Procedure and Rule 11 of the Federal Rules of Civil Procedure) require a good faith basis to assert a trade secret misappropriation claim at the time of filing a lawsuit. Yet trade secret holders may have a good faith basis to file a lawsuit without knowing the full extent of which particular trade secrets were misappropriated. For example, an employee may have resigned without advance notice and circumstances may show that the employee took company trade secrets for use in a competing business. Computer records may reveal that a departing employee downloaded or printed volumes of trade secret specifications and designs in the middle of the night prior to resigning, likely without any reason other than for use in future competitive employment. While these circumstances may point to misappropriation of some particular trade secrets, other trade secrets accessible to the departing employee also could have been misappropriated. In this situation, the tension that arises is that upon filing the complaint the plaintiff can only identify some of the trade secrets that may have been misappropriated. The plaintiff may want discovery to learn the full extent of the misappropriation. The defendant may want to avoid discovery of undetected wrongdoing.

§ 11.03 Requirements Under California Code of Civil Procedure Section 2019.210 and Ninth Circuit Law

Because complaints are publicly available in courthouse records, they rarely disclose the specific trade secret information at issue. Once litigation is filed, California law requires that trade secret plaintiffs identify the allegedly misappropriated trade secrets with "reasonable particularity" pursuant to section 2019.210 of the Code of Civil Procedure. Cal. Civ. Proc. Code § 2019.210 (operative July 1, 2005, and previously numbered as section 2019(d) of the California Code of Civil Procedure). This statute requires that plaintiffs identify their trade secrets before they can commence discovery relating to the trade secrets. *Id.* The plaintiff has the burden of proof to identify trade secrets with reasonable particularity. *MAI Sys. Corp. v. Peak Computer, Inc.*, 991 F.2d 511, 522 (9th Cir. 1993).

In 2020, the Ninth Circuit indicated that a particularity requirement applies to pre-discovery disclosure of trade secrets in federal court as well, though it remains to be seen precisely what level of particularity applies in federal court, whether the requirement serves the same discovery gating function as section 2019.210, and the extent to which it differs depending on whether the plaintiff brings claims under CUTSA or the DTSA. *See InteliClear, LLC v. ETC Glob. Holdings, Inc.*, 978 F.3d 653, 658 (9th Cir. 2020) (reversing summary judgment for defendant that was based on plaintiff's purported failure to identify trade secrets adequately prior to discovery on plaintiff's CUTSA and DTSA claims). In *InteliClear*, the Ninth Circuit found "a triable issue of fact as to whether [plaintiff] sufficiently identified its trade secrets under both the federal statutory standard," defined as sufficient particularity (seemingly drawn from both the DTSA and federal case law predating the DTSA), "and the state statutory standard" (reasonable particularity under section 2019.210). *Id.* at 658 n.1. The court did not, however, decide which standard should apply. *Id.*

In practice, the process of trade secret identification often consumes an inordinate amount of the parties' time and resources. Unfortunately, it is the uncommon case where the plaintiff comes forward with a specific list of trade secrets and the defendant acknowledges that the plaintiff identified the trade secrets with sufficient particularity.

Often in trade secret disputes, plaintiffs resist identifying their trade secrets with any real particularity. Parties commonly fight over what constitutes the requisite level of particularity. One reason for such disputes is that section 2019.210 does not define "reasonable particularity," and case law sheds little light on the issue. Case law, in fact, suggests that section 2019.210 is purposefully vague so that the law remains flexible for the "court to achieve a just result depending on the facts, law, and equities" of a particular case. *Advanced Modular Sputtering, Inc. v. Superior Court*, 132 Cal. App. 4th 826, 835 (2005). On the federal side, the Federal Rules of Civil Procedure contain no analogue to section 2019.210, and the DTSA does not discuss particularity.

§ 11.04 The Trade Secret Plaintiff's Mindset

Trade secret holders often are quick to conclude that former employees or business partners misappropriated their trade secrets. Trade secret litigation has an emotional aspect to it by virtue of the fact that it often arises from a setting where (a) a valuable employee departs to work at a direct competitor in a similar position, or (b) two companies share trade secrets under a nondisclosure agreement in connection with a potential joint venture, and one party discovers that the other party pursued the opportunity for itself. Plaintiffs often believe that misappropriation "must have occurred" for the other party to have taken the same position in a competing company, or for the other company to have been able to capitalize on a business opportunity. Trade secret holders often point to how quickly the defendant brought a competing service or product to market as proof that the former employee or former partner could not have independently developed the trade secret information.

Plaintiffs sometimes resist identifying their trade secrets because of concern that doing so will harm their case or lead to further misuse of their trade secrets. Plaintiffs might fear that designating trade secrets too broadly could result in the designated information being deemed "generally known to the public" and not protectable. Conversely, plaintiffs may worry that designating trade secrets too narrowly could result in the defendant showing that it does not use those precise methods, techniques, processes, and the like, leading to a finding of no misappropriation. As a result, plaintiffs sometimes attempt to delay the ultimate identification of their trade secrets in litigation.

§ 11.05 The Trade Secret Defendant's Mindset

Defendants accused of misappropriation often react with surprise. Employees who changed jobs to work for competitors regularly state that they believed that they had the right to change employment. Employees maintain that California is a "right to work" state where employers cannot prevent employees from working for a competitor. Employees charge that if they were prevented from using any information they learned while at their prior employer, they would be unable to work in their chosen field. Employees demand to know what information from their prior employer constitutes trade secret information that they allegedly misappropriated in their work at the new employer.

In trade secret lawsuits arising from aborted joint ventures, defendant companies state that, although they explored working with the plaintiff, they decided to carry out their business on their own. The defendant companies hold firm that they merely were exercising their freedom to proceed on their own and that they never used any proprietary information learned from the plaintiff. Defendants say that they cannot understand what the plaintiff could claim as its trade secrets, as the only information discussed between them was common knowledge in the industry. Defendants often react to trade secret claims by stating that the plaintiff company never disclosed any information that could qualify as trade secret information. Defendants also have concern that plaintiffs who delay identifying their trade secrets want to obtain discovery regarding the defendant's technology so that they can tailor the identification of their own trade secrets to match.

§ 11.06 The Need for Trade Secret Identification

In trade secret cases other than when the defendants confess that they stole trade secrets (which rarely occurs but does happen from time to time), defendants usually insist that they need to know the specific trade secrets that they are accused of misappropriating. This need arises because trade secrets are seldom defined between two parties prior to a dispute arising.

Confusion over the specifics of the claimed trade secrets lasts far longer than it should in many disputes. This inevitably increases the costs of litigation for all involved. Despite the California requirement that plaintiffs identify trade secrets at the front end of a lawsuit, parties often fight over the identification of trade secrets up through trial. Disputes over trade secret designations even continue on appeal in some cases.

Some plaintiffs delay providing any real specificity until they obtain discovery from the defendant. Those plaintiffs might then unscrupulously designate their trade secrets in a manner to capture what they found through discovery. That is the exact hazard that California law seeks to prevent.

Some plaintiffs designate trade secrets as broadly as "customer information," "software programs," "processes for etching wafers," or "manufacturing expertise for semiconductors." Where descriptions merely identify the *topic* of the trade secrets, but do not give the defendant notice of the scope of the trade secret, they ordinarily should not be deemed sufficient to meet the particularity required by section 2019.210 or Ninth Circuit precedent. Situations may exist, though, where a plaintiff's identification of categories of trade secrets together with exemplary documents provides sufficient notice to the defendant. *See infra* at section 11.13.

§ 11.07 The Precursor to Section 2019.210—*Diodes v. Franzen*

Prior to the adoption of section 2019.210 of the California Code of Civil Procedure (and its predecessor, section 2019(d)), the case of *Diodes, Inc. v. Franzen*, 260 Cal. App. 2d 244 (1968) addressed the necessity that plaintiffs identify their trade secrets. In *Diodes*, the court held that the plaintiff's description of its trade secret as a "diode manufacturing process" failed to state a claim. *Id.* at 252 n.1, 258. The court affirmed the lower court, which had sustained the defendant's demurrer without leave to amend. The appellate court recognized that one need not "spell out the details" of the claimed trade secret in a complaint in order to avoid a demurrer. *Id.* at 252. The court held, though, that a trade secret plaintiff must plead facts showing the existence of subject matter capable of protection as trade secret. *Id.* Bare legal conclusions that a trade secret exists are inadequate to meet pleading standards. The plaintiff "should describe the subject matter of the trade secret with sufficient particularity to separate it from matters of general knowledge in the trade or of special knowledge of those persons who are skilled in the trade . . . ." *Id.* at 253. Defendants are entitled to "ascertain at least the boundaries within which the [trade] secret lies." *Id.* The plaintiff's disclosure must provide the defendant "reasonable notice of the issues which must be met at the time of trial" and "reasonable guidance in ascertaining the scope of appropriate discovery." *Id.*

Diodes remains good law despite the fact that it predates California's adoption of the UTSA. The court in *Farhang v. Indian Inst. of Tech., Kharagpur*, No. C-08-02658 RMW, 2010 WL 2228936 (N.D. Cal. June 1, 2010), applied *Diodes* to dismiss a claim for trade secret misappropriation. In *Farhang*, the defendant challenged a second amended complaint for failure to allege sufficient facts showing the existence of a trade secret. *Id.* at *12. In granting the motion, the court cited *Diodes* for the proposition that the vague description of a category of trade secrets in the complaint did not describe the subject matter with sufficient particularity to separate it from matters of general knowledge in the trade or of special knowledge of those persons who are skilled in the trade. *Id.* at *13–14.

§ 11.08 Section 2019.210 of the California Code of Civil Procedure

Section 2019.210 of the California Code of Civil Procedure codifies the principles from *Diodes, Inc. v. Franzen*, 260 Cal. App. 2d 244 (1968). Section 2019.210 provides:

> In any action alleging the misappropriation of a trade secret under the Uniform Trade Secrets Act (Title 5 (commencing with Section 3426) of Part 1 of Division 4 of the Civil Code), before commencing discovery relating to the trade secret, the party alleging the misappropriation shall identify the trade secret with reasonable particularity subject to any orders that may be appropriate under Section 3426.5 of the Civil Code.

Cal. Civ. Proc. Code § 2019.210. Section 2019.210 actually builds on the holding in *Diodes* by requiring disclosure and identification of trade secrets as a prerequisite to the plaintiff commencing discovery relating to the trade secrets. Thus, section 2019.210 sets the timing and requirements for the identification of trade secrets.

§ 11.09 Policies Behind Section 2019.210

The case *Computer Econ., Inc. v. Gartner Group, Inc.*, 50 F. Supp. 2d 980 (S.D. Cal. 1999), contains a comprehensive discussion of the policies behind section 2019.210. This opinion cites four primary purposes of section 2019.210: (1) "it promotes well-investigated claims and dissuades the filing of meritless trade secret complaints;" (2) it prevents plaintiffs from conducting "fishing expeditions" in discovery as a means to obtain the defendant's trade secrets; (3) it assists the court in "framing the appropriate scope of discovery;" and (4) "it enables defendants to form complete and well-reasoned defenses" and ensures that defendants "need not wait until the eve of trial to" defend effectively against trade secret claims. *Id.* at 985 (citation omitted). The decision in *Computer Econ.* details the many reasons why the California Legislature adopted section 2019.210, such as trade secret claims being "especially prone to discovery abuse since neither the court nor the defendant can delineate the scope of permissible discovery without an identification of plaintiff's alleged trade secrets." *Id.* at 992.

§ 11.10 Applicability of Section 2019.210 in Federal Court

No consensus has emerged among federal district courts in California regarding whether section 2019.210 applies in federal court. Courts in the Northern District have tended to require trade secret plaintiffs to comply with the rule, reasoning that doing so is proper under the *Erie* doctrine, comports with the court's authority to control the timing and sequence of discovery and issue protective orders, and dissuades forum shopping. *See Soc. Apps, LLC v. Zynga, Inc.*, No. 4:11-CV-04910 YGR, 2012 WL 2203063, at *1–2 (N.D. Cal. June 14, 2012). Courts in the Eastern District generally have not applied section 2019.210, on the ground that it constitutes a state rule of civil procedure that would impose an otherwise un-mandated sequence to discovery in federal court. *See Proven Methods Seminars, LLC v. Am. Grants & Affordable Hous. Inst.*, No. CIV S-07-1588 WBS EFB, 2008 WL 282374, at *2–3 (E.D. Cal. Jan. 31, 2008); *see also Funcat Leisure Craft, Inc. v. Johnson Outdoors, Inc.*, No. S-06-0533 GEB GGH, 2007 WL 273949, at *1–3 (E.D. Cal. Jan. 29, 2007).

Courts in the Central and Southern Districts of California have displayed more variability. *Compare M/A-COM Tech. Sols., Inc. v. Litrinium, Inc.*, No. SACV1900220JVSJDEX, 2019 WL 4284523, at *1–2 (C.D. Cal. June 11, 2019) (declining to undertake an analysis under *Erie* and instead holding that "under the particular facts of this case, the procedural requirements of Section 2019.210 are warranted and appropriate to assist in the orderly and expeditious handling of discovery"); *and Computer Econ., Inc. v. Gartner Group, Inc.*, 50 F. Supp. 2d 980, 988–89 (S.D. Cal. 1999) (ruling that section 2019.210 (then known as section 2019(d)) applied to a trade secret case pending in district court on diversity jurisdiction) *with Conversion Logic, Inc. v. Measured, Inc.*, No. CV195546ODWFFMX, 2020 WL 2046391, at *1–2 (C.D. Cal. Jan. 16, 2020) ("Section 2019.210 imposes burdens on discovery that conflict with the liberal discovery scheme of the Federal Rules of Civil Procedure. Therefore, the Court finds that Federal Rule of Civil Procedure 26, and not section 2019.210, controls the timing of the commencement of discovery in this action."); *Freeman Inv. Mgmt. Co., LLC v. Frank Russell Company*, 2015 WL 13828591, at *3 (S.D. Cal. July 30, 2015) (same).

The Ninth Circuit has yet to decide this issue directly, and the impact of its decision in *InteliClear, LLC v. ETC Global Holdings, Inc.*, 978 F.3d 653 (9th Cir. 2020) remains to be seen. In

InteliClear, defendant ETC Global Holdings ("ETC") moved for summary judgment on InteliClear's CUTSA and DTSA claims the day after discovery opened—before any discovery had taken place—on the ground that InteliClear failed to identify the trade secrets at issue with the requisite particularity. The Ninth Circuit analyzed InteliClear's CUTSA and DTSA claims together, and discussed both section 2019.210's reasonable particularity requirement and a federal "sufficient particularity" requirement. *Id.* at 657-68. Regarding the former standard, the court acknowledged that federal courts have applied 2019.210, specifically citing *Social Apps, LLC v. Zynga, Inc.*, No. 4:11-CV-04910 YGR, 2012 WL 2203063 (N.D. Cal. June 14, 2012), as an example. *InteliClear*, 978 F.3d at 658 n.1 ("Federal courts have applied the state provision in federal cases."). Regarding the "sufficient particularity" standard, the court explained that to prove ownership of a trade secret, a plaintiff "should describe the subject matter of the trade secret with sufficient particularity to separate it from matters of general knowledge in the trade or of special knowledge of those persons ... skilled in the trade." *Id.* at 658 (quoting *Imax Corp. v. Cinema Techs.*, Inc., 152 F.3d 1161, 1164 (9th Cir. 1998)). The court deemed summary judgment inappropriate without determining whether a "reasonable particularity" or "sufficient particularity" standard should apply, finding "a triable issue of fact as to whether InteliClear sufficiently identified its trade secrets under both the federal statutory standard and the state statutory standard." *Id.* at 658 n.1. The court further explained, "it is not fatal to InteliClear's claim that its hedging language left open the possibility of expanding its identifications later. InteliClear's burden is only to identify at least one trade secret with sufficient particularity to create a triable issue." *Id.* at 659.

The Ninth Circuit also reversed the district court's denial of InteliClear's Rule 56(d) request to defer the summary judgment ruling until after discovery. *Id.* at 664. The court opined:

> Refining trade secret identifications through discovery makes good sense. The process acknowledges the inherent tension between a party's desire to protect legitimate intellectual property claims and the need for intellectual property law to prevent unnecessary obstacles to useful competition. Other courts have recognized that plaintiffs in trade secret actions may have commercially valid reasons to avoid being overly specific at the outset in defining their intellectual property.

Id. at 662 (citing *IDX Sys. Corp. v. Epic Sys. Corp.*, 285 F.3d 581, 583 (7th Cir. 2002)).

The Ninth Circuit's decision in *InteliClear* suggests different avenues that California district courts may take in addressing trade secret identification in CUTSA and DTSA claims:

- Courts may relax the gating requirement of trade secret identification, allowing more flexibility in a plaintiff amending and refining its identification during discovery. This could prove especially helpful to plaintiffs in cases with strong evidence of misappropriation coupled with trade secrets that do not bear easy identification, such as where a former employee downloads a large volume of trade secret information before joining a competitor.

- More district courts may apply section 2019.210, given the Ninth Circuit's acknowledgment of that practice with apparent approval (or at least not disapproval).

- Even where a district court does not apply section 2019.210, it may nevertheless require that a claimant identify trade secrets with "sufficient particularity."
- Courts may require pre-discovery disclosure of trade secrets in DTSA cases, despite the absence of any provision parallel to section 2019.210 in the DTSA or Federal Rules.

§ 11.11 Defining Reasonable and Sufficient Particularity

The following cases provide the legal standards for reasonable and sufficient particularity in trade secret cases. Lower courts frequently cite these cases in deciding sufficiency of trade secret identification.

- In *Advanced Modular Sputtering, Inc. v. Superior Court*, 132 Cal. App. 4th 826, 835 (2005), the court held that "reasonable particularity" in section 2019.210 means "that the plaintiff must make some showing that is reasonable, *i.e.*, fair, proper, just and rational" under all of the circumstances to "allow the trial court to control the scope of subsequent discovery, protect all parties' proprietary information, and allow them a fair opportunity to prepare and present their best case or defense at a trial on the merits." *Id.* at 836. The court further stated that "reasonable particularity" does not mean that the claimant "has to define every minute detail of its claimed trade secret at the outset of the litigation." *Id.* at 835. The *Advanced Modular* court specifically stated that the statute does not require "a miniature trial on the merits of a misappropriation claim before discovery may commence." *Id.* at 835–36.
- In *Brescia v. Angelin*, 172 Cal. App. 4th 133 (2009), the court held that section 2019.210 does not necessarily require that a trade secret claimant explain in its designation how the trade secret differs from the general knowledge of skilled persons in the relevant field. *Id.* at 138. The court held that "such an explanation is required only when, given the nature of the alleged secret or the technological field in which it arises, the details provided by the claimant to identify the secret are themselves inadequate to permit the defendant to learn the boundaries of the secret and investigate defenses or to permit the court to understand the designation and fashion discovery." *Id.* The court further held that a trade secret designation under section 2019.210 should be construed liberally "and reasonable doubts regarding its adequacy are to be resolved in favor of allowing discovery to go forward." *Id.*
- In *InteliClear, LLC v. ETC Glob. Holdings, Inc.*, 978 F.3d 653 (9th Cir. 2020), the court explained that "[t]o prove ownership of a trade secret, plaintiffs 'must identify the trade secrets and carry the burden of showing they exist,'" *id.* at 658 (quoting *MAI Sys. Corp. v. Peak Computer, Inc.*, 991 F.2d 511, 522 (9th Cir. 1993)), which requires that plaintiffs "'describe the subject matter of the trade secret with sufficient particularity to separate it from matters of general knowledge in the trade or of special knowledge of those persons ... skilled in the trade.'" *Id.*

(quoting *Imax Corp. v. Cinema Techs., Inc.*, 152 F.3d 1161, 1164 (9th Cir. 1998). To describe trade secrets with sufficient particularity, "[p]laintiffs must 'clearly refer to tangible trade secret material' instead of referring to a 'system which *potentially* qualifies for trade secret protection.'" *Id.* (quoting *Imax Corp.*, 152 F.3d at 1167). "Plaintiffs may not simply rely upon 'catchall' phrases or identify categories of trade secrets they intend to pursue at trial." *Id.* (citing *Imax*, 152 F.3d at 1167; *X6D Ltd. v. Li-Tek Corps.* Co., No. 10-cv-2327-GHK-PJWx, 2012 WL 12952726, at *6 (C.D. Cal. Aug. 27, 2012)). Finally, "[i]t is inadequate for plaintiffs to 'cite and incorporate by reference hundreds of documents that purportedly reference or reflect the trade secret information.'" *Id.* (citing *X6D Ltd.*, 2012 WL 12952726, at *6; *IDX Sys. Corp. v. Epic Sys. Corp.*, 165 F. Supp. 2d 812, 819 (W.D. Wis. 2001)).

§ 11.12 Specific Examples of Trade Secret Identification

Few cases discuss courts' detailed assessment of plaintiffs' identification of trade secrets. Decisions on the topic redact references to the specifics of the dispute due to the putative nonpublic nature of the claimed trade secrets. The following cases (some decided under *Diodes* or section 2019(d)) are instructive.

- In *Whyte v. Schlage Lock Co.*, 101 Cal. App. 4th 1443 (2002), decided under Diodes, 260 Cal. App. 2d 244 (1968), not section 2019.210, the court addressed the trade secret holder's identification of trade secrets among many issues in reviewing the denial of an application for preliminary injunction. The court found that the party claiming trade secret misappropriation identified all but one category of trade secrets with the requisite particularity. Id. at 1453. The court stated that at the preliminary injunction stage a trade secret claimant must satisfy the Diodes test for: (1) separating the subject matter of the trade secret from matters of general knowledge in the trade or of special knowledge of those skilled in the trade, and (2) permitting the defendant to ascertain the boundaries of the trade secret. Whyte, 101 Cal. App. 4th at 1453. The court found that the trade secret claimant met these standards and that its briefing and declarations removed any doubt about the boundaries of the trade secrets. For one category, though, the court found that the identification of "new product information" was too broad because it did not differentiate between truly secret information, such as actual formulas and product design, and other new product information that had been disclosed publicly. Id. at 1454.

- In *Excelligence Learning Corp. v. Oriental Trading Co.*, No. 5:03-CV-4947 JF (RS), 2004 WL 2452834, at *1–9 (N.D. Cal. June 14, 2004), the court evaluated the plaintiff's compliance with the statute then known as section 2019(d) in the context of a motion to compel discovery brought by the plaintiff and a concurrent motion for protective order brought by the defendant. The court noted that while 2019(d) was not binding, it would apply the rule given the absence of a parallel trade secret discovery provision in the Federal Rules of Civil Procedure. Id. at *3 n.3. The plaintiff contended that it sufficiently identified its trade secrets in its first amended complaint and interrogatory responses. Id. at *3. The defendant claimed that the supposed trade secrets failed to meet the requirements for a trade secret because they were publicly available or known to those in the trade. Id. The court ruled that the plaintiff's disclosures met the "minimum threshold requirements of the California trade secrets discovery statute." Id. at *4. In the ruling in the plaintiff's favor, the court referenced the combination of the plaintiff's pleadings, discovery responses, and supplemental disclosures. Id. The court also noted that the defendant's arguments addressed the merits rather than the plaintiff's discovery responsibility to identify the claimed trade secrets. Id. at *3–4.

- The court in *Neothermia Corp. v. Rubicor Med.*, Inc., 345 F. Supp. 2d 1042 (N.D. Cal. 2004), held that the plaintiff satisfied the statute then known as section 2019(d) through its interrogatory responses and declarations. Id. at 1044.

- In *WeRide Corp. v. Kun Huang*, 379 F. Supp. 3d 834 (N.D. Cal. 2019), modified in part, No. 5:18-CV-07233-EJD, 2019 WL 5722620 (N.D. Cal. Nov. 5, 2019), the court found that the plaintiff's trade secret identification, filed with its motion for a preliminary injunction, complied with section 2019.210. Id. at 847 (explaining that because plaintiff met section 2019.210's requirements, the court need not decide whether section 2019.210 applied to the plaintiff's DTSA claims as well as those under CUTSA). The court reasoned that plaintiff WeRide's 20-page filing, which described 10 trade secrets comprised of "source code for certain of WeRide's HD mapping, fusion sensor-based localization, and state machines capabilities," was sufficient even though WeRide did not, as the defendant wanted, identify the specific source code. Id. at 846. The court offered the following example to illustrate the sufficiency of WeRide's disclosure: "WeRide identifies its HD mapping algorithms as its second trade secret. WeRide specifies that it is not referring to HD mapping algorithms generally, but to 'the unique algorithms used by WeRide's autonomous vehicles to create HD Maps.' WeRide then provides the factors a developer must consider in generating such maps, and describes the process WeRide uses to create the algorithms." Id. at 846-47 (internal citation omitted).

The California Court of Appeal's decision in *Perlan Therapeutics, Inc. v. Superior Court*, 178 Cal. App. 4th 1333 (2009), offered additional direction on trade secret identification under section 2019.210, following *Brescia v. Angelin*, 172 Cal. App. 4th 133 (2009), and *Advanced Modular Sputtering, Inc. v. Superior Court*, 132 Cal. App. 4th 826 (2005).

Perlan Therapeutics, Inc. had developed an "anti-viral protein-based therapeutic" nasal spray for the prevention and treatment of the common cold. *Perlan Therapeutics, Inc. v. Superior Court*, 178 Cal. App. 4th at 1337. Its founder eventually left and formed another company, NexBio, Inc., to develop protein therapies for influenza. *Id.* In connection with its trade secret misappropriation claim against NexBio and other defendants, Perlan submitted a trade secret statement pursuant to section 2019.210. *Id.* at 1337–38. Defendants obtained protective orders precluding Perlan from conducting discovery on its trade secret claim because Perlan's initial and amended trade secret statements were deemed inadequate. *Id.* Following the trial court's issuance of the protective order as to Perlan's amended trade secret statement, Perlan petitioned the Court of Appeal for a writ of mandate or prohibition to the trial court, directing it to accept Perlan's trade secret statement as sufficient and allow it to commence discovery. *Id.* at 1336.

Reviewing the trial court's decision for abuse of discretion, the Court of Appeal denied Perlan's writ request, finding that the trial court was justified in holding that Perlan's amended trade secret statement had failed to clearly identify all of the trade secrets at issue. *Id.* at 1354. Perlan's amended trade secret statement consisted of a "preliminary statement" and "general objections," followed by four pages of text that largely repeated the allegations in the operative complaint and included additional detail that was publicly available. *Id.* at 1338–39. While Perlan summarized its trade secrets as "the Charles Invention, Perlan's Protein Multimerization Process, and Perlan's unique idea [concerning sialidase], and all related research, development, advancements, improvements and processes related thereto," the Court concluded that Perlan "did not identify its trade secrets with absolute precision," nor did it describe with sufficient particularity "how its secrets differed from publicly available knowledge." *Id.* at 1339, 1352. Perlan's inclusion of legal objections, factual allegations and reservations of right, characterized by the Court as "surplusage," as well as its references to "hundreds of pages of extra documents" were additional bases supporting the trial court's protective order. *Id.* at 1352.

The *Perlan* decision, which discusses the analytical principles derived from *Brescia* and *Advanced Modular Sputtering* and their application to the Perlan trade secret statement, provides guidance on how courts will scrutinize trade secret statements, and emphasizes that trial courts have broad discretion under section 2019.210 to determine whether a trade secret statement is sufficiently particular. It also illustrates that no single factor compels the outcome on the sufficiency of a trade secret disclosure.

Although not specifically in the context of a section 2019.210 trade secret disclosure statement, the federal trial court in *Mattel, Inc. v. MGA Entm't, Inc.*, 782 F. Supp. 2d 911, 968–70 (C.D. Cal. 2011) provided an instructive analysis of the sufficiency of plaintiff Mattel's trade secret identification allegations at the summary judgment stage. The court held as vague the following alleged trade secrets:

> Mattel's "forecasting process," which "consists of measuring the market viability of a particular product through customer focus groups, communicating that information to the company's marketing and pricing teams, and attempting to produce the optimal number of goods." *Id.* at 967–68. The court held that, as described, "the concept of projecting sales through market research and communication with the company is general, intuitive, and . . . derives no independent economic value from its secrecy." *Id.* at 968.
>
> Mattel's "demand planning process," which entails "a series of inputs and outputs." *Id.* at 968. The court found the allegations identifying this trade secret "nebulous" and lacking in particularity. *Id.*
>
> "Mattel's International Data Warehouse," which is "used to 'store and calculate data relating to the business of Mattel's international subsidiaries.'" *Id.* at 969. The court

> deemed the description of this alleged trade secret "impermissibly vague" and "based upon an inflated approximation of the value obtained from storing and processing common sales-related variables." *Id.* at 970.
>
> "Information concerning the 'OMNI [ ] order management system' purchased and customized by Mattel to assist with 'processing, allocating and executing orders.'" *Id.* at 970. The court held that Mattel's description of the system as customizable and customized was vague, "preclud[ing] the Court from effectively determining whether information about the OMNI system derives independent economic value from not being generally known...." *Id.*

In *Loop AI Labs Inc. v. Gatti*, 195 F. Supp. 3d 1107 (N.D. Cal. 2016), a federal district court provided a thorough analysis of plaintiff Loop AI's trade secret identification in finding that Loop AI failed to comply with the court's earlier order that it provide a trade secret disclosure meeting the reasonable particularity standard of section 2019.210. The court provided a detailed analysis of its reasoning, attributable at least in part to Loop AI's decision not to file its trade secret identification under seal, which the court noted was a "telling indication" that the identification fell short of the reasonable particularity standard. *Id.* at 1113.

The court reasoned that the plaintiff's disclosure—55 paragraphs that "read[] like an inventory of categories of Plaintiff's scientific or strategic business information"—was insufficient for several reasons, including that it relied on references to pleadings and other filings, *id.* at 1112-14, offered nothing more than a "listing of general concepts or categories of information," *id.* at 1115, "resemble[d] an effort to categorize every piece of information or know-how that could potentially have value to the company," *id.* at 1114, and "read more like requests for production of documents rather than trade secret disclosures." *Id.* at 1115. The court further criticized plaintiff's use of "catchall" wording, *id.* at 1115, and noted plaintiff's failure to offer any supporting expert declarations, explaining that while such declarations are not required, they are often used in cases that involve technical or scientific information. *Id.* at 1113. The magistrate judge deciding the issue deferred to the district court regarding the appropriate sanction for Loop AI's failure, and the district court ultimately dismissed Loop AI's claims for a variety of reasons, including the failure to provide an adequate trade secret disclosure. *See Loop AI Labs Inc. v. Gatti*, No. 15-CV-00798-HSG, 2017 WL 934599 (N.D. Cal. Mar. 9, 2017), *aff'd*, 742 F. App'x 286 (9th Cir. 2018). The court identified the following specific descriptions as insufficient:

> "All information and documents identified by Plaintiff as containing its trade secrets at issue in this case in response to discovery propounded by or sought by any defendant, as well as the information and documents identified in Plaintiff['s] ... First Amended Complaint and Second Amended Complaint," and "[a]ll information and documents identified with particularity in Plaintiff's documents produced to the Defendants at Bates Numbers Loop-00019679 to Loop-00020223," where the court had "already rejected Plaintiff's prior attempt to rely on the pleadings and other filings to satisfy its trade secret disclosure obligations," and "the specified bates range identifie[d] two declarations previously publicly filed in this litigation." *Id.* at 1113-14.

"Application of Plaintiff's technology to the analysis of big data generally owned by medium to large companies and governmental entities (including the target customers and partners from among those types of entities) with large volumes of structured and unstructured data from multiple sources and in need of quickly performing analyses of the data and obtain actionable inputs or results that can quickly be used for a variety of applications in various fields including customer relationship management, customer experience needs." *Id.* at 1114.

"Plaintiff's confidential information regarding the generation of semantics from structured and unstructured text data." *Id.*

"Plaintiff's confidential modeling and discussions regarding its development and experimentation of supervised and unsupervised artificial intelligence technology." *Id.*

"[A]ctual and prospective investors and partners . . . key contact information . . . at a large Japanese technology company . . . key contacts at a major telephone company . . . confidential target partner, client, investor, supplier, employee, consultant, advisor information . . . and key service providers." *Id.* at 1115 (explaining that while this information "theoretically could constitute protectable facts . . . Plaintiff's disclosure was unaccompanied by any supporting documentation, and there is no indication that Plaintiffs identified these claimed trade secrets with more specificity," leaving Defendants to guess at the secret companies and individuals).

"Plaintiff's confidential information, including regarding problems experienced with certain tests . . ." *Id.*

"All information stored in Plaintiff's Apple MacBook Air computer ... assigned to Anna Gatti in 2012 for use in conjunction with Plaintiff's business . . . [a]ll information stored in Plaintiff's data accounts used by Gatti while she purported to work as Plaintiff's CEO and President," and "Plaintiff's information sent to Defendant Gatti's email address while she was working for Plaintiff, which Gatti improperly forwarded to her personal email account . . ." *Id.* at 1115-16.

"Plaintiff's confidential patent application provided to Gatti on May 29, 2014, as set forth at Loop-00020163-66." *Id.* at 1116 (noting that Loop AI failed to "specify which portion of the application describes the claimed secret").

Loop AI Labs Inc. v. Gatti once again demonstrates that the sufficiency of a trade secret disclosure depends on the facts of the individual case, a concept which the court reiterated: "Review of the case law cited in the moving papers, as well as the court's own research, makes clear that there is no bright-line rule governing the level of particularity required by section 2019.210." *Id.* at 1111 (citations omitted).

Presumably because the opinions in the preceding cases are public, the trade secrets are referenced by topic only. Still, these opinions are instructive regarding best practices for drafting trade secret identifications.

While no single factor can be relied upon to establish sufficiency or lack thereof of a trade secret disclosure, litigants and courts have the series of three important California state court appellate cases (*Advanced Modular Sputtering, Brescia*, and *Perlan Therapeutics*), as well as numerous decisions from the Ninth Circuit and federal district courts to guide them on the process for identifying trade secrets in discovery.

§ 11.13 Trade Secret Identification in Cases of Theft of Electronic Files

The specific facts of cases may warrant a relaxation of the requirement for designating trade secrets with particularity. For example, some trade secret lawsuits arise from mass downloading of electronic files by wrongdoers, such as soon-to-be departing employees. At times, these cases are referred to as "midnight download" cases because the wrongdoers often engage in their misconduct late in the evening and shortly before departing their employer. In these cases, the former employer who discovers the mass downloading has an immediate need for return of its electronic files and accompanying injunctive relief. Courts faced with this situation may relax the requirement for identification of the claimed trade secrets for a variety of reasons. In addition to the need for prompt injunctive relief, the equities of the situation may not favor requiring that the plaintiff catalog or schedule all the trade secrets found in thousands of stolen electronic files.

Case authorities support less specificity – and reference to documents – in a company's trade secret identification in different situations. In *Cisco Sys., Inc. v. Chung*, No. 19-CV-07562-PJH, 2020 WL 7495085, at *10 (N.D. Cal. Dec. 21, 2020), *reconsideration denied*, No. 19-CV-07562-PJH, 2021 WL 981048 (N.D. Cal. Mar. 16, 2021), the court recognized that citation to specific documents in a trade secret disclosure can provide sufficient detail to allow the defendant to investigate the claims against them. In *Genentech, Inc. v. JHL Biotech, Inc.*, No. C 18-06582 WHA, 2019 WL 1045911 (N.D. Cal. Mar. 5, 2019), the court found a trade secret disclosure sufficient where the plaintiff listed categories of misappropriated trade secrets along with identification of exemplary documents containing the trade secret information. In approving Genentech's trade secret disclosure at the preliminary injunction stage, the court wrote:

> The statement explains that Genentech memorialized the aforementioned material in various documents allegedly misappropriated by defendants, including Genentech's Standard Operating Procedures (SOPs), Test Procedures, Validation Protocols, Validation Reports, Qualification Protocols, Qualification Reports, and Technical Reports. [] It then identifies exemplary documents (which are attached as exhibits) that contain the trade secret information. For example, Genentech identifies [Redacted] as an example document containing trade secret information related to testing the purity of Pulmozyme. [Redacted]"

Id. at *17–18 (noting, however, that "the categories of trade secrets within Genentech's statement risk vagueness at their outer edges" and framing injunctive relief accordingly).

In ruling that a trade secret designation was sufficient, the court in *Telswitch, Inc. v. Billing Solutions Inc.*, No. C12-00172 EMC (LB), 2012 WL 3877645, at *1-3 (N.D. Cal. September 6, 2012) allowed a designation that claimed trade secret rights in a database structure depicted in an attached diagram depicting numerous tables and fields. Notably, the foregoing cases are all filed in federal court and not state court.

In *InteliClear, LLC v. ETC Glob. Holdings, Inc.*, 978 F.3d 653, 658 (9th Cir. 2020), the Ninth Circuit wrote that at summary judgment "InteliClear's burden is only to identify at least one trade secret with sufficient particularity to create a triable issue." *Id.* at 659. Under the holding in *InteliClear*, trade secret plaintiffs in federal court may find more receptive audiences to the position that not all cases warrant identification of all claimed trade secrets in a pre-discovery disclosure. The 2020 holding in *InteliClear* casts doubt on the remaining viability of the Ninth Circuit's reasoning in 1998 in *Imax Corp. v. Cinema Techs.*, Inc., 152 F.3d 1161, 1166 (9th Cir. 1998) where the court criticized the plaintiff's reference to documents in articulating the claimed trade secrets.

§ 11.14 Recommended Methods of Identifying Trade Secrets

Based on the California statutory requirement and governing case law, the following examples may provide some guidance for identifying trade secrets in litigation.

Less Specific	**More Specific**	**Notes**
Trade secrets relating to acceptable ranges of material properties of plaintiff's elastomeric infusion pump bladders, such as acceptable ranges for the tensile strength of the elastomeric material.	The unique ranges of acceptable tensile strength were compiled through years of plaintiff's internal testing, experimentation, and data collection, and while certain individual acceptable tensile strength values may be known to those skilled in the trade, plaintiff's compiled range of acceptable tensile strength values are not generally known to those skilled in the trade.	This example comes from *I-Flow Corp. v. Apex Med. Techs., Inc.*, No. 07cv1200-DMS(NLS), 2008 WL 2233962, *4-5 (S.D. Cal. May 23, 2008) (conducting a line-by-line comparison of the text in the left column, from plaintiff's original description that failed to distinguish trade secrets from general knowledge in the field, and the right column, with an amended description that the court found adequate.
"[C]hipset products [that] implement USB (Universal Serial Bus) 3.0 technology, including but not limited to PCIE . . . , SATA . . . , USB . . . 1.1 and 2.0, and SSC . . . technologies."	Analog designs and schematics that implement a list of specific USB 3.0 technologies for identified chipset products.	This example comes from *Via Techs., Inc. v. Asus Computer Int'l*, No. 14-CV-03586-BLF, 2016 WL 1056139, at *2-3 (N.D. Cal. Mar. 17, 2016) (explaining that "[e]very time [plaintiff] identifies a trade secret with any particularity, it hides that identification in layers of hedging. For instance, [plaintiff's] trade secrets "include, but are not limited to," the technologies that its products implement).
Multi-prong business expansion plan and multi-step sales strategy	Multi-prong business expansion plan and multi-step sales strategy aimed at capturing market share for certain sorts of products, accompanied	This example comes from *Cisco Sys., Inc. v. Chung*, No.

aimed at capturing market share for certain sorts of products	by citations to specific, produced documents elaborating on the two projects	19-CV-07562-PJH, 2020 WL 7495085 at *10 (N.D. Cal. Dec. 21, 2020), *reconsideration denied*, No. 19-CV-07562-PJH, 2021 WL 981048 (N.D. Cal. Mar. 16, 2021) (rejecting defendant's argument that disclosure was insufficient, reasoning that inclusion of citations to specific documents "provides [defendants] sufficient detail about these projects to investigate the claims against them as they pertain to that information")
Software	"[I]nformation regarding the steps taken by [plaintiff] to develop [the computer game at issue], how [plaintiff's] employees authored approximately 240,000 lines of Lua code to implement [plaintiff's] development efforts, how the particular code embodied in [the computer game] is unique to [plaintiff] and not generally known, and a description of [plaintiff's] efforts to keep its Lua code confidential."	This example comes from *Lilith Games (Shanghai) Co. v. uCool, Inc.*, No. 15-CV-01267-SC, 2015 WL 4149066, at *5 (N.D. Cal. July 9, 2015) (finding disclosure described in column two sufficient under section 2019.210)

Bear in mind that although most would agree that the descriptions in the left column above are inadequate under section 2019.210, not all would agree that the descriptions in the middle column provide sufficient "particularity." Reasonable people can disagree about the specificity of descriptions in any particular case.

The specificity required for a trade secret designation may depend on the type of trade secret. One court stated that where the trade secret consists of incremental variations on, or advances in, the state of the art in a highly specialized technical field, a "more exacting level of particularity may be required to distinguish the alleged trade secrets from matters already known to persons skilled in that field." *Advanced Modular Sputtering, Inc. v. Superior Court*, 132 Cal. App. 4th 826, 836 (2005). Thus, the specificity required in any given matter will depend on the circumstances of the individual matter and the nature and type of trade secret information in that case.

Furthermore, litigants should bear in mind that even when the requirement of section 2019.210 is met, it is not a functional substitute for discovery. Defendants will most often need to probe the identity and parameters of the designated trade secrets in depositions, written discovery, and expert discovery. The trade secret identification should, though, provide clear guidance as to the nature of the trade secrets at issue in the case in a way that separates them from general knowledge in any given trade, and which provides notice to the defendant of the case that it must defend.

§ 11.15 Ramifications of Failing to Identify Trade Secrets with Sufficient Particularity

The consequences of failing to comply with section 2019.210 can range from restrictions on discovery to the granting of summary judgment against the trade secret claimant. The plain language of section 2019.210 provides that a plaintiff shall identify its trade secrets with reasonable particularity before commencing discovery related to the trade secrets. Cal. Civ. Proc. Code § 2019.210. Thus, defendants can attempt to obtain a protective order preventing the plaintiff from taking discovery on the trade secret claim prior to identifying trade secrets with the requisite particularity. *See, e.g.*, *Perlan Therapeutics, Inc. v. Superior Court*, 178 Cal. App. 4th 1333 (2009) (plaintiff's failure to identify trade secrets with reasonable particularity supported protective order precluding plaintiff from pursuing discovery relating to its claimed trade secrets).

The ultimate consequences of failing to identify trade secrets with sufficient particularity can be as drastic as the court striking the allegations or the plaintiff losing summary judgment. In *Quintara Biosciences, Inc. v. Ruifeng Biztech Inc.*, No. C 20-04808 WHA, 2021 WL 965349 at *4 (N.D. Cal. March 13, 2021), the district court struck allegations deemed noncompliant with the court's prior order directing plaintiff to disclose its asserted trade secrets with particularity. *See also*, *Quintara Biosciences, Inc. v. Ruifeng Biztech Inc.*, No. C 20-04808 WHA, 2021 WL 2166880 (N.D. Cal. May 27, 2021) (district court's response to mandamus petition).

In *Imax Corp. v. Cinema Techs.*, 152 F.3d 1161, 1162 (9th Cir. 1998), the Ninth Circuit affirmed summary judgment for the defendant on a trade secret claim based on the plaintiff's failure to designate trade secrets with sufficient specificity. Although *Imax* is not a section 2019.210 case, the same principles apply. In the district court, the defendant had moved to compel responses to interrogatories seeking identification and specification of Imax's trade secrets. *Id.* at 1165. The defendant obtained an order that Imax provide "complete, written responses" specifying any trade secrets that the defendant allegedly misappropriated. *Id.* In response to the court order, Imax served a general, nonspecific description of its purported trade secrets as: "the design of the cam unit, *including every dimension and tolerance that defines or reflects that design* . . . [and] *the design of the film arms, including every dimension and tolerance that defines or reflects that design*." *Id.* at 1166 (emphasis original).

The defendant moved for summary judgment on the misappropriation claim, based in part on Imax's failure to specifically identify its purported trade secrets (the "dimensions and tolerances" of the projector) as ordered by the court. *Id.* at 1164. In opposition, Imax argued that it accompanied its written designation with other material specifying all of the "dimensions and tolerances" it claimed as trade secrets. *Id.* at 1165. The district court dismissed Imax's position in oral argument, stating: "[the designation] doesn't give me the trade secret. [It] gives me something that leads me to the trade secret, where I go someplace else." *Id.* at 1166. The district court also found it unimportant that Imax specified its alleged trade secrets in depositions. *Id.* at 1167 (noting that the depositions were taken prior to the court order requiring supplemental responses). The court ruled that "because Imax did not identify the precise numerical dimensions and tolerances in its [court-ordered designation], Imax failed to carry its burden of identifying for the court exactly what dimensions and tolerances it claimed as trade secrets." *Id.* at 1166. As a result, the district court granted the defendant's motion for summary judgment. *Id.* at 1170.

The Ninth Circuit affirmed, noting that under existing precedent a plaintiff asserting trade secret misappropriation must describe the subject matter of the trade secret with sufficient particularity to separate it from matters of general knowledge in the trade. *Id.* at 1164–65 (citing *Universal Analytics v. MacNeal-Schwendler Corp.*, 707 F. Supp. 1170, 1177 (C.D. Cal. 1989), *aff'd*, 914 F.2d 1256 (9th Cir. 1990)). The court specifically stated that Imax's designation was insufficient because it did not "*clearly refer* to tangible trade secret material. Rather, it [referred] to a patented projector system which *potentially* qualifies for trade secret protection." *Id.* at 1167 (citing *Henry Hope X-Ray Prods., Inc. v. Marron Carrel, Inc.*, 674 F.2d 1336, 1342 (9th Cir. 1982)). The Ninth Circuit agreed that it made no difference that Imax specifically described its trade secrets in various documents, depositions, and reports. *Id.* at 1167-68. Because Imax did not identify the specific "dimensions and tolerances" it claimed as trade secrets in its court-ordered designation, the Ninth Circuit refused to consider them and upheld the district court's summary judgment on the trade secret claim. *Id.* at 1168, 1170.

While *InteliClear, LLC v. ETC Global Holdings, Inc.*, 978 F.3d 653 (9th Cir. 2020), may provide plaintiffs with some flexibility given the Ninth Circuit's holding that, on summary judgment, the plaintiff's "burden is only to identify at least one trade secret with sufficient particularity to create a triable issue," *id.* at 659, the court cabined this ruling by noting that "no discovery whatsoever had occurred." *Id.* Other recent decisions issued in the summary judgment context likewise indicate that waiting too long to provide a particularized description of trade secrets may be fatal.

In *Coast Hematology-Oncology Assocs. Med. Grp., Inc. v. Long Beach Mem'l Med. Ctr.*, 58 Cal. App. 5th 748 (2020), California's Second District Court of Appeal affirmed summary adjudication on the plaintiff's trade secret claims related to medical codes, reasoning that the plaintiff waited too long to fix issues with its trade secret identification. Specifically, the plaintiff failed to include the medical code trade secrets in its section 2019.210 designation. *Id.* at 758. The plaintiff claimed, however, that it had requested leave from the trial court in its summary judgment briefing to amend its trade secret designation to add the medical codes, and that it had not identified the codes as trade secrets sooner because the defendant's delay in providing discovery responses prevented it from discovering their misappropriation. *Id.* at 759-60. The court rejected this argument, noting that the plaintiff made no showing of discovery abuse, and explaining: "[I]t destroys the utility of the summary judgment procedure for the plaintiff to wait until *after* the defense has filed its summary judgment motion to announce there is a new secret the plaintiff would like to define." *Id.* at 759.

In *Pixion, Inc. v. PlaceWare Inc.*, 421 F. Supp. 2d 1233, 1242 (N.D. Cal. 2005), the court refused to allow the plaintiff to defend against a summary judgment motion by asserting trade secrets other than what it disclosed in its trade secret designation. The plaintiff had previously represented that it designated a complete statement of its trade secrets. *Id.* The court stated: "Allowing Pixion to defend against summary judgment by asserting now that its method is secret even if the functionality disclosed is not would defeat the purposes of § 2019(d), limiting both PlaceWare's ability to defend against the trade secret claim and the Court's ability to review the issue of secrecy." *Id.*

The court in *Universal Analytics* and *Postx Corp. v. Secure Data in Motion, Inc.*, No. C 02-04483 SI, 2004 WL 2663518, at *3 (N.D. Cal. Nov. 20, 2004) also granted summary judgment to defendants based on the plaintiffs' failure to identify trade secrets with particularity. Note, though, that the *Universal Analytics* decision cites to *Diodes, Inc. v. Franzen*, 260 Cal. App. 2d 244 (1968), rather than to section 2019.210.

Failing to identify trade secrets properly also can result in negative outcomes at the pleading stage, as discussed *supra* Chapter 8.

§ 11.16 Tips for Plaintiffs Identifying Trade Secrets

- **Planning.** Plaintiffs and their counsel ought to articulate their trade secrets in writing prior to filing suit. Too few counsel actually do this. This process fleshes out the strengths and weaknesses of a trade secret complaint. This exercise benefits plaintiffs by leading to more targeted and efficient assertion of claims. Plaintiffs should see in black and white what it is that they contend is a trade secret and what discovery will be fair game against them. Through this process, some plaintiffs may even discover that pursuing the lawsuit may not be in their own best interests.

- **Assessing Causes of Action.** Plaintiffs ought to consider pursuing their lawsuit without a claim for trade secret misappropriation. In some instances, claims such as breach of contract or unfair competition can suffice to pursue one's claims. Some courts will find that breach of contract and unfair competition claims do not trigger the identification of trade secrets requirement under section 2019.210. The language of section 2019.210 begins: "In any action alleging the misappropriation of a trade secret under the Uniform Trade Secrets Act." Cal. Civ. Proc. Code § 2019.210. Even in the absence of a trade secret claim, though, a court may still order compliance with section 2019.210. In *Neothermia Corp v. Rubicor Med., Inc.*, 345 F. Supp. 2d 1042, 1043–44 (N.D. Cal. 2004), the court ruled that section 2019.210 applied to claims for breach of a nondisclosure agreement on grounds that the claim asserted trade secret misappropriation as defined under California's UTSA.

In cases combining a trade secret claim with other claims, courts differ on whether section 2019.210 governs the other causes of action. The court in *Advanced Modular Sputtering, Inc. v. Superior Court*, 132 Cal. App. 4th 826, 830, 834 (2005), held in a case of first impression that section 2019.210 "extends to any cause of action which relates to the trade secret" (but recognizing that an action could allege misappropriation in some causes of action but not in others). The court in *Bryant v. Mattel, Inc.*, Nos. C 04-09049 SGL (RNBx), CV 04-09059, CV 05-2727, 2007 WL 5430888, at *4 n.3 (C.D. Cal. May 18, 2007), looked at the issue from a different perspective, and found section 2019.210 inapplicable to discovery requests relevant to claims other than the claim for trade secret misappropriation (such as the claim for copyright infringement). The court in *Bryant* distinguished *Advanced Modular* by stating that not all of Mattel's claims were "factually dependent" on the trade secret claim. *Id.* Thus, the manner in which a plaintiff positions claims in the case may influence the applicability of section 2019.210 to non-trade secret causes of action.

- **Drafting the Trade Secret Complaint.** Plaintiffs should strive to describe their trade secrets in their complaint with sufficient factual detail to separate the trade secrets from matters of general knowledge, but without divulging secret information in the complaint. The complaint should contain a detailed factual basis for the trade secret claim, including publicly known information regarding the trade secrets such as specific products, product lines, or customers. Be careful not to disclose the precise trade secrets in the complaint to avoid losing trade secret protection by virtue of a publicly available court filing.

- **Preparing the Section 2019.210 Trade Secret Designation.** Be sure that a court-approved protective order is in place prior to disclosure of the specific trade secrets to defense counsel, as discussed *supra* Chapter 10. The trade secret designation should contain detailed but concise identification of all trade secrets in dispute. Identify what information was not publicly known and only became known by the defendant through the misappropriation. Describe the subject matter of the trade secrets with sufficient particularity to separate them from matters of general knowledge in the trade or of special knowledge of those persons who are skilled in the trade, but avoid being painted into a corner with an unnecessarily narrow identification of trade secrets. Be sure to provide enough information to enable a court to determine that the designated information can constitute protectable trade secrets, that the plaintiff has provided a meaningful road map for discovery, and that the defendant can ascertain how to prepare its defense. Be mindful that too narrow or too broad an identification can make summary judgment more attainable for the defendant. Do not simply refer to attached materials that describe the trade secrets.

- **Limit "Surplusage."** Recognize that a court will see preliminary statements, general objections and other qualifications as boilerplate jargon that does not comply with section 2019.210. *See Perlan Therapeutics, Inc. v. Superior Court*, 178 Cal. App. 4th 1333, 1350 (2009) (court criticized the plaintiff for hiding alleged trade secrets in "plain sight" by burying the information in surplusage and voluminous attachments).

- **Expert Involvement.** Plaintiff's counsel should involve an independent expert witness in the preparation or review of the trade secret designation. In court disputes over the specificity of a trade secret designation, courts may look to expert witness declarations on the adequacy of a designation and the distinction of the asserted trade secret from the prior art or generally known information. *See Advanced Modular*, 132 Cal. App. 4th at 836.

- **Discovery.** Case law does not necessarily limit a plaintiff at time of summary judgment or trial to trade secrets listed in a trade secret designation under section 2019.210. The precise specifications and boundaries of trade secrets must be disclosed during discovery if not previously disclosed. Failure to provide this information or failure to comply with discovery orders on the subject may result in summary judgment for the defendant (and possibly sanctions and an award of attorneys' fees). In addition, plaintiffs should consider whether taking depositions of the defendant's witnesses would help to establish that certain types of information are not generally known in the industry.

- **Court Proceedings on the Merits.** At an injunction hearing, a summary judgment motion, and at trial, courts will require identification of the claimed trade secrets. Without identification of trade secrets, courts cannot determine probability of success or rule on the merits (or lack of merits). The level of specificity may vary at an injunction hearing versus at trial. Courts differ in whether they allow plaintiffs to expand upon or vary from their previously designated trade secrets at the time of hearings on the merits.

§ 11.17 Tips for Defendants Seeking Identification of Trade Secrets in Litigation

The defendant's goals include having the plaintiff commit to a position on the trade secrets at issue in the case before the plaintiff takes discovery from the defendant on the alleged trade secrets. Otherwise, an obvious hazard is that the plaintiff could take discovery from the defendant, learn the defendant's techniques, and then disingenuously claim that it was the original owner of those "trade secrets." The defendant's methods for pinning down the plaintiff include the following:

- **Demurrer or Motion to Dismiss.** Defendants could demur or move to dismiss a complaint if the allegations fail to separate the claimed trade secret subject matter from areas of general or special knowledge in the trade and if the complaint does not allow the defendant to ascertain the boundaries in which the trade secret lies or allow reasonable notice of the issues.

- **Motion for More Definite Statement.** In federal court, defendants can move for a more definite statement under Rule 12(e) of the Federal Rules of Civil Procedure if the plaintiff did not meet the pleading requirements to allege information capable of protection as a trade secret. *Resonance Tech., Inc. v. Koninklijke Philips Elecs., N.V.*, No. CV 08-2580 PSG (PLAx), 2008 WL 4330288, at *3–4 (C.D. Cal. Sept. 17, 2008) (complaint asserted patented information as trade secret).

- **Resist Discovery.** If the plaintiff's identification is too broad or vague, the defendant may wish to resist discovery until plaintiff divulges its alleged trade secrets with sufficient particularity. Defendants can move for a protective order prohibiting the plaintiff from engaging in discovery relating to the trade secrets until it identifies the trade secrets with reasonable particularity. One benefit of moving for a protective order (rather than simply objecting to the discovery and leaving the plaintiff to move to compel discovery) is that the defendant becomes the first party to frame the issue for the court. In some courts, a defendant can simply object in writing to the discovery requests and leave it to the plaintiff to move to compel, which is the path some resource-constrained defendants elect.

- **Written Demand for Identification of Trade Secrets.** Defendants can serve a written discovery request for the identification of trade secrets under section 2019.210 of the California Code of Civil Procedure. This may accelerate the discovery process in trade secret cases.

- **Case Management Order.** In federal court, a defendant can seek a case management order under Rule 26(c) of the Federal Rules of Civil Procedure and the court's inherent discretion to manage its own discovery. Such an order can require a plaintiff to disclose and designate trade secrets. *Applied Materials, Inc. v. Advanced Micro-Fabrication Equip. (Shanghai) Co.*, No. C 07-5248 JW (PVT), 2008 WL 183520, at *1 (N.D. Cal. Jan. 18, 2008).

- **Interrogatories.** Defendants ought to consider serving interrogatories seeking the identification of trade secrets and asking that the plaintiff identify the entire content of the purported trade secrets. Defendants should demand that the plaintiff identify its trade secrets with as much precision and as narrowly as possible to limit further discovery and to set the stage for summary judgment.

- **Depositions and Expert Discovery.** Defendants are urged to consider deposing the most knowledgeable people regarding the identification of the plaintiff's trade secrets. Deponents include plaintiffs, company employees, corporate designees, and experts. The goals for the depositions include pinning the witnesses down, narrowing further discovery, and preparing for summary judgment and trial.

- **Motion to Compel.** If the plaintiff fails to provide a satisfactory identification of trade secrets, the defendant may move to compel a further identification. Defendants seeking a further identification should consider filing an expert witness declaration in support of the motion, attesting to any vagueness of the asserted trade secret information or another problem with distinguishing the identified information from the prior art. Defendants should not be shy about moving to compel further responses to incomplete answers to trade secret discovery. At some point, evasive discovery responses by the plaintiff regarding the identification of trade secrets may suffice to warrant summary judgment in the defendant's favor.

- **Motion for Summary Judgment.** As an alternative to filing motions seeking a more specific identification of trade secrets, a defendant may choose simply to move for summary judgment. Some courts will decide at summary judgment that a trade secret designation fails to identify any protectable trade secret. *See Canter v. West Pub. Co, Inc.*, 31 F. Supp. 2d 1193, 1203 (N.D. Cal. 1999); and *infra* Chapter 14 for further discussion of summary judgment. Remaining silent regarding deficiencies in a plaintiff's trade secret identification until summary judgment, however, could provide a basis for its denial. *See Fortinet, Inc. v. Sophos, Inc.*, No. 13-CV-05831-EMC, 2015 WL 5971585, at *2 (N.D. Cal. Oct. 14, 2015) (noting, in order denying summary judgment based on inadequacy of trade secret identification, that defendant "has already accepted [plaintiff's] trade secret disclosure for discovery purposes").

Plaintiffs who have delayed identifying their trade secrets with particularity sometimes come forward with more specific information in opposition to a motion for summary judgment. In this circumstance, if the defendant does not win summary judgment, at least it obtains the requisite specificity regarding the plaintiff's trade secrets at this time.

- **Motions in Limine.** On occasion, a plaintiff will first identify its trade secrets close to trial. Defendants in this position may file motions in limine that seek to exclude evidence at trial of trade secrets that were not designated properly and timely.

Making the plaintiff commit to an identification has multiple potential benefits: (1) it may limit the scope of discoverable information; (2) it may make it more likely that the plaintiff's specificity will lead to useful knowledge of the differences existing between the plaintiff's trade secrets and the defendant's technology or other information; and (3) it may narrow the issues for summary judgment and trial.

§ 11.18 Conclusion

Although the identification of trade secrets in litigation is an art and not a science, it should not be a mystery or a game. By following the guidelines set forth above, parties are better positioned to get past the rhetoric ("They must have stolen our trade secrets!") and get to the business of evaluating the validity of the trade secret and misappropriation claim.

Chapter 12
INJUNCTIONS

By: Rebecca ("Bec") Edelson, Esq.
and Seth M. Gerber, Esq.

---

§ 12.01 Injunctive Relief Under The CUTSA and The DTSA

A. Statutory Provisions

The California Uniform Trade Secrets Act (CUTSA) and the federal Defend Trade Secrets Act (DTSA) both authorize injunctions to prohibit misappropriation. *See* Cal. Civ. Code § 3426.2(a); 18 U.S.C. § 1836(b)(3)(A)(i). The DTSA also provides for *ex parte* seizure orders but only in extraordinary circumstances. *See* 18 U.S.C. § 1836(b)(2).

Under the CUTSA, a court may enjoin any actual or threatened misappropriation of a trade secret, Cal. Civ. Code § 3426.2(a), and, if appropriate under the circumstances, order affirmative acts to protect a trade secret, Cal. Civ. Code § 3426.2(c). The DTSA is comparable. 18 U.S.C. § 1836(b)(3)(A)(i) & (ii).

Even when the trade secret has ceased to exist, an injunction may be used to eliminate commercial advantage derived from the misappropriation. Cal. Civ. Code § 3426.2(a); *see also ELT Sight, Inc. v. EyeLight, Inc.*, No. 19-cv-5545, 2020 WL 7862134, at *29 (C.D. Cal. Aug. 28, 2020) (addressing the "head start" issue in ruling on a preliminary injunction based on CUTSA and DTSA claims).

If a court determines that issuance of an injunction would be unreasonable to prevent future use of the trade secret, the CUTSA authorizes courts to "condition future use upon payment of a reasonable royalty for no longer than the period of time the use could have been prohibited." Cal. Civ. Code § 3426.2(b). The DTSA further provides that if exceptional circumstances render an injunction inequitable, the court can condition future use of the trade secret upon payment of a reasonable royalty for no longer than the period of time for which such use could have been prohibited. 18 U.S.C. § 1836(b)(3)(A)(iii).

The DTSA provides that: (1) the injunctions cannot prevent a person from entering into an employment relationship; (2) injunctions that place conditions on employment shall be based on evidence of threatened misappropriation and not merely on the information that the person knows (often referred to as the inevitable disclosure doctrine, which posits that a former employee will inevitably use a former employer's trade secrets at a new job); and (3) injunctions shall not conflict with applicable state law prohibiting restraints on the practice of a lawful profession, trade, or business. 18 U.S.C. § 1836(b)(3)(A)(i). The CUTSA contains no comparable provision related to employees. But, *see infra* Sections 12.02.B and 12.05.

B. Legal Standards to Obtain an Injunction

1. California Standard

General principles applicable to injunctions apply to trade secret matters. *DVD Copy Control Ass'n, Inc. v. Bunner* (*DVD Copy Control I*), 116 Cal. App. 4th 241, 250 (2004); *Whyte v. Schlage Lock Co.*, 101 Cal. App. 4th 1443, 1449 (2002). Notwithstanding the parties' prior agreement that injunctive relief shall issue, courts may still require the party seeking the injunction to establish what is ordinarily required for injunctive relief to issue. *Grail Semiconductor, Inc. v. Mitsubishi Elec. & Elecs. USA, Inc.*, 225 Cal. App. 4th 786, 801 (2014).

a. TRO

The standard for obtaining a temporary restraining order (TRO) under California law is:

> [N]o more than a review of the conflicting contentions to determine whether there is a sufficiency of evidence to support the issuance of an interlocutory order to keep the subject of litigation in status quo pending a full hearing to determine whether the applicant is entitled to a preliminary injunction.

Landmark Holding Group, Inc. v. Superior Court, 193 Cal. App. 3d 525, 528 (1987). A TRO may be granted based upon a verified complaint or declarations which show satisfactory grounds exist for the order. Cal. Code Civ. Proc. § 527(a), (c). An *ex parte* application for a TRO must comply with California Rules of Court 3.1200-3.1207; *see also* Cal. Code Civ. Proc. § 527(c).

b. Preliminary Injunction

"A preliminary injunction may be granted at any time before judgment upon a verified complaint, or upon affidavits if the complaint in the one case or the affidavits in the other, show satisfactorily that sufficient grounds exist therefor." Cal. Code Civ. Proc. § 527(a).

The purpose of a preliminary injunction is to preserve the status quo pending a final decision on the merits. *Major v. Miraverde Homeowners Ass'n*, 7 Cal. App. 4th 618, 623 (1992).

The Civil Code lays out four instances in which a preliminary injunction may issue. Cal. Civ. Code § 3422. The court may issue an injunction to prevent the breach of an obligation existing in favor of the applicant:

> 1. Where pecuniary compensation would not afford adequate relief;
>
> 2. Where it would be extremely difficult to ascertain the amount of compensation [that] would afford adequate relief;
>
> 3. Where the restraint is necessary to prevent a multiplicity of judicial proceedings; or,
>
> 4. Where the obligation arises from a trust.

Id.

"In deciding whether to issue a preliminary injunction, a court must weigh two 'interrelated' factors: (1) the likelihood that the moving party will ultimately prevail on the merits and (2) the relative interim harm to the parties from issuance or nonissuance of the injunction." *Butt v. State of California*, 4 Cal.4th 668, 677-78 (1992); *see also DVD Copy Control I*, 116 Cal. App. 4th at 250 (noting that the CUTSA's authorization of injunctive relief does not relieve the movant's burden to demonstrate both that it is likely to succeed on the merits and that the balance of harms weighs in its favor).

"[T]he greater the plaintiff's showing on one, the less must be shown on the other to support an injunction. [Citation.]" *Butt*, 4 Cal.4th at 678.

A party seeking injunctive relief must show the absence of an adequate damages remedy at law. Cal. Code Civ. Proc. § 526(a)(4); *see also Tahoe Keys Property Owners' Assn. v. State Water Resources Control Bd.*, 23 Cal. App. 4th 1459, 1471 (1994).

The judge must require an undertaking, or a bond or deposit into the court, when granting any preliminary injunction. Cal. Code Civ. Proc. §§ 529(a), 995.210(b), 995.710; Cal. Rules of Ct. 3.1130.

A court's preliminary injunction ruling is not a final adjudication of the merits. *Cohen v. Board of Supervisors*, 40 Cal.3d 277, 286 (1985). "'The denial of a preliminary injunction does not require any statement of decision or explanation.' [Citation.] '[T]he fact that the court's conclusion is set forth in a summary fashion does not mean the court failed to engage in the requisite analysis, or that its analysis was incorrect.' [Citation.]" *Whyte v. Schlage Lock Co.*, 101 Cal. App. 4th 1443, 1450-51 (2002).

c. Permanent Injunction

A permanent injunction is a final judgment on the merits that a plaintiff has prevailed on a cause of action against a defendant and that equitable relief is appropriate. *Dawson v. East Side Union High School Dist.*, 28 Cal. App. 4th 998, 1041 (1994); *Art Movers, Inc. v. Ni West, Inc.*, 3 Cal. App. 4th 640, 646 (1992).

California Civil Code section 3422 allows a court to grant a permanent injunction "to prevent the breach of an obligation existing in favor of the applicant: [¶] 1. Where pecuniary compensation would not afford adequate relief; [¶] 2. Where it would be extremely difficult to ascertain the amount of compensation [that] would afford adequate relief; [¶] 3. Where the restraint is necessary to prevent a multiplicity of judicial proceedings; or, [¶] 4. Where the obligation arises from a trust." "The first two grounds 'embody the requirement that to obtain an injunction a plaintiff ordinarily must show that the defendant's wrongful acts threaten to cause irreparable injury, meaning injury that cannot adequately be compensated in damages.'" *DVD Copy Control Ass'n, Inc. v. Kaleidescape, Inc.*, 176 Cal. App. 4th 697, 722 (2009) (*quoting Syngenta Crop Protection, Inc. v. Helliker*, 138 Cal. App. 4th 1135, 1167 (2006)).

"[T]o say that the harm is irreparable is simply another way of saying that pecuniary compensation would not afford adequate relief or that it would be extremely difficult to ascertain the amount that would afford adequate relief." *Kaleidescape*, 176 Cal. App. 4th at 722.

2. Federal Standard

a. TRO

Rule 65 of the Federal Rules of Civil Procedure provides for the issuance of TROs and preliminary injunctions in federal court. A party seeking a TRO must satisfy the same requirements that it must satisfy to obtain a preliminary injunction. *See Henry Schein, Inc. v. Cook*, 191 F. Supp. 3d

1072, 1076 (N.D. Cal. 2016). *See* Section 12.01.B.2.b below for a discussion of requirements for issuance of a preliminary injunction.

A plaintiff seeking the issuance of an *ex parte* TRO must show "[t]hat immediate and irreparable injury, loss, or damage will result to the movant before the adverse party can be heard in opposition" and provide a certification of "efforts made to give notice and the reasons why it should not be required." Fed. R. Civ. P. 65(b)(1).

The purpose of a TRO is to preserve the status quo and prevent irreparable harm "just so long as is necessary to hold a hearing, and no longer." *Cutera, Inc. v. Lutronic Aesthetics, Inc.*, 444 F. Supp. 3d 1198, 1204 (E.D. Cal. 2020) (CUTSA and DTSA claims asserted) (*quoting Granny Goose Foods, Inc. v. Brotherhood of Teamsters*, 415 U.S. 423, 439 (1974)); *Samick Music Corp. v. Gordon*, Case No. SACV 20-395-GW-JDEx, 2020 WL 3210613, at *3 (C.D. Cal. March 26, 2020). "The status quo ante litem refers not simply to any situation before the filing of a lawsuit, but instead to 'the last uncontested status which preceded the pending controversy.'" *GoTo.com, Inc. v. Walt Disney Co.*, 202 F.3d 1199, 1210 (9th Cir. 2000) (quotation omitted). "[A]n injunction may issue both to prohibit a departure from the status quo and to restore the parties to a prior status quo." *ELT Sight, Inc. v. EyeLight, Inc.*, No. LA CV19-05545 JAK (RAOx), 2020 WL 7862134, at *26 (C.D. Cal. Aug. 28, 2020) (CUTSA and DTSA claims asserted).

Select decisions granting TROs under the DTSA include:

- *Cutera, Inc. v. Lutronic Aesthetics, Inc.*, 444 F. Supp. 3d 1198, 1204-1214 (E.D. Cal. 2020) (granting TRO and preservation order, addressing the legal requirements at length; observing no material difference between the CUTSA and the DTSA for purposes of the TRO application).

- *Henry Schein Inc. v. Cook,* 191 F. Supp. 3d 1072, 1076-79 (N.D. Cal. 2016) (same; however, the court denied the portion of the injunction that sought to direct a forensics expert to obtain images of the defendant's personal devices).

- *H.Q. Milton, Inc. v. Webster*, 2017 U.S. Dist. LEXIS 193646, at *15, 2017 WL 5625929 (N.D. Cal. Nov. 22, 2017) (granting TRO; "To the extent [defendant] argues that such an injunction would harm defendants' fledgling company, that argument implicitly concedes [that plaintiff's] confidential information was being used and [that argument] therefore does not weigh in favor of defendants.").

- *Trulite Glass and Aluminim Solutions, LLC v. Smith*, 2016 WL 5858498, at *1 (E.D. Cal. Oct. 6, 2016) (granting a TRO, ordering defendants to provide written certification that they have returned or destroyed all of plaintiff's information in their possession, and enjoining defendants from directly or indirectly initiating contact with any of plaintiff's known customers for six months).

- *Panera, LLC v. Nettles*, 2016 WL 4124114, at *4 (E.D. Mo. Aug. 3, 2016) (court granted a TRO where (among other reasons) defendant "was privy to and worked extensively with Panera's trade secrets . . ." and because the defendant's "deletion of the documents in his possession, and return of his computer to 'factory state' gives rise to a strong inference of irreparable harm.").

- *Complete Statistical Servs., LLC v. Rulh*, No. 18-cv-3799, 2018 WL 3970750, at *1 (E.D. La. Apr. 12, 2018) (granting a TRO without notice, enjoining the defendants from using or disclosing plaintiff's intellectual property, and ordering defendants to return all of plaintiff's intellectual property).

- *Earthbound Corporation v. MiTek USA, Inc.*, No. C16-1150 RSM, 2016 WL 4418013, at *10 (W.D. Wash. Aug. 19, 2016) (granting TRO; evidence showed that defendants used plaintiffs' trade secret information shared under an NDA to underbid a client project).

For examples of decisions where a TRO requested under the DTSA was denied, *see Phyllis Schlafly Revocable Trust v. Cori*, No. 4:16CV01631 JAR, 2016 U.S. Dist. LEXIS 155409 (E.D. Mo. Nov. 9, 2016) (plaintiffs failed to show likelihood of success based on conflicting evidence of ownership of the database at issue, and plaintiffs failed to show threat of irreparable harm); *GTO Access Systems, LLC v. Ghost Controls, LLC*, No. 4:16-cv-355-WS-CAS, 2016 WL 4059706 (N.D. Fla. Jun. 20, 2016) (the plaintiff's motion lacked identification of specific harm and failed to demonstrate any immediate and irreparable harm, and that the plaintiff was untimely in bringing its motion).

See Section 12.08 for a discussion of the DTSA *ex parte* seizure orders.

b. Preliminary Injunction

"A preliminary injunction is an extraordinary remedy never awarded as a matter of right." *Winter v. Natural Res. Def. Council, Inc.*, 555 U.S. 7, 24 (2008). It "may only be awarded upon a clear showing that the plaintiff is entitled to such relief." *Id.* at 22.

"[T]he purpose of a preliminary injunction is to preserve the status quo between the parties pending a resolution of a case on the merits." *McCormack v. Hiedeman*, 694 F.3d 1004, 1019 (9th Cir. 2012).

A district court should issue a preliminary injunction only "upon a clear showing that the plaintiff is entitled to relief." *Winter v. Natural Res. Def. Council, Inc.*, 555 U.S. 7, 22 (2008). This requires the federal court to make findings of fact and conclusions of law. *Perfect 10, Inc. v. Amazon.com, Inc.*, 508 F.3d 1146, 1157 (9th Cir. 2007); *see also Hicks v. Neal*, No. C 12-2207 SI (pr), 2012 WL 3791399, at *3 (N.D. Cal. Aug. 31, 2012) ("In other words, the movant has to demonstrate, not merely allege, his entitlement to a preliminary injunction . . . [A]llegations that may be sufficient for pleading purposes simply are not enough to prove his entitlement to a preliminary injunction.").

To obtain a preliminary injunction in federal court, the moving party must establish: (1) it is likely to succeed on the merits of its underlying claims; (2) it is likely to suffer irreparable harm unless the requested preliminary injunctive relief is granted; (3) the balance of the equities between the parties tips in its favor; and (4) that an injunction is in the public interest. *Am. Trucking Ass'ns, Inc. v. City of Los Angeles*, 559 F.3d 1046, 1052 (9th Cir. 2009) (*citing Winter*, 555 U.S. at

20). This "requires the plaintiff to make a showing on all four prongs." *Alliance for the Wild Rockies v. Cottrell*, 632 F.3d 1127, 1135 (9th Cir. 2011).

"In each case, courts must balance the competing claims of injury and must consider the effect on each party of the granting or withholding of the requested relief." *Winter*, 555 U.S. at 24; *see also Henry Schein, Inc.*, 191 F. Supp. 3d at 1076.

"The elements of [this] test are balanced, so that a stronger showing of one element may offset a weaker showing of another. For example, a stronger showing of irreparable harm to [the movant] might offset a lesser showing of likelihood of success on the merits." *Alliance for the Wild Rockies*, 632 F.3d at 1131; *WeRide Corp. v. Kun Huang*, 379 F. Supp. 3d 837, 846 (N.D. Cal. 2019).

After *Winter*, the Ninth Circuit refined its "sliding scale" approach, which balanced the elements of the test for issuance of a preliminary injunction. Under this alternative test, where a plaintiff establishes "serious questions going to the merits," and demonstrates "a balance of the hardships that tips sharply towards the plaintiff," a preliminary injunction is warranted "so long as the plaintiff also shows that there is a likelihood of irreparable injury and that the injunction is in the public interest." *ELT Sight, Inc. v. EyeLight, Inc.*, No. LA CV19-05545 JAK (RAOx), 2020 WL 7862134, at *10 (C.D. Cal. Aug. 28, 2020) (*citing Alliance for the Wild Rockies*, 632 F.3d at 1135).

The Ninth Circuit's "serious questions" test (a lower standard than proving a likelihood of success on the merits) survived *Winter's* holding provided that the balancing of the equities tips "sharply" in favor of the movant and the other two *Winter* factors –irreparable harm and the public interest – are satisfied. *See Farris v. Seabrook*, 677 F.3d 858, 864-65 (9th Cir. 2012). "The Ninth Circuit has held that courts may 'balance' the elements of the preliminary injunction test . . . so that a stronger showing of one element may offset a weaker showing of another." *WeRide Corp.*, 379 F. Supp. 3d at 846; *see also Pyro Spectaculars North, Inc. v. Souza*, 861 F. Supp. 2d 1079, 1087 (E.D. Cal. 2012) (applying this standard).

For examples of cases in which the court granted injunctive relief under the DTSA, see:

- *Henry Schein, Inc. v. Cook*, No. 16-CV-03166-JST, 2016 WL 3418537, at *11 (N.D. Cal. June 22, 2016) (barring defendant from using any of plaintiff's confidential or trade secret information, but declining to prohibit defendant from soliciting the plaintiff's customers).

- *WeRide Corp. v. Kun Huang*, 379 F. Supp. 3d 834, 853 (N.D. Cal. 2019) (granting a preliminary injunction; WeRide had established that it was likely to suffer irreparable harm from defendants' misappropriation of trade secrets (including source code) by giving defendants "an unfair advantage in the nascent autonomous vehicle industry.").

- *Allstate Insurance Company v. Rote*, No. 3:16-cv-01432-HZ, 2016 WL 4191015 (D. Or. Aug. 7, 2016) (partially granting injunctive relief because proof of former Allstate agent's retention of confidential information supported likelihood of success).

- *Engility Corporation v. Daniels*, No. 16-cv-2473-WJM-MEH, 2016 U.S. Dist. LEXIS 166737 (D. Colo. Dec. 2, 2016) (granting preliminary injunction in part; plaintiff demonstrated that former program manager retained electronic trade secret information during and after formation of competing enterprise).

- *Vendavo Inc. v. Long*, 397 F. Supp. 3d 1115, 1142 (N.D. Ill. 2019) (granting a preliminary injunction because plaintiff showed that the defendant, a former key employee, misappropriated "specific knowledge about contacts at current and prospective clients that would be invaluable to [her current employer and plaintiff's competitor] as they seek to broaden their presence in the pricing software marketplace.").

- *Gallagher Benefit Services, Inc. v. Richardson*, No. 6:19-cv-427, 2020 WL 1435111 (E.D. Tex. Mar. 24, 2020) (granting preliminary injunction in part, prohibiting defendants from soliciting any of plaintiff's accounts for which defendants had performed services during the two-year period preceding their termination by plaintiffs, prohibiting defendants from using plaintiff's trade secret information, and ordering defendants to turn over all of plaintiffs' trade secret information still in their possession).

- *Intertek Testing Services, N.A., Inc. v. Pennisi*, 443 F. Supp. 3d 303 (E.D.N.Y. 2020) (granting preliminary injunction, ordering defendants not to use or disclose any of plaintiffs' trade secret information, and prohibiting defendants from engaging in any business competitive with plaintiff until final disposition of the action).

- *Peoplestrategy, Inc. v. Lively Employer Services, Inc.*, No. 3:20-cv-2640, 2020 WL 7869214 (D.N.J. Aug. 28, 2020) (enjoining former employees of plaintiff and their current employer from using or disclosing plaintiff's information related to payroll services, employee benefits services, and 401k services).

- *ELT Sight, Inc. v. EyeLight, Inc.*, No. 19-cv-5545, 2020 WL 7862134, at *33 (C.D. Cal. Aug. 28, 2020) (granting preliminary injunction on counterclaims; prohibiting counterclaim defendants from having any contact with certain representatives from two third parties interested in acquiring counterclaim plaintiff for a period of eight months, but rejecting the request that counterclaim defendants cease all development and commercialization activity as not sufficiently tailored to the protection of the subject trade secrets).

By contrast, for examples of decisions denying preliminary injunctive relief in DTSA cases, see:

- *Phyllis Schlafly Revocable Trust v. Cori*, No. 4:16CV01631 JAR, 2016 U.S. Dist. LEXIS 155409 (E.D. Mo. Nov. 9, 2016) (plaintiffs failed to show likelihood of success based on conflicting evidence of ownership of the database at issue, and plaintiffs failed to show threat of irreparable harm).

- *Highland Consulting Group, Inc. v. Soule*, No. 9:19-cv-81636, 2020 WL 1272516 (S.D. Fla. Mar. 17, 2020) (granting a preliminary injunction as to plaintiffs' breach of contract claims, but denying plaintiff's request for a preliminary injunction with respect to its DTSA claim).

- *Digital Mentor, Inc. v. Ovivo USA, LLC,* No. 17-cv-1935, 2018 WL 993944, at *2 (W.D. Wa. Feb. 21, 2018) (denying the preliminary injunction because plaintiff "fail[ed] to identify what this algorithm is, and what about [plaintiff's] interaction with users is a trade secret.").

c. Permanent Injunction

A federal court may issue a permanent injunction after there has been a determination on the merits that a plaintiff has prevailed on a cause of action against a defendant and that equitable relief is appropriate. *Brocade Commc'ns Sys., Inc. v. A10 Networks, Inc.*, No. C 10-03428 (PSG), 2013 WL 890126, at *3 (N.D. Cal. Jan. 23, 2013). Thus, to prevail in federal court on a request for a permanent injunction to protect trade secrets, a plaintiff must show irreparable harm, which includes a showing that remedies at law are inadequate, and that other equitable considerations warrant entry of an injunction. *Brocade*, 2013 WL 890126, at *3.

§ 12.02 Likelihood of Success

A. Elements of a Trade Secret Case

In order to obtain a preliminary injunction, a trade secret plaintiff must establish a likelihood of success (or, in federal court, "serious questions") as to the merits of its claim for misappropriation of trade secrets. *See DVD Copy Control Ass'n, Inc. v. Bunner* (*DVD Copy Control I*), 116 Cal. App. 4th 241, 250 (2004).

The elements of a claim for misappropriation of trade secrets under the DTSA are similar to those under the CUTSA. *Alta Devices, Inc. v. LG Elecs., Inc.*, 343 F. Supp. 3d 868, 877 (N.D. Cal. 2018). Under both statutes, a plaintiff must allege that: "(1) the plaintiff owned a trade secret; (2) the defendant misappropriated the trade secret; and (3) the defendant's actions damaged the plaintiff." *Id.*

The moving party's "first hurdle" in obtaining the injunction is to show that the information it seeks to protect is currently a trade secret. *DVD Copy Control I*, 116 Cal. App. 4th at 251-52; *Mike Ferry Organization, Inc. v. Grote*, No. SACV 13-835 JLS (SSx), 2014 WL 12561606, at *4 (C.D. Cal. Feb. 19, 2014) (concluding plaintiff unable to show likelihood of success where plaintiff engaged in a pattern of activities encouraging the public disclosure of, and itself disclosing, the identifies of its clients).

The fact that the former trade secret has become public knowledge, however, would not necessarily prevent the issuance of an injunction prohibiting activities other than disclosure. *See DVD Copy Control I*, 116 Cal. App. 4th at 251-54 ("If the trade secret has already entered the public domain, an injunction may be appropriate to remedy any head start or other unfair advantage acquired by the defendant as a result of the appropriation."); Cal. Civ. Code § 3426.2(a) (providing that even when the trade secret has ceased to exist, an injunction may be used "to eliminate commercial advantage" derived from the misappropriation). *See also O2 Micro Int'l Ltd. v. Monolithic Power Sys., Inc.*, 399 F. Supp. 2d 1064, 1070 (N.D. Cal. 2005) (addressing the availability of an injunction to eliminate commercial advantage derived from misappropriation).

"For purposes of preliminary injunction, the party seeking injunctive relief must 'describe the subject matter of the trade secret with sufficient particularity to separate it from matters of general knowledge in the trade or of special knowledge of those persons who are skilled in the trade, and to permit the defendant to ascertain at least the boundaries within which the secret lies.'" *Agency Solutions.Com, LLC v. TriZetto Group, Inc.*, 819 F. Supp. 2d 1001, 1016 (E.D. Cal. Sept. 13, 2011) (*quoting Diodes, Inc. v. Franzen,* 260 Cal. App. 2d 244, 253 (1968)). "It is crucial to any CUTSA cause of action – and any defense – that the information claimed to have been misappropriated be clearly identified." *Agency Solutions.Com, LLC*, 819 F. Supp. 2d at 101. For other decisions addressing this issue, *see Spolar v. Discovery Communications, LLC*, No. 2:20-cv-08837-SVW-MAA, 2020 WL 7222807, at *5 (C.D. Cal. Oct. 2, 2020); *Waymo LLC v. Uber Techs. Inc.*, No. C 17-00939 WHA, 2017 WL 2123560, at *1, 11 (N.D. Cal. May 11, 2017); *ReadyLink Healthcare v. Cotton*, 126 Cal. App. 4th at 1018; *Extreme Reach, Inc. v. SpotGenie Partners, LLC*, No. CV 13-07563-DMG (JCGx), 2013 WL 12081182, at 1-2 (C.D. Cal. Nov. 22, 2013); *Pyro Spectaculars N. Inc. v. Souza*, 861 F. Supp. 2d 1079, 1082-83 (E.D. Cal. 2012). *See also* Chapter 11, which addresses identifying alleged trade secrets in misappropriation litigation.

B. Actual or Threatened Misappropriation and the Inevitable Disclosure Doctrine

Ordinarily, an injunction may not issue unless the threatened misconduct is imminent. "An injunction cannot issue in a vacuum based on the proponent['s] fears about something that may happen in the future. It must be supported by actual evidence that there is a realistic prospect that the party enjoined intends to engage in the prohibited activity." *Korean Phila. Presbyterian Church v. Cal. Presbytery*, 77 Cal. App. 4th 1069, 1084 (2000) (*citing* Cal. Civ. Proc. Code § 526(a)(3)). Thus, "[a]n injunction properly issues only where the right to be protected is clear, [and] injury is impending and so immediately likely as only to be avoided by issuance of the injunction." *East Bay Mun. Util. Dist. v. Dep't of Forestry & Fire Prot.*, 43 Cal. App. 4th 1113, 1126 (1996) (citation omitted).

California has rejected the doctrine of "inevitable disclosure," which would allow a court to enjoin less than imminently threatened misappropriation of trade secrets based on the nature of the defendant's new job position. *See Whyte v. Schlage Lock Co.*, 101 Cal. App. 4th 1443, 1458-64 (2002)*; see also FLIR Systems, Inc. v. Parrish*, 174 Cal. App. 4th 1270, 1277 (2009) ("The doctrine of inevitable disclosure is not the law in California."). Mere "speculation that a departing employee may misappropriate and use a trade secret in a startup business will not support an injunction." *FLIR*, 174 Cal. App. 4th at 1277 (*citing Cont'l Car-Na-Var Corp. v. Moseley*, 24 Cal. 2d 104, 107-08 (1944), and *Globespan, Inc. v. O'Neill,* 151 F. Supp. 2d 1229, 1235 (C.D. Cal. 2001)). For other federal decisions outside California which reject the doctrine of inevitable disclosure, *see ELT Sight, Inc. v. EyeLight, Inc.*, No. 19-cv-5545, 2020 WL 7862134, at *25 (C.D. Cal. Aug. 28, 2020); *Bayer Corp. v. Roche Molecular Sys., Inc.*, 72 F. Supp. 2d 1111, 1112 (N.D. Cal. 1999); *Brocade*, 2013 WL 890126, at *4. *See also* Section 12.05 below for a discussion of the DTSA case law regarding the doctrine of inevitable disclosure.

Although the plaintiff cannot rely solely on the nature of the defendant employee's new job to demonstrate threatened misappropriation, the plaintiff can offer other facts to support existence of threatened misappropriation, such as that the defendant has engaged in misconduct in the past. *See, e.g., ReadyLink Healthcare v. Cotton*, 126 Cal. App. 4th 1006, 1023 (2005) (the defendant had stolen plaintiff's proprietary information in the past to assist one of plaintiff's competitors, the defendant had the continued ability to misuse the plaintiff's proprietary information, and the defendant had animosity towards the plaintiff; "If it is true that [the defendant] is not a threat because he is not working in the healthcare staffing business, then the preliminary injunction should have no impact on him.").

§ 12.03 Irreparable Injury

The party seeking relief must show that it is "likely" to suffer irreparable harm in the absence of preliminary injunctive relief; a mere "possibility" of irreparable harm is not sufficient. *Winter*, 555 U.S. at 22; *Alliance for the Wild Rockies v. Cottrell*, 632 F.3d 1127, 1131 (9th Cir. 2011); *Am. Trucking Ass'ns, Inc. v. City of Los Angeles*, 559 F.3d 1046, 1052 (9th Cir. 2009); *Kovesdy v. Kovesdy*, No. C 10-02012 (SBA), 2010 WL 3619826, at *7 (N.D. Cal. Sept. 13, 2010) (conclusory assertions insufficient to satisfy burden of showing a likelihood of irreparable injury).

"Alleged harm that is remote or speculative will not be considered irreparable; rather, the movant must demonstrate that the threatened harm is imminent." *ELT Sight, Inc. v. EyeLight, Inc.*, No. LA CV19-05545 JAK (RAOx), 2020 WL 7862134, at *25 (C.D. Cal. Aug. 28, 2020) (*quoting Lilith Games (Shanghai) Co. Ltd. v. UCool, Inc.*, No. 15-CV-01267-SC, 2015 WL 5591612, at *10 (N.D. Cal. Sept. 23, 2015)).

"Irreparable harm is traditionally defined as harm for which there is no adequate legal remedy, such as an award of damages." *Genesis 1 Oil Services LLC v. Wisemann Group, LLC*, No. 8:20-cv-02114-JLS-ADS, 2021 WL 1110594, at *8 (C.D. Cal. March 23, 2021) (*quoting Arizona Dream Act Coalition v. Brewer*, 757 F.3d 1053, 1068 (9th Cir. 2014)). "It is well established that monetary injury is not 'irreparable harm.'" *Javo Beverage Co., Inc. v. California Extraction Ventures, Inc.*, 19-CV-1859-CAB-WVG, 2020 WL 886527, at *5 (S.D. Cal. Feb. 2, 2020) (*citing Los Angeles Memorial Coliseum Comm'n v. NFL*, 634 F.2d 1197, 1202 (9th Cir. 1980)); *see also Intel Corp. v. Hamidi*, 30 Cal. 4th 1342, 1352 (2003) (plaintiff seeking injunction "must ordinarily show that the defendant's wrongful acts threaten to cause *irreparable* injuries, ones that cannot be adequately compensated in damages"); *Citcon USA, LLC v. Riverpay, Inc.*, No. 18-cv-2585-NC, 2020 WL 5365980, at *6 (N.D. Cal. Sept. 8, 2020) (plaintiff failed to show why a $1.5 million jury award was an inadequate remedy at law).

A delay in seeking injunctive relief weighs against a finding of irreparable harm. *Garcia v. Google, Inc.*, 786 F.3d 733, 746 (9th Cir. 2015) (holding that the district court did not abuse its discretion by finding a month's long delay in seeking an injunction undercut her claim of irreparable harm); *Oakland Tribune, Inc. v. Chronicle Publ'g Co.*, 762 F.2d 1374, 1377 (9th Cir. 1985) ("Plaintiff's long delay before seeking a preliminary injunction implies a lack of urgency and irreparable harm."); *Lydo Enters., Inc. v. City of Las Vegas*, 745 F.2d 1211, 1213 (9th Cir. 1984) ("A delay in seeking a preliminary injunction is a factor to be considered in weighing the proprietary of relief"); *Applied Materials, Inc. v. LTD Ceramics, Inc.*, No. C-01-20478-JF(PVT), 2002 WL 971721, at *2 (N.D. Cal. Mar. 22, 2002) (denying plaintiff's motion for preliminary injunction where plaintiff "waited a year after it began its investigation before filing suit, and then waited an additional seven months" before filing a motion for preliminary injunction). "However, a reasonable delay caused by a plaintiff's good faith efforts to investigate an infringement will not" preclude injunctive relief. *CyberMedia, Inc. v. Symantec Corp.*, 19 F. Supp. 2d 1070, 1078 (N.D. Cal. 1998).

Even after *Winter*, some courts have relied on a "presumption" of irreparable harm in the context of trade secret misappropriation. *See, e.g., Allergan, Inc. v. Merz Pharmaceuticals, LLC*, No. SACV 11-446 AG (Ex), 2012 WL 781705, at *13 (C.D. Cal. March 9, 2012); *Vinyl Interactive, LLC v. Guarino*, No. C 09-0987 (CW), 2009 WL 1228695, at *8 (N.D. Cal. May 1, 2009) ("The Court presumes that Vinyl will suffer irreparable harm if its proprietary information is misappropriated.") (citation omitted).

However, other courts have concluded that after *Winter* and *eBay, Inc. v. MercExchange, LLC*, 547 U.S. 388, 394 (2006), they may no longer presume irreparable harm for the purpose of granting injunctive relief. *See Cutera, Inc. v. Lutronic Aesthetics, Inc.*, 444 F. Supp. 3d 1198, 1208 (E.D. Cal. 2020); *7-Eleven, Inc. v. Dhaliwal*, No. 12-CV-02276-KJM-GGH, 2012 WL 5880462, at *6-7 (E.D. Cal. Nov. 21, 2012); *TMX Funding, Inc. v. Impero Techs., Inc.*, No. C 10-00202 JF (PVT), 2010 WL 2077011, at *7 (N.D. Cal. May 21, 2010).

Yet, even without the benefit of a presumption of irreparable harm, some courts have found that "'intangible injuries, such as damage to ongoing recruitment efforts and goodwill, can qualify as irreparable harm' in the context of trade secrets misappropriation." *TMX Funding,* 2010 WL 2077011, at *7; *Cutera, Inc. v. Lutronic Aesthetics, Inc.*, 444 F. Supp. 3d 1198, 1204-1214 (E.D. Cal. 2020); *ELT Sight, Inc. v. EyeLight, Inc.*, No. 19-cv-5545, 2020 WL 7862134, at *25 (C.D. Cal. Aug. 28, 2020); *Accredability, LLC v. Accreditsoft*, No. CV 18-5969-DMG (FFMx), 2019 WL 4137409, at *3 (C.D. Cal. May 10, 2019); *Stuhlbarg Int'l Sales Co. v. John D. Brush & Co.*, 240 F.3d 832, 841 (9th Cir. 2001) (evidence of threatened loss of prospective customers or goodwill supports irreparable harm finding); *Genentech, Inc. v. JHL Biotech, Inc.*, No. C 18-06582 WHA, 2019 WL 1045911, at *18 (N.D. Cal. March 5, 2019) (finding irreparable harm where the improper use of confidential Genentech documents filled with proprietary negative know-how would be "virtually untraceable," thereby making the task of identifying and enjoining which of defendant's biosimilars used Genenetech's trade secrets, if Genenetech were to prevail at trial, a "bone-crushing endeavor.").

At least one case has stated "an intention to make imminent or continued use of a trade secret or to disclose it to a competitor will almost always certainly show irreparable harm." *Sun Distrib. Co., LLC v. Corbett*, No. 18-cv-2231-BAS-BGS, 2018 WL 4951966, at *7 (C.D. Cal. Oct. 12, 2018).

Although "loss of control over business reputation and damage to goodwill could constitute irreparable harm," a court's finding of such harm cannot be "grounded in platitudes rather than evidence." *Cutera, Inc. v. Lutronic Aesthetics, Inc.*, 444 F. Supp. 3d 1198, 1208 (E.D. Cal. 2020) (*quoting Herb Reed Enters., LLC v. Fla Entm't Mgmt., Inc.*, 736 F.3d 1239, 1249 (9th Cir. 2013)).

§ 12.04 Scope of the Injunction

A. Duration of the Injunction

Generally, there is "no time limitation on the duration of injunctive relief as to use of . . . trade secret information." *ReadyLink Healthcare v. Cotton*, 126 Cal. App. 4th 1006, 1021 (2005).

"[T]he appropriate duration for the injunction should be the period of time it would have taken [the defendant], either by reverse engineering or by independent development, to develop [the product] legitimately without use of [plaintiff's] trade secrets." *Lamb-Weston, Inc. v. McCain Foods, Ltd.*, 941 F.2d 970, 974 (9th Cir. 1991) (*quoting K-2 Ski Co. v. Head Ski Co.*, 506 F.2d 471, 474 (9th Cir. 1974)); *see also Winston Research Corp. v. Minn. Mining & Mfg.*, 350 F.2d 134, 142 (9th Cir. 1965) ("[T]he appropriate injunctive period is that which competitors would require after public disclosure to develop a competitive machine."); *Am. Paper & Packaging Prods., Inc. v. Kirgan*, 183 Cal. App. 3d 1318, 1326 (1986); *DVD Copy Control I*, 116 Cal. App. 4th 241, 251-52 (2004); *Brocade Commc'ns Sys., Inc. v. A10 Networks, Inc.*, No. C 10-03428 (PSG), 2013 WL 890126, at *4 (N.D. Cal. Jan. 23, 2013).

See also Section 12.01.A above (addressing injunctions to eliminate the unfair head start).

B. Scope and Specificity of the Injunction

An injunction that is overbroad is defective. *See Components for Research, Inc. v. Isolation Prods., Inc.*, 241 Cal. App. 2d 726, 730 (1966) (the injunction went beyond precluding trade secret misappropriation); *see also Whyte v. Schlage Lock Co.*, 101 Cal. App. 4th 1443, 1453-54 (2002) (injunction was too broad to enforce because it did not differentiate between true trade secrets and product information that had been publicly disclosed); *Ret. Group v. Galante*, 176 Cal. App. 4th 1226, 1238-1239 (2009) (injunction ran afoul of section 16600 of the California Business and Professions Code and since another portion of the preliminary injunction already granted the full range of trade secret protection to which the provider was entitled); *Western Directories, Inc. v. Golden Guide Directories, Inc.*, No. C 09-1625 (CW), 2009 WL 1625945, at *7 (N.D. Cal. June 8, 2009) (rejecting as overbroad a category of requested injunctive relief that would have essentially shut down the defendant's business and wiped out the plaintiff's competition altogether).

An injunction also may be challenged on the ground of vagueness. *Whyte*, 101 Cal. App. 4th at 1453 (injunction must describe the subject matter of the trade secret with sufficient particularity to separate it from matters of general knowledge in the trade or of special knowledge of those persons who are skilled in the trade, and to permit the defendant to ascertain at least the boundaries within which the secret lies); *Brocade*, 2013 WL 890126, at *10 ("When fashioning an injunction, the court remains obligated to state the terms of the injunction specifically and 'describe in reasonable detail—and not be referring to the complaint or other document—the act or acts restrained or required.'"); *see also Genentech, Inc. v. JHL Biotech, Inc.*, No. C 18-06582 WHA, 2019 WL 1045911, at *18 (N.D. Cal. March 5, 2019) (provisional relief granted where defendant did not contest over half of the exhibits attached to Genentech's Statement Regarding Trade Secrets or contest that compilations of the supposedly public information in the form of a single document are not readily accessible); *cf., Global Protein Products, Inc. v. Le*, 42 Cal. App. 5th 352, 366, 369-70 (2019) (rejecting that the stipulated permanent injunction was "too vague"). *See also* Section 12.02.A above (addressing the requirement that moving party identify the alleged trade secrets).

An injunction need not disclose the actual trade secret to be sufficiently precise. *See ReadyLink*, 126 Cal. App. 4th at 1026.

§ 12.05 Public Interest (Including But Not Limited to the Policy in Favor of Employee Mobility)

"In exercising their sound discretion, courts of equity should pay particular regard for the public consequences in employing the extraordinary remedy of injunction." *Winter*, 555 U.S. at 24 (*quoting Weinberger v. Romero-Barcelo*, 456 U.S. 305, 312 (1982)).

Thus, injunctions should not issue if they place the public at risk. *See Shoemaker v. County of Los Angeles*, 37 Cal. App. 4th 618, 634 (1995) (denying injunction where it would have put the health of the community at risk).

Generally, "[p]rotection of trade secrets benefits the public interest." *Extreme Reach, Inc. v. Spotgenie Partners, LLC*, No. CV 13-07563-DMG (JCGx), 2013 WL 12081182, at *9 (C.D. Cal. Nov. 22, 2013) (*citing Kewanee Oil Co. v. Bicron Corp.*, 416 U.S. 470, 483 (1974); *Accredability, LLC v. Accreditsoft*, No. 18-5969-DMG (FFMx), 2019 WL 4137409, at *3 (C.D. Cal. May 10, 2019); *Chartwell Staffing Services Inc. v. Atlantic Solutions Group Inc.*, No. 8:19-cv-00642-JLS-JDE, 2019 WL 2177262, at *11 (C.D. Cal. May 20, 2019); *Genentech, Inc. v. JHL Biotech, Inc.*, No. C 18-06582 WHA, 2019 WL 1045911, at *20 (N.D. Cal. March 5, 2019).

However, in cases where former employees are accused of misappropriating trade secrets, the court may consider the following competing public interests:

> [There is] a "settled … policy in favor of open competition and employee mobility," …. On the other hand, the state also has a strong policy in favor of protecting trade secrets. ….

Pyro Spectaculars N. Inc. v. Souza, 861 F. Supp. 2d 1079, 1092 (E.D. Cal. 2012) (citations omitted). *See also* Chapter 4 (addressing contractual restrictive covenants).

An injunction implicating policy in favor of open competition and employee mobility may be closely scrutinized. *See e.g., Retirement Group v. Galante*, 176 Cal. App. 4th 1226, 1238 (2009); *Fillpoint, LLC v. Maas*, 208 Cal. App. 4th 1170, 1173 (2012); Cal. Bus. & Prof. Code § 16600. A few federal courts have found such narrow non-solicitation clauses appropriate to prevent the misuse of trade secrets. *See, e.g., Pyro Spectaculars,* 861 F. Supp. 2d at 1098; *Fidelity Brokerage Servs. LLC v. McNamara,* No. 11 CV 1092 MMA (RBB), 2011 WL 2117546, at *2-8 (S.D. Cal. May 27, 2011); *Asset Marketing Systems, Inc. v. Gagnon*, 542 F.3d 748, 758 (9th Cir. 2008) ("Under California law, non-competition agreements are unenforceable unless necessary to protect an employer's trade secret"). Other courts have called into question or rejected the so-called common law "trade secret" exception to section 16600 or concluded that noncompete/nonsolicitation provisions at issue were not necessary to protect trade secrets and, therefore, void and unenforceable. *See, e.g., Henry Schein, Inc.*

v. Cook, No. 16-cv-03166-JST, 2016 U.S. Dist. LEXIS 81369, at *18 (N.D. Cal. June 22, 2016) (denying preliminary injunction in part, finding nonsolicitation provision unenforceable because there are separate clauses independently requiring defendant from refraining from revealing or otherwise misusing trade secrets); *see also* Chapter 4, which also addresses the trade secret exception.

The DTSA expressly addresses the public policy in favor of employee mobility. It requires that injunctions do not violate certain employment rights. See Section 12.01.A above citing 18 U.S.C. § 1836(b)(3)(A)(i). *See also ELT Sight, Inc. v. EyeLight, Inc.*, No. 19-cv-5545, 2020 WL 7862134, at *25 (C.D. Cal. Aug. 28, 2020) (application of the inevitable disclosure doctrine in California has been rejected by courts there addressing DTSA claims); *UCAR Technology (USA) Inc. v. Yan Li,* No. 5:17-cv-01704, 2017 WL 6405620, at *3 (N.D. Cal. Dec. 15, 2017) (dismissing plaintiff's misappropriation claims "[t]o the extent the complaint relies on these types of 'inevitable disclosure' allegations").

Nevertheless, some courts outside of California have issued injunctions restricting employment and/or considered inevitable disclosure in the DTSA injunction proceedings. *See, e.g.*, *Sunbelt Rentals, Inc. v. Love*, No. 20-cv-17611, 2021 WL 82370, *68 (D.N.J. Jan. 11, 2021); *Vendavo Inc. v. Long*, 397 F. Supp. 3d 1115, 1146 (N.D. Ill. 2019).

§ 12.06 The First Amendment

"Temporary restraining orders and permanent injunctions—*i.e.,* court orders that actually forbid speech activities – are classic examples of prior restraints." *Alexander v. United States*, 509 U.S. 544, 550 (1993).

Injunctions issued to prevent trade secret misappropriation are subject to scrutiny under the free speech clauses of the United States and California Constitutions. *DVD Copy Control Ass'n, Inc. v. Bunner* (*DVD Copy Control II*), 31 Cal. 4th 864, 870, 877-86 (2003) (finding that the information in dispute was not protected by the First Amendment).

"Whether and how the prior restraint doctrine applies to protectable trade secrets – especially those covering matters of public concern – remains murky." *Spolar v. Discovery Communications, LLC*, No. 2:20-cv-08837-SVW-MAA, 2020 WL 7222807, at *10 (C.D. Cal. Oct. 2, 2020) (DTSA case).

§ 12.07 Bonds

A. California Standard

Section 529(a) of the California Code of Civil Procedure provides: "On granting an injunction, the court or judge must require an undertaking on the part of the applicant . . . " Cal. Civ. Proc. Code § 529(a). That requirement is mandatory, and "[n]othing in the statute conditions the trial court's obligation to require such an undertaking upon a request from the parties." *ABBA Rubber Co. v. Seaquist*, 235 Cal. App. 3d 1, 10 (1991). Thus, a "restrained party does not waive its right to that statutorily mandated protection by failing to affirmatively request it." *Id.* at 11.

The defendants are entitled to an undertaking in an amount sufficient to pay "any damages . . . [they] may sustain by reason of the injunction, if the court finally decides that the applicant was not entitled to the injunction." Cal. Civ. Proc. Code § 529(a). "[T]he trial court's function is to estimate the harmful effect which the injunction is likely to have on the restrained party, and to set the undertaking at that sum." *ABBA Rubber*, 235 Cal. App. 3d at 14. "When an injunction restrains the operation of a business, foreseeable damages include 'the profits which [the operator] would have made had he not been prevented by the injunction from carrying on his business.'" *Id.* (*quoting Lambert v. Haskell*, 80 Cal. 611, 618 (1889)). In calculating the amount of the undertaking, the trial court must also consider "the attorney's fees and expenses to be incurred in either prosecuting an appeal of the preliminary injunction, or defending at trial against those causes of action upon which the preliminary injunctive relief had been granted." *ABBA Rubber*, 235 Cal. App. 3d at 16.

The procedure to object to an undertaking is set forth in section 995.930 of the California Code of Civil Procedure.

B. Federal Standard

Rule 65(c) of the Federal Rules of Civil Procedure requires that, as a condition of the issuance of a restraining order or preliminary injunction, the applicant must provide security in such sum as the district court deems proper for payment of such costs and damages as may be incurred or suffered by any party found to have been wrongfully enjoined or restrained.

The Ninth Circuit has "recognized Rule 65(c) invests the district court 'with discretion as to the amount of security required, if any.'" *Fidelity Brokerage Servs. LLC v. McNamara*, No. 11 CV 1092 (MMA) (RBB), 2011 WL 2117546, at *7 (S.D. Cal. May 27, 2011) ("The district court may [therefore] dispense with the filing of a bond when it concludes there is no realistic likelihood of harm to the defendant from enjoining his or her conduct.") (quotation omitted); *see also ELT Sight, Inc. v. EyeLight, Inc.*, No. 19-cv-5545, 2020 WL 7862134, at *33 (C.D. Cal. Aug. 28, 2020) ("Given the scope of the preliminary injunction granted here and the minimal likelihood of harm to [non-moving parties], no bond is required.").

§ 12.08 Civil Seizure Orders Under The DTSA

The DTSA allows a plaintiff to request that a district judge grant an order directing that federal law enforcement officials seize property when necessary to prevent the propagation or dissemination of trade secrets. 18 U.S.C. § 1836(b)(2). To curtail potential abuse, the DTSA requires stringent proof of the necessity and propriety of a civil seizure.

The "*ex parte*" nature of the request means that the remedy can be sought without notice to the defendant or any other alleged wrongdoer. For a plaintiff to secure a seizure order without notice to the defendant, the plaintiff should consider filing its complaint under seal.

In a civil seizure order, the court directs a federal marshal to seize property from a third party pending further order of the court. During the pendency of the seizure, the seized property is held at the court without any party having access to it unless otherwise allowed by court order.

The civil seizure remedy can provide immediate relief to stop further dissemination of trade secret information. Prompt seizure of property can aid in combating misappropriation and mitigating loss to companies.

The applicant seeking a civil seizure must establish the following through an affidavit or a verified complaint: (1) inadequacy of an injunction or other equitable relief; (2) irreparable harm; (3) the balance of harms favors the applicant; (4) likelihood of success; (5) the target possesses the trade secret and the property to be seized; (6) the request describes the property with reasonable particularity; (7) the target would destroy the property if the applicant proceeded with notice; and (8) the applicant has not publicized the requested seizure. For the complete text of the DTSA's requirements for an *ex parte* civil seizure request, *see* 18 U.S.C. § 1836(b)(2)(A)(ii).

For the seizure order to issue, the court must find that it "clearly appears" from "specific facts" that the requirements for a civil seizure are met. The DTSA imposes various requirements: (1) the court must render findings of fact and conclusions of law; (2) the order shall be the narrowest seizure necessary for the situation and direct that the seizure be conducted so as to minimize interruption of the business operations of third parties and, to the extent possible, not interrupt the legitimate business operations of the person accused of misappropriation; (3) the order shall protect the seized property from disclosure by prohibiting access by the applicant or the person against whom the order is directed, and prohibiting copies of the seized property until such parties have an opportunity to be heard in court; (4) the order shall guide law enforcement on execution of the seizure including hours during which the seizure may be executed and whether force may be used to access locked areas; (5) the court shall set a hearing date within 7 days from issuance of the order for consideration of the facts supporting the findings of fact and conclusions of law necessary to support the seizure order, and for consideration of dissolution or modification of the order; and (6) the order shall require that the applicant provide the security determined adequate by the court for payment of damages that may be owed for wrongful or excessive seizure or attempted seizure. For the full text of the DTSA's requirements for a civil seizure order, *see* 18 U.S.C. § 1836(b)(2)(B).

The only known seizure order granted in the first year following enactment of the DTSA came from the Southern District of New York in an unpublished opinion. In *Mission Capital Advisors LLC v. Romaka*, No. 1:16-cv-05878-LLS (S.D.N.Y. July 29, 2016), the court ordered seizure of the plaintiff's Contact Lists from the defendant's computer. Based on a record of forensic evidence and false representations regarding deletion of data, the court found that extraordinary circumstances warranted seizure. *Id.* at 2-6. The court conditioned the seizure on payment of fees for the cost of the U.S. Marshal and a neutral technical expert as well as posting of a bond. *Id.* at 5.

Since then, there have been few plaintiffs that obtained seizure orders. *See, e.g.,*

- *Vice Capital, LLC v. CBD World, LLC*, No. 18-cv-566, 2018 WL 8786293 (W.D. Ok. Jun. 20, 2018) (granting an order for the seizure of plaintiff's trade secret material from defendant, including a list of customers of plaintiff's CBD products).

- *Solar Connect, LLC v. Endicott*, No. 2:17-cv-1235, 2018 WL 2386066 (D. Utah Apr. 6, 2018) (granting a seizure order for the imaging of computers and computer devices).

- *The Ruby Slipper Café, LLC v. CB Hospitality, LLC et al.*, No. 18-cv-1548 (E.D. La. Sep. 30, 2019) (directing the seizure from defendant of plaintiff's recipes but denying plaintiff's request for the seizure and copying of defendant's computers).

- *Travis Lynn Shumway et al. v. James Linn Wright et al.*, No. 4:19-cv-58, 2019 U.S. Dist. LEXIS 148882; 2019 WL 8137119 (D. Utah Aug. 26, 2019) (ordering the seizure of defendants' computers and electronic devices containing plaintiffs' trade secret material, including their customer and patient lists, based in part on defendants' demonstrated willingness to hide information and provide false and misleading information, including false information to conceal their identity and involvement in business entities).

For examples of denials of seizure requests, *see:*

- *OOO Brunswick Rail Management v. Sultanov*, No. 5:17-cv-00017-EJD, 2017 WL 67119, *2 (N.D. Cal. Jan. 6, 2017) (in rejecting the seizure requests, the court instead ordered document preservation and delivery of devices to the court at the time of a scheduled preliminary injunction hearing).

- *Dazzle Software II, LLC v. Kinney*, No. 2:16-cv-12191 (E.D. Mi. Jul. 18, 2016) (denying seizure request but ordering expedited discovery).

- *Hayes Healthcare Services, LLC v. Meacham*, No. 19-cv-60113, 2019 WL 2637053 (S.D. Fla. Feb. 1, 2019) (granting an injunction requiring defendants to return and cease use of all of plaintiffs' trade secret information, but denying plaintiffs' request for a seizure order).

- *Balearia Caribbean Ltd., Corp v. Calvo*, No. 16-23300-CIV-WILLIAM, (S.D. Fla. Aug. 5, 2016) (the court denied the seizure request based on a failure to satisfy the "extraordinary circumstances" test and instead issued a temporary restraining order).

- *Jones Printing LLC v. Adams Lithographing Co.*, No. 1:16-cv-442 (E.D. Tenn. Nov. 3, 2017) (denying the seizure order request without prejudice because the plaintiff's alleged facts were "largely conclusory in nature" and the plaintiff did not show the extraordinary circumstances warranting a seizure).

Subsequent to the initial contested seizure hearing, either the defendant or any person harmed by the order may move the court at any time to dissolve or modify the seizure order. 18 U.S.C. § 1836(b)(2)(F)(iii). Additionally, anyone claiming an interest in the seized property may make a motion at any time to encrypt any seized material that is stored on a storage medium. 18 U.S.C. § 1836(b)(2)(H).

A federal law enforcement officer shall serve the civil seizure order and carry out the seizure pursuant to the order. The applicant may not participate in the seizure. If needed, a technical expert unaffiliated with the applicant may assist the law enforcement officer with the seizure. For a technical expert to assist, the court must determine that the expert will aid the efficient execution of the seizure and minimize the burden of the seizure. 18 U.S.C. § 1836(b)(2)(E).

The civil seizure statute contains requirements for handling seized property. 18 U.S.C. § 1836(b)(2)(D). Seized materials shall be taken into the custody of the court and secured from access during the period of seizure. *Id.* Any seized materials on a storage medium shall not be connected to a network or the Internet without both parties' consent prior to the court's hearing on the matter. *Id.* If warranted, the court may appoint a special master to locate and isolate all misappropriated trade secret information in the seized property, in order to facilitate the return of the unrelated property and data to the person subject to the seizure. *Id.*

Anyone who suffers damage from wrongful or excessive seizure of property has a cause of action against the applicant for damages caused by the improper seizure. 18 U.S.C. § 1836(b)(2)(G). These damages may include such relief as may be appropriate, including damages for lost profits, cost of materials, and loss of good will. *Id.* Upon a showing that the seizure was sought in bad faith, the court can award punitive damages. The injured party may also recover reasonable attorneys' fees and prejudgment interest. 18 U.S.C. § 1836(b)(2)(G), 15 U.S.C. § 1116(d)(11). The injured party's recovery is not limited by the amount of the security posted by the applicant pursuant to the court's seizure order. *Id.*

§ 12.09 Enforcement by Contempt Proceedings

A. California Standard

A trial court may enforce an injunction to protect trade secrets through contempt proceedings. Cal. Civ. Proc. Code §§ 1209-1222. Even though contempt proceedings are denominated civil, these proceedings are criminal in nature because of the penalties available to the judge. *In re Koehler,* 181 Cal. App. 4th 1153, 1158-59 (2010). In a contempt proceeding based on a violation of a court order, the moving party must establish each of the following elements: (1) facts establishing the court's jurisdiction (*e.g.*, personal service, validity of the court order allegedly violated, etc.), (2) defendant's knowledge of the order disobeyed, (3) defendant's ability to comply, and (4) defendant's willful disobedience of the court order. *Id.*

"A party may successfully defend against the enforcement of an injunction on the ground that the injunction is invalid only in the narrow circumstance in which the party can demonstrate that the injunction was beyond the trial court's jurisdiction to issue in the first instance." *Wanke, Indus., Commercial, Residential, Inc. v. Superior* Court, 209 Cal. App. 4th 1151, 1177 (2012) (stating that a showing that the trial court erred in issuing the injunction would not be sufficient to demonstrate that the court acted in "excess of its jurisdiction" in doing so).

B. Federal Standard

Civil contempt "consists of a party's disobedience to a specific and definite court order by failure to take all reasonable steps within the party's power to comply." *Verigy US, Inc. v. Mayder*, No. C-07-04330 (RMW), 2008 WL 2128145, at *3 (N.D. Cal. May 20, 2008) (*quoting In re Dual-Deck Video Cassette Recorder Antitrust Litig.*, 10 F.3d 693, 695 (9th Cir. 1993)).

"The standard for finding a party in civil contempt is well settled: The moving party has the burden of showing by clear and convincing evidence that the [nonmoving party] violated a specific and definite order of the court." *FTC v. Affordable Media, LLC,* 179 F.3d 1228, 1239 (9th Cir. 1999) (quotation omitted).

"But a person should not be held in contempt if his action appears to be based on a good faith and reasonable interpretation of the court's order." *Dual-Deck,* 10 F.3d at 695.

Thus, a party seeking contempt sanctions must show "(1) a violation of the order, (2) beyond substantial compliance, (3) not based on a good faith and reasonable interpretation of the order, (4) by clear and convincing evidence." *Verigy,* 2008 WL 2128145, at *5 (*citing Dual-Deck,* 10 F.3d at 695).

The district court has the inherent power to impose a remedy for contempt. *Verigy,* 2008 WL 2128145, at *8 (court extended the preliminary injunction for an additional four months). The judge is "solely responsible for identifying, prosecuting, adjudicating, and sanctioning the contumacious conduct." *Id.* (*quoting Int'l Union v. Bagwell,* 512 U.S. 821, 831 (1994)).

Any award of sanctions must be compensatory and limited to the plaintiff's "actual loss" for "injuries which result from the noncompliance." *Id.* (*quoting In re Crystal Palace Gambling Hall, Inc.,* 817 F.2d 1361, 1366 (9th Cir. 1987)).

§ 12.10 Dissolution

A. California Standard

Cal. Code Civ. Proc. section 533 provides that "[i]n any action, the court may on notice modify or dissolve an injunction or temporary restraining order upon a showing that there has been a material change in the facts upon which the injunction or temporary restraining order was granted, that the law upon which the injunction or temporary restraining order was granted has changed, or that the ends of justice would be served by the modification or dissolution of the injunction or temporary restraining order."

Cal. Code Civ. section 3426.2, subdivision (a) provides that "[u]pon application to the court, an injunction shall be terminated when the trade secret has ceased to exist, but the injunction may be continued for an additional period of time in order to eliminate commercial advantage that otherwise would be derived from the misappropriation."

The dissolution of an injunction is subject to the trial court's discretion. *Global Protein Products, Inc. v. Le*, 42 Cal. App. 5th 352, 366, 368 (2019) (holding that there was sufficient evidence to support the trial court's implied determination, in declining to dissolve the injunction, that the plaintiff's trade secret remained a trade secret).

B. Federal Standard

Where a TRO was issued without notice, the application to modify or dissolve may be heard on two days' notice, or even less if prescribed by the court. Federal Rule of Civil Procedure Rule 65(b)(4).

The trial court retains the power to modify a preliminary injunction at any time on consideration of new facts. *A&M Records, Inc. v. Napster, Inc.*, 284 F.3d 1091, 1098 (9th Cir. 2002).

Some courts hold modification or dissolution is typically proper only if there has been a significant change in fact or law that would render the original injunction inequitable. *Alto v. Black*, 738 F3d 1111, 1120 (9th Cir. 2013) (standard: "significant change in facts warrants revision or dissolution of the injunction"; denial of dissolution of preliminary injunction affirmed); *Flores v. Huppenthal*, 789 F.3d 994, 1001, 1008 (9th Cir. 2015) (it may be an abuse of discretion for a court to refuse to modify an injunction if there has been a significant change in factual conditions or the law that renders its continued enforcement detrimental to the public interest; continued enforcement of the permanent injunction was not justified under the circumstances there).

Chapter 13
DAMAGES AND OTHER MONETARY RELIEF FOR TRADE SECRET MISAPPROPRIATION

By: Rebecca ("Bec") Edelson, Esq.
and M. Alim Malik, Esq.

---

§ 13.01 Introduction to CUTSA Monetary Remedies

California's Uniform Trade Secrets Act (CUTSA), Cal. Civ. Code §§ 3426.1-3426.11, provides broad monetary relief for trade secret misappropriation, including damages for the actual loss caused by the misappropriation, recovery of unjust enrichment, reasonable royalties, exemplary damages, and attorneys' fees. *See id.* §§ 3426.3-3426.4.

Section 3426.3 of the California Civil Code states:

> (a) A complainant may recover damages for the actual loss caused by misappropriation. A complainant also may recover for the unjust enrichment caused by misappropriation that is not taken into account in computing damages for actual loss.
>
> (b) If neither damages nor unjust enrichment caused by misappropriation are provable, the court may order payment of a reasonable royalty for no longer than the period of time the use could have been prohibited.
>
> (c) If willful and malicious misappropriation exists, the court may award exemplary damages in an amount not exceeding twice any award made under subdivision (a) or (b).

Id. § 3426.3.

Section 3426.4 of the California Civil Code states:

> If a claim of misappropriation is made in bad faith, a motion to terminate an injunction is made or resisted in bad faith, or willful and malicious misappropriation exists, the court may award reasonable attorney's fees and costs to the prevailing party. Recoverable costs hereunder shall include a reasonable sum to cover the services of expert witnesses, who are not regular employees of any party, actually incurred and reasonably necessary in either, or both, preparation for trial or arbitration, or during trial or arbitration, of the case by the prevailing party.

Id. § 3426.4.

Trade secret claims may be filed in conjunction with other claims, but the claimant is not entitled to recover twice for the same injury. *See Robert L. Cloud & Assocs., Inc. v. Mikesell*, 69 Cal. App. 4th 1141, 1150-51 (1999) (concluding that although section 3426.7 does not affect any other civil remedies that may be available, it does not authorize a "double recovery").

Even after a claim for misappropriation has accrued, *see supra* Chapter 9, the amount of damages, unjust enrichment, or a reasonable royalty may continue to increase where the misappropriation continues or is repeated. *Cadence Design Sys., Inc. v. Avant! Corp.*, 29 Cal. 4th 215, 225-26 (2002).

§ 13.02 CUTSA Damages

The CUTSA provides that a plaintiff may recover for the actual loss caused by misappropriation. Cal. Civ. Code § 3426.3(a). Thus, trade secret holders can recover whatever losses they can demonstrate were caused by the misappropriation.

"Damages for misappropriation of trade secrets must have a reasonable basis but need not be calculated with absolute precision." *Roadrunner Transportation Servs., Inc. v. Tarwater*, No. SACV101534AGMLGX, 2013 WL 12171729, at *2 (C.D. Cal. Aug. 9, 2013); *accord CTC Glob. Corp. v. Huang*, No. SACV1702202AGKESX, 2019 WL 4148184, at *7 (C.D. Cal. July 29, 2019).

A party that owned the trade secret at the time of the misappropriation can bring an action for damages even if it sold the trade secret before filing the misappropriation action. *See Jasmine Networks, Inc. v. Superior Court*, 180 Cal. App. 4th 980, 993, 996 (2009).

§ 13.03 CUTSA Unjust Enrichment

The CUTSA suggests a hierarchy of recovery—first, damages; second, unjust enrichment; and third, royalties. *See* Cal. Civ. Code § 3426.3 (recovery for unjust enrichment is limited to what "is not taken into account in computing damages for actual loss" and a reasonably royalty may be ordered only where "neither damages nor unjust enrichment caused by misappropriation are provable"); *cf., Ajaxo Inc. v. E*Trade Grp., Inc.*, 135 Cal. App. 4th 21, 62 (2005) ("The selection of which measure of damages to apply is left to the sound discretion of the trier of fact.").

The trade secret holder is not permitted to obtain a double recovery for actual damages and unjust enrichment that overlap. *See* Cal. Civ. Code § 3426.3(a).

In some cases, the misappropriator's unjust enrichment may be offered as a measure of the trade secret holder's actual damages. *See Klamath-Orleans Lumber, Inc. v. Miller*, 87 Cal. App. 3d 458, 466 (1978). On the other hand, courts have rejected the proposition that the amount of a defendant's gain from the misappropriation is always equivalent to the value of a plaintiff's alleged loss. *See Unilogic, Inc. v. Burroughs Corp.*, 10 Cal. App. 4th 612, 627-28 (1992) (claimant failed to introduce evidence of unjust enrichment).

The misappropriator's unjust enrichment need not be proven with precision. Instead, a "reasonable approximation" is sufficient. *Morlife, Inc. v. Perry*, 56 Cal. App. 4th 1514, 1528 (1997) ("We cannot say the court's determination [of the amount of enrichment] was arbitrary or not supported by substantial evidence" where the trial court applied a thirty-three percent figure to defendants' combined earnings, reflecting that thirty-three percent of the plaintiff's business during the first six months was derived from work for misappropriated former customers of plaintiff).

Nevertheless, the unjust enrichment must be adequately supported by the evidence. *Ajaxo Inc.*, 135 Cal. App. 4th at 63 (concluding that "there was substantial evidence from which the jury could have concluded that [the defendant] was unjustly enriched").

When determining unjust enrichment, the court will look to the misappropriator's net profits from the misappropriation rather than its gross profits. *See Klamath-Orleans*, 87 Cal. App. 3d at 467 (reversing the judgment where the jury ignored the cost to the defendant of bookkeeping and office management in determining the defendant's unjust enrichment from the misappropriation).

§ 13.04 CUTSA Royalties

The CUTSA provides: "If neither damages nor unjust enrichment caused by misappropriation are provable, the court may order payment of a reasonable royalty for no longer than the period of time the use could have been prohibited." Cal. Civ. Code § 3426.3(b).

Thus, a reasonable royalty is recoverable only if neither actual damages nor unjust enrichment are provable. *Cacique, Inc. v. Robert Reiser Co.*, 169 F.3d 619, 623 (9th Cir. 1999) (holding that trade secret claimant could not recover reasonable royalty under circumstances where it could establish unjust enrichment); *Robert L. Cloud & Assocs. v. Mikesell*, 69 Cal. App. 4th 1141, 1149 (1999); *Morlife, Inc. v. Perry*, 56 Cal. App. 4th 1514, 1529 (1997); *see also SkinMedica, Inc. v. Histogen Inc.*, 869 F. Supp. 2d 1176, 1198 (S.D. Cal. 2012) (rejecting on summary judgment that a reasonable royalty was unavailable as a matter of law and noting that the required "independent economic value" of the trade secret could be inferred by defendant's own conduct, i.e., her attempt to patent the information herself "casts doubt upon her statement that she believed the information lacked value irrespective of the PTO rejection of those applications"); *see also In re Sotera Wireless, Inc.*, 794 F. App'x 625, 628 (9th Cir. 2020) ("[B]ecause the court awarded unjust enrichment damages ..., it did not err by failing to expressly address whether royalties were warranted").

When damages and unjust enrichment are unprovable, either as a matter of fact or of law, reasonable royalties may be awarded. *Ajaxo, Inc. v. E*Trade Fin. Group, Inc.*, 187 Cal. App. 4th 1295, 1310-13 (2010); *Altavion, Inc. v. Konica Minolta Sys. Lab'y, Inc.*, 226 Cal. App. 4th 26, 66-68 (2014). However, even if they are unprovable, that does not mean that the trial court is required to make a reasonable royalty award. *Ajaxo, Inc. v. E*Trade Fin. Group, Inc.*, 48 Cal. App. 5th 129, 165 (2020) (recognizing the trial court's discretion in that regard).

"Under California's head start rule, codified in section 3426, a court may order payment of a reasonable royalty for no longer than the period of time the use could have been prohibited." *Ajaxo, Inc. v. E*Trade Fin. Corp.*, 48 Cal. App. 5th 129, 154 (2020). The payment of a reasonable royalty for future use of the trade secret is available only when the court does not issue an injunction prohibiting such future use under section 3426.2. *Robert L. Cloud*, 69 Cal. App. 4th at 1150.

The "Georgia-Pacific" factors applied in determining a reasonable royalty for use of a patented invention may also be used in determining a reasonable royalty for use of trade secrets. *Ajaxo, Inc. v. E*Trade Fin. Group, Inc.*, 48 Cal. App. 5th 129, 161-162, 187-192 (2020); *see also O2 Micro Int'l Ltd. v. Monolithic Power Sys. Inc.*, 399 F. Supp. 2d 1064, 1078 (N.D. Cal. 2005) (relying on Georgia-Pacific factors, the court determined that a royalty of $900,000 was appropriate), *judgment amended by* 420 F. Supp. 2d 1070 (N.D. Cal. 2006).

The court may also consider a party's spoliation of evidence in the royalty award determination. *Ajaxo, Inc. v. E*Trade Fin. Group, Inc.*, 48 Cal. App. 5th 129, 168-173 (2020). *See also* Chapter 23 (Spoliation).

In determining the amount of the reasonable royalty, the court also may apportion value use of the trade secret and value of use of non-trade secrets. *Ajaxo, Inc. v. E*Trade Fin. Group, Inc.*, 48 Cal. App. 5th 129, 168-171 (2020).

§ 13.05 CUTSA Exemplary Damages

Under the CUTSA, exemplary damages are permitted if "willful and malicious misappropriation exists" but are limited to an amount not to exceed twice the damages, unjust enrichment, or reasonable royalty awarded. Cal. Civ. Code § 3426.3(c). *See, e.g.*, *Ajaxo Inc. v. E*Trade Grp.*, 135 Cal. App. 4th 21, 53 (2005) ("There was substantial evidence to support the jury verdict that [the defendant] willfully and maliciously misappropriated [the plaintiff's] trade secrets.").

Willful and malicious misappropriation must be proven by clear and convincing evidence according to *Citcon USA, LLC v. RiverPay, Inc.*, No. 18-CV-2585-NC, 2020 WL 5365980, at *4 (N.D. Cal. Sept. 8, 2020).

The trial court's discretion in setting the level of exemplary damages under section 3426.3(c) is "wide" but not unfettered and any award still must be "appropriate" in light of the circumstances. *See Robert L. Cloud & Assocs. Inc. v. Mikesell*, 69 Cal. App. 4th 1141, 1151, 1152, 1153 n.8 (1999) (finding that since there was no evidence of the defendant's personal financial condition or net worth, the award of punitive damages could not stand).

A district court has held that even where no compensatory damages have been awarded, three factors must be considered in determining whether to award exemplary damages for misappropriation of trade secrets: "(1) the nature of the misconduct; (2) amount of compensatory damages; and (3) the defendant's financial condition." *O2 Micro Int'l Ltd. v. Monolithic Power Sys. Inc.*, 399 F. Supp. 2d 1064, 1079-1080 (N.D. Cal. 2005), *judgment amended by* 420 F. Supp. 2d 1070 (N.D. Cal. 2006). *Cf. Mattel, Inc. v. MGA Entm't, Inc.,* 801 F. Supp. 2d 950, 954 (C.D. Cal. 2011) ("though exemplary damages equal to twice the compensatory award may be awarded in cases involving purely economic loss, such an award is not justified here").

§ 13.06 CUTSA Attorneys' Fees

The CUTSA provides that, where "a claim of misappropriation is made in bad faith, a motion to terminate an injunction is made or resisted in bad faith, or willful and malicious misappropriation exists, the court may award reasonable attorney's fees and costs to the prevailing party." Cal. Civ. Code § 3426.4.

Willful and Malicious Misappropriation. Although ordinarily the "willful and malicious misappropriation" predicate will rest on a finding made by the trier of fact after a trial, it is possible that the court will be required to make that determination upon a motion for attorneys' fees. *See Khavarian Enters., Inc. v. Commline, Inc.*, 216 Cal. App. 4th 310, 317, 320, 325-328 (2013) ("Nor is it unlawful or procedurally impossible for parties [which have settled the claim before trial] to ask a trial court to act as fact finder postsettlement and decide whether defendants engaged in willful and malicious misappropriation of trade secrets").

Bad Faith. "Bad faith" for purposes of section 3426.4 requires both objective speciousness of the plaintiff's claim, as opposed to frivolousness, and its subjective bad faith in bringing or maintaining the claim. *Cypress Semiconductor Corp. v. Maxim Integrated Products, Inc.*, 236 Cal.App.4th 243, 260 (2015). *See also Gemini Aluminum Corp. v. Cal. Custom Shapes, Inc.*, 95 Cal. App. 4th 1249, 1262, 1264 (2002) (holding the trial court did not abuse its discretion in finding "both objective speciousness and subjective bad faith" where, despite the lack of proof of any economic value, the plaintiff persisted with its misappropriation claims). "But it does not follow, and is not the case, that a subjective belief in the merits will bar a fee award where an objectively specious claim is found on substantial evidence to have been maintained for an improper purpose." *Cypress Semiconductor Corp.*, 236 Cal. App. 4th 243 at 268 (holding there was sufficient evidence of an improper purpose to affirm the fees award against the plaintiff).

"Objective speciousness exists where the action superficially appears to have merit but there is a complete lack of evidence to support the claim." *FLIR Sys., Inc. v. Parrish*, 174 Cal. App. 4th 1270, 1276 (2009) (citations omitted). To establish objective speciousness, the defendant need not prove that the misappropriation claim was frivolous. *Id.* Rather, in *FLIR,* objective speciousness was established by: (1) evidence that the plaintiffs had an anticompetitive motive in filing the lawsuit; and (2) the lack of evidence of damages, misappropriation or threatened misappropriation (to be distinguished from speculation based on the inevitable disclosure doctrine, which California law has rejected). *Id.* at 1276-78. *See also Cypress Semiconductor Corp. v. Maxim Integrated Products, Inc.*, 236 Cal. App. 4th 243, 264 (2015) ("Nothing in the complaint, and nothing submitted by Cypress since filing the complaint, lends any color to the naked assertion that Maxim was pursuing Cypress employees with the object of extracting trade secrets from them.").

"Subjective bad faith may be inferred by evidence that [the plaintiff] intended to cause unnecessary delay, filed the action to harass [the defendants], or harbored an improper motive." *FLIR Sys.,* 174 Cal. App. 4th at 1278 (citations omitted). The timing of the action may raise an inference of bad faith. *Id.* Similar inferences may be made where the plaintiff proceeds to trial after the action's fatal shortcomings are revealed by opposing counsel. *Id.*

A plaintiff's reliance on the defendant's download of technical data onto a portable hard drive does not necessarily establish good faith. *FLIR Sys.,* 174 Cal. App. 4th at 1279-1280 ("Subjective bad faith was established by the contradictory testimony of [the plaintiffs'] executives .... [They] testified that [defendants] were trustworthy, would not do anything wrong, and should have been allowed to start a new company.").

A plaintiff's failure to identify the alleged trade secrets at issue may also be used to establish bad faith. *FLIR Sys.,* 174 Cal. App. 4th at 1281. *See also Gabriel Technologies Corp. v. Qualcomm Inc.*, No. 08cv 1992 AJB (MDD), 2013 WL 410103, *7-*8 (S.D. Cal. Feb. 11, 2013) (awarding $12.4 million in attorneys' fees against the plaintiff, where the plaintiff "made seven failed attempts to articulate their trade secrets," and the plaintiff continued to pursue trade secret claims after having been "notified of their evidentiary deficiencies by two magistrate judges and one district court judge.").

A plaintiff's request for an overbroad injunction also may be used as evidence of bad faith. *FLIR Sys.,* 174 Cal. App. 4th at 1281 ("Among other things, the proposed injunction barred [defendants] from developing certain products for a 12 month period even if [they] did not use [the plaintiffs'] technology or trade secrets. It was an unlawful restraint on trade (Cal. Bus. & Prof. Code § 16600) and strong evidence of subjective bad faith.").

The plaintiff's settlement positions may also be used as evidence of bad faith according to the court in the *FLIR Sys.* case. *FLIR Sys.,* 174 Cal. App. 4th at 1282.

That the trial court ruled on motions in the favor of the party's whose bad faith is being determined does not necessarily preclude a finding of bad faith. *FLIR Sys.,* 174 Cal. App. 4th at 1282-84.

The defendant does not need to establish that there was no misappropriation to support a finding of bad faith against the plaintiff. *SASCO v. Rosendin Elec., Inc.*, 207 Cal. App. 4th 837, 848 (2012).

Discretionary Nature. A request for an attorneys' fee award is entrusted to the trial court's discretion and will not be overturned by the court of appeal "in the absence of a manifest abuse of discretion, a prejudicial error of law, or necessary findings not supported by substantial evidence". *See Yield Dynamics, Inc. v. Tea Sys. Corp.*, 154 Cal. App. 4th 547, 577-78 (2007). The trial court's discretion also includes whether or not to hold a hearing. *FLIR Sys., Inc. v. Parrish*, 174 Cal. App. 4th 1270, 1284-85 (2009) (affirming the $1,352,000 attorneys' fees award below).

Attorneys' fees are not necessarily mandatory under the CUTSA even if the jury finds willful and malicious misappropriation. *O2 Micro Int'l Ltd. v. Monolithic Power Sys. Inc.*, 399 F. Supp. 2d 1064, 1080 (N.D. Cal. 2005), *judgment amended by* 420 F. Supp. 2d 1070 (N.D. Cal. 2006)); *see also Mattel, Inc. v. MGA Ent., Inc.*, 801 F. Supp. 2d 950, 953 (C.D. Cal. 2011) (noting that while some courts treat a jury finding of willful and malicious misappropriation as support for the "maximum possible amount in exemplary damages," the trial court must make its own "independent evaluation" of the nature of misconduct supporting a punitive damage award).

Prevailing Party. There is authority that a party need not prevail on all issues to qualify as a "prevailing party" under section 3426.4. *See Mattel, Inc. v. MGA Entm't, Inc.,* 801 F. Supp. 2d 950, 958 (C.D. Cal. 2011) ("Though MGA did not obtain an unblemished outcome, it cannot be disputed that an $85 million award and a finding of malice represents a significant victory, and that MGA is therefore entitled to the fees it incurred prosecuting the underlying trade secrets claim."); *BladeRoom Grp. Ltd. v. Emerson Elec. Co.*, No. 5:15-CV-01370-EJD, 2020 WL 1677328, at *11 (N.D. Cal. Apr. 6, 2020) (appeal pending) (awarding BladeRoom approximately $24.5 million in attorney fees and costs; "[t]hat BladeRoom did not pursue or obtain misappropriation findings at trial on all of its trade secrets in no way diminishes BladeRoom's success at trial").

Further, the fact that a plaintiff voluntarily dismisses the action does not necessarily preclude an attorneys' fees award against it. *See Cypress Semiconductor Corp. v. Maxim Integrated Products, Inc.*, 236 Cal.App.4th 243, 253–55 (2015) (defendants were the prevailing party even though the plaintiffs voluntarily dismissed their CUTSA action without prejudice after the defendants had demurred generally to the complaint, but before the demurrer was ever heard; "[t]he only plausible explanation for Cypress's dismissal … is that it feared a determination on the merits"); *SASCO v. Rosendin Elec., Inc.*, 207 Cal. App. 4th 837, 845-848 (2012) (plaintiff dismissed the action while a summary judgment motion against it was pending); *Khavarian Enters., Inc. v. Commline Inc.*, 216 Cal. App. 4th 310, 320-325 (2013) (voluntary dismissal pursuant to a settlement). *Cf.*, Cal. Civ. Code § 1717(b)(2) (where a cause of action has been voluntarily dismissed, there shall be no prevailing party for purpose of recovering attorneys' fees under a contract).

Pleading. Section 3426.4 may not be invoked as a basis to recover attorneys' fees where the operative pleading does not allege a claim for misappropriation of trade secrets under the CUTSA. *Cytodyn, Inc. v. Amerimmune Pharmaceuticals Inc.*, 160 Cal. App. 4th 288, 300 (2008) ("because Cytodyn's complaint cannot be read to allege a cause of action for misappropriation of trade secrets, we are compelled to conclude the trial court erred in awarding attorney fees under section 3426.4."); *but see Indigo Grp. USA, Inc. v. Polo Ralph Lauren Corp.,* No. CV-11-5883-MWF (CWX), 2014 WL 12573380, at *8 (C.D. Cal. Mar. 17, 2014), aff'd, 749 F. App'x 639 (9th Cir. 2019) (while there was no facial claim for trade secrets misappropriation, section 3426.4 fees held available where plaintiff pled breach of confidence claim which was preempted under the CUTSA).

Amount of Fees Award. The trial court has discretion in determining the reasonableness of the amount of the attorneys' fees requested under section 3426.4. *Altavion, Inc. v. Konica Minolta Systems Laboratory, Inc.*, 226 Cal. App. 4th 26, 72-73 (2014) (the trial court makes its determination of what constitutes "reasonable attorney fees" after consideration of a number of factors, including the nature of the litigation, its difficulty, the amount involved, the skill required in its handling, the skill employed, the attention given, the success or failure, and other circumstances in the case.). *See also Sandler Partners, LLC v. Masergy Commc'ns, Inc.*, No. CV 19-6841-JFW(MAAX), 2020 WL 7347869, at *1 (C.D. Cal. Sept. 30, 2020) (awarding attorneys' fees to defendant in the amount of $126,834.00 pursuant to § 3426.4 and rejecting plaintiff's argument that only $49,990 should have been awarded; "If opposing counsel cannot come up with specific reasons for reducing the fee request that the district court finds persuasive, it should normally grant the award in full, or with no more than a haircut").

Apportionment of Fees Among Claims. The apportionment of fees between those related to the trade secret claim and those unrelated to the trade secret claim "is within the trial court's discretion." *VSL Corp. v. Gen. Techs., Inc.*, 46 U.S.P.Q.2d (BNA) 1356, 1361 (N.D. Cal. 1998) (citing *Abdallah v. U.S. Sav. Bank*, 43 Cal. App. 4th 1101, 1111 (1996)). "When fees and claims are 'inextricable [sic] intertwined' rendering them impracticable to divide, all fees may be awarded." *Id.* (citing *Abdallah*, 43 Cal. App. 4th at 1111). "[A]ttorneys' fees need not be apportioned when the work was performed on an issue common to both a fee-shifting and an 'ordinary' cause of action." *Id.* (citing *Abdallah*, 43 Cal. App. 4th at 1111); *cf. Mattel, Inc. v. MGA Entm't, Inc.,* 801 F. Supp. 2d 950, 957 (C.D. Cal. 2011) ("Contrary to MGA's argument, most of the time spent on its affirmative claims between 2004 and 2010 did not advance its successful claim for trade secret misappropriation.").

Fees on Appeal. Section 3426.4 can also be invoked as a basis to recover attorneys' fees incurred in connection with an appeal. *Gemini Aluminum*, 95 Cal. App. 4th at 1264. Interestingly, it is unclear from that opinion whether such fees are recoverable only if "bad faith" is found in accordance with section 3426.4. The opinion suggests that a party can recover attorneys' fees incurred on appeal merely if it is the "prevailing party on appeal." *Id.* On the other hand, although the court of appeal did not mention it in connection with its discussion of the recovery of attorneys' fees on appeal, the non-prevailing party in that case had been found to have acted in bad faith. *Id.* at 1255. *See also SASCO v. Rosendin Elec., Inc.*, 207 Cal. App. 4th 837, 849, 143 Cal. Rptr. 3d 828, 837 (2012), *as modified on denial of* reh'g (Aug. 7, 2012) ("We agree with defendants that they are entitled to reasonable attorney fees incurred on appeal. Defendants are "the prevailing part[ies] on appeal, and thus [they] are entitled to fees under section 3426.4. 'Although this court has the power to fix attorney fees on appeal, the better practice is to have the trial court determine such fees.'") (citing *Gemini*, supra, 95 Cal. App. 4th at p. 1264).

§ 13.07 DTSA Monetary Remedies

The Defend Trade Secrets Act (DTSA), 18 U.S.C. § 1836 *et seq.*, provides a range of monetary relief for trade secret misappropriation. 18 U.S.C. § 1836(b)(3)(B). As with claims asserted under the CUTSA, DTSA violations can give rise to actual damages, unjust enrichment, royalties, exemplary damages and attorneys' fees. 18 U.S.C. § 1836(b)(3)(B)-(D).

As the DTSA was enacted only in May 2016, there are not an abundant number of cases construing Section 1836. We address below some of the case law that exists.

A. Damage, Unjust Enrichment, and Royalty

The DTSA allows for the same three forms of monetary damages as the CUTSA. Actual damages, unjust enrichment, and royalty are all recognized forms of damages in DTSA cases. 18 U.S.C. § 1836(b)(3)(B). The DTSA provides for recovery of damages as follows:

- Damages for actual loss caused by the misappropriation of the trade secret;
- Damages for any unjust enrichment caused by the misappropriation of the trade secret that is not addressed in computing damages for actual loss; and
- In lieu of damages measured by any other methods, the damages caused by the misappropriation may be measured by imposition of liability for a reasonable royalty for the misappropriator's unauthorized disclosure or use of the trade secret.

While the DTSA allows for the same three forms of damages as the CUTSA, under the CUTSA a plaintiff can recover royalty damages only "[i]f neither damages nor unjust enrichment caused by misappropriation are provable." Cal. Civ. Code § 3426.3. By contrast, according to some courts, the DTSA does not require a finding that other damage forms are unprovable in order to obtain a royalty recovery. *Bus. Sols. LLC v. Ganatra*, No. SACV181426DOCKESX, 2020 WL 1279209, at *4 (C.D. Cal. Jan. 22, 2020) ("Under the CUTSA, a court can award damages for actual loss, unjust enrichment, and, if neither are provable, "a reasonable royalty for no longer than the period of time the use could have been prohibited"). The same measures are available under the DTSA, but it is not necessary to find that actual loss or unjust enrichment is unprovable before a reasonable royalty can be awarded"). *Cf., DiscoveryOrg Data, LLC v. Bitnine Glob., Inc.*, No. 19-CV-08098-LHK, 2020 WL 6562333, at *9 (N.D. Cal. Nov. 9, 2020) ("The DTSA permits an award of 'a reasonable royalty for the misappropriator's unauthorized disclosure or use of the trade secret' 'in lieu of damages measured by any other methods.' 18 U.S.C. § 1836(b)(3)(B)(ii). … Plaintiff acknowledges that a reasonable royalty is appropriate here because Plaintiff did not have access to discovery in order to prove actual loss or unjust enrichment" on its motion for default judgment).

"Unjust enrichment damages include what the parties call "avoided costs" -- i.e. the development costs that [defendant] avoided incurring when it misappropriated [plaintiff's] trade secrets. These avoided costs are recoverable as damages for unjust enrichment under the DTSA …." *Syntel Sterling Best Shores Mauritius Limited, et al., v. The Trizetto Group, Inc.,* No. 15 CIV. 211 (LGS), 2021 WL 1553926, at *6 (S.D.N.Y. Apr. 20, 2021).

While a DTSA claim may be filed in conjunction with other claims, the claimant is not entitled to double recovery. *See Motorola Sols., Inc. v. Hytera Commc'ns Corp.*, No. 1:17-CV-1973, 2020 WL 6554645, at *14 (N.D. Ill. Oct. 19, 2020) (rejecting defendant's claim that the jury verdict awarded a double recovery by allowing disgorgement (actual losses - calculated by the jury as lost profits worth $136.6 million), along with avoided research and development costs (roughly $73.6 million)); *Syntel Sterling Best Shores Mauritius Limited, et al., v. The Trizetto Group, Inc.,* No. 15 CIV. 211 (LGS), 2021 WL 1553926, at *7 (S.D.N.Y. Apr. 20, 2021) ("The DTSA expressly permits the award of both actual loss and unjust enrichment, as long as there is no double counting") (citing *Lightning Box Games Pty, Ltd. v. Plaor, Inc.*, No. 17-CV-03764-EDL, 2017 WL 7310782, at *11 (N.D. Cal. Dec. 29, 2017)), report and recommendation adopted, No. 17-CV-03764-WHO, 2018 WL 3069296 (N.D. Cal. Feb. 27, 2018) ("The Court declines to recommend an additional award of $66,008 in damages under the DTSA, as this would essentially constitute double recovery for the same allegedly unlawful misappropriation of trade secrets. At the hearing, Plaintiff conceded that recovery under … the … DTSA was not warranted for this reason").

For a case where the court denied alleged damages as a type of damages not authorized by the DTSA. *See Mtivity, Inc. v. Off. Depot, Inc.*, No. 1:19-CV-5094-FB-RML, 2021 WL 969124, at *9 (E.D.N.Y. Mar. 16, 2021) ("[The DTSA] does not ….provide for the type of damages Mtivity seeks, i.e. 'damages based on the cost to create the application, the cost for data migration and employee costs.' …. Because these types of damages are not explicitly covered by the statute, and it is unclear how the alleged improper disclosure caused Mtivity to incur them, Mtivity has failed to plead a cognizable harm").

For a case denying lost profits, see *Herrmann Int'l, Inc. v. Herrmann Int'l Eur.,* No. 1:17-CV-00073-MR, 2021 WL 861712, at *21 (W.D.N.C. Mar. 8, 2021) ("While the Plaintiffs' evidence shows an established history of consistent profits between 2011 and 2013, the Court cannot conclude on this record that the Defendants are responsible for the Plaintiffs' lost profits from 2014 to 2016 when accounting for the unexplained loss of IBM's business prior to the breach of contract or the seizure of the server.").

B. Exemplary Damages and Attorneys' Fees

The DTSA allows for recovery of exemplary damages upon a showing of willful and malicious misappropriation. A court may award exemplary damages in an amount not more than two times the amount of the compensatory damages awarded. 18 U.S.C. § 1836(b)(3)(C).

The DTSA also allows the court to award reasonable attorneys' fees to the prevailing party upon determination that a claim of misappropriation was made in bad faith, a motion to terminate an injunction was made or opposed in bad faith, or the trade secret was willfully and maliciously misappropriated. 18 U.S.C. § 1836(b)(3)(D).

Under the DTSA, a dismissal without prejudice does not establish a prevailing party for the purposes of an attorneys' fees award. *Physician's Surrogacy, Inc. v. German*, 311 F. Supp. 3d 1190, 1196–97 (S.D. Cal. 2018) (voluntary dismissal without prejudice does not establish prevailing party status and defendants are therefore ineligible for an award of attorneys' fees under the DTSA); *Dunster Live, LLC v. LoneStar Logos Management Company, LLC.*, 908 F.3d 948, 950 (5th Cir. 2018) (dismissal without prejudice of the DTSA case did not support prevailing party attorney fee award). *See also CleanFish, LLC v. Sims*, No. 19-CV-03663-HSG, 2020 WL 7353462, at *1 (N.D. Cal. Dec. 15, 2020) (denying defendant's motion for attorneys' fees and costs even though Court dismissed without leave to amend plaintiff's claims for the DTSA violations; "weaknesses do not establish objective speciousness. … the Court's motion to dismiss order also does not establish speciousness. … Plaintiff's decision to pursue its claims despite Defendant's insistence that the claims lacked merit does not establish subjective bad faith").

The DTSA requires employers to provide certain notices of whistleblower immunity provisions in order to qualify for a potential award of attorneys' fees or exemplary damages. 18 U.S.C. § 1833(b). In the event a plaintiff asserting a DTSA violation has not complied with the whistleblowing notice requirement (*see* Chapter 6), the plaintiff may not be awarded exemplary damages or attorney fees under subparagraph (C) or (D) of section 1836(b)(3). *See, e.g., Quintara Biosciences, Inc. v. Ruifeng Biztech Inc.*, No. C 20-04808 WHA, 2020 WL 6118494, at *3 (N.D. Cal. Oct. 16, 2020) (concluding, in part, that plaintiff may not recovery exemplary damages or attorneys' fees where the employment agreement did not include the relevant whistleblower protection notice pursuant to 18 U.S.C. § 1833(b)); *Xoran Holdings LLC v. Luick*, No. 16-13703, 2017 WL 4039178, at *7 (E.D. Mich. Sept. 13, 2017) (where employer failed to provide notice of the DTSA employee whistleblower immunity provisions, it could not recover attorneys' fees or exemplary damages on the DTSA claim).

For some additional cases that address attorneys' fees or exemplary damages under the DTSA, *see*:

- *Accredability, LLC v. Accreditsoft*, No. CV185969DMGFFMX, 2019 WL 4137409, at *4 (C.D. Cal. May 10, 2019) (denying plaintiff's request for $97,926 in attorneys' fees and $637 in costs on the ground that plaintiff failed to demonstrate that the appropriation was "malicious").
- *Swarmify, Inc. v. Cloudflare, Inc.*, No. C 17-06957 WHA, 2018 WL 4680177, at *2 (N.D. Cal. Sept. 28, 2018) ("courts generally adopt a two-pronged standard for the evaluation of [claims of bad faith]"); citing *Farmers Edge Inc. v. Farmobile, LLC*, No. 8:16CV191, 2018 WL 3747833, at *6 (D. Neb. Aug. 7, 2018) (party seeking an award of attorneys' fees under DTSA must show (1) the objective speciousness of opposing party's claim, and (2) the subjective bad faith of the opposing party in bringing or maintaining the action for an improper purpose) (citation omitted).

- *Zeetogroup, LLC v. Fiorentino*, No. 19-CV-458 JLS (NLS), 2020 WL 886866, at *4 (S.D. Cal. Feb. 24, 2020) (exemplary damages unavailable when based solely on defendant's alleged violation of preliminary injunction, "Plaintiffs ... are not yet the prevailing party for purposes of the statute [having only succeeded in obtaining a preliminary injunction]").

- *Motorola Sols., Inc. v. Hytera Commc'ns Corp.*, No. 1:17-CV-1973, 2020 WL 6554645, at *12, *15 (N.D. Ill. Oct. 19, 2020) (exemplary damages award of $418 million on a compensatory damages award of $346 million was supported by the evidence showing intentional bad faith acts, and the amount was comparable to similar awards).

- *DiscoverOrg Data, LLC v. Bitnine Glob., Inc.*, No. 19-CV-08098-LHK, 2020 WL 6562333, at *10 (N.D. Cal. Nov. 9, 2020) (plaintiff entitled to exemplary damages given defendant's willful and malicious misappropriation - "instead of buying its own valid subscription, Defendant used the login credentials of other subscribers [to access Plaintiff's password protected database]. ... Defendant then downloaded hundreds of thousands of records from the database, and used those records for its own sales and marketing purposes…").

- *Lightning Box Games Pty, Ltd. v. Plaor, Inc.*, No. 17-CV-03764-EDL, 2017 WL 7310782, at *11 (N.D. Cal. Dec. 29, 2017), report and recommendation adopted, No. 17-CV-03764-WHO, 2018 WL 3069296 (N.D. Cal. Feb. 27, 2018) ("…the Court declines to find that Plaor willfully and maliciously misappropriated Plaintiff's trade secrets. There is no evidence to support that finding, aside from conclusory allegations ….").

C. Relying on UTSA Case Law in DTSA Litigation

While the DTSA body of law is developing, courts addressing monetary remedies under section 1836 may look to case law addressing similar remedies under state UTSA statutes. *See, e.g., Corelogic Sols., LLC v. Credifi Corp.,* No. 820CV01676FLADFMX, 2021 WL 1156860, at *8 (C.D. Cal. Jan. 29, 2021) ("The DTSA is largely modelled after …UTSA … and a misappropriation claim under the DTSA is materially the same as the corresponding claim under [the CUTSA] …. "Accordingly, federal district courts in California have applied California's trade secret case law to causes of action brought under the federal DTSA.") (citing *Deerpoint Grp., Inc. v. Agrigenix, LLC*, 345 F.Supp.3d 1207, 1227 (E.D. Cal. 2018); *Founder Starcoin, Inc. v. Launch Labs, Inc.*, 2018 U.S. Dist. LEXIS 113737, at *10 (S.D. Cal. July 9, 2018); *Calendar Research LLC v. StubHub, Inc.*, 2020 U.S. Dist. LEXIS 112361, at *9 & n.5 (C.D. Cal. May 13, 2020)"). *See also CleanFish, LLC v. Sims*, No. 19-CV-03663-HSG, 2020 WL 7353462, at *1 (N.D. Cal. Dec. 15, 2020). *But see Dunster Live, LLC v. LoneStar Logos Management Company, LLC.*, 908 F.3d 948, 950 (5th Cir. 2018) (rejecting the argument that it should look to state UTSA case law rather the other federal fee statutes interpreting the term "prevailing party").

Chapter 14
SUMMARY JUDGMENT AND SUMMARY ADJUDICATION IN TRADE SECRET CASES

By: Rebecca ("Bec") Edelson, Esq.
and John V. Picone III, Esq.

---

§ 14.01 Introduction

Despite the typically fact-intensive nature of trade secret claims, motions for summary judgment or summary adjudication can be granted at times. For example, in *API Ams. Inc. v. Miller*, the court granted the plaintiff's motion for summary judgment on its DTSA and Kansas Uniform Trade Secrets Act causes of action, arguing it had established all necessary elements of its misappropriation claims. 380 F. Supp. 3d 1141, 1147-50 (D. Kan. 2019). In evaluating plaintiff's DTSA claim, the court referenced summary judgment case law from other courts within the Tenth Circuit because there were no controlling decisions regarding establishing entitlement to summary judgment on a DTSA misappropriation claim. *Id.* at 1148, n. 5. Thus, given that DTSA is relatively new, courts may look to state UTSA decisions for guidance.

The California practitioner should keep in mind that it is more difficult to obtain in state court summary adjudication of particular issues that do not resolve an entire cause of action than it is in federal court. *Compare* Fed. R. Civ. P. § 56, *with* Cal. Civ. Proc. Code § 437c.

This chapter addresses summary judgment or summary adjudication in the context of trade secret misappropriation claims.

§ 14.02 The Existence of a Trade Secret

Although it is ordinarily a question of fact whether information constitutes a trade secret, a court may grant summary judgment on the issue in some circumstances (for example, when it cannot be controverted that the alleged trade secret information is not secret or is easily obtainable). In *Self Directed Placement Corp. v. Control Data Corp.*, 908 F.2d 462, 465 (9th Cir. 1990), the Ninth Circuit, applying CUTSA, ruled that "the district court correctly held as a matter of law that the [alleged trade secrets] . . . were not secret and were a matter of common public knowledge." *See also Source Prod. & Equipment Co., Inc. v. Schehr*, 2019 WL 4752058, at *7 (E.D. La. Sept. 30, 2019) (granting summary adjudication against plaintiff, finding certain of the alleged trade secrets were not trade secrets under DTSA; "It is the plaintiff's burden to prove that a trade secret exists and identify what information is known to the trade and which is not"); *CMI Roadbuilding, Inc. v. Iowa Parts, Inc.*, 2017 WL 6210920, at *12 (N.D. Iowa Dec. 8, 2017) (granting summary judgment to defendant on DTSA claim where plaintiff failed to maintain secrecy of its alleged trade secrets); *Care Servs. Mgmt., LLC v. Premier Mobile Dentistry of VA, LLC*, 2020 WL 5797974, at *6 (M.D. Tenn. Sept. 29, 2020) (defendant was entitled to summary judgment on the DTSA claim because plaintiffs had intentionally shared the information with third parties).

Similarly, courts have summarily adjudicated that the alleged misappropriated information is trade secret. *See, e.g., MAI Sys. Corp. v. Peak Computer Inc.*, 991 F.2d 511, 521-22 (9th Cir. 1993) (claim asserted under CUTSA; affirming that portion of the district court's summary adjudication that certain of the allegedly misappropriated information qualified as trade secrets.),

However, courts also have found triable issues of fact exist regarding whether information was trade secret, precluding summary judgment. *See, e.g., San Jose Constr., Inc. v. S.B.C.C., Inc.*, 155 Cal. App. 4th 1528, 1542-43 (2007) (the information, although known on a piecemeal basis to a number of parties, was not necessarily "readily ascertainable in the circumstances presented."); *SkinMedica, Inc. v. Histogen, Inc.*, 869 F. Supp. 2d 1176, 1192-96 (S.D. Cal. 2012) (claim asserted under CUTSA; denying the defendant's motion for summary judgment where there were triable issues of fact as to whether the alleged trade secrets had independent economic value from not being generally known).

Summary judgment may be granted against a trade secret claimant if it fails to identify the trade secret properly or with care. *See Imax Corp. v. Cinema Techs., Inc.*, 152 F.3d 1161, 1164-68 (9th Cir. 1998) (applying CUTSA); *Pixion, Inc. v. PlaceWare Inc.*, 421 F. Supp. 2d 1233, 1242 (N.D. Cal. 2005) (CUTSA case; "[a]llowing Pixion to defend against summary judgment by asserting now that its method is secret [in the face of the "reasonable particularity" requirement,] . . . would defeat the purposes of [Cal. Civ. Proc. Code] § 2019(d)[, the current § 2019.210]."). *But see SkinMedica*, 869 F. Supp. 2d at 1190 n. 6 (summary judgment denied because trade secrets were adequately described in answers to interrogatories and in expert reports). *See supra* Chapter 11 regarding the duty to identify the trade secret with reasonable particularity.

A trade secret claimant may also be denied summary judgment if it fails to identify the alleged trade secret adequately. *See MAI Sys.*, 991 F.2d at 521-23; *Mattel, Inc. v. MGA Entm't, Inc.*, 782 F. Supp. 2d 911, 960, 968, 970 (C.D. Cal. 2011) (CUTSA case; descriptions "vague" and "nebulous").

The Ninth Circuit overruled a grant of summary judgment against the plaintiffs based on (among other grounds) plaintiffs' claimed failure to identify adequately the alleged trade secrets claimed to have been misappropriated under CUTSA and DTSA. *InteliClear, LLC v. ETC Glob. Holdings, Inc.*, 978 F.3d 653, 655 (9th Cir. 2020). The Ninth Circuit held that there was a genuine issue of fact whether a reasonable jury could conclude that the "uniquely designed tables, columns, account number structures, methods of populating table data, and combination or interrelation thereof, are protectable trade secrets." *Id.*, at 659. The Court reasoned that "[a]t this stage, particularly where no discovery whatsoever had occurred, it is not fatal to InteliClear's claim that its hedging language left open the possibility of expanding its identifications later. InteliClear's burden is only to identify at least one trade secret with sufficient particularity to create a triable issue." *Id.* The Court emphasized its holding was tied to the particular facts of the case and "[r]efining trade secret identifications through discovery makes good sense. The process acknowledges the inherent tension between a party's desire to protect legitimate intellectual property claims and the need for intellectual property law to prevent unnecessary obstacles to useful competition." *Id.* at 662; *Cf. Next Payment Solutions, Inc. v. CLEAResult Consulting, Inc.*, 2019 WL 955354, at *21-*23 (DTSA case; broad categories of trade secret information "were enough to survive a motion to dismiss, . . . but the question at the summary judgment stage is whether [p]laintiff has provided enough evidence identifying a concrete trade secret to create a triable issue as to whether [d]efendant misappropriated that trade secret"); *Calendar Research LLC v. StubHub, Inc.*, 2020 WL 4390391, at *5 (C.D. Cal. May 13, 2020) (granting summary judgment to defendant on DTSA claim where plaintiff failed to sufficiently define its trade secrets); *OsteoStrong Franchising, LLC v. Richter*, 2020 WL 4584007, at *5 (D.N.M. Aug. 10, 2020) (same).

§ 14.03 Misappropriation

The issue of misappropriation is ordinarily a factual matter, precluding summary judgment. *See, e.g., MAI Sys. Corp. v. Peak Computer Inc.*, 991 F.2d 511, 521-22 (9th Cir. 1993) (CUTSA case). Thus, the court denied a defendant's motion for a no-misappropriation adjudication in the *SkinMedica* litigation. *See* 869 F. Supp. 2d at 1197 ("[Defendant's] scattershot attempt to disclaim use of various elements of the claimed trade secrets does not foreclose the possibility that [defendant's] process was not substantially derived from the claimed trade secrets, even if it differed in specifics from the process described therein."). *See also S.O.S., Inc. v. Payday, Inc.*, 886 F.2d 1081, 1090 (9th Cir. 1989) (reversing summary judgment; "There is a genuine issue of fact as to whether the contract gave [defendant] a right to possess only a protected copy of the software if it elected to process its customers' work on its own computer, or whether [defendant] was entitled to possess an unprotected copy.").

While misappropriation is generally a factual matter, the issue of misappropriation can give rise to a summary judgment in some circumstances where the facts are not controverted. *See, e.g.*, *Silvaco Data Sys. v. Intel Corp.*, 184 Cal. App. 4th 210, 224-30 (2010), *disapproved on other grounds by Kwikset Corp. v. Superior Court*, 51 Cal. 4th 310 (2011) (summary judgment on trade secret misappropriation claim in favor of defendant appropriate where it was uncontroverted that the defendant never possessed or had knowledge of the alleged trade secret); *Gibson-Homans Co. v. Wall-Tite, Inc.*, No. 92 2750 JGD, 1992 WL 512411, at *4 (C.D. Cal. Oct. 27, 1992) (CUTSA case) (granting defendant's motion for summary judgment based upon the lack of evidence of any misappropriation; "since defendants have not used the formulas or otherwise impaired their commercial benefit to plaintiff, no misappropriation has occurred."); *Sapienza v. Trahan*, 2018 WL 4440897, at *8 (W.D. La. Sept. 17, 2018) (granting defendants summary judgment on DTSA claim where there was no evidence of misappropriation); *Capricorn Mgmt. Sys., Inc. v. Gov't Employees Ins. Co.*, 2020 WL 1242616, at *9 (E.D.N.Y. Mar. 16, 2020) (granting defendants' motion for summary judgment on DTSA claim because plaintiff failed to raise a triable issue of fact as to any alleged trade secret's misappropriation by defendants); *Call One, Inc. v. Anzine*, 2018 WL 2735089, at *9 (N.D. Ill. June 7, 2018) (granting summary judgment to defendant on DTSA claim where plaintiff presented no facts from which a reasonable jury could conclude the defendant had misappropriated the plaintiff's trade secret); *see also*, *Keystone Transp. Solutions, LLC v. Nw. Hardwoods, Inc.*, 2019 WL 1756293, at *6 (W.D. Va. April 19, 2019) (denying defendants' summary judgment under the DTSA because simply replicating a business model is the kind of "extensive circumstantial evidence" that would create a material issue of fact regarding whether misappropriation occurred).

A misappropriation claim cannot be based solely on speculation that the defendants "must be" misappropriating or "must have" misappropriated the trade secrets because they are working in a similar area or technology and the competitor made improvements to its product. *See Universal Analytics, Inc. v. MacNeal-Schwendler Corp.* 707 F. Supp. 1170, 1177-78 (C.D. Cal. 1989), *aff'd*, 914 F.2d 1256 (9th Cir. 1990) (decided under CUTSA). Courts have granted summary judgment in the defendant's favor on this basis. For example, in *Hooked Media Group, Inc. v. Apple Inc.,* 55 Cal. App. 5th 323, 332-333 (2020), in affirming summary judgment in favor of defendant on the ground that the plaintiff could not prove misappropriation, the Court of Appeals reasoned that:

- while inferential evidence can be used to prove misappropriation, Hooked's evidence only "suggest[ed] the engineers drew on knowledge and skills they gained from Hooked to develop a product for their new employer" which was permitted by "California's policy favoring free mobility for employees";

- "evidence that Apple hired engineers with knowledge of Hooked's trade secrets and that the engineers inevitably would have relied on that knowledge in their work for Apple does not support a claim for improper acquisition of a trade secret";

- "[m]ere possession of trade secrets by a departing employee is not enough for an injunction[,]" citing *FLIR Sys., Inc. v. Parrish*, 174 Cal. App. 4th 1270, 1279 (2009).

See also Wyatt Tech. Corp. v. Malvern Instruments Inc., No. CV 07–08298 DDP (MANx), 2009 WL 2365647, at *18-19 (C.D. Cal. July 29, 2009) (granting summary adjudication in defendant's favor; a defendant's access to alleged trade secret information while an employee before reentering the market in competition with his former employer is not sufficient to create a triable issue of fact as to whether defendants used the trade secret financial information.); *Danjaq LLC v. Sony Corp.*, No. CV 97-8414-ER (MCX), 1999 WL 317629, at *1 (C.D. Cal. Mar. 11, 1999) (CUTSA case; "Plaintiffs cannot create a factual dispute through their mere speculation . . . ."); *Gibson-Homans*, 1992 WL 512411, at *5 ("There is no evidence to suggest that defendants intend to use or disclose to other competitors the . . . formulas[;] [i]f in the future the threat of misappropriation becomes real, plaintiff will have a remedy under [Cal. Civ. Code] § 3426.2.").

See also supra Chapter 12 discussing the inevitable disclosure doctrine. *But see supra* Chapter 2 discussing the sufficiency of circumstantial evidence and reasonable inferences to prove misappropriation.

In addition to summarily adjudicating the lack of any misappropriation, a court can also summarily adjudicate in some circumstances that misappropriation occurred as a matter of law. For example, in *MAI Sys.*, the Ninth Circuit affirmed that portion of the district's court's summary judgment adjudicating that the defendant misappropriated the trade secret customer information. *MAI Sys.*, 991 F.2d at 521-22 (misappropriation by solicitation of customers using trade secret information).

§ 14.04 Defenses

Affirmative defenses to a misappropriation claim may also be subject to summary judgment. For example, the court in *HiRel Connectors, Inc. v. United States*, 465 F. Supp. 2d 984, 990-91 (C.D. Cal. 2005), granted summary judgment on the plaintiff's trade secret claims against a subset of defendants based upon the expiration of the three-year statute of limitations for CUTSA claims. *See also*, *Array Techs., Inc. v. Mitchell*, 2020 WL 1976374, at *2 (D.N.M. April 24, 2020) (granting plaintiff's summary judgment to defendants' unclean hands defense to a DTSA claim).

§ 14.05 Remedies

Remedies can be the subject of a summary adjudication motion. For example, in *SkinMedica, Inc. v. Histogen, Inc.*, 869 F. Supp. 2d 1176 (S.D. Cal. 2012), the defendant sought summary adjudication of the plaintiff's claim for a reasonable royalty, the only monetary remedy sought by the plaintiff. *Id.* at 1197. However, the court denied the motion, as it could not determine that damages and unjust enrichment were provable such that a royalty would be an unavailable remedy. *Id.* at 1197-98.

§ 14.06 Conclusion

Although more frequently than not triable issues of fact preclude summary judgment in trade secret cases, the practitioner should always consider whether the case is the exception to this generalization. Under appropriate circumstances, it is possible to obtain summary judgment of a trade secret claim. Moreover, even if summary judgment of the entire claim is unavailable, the practitioner should always consider whether a summary adjudication of a particular issue would be helpful to resolve the case.

Chapter 15
INTERSECTION OF TRADE SECRETS AND OTHER FORMS OF INTELLECTUAL PROPERTY

By: Robert B. Milligan, Esq.,
Anthony J. Orler, Esq.,
and Puya Partow-Navid, Esq.

---

§ 15.01 Introduction

In addition to trade secrets, other important forms of intellectual property protection include patents, copyrights, and trademarks. In certain circumstances, contracts and the law of unfair competition can also be used to protect intellectual property. This chapter examines the key differences and similarities between trade secrets and these other forms of intellectual property protection. This chapter also provides the reader with guidance regarding which form (or forms) of intellectual property protection may be suited for particular situations. A full discussion of the substantive law of these other forms of intellectual property is beyond the scope of this chapter.

A. Patents

Title 35 of the U.S. Code governs the prosecution, rights, and infringement of patents. An issued patent provides its owner with the right to exclude others from making, using, offering to sell, selling, or importing the invention claimed by the patent. 35 U.S.C. § 271(a) (2010). These exclusionary rights are limited in duration to the term of the patent. *Ibid.* For applications filed on or after June 8, 1995, the patent term is twenty years from the first filing date of the patent application. *Id.* § 154. Not every invention is patentable. An invention must be new, useful, and not obvious to "one skilled in the art." Id., §§ 102-103. Additionally, the invention must be directed to patent-eligible subject matter. 35 U.S.C. § 101 defines patent-eligible subject matter as "any new and useful process, machine, manufacture, or composition of matter, or any new and useful improvement thereof." Ibid. The broad statutory recitation of patent-eligible subject matter is also subject to several judicially-created exceptions. Based on these judicially-created exceptions, laws of nature, natural phenomena, and abstract ideas are not patentable. *Alice Corp. v. CLS Bank Int'l.*, 573 U.S. 208 (2014).

An invention may be protected by patent law as well as trade secret law. The principles behind these different forms of intellectual property, however, may render patents and trade secrets mutually exclusive for a specific aspect of the invention. Patent law confers exclusive rights to the patent owner in exchange for disclosing the invention to the public. Once the patent term expires, a person skilled in the art should be able to make, use, and sell the invention from the patent disclosure. *Id.* § 112(a).

For competitive reasons or other reasons, an inventor may be reluctant to provide such a complete and enabling disclosure of the invention. Additionally, or alternatively, the inventor may want to withhold certain aspects of the invention as a trade secret. The withholding of information in the specification may be cause for rejection of the application during prosecution under 35 U.S.C. § 112(a) as not providing the "best mode" of practicing the invention. If the withholding is severe enough, the patent may also be held invalid under 35 U.S.C. § 112(a) as not enabling the disclosure.

On the other hand, one aspect of a single product may be protected using patent law, and another aspect of the product may be protected using trade secret law. For example, a patent may claim and cover a product that uses a specific component that may be made in several different ways. The method used to manufacture the component may also constitute a second invention that can be separately patented or protected as a trade secret.

Patents and trade secrets may also be used to protect the same invention nonconcurrently. Specifically, an inventor may keep the invention confidential, thereby protecting the invention as a trade secret, and then later file for and obtain patent protection for the invention. By delaying the filing for patent protection, however, the inventor risks losing patent rights as well as trade secret rights.

Patent applications filed prior to March 16, 2013 are examined and litigated under a "first to invent" approach. *See* 35 U.S.C. § 102(a)(2) (2011). Under the "first to invent" approach, patent protection may be available for an invention developed by a first inventor, even if the first inventor was not the first applicant to file a patent application directed to the invention. As of March 16, 2013, the United States joined the remainder of the world in a "first to file" patent system. Under the "first to file" patent system, patent protection is no longer available for an invention once a patent application for that invention is filed at the Patent Office, even if the inventor of the patent application was not the first inventor.

Further, patent applications are often published fourteen to eighteen months after filing. The publication of the patent application is considered a "disclosure" of the invention to the public, negating any trade secret protection for third parties. Because patent applications are often published before a patent is granted, a worst-case scenario is that the patent application is published, but a patent is never granted; therefore, both patent and trade secret protection for the invention would be lost.

The owner of an invention must make a careful determination regarding whether to seek patent protection or to rely instead on trade secret protection, with possibly longer-term protection and concomitant risks. The decision requires a thoughtful multi-pronged analysis which considers the nature of the specific invention and the owner's commercial objectives. Additional factors for an owner to consider may include the likelihood of obtaining a patent as well as the costs of obtaining and enforcing a patent.

Arguably, the most important factor to consider is the nature of the invention. A trade secret does not provide protection against independent development or legal reverse engineering, but a patent does protect against such events. *Chicago Lock Co. v. Fanberg*, 676 F.2d 400, 404 (9th Cir. 1982) ("Trade secrets do not enjoy the absolute monopoly protection afforded patented processes, for example, and trade secrets will lose their character as private property when the owner divulges them or when they are discovered through proper means."). Therefore, if the nature of the invention may likely be developed independently or the invention may readily be discovered through examination or reverse engineering, then a patent would likely provide greater protection for the invention than simply maintaining the invention as a trade secret.

If reverse engineering or independent development of the invention would be difficult, such as an improved process for producing products, then trade secret protection may provide the best protection. In addition, if the patent disclosure would allow others to readily design around the patent claims, then protecting the invention as a trade secret may be the better approach.

Another factor to consider is the subject matter of the invention. If a particular invention falls within the various types of subject matter that are not patent eligible, then trade secret protection may be the only available approach. As discussed, patent ineligible subject matter includes laws of nature, natural phenomena, and abstract ideas. *See Diamond v. Diehr,* 450 U.S. 175, 185 (1981); *Alice* 573 U.S. 208 (2014). Abstract ideas have been held to include mathematical concepts, certain methods of organizing human activity, and mental processes. *See* MPEP § 2106.04.

In deciding whether to apply for patent protection or maintain a discovery as a trade secret, it is also important to remember that trade secret law does not protect against independent development. If a second inventor were to independently make the same discovery, absent patent protection, the first inventor has no recourse against the second inventor. Even outside the patent filing process, if the second inventor publicly discloses the details of the discovery, the first inventor would lose trade secret protection for his discovery.

It is also important to consider the commercially valuable life of the invention. If the invention has an expected useful life significantly longer than the twenty-year term of a patent, then it may be advisable to protect the invention as a trade secret. The useful life of the invention should also be considered in light of the likelihood of independent development or discovery through reverse engineering to determine whether to select patent or trade secret protection.

Because trade secret protection automatically attaches to any information that derives independent economic value from being secret and is the subject of reasonable efforts to protect its secrecy, the ability to even obtain a patent should also be reviewed. Before a patent is granted on an invention, the application must be reviewed by the Patent Office and determined to be in statutory compliance. Further, the invention must be considered new, not obvious in view of the prior art, and useful. In short, the information may not qualify for protection under the patent laws.

The patenting process may take several years to ripen into an issued patent, and the scope of protection may change between the beginning of the process and the issuance. Until the patent issues, the owner has no mechanism for enforcing his rights under the patent laws. Therefore, if it appears likely that the inventor may not be able to obtain a patent, or it may take too long to obtain useful patent enforcement, then protecting the invention as a trade secret may be the better approach.

During the patent examination process, the scope of patent protection may change. What the inventor originally thought was new and nonobvious may turn out to be part of the public domain or part of someone else's patent. The scope of the public domain is not limited to U.S. publications. Rather, the patent examination process may consider any publication as prior art that may be cited against the patent application. To continue the patent process, inventors often change the scope of the monopoly they seek by reducing the protection covered by the patent claims. However, the changes made during the examination process are open to the public after the patent issues, which may make it easier for others to avoid patent infringement. Further, narrower patent claim coverage may make patent enforcement more difficult. In such cases, trade secret protection may be preferable.

Moreover, it is important to also consider the costs of obtaining and maintaining a patent. The costs involved in applying for, obtaining, and maintaining a patent are typically high—perhaps prohibitively so for some inventors or companies. The exact costs involved in obtaining a patent vary depending on a number of factors, including: the complexity of the invention, the field of the invention, an amount of prior art in the field, and attorney/patent agent fees. The fees for drafting a patent application can range from $5,000 to $30,000 or more, depending on the invention. Fees associated with prosecuting the application to issuance can amount to $10,000 or more, depending on the course through the United States Patent and Trademark Office (USPTO). In addition, the USPTO charges filing, prosecution-related, and maintenance fees ranging from several hundred to a few thousand dollars. Obtaining a patent in countries other than the United States will have additional fees in similar fee ranges per country where protection is sought. In contrast, protecting a trade secret does not require the same initial costs; however, depending on the nature of the trade secret, the owner may find it necessary to spend a significant amount on security costs and other expenses to protect the trade secret.

B. Copyrights

Copyright protection applies to any "original work of authorship" automatically upon becoming "fixed in any tangible medium of expression." 17 U.S.C. § 102(a) (2009). Exclusive rights provided to an owner of a copyrighted work include the right to reproduce, distribute copies, prepare derivative works and publicly display or perform the copyrighted material. In contrast to trade secret protection, copyright protection extends to published and unpublished works, and is limited to the particular expression of the work as opposed to the idea embodied in the work. There is no requirement that there be "public use" of the work for there to be copyright protection. Moreover, copyright law provides protection for only a limited term. For work created on or after January 1, 1978, and the author is a natural person, the term is a fixed period of time beyond the length of the author's life. If the author is a business entity (e.g. corporation) or anonymous, the term is fixed based on whether the work has been published or not. For works created prior to January 1, 1978, there is a more complex system based on whether and when the work was published. Copyright law and trade secret law are similar in that neither provides protection against independent development. Copyright infringement requires a showing of impermissible copying. Direct evidence of copying is usually unavailable, so infringement is often established through proof of access to the original work and substantial similarity between the original work and the alleged copy.

Copyright law and trade secret law can be used to protect the same information. A common example is found in computer programs where the owner may choose to assert copyright protection for programs describing or embodying trade secrets while the underlying trade secrets themselves (such as an algorithm) remain confidential. This is made possible by the Copyright Office, which specifically allows for a copyright owner to deposit a redacted specimen to avoid disclosing its trade secrets. *See* U.S. Copyright Office, Circular 61: Copyright Registration for Computer Programs, *available at* https://www.copyright.gov/circs/circ61.pdf (March 2021). However, because software can be protected under both trade secret law and copyright law, a trade secret claim for the misappropriation of software (or any other copyrighted work) may be preempted by copyright law. *See supra* Chapter 9.

C. Trademarks

Trademarks are words, names, logos, or other symbols that identify goods as originating from a single source. Trademarks are used to distinguish the goods from those manufactured or sold by other sources. Trademark rights are created by using the designation in the marketplace in connection with certain goods or services. Federal trademark law (15 U.S.C. §§ 1051-1072 (2009)) provides benefits and protections for those trademarks that are used in manner that falls under the Commerce Clause of U.S. Constitution. State law provide protection for trademarks in that specific state. Traditionally, the goal of trademark law has been to prevent deception, confusion, or mistake as to the origin of goods and services. The legal protection of a trademark thus serves to both protect the consumer from confusion and deception while also protecting the market and goodwill of the trademark owner. Similar to trade secrets, trademarks have an indefinite duration that continues so long as the mark is used in connection with the designated goods or services.

Trademarks are a very different type of intellectual property than trade secrets. Trademarks are valuable because they allow the public to identify the source of goods and protect the goodwill a company has acquired. Trade secrets are valuable because they are specifically kept secret from the public, thereby providing the owner with a competitive advantage over others.

D. Unfair Competition Laws

Historically, the common law has provided remedies for wrongful acts that could also be the basis for a trade secret misappropriation claim. *Balboa Ins. Co. v. Trans Global Equities*, 218 Cal. App. 3d 1327, 1342 (1990). Examples of such claims include unfair competition, breach of fiduciary duty, interference, and conversion.

In an often-cited decision, the California Court of Appeal held that such common law claims, if based on the same nucleus of facts as a trade secret claim, are preempted even if the trade secret claim itself ultimately is unsuccessful. *K.C. Multimedia, Inc. v. Bank of Am. Tech. & Operations, Inc.*, (171 Cal. App. 4th 939, 958-959 (2009). *But see Imax Corp. v. Cinema Techs., Inc.*, 152 F.3d 1161, 1169 (9th Cir. 1998) (holding that under then-existing California law, "a plaintiff can maintain a common law unfair competition claim regardless of whether it demonstrates a legally protectable trade secret"). *See supra* Chapter 9.

E. Contracts

A duty to protect the confidential nature of a trade secret may be implied under common law, implied because of a relationship between parties, or imposed under a contractual relationship. Contracts such as nondisclosure or confidentiality agreements are often used to protect the confidential nature of a trade secret, either through imposition of a duty of confidentiality or by expansion of an already existing implied duty of confidentiality. Moreover, a breach of such an agreement can be the type of "improper means" necessary for a claim of trade secret misappropriation. *See supra* Chapter 2.

In addition to imposing confidentiality obligations, contracts can be used to protect trade secrets in other ways. For example, products embodying trade secrets, such as software products, are often licensed as opposed to sold. Since trade secret law does not protect against reverse engineering, a contractual promise to not reverse engineer a product should be part of any license or agreement governing the use of such product. If a product is reverse engineered to acquire a trade secret, in contravention of an agreement governing the use of the product, this reverse engineering becomes the type of "improper means" that can form the basis for a trade secret misappropriation claim as well as a breach of contract claim. *See supra* Chapter 2.

Confidentiality agreements can also help protect the patentability of nonfiled patentable inventions. Specifically, confidentiality agreements should always be used to protect an invention for which a patent is desired but not yet applied for because these agreements help avoid the effects of the "public use" and "on sale" doctrines which can prevent an inventor from obtaining a patent. *See* 35 U.S.C. § 102(a)(1) (2011).

§ 15.02 Comparison Chart of Intellectual Property Rights

	Trade Secret	Patent	Copyright	Trademark
Subject Matter	Any information that derives independent economic value from not being known or generally ascertainable and is the subject of reasonable efforts to protect its secrecy	Any new, useful and nonobvious process, machine, manufacture, composition of matter, or improvements thereto	Original works of authorship once fixed in a tangible medium of expression; including literary, musical, dramatic, chronographic, pictorial, audiovisual, sound recordings, and architectural works	Words, names, symbols, and other indicia of source or origin
Term	Indefinite so long as it remains secret	Limited term, generally twenty years from filing date	Limited term based on life of the author	Indefinite so long as the mark is used
Protects Against	Wrongful acquisition, use, or disclosure of the trade secret	Making, using, selling, offering for sale, or importing the claimed invention (even if independently developed by another)	Copying, distributing, preparing derivative works, or publicly displaying or performing the copyrighted work	Use of a copy, counterfeit, or imitation of a trademark that is likely to cause confusion or mistake or to deceive
Potential Remedies	Damages (actual damages, unjust enrichment, or reasonable royalty); exemplary damages; attorneys' fees; injunction	Damages (reasonable royalty or lost profits); increased damages attorneys' fees; injunction	Damages (actual damages, infringer's profits, or statutory damages); attorneys' fees; injunction; reasonable royalty	Damages (actual damages or infringer's profits); increased damages; attorneys' fees; injunction
Applicable Laws	State laws; Cal. Civ. Code § 3426 et seq.; 18 U.S.C. §§1832 et seq.	35 U.S.C. §§ 101 et seq.	17 U.S.C. §§ 101 et seq.	State laws; 15 U.S.C. § 1051 et seq.

Chapter 16
THE TRADE SECRET PRIVILEGE

By: Rebecca ("Bec") Edelson, Esq.
and Philip H.R. Nevinny, Esq.

---

§ 16.01 Section 1060 of the California Evidence Code—The Trade Secret Privilege

A. The Privilege and its Potential Waiver

Practitioners who represent trade secret holders should familiarize themselves with section 1060 of the California Evidence Code. Cal. Evid. Code § 1060. This statutory provision establishes a privilege that can be invoked to protect a trade secret in litigation, providing that "the owner of a trade secret has a privilege to refuse to disclose the secret, and to prevent another from disclosing it, if the allowance of the privilege will not tend to conceal fraud or otherwise work injustice." *Id.*

Practitioners should assert the privilege as soon as it is appropriate to do so. If not timely asserted, the privilege could be waived. *Stadish v. Superior Court*, 71 Cal. App. 4th 1130, 1141 (1999) (holding that the holder of the trade secret waived the trade secret privilege by failing to assert the privilege in response to a document demand, and then allowing opposing counsel to review forty boxes of documents before claiming the privilege).

Even if a trade secret holder failed to timely assert the privilege in response to a discovery request and, even if a trade secret holder provided the trade secret information to the party seeking the discovery, the trade secret holder may be able to obtain a protective order to govern the use and disclosure of the trade secret information. *Id.* at 1144. Nevertheless, the better practice is always to assert the privilege whenever it is applicable in order to avoid any claims of waiver.

B. The Purpose of the Privilege

The purpose of the trade secret privilege is to protect the confidentiality of trade secret information, so long as the privilege is not used to shield wrongful conduct. According to the Law Revision Commission Comment to section 1060:

> This privilege is granted so that secret information essential to the continued operation of a business or industry may be afforded some measure of protection against unnecessary disclosure . . . . Nevertheless, there are dangers in the recognition of such a privilege . . . . [D]isclosure of the matters protected by the privilege may be essential to disclose unfair competition or fraud or to reveal the improper use of dangerous materials by the party asserting the privilege. Recognizing the privilege in such cases would amount to a legally sanctioned license to commit the wrongs complained of, for the wrongdoer would be privileged to withhold his wrongful conduct from legal scrutiny.
>
> Therefore, the privilege exists under this section only if its application will not tend to conceal fraud or otherwise work injustice.

Cal. Evid. Code § 1060 cmt.

C. The Scope of the Privilege

The trade secret privilege is not absolute – instead, it is a qualified privilege. *Upjohn Co. v. Hygieia Biological Labs.*, 151 F.R.D. 355, 358 (E.D. Cal. 1993) ("'[T]here is no absolute privilege for trade secrets and similar confidential information.' 'The courts have not given trade secrets automatic and complete immunity against disclosure, but have in each case weighed their claim to privacy against the need for disclosure. Frequently, they have been afforded a limited protection.'") (citations omitted); *see also* Cal. Evid. Code § 1060 cmt. ("The limits of the privilege are necessarily uncertain and will have to be worked out through judicial decisions.").

The court must balance the need for protecting the trade secrets against the needs of the litigation. *Bank of Am., N.A. v. Hensley Props., L.P.,* No. CIV S-07-1584 GEB (EFB), 2008 WL 3272077, at *3 (E.D. Cal. Aug. 6, 2008) (citing *Davis v. Leal*, 43 F. Supp. 2d 1102, 1110 (E.D. Cal. 1999), and *Raymond Handling Concepts Corp. v. Superior Court*, 39 Cal. App. 4th 584, 590 (1995)).

According to the plain language of section 1060, the privilege cannot be used to protect a trade secret if such protection will tend to conceal "fraud" or "otherwise work injustice." *See, e.g.*, *Steiny & Co. v. Cal. Elec. Supply Co.*, 79 Cal. App. 4th 285, 292 (2000) (holding that the owner of a trade secret has "the right to stand on the privilege, but not the right to proceed with [its] claim while at the same time insisting on withholding key evidence" and that "[w]here privileged information goes to the heart of the claim, fundamental fairness requires that it be disclosed for the litigation to proceed"); *State Farm Fire & Cas. Co. v. Super. Ct.*, 54 Cal. App. 4th 625, 651 (1997) (applying the fraud exception to hold that alleged trade secret information was subject to discovery).

The "work injustice" exception does not apply to protect information generally relevant to the subject matter of an action or information helpful to the preparation of a case. Instead, for that exception to apply, the information must be "essential" to the prosecution or defense of the case:

> Failure to disclose the information would "work an injustice" [where] one side would have evidence—reasonably believed to be *essential* to a fair resolution of the lawsuit—which was denied the opposing party.

Bridgestone/Firestone, Inc. v. Super. Ct., 7 Cal. App. 4th 1384, 1391 (1992) (emphasis added) (involving plaintiffs in a product liability suit who failed to show need for disclosure of formulas of a rubber compound for which the manufacturer asserted trade secret privilege; nothing in the record demonstrated the necessity of the formula to prove theories of recovery); *cf. Hypertouch, Inc. v. Super. Ct.*, 128 Cal. App. 4th 1527, 1555 (2005) (observing that if it could be established that defendant's trade secret database identified members of the class plaintiff was otherwise unable to identify to give class notice, the trial court may wish to consider whether, in light of defendant's spoliation of evidence, it would "work injustice" to allow the defendant to maintain the secrecy of the database) (citing *Upjohn Co. v. Hygieia Biological Labs.*, 151 F.R.D. 355, 358 (E.D. Cal. 1993), and *Bridgestone/Firestone, Inc,* 7 Cal. App. 4th at 1391).

Even after the court determines that trade secret information is essential to the fair resolution of the case, the analysis continues. The court is required to balance the competing interests in determining whether disclosure is appropriate and under what conditions:

> [A] court is required to order disclosure of a trade secret unless, after balancing the interests of both sides, it concludes that under the particular circumstances of the case, no fraud or injustice would result from denying disclosure. What is more, in the balancing process the court must necessarily consider the protection afforded the holder of the privilege by a protective order as well as any less intrusive alternatives to disclosure proposed by the parties.

Bridgestone/Firestone, 7 Cal. App. 4th at 1393; *see also Davis*, 43 F. Supp. 2d at 1110.

D. The Shifting Burdens

In addition to defining the above balancing test, the court in *Bridgestone/Firestone* identified the shifting burdens of proof that must be met in connection with determining whether the trade secret privilege should be applied.

A party claiming the privilege has "the burden of establishing its existence." *Bridgestone/Firestone*, 7 Cal. App. 4th at 1393. "[W]hile the burden of making a *prima facie* showing of the particularized need for [disclosure of] a trade secret is on the party seeking discovery, the trial court need not ignore evidence presented by the opposing party on the question whether the information sought is a trade secret." *Id.* at 1395. *See also Amgen Inc. v. Health Care Services*, 47 Cal.App.5th 716, 735 (2020) (trade secret privilege could not prevent production in response to a request made under the California Public Records Act (("CPRA") CAL. GOV. CODE, § 6250 *et seq.*) where the subject pricing information had previously been disclosed to others without imposing any restrictions on disclosure or use).

If that initial burden on the party claiming the privilege is met,

> [T]he party seeking discovery [of a trade secret] must make a *prima facie*, particularized showing that the information sought is relevant and necessary to the proof of, or defense against, a material element of one or more causes of action presented in the case, and that it is reasonable to conclude that the information sought is essential to a fair resolution of the lawsuit. It is then up to the holder of the privilege to demonstrate [any claimed disadvantages of a protective order].

Id. at 1393. Either party may propose or oppose less intrusive alternatives to disclosure, but the trade secret claimant has the burden "to demonstrate that an alternative to disclosure will not be unduly burdensome to the opposing side and that it will maintain the same fair balance in the litigation that would have been achieved by disclosure." *Id*; *see also Davis*, 43 F. Supp. 2d at 1110 ("The party asserting the privilege has the initial burden of establishing the existence of the privilege; the burden would then shift to the party seeking the information to justify the need for the information despite the privilege."); *Upjohn*, 151 F.R.D. at 358 ("In order to resist discovery of a trade secret, a party must first demonstrate by competent evidence that the information sought through discovery is a trade secret and that disclosure of the secret might be harmful. If this showing is made, 'the burden shifts to the party seeking discovery to establish that the disclosure . . . is relevant and necessary to the action.'") (citations omitted).

In a suit by a jeans manufacturer against a retailer for sale of stolen property, unfair competition, fraud, and conspiracy, the trial court was within its discretion in concluding that the trade secret privilege applied to the identities of the suppliers who had sold the manufacturer's merchandise to the retailer, even if a protective order could have been used to prevent the retailer's other competitors from learning its trade secrets regarding the identities of its suppliers, since the manufacturer was in indirect competition with the retailer as well. *Citizens of Humanity, LLC v. Costco Wholesale Corp.*, 171 Cal. App. 4th 1, 14 (2009), *disapproved on other grounds by Kwikset Corp. v. Superior Court*, 51 Cal. 4th 310, 335-37 (2011). The manufacturer distributed its merchandise to the retailer's direct competitors, and it was likely that if it could identify which of its customers was selling jeans to the retailer, the manufacturer would attempt to cut off the retailer's line of supply. *Id.*

§ 16.02 The Assertion of the Trade Secret Privilege by Motion for Protective Order Under Section 3426.5 of the California Civil Code and Section 2017.020 of the California Code of Civil Procedure

In addition to asserting the trade secret privilege as the basis to prevent discovery (through, for example, objections to a document demand or deposition question, or a motion to quash a subpoena), the trade secret holder can also invoke the trade secret privilege to move for a protective order under section 3426.5 of the California Civil Code and section 2017.020 of the California Code of Civil Procedure. Cal. Civ. Code § 3426.5; Cal. Code Civ. Proc. § 2017.020. Notably, certain civil discovery statutes expressly authorize a protective order that provides "that a trade secret or other confidential research, development, or commercial information not be disclosed or be disclosed only in a certain way." *See, e.g.*, Cal. Code Civ. Proc. § 2030.090(b)(6) (governing interrogatories); *id.* § 2031.060(b)(5) (governing requests for production). Procedures for such protective orders are discussed *supra* in Chapter 10.

§ 16.03 The Assertion of the Trade Secret Privilege by a Motion for a Protective Order Under Section 1061 of the California Evidence Code

Section 1061 of the California Evidence Code provides detailed procedures for an owner of a trade secret to assert the trade secret privilege in a criminal proceeding. Cal. Evid. Code § 1061. Although section 1061 purports to govern criminal proceedings, at least one court has held that "[i]n order to determine whether good cause exists [for a protective order under the civil discovery statutes], Evidence Code section 1061 should be followed." *Stadish v. Super. Ct.*, 71 Cal. App. 4th 1130, 1144 (1999). Therefore, consider section 1061 of the California Evidence Code when attempting to obtain a protective order in civil litigation.

Section 1061 of the California Evidence Code authorizes the owner of an alleged trade secret to file a motion for protective order for its protection during litigation. Cal. Evid. Code § 1061(b)(1). The party seeking a protective order has the ultimate burden to demonstrate by a preponderance of the evidence that the requested order is proper. *Id.* § 1061(b)(3).

In terms of the contents of such a motion, "[t]he motion shall include an affidavit based upon personal knowledge listing the affiant's qualifications to give an opinion concerning the trade secret at issue, identifying, without revealing, the alleged trade secret . . . and presenting evidence that the secret qualifies as a trade secret under [section 3426.1(d) of the Civil Code]." *Id.* § 1061(b)(1).

Section 1061 in turn authorizes any party to oppose the request for the protective order, based upon affidavits supported by personal knowledge. *Id.* § 1061(b)(2). Such "affidavits shall be filed under seal, but shall be provided to the owner of the trade secret and to all parties in the proceeding." *Id.* The affidavits are not to be disclosed to persons other than counsel of record without prior court approval. *Id.*

The court may rule on the requested protective order without holding an evidentiary hearing. *Id.* § 1061(b)(3). The court does, however, have the discretion to hold an *in camera* evidentiary hearing concerning disputed articles with only the owner of the trade secret, the party seeking disclosure of the trade secret, and counsel present. *Id.* In such an in camera hearing, "the parties' right to examine witnesses shall not be used to obtain discovery, but shall be directed solely toward the question of whether the alleged trade secret qualifies for protection." *Id.*

Based on the motion and opposition, as well as any oral argument, the court decides what (if any) protective order is appropriate. *Id.* § 1061(b).

Section 1061 provides various examples of potential protective order provisions, including but not limited to the following: (i) the trade secret may be disseminated only to counsel for the parties; (ii) the party seeking disclosure of the trade secret may view the secret only in the presence of its counsel or at counsel's offices; (iii) any party seeking to show the trade secret to any person (such as experts) provided under the protective order must first obtain court approval to do so; (iv) the person receiving the trade secret must sign a copy of the protective order and agree to be bound by its terms; and (v) no article disclosing the trade secret may be filed or otherwise made a part of the court record available to the public without court approval and notice to the owner of the secret. *Id.* § 1061(b)(4). For other potential protective order provisions, *see supra* Chapter 10. The statute also provides a catch-all protection for trade secrets, providing that the court may issue "[o]ther orders as the court deems necessary to protect the integrity of the trade secret." *Id.* § 1061(b)(4)(E).

It is important to note, however, that issuance of an order under this statute "shall not be construed as a determination that the alleged trade secret is or is not a trade secret." *Id.* § 1061(c). "Such a ruling shall not have any effect on any civil litigation." *Id.*

§ 16.04 The Assertion of the Trade Secret Privilege by a Request for Sealing of Records Under Rules 2.550-2.551 of the California Rules of Court

As stated above, the trade secret privilege can be invoked as a potential basis to request that records containing trade secrets or proceedings concerning them be sealed. Rules 2.550-2.551 of the California Rules of Court address the sealing of "discovery materials that are used at trial or submitted as a basis for adjudication of matters other than discovery motions or proceedings" unless the "records . . . are required to be kept confidential by law." Cal. Ct. R. 2.550(a)(2-3). An argument could be made that Rules 2.550-2.551 do not apply to trade secrets and that documents including trade secret information can be sealed without regard to these rules, because section 3426.5 of the California Civil Code expressly provides that the court shall preserve the secrecy of an alleged trade secret by reasonable means. The Advisory Committee comments suggest, however, that these rules do apply to trade secrets. Citing *NBC Subsidiary (KNBC-TV) v. Superior Court*, 20 Cal. 4th 1178, 1222 n.46 (1999), the Advisory Committee comments note that "[c]ourts have found that, *under appropriate circumstances*[,] . . . trade secrets[,] . . . when properly asserted and not waived, *may* constitute [the] 'overriding interests' [required for closing or sealing a record under Rule 2.550]." Cal. Ct. R. 2.550 advisory comm. cmts. (emphases added). *See also McGuan v. Endovascular Techs., Inc.*, 182 Cal. App. 4th 974, 988 (2010) ("Courts have found that the protection of trade secrets is an interest that can support sealing records in a civil proceeding.") (citation omitted), *cert. denied*, 131 S. Ct. 822 (2010). Thus, a party seeking to seal records or proceedings regarding trade secrets may be required to follow the procedures set forth in Rules 2.550-2.551.

Even if a court has issued an order to seal records in a particular case, it has the authority to unseal those records if it concludes that granting access would be in the public interest. *See, e.g.*, *In re Providian Credit Card Cases*, 96 Cal. App. 4th 292 (2002) (upholding the lower court's unsealing of records claimed to contain trade secrets upon intervenor news corporation's motion for reconsideration of the protective order permitting the sealing of the records). *See also In re Marriage of Nicholas*, 186 Cal. App. 4th 1566, 1574 (2010) (a trial court has continuing jurisdiction to modify prior sealing orders entered in the case even though prior sealing orders were not appealed and the time for appeal had lapsed); *Sorenson v. Super. Ct.*, 219 Cal. App. 4th 409, 422 (2013) (a court has discretion to grant access to files previously deemed sealed).

See Chapter 10 *supra* for a further discussion of sealing requests.

Chapter 17
FIRST AMENDMENT ACCESS AND TRADE SECRETS
By: Tenaya Rodewald, Esq.

---

§ 17.01 Introduction

U.S. common law and the First Amendment to the U. S. Constitution provide a presumptive right of public access to civil court proceedings and documents. *NBC Subsidiary (KNBC-TV), Inc. v. Super. Ct.*, 20 Cal. 4th 1178, 1212 (1999); *Richmond Newspapers, Inc. v. Virginia*, 448 U.S. 555, 564-74 (1980). "For many centuries, both civil and criminal trials have traditionally been open to the public." *Gannett Co. v. DePasquale*, 443 U.S. 368, 386 n.15 (1979) (citation omitted). This tradition of openness "is no quirk of history; rather it has long been recognized as an indispensable attribute of an Anglo-American trial." *Richmond Newspapers*, 448 U.S. at 569.

The law protects the public's right of access to court records and proceedings. *NBC Subsidiary*, 20 Cal. 4th at 1208 & n.25, 1211 n.27, 1218-19; *see also* Cal. Const. art. I, § 3(b); Cal. Ct. R. 2.550, 2.551. Yet, *NBC Subsidiary* recognizes that trade secrets are an exception to this rule. 20 Cal. 4th at 1208. The California Uniform Trade Secrets Act ("CUTSA") dictates that in trade secret actions, "alleged" trade secrets shall be maintained in confidence and may be sealed from the public record. Cal. Civ. Code § 3426.5. Similarly the Defend Trade Secrets Act ("DTSA") provides that "[i]n any prosecution or other proceeding under this chapter, the court shall enter such orders and take such other action as may be necessary and appropriate to preserve the confidentiality of trade secrets, consistent with the requirements of the Federal Rules of Criminal and Civil Procedure, the Federal Rules of Evidence, and all other applicable laws." 18 U.S.C. § 1835(a).

A trade secret is information that derives economic value from not being generally known, and is subject to reasonable security measures. *See* Chapter 1; *see also* Fed. R. Civ. P. § 26(c); *Fed. Open Mkt. Comm. v. Merrill*, 443 U.S. 340, 361 (1979). Parties sometimes try to shield information that is not trade secret. Disputes regarding the sealing of court records may arise not only in misappropriation actions, but also in other types of litigation. Under federal and California law, an order improperly sealing information may be challenged by the public or press. *See, e.g.*, *Copley Press, Inc. v. Super. Ct.*, 63 Cal. App. 4th 367, 370-72 (1998); *Hagestad v. Tragesser*, 49 F.3d 1430, 1432, 1434 (9th Cir. 1995); *Associated Press v. U.S. Dist. Court*, 705 F.2d 1143, 1145 (9th Cir. 1983); *see also Leucadia, Inc. v. Applied Extrusion Techs., Inc.*, 998 F.2d 157, 158, 167-68 (3d Cir. 1993).

This chapter addresses the tension between the right of access to court proceedings and records, and the need for businesses to protect their trade secrets, the common law and constitutional rights of access to court proceedings and records, and California's adoption of court rules paralleling the First Amendment test for protecting public access. It also provides guidance regarding how the courts have applied the right of access in cases involving alleged trade secrets. *See also* Chapter 12, which addresses First Amendment rights in the context of trade secret injunctions.

§ 17.02 Common Law and First Amendment Rights of Access in Federal Courts

A. The Common Law Right of Access

As Chief Justice Burger observed, "a presumption of openness inheres in the very nature of a [ ] trial under [our] system of justice." *Richmond Newspapers, Inc. v. Virginia*, 448 U.S. 555, 573 (1980). The American tradition of access to courts predates the Constitution. *Leucadia, Inc. v. Applied Extrusion Techs., Inc.*, 998 F.2d 157, 161 (3d Cir. 1993). The U.S. Supreme Court recognizes a common law right to "inspect and copy public records and documents, including judicial records and documents." *Nixon v. Warner Commc'ns, Inc.*, 435 U.S. 589, 597 (1978) (footnote omitted). The right is "beyond dispute," and applies in both civil and criminal cases, and to both court proceedings and judicial records. *Leucadia*, 998 F.2d at 161 (citations omitted); *see also Hagestad v. Tragesser*, 49 F.3d 1430, 1434 (9th Cir. 1995); *Associated Press v. U.S. Dist. Court*, 705 F.2d 1143, 1145 (9th Cir. 1983) ("There is no reason to distinguish between pretrial proceedings and the documents filed in regard to them.").

Many justifications recognize a common law right of access, including by keeping a "watchful eye on the workings of public agencies," *Nixon*, 435 U.S. at 598, publishing "information concerning the operation of government," *id.*, and "preserving the integrity of the law enforcement and judicial processes." *United States v. Hickey*, 767 F.2d 705, 708 (10th Cir. 1985). As California's Supreme Court explained:

> If public court business is conducted in private, it becomes impossible to expose corruption, incompetence, inefficiency, prejudice, and favoritism. For this reason traditional Anglo-American jurisprudence distrusts secrecy in judicial proceedings and favors a policy of maximum public access to proceedings and records of judicial tribunals." . . . [T]he high court has "repeatedly recognized the salutary function served by the press in encouraging the fairness of trials and subjecting the administration of justice to the beneficial effects of public scrutiny.

NBC Subsidiary (KNBC-TV), Inc. v. Super. Ct., 20 Cal. 4th 1178, 1212 n.28 (1999) (quoting *Estate of Hearst*, 67 Cal. App. 3d 777, 784 (1997) and *Brian W. v. Superior Court*, 20 Cal. 3d 618, 625 (1978)).

The common law right is not absolute, but it may not be denied without careful consideration. *Mary R. v. B. & R. Corp.*, 149 Cal. App. 3d 308, 317 (1983). Courts must "start with a strong presumption in favor of access," which may only be overcome "'on the basis of articulable facts known to the court, not on the basis of unsupported hypothesis or conjecture.'" *Hagestad*, 49 F.3d at 1434 (citation omitted). The court can deny access only if all relevant factors have been taken into consideration and there is a compelling reason to do so. *Id.*

B. First Amendment Right of Access

Since 1980, the U.S. Supreme Court has repeatedly held that the First Amendment also guarantees the public and the press the right of access to judicial proceedings. *See Press-Enterprise v. Superior Court* (*Press-Enterprise I*), 464 U.S. 501, 509 and n. 8 (1984); *Richmond Newspapers, Inc. v. Virginia*, 448 U.S. 555, 580 (1980); *see also, e.g., El Vocero de Puerto Rico v. Puerto Rico*, 508 U.S. 147, 150-51 (1993). The primary foundation on which this right is based is the recognition that access provides assurance that proceedings are conducted fairly. *Richmond Newspapers*, 448 U.S. at 569-70. The Ninth Circuit more recently explained:

> The presumption of access to judicial proceedings flows from an "unbroken, uncontradicted history" rooted in the common law notion that "justice must satisfy the appearance of justice." Openness in judicial proceedings "enhances both the basic fairness of the [proceeding] and the appearance of fairness so essential to public

> confidence in the system," and forms "an indispensable predicate to free expression about the workings of government." "The right of access is thus an essential part of the First Amendment's purpose to 'ensure that the individual citizen can effectively participate in and contribute to our republican system of self-government.'"

Courthouse News Serv. v. Planet (*Planet II*), 947 F.3d 581, 590 (9th Cir. 2020) (citations omitted).

The U.S. Supreme Court has applied the right to a variety of criminal proceedings, including preliminary hearings (*Press-Enterprise v. Superior Court* (*Press-Enterprise II*), 478 U.S. 1, 7 (1986)), voir dire (*Press-Enterprise I*, 464 U.S. at 508-10), and trials (*Richmond Newspapers*, 448 U.S. at 580). The Ninth Circuit has expressly applied the right to judicial documents and records. *Seattle Times Co. v. U.S. Dist. Court*, 845 F.2d 1513, 1515-16 (9th Cir. 1988); *Associated Press v. U.S. Dist. Court*, 705 F.2d 1143, 1147 (9th Cir. 1983).

Although the U.S. Supreme Court has not specifically held that the First Amendment right of access applies to civil cases, "the federal courts of appeals have widely agreed that it extends to civil proceedings and associated records and documents." *Courthouse News Serv. v. Planet* (*Planet I*), 750 F.3d 776, 786 (9th Cir. 2014) (collecting cases). "Indeed, every circuit to consider the issue has uniformly concluded that the right applies to both civil and criminal proceedings." *Planet II*, 947 F.3d at 590 and n.3. Accordingly, although "the First Amendment does not explicitly mention a right of access to court proceedings and documents, the courts of this country recognize a general right to inspect and copy public records and documents, including judicial records and documents, and that this right extends to civil complaints." *Id.* at 591 (internal quotations and citation omitted).

The constitutional right of access has been applied to records pertaining to a variety of pre-trial proceedings. *See, e.g.*, *Planet II*, 947 F.3d at 597 (complaints); *In re Providian Credit Card Cases*, 96 Cal. App. 4th 292, 297-98 (2002) (documents filed in opposition to motion to certify class); *N.Y. Civil Liberties Union v. N.Y.C. Transit Auth.*, 684 F.3d 286, 298 (2d Cir. 2012) (administrative civil infraction hearings); *Rushford v. New Yorker Magazine*, 846 F.2d 249, 253 (4th Cir. 1988) (documents filed in connection with a summary judgment motion); *Brown & Williamson Tobacco Corp. v. Fed. Trade Comm'n*, 710 F.2d 1165, 1176 (6th Cir. 1983) (administrative record and other documents filed in connection with pretrial motions); *In re Cont'l Ill. Sec. Litig.*, 732 F.2d 1302, 1308-09 (7th Cir. 1984) (report of special litigation committee formed to evaluate shareholder derivative claims, filed in connection with motion to terminate claims).

C. Access with Respect to Discovery Materials Not Filed with the Court

The First Amendment right of access generally does not apply to materials exchanged in discovery but never filed with the court. *See* Cal. Ct. R. 2.550(a)(3); *Foltz v. State Farm Mut. Auto. Ins. Co.*, 331 F.3d 1122, 1134 (9th Cir. 2003); *Phillips v. Gen. Motors Corp.*, 307 F.3d 1206, 1213 (9th Cir. 2002).

This does not mean, however, that discovery materials are not subject to any right of public access, at least under federal law. The Ninth Circuit has held, "[i]t is well-established that the fruits of pretrial discovery are, in the absence of a court order to the contrary, presumptively public." *San Jose Mercury News v. U.S. Dist. Court*, 187 F.3d 1096, 1103 (9th Cir. 1999). Rule 26(c) of the

Federal Rules of Civil Procedure requires that "good cause" be shown to justify imposing protective orders limiting disclosure of or access to discovery materials. "A party asserting good cause bears the burden, for each particular document it seeks to protect, of showing that specific prejudice or harm will result if no protective order is granted." *Foltz*, 331 F.3d at 1130.

Some courts have held that the public has no affirmative right to seek or obtain access to unfiled discovery materials under Rule 26(c). *Bond v. Utreras,* 585 F.3d 1061, 1076 (7th Cir. 2009) ("[N]othing in Rule 26(c)—either standing alone or when read in conjunction with the current version of Rule 5(d)—confers substantive rights upon third parties seeking access to the fruits of discovery."); *SEC v. TheStreet.com*, 273 F.3d 222, 233 n. 11 (2d Cir. 2001) (amended version of Rule 5(d) "provides no presumption of filing of all discovery materials, let alone public access to them"). However, the Ninth Circuit has continued to hold that Rule 26(c) at least imposes a requirement for showing good cause in order to justify preventing a party to the litigation from disclosing materials produced in discovery and never filed with the court. *In re Roman Catholic Bishop of Portland in Oregon*, 661 F.3d 417, 423-25 (9th Cir. 2011). In addition, the Ninth Circuit continues to recognize that parties to other litigation have a right to obtain access to unfiled discovery materials upon showing that it is relevant to the other litigation. *Blum v. Merrill Lynch Pierce Fenner & Smith Inc.*, 712 F.3d 1349, 1355 (9th Cir. 2013).

§ 17.03 Federal Test for Sealing Court Records and Proceedings

Information that is alleged to constitute a trade secret may be sealed even though included in documents filed with the court in the course of pre-trial proceedings or trial. As noted, the DTSA specifically contemplates orders and measures "appropriate to preserve the confidentiality of trade secrets, consistent with the requirements of the Federal Rules of Criminal and Civil Procedure, the Federal Rules of Evidence, and all other applicable laws." 18 U.S.C. § 1835(a).

However, given the common law and First Amendment rights of access described above, stringent standards must be met before criminal or civil documents or proceedings may be sealed.

A. The Test For Sealing Applied to Most Requests to Seal in Civil Actions

The Ninth Circuit has held that in most circumstances, documents and information filed with the court in civil actions cannot be sealed absent a showing of "compelling reasons" that overcome the strong presumption of public access, and even then, any sealing order must be narrowly tailored to further the compelling interest. *See Kamakana v. City & County of Honolulu*, 447 F.3d 1172, 1180 (9th Cir. 2006) (sealing request "must meet the high threshold of showing that 'compelling reasons' support secrecy"); *Center for Auto Safety v. Chrysler Group, LLC*, 809 F.3d 1092, 1096-97 (9th Cir. 2016) (noting that "stringent standard" for sealing documents reflects a "strong preference for public access").

Under this test, "a strong presumption in favor of access is the starting point" of the analysis. *Kamakana*, 447 F.3d at 1178 (9th Cir. 2006) (internal quotation marks and citation omitted). A party seeking to seal a judicial record then bears the burden of overcoming this presumption by articulating compelling reasons supported by specific factual findings that outweigh the presumption of public access. *Id.* at 1178-79; *United States v. Lopez*, 818 F. App'x 654, 656 (9th Cir. 2020) (a sealing request must "articulate a compelling justification, supported by particular facts."). The Ninth Circuit has rejected "speculative arguments" as to the prejudice that a party would suffer if the records were not sealed, and the court may not rely on "hypothesis or conjecture" in issuing rulings regarding sealing. *United States v. Carpenter*, 923 F.3d 1172, 1179-80 (9th Cir. 2019); *Ctr. for Auto Safety*, 809 F.3d at 1096-97 (A court may seal records "only when it finds 'a compelling reason and articulate[s] the factual basis for its ruling, without relying on hypothesis or conjecture.'" (citation omitted).) Thus, a party seeking to seal may not rely on general assertions that the information is 'confidential' or a 'trade secret,' but must support its application for sealing with specific facts establishing compelling reasons for sealing.

Finally, "[t]he mere fact that the production of records may lead to a litigant's embarrassment, incrimination, or exposure to further litigation will not, without more, compel the court to seal its records." *Kamakana*, 447 F.3d at 1179; *Oliner v. Kontrabecki*, 745 F.3d 1024, 1026 (9th Cir. 2014) (the party seeking sealing must show that "'disclosure will work a clearly defined and serious injury to the party seeking'" sealing, and that injury has to be more than embarrassment) (citation omitted).)

In sum, maintaining the confidentiality of trade secrets can be a compelling reason justifying sealing. *Elec. Arts, Inc. v. United States Dist. Court (In re Elec. Arts, Inc.)*, 298 F. App'x 568, 569-70 (9th Cir. 2008). However, a party seeking sealing should expect have to submit declarations or other evidence—specific facts—to support the conclusion that the material sought to be sealed constitutes trade secrets, and non-speculative arguments that it would suffer clearly defined and serious injury to its competitive standing if the information were made public.

As noted, the foregoing test is applied in most circumstances when a party seeks to seal material submitted in the course of civil litigation.

B. The Test for Sealing Applied to Discovery Materials Attached to "Tangential" Motions

When discovery material is submitted in connection with a motion that is only "tangentially related to the underlying cause of action," such as a civil discovery motion, the material may be sealed if the party requesting sealing meets a lower "good cause" standard. *Center for Auto Safety*, 809 F.3d at 1097, 1099. The good cause standard derives from Federal Rule of Civil Procedure 26(c), which permits a court to issue a protective order upon a showing of good cause. *Id.* at 1097.

Under the "good cause" standard, the party requesting sealing must make a "particularized showing" that "specific prejudice or harm will result" if the information is disclosed. *Phillips ex rel. Estates of Byrd v. Gen. Motors Corp.,* 307 F.3d 1206, 1210-11 (9th Cir. 2002). "'Broad allegations of harm, unsubstantiated by specific examples of articulated reasoning'" will not suffice. *Id.* at 1211(citation omitted). Furthermore, "[i]f a court finds particularized harm will result from disclosure of information to the public, then it balances the public and private interests to decide whether" sealing is required. *Id.*; *see also, e.g., Foltz v. State Farm Mut. Auto. Ins. Co.*, 331 F.3d 1122, 1131 (9th Cir. 2003) ("'The burden is on the party requesting a protective order to demonstrate that

(1) the material in question is a trade secret or other confidential information within the scope of Rule 26(c), and (2) disclosure would cause an identifiable, significant harm.'") (citation omitted).

It is worth noting as well, that when challenged, sealing based on stipulated protective orders may not withstand claims of right of public access. *Foltz*, 331 F.3d at 1137-38 (vacating sealing order because it was based on a stipulated protective order, which, standing alone, did not create a "compelling" reason for sealing court records). "Such blanket orders are inherently subject to challenge and modification, as the party resisting disclosure generally has not made a particularized showing of good cause with respect to any individual document." *San Jose Mercury News v. U.S. Dist. Ct.*, 187 F.3d 1096, 1103 (9th Cir. 1999).

§ 17.04 California's Presumptively Open Courts

The California Supreme Court has followed the majority of federal circuits in recognizing a constitutional right of access to civil judicial proceedings. *See NBC Subsidiary (KNBC-TV), Inc. v. Super. Ct.*, 20 Cal. 4th 1178, 1208 n.25, 1209-10 (1999) (the First Amendment right of access applies "to ordinary civil trials and proceedings" and to "civil litigation documents filed in court as a basis for adjudication.").

Under California law, courts may not blindly accept the parties' representations regarding the need for confidentiality. Because records as filed are maintained by the clerk of the court, courts should "engage in independent review of that matter," and enter findings to justify its sealing of the records. *Huffy Corp. v. Super. Ct.*, 112 Cal. App. 4th 97, 105 (2003). In *Huffy*, the appellate court held that a stipulated sealing order that lacked factual findings failed to comply with the requirement that findings be identified. *Id.* The court also found that the trial court's sealing order unnecessarily "seal[ed] thousands of pages of routine legal argument concerning insurance coverage, notices of motion, lengthy separate statements of undisputed and disputed facts, proofs of service, and lodged documents including appellate court documents." *Id.*; *see also H.B. Fuller Co. v. Doe*, 151 Cal. App. 4th 879, 891 (2007); Cal. Ct. R. 2.550(d), (e) as well as Chapter 10.

§ 17.05 California State Court Test for Sealing Court Records

The standard for sealing court records under California law parallels the requirements imposed under the First Amendment. *NBC Subsidiary (KNBC-TV), Inc. v. Super. Ct.*, 20 Cal. 4th 1178, 1212 (1999) ("We conclude . . . the First Amendment provides a right of access to ordinary civil trials and proceedings, that constitutional standards governing closure of trial proceedings apply in the civil setting," and so any order closing court proceedings "must, accordingly, be interpreted in a manner compatible with those standards."). In *NBC Subsidiary*, the California Supreme Court established a four part "overriding interest" test that must be satisfied before courtroom proceedings are closed or records are sealed. *Id.* at 1217-18. Any party seeking to deny access to documents bears a heavy burden. Before access can be denied, the overriding interest test requires that the trial court hold a hearing and expressly find that:

(i) there exists an overriding interest supporting closure and/or sealing;

(ii) there is a substantial probability that the interest will be prejudiced absent closure and/or sealing;

(iii) the proposed closure and/or sealing is narrowly tailored to serve the overriding interest; and

(iv) there is no less restrictive means of achieving the overriding interest.

Id.

Following the California Supreme Court's decision in *NBC Subsidiary*, California Rules of Court were adopted that codify the public's right of access to most court records. Cal. Ct. R. 2.550, 2.551. Any closure order must be supported by specific factual findings and by a detailed discussion of what interest is being protected and why less restrictive alternatives do not adequately protect that interest. *See NBC Subsidiary*, 20 Cal. 4th at 1225; *see also* Cal. Ct. R. 2.550(d) (listing the *NBC Subsidiary* factors as express findings that the court must make in order to seal records). Specifically, any sealing order must:

> (A) [s]pecifically state the facts that support the findings [required by Cal. Ct. R. 2.550(d)]; and (B) [d]irect the sealing of only those documents and pages, or, if reasonably practicable, portions of those documents and pages, that contain the material that needs to be placed under seal. All other portions of each document or page must be included in the public file.

Cal. Ct. R. 2.550(e)(1) (emphasis added). *See also* Chapter 10.

In re Providian Credit Card Cases was class action litigation that did not involve misappropriation of trade secret allegations. *In re Providian Credit Card Cases*, 96 Cal. App. 4th 292 (2002). Nevertheless, the defendant credit card companies claimed that certain materials contained trade secrets, and sought to seal the records on that basis. The case therefore addresses the sealing of trade secrets in some detail. The *Providian* court engaged in a document-by-document review of the documents that the defendants sought to seal. *Id.* at 303-08. However, the defendants failed to meet the stringent requirements for sealing including because they failed to establish any specific trade secret information in the documents, and defendants' declarations were "conclusionary and lacking in helpful specifics." *Id.* at 305, 308-09. Where documents, such as telemarketing scripts, had been made available to the public, the *Providian* court rejected the defendants' claim of trade secret status. *Id.* at 305. In unsealing those records, the *Providian* court noted: "Even if it is possible that a fragment here or a paragraph there might qualify as a trade secret, defendants spurned such a line-by-line approach. They cannot now fault the trial court for following their lead." *Id.* at 309. By contrast, in *McGuan v. Endovascular Technologies, Inc.*, 182 Cal. App. 4th 974 (2010), *cert. denied*, 131 S. Ct. 822 (2010), the court upheld sealing. The court relied on *In re Providian* and applied the definition of trade secrets in section 3426.1(d) of the California Civil Code to uphold the sealing of trade secret material. *Id.* at 988. The court affirmed the trial court's finding that sealing of records describing the details of defendants' confidential "quality system procedures, complaint handling procedures, device tracking procedures, process validation procedures, and corrective action procedures" was justified. *Id.* In particular, the trial court's findings in support of sealing were "supported by substantial evidence" including defendants' declarations detailing how the information constituted trade secrets and would cause defendants competitive harm if disclosed. *Id.* at 988-89.

In an action alleging the misappropriation of trade secrets, information alleged to constitute a trade secret may be sealed. Section 3426.5 of the California Civil Code, enacted in 1984, was taken directly from the Model Uniform Trade Secrets Act without revision. It provides that, in an action for misappropriation, the court "shall preserve the secrecy of an alleged trade secret by reasonable means, which may include . . . sealing the records of the action." Cal. Civ. Code § 3426.5; *see also* Model Uniform Trade Secrets Act § 5. *See also* Chapters 10 and 16. Although the use of the term "alleged trade secret" indicates that sealing may occur even though the owner has not definitively established that the material sought to be sealed is a trade secret, this does not mean that the proponent of sealing bears no burden. As explained above, there is a constitutional right of public access to court records. Although no published California opinions directly address the interaction of California Civil Code Section 3426.5 and the constitutional right of access, the constitutional right of access cannot be disregarded. Thus, even in cases alleging misappropriation of trade secrets where Section 3426.5 applies, there should be some basis for a claim that material sought to be sealed qualifies as trade secret. And indeed, one court rejected the "premise that merely by filing a pleading characterizing certain information as a trade secret, a party can compel the courts to withhold that information from the public record until such time as it finally adjudged not to be a trade secret." *Cypress Semiconductor Corp. v. Maxim Integrated Prods., Inc.*, 236 Cal. App. 4th 243, 255 (2015) (upholding trial court's refusal to seal information that was not a colorable trade secret). Accordingly, a party seeking sealing risks having a request for sealing rejected if the party fails to provide evidence establishing the existence of a colorable trade secret and the need for sealing.

§ 17.06 Conclusion

The right of public access to judicial proceedings and documents plays a critical role in the proper functioning of the American judicial system. The right to protect legitimate trade secrets is also compelling. Thus, the sealing of court records can be used to protect legitimate trade secrets, although the right of access to court proceedings prevents the trade secret exception from being used to seal merely confidential information (that does not qualify as a trade secret) or embarrassing information.

Whether under California or federal law, the standard that must be met before judicial records can be sealed is high. Parties seeking sealing should be prepared to submit evidence demonstrating and explaining how the material sought to be sealed qualifies as trade secret and addressing the appropriate Ninth Circuit or California test for sealing. Provided parties are able to do so, trade secrets can meet the exacting standards for sealing.

Chapter 18
PROTECTING TRADE SECRETS WHEN CONTRACTING WITH THE FEDERAL GOVERNMENT

By: Keith R. Szeliga, Esq.

---

§ 18.01 Statutory Protections

A. Trade Secrets Act

Under the Federal Trade Secrets Act (the Act), 18 U.S.C. § 1905, officers and employees of the United States (or any department or agency thereof) are prohibited from publishing, divulging, or disclosing (unless authorized by law) information that, in relevant part, "relates to . . . trade secrets, processes, operations, style of work, or apparatus . . . ." if that information came "to [them] in the course of [their] employment or official duties . . . ." 18 U.S.C. § 1905. A violation of this Act can result in a fine, imprisonment up to one year, or both, and removal from office or employment. *Id.* A private party my file an action under the Administrative Procedure Act (the APA), 5 U.S.C. § 701 *et seq.*, to enjoin the government from disclosing information protected by the Trade Secrets Act. *See Chrysler Corp. v.* Brown, 441 U.S. 281, 317-318, 99 S.Ct. 1705, 1725-1726, 60 L.Ed.2d 208 (1979) (owner of trade secret was entitled to APA review of agency's decision to disclose information in alleged violation of the Trade Secrets Act); *Megapulse, Inc. v. Lewis*, 672 F.2d 959, 964-966 (D.C. Cir. 1982) (fact that technical data was delivered under a contract did not deprive the district court of jurisdiction to enjoin disclosure under the APA in alleged violation of the Trade Secrets Act).

The Trade Secrets Act prohibits the disclosure of more than trade secrets. Courts have interpreted the Act to prohibit the unauthorized disclosure of all data protected by Exemption 4 to the Freedom of Information Act, 5 U.S.C. § 552, which applies broadly to "matters that are trade secrets and commercial or financial information obtained from a person and privileged or confidential." 5 U.S.C. § 552(b)(4); *see CAN Fin. Corp. v. Donovan*, 830 F.2d 1132, 1151-1152 (D.C. Cir. 1987) ("the scope of the Act is at least co-extensive with that of Exemption 4 of FOIA"). Thus, in evaluating whether the Trade Secrets Act protects against the disclosure of particular information, it is helpful to analyze precedent interpreting FOIA Exemption 4 rather than looking only to trade secret law.

The scope of protection under the Trade Secrets Act and Exemption 4, although broad, is not unlimited. The Act does not prohibit the disclosure of information that is publicly available or that the owner has not maintained confidential. *See Alcolac, Inc. v. Wagoner*, 610 F.Supp. 745, 748-750 (W.D. Mo. 1985) (documents submitted pursuant to application for hazardous waste facility permit were not protected under the Act because, *inter* alia, the plaintiff failed to make a satisfactory showing that it had taken reasonable measures to protect the confidentiality of the information and that the information was not obtainable by other legitimate means without the plaintiff's consent). The Act also permits the disclosure of trade secrets pursuant to a license because it prohibits disclosures only to the extent "not authorized by law." 18 U.S.C. § 1905. For example, the government's disclosure of information in which the government has unlimited license rights cannot violate the Trade Secrets Act because the government has the right to disclose it. *See Conax Florida Corp. v. United States*, 641 F.Supp. 408, 414-15 (D.D.C. 1986), *aff'd by* 842 F.2d 1124 (D.C. Cir. 1987).

Government employees often contend that there is no need for them to execute nondisclosure agreements (NDAs) because they are bound by the Trade Secrets Act. The Act, however, provides less protection for trade secrets than most NDAs. For example:

- The Act does not to limit the disclosure of trade secrets *within the government*. *See Emerson Elec. Co. v. Schlesinger*, 609 F.2d 898, 907 (8th Cir. 1979) ("We seriously doubt whether § 1905 was intended to prohibit any interagency information disclosures."). This is significant because there are more than 2 million federal employees, all of whom are potential recipients of trade secrets disclosed to the government.

- The Act does not prohibit the *use* of trade secrets by government employees. This is problematic when the trade secret that has been disclosed is of a type that the government is capable of using without assistance from third party contractors.

- The Act does not require government employees to exercise reasonable care to protect trade secrets from inadvertent disclosure or unauthorized access by third parties.

- The Act does not create a private right of action. *See Bruce v. United States*, 621 F.2d 914, 918 (8th Cir. 1980) (citing *Chrysler Corp.*, 441 U.S. at 316). Damages for the unlawful disclosure of trade secrets are not available under the Act.

B. Federal Tort Claims Act

The Federal Tort Claims Act (the FTCA) is a federal statute that allows private parties to pursue certain tort claims against the government for the "negligent or wrongful act or omission of any employee of the Government while acting within the scope of his office or employment…." 28 U.S.C. § 1346(b)(1). The grant of jurisdiction and waiver of sovereign immunity under the FTCA are subject to several important exceptions. *See* 28 U.S.C. § 2680.

Courts have held that the FTCA waives the government's sovereign immunity for misappropriation trade secret claims. *See Jerome Stevens Pharmaceuticals, Inc. v. Food & Drug Admin.*, 402 F.3d 1249, 1252-1255 (D.C. Cir. 2005) (misappropriation of trade secret claims against the government were not barred by either the discretionary function exception or the intentional tort exception to the FTCA); *Kramer v. United States Dep't of the Army*, 653 F.2d 726, 729-730 (2d Cir. 1980) (plaintiff's putative conversion claim for the government's disclosure of its supplier's identity to a competitor should have been viewed as a cause of action for misappropriation of trade secret over which district court had jurisdiction under the FTCA). Although federal district courts have exclusive jurisdiction over FTCA claims, they must apply "the law of the place where the act or omission occurred." 28 U.S.C. § 1346(b)(1). Thus, trade secret misappropriation claims against the government under the FTCA are governed by state trade secret law. *Id.*; *see also Kramer*, 653 F.2d at 729-730 (applying New York law to misappropriation of trade secret claim under the FTCA).

Although misappropriation of trade secret claims under the FTCA are governed by state law, the FTCA limits the remedies available against the government. The only relief provided for in the FTCA is monetary damages; injunctive relief is not available. *Compare* 28 U.S.C. § 1346(b) *with* Cal. Civ. Code § 3426.2; *see also Talbert v. United States*, 932 F.2d 1064, 1065-66 (4th Cir. 1991) (noting that courts lack jurisdiction to award non-monetary relief under the FTCA). Further, the FTCA precludes the recovery of punitive damages, which would render multiple damages for willful and malicious misappropriation unavailable. *Compare* 28 U.S.C. § 2674 *with* Cal. Civ. Code. § 3426.3(c).

The FTCA bars claimants from brining suit in federal court until they have exhausted their administrative remedies. *McNeil v. United States*, 508 U.S. 106, 113, 113 S.Ct. 1980, 124 L.Ed.2d 21 (1993). Thus, with certain exceptions, a plaintiff may not institute an FTCA action against the government until: (1) the plaintiff has first "presented the claim to the appropriate Federal agency" and (2) that agency has "finally denied" the plaintiff's claim. 28 U.S.C. § 2675(a); *see also Lopez v. United States*, 823 F.3d 970, 977 (10th Cir. 2016) (district court lacked jurisdiction over FTCA suit where plaintiff's administrative claim did not provide the government with adequate notice of the relevant facts). If the claimant and the agency agree on a settlement, no further litigation occurs. 28 U.S.C. § 2672. If no settlement is reached, the agency generally will deny the claim. The failure of an agency to issue a final decision on the claim within six months may be treated as a deemed denial, and the claimant may file suit in federal district court before the administrative claim has been denied. *Id.* § 2675(a).

The statute of limitations under the FTCA is shorter than the statute of limitations for misappropriation of trade secret under the laws of most states. Ordinarily, a claimant has only two years from the date of the misappropriation to file an administrative claim. *Id.* § 2401(b). If the claim is denied, the claimant has six (6) months from the date the agency mails the denial to file suit in federal district court. *Id.* The failure to meet either of these deadlines generally bars the claim. *Id.*

Jurisdictional issues may arise when the alleged misappropriation of trade secret bears a close nexus to a government contract. The FTCA vests subject matter jurisdiction for the *tort* of misappropriation of trade secrets in federal district court. The FTCA does not, however, extend the district courts' subject matter jurisdiction to claims sounding in contract, over which the Tucker Act, 28 U.S.C. § 1491(a), affords the Court of Federal Claims (the COFC) has exclusive jurisdiction. Thus, when a misappropriation of trade secret claim arises under or relates to a contract, the district court has broad discretion to determine whether the cause of action is actually one sounding in contract that must be litigated at the COFC. *See U.S. Marine v. United States*, 722 F.3d 1360 (Fed. Cir. 2013). This is significant because may view district courts as a more favorable forum for private parties litigating against the government.

§ 18.02 Nondisclosure Agreements with the Federal Government

A. Applicability

The Federal Acquisition Regulation (FAR) and the Defense Federal Acquisition Regulation Supplement (DFARS) include protections for trade secrets submitted to the government in formal proposals for and deliverables under procurement contracts. These protections, addressed in Sections 18.03 and 18.04 below, do not apply to informal exchanges of information such as those that might occur in the early stages of marketing a technology to the government. To protect trade secrets outside the formal procurement process, companies seeking to do business with the federal government, where possible, may wish to obtain NDAs. Although the government typically resists signing NDAs as a matter of policy, the government may be more inclined to sign an NDA to receive access highly valued and sought after technology that cannot otherwise be obtained.

In addition, the data rights regulations require agencies to enter into NDAs with third parties before disclosing trade secret information. 48 C.F.R. §§ 52.227-14 (Alternates II and III), 227.7103-7, 252.227-7025(b). The standard form NDAs for Department of Defense (DoD) entities identify the owners of the technical data or computer software to be disclosed to the government as third party beneficiaries, so they have an immediate recourse in the event of misappropriation, rather than having to seek redress through their government customer. *Id.* §§ 227.7103-7, 252.227-7025(b). The data rights regulations applicable to civilian agencies do not include a standard form NDA. Accordingly, where possible, it is advantageous for a company to enter into an NDA directly with any entity to which its proprietary technical data or computer software will be disclosed.

B. Enforceability

An NDA with the government will be enforceable only if the government employee who signed the NDA has actual authority – not merely apparent authority – to bind the government. *See Liberty Ammunition, Inc. v. United* States, 835 F.3d 1388 (Fed. Cir. 2016). Most government employees do not have such authority.

In *Liberty Ammunition*, the court held that a Lieutenant Colonel lacked the authority to bind the government to an NDA. *Id.* at 1401-1402. There was no dispute that the Lieutenant Colonel did not have express actual authority, but the plaintiff argued that he had implied actual authority to bind the government because the execution of NDAs was integral to his job responsibilities. *Id.* The court rejected this argument even though the Lieutenant Colonel's job responsibilities included weekly meetings with industry representatives pitching products to the government. *Id.* The court held that implied actual authority did not exist because that the Lieutenant Colonel had signed only five NDAs over a two-year period demonstrated that the execution of NDAs was not necessary for the performance of his job responsibilities. *Id.*

Liberty Ammunition teaches the importance of ensuring that an NDA with the government is signed by a warranted contracting officer with express actual authority to bind the government. In all other cases, there is a significant risk that the NDA will not be enforceable against the government.

C. Practical Pointers

The following are suggestions for negotiating an NDA with the government.

- Draft the NDA to be as short and simple as possible. Avoid jargon and "nice to have" but unnecessary boilerplate terms.
- Avoid terms that the government is unlikely to accept, *e.g.*, choice of law/forum, and indemnification. Some of these terms are unenforceable even if the government accepts them.
- Do not overreach—government officials must feel comfortable with the obligations of the NDA before they will sign it. Obtaining the government's agreement to any NDA is an accomplishment.

- If the government will not agree to an NDA, consider characterizing the agreement as a license. Granting a narrow license for evaluation purposes only may be able to accomplish the same objective as an NDA.

- Confirm that the government employee signing the NDA is a contracting officer. If the government employee is not a contracting officer, assume there is a very high likelihood that the NDA will be unenforceable

In cases where the government refuses to enter into an NDA prior to the submission of a formal proposal, a company must balance the potential for obtaining government business against the risk of losing valuable trade secret protection. Even where the parties have entered into an NDA, managing the type of information disclosed to the government and placing the government on notice that information is being submitted with the expectation of confidentiality is critical to managing risk. The following are practical pointers to protect trade secrets, whether or not the government is willing to enter into an NDA with the company:

- Establish an internal review and approval process to centralize control over the disclosure of information to the government.

- Provide summary information, rather than detailed trade secret information, to the government when practicable.

- If it becomes necessary to provide more detailed information to the government, consider presenting the information orally or allowing the government to review information without taking away presentation materials or documents.

- Provide written notice to the government, prior to or contemporaneous with each disclosure, that the information is being submitted with an expectation of confidentiality.

- Include an appropriate restrictive legend, similar to the following, on each page that contains trade secret information: "CONTAINS INFORMATION THAT IS CONFIDENTIAL AND PROPRIETARY TO XYZ, INC. / MAY NOT BE DISCLOSED OUTSIDE THE U.S. GOVERNMENT WITHOUT THE WRITTEN PERMISSION OF XYZ, INC. / MAY BE USED BY THE U.S. GOVERNMENT FOR EVALUATION PURPOSES ONLY / EXEMPT FROM DISCLOSURE UNDER THE FREEDOM OF INFORMATION ACT / PROTECTED FROM DISCLOSURE UNDER THE TRADE SECRETS ACT, 18 U.S.C. §1905."

- Consider submitting an unsolicited proposal, for which the FAR provides additional protections.

- If the information is too valuable, and the risk is too high, refuse to disclose the information to the government without an NDA.

Note that these pointers do not apply to the submission of formal proposals for procurement contracts or deliverables under procurement contracts. The remaining sections of this chapter address the protection of trade secrets in those contexts.

§ 18.03 Protection of Trade Secrets Contained in Proposals Submitted to the Federal Government

The regulations governing the submission of proposals for procurement contracts with the government include provisions that protect trade secret information. For example, the standard instructions for the submission of proposals in negotiated procurements require offerors to include the following restrictive legend on the title page of any proposal that contains information that they do not want the government to disclose to the public or use for any purpose other than evaluation of the proposal:

> This proposal includes data that shall not be disclosed outside the Government and shall not be duplicated, used, or disclosed—in whole or in part—for any purpose other than to evaluate this proposal. If, however, a contract is awarded to this offeror as a result of—or in connection with—the submission of this data, the Government shall have the right to duplicate, use, or disclose the data to the extent provided in the resulting contract. This restriction does not limit the Government's right to use information contained in this data if it is obtained from another source without restriction. The data subject to this restriction are contained in sheets [insert numbers or other identification of sheets]

48 C.F.R. § 52.215-1(e). The FAR also requires offerors to mark each sheet of the proposal that contains information they wish to restrict with the following legend: "Use or disclosure of data contained on this sheet is subject to the restriction on the title page of this proposal." *Id.* The FAR prescribes similar restrictive legends for unsolicited proposals. *Id.* § 15-609.

The government's use or disclosure of proposal data in violation of these prohibitions may give rise to an action for breach of an implied-in-fact contract. *See Research, Analysis, & Development, Inc. v. United States*, 8 Cl. Ct. 54, 58-61 (1985) (implied in fact contract existed that obligated the government to safeguard proprietary information contained in the contractor's unsolicited proposal). Such a cause of action will not be available, however, if the company has not complied strictly with the applicable solicitation or regulatory requirements. *See Xerxe Group, Inc. v. United States*, 278 F.3d 1357, 1358-1359 (2002). In *Xerxe*, the contractor had placed the required restrictive legend on the title page of its unsolicited proposal but neglected to place the shorter legend on each page that contained data that was subject to the restriction on the title page. *Id.* at 1358. The court concluded that the contractor could not recover damages from the government because, *inter alia*, the contractor had failed to comply with all of the applicable marking requirements. *Id.* at 1359-1360.

In addition to the protections afforded by the FAR, the government is prohibited by statute from releasing a proposal under the Freedom of Information Act (the FOIA), 5 U.S.C. § 552, unless that proposal has been incorporated by reference into the resulting contract. 41 U.S.C. § 253b(m). This prohibition applies to all proposals, whether or not they are submitted by successful or unsuccessful bidders. *Sinkfield v. U.S. Department of Housing and Urban Development*, No. 10-885, 2012 WL 893876, at *5 n.4 (S.D. Ohio March 15, 2012). Moreover, the statute bars the disclosure of contractor proposal submissions in their entirety, without the need to engage in laborious line-by-line redactions. *Hodes v. U.S. Department of Treasury*, 967 F.Supp. 2d 369, 375 (D.D.C. 2013).

§ 18.04 The Data Rights Regulations

In order to protect a company's trade secrets when delivering information to the federal government, companies must fully comply with the requirements of the applicable statutes and regulations. For most government contracts, these regulations are found in the FAR or DFARs. The "data rights" regulations apply to trade secret or copyrightable material such as a company's technical data, including schematics, diagrams, designs or drawings, or processes, as well as computer software. The data rights clauses found in the FAR are applicable to civilian agency procurements, while the DFARS clauses are applicable to procurements by DoD components.

A. Technical Data and Computer Software

Generally, companies own the material created by their employees in the course of performing government contracts, including both technical data and computer software. 17 U.S.C. § 201(b); *see also id.* § 101 (definition of "work made for hire").

The term "technical data" is broadly defined by the regulations as recorded information, regardless of the form or method of the recording, of a scientific or technical nature (including computer software documentation). 48 C.F.R. §§ 52.227-14(a), 252.227-7013(a)(15). The term "technical data" does not include computer software or data incidental to contract administration, such as financial or management information. *Id.* §§ 52.227-14(a), 252.227-7013(a)(15).

The term "computer software" includes computer programs, source code, source code listings, object code listings, design details, and related material that would enable the software to be reproduced, recreated, or recompiled. *Id.* §§ 52.227-14(a), 252.227-7013(a)(3). Computer software does not include computer databases or computer software documentation, which is considered technical data. *Id.*

B. Types of License Rights

When technology is developed under a government contract, the scope of the government's license to use or disclose technical data and computer software is generally determined by the source of the funding, commonly referred to as the Follow the Funds Test. *Id.* §§ 27.401, 52.227-14(a), 227.7103-5, 227.7203-5. For purposes of applying the test, the FAR identifies the relevant categories as developed at private expense and developed at government expense. *Id.* §§ 27.401, 52.227-14(a). The DFARS identifies three categories: (1) exclusively at government expense, (2) exclusively at private expense, or (3) with mixed government and private funding. *Id.* § 227.7103-5, 227-7203-5, 252.227-7013(a), 252.227-7014(a).

1. Unlimited Rights

Where technology is developed with government funds (or under the DFARS "exclusively" with government funds), the government receives "unlimited rights." *Id.* §§ 27.401, 52.227-14(a), 227.7103-5(a), 227.7203-5(a), 252.227-7013(b)(1)(i), 252.227-7014(b)(1)(i). The government also obtains unlimited rights in technical data created exclusively with government funds under a contract that does not require the development, manufacture, construction, or production of items, components, or processes. *Id.* §§ 227.7103-5(a)(3), 252.227-7013(b)(1)(iii). As defined in the DFARS, development exclusively with government funds means development was not accomplished exclusively or partially at private expense. *Id.* § 252.227-7013-(a)(9), 252.227-7013(b)(9). In other words, the technology was developed directly in the performance of government contracts. The FAR does not define development at private expense but it is understood to have the same meaning.

Unlimited rights allow the government to use, modify, reproduce, perform, display, release, or disclose technical data or computer software in any manner, and for any purpose whatsoever, and to have or authorize others to do so as well. *Id.* §§ 27.401, 52.227-14(a), 252.227-7013(a)(16), 252.227-7014(a)(16). Unlimited rights allow the government to provide a company's technical data or computer software to a competitor who could use this data to compete against the company in future procurements by the government or in the commercial marketplace. *See HiRel Connectors, Inc. v. United States*, 2006 WL 3618007, at *6 (C.D. Cal. Sept. 5, 2006) (Government was entitled to disclose unlimited rights data publicly in a solicitation) ; *Plainville Elec. Products Co. v. Bechtel Bettis, Inc.*, 2009 WL 801639, at (D. Conn. Mar. 26, 2009) (unlimited rights included "the right to use and distribute the data to whomever it wanted and however it wanted.").

Given the broad scope of an unlimited rights license, several courts have held that a contractor's grant of unlimited rights in technical data or computer software to the Government negates trade secret protection. *See, e.g., Secure Servs. Tech., Inc. v. Time and Space Processing, Inc.*, 722 F. Supp. 1354, 1359-60 (E.D. Va. 1989); *L-3 Communications Westwood Cor. v. Robichaux*, 2008 WL 577560, at *6-8 (E.D. La. Feb. 29, 2008); *HiRel Connectors, Inc. v. United States*, 2005 WL 4958589, at *4 (C.D. Cal. Jan. 4, 2005). *But see Imi-Tech Corp. v. Gagliani*, 691 F. Supp. 214, 231 (S.D. Cal. 1986) (whether the Government has unlimited rights "does not provide a defense…under California trade secret law…."); *Lockheed Martin Corp. v. L-3 Communications Corp.*, 2008 WL 4791804, *8 (N.D. Ga. Sept. 30, 2008) ("[e]ven assuming arguendo that the government is free to provide the P-3 data to any third party, there is no evidence that the government provided the data to [the private defendants'] predecessors without restriction.").

It should be noted that the government also obtains unlimited rights in certain other categories of technical data and computer software, regardless of the source of funding. Examples include: (1) studies, analyses, and test data produced for a contract and specified as an element of performance, (2) form, fit, and function data, which describe the required physical, functional, and performance characteristics of an item, component, or process to the extent necessary to permit identification of physically and functionally interchangeable items, and (3) technical data necessary for installation, operation, maintenance, or training purposes (including computer software documentation). *Id.* §§ 27.404-1, 52.227-14(b)(1), 227-7103-5(a), 227.7203-5(a), 252.227-7013(b)(1), 252.227-7014(b)(1). Companies should take care to ensure that they do not inadvertently include trade secrets in such deliverables.

2. Limited/Restricted Rights

Development exclusively at private expense occurs if development is accomplished entirely with costs charged to indirect cost pools (such as independent research and development or overhead), costs not allocated to a government contract (such as the company's own capital or the cost of performing contracts for parties other than the government), or any combination of the foregoing. *Id.* §§ 252.227-7013(a)(11); 252.227-7014(a)(11). The source of funding for development is determined by the proper accounting treatment of costs. Thus, if development occurs directly in the performance of a government contract, the cost of development is considered to be at government expense, and the contractor cannot establish development at private expense by choosing to pay for the work itself or allocating the cost of the work to an indirect cost pool.

The government generally obtains "limited rights" in technical data pertaining to items, components or processes developed at private expense (or under the DFARS technical data developed "exclusively" at private expense) and technical data created exclusively at private expense in the performance of a contract that does not require the development, manufacture, construction, or production of items, components or processes. *Id.* §§ 27.401, 227.7103-5(c)(1), 252.227-7013(b)(3)(i). Limited rights allow the government to use, modify, reproduce, release, perform, display, or disclose technical data, in whole or in part, within the Government." *Id.* §§ 52.227-14(g)(3) (Alternate II), 252.227-7013(a)(14). The government may not, without the contractor's permission, release or disclose limited rights technical data outside the government, use the technical data for manufacturer, or authorize the technical data to be used by another party, subject to certain narrow exceptions, such as for emergency repair and overhaul services or covered government support contractors. *Id.* In cases where limited rights data are permitted to be disclosed to third parties, the government is required to obtain a nondisclosure agreement. *Id.* § 52.227-14(g)(3) (Alternate II), 252.227-7013(a)(14)(ii).

The government obtains restricted rights in noncommercial computer software developed exclusively at private expense and required to be delivered to the government under a contract. *Id.* §§ 27.401, 227-7201-5(c)(1), 252.227-7014(b)(3)(i). Restricted rights include the rights for the government to use a computer program on a single computer, transfer a computer program to another government agency, copy a computer program for archival or backup purposes, and modify a computer program and obtain restricted rights in the modification. *Id.* §§ 52.227-14(g)(4) (Alternate III), 252.227-7014(a)(15). In addition, the government may disclose restricted rights computer software to third parties under very limited circumstances, such as to diagnose and correct deficiencies in a computer program, to combine or merge a computer program with other programs, to respond to urgent tactical situations, and to enable emergency repair and overhaul services. *Id.* In each case, the third party contractor that receives the restricted rights software is subject to a prohibition on further use and disclosure. *Id.*

The common feature of limited and restricted rights licenses is that they are not broad enough to allow the government to disclose trade secrets to other contractors to procure competing products or services. Unlike the grant of unlimited rights, limited and restricted rights are compatible with reasonable measures to keep information secret and, thus, continued trade secret protection.

3. Government Purpose Rights

Where technical data is developed through a combination of government and private funding, and the contract is with a DoD entity, the government receives "government purpose rights." *Id.* §§ 227.7103-5(b)(1), 227-7104-5(b)(1), 252.227-7013(b)(2), 252.227-7014(b)(2). The FAR does not provide for government purpose rights for civilian agencies.

Government purpose rights allow the government to use or disclose the technical data or computer software, either within the government or outside the government, but only for government purposes. *Id.* §§ 252.227-7013(a)(12), 252.227-7014(a)(12). Government purposes are defined to include any activity in which the government is a party, including competitive procurements, but do not include the right to use, modify, or disclose technical data or computer software for commercial purposes. *Id.* §§ 252.227-7013(a)(11), 252.227-7014(a)(11). Government purpose rights convert to unlimited rights after a fixed period, typically five (5) years. *Id.* §§ 227.7103-5(b)(2), 227.7203-5(b)(2), 252.227-7013(b)(2), 252.227-7014(b)(2).

4. Analyzing the Source of Funds

If a company develops a product exclusively at private expense, and then accepts government funds to develop a new component, there are two ways to conceptualize the source of funding. At the macro level, one might view the modified product as a whole as being developed with mixed funding since the government paid for the development of the new component. This approach would result in the government obtaining government purpose rights in data pertaining to the entire modified product, thus enabling the government to re-procure the entire product from the company's competitors.

This harsh result is not required because the source of funds determination is to be made at the lowest practicable level. This concept is articulated in the DFARS as follows:

> The determination of the source of development funds for technical data pertaining to items, components, or processes should be made at any practical sub-item or sub-component level or for any segregable portion of a process. Contractors may assert limited rights in a segregable sub-item, sub-component or portion of a process which otherwise qualifies for limited rights….

Id. § 227.7103-4(b). Thus, instead of obtaining government purpose rights in technical data pertaining to the entire modified product, the government would obtain limited rights in data pertaining to components developed at private expense, and unlimited rights in data pertaining to components developed with mixed funding. If the components for which the government received limited rights would be difficult to duplicate, then the government's unlimited rights in data pertaining to the other components would not, as a practical matter, allow a competitor to duplicate the company's technologies.

Similar analysis applies to the source of funds determination for computer software:

> The determination of the source of funds used to develop computer software should be made at the lowest practicable segregable portion of the software or documentation

> (e.g., a software sub-routine that performs a specific function). Contractors may assert restricted rights in a segregable portion of computer software which otherwise qualifies for restricted rights.

Id. § 227.7203-4(b). By applying this doctrine of segregability, it may be possible to a company to accept government funding for modifications to privately developed technologies without granting the government sufficiently broad license rights to provide the company's trade secrets to other contractors to procure competing products.

5. Other Types of Government Rights

In addition to the rights discussed above, there are three other important types of government rights that must be considered: (1) specifically negotiated license rights, (2) Small Business Innovation and Research (SBIR) data rights, and (3) commercial license rights

a. Specifically Negotiated License Rights

The DFARS expressly permit the parties to enter into a customized license where the rights received by the government are tailored to fit the particular circumstances. *Id.* §§ 227.7103-5(d), 227.7203-5(d). The FAR likewise acknowledges that license rights may be negotiated. *Id.* § 27.406-1(a). Specifically negotiated license rights allow the parties with flexibility to deviate from the strict "follow-the-funding" approach and allows the government and the company to negotiate the specific terms of the license to be provided to the government. *Id.* § 227.7103-5(d), 227.7203-5(d). Common examples of specifically negotiated license rights include agreements to furnish government purpose rights rather than unlimited rights, provide for tiered licenses under with the government's rights expand over time, or to negotiate license rights limited to a particular agency or program.

There are, however, certain limitations. While specifically negotiated license rights may be modified pursuant to mutual agreement, the result of negotiations may not provide the government with less than limited or restricted rights, depending on whether technical data or software is at issue. *Id.* § 227.7103-5(d)(1), 227.2203-5(d).

b. Small Business Innovation Research (SBIR) Data Rights

SBIR Data Rights apply only to contracts awarded under the Small Business Innovation Research Program. *Id.* §§ 27.409(h), 227.7104(a), 227.7204. The rights provided to small businesses under this program are generally more favorable than would otherwise be the case. For example, even where development is funded by the government, under the SBIR program, small businesses are allowed to impose restrictions for a period of four or five years on the unlimited rights the government would otherwise receive. *Id.* §§ 52.227-20(d), 252.227-7018(a)(19). During those four or five years, the government obtains limited or restricted rights rather than unlimited rights. Following the five-year period, the government receives unlimited rights to the data or software. *Id.*

c. Government Rights in Commercial Computer Software

The government is required to acquire commercial computer software under a contractor's standard commercial license to the extent such licenses are consistent with federal law and otherwise satisfy the government's needs. *Id.* §§ 12.212, 227.7202-3(a); *but see id.* § 52.227-19 (providing license terms for commercial computer software when a standard commercial license is not used). If the government has a need for additional license rights, it must negotiate with the contractor to determine if there are acceptable terms for transferring such rights. *Id.* §§ 12.212(b), 227.7202-3(b). The specific license rights provided to the government must be enumerated in the contract or an addendum. *Id.* § 227.7202-3(b).

Notwithstanding the preference for commercial license rights in computer software, companies should be aware that there are certain common commercial terms that the government either cannot accept because they violate federal law or may not accept as a matter of policy. Common examples of such terms include:

- Any provision requiring the application of any law other than federal law;
- Any provision requiring dispute resolution in a specific forum or venue that is different from that prescribed by federal law;
- Any provision prescribing a different time period for bringing an action than that prescribed by federal law;
- Any provision allowing the contractor unilaterally to revoke, terminate, or suspend the license;
- Any provision providing for binding arbitration unless specifically authorized by agency guidance;
- Any provision for equitable or injunctive relief, attorneys fees, cost or interest that is not explicitly provided for by statute;
- Any provision permitting the contractor to make unilateral changes to material terms;
- Any provision for automatic renewals without prior express consent;
- Any provision requiring indemnification from the government; and
- Any provision that purports to permit the contractor to sign the agreement without government consent.

The best practice is for a company to create a version of its standard commercial license that excludes such terms or to include in its standard commercial terms a provision indicating that such provisions do not apply to government customers. Some companies include a provision in their standard commercial license stating that commercial computer software is licensed to the government pursuant to FAR 52.227-19, Commercial Computer Software. That practice should be carefully considered, however, because FAR 52.227-19 affords far less protection for commercial computer software than most standard commercial computer software licenses.

C. Requirements for Protecting Data Rights

1. Listing Data in Pre-Award Assertions

Proposals submitted to military agencies are required to include a standard form attachment that identifies technical data and computer software to be furnished with less than unlimited rights. *Id.* §§ 252.227-7013(e), 252.227-7014(e), 252.227-7017. Technical data and computer software not listed on this form generally must be delivered with unlimited rights. *Id.* §§ 252.227-7013(e)(2), 252.227-7014(e)(2). A contractor may add assertions after award only if the failure to identify the data prior to award was based on lack of information regarding the need to use the data or an inadvertent omission. *Id.* §§ 252.227-7013(e)(3), 252.227-7014(e)(3). In the case of an inadvertent omission, a contractor may not be permitted to assert proprietary rights if the receipt of unlimited rights in the omitted data was a significant factor in selecting the contractor for award. *Id.*

Identifying technical data or computer software on the assertions list places the government on notice that the contractor is asserting the right to deliver the technical data or computer software with less than unlimited rights. The government's rights in technical data and computer software, however, ultimately are determined by the data rights clauses included in the contract, not the pre-award assertions table. *Id.* §§ 227-7103-10(a)(4), 227-7203-10(a)(4). For example, asserting limited rights in technical data pertaining to items, components, or processes developed exclusively at government expense (or in computer software developed exclusively at government expense) will not change the unlimited rights in such technical data or computer software allocated to the government under the terms of the contract.

2. Withholding and Marking Requirements

The standard data rights clause for civilian agencies allows contractors to protect limited rights data and restricted rights computer software by withholding them from delivery and providing the government with form, fit, and function data instead. *Id.* § 52.227-14(g). The delivery of limited rights technical data and restricted rights computer software is required for most civilian agencies only if the solicitation or contract includes Alternate II or Alternate III to the standard clause. *Id.* For defense agencies, there is no option to withhold limited rights technical data or restricted rights computer software.

For both civilian and defense agencies, data delivered with less than unlimited rights must be marked with an appropriate restrictive legend. *Id.* §§ 52.227-14(g) (Alternate II and III), 227.7103-10(b), 227.7203-10(b), 252.227-7013(f), 252.227-7014(f). The regulations require a different restrictive legend for each type of license right, and the contractor must comply strictly with the prescribed language.

The government obtains unlimited rights in data furnished without the prescribed restrictive legend, even if that data otherwise would qualify for delivery with limited or restricted rights. *Id.* §§ 27.404-5(b)(1), 52.227-14(f)(1), 227.7103-10(c), 227.7203-10(c); *see also Gen. Atronics Corp.*, ASBCA No. 49196, 2002 WL 450441 (Mar. 19, 2002) (government obtained unlimited rights in software that lacked the restricted rights legend); *see also Ervin & Assocs., Inc. v. United States*, 59 Fed. Cl. 267, 297 (Fed. Cl. 2004) (contractor's failure to mark data with the limited rights notice resulted in the government obtaining unlimited data rights). A contractor may add a legend to unmarked data within six months after delivery, but the government will not be liable for use or disclosure of any data that were not marked. 48 C.F.R. §§ 27.404-5(b)(1), 52.227-14(f)(2), 227.7103-10(c)(2), 227.7203-10(c)(2), 252.227-7013(c)(2), 252.227-7014(c)(2). What particular legends may be used with unlimited rights data is an open question currently. *See Boeing Co. v. Secretary of Air Force*, 983 F.3d 1321 (Fed. Cir. 2020).

The DFARS provide detailed instructions for marking technical data and computer software. Those instructions also serve as best practices for civilian agencies. Appropriate restrictive legend should appear on the transmitted document or storage container and, for printed material, on each page that contains data furnished with less than unlimited rights. *Id.* §§ 252.227-7013(f)(1), 252.227-7014(f)(1). When only a portion of a page is subject to the asserted restriction, the contractor is required to identify that portion by circling, underscoring, making a note, or some other method. *Id.* § 252.227-7013(f)(1). For computer software, it is advisable to include the legend in as many locations as practicable, including boot screens, windows of programs, help menus, related documentation, packaging, and the physical media on which the software resides. The legend, however, must not obstruct the operation of the software or its intended use. *Id.* § 252.227-7014(f)(1)

The regulations do not require restrictive legends for technical data pertaining to commercial items or commercial computer software. However, it is advisable to include such a legend so that the user knows that the data have been furnished with commercial, rather than unlimited, license rights.

3. Proof of Development at Private Expense

If the government challenges a company's assertion of proprietary rights in data, the company will have the burden to justify that it was entitled to deliver the data with less than unlimited rights. *Id.* §§ 52.227-14(e), 252.227-19, 252.227-7037. Thus, it is incumbent upon contractors to maintain evidence sufficient to establish development at private expense. Although the regulations do not specific what records are required for this purpose, it is advisable to create and maintain at least the following documents:

- A memorandum that documents the baseline technology, describes the nature of the planned development, and creates a separate account number for the development effort;
- Records of all costs charged to the separate development account;
- Periodic status reports on the progress of the development effort;
- Records of all significant tests performed and the design status at the time of testing;
- Engineering, laboratory, and project management logs and journals; and
- Copies of all contracts under which products incorporating the relevant technology are delivered, modified, tested, or enhanced.

D. Strategies for Maximizing and Protecting Rights to Intellectual Property

Companies that do business with the federal government should develop and implement strategies to maximize the protection of their trade secrets. These strategies should include steps to maximize government funding while allowing the company to protect and profit from its development efforts. Below are some examples of such strategies:

- Identify core items, components, processes, or software that offers long-term competitive advantages. The best candidates will be useful to the government, not have readily available substitutes, and be difficult to reverse engineer.

- Develop the core items, components, processes, or software exclusively at private expense. Remember that private expense includes indirect costs, such as independent research and development, even if such costs are ultimately allocated to government contracts.

- Maintain adequate documentation to prove that the core items, components, processes, or software were developed at private expense. There is no fixed duration on trade secret protection, such documents should be maintained indefinitely.

- Do not accept any government funding to further develop or modify the core items, components, processes, or software. Review government statements of work carefully to ensure they do not require further development.

- Ensure that any improvements developed with government funding are segregable from the core technology. This may not be the most elegant engineering approach but is necessary to avoid contaminating the core items, components, processes, or computer software with government funding.

- Review the data rights clauses contained in solicitations carefully. Some standard FAR and DFARS clauses, such as the Special Works clauses, afford the government broader rights. Some agencies have different standard clauses. It has become increasingly common to find poorly drafted data rights clauses in statements of work, where they do not belong.

- List all data to be delivered with less than unlimited rights in the pre-award assertions table. But remember that the purpose of these listings is to provide notice to the government, and that they are not determinative of the government's license rights.

- When doing business with civilian agencies, withhold limited rights technical data and restricted rights computer software and furnish form, fit, and function data instead, if permitted.

- Include the appropriate restrictive legend on all data to be delivered with less than unlimited rights. Consider delivering data through a single point of contact who is trained to use appropriate markings and ensure that overly broad data deliveries are not being made.

- The government obtains unlimited rights in certain categories of data, such as manuals and test reports, regardless of the source of funding. Avoid including trade secrets in such documents.

- Deliver no more data than necessary. The government can only require delivery of data identified in the contract as deliverable and, if the contract includes a Deferred Ordering or Additional Data clause, data first generated in performance of the contract.

- The data rights regulations only protect data. They do not prohibit the government from reverse engineering items, components, or processes, or providing your products to competitors for them to reverse engineer.

- Consult with company intellectual property representatives or legal counsel if there are any questions regarding the government's rights to intellectual property.

Following these tips may reduce the risk of losing valuable trade secret protection for proprietary technologies.

Chapter 19
COMPELLED DISCLOSURE BY REGULATION: MAKING SURE BIG BROTHER KEEPS YOUR SECRETS
By: Joanna R. Mendoza, Esq.

---

§ 19.01 Introduction

Many different types of regulations, both state and federal, have been put in place to control and regulate various aspects of business with the government taking on the role of the public watchdog. The number of regulations requiring a business to submit sensitive, proprietary information in order to operate, perform services, and sell various products are too numerous and complex to address individually. It goes without dispute that the State of California, in many contexts, may require a business to submit trade secret information to the government as a requirement of doing business in this state. This creates a practical problem for regulated businesses that rely on maintaining the secrecy of their valuable proprietary information: How does a business ensure that these same government agencies do not disclose the trade secret information to the public and thereby destroy their value as intellectual property? How can a business prevent a competitor from gaining access to sensitive proprietary information submitted to the government that would give the competitor an advantage?

This chapter attempts to address these issues. When addressing a business' concerns regarding required disclosures to the government, it should be kept in mind that although intellectual property law and issues have been around for quite some time, many of the concepts relating to intellectual property law are in many respects only now coming within the purview of government agencies. While some government agencies are clearly well versed in the existence and importance of intellectual property, others find the concepts new and have difficulty applying them in the context of governmental regulation. This disparity in the levels of understanding has resulted in nearly identical disparity in the application of laws designed to protect against disclosure of trade secrets that are submitted to the government. It is more difficult for agencies not as familiar with intellectual property laws to accurately weigh the interests of the property holder against the competing public policy of free and open access to information concerning its conduct. With these considerations in mind, this chapter discusses how to minimize a business' exposure to potential disclosure of its compelled submissions, what to do when a competitor seeks to acquire trade secret information from a government agency, and what remedies are in place for improper disclosure by a government agency.

§ 19.02 Reducing the Risk of Disclosure at the Time of Submitting Trade Secrets to the Government

Whereas a business can always choose *not* to contract with the government, it does not have a say in whether it will be regulated by it. It is certainly an uncomfortable task for a business to entrust its most precious secrets to a third party. It is also certainly of no comfort that, in the case of the government, the third party to whom the business must submit its most sensitive information operates upon the basic presumption that the public generally should be allowed access to all information in its possession. To the extent that trade secret information *must* be submitted by a regulated business to a governmental agency, several steps may be taken to reduce the possibility that the government will publicly disclose its trade secrets.

- **Enter Into a Nondisclosure Agreement (NDA) With the Agency.** Request that the agency enter into an NDA, as previously suggested and discussed in some detail. *See supra* Chapter 18. By signing such an agreement, the agency acknowledges the confidential nature of the material presented and agrees to treat it as trade secret information. The agency may be able to use the existence of an NDA as a basis for refusing to disclose sensitive information in response to a Freedom of Information Act (FOIA) request. *See Billington v. U.S. Dep't of Justice*, 69 F. Supp. 2d 128, 136 (D.D.C. 1999), *aff'd in part, vacated in part*, 233 F.3d 581 (D.C.Cir. 2000) *remanded to* 245 F. Supp. 2d 79 (D.D.C. 2003), *reconsideration granted in part*, 301 F. Supp. 2d 15, 21-22 (D.D.C. 2004). In the *Billington* case, the Department of Justice (DOJ) withheld information requested pursuant to a FOIA request which had been obtained from foreign governments based upon explicit or implied confidentiality agreements. Exemption 1, 5 U.S.C. § 552(b)(1), (2) (2020). Under Exemption 7(D), 5 U.S.C. § 552(b)(7)(D), the DOJ was allowed to withhold the identity of an informant if there was an understanding that the communication would remain confidential. The case provides that, to invoke Exemption 7(D), an agency must show either that a source provided the information to the agency under express assurances of confidentiality or that the circumstances support an inference of confidentiality. *See also U.S. Dep't of Justice v. Landano*, 508 U.S. 165, 172 (1993).

- **Only Submit Trade Secret Information If *Absolutely* Necessary.** This may seem obvious on its face, but a number of businesses do not take the time to learn what they *do not* need to submit to an agency that is regulating it and still be in compliance. For many it is easier, to ensure they are in compliance with the law, to submit more information rather than less. Such a practice may work in general to avoid being out of compliance, but when it comes to protecting company trade secrets, the time should be taken to determine the minimal amount of information necessary to submit to be in compliance. For example, Occupational Safety and Health Administration (OSHA) regulations allow a manufacturer to withhold secret chemical formulations from a Material Safety Data Sheet, 29 C.F.R. § 1910.1200(i)(1) (2012), thereby shielding the manufacturer from a claim of recklessness in causing injuries that might have been prevented by a more complete warning. *Boyette v. L.W. Looney & Son, Inc.*, 932 F. Supp. 1344, 1348 (D. Utah 1996). Be aware of any special regulations that allow a business to avoid submitting trade secret information.

- **Be Aware of and Follow the Rules Imposed by the Agency for Submitting Confidential Information.** Many agencies have specific requirements or rules for submission of confidential material to help ensure it is not inadvertently disclosed by the agency. It is important to know whether there are any such rules and, if so, ensure that they are complied with. Several state agencies have addressed the submission of confidential information within specific regulatory language. *See, e.g.*, Cal. Code Reg. tit. 10, § 102.203 (2021) (investments); Cal. Code Reg. tit. 17, § 91011 (2021) (Air Resources Board); and Cal. Code Reg. tit. 28, § 1007(b) (2021) (managed health care). For example, submissions made to the U.S. Copyright Office that contain trade secret information should be submitted under a "special relief" application evidencing the need for confidential treatment. 37 C.F.R. § 202.20(d) (2021). In addition, at least one California agency, the Department of Pesticide Regulation, has set forth statutory guidelines for the submission of trade secret information by registrants or applicants. Cal. Gov't Code § 6254.2.

- **Mark All Confidential Submissions Conspicuously and Often.** Reduce the possibility of disclosures by the agency by liberally using conspicuous markings, stamps, or legends clearly identifying the material being submitted as "confidential," "proprietary" or "trade secret." Keep in mind that information originally intended for one agency may be provided to other agencies, and the markings that a business provides on its submissions ultimately may be the only indication that certain information is proprietary. Keep in mind, also, that portions of a submission may become separated from each other. In such an event it would not be effective to have only marked the first page of a submission—marking every appropriate page is important to ensure adequate notice of confidentiality.

- **Separate Nonconfidential Submissions, If Possible.** Keep confidential information separated from nonconfidential information to the extent possible in order to reduce the possibility of errors made in the disclosure process.

§ 19.03 Preventing Disclosure of Trade Secrets Submitted to Government Agencies

The manner in which one would go about preventing disclosure of trade secrets by a government agency depends on the means used to acquire the information. The initial step usually involves convincing the agency that the records requested are protected from disclosure by statute or applicable case law. Even if the agency agrees that the information sought is trade secret, however, the agency may conclude that some other public interest trumps the interest of the owner of the trade secret. For example, the U.S. Environmental Protection Agency ruled according to the Federal Register dated February 7, 2014 that it will not accept any confidential business information claims for hazardous waste manifests, classifying the shipment documents as public information. This was over protests that the information disclosed may permit competitors to discover valuable trade secrets (e.g., chemical mixtures used in connection with products; customer lists). Assuming that the information submitted to the government is protectable by law, a business owner needs to be prepared to establish both that its information deserves protection, and that the business owner's interest should be weighed favorably against any public policy that otherwise supports disclosure.

A. Modes of Access to Records Held by a Government Agency

An individual or business can access records filed with a government agency usually through one of two means, depending upon whether there is pending litigation—a public records request or a subpoena. Another mode of access is available only to legislative bodies, but a business should nevertheless be made aware of that possibility.

1. Freedom of Information Act (FOIA) Request

- **FOIA Often Used for Anticompetitive Purposes.** Despite its virtuous intentions, the FOIA has at times, since its inception in 1966, been used by businesses as a means to acquire a competitor's data, as well as by foreign governments to acquire access to technology and information not being developed within their own countries. One of the better known instances of agency disclosure of trade secrets due to a FOIA request was when the Environmental Protection Agency (EPA), in response to a FOIA request, mistakenly released Monsanto's half-billion dollar secret formula to the herbicide "Roundup." *See Ruckelshaus v. Monsanto Co.*, 467 U.S. 986 (1984).

- **Request Must Be Made in Accordance With Statutory Requirements.** The requester must describe the records being sought with sufficient particularity that the agency can understand what is being requested. 5 U.S.C. § 552(a)(3)(A) (2020). Furthermore, the request must be "made in accordance with published rules stating the time, place, fees (if any), and procedures to be followed." *Id.* In some cases the cost to the person or entity requesting the records may effectively prevent access to the information. *See, e.g., OSHA Data/CIH, Inc. v. U.S. Dep't of Labor*, 220 F.3d

153, 156 (3d Cir. 2000) (involving an agency that charged $1.7 million as a condition to considering a FOIA request due to the cost of the evaluation of the information's confidentiality).

- **Records Requested Under FOIA Must Be Produced by Agency Without Significant Delay.** The mandate of the law requires that the agency make available information in its possession to the requester within a reasonably short period of time. 5 U.S.C. § 552(a)(3)(A) (2020). This means that the time within which one must respond and attempt to prevent disclosure is often very limited.

- **Trade Secrets Are Specifically Exempt From Disclosure.** Trade secrets may be protected from disclosure pursuant to the specific exemption found within the FOIA, 5 U.S.C. § 552(b)(3)-(4) (2020), read in conjunction with the Trade Secrets Act, which prohibits government employees from disclosing trade secrets "to any extent not authorized by law." 18 U.S.C. § 1905 (2009). Together, these statutory schemes provide the basis for a claim by the owner of a trade secret that the material it has submitted to the government agency qualifies under the applicable exemptions and should be protected against disclosure. Such exemptions, however, are narrowly construed. *Dept of Interior v. Klamath Water Users Protective Ass'n*, 532 U.S. 1, 8 (2001)

- **"Vaughn" Index Must Be Prepared by Agency If Documents Withheld.** When the government prohibits disclosure on the basis of a trade secret exemption, the federal agency will need to make available a "Vaughn" index (similar to a privilege log) to show what portions of the information may be segregable and properly produced. *Vaughn v. Rosen*, 484 F.2d 820, 825-28 (D.C.C. 1973); *See Judicial Watch, Inc. v. U.S. Dep't of Commerce*, 83 F. Supp. 2d 105, 109 (D.D.C. 1999). A "Vaughn" index must describe the documents withheld or redacted and the specific FOIA exemption(s) invoked, and it must also explain why each exemption applies. *Prison Legal News v. Samuels*, 787 F.3d 1142, 1145 n.1 (D.C.C. 2015).

- **Exception to "Vaughn" Index Requirement.** There is an exception to the "Vaughn" requirement when merely confirming or denying the existence of certain records would itself reveal protected information. *Nation Magazine v. U.S. Customs Serv.*, 71 F.3d 885, 893 (D.C.Cir. 1995). This is known as a "Glomar" response. *See Marino v. DEA*, 685 F.3d 1076, 1078 n. 1 (D.C.Cir. 2012). For such a response to be appropriate it must be established that revealing the very existence of records would cause harm cognizable under a FOIA exception. *Wolf v. CIA*, 473 F.3d 370, 374 (D.C.Cir. 2007). The court will then weigh the public interest in the release of the information against the interest in nondisclosure to determine if the exemption supports a "Glomar" response. *PETA v. Nat'l Inst. Of Health*, 745 F.3d 535, 541 (D.C.Cir. 2014).

2. California Public Records Act (PRA) Request

- **Construction of the PRA Is Parallel to the FOIA.** The California Supreme Court has held that the PRA and the FOIA should receive a parallel construction. *Am. Civil Liberties Union Found. v. Deukmejian*, 32 Cal.3d 440, 447-49 (1982). Hence, while certain aspects of the statutory schemes are different, for the most part much of the law relating to implementation of the FOIA is applicable to California's PRA.

- **General Procedure for a PRA Request.** Upon receipt of a request reasonably describing identifiable records, the agency is required to promptly make the nonexempt records available "upon payment of fees covering direct costs of duplication, or a statutory fee if applicable." Cal. Gov't Code § 6253(b).

- **Public Agency Must Assist in Identifying Records Sought.** California law specifically provides that, when a member of the public requests public records, the public agency has a duty "to assist the member of the public make a focused and effective request that reasonably describes an identifiable record." Cal. Gov't Code § 6253.1(a). This includes describing the information technology and the physical location where the records are kept, as well as providing suggestions for overcoming any practical basis for denying records or information sought. *Id.* However, if the agency determines that the request should be denied solely on the basis of an exemption listed in section 6254 of the California Government Code, the public agency is not required to assist to the extent otherwise dictated by the statute. Cal. Gov't Code § 6253.1(d).

- **Agency Has Ten Days to Determine Whether Records Requested Under PRA Are Disclosable Public Records.** Unless "unusual circumstances" are present, the agency generally only has ten days after receipt of a request to "determine whether the request, in whole or in part, seeks copies of disclosable public records in the possession of the agency and shall promptly notify the person making the request of the determination and the reasons therefor." Cal. Gov't Code § 6253(c). If it is determined that the agency has disclosable public records to produce, it is to provide the requester with "the estimated date and time when the records will be made available." *Id.*

- **Trade Secrets Are Not *Specifically* Enumerated as Being Exempt From Disclosure.** Unlike the FOIA, trade secrets are not specifically identified as exempt under the PRA. *See* Cal. Gov't Code § 6254. The PRA at section 6254(k) of the California Government Code specifically exempts "[r]ecords, the disclosure of which is exempted or prohibited pursuant to federal or state law, including, but not limited to, provisions of the Evidence Code relating to privilege." Cal. Gov't Code § 6254(k). Hence, trade secrets are arguably exempt from disclosure due to the trade secret privilege set out in section 1060 of the California Evidence Code. *Cal. School Employees Ass'n. v. Sunnyvale Elementary School Dist. of Santa Clara Cnty.*, 36 Cal. App. 3d 46, 65-66 (1973) (holding that the PRA exception in favor of privileged material is broad enough to include trade secrets).

- **Trade Secrets Submitted for the Purpose of Retaining, Locating, or Expanding Private Company Facilities *Are* Specifically Identified as Exempt.** Under section 6254.15 of the California Government Code, corporate financial records, proprietary information, and trade secrets, all of which have been "furnished to a government agency by a private company for the purpose of permitting the agency to work with the company in retaining, locating, or expanding a facility within California" are not deemed to be "public records" subject to disclosure. Cal. Gov't Code § 6254.15.

- **California Does Not Require "Vaughn" Index Type Listing To Be Prepared By The Agency.** Unlike the FOIA, California law does not require that the public agency prepare an inventory of records that were potentially responsive to a PRA request but were withheld on the basis that they revealed information that was exempt from disclosure. *Haynie v. Super. Ct.*, 26 Cal. 4th 1061 (2001). The California Supreme Court has determined that this type of listing was not mandated by the Act, and that to require such a list could "satellite litigation over the adequacy of its descriptions of the documents exempt from disclosure." *Id.* at 1074-75.

3. Subpoena

An alternative to a PRA request is the issuance of a subpoena to the agency as a third party to pending litigation. There is no legal authority that states that one may acquire through a subpoena to a governmental agency something that cannot be acquired through a PRA or FOIA request or the discovery statutes in general. At least one known federal agency has treated a subpoena as a FOIA, and treated disclosure under the subpoena identical to its handling of FOIA requests—the exact procedure for FOIA requests was followed and the date of production was ignored in place of the dates to produce as required by the statutory scheme. 7 C.F.R. § 1.215 (2020). However, each agency may treat the receipt of a subpoena differently, and there is no guarantee that the protections afforded the submitter through the FOIA and PRA will be instituted when the request comes by way of subpoena rather than a FOIA or PRA request.

If a party to litigation seeks submitted records of the opposing party in that litigation, by issuance of a subpoena to a government agency rather than by way of standard discovery requests to the submitting party, it can be assumed that the purpose is to get additional, and perhaps undiscoverable, information. The only likely circumstance that would warrant the use of a subpoena to the government agency for copies of the submitting party's records would be in a situation where the records sought are no longer in the possession of the party itself. It could otherwise be used as a means to circumvent discovery limitations, where a competitor can hope that the agency discloses more information than would otherwise be disclosed by the competing party in response to discovery requests.

Given the procedures provided by California Evidence Code to protect privileged information (*see* Chapter 16), it has been noted that "[s]uch procedures would be nullified if . . . the same information, or information leading to it, could be obtained as a matter of right" through the public agency holding that information for other purposes. *City of Hemet v. Superior Court*, 37 Cal. App. 4th 1411, 1425 (1995) (citation omitted).

4. Congressional or Legislative Access

There is an additional risk of disclosure in the event that the agency is called upon by Congress or the state Legislature to give access to its files. One court has specifically noted that, so long as the congressional inquiry lies within the broad scope of its power, injunctive relief is not available to prevent disclosure, even when the committee seeking access to the files has a record of indiscretions and refuses to agree to hold the information in confidence. *Ashland Oil, Inc. v. Fed. Trade Comm'n*, 409 F. Supp. 297, 308-09 (D.D.C. 1976), *aff'd*, 548 F.2d 977 (D.C.Cir. 1976).

B. Procedures Available for Preventing Disclosure

It is often the regulatory practice that a business is notified by the governmental agency that a request for records has been made by a third party to be disclosed by the agency either under the FOIA (federal agencies) or the PRA (state agencies). This provides the business with an opportunity to assert any objections it may have to disclosure of sensitive information and ensure protection of its trade secrets. If the request for records comes through a form other than a record request, such as a subpoena during the course of other litigation, the agency receiving the subpoena may or may not treat it as it would a record request. However, with a subpoena, the business whose records have been sought may also have the opportunity to assert objections and attempt to prevent disclosure. In either situation it may be necessary to seek court intervention. The agency itself, however, does not always have that option.

1. Objections to FOIA Disclosure

In 1987 President Ronald Reagan signed Executive Order No. 12600 entitled "Predisclosure Notification Procedures for Confidential Commercial Information," which ordered each federal agency subject to the FOIA to "establish procedures to notify submitters of records containing confidential commercial information . . . when those records are requested under the [FOIA]." Exec. Order No. 12600, 52 Fed. Reg. 23,781 (June 23, 1987). The agency is to provide the submitter notice if it determines either that (1) the record requests seek information already designated as "confidential" by the submitter, or (2) the agency has reason to believe that the request seeks information that "could reasonably be expected to cause substantial competitive harm." *Id.* This establishes the clear benefit of identifying trade secret and confidential information submitted to the agency *at the time of submission*—the submitter is not leaving the determination of what is likely to cause competitive harm to the agency upon receipt of a FOIA request.

- **Overview of FOIA Procedure for Objecting to Disclosure of Records.** Upon receipt of notification of a FOIA request by the agency, the submitter is to be provided "a reasonable period of time . . . [to] object to the disclosure of any specified portion of the information and to state all grounds upon which disclosure is opposed." *Id.* The agency must also notify the requester that it is giving the submitter of the records an opportunity to comment upon the propriety of disclosure, as well as notification to the requester of the agency's final decision regarding the application of exemptions to the records request. *Id.* Notice is not necessary, however, if certain circumstances exist, such as prior publication of the data or the existence of another law that requires disclosure. *Id.* The agency must give careful consideration to all grounds specified by the submitter for nondisclosure. *Id.* If the agency decides that disclosure is appropriate despite the protestations of the submitter, a written statement briefly stating why the submitter's objections were not sustained must be provided by the agency. *Id.* The process is designed to move very rapidly, and the submitter of information should adhere to the agency time limitations or risk disclosure.

- **Applying the Relevant FOIA Exemptions to Records Requested.** When presented with a request for records submitted with a government agency, a business will need to go through the documentation and argue how each particular aspect of the information contained in those records falls within the exemptions to disclosure under the FOIA. It is the burden of the business whose government submitted records are being sought to establish for the federal agency what documents that fall within the request are exempt from disclosure.

- **Submitter Must Convince Agency That the Records Requested Contain Either Trade Secret or Confidential Information.** In order to assert protection against disclosure of proprietary or sensitive commercial information, the statutory scheme of the FOIA sets forth two applicable exemptions to disclosure, which state, respectively, as follows:

> (b) [FOIA disclosure] does not apply to matters that are—
>
>> (3) specifically exempted from disclosure by statute . . . provided that such statute (A) requires that the matters be withheld from the public in such a manner as to leave no discretion on the issue, or (B) establishes particular criteria for withholding or refers to particular types of matters to be withheld; [and]
>>
>> (4) trade secrets and commercial or financial information obtained from a person and privileged "or" confidential[.]

5 U.S.C. § 552(b)(3)-(4) (2020).

The purpose of the exemptions for trade secrets and confidential information is to not only ensure the competitive position of the citizen-provided information to the agency, but also to encourage cooperation with the government by persons who have information which is useful to government officials. *Shermco Indus., Inc. v. Sec'y of Air Force*, 613 F.2d 1314, 1317 (5th Cir. 1980). If confidential and trade secret records were subject to disclosure by the public agency to a competitor, "the results would probably be so inconsistent that the effect would be to discourage candor due to the apprehension of disclosure." *Hemet*, 37 Cal. App. 4th at 1428 n.18. If, however, licensees fear that this information will be disseminated to competitors, then they are less likely to disclose their sensitive trade secret or other confidential information. *Id.* at 1429 n.19 (noting that "citizens who believe that their records, or information they have provided, will be absolutely confidential [should not] be obliged to submit to routine judicial perusal of the information" or threat of disclosures). This reminder of the basis for the exemptions may be useful to the submitter of information when responding to a FOIA request.

- **Trade Secret Information Is Narrowly Defined.** The term "trade secret" as used in the FOIA is not identical to the definition set forth in California's Uniform Trade Secret Act found at section 3426.1(d) of the California Civil Code. Rather, in 1983, the United States Court of Appeals, District of Columbia Circuit, held that the term "trade secret" is to be defined in its "common law sense, which incorporates a direct relationship between the information at issue and the productive process." *Pub. Citizen Health Research Grp. v. Food & Drug Admin.*, 704 F.2d 1280, 1288 (D.C. Cir. 1983). This narrow interpretation has been accepted as authoritative. *See, e.g.*, *Anderson v. Dep't of Health & Human Servs.*, 907 F.2d 936, 944 (10th Cir. 1990).

- **Unintended Waiver of Trade Secret Status Is Possible.** If a submitting company reveals its trade secret to the government in a submission made as a precondition for a license, secrecy is waived when subsequent disclosure occurs under statutory powers known to the submitter at the time of the submission. *Ruckelshaus v. Monsanto Co.*, 467 U.S. 986 (1984) (holding no uncompensated taking in violation of the Fifth Amendment of Monsanto's trade secret property interest in pesticide test data by internal governmental use, by use in connection with application from another, or by disclosure after ten years, because all of these were allowed by statute in effect when data were submitted). However, secrecy is *not* waived when a subsequent disclosure violates statutory requirements which clearly mandated that the government preserve the secrecy. *Id.* If the agency inadvertently discloses the trade secret, the trade secret status is not lost. *Masonite Corp. v. Cnty. of Mendocino Air Quality Mgmt. Dist.*, 42 Cal. App. 4th 436 (1996).

- **Confidential Information Exemption Expands the Scope of Protection Against Disclosure.** Information need not fall within the limited and narrow definition of a trade secret to be protected against disclosure under the exemptions provided by the FOIA. Under the FOIA, an agency is not to disclose any matters that are deemed "commercial or financial information obtained from a person and privileged or confidential." 5 U.S.C. § 552(b)(4) (2020).

The United States Supreme Court has set forth a single test for determining whether information is deemed "confidential" under Exemption 4 of the FOIA, regardless of whether the information is provided to the government voluntarily or involuntarily. *Food Marketing Institute v. Argus Leader Media*, __ U.S. __, 139 S.Ct. 2356 (2019). Under the Supreme Court's analysis "commercial or financial" information is considered confidential for the purposes of Exemption 4 when it is "both customarily and actually treated as private by its owner," and, perhaps as well, "provided to the government under an assurance of privacy. *Id.* at 2366. While the Supreme Court did not ultimately decide whether the assurance of privacy is necessary to be established for information to be confidential within the meaning of Exemption 4, at least one lower court has since concluded that the submitter of information may be required to so establish such governmental assurance of privacy. *Id.* at 2363; *Ctr. For Investigative Reporting v. U.S. Customs and Border Prot.*, 436 F.Supp.3d 90, 109, n.9 (D.C.C. 2019); see also *Am. Small Bus. League v. U.S. Dep't of Def.*, 411 F.Supp.3d 824, 829 (N.D. Cal. 2019) (It remains an open question as to whether a showing of assurance of privacy by the government is required to establish confidentiality of information following the *Food Marketing* decision). When seeking to establish an assurance of privacy, Exemption 4 does not require written documentation or express assurances by the government – an implied promise of confidentiality suffices. *Food Marketing Institute*, 139 S.Ct. at 2363; *Am. Small Bus. League*, 411 F.Supp.3d at 834.

In addition to the two-part test to determine "confidentiality," in order to invoke Exemption 4 it is necessary to establish that "foreseeable harm" will be caused by disclosure. The "foreseeable harm" requirement was codified under the FOIA Improvement Act of 2016, and by its terms it allows a federal agency to withhold information under an exemption "only if the agency reasonably foresees that disclosure would harm an interest protected by an exemption" or "disclosure is prohibited by law." 5 U.S.C. § 552(a)(8)(A)(i) (2020). Thus, even if an exemption applies, the agency is required to release information "if disclosure would not reasonably harm that exemption-protected interest – given its age, content, and character – and its disclosure is not prohibited by law." *Am. Small Bus. League*, 411 F.Supp.3d at 835. A submitter will have to explain how disclosing the information, in whole or part, would harm an interest protected by Exemption 4, such as by causing "genuine harm to [the submitter's] economic or business interests." *Food Marketing Institute*, 139. S.Ct. at 2369; *Ctr. for Investigative Reporting*, 436 F.Supp.3d at 113.

Simply because some part of a record qualifies for Exemption 4, however, does not mean the entire record can be withheld. The FOIA requires that "[a]ny reasonably segregable portion of a record shall be provided to any person requesting such record after deletion of the portions which are exempt" from disclosure. 5. U.S.C. § 552(b) (2020); see also 5 U.S.C. § 552(a)(8)(A)(ii)(II) (2020) ("An agency shall…take reasonable steps necessary to segregate and release nonexempt information."). The FOIA Improvement Act of 2016 expanded the agency obligations with respect to segregability by providing that "[a]n agency shall … (I) consider whether partial disclosure of information is possible whenever the agency determines that a full disclosure of a requested record is not possible…and (II) take reasonable steps necessary to segregate and release nonexempt information." 5. U.S.C. § 552(a)(8)(A)(ii) (2020).

If any agency is unable to segregate exempt information, it must "provide the court with its reasons – as opposed to its simple conclusion – for its inability to segregate non-exempt portions of the documents, and also provide the court with a description of what proportion of the information in a document is non-exempt, and how that material is dispersed throughout the document." *Lawyers' Comm. For Civil Rights of San Francisco Area v. Dep't of the Treasury*, 2008 WL 4482855 (N.D. Cal. 2008); *Am Small Bus. League*, 411 F.Supp.3d at 836. This information is properly set forth in the "Vaughn" index.

Finally, with regard to the statutory exemption for privileged information found within 5 U.S.C. § 552(b)(4) (2020), the privilege must be of the type not otherwise referred to in the exemption, such as the attorney-client and work product privileges. *See Anderson*, 907 F.2d at 945. Hence, this aspect is arguably repetitive of the exemption at § 552(b)(3) because such privileges are all found within the California Evidence Code.

- **Application of the Trade Secrets Act to the Record Request.** It can be argued that the FOIA exemptions should be read in conjunction with the Trade Secrets Act, which prohibits government employees from disclosing trade secrets "to any extent not authorized by law." 18 U.S.C. § 1905 (2020). However, it does not qualify as a withholding statute under § 552(b)(3) of the FOIA since the Trade Secrets Act does not provide any substantive right to withhold.

- **The Trade Secrets Act Does Not Provide Additional Protection.** If any statute, including the FOIA provisions, allows an agency to disclose the information at issue then the express language of the Trade Secrets Act provides that there is no liability for such disclosure under the Act. *See* 18 U.S.C. § 1905 (2020); *9 to 5 Org. for Women Office Workers v. Bd. of Governors of Fed. Reserve Sys.*, 721 F.2d 1 (1st Cir. 1983) (holding that if disclosure is not prohibited under FOIA, then disclosure will also not be a violation of the Trade Secrets Act). Nevertheless, the Trade Secrets Act may provide additional incentive for the agency personnel to correctly apply the exemptions under FOIA and prohibit disclosure if such an exemption applies. Furthermore, if the information would be discoverable in a civil suit under the Federal Rules of Civil Procedure, it cannot be said to be confidential information under the Trade Secrets Act since the terms of the Act permit disclosure authorized by law. *Exch. Nat'l Bank of Chicago v. Abramson*, 295 F. Supp. 87 (D.C. Minn. 1969). This is true even if the information is otherwise exempt from disclosure under the FOIA. *Pleasant Hill Bank v. United States*, 58 F.R.D. 97, 99-100 (W.D. Mo. 1973).

- **A Violation of the Trade Secrets Act Requires Knowledge or Intent.** Appropriate culpability for violation of the Trade Secrets Act must include knowledge that the information disclosed by the federal employee was, in fact, confidential. *United States v. Wallington*, 889 F.2d 573, 578 (5th Cir. 1989). Hence, it may be beneficial for the trade secret submitter to put the federal agency on notice of the claim of confidentiality at the earliest opportunity.

2. Objections to PRA Disclosure

- **Reliance Upon Evidentiary Trade Secret Privilege to Prevent Disclosure.** Section 6254 of the California Government Code sets forth the exclusions to the disclosure requirements set forth in the PRA. The burden is on the party whose records are sought to establish that one or more of the exclusions enumerated in section 6254 are applicable to prevent disclosure. Again, trade secret information is not specifically enumerated, but it is generally understood that subsection (k) ordinarily precludes its disclosure in that it provides that records in the possession of governmental authorities shall not be disclosed under the California PRA if "disclosure [] is exempted or prohibited pursuant to *federal or state* law" (emphasis added). Cal. Gov't Code § 6254(k). *See County of Los Angeles v. Superior Court*, 82 Cal. App. 4th 819, 828-29 (2000) (holding that documents that are normally privileged cannot be obtained through a PRA request); *Hemet*, 37 Cal. App. 4th at 1428 (holding that to allow disclosure of trade secrets would make the privilege set forth in section 1060 of the California Evidence Code illusory at best). *See* Chapter 16 for a discussion of the trade secret privilege.

- **Special Statutory Provisions for Department of Pesticide Regulation (DPR).** As a testament to the length of time the DPR has been dealing with registrant's trade secrets, as well as a reflection upon the industry lobbying interests represented in state government, the DPR has set forth by statute the requirements for protesting disclosure of trade secret information sought by way of a PRA request. Cal. Gov't Code § 6254.2. There is a balancing act that is applied by the DPR between the public interest to learn about pesticides used in the environment and what may be contained in those pesticides and the desire of the pesticide manufacturers to maintain the secrecy of their formulations.

Under the statutory provisions, after receipt of notification from the DPR director that data submitted is not considered to be trade secret, the manufacturer has thirty days "to provide the director with a complete justification and statement of the grounds on which the trade secret privilege is claimed." Cal. Gov't Code § 6254.2(d). The definition of a trade secret for DPR's purposes is controlled entirely by the federal statutory scheme set forth in the Insecticide, Fungicide, and Rodenticide Act, 7 U.S.C. § 136h(d)(1) (2020). If the data is not disclosable under the federal act then it is deemed a trade secret for purposes of the DPR filings.

In order to ensure that the director of the DPR does not knowingly disclose information to a competitor, any person requesting a registrant's/applicant's information from the director of DPR must execute a document entitled "Affirmation of Status" which states that the requester does not seek access to the information for competitive purposes. Cal. Gov't Code § 6254.2(h). However, if an officer or employee of the state willfully discloses the information in violation of the code, the code provides for criminal prosecution in a manner very similar to the Trade Secrets Act discussed above. Cal. Gov't Code § 6254.2(l).

Regardless of its trade secret status, the director may disclose the information "to any person in connection with a public proceeding conducted under law or regulation, if the director determines that the information is needed to determine whether a pesticide, or any ingredient of any pesticide, causes unreasonable adverse effects on health or the environment." Cal. Gov't Code § 6254.2(i). In other words, the evidentiary trade secret privilege is not absolute, and in some circumstances the equitable and public policy considerations will outweigh the privilege and require disclosure. If such information is disclosed, the director is required to provide the identity of the requester to the submitter. Cal. Gov't Code § 6254.2(j).

- **Exempted Provisions Are Merely Permissive, Not Mandatory.** California case law established that the exemptions identified within the statutory scheme are not absolute in their ability to prevent disclosure. *Black Panther Party v. Kehoe*, 42 Cal. App. 3d 645 (1974). The balancing test to be used has been codified in section 6255 of the California Government Code, which provides:

> The agency shall justify withholding any record by demonstrating that the record in question is exempt under express provisions of this chapter or that on the facts of the particular case the public interest served by not disclosing the record clearly outweighs the public interest served by disclosure of the record.

See San Gabriel Tribune v. Superior Court, 143 Cal. App. 3d 762, 776-77 (1983) (stating that the privilege that section 6254(k) incorporates is conditional and not absolute, and applied only on a clear showing that disclosure is against the public's interest). *See also Lorig v. Med. Bd.*, 78 Cal. App. 4th 462, 466-67 (2000) (holding that disclosure serves significant public interests); *Uribe v. Howie*, 19 Cal. App. 3d 194, 206-09 (1971) (stating that even if reports sought for disclosure contained trade secrets, the balancing of interests doctrine required disclosure in the public interest).

Section 6255 of the California Government Code serves as a residuary statutory exemption for balancing privacy interests with the public's interest in access. The same balancing test can also be used, therefore, to *withhold* a record from disclosure: the public's right to disclosure is also not absolute and the public interest served by not making a record public may be deemed to outweigh the public interest served by disclosure. *City of San Jose v. Super. Ct.*, 74 Cal. App. 4th 1008 (1999). Hence, while arguing against disclosure, it is to the advantage of the submitter to provide a convincing argument as to why the balancing test set forth in section 6255 of the California Government Code weighs in favor of withholding the records requested.

- **Requesting Party May Bring Action Under PRA to Require Disclosure.** If the government agency has agreed to withhold documents on the claim of privilege (under section 6254(k)), the requesting party may always choose to initiate proceedings in superior court under section 6258 of the California Government Code, which provides for injunctive relief, declaratory relief or writ of mandate to obtain disclosure of a public record or class of public records. Cal. Gov't Code § 6258. Upon the initiation of such a proceeding, it is the burden of "the agency to justify withholding the record on the basis of an express exemption or on a showing that public interest served in nondisclosure outweighs the public interest in disclosure." *San Gabriel Tribune*, 143 Cal. App. 3d at 780; *accord Black Panther Party*, 42 Cal. App. 3d at 657. If the government agency is unable to meet its burden of proof, the party that initiated the litigation seeking disclosure of the records will be able to recover its attorneys' fees and costs from the agency under section 6259 of the California Government Code. *Belth v. Garamendi*, 232 Cal. App. 3d 896, 899-900 (1991) (an award of costs and attorneys' fees pursuant to this provision is mandatory if the plaintiff prevails). Only if the plaintiff's case is *clearly frivolous* can the agency recover its own attorneys' fees and costs. Cal. Gov't Code § 6259(d). The agency is much more likely to agree to withhold records if the submitter has provided it with a strong argument in support of the application of the trade secret privilege, as well as a strong argument with regard to the balancing test—such arguments will go a long way in convincing the agency it will likely prevail if challenged in court and, as a result, will not be ordered to pay attorneys' fees incurred by the requesting party.

In keeping with the legislative objective of an expedited process, the PRA directs the trial court to reach a decision as soon as possible, Cal. Gov't Code § 6258, and appellate review is limited to a petition for extraordinary writ in order to provide expedited appellate review, Cal. Gov't Code § 6259(c). The California Supreme Court has since held that trial court orders directing or refusing disclosure of public records pursuant to the PRA are reviewable on their merits in the context of a petition for issuance of extraordinary writ of review, addressing the inapplicability of prior case authority which indicated that matters could only be reviewed to determine whether the trial court acted in excess of jurisdiction. *Times Mirror Co. v. Super. Ct.*, 53 Cal. 3d 1325, 1336 (1991).

3. Administrative Procedure Act (APA) Review—"Reverse FOIA"

If a federal agency has indicated that it intends to disclose information identified to be trade secret by the submitter of that information, review of that agency's decision can be sought by the submitter under the Administrative Procedure Act (APA), also known as a reverse FOIA action. 5 U.S.C. § 702 (2020). *See also Campaign for Family Farms v. Glickman*, 200 F.3d 1180, 1184 (8th Cir. 2000). This is the only legal avenue to prevent disclosure under FOIA, since the United States Supreme Court has ruled that there is no private right of action implied under the FOIA or the Trade Secrets Act. *Chrysler Corp. v. Brown*, 441 U.S. 281, 316-18 (1979). The APA provides that a reviewing court may overturn an agency action which is "arbitrary, capricious, an abuse of discretion, or otherwise not in accordance with law." 5 U.S.C. § 706(2)(A) (2020). The United States Supreme Court held that "any disclosure that violates § 1905 [of the Trade Secrets Act] is 'not in accordance with law.'" *Chrysler*, 441 U.S. at 318.

4. No California Direct Counterpart to Reverse FOIA Action

- **Submitter *May* Be Able to Proceed With Action for Injunctive or Declaratory Relief to Stop Disclosure.** A party's right to seek a judicial determination precluding a public agency from disclosing documents pursuant to the California PRA has not yet been specifically addressed by a California court. While a reverse FOIA under the APA can be used to preclude disclosure under FOIA there is no California counterpart to that statute.

While there is no direct authority that precludes a submitter from seeking injunctive relief against an agency in order to prevent disclosure of information claimed by the submitter to be exempt from disclosure under the PRA, several cases addressing PRA disclosure indicate that declaratory or injunctive relief by the submitter is a standard procedure sought to prevent disclosure by the agency to whom a PRA request has been made. *See, e.g.*, *Masonite Corp. v. Super. Ct.*, 25 Cal. App. 4th 1045 (1994) (explaining that declaratory relief or injunctive relief is specifically authorized under section 44346(c) of the California Health and Safety Code in action involving disclosure of information submitted to county Air Quality Management District in conjunction with reporting obligations under the Air Toxics "Hot Spots" Information and Assessment Act of 1987); *Lorig*, 78 Cal. App. 4th 462 (involving an action for injunctive and declaratory relief).

- **State Agency Cannot Initiate Action to Determine Its Obligations Under the PRA.** The California Supreme Court has addressed the issue of an agency's right to initiate a declaratory relief action under the PRA. *Filarsky v. Super. Ct.*, 28 Cal. 4th 419 (2002). The court concluded therein that

> [T]he Legislature set forth in Government Code sections 6258 and 6259 the exclusive procedure for litigating the issue of a public agency's obligation to disclose records to a member of the public . . . and these provisions do not authorize a public agency in possession of the records to seek a judicial determination regarding its duty of disclosure.

Id. at 423; *accord City of Santa Rosa v. Press Democrat*, 187 Cal. App. 3d 1315, 1323-24 (1986).

- **California Supreme Court's Reasoning for Denying Agency Right of Action May Apply to Preclude a Submitter's Right of Action.** With regard to a submitter's right to initiate an action, the California Supreme Court stated that it did not have the occasion in *Filarsky* "to determine whether a third party possesses the right to seek a judicial ruling precluding a public agency from disclosing documents pursuant to the CPRA." *Filarsky*, 28 Cal. 4th at 431. The court recognized that the reverse FOIA action available in a federal context is available because it is specifically authorized by the APA, 5 U.S.C. § 702 (2020), but there is no specific California counterpart to the APA. The court confirmed that the U.S. Supreme Court has specifically found that the FOIA itself does not provide a cause of action to prohibit disclosure—only an action to compel disclosure similar to that provided by the PRA. *Filarsky*, 28 Cal. 4th at 431.

Part of the reasoning in the *Filarsky* case prohibiting an agency from initiating an action to determine its rights and obligations of disclosure under the PRA applies equally to the situation where a submitter would initiate an action to prohibit disclosure of its information by a public agency—the statutory scheme only provides for the requester to initiate an action under the PRA. Cal. Gov't Code § 6258; *Filarsky*, 28 Cal. 4th at 426 ("The plain language of this provision contemplates a declaratory relief proceeding commenced only by an individual or entity seeking disclosure of public records . . . ."). Furthermore, the fact that a submitter could initiate a declaratory relief action under section 1060 of the California Code of Civil Procedure would cause a similar delay in the disclosure period that would be caused by an agency-initiated action that the Act is designed to prevent. Included in that additional delay not contemplated by the PRA is the possibility of the right to an appeal after a declaratory relief action is heard, which is not otherwise available under the PRA.

- **Due Process and Takings Clause May Ultimately Prevail to Allow a Submitter's Action to Preclude Disclosure.** The *Filarsky* court was not provided with the opportunity to weigh the interests of the submitter and the property rights associated with trade secrets that would be lost due to improper disclosure—an interest that a public agency does not have in the outcome of a PRA disclosure. It is uncertain how the California Supreme Court would adjust its reasoning given this other factor implicating due process and property rights. *See Ruckelshaus v. Monsanto Co.*, 467 U.S. 986 (1984) (involving a submitter who sought injunctive and declaratory relief to prohibit disclosure on the basis that provisions of law effected a "taking" in violation of the Fifth Amendment). There is no evidence that the California Legislature, in drafting the PRA, intended that a submitter *not* be given the opportunity to protect its trade secrets from inadvertent disclosure by a public agency. In fact, that portion of the PRA exempting trade secrets from disclosure suggests that the California Legislature intended for submitters to have the opportunity to protect against the loss of trade secret protection.

5. Motion for Protective Order and Motion to Quash

- **Standard Discovery Motions Are Available If the Subpoena Process Is Used Rather Than a PRA Request.** If the request for disclosure is made in the form of a subpoena to the government agency in the course of litigation, the party whose records are sought by the subpoena may pursue a motion for protective order to limit or prohibit disclosure of information ordinarily prohibited by discovery statutes. *See* Chapter 10. Alternatively, a motion to quash may be used against the subpoena. The evidentiary privilege under section 1060 of the California Evidence Code (*see* Chapter 16) should be raised as a basis for either precluding disclosure altogether or for articulating a protective order that prevents use and disclosure of the trade secret information outside of the scope of the litigation.

- **Submitter May Attempt to Persuade the Agency to Withhold Information As If Subpoena Were a PRA Request.** If the submitter is seeking to have all such information withheld from the requesting party, the submitter may attempt to treat the subpoena as it would a FOIA or PRA request and assert the exemption for privileged trade secret information in a request to the agency that it not produce the information. However, it is not certain whether the agency will treat the subpoena as it would a PRA request. It is the author's experience that this is highly dependent on the agency—whereas the United States Department of Agriculture (USDA) has treated a subpoena as a FOIA request, the California Department of Food and Agriculture has refused to treat a subpoena as a PRA request. The result was that the federal agency agreed not to disclose trade secret and confidential information responsive to the subpoena insofar as FOIA prohibits such disclosure, while the California agency produced such information over the objections of the submitter. There is no uniform policy applied by the different agencies, leaving the issue of disclosure highly dependent upon the individuals in the agency to whom one is required to raise such concerns.

- **Submitter May Argue That Compliance With Section 2019.210 of the California Code of Civil Procedure Is Required Prior to Disclosure.** If the underlying case involves a question of trade secret misappropriation, and the subpoena seeks the trade secrets of the defendant that have been confidentially submitted to a government agency, the defendant may attempt to argue in a motion to quash or motion for protective order that the provisions of section 2019.210 of the California Code of Civil Procedure must first be complied with before any such disclosure is appropriate. Section 2019.210 of the California Code of Civil Procedure requires that the plaintiff in a trade secret misappropriation action identify, with sufficient particularity, the trade secrets that have allegedly been stolen by the defendant before discovery can proceed. *See* Chapters 10 and 11 for a discussion of this requirement. One may attempt to invoke this precondition to discovery when communicating with the public agency, relying upon the provisions of the FOIA and the PRA that prohibit disclosure of information which is otherwise prohibited by law. 5 U.S.C. § 552(b)(3) (2009); Cal. Gov't Code § 6254(k).

§ 19.04 Remedies for Improper Disclosure

A. Action for Injunction to Prevent Further Disclosures/Use and Damages Against Recipient

Once the government agency has released information under either the FOIA or the PRA, it may be possible to limit the damage incurred by seeking injunctive relief to prevent the requesting party from using the information for improper purposes or further disclosing the information in a way that would cause additional damage to the submitter. Even if the information was disclosed mistakenly by a government agency, the recipient of the information received by accident does not evade liability if the recipient was aware that the disclosure was a mistake. *See Williams v. Curtiss-Wright Corp.*, 681 F.2d 161, 164 (3d Cir. 1982).

B. Action for Damages Against the Government

1. Claim for Compensation Under the Tucker Act, 28 U.S.C. § 1491 (2009), or Fifth Amendment

Claims for compensation arising out of improper disclosure of trade secret information exempt from disclosure under the FOIA or the PRA may be made under the Tucker Act (for breach of an implied or express contract of confidentiality), or under the Fifth Amendment to the United States Constitution (based upon a theory of a taking without compensation). *See, e.g.*, *Ruckelshaus v. Monsanto Co.*, 467 U.S. 986, 1010-12 (1984); *Lariscey v. United States*, 949 F.2d 1137, 1142 (Fed. Cir. 1991), *vacated*, 962 F.2d 1047 (Fed Cir. 1992), *aff'd en banc*, 981 F.2d 1244 (Fed. Cir 1992) (holding that in a claim against government for uncompensated use, a prisoner has a property right in an invention made in prison); *Syngenta Crop Prot., Inc. v. Helliker*, 138 Cal. App. 4th 1135, 1167 (2006), *review denied* (the takings clauses of the U.S. and California Constitutions "protect not only tangible property, but also intangible trade secret property rights protected by state law").

Therefore, if the owner submits its trade secret information to a government agency with a "reasonable investment-backed expectation" that it will be protected from disclosure or use, the government may only disclose the information if it compensates the owner. *Ruckelshaus*, 467 U.S. at 1010-12; *Syngenta*, 138 Cal. App. 4th at 1170-71 (submitter of data with Dept. of Pesticide Regulation did not prove a basis for "reasonable investment-backed expectation of confidentiality," such that no support could be found for a taking claim under either the Fifth Amendment or the California Constitution).

2. No State Immunity for Deliberate Disclosure to Competitor or for Statutorily Required Disclosure

There is no state immunity for deliberate disclosure of trade secrets to a competitor because the conduct is deemed "operational" (*i.e.*, not inherent in policy or planning, but more like an implementation) rather than "discretionary" (involving fundamental policy decisions). *Discovery Experimental & Dev., Inc. v. State Dep't of Health & Rehabilitative Servs.*, 735 So.2d 516, 518 (Fla. App. 1999). Where a state statute forces revelation of trade secrets as a condition of permitting the sale of a product (for example, licensing), the takings clause of the Fifth Amendment is triggered.

Philip Morris, Inc. v. Harshbarger, 159 F.3d 670 (1st Cir. 1998) (affirming preliminary injunction against Massachusetts statute requiring cigarette manufacturers to disclose additives). In *Syngenta*, the Department of Pesticide Regulation provided data to another applicant without that owner's consent. The court found that such conduct by the agency could constitute misappropriation under the Uniform Trade Secrets Act if the data qualified as a trade secret and the department personnel knew or had reason to know that it obtained the data under circumstances giving rise to a duty to limit its use of the data. *Syngenta*, 138 Cal. App. 4th at 1172-73.

Chapter 20
LICENSING OF TRADE SECRETS AND KNOW-HOW

By: Kevin D. DeBré, Esq.

---

§ 20.01 Introduction

Owners of trade secrets often need to share them with others. For example, they may have a reason to disclose trade secret manufacturing techniques, pharmaceutical formulations and computer source code to independent contractors, suppliers, customers, business partners, potential investors and their own employees. Many times, these relationships are governed by a written agreement— but not always.

This chapter explains why parties may enter into trade secret licenses and what they may seek to accomplish by doing so. The second and third sections describe reasons for memorializing trade secret licenses in writing and some scenarios in which trade secret licenses are granted. The fourth and fifth sections describe provisions that typically are included in trade secret licenses. The last section discusses other considerations when drafting trade secret licenses.

§ 20.02 Reasons for Entering into a Trade Secret License

A trade secret license helps to preserve the protection of trade secrets that the owner discloses to a third party. To preserve their rights in trade secrets, owners must use reasonable efforts to maintain the secrecy of their trade secrets. *See supra* Chapter 1. A written license agreement that requires the recipient of a trade secret to keep it in confidence evidences the owner's reasonable efforts to maintain secrecy. Requiring recipients of a trade secret to sign a confidentiality agreement in advance of their access to the trade secret reinforces the secret nature of the disclosed information. *Fabkom, Inc. v. R.W. Smith & Assocs.*, No. 95 Civ. 4552 (MBM), 1996 U.S. Dist. LEXIS 13686, at *20 (S.D.N.Y Sept. 18, 1996). License agreements often are used to protect trade secrets contained within software code. Software license agreements usually contain provisions requiring the licensee to keep the licensed software in confidence. By requiring customers to enter into a license agreement imposing confidentiality requirements, a trade secret owner arguably demonstrates reasonable efforts to protect trade secrets contained within the code of the licensed software program and embodied within the program's sequence, structure and organization. *Compuware Corp. v. Serena Software Int'l, Inc.*, 77 F. Supp. 2d 816, 822 (E.D. Mich. 1999). Trade secret protection may be lost by providing trade secrets to a third party without a confidentiality agreement. *See Gemisys Corp. v. Phoenix Am., Inc.*, 186 F.R.D. 551, 562 (N.D. Cal. Mar. 18, 1999).

A trade secret license agreement may also help establish the recipient's duty of confidentiality or the existence of a confidential or fiduciary relationship between the trade secret owner and the recipient. Evidencing such a duty or relationship is particularly important for protecting trade secrets where an implied duty of confidentiality, such as an employee's duty to maintain the confidentiality of his employer's information, does not exist.

In addition, a trade secret license can reduce the risk of a dispute occurring over the use of a trade secret within a business relationship. By identifying the trade secrets disclosed by each party and the parties' respective duties of confidentiality, a trade secret license helps to minimize the risk of a party's inadvertent misuse or disclosure of the other party's trade secret.

§ 20.03 Types of Trade Secret License Agreements

Trade secret licenses arise in a wide variety of circumstances and are embodied in many different types of agreements. A few examples are:

- **Secrecy Agreements.** Potential licensees often require access to the trade secrets before signing an agreement to license them. Providing preliminary access for a limited period of time enables the recipient to evaluate the secret and its commercial value in order to determine whether to license it and how much to pay for the license. A secrecy agreement aims to prevent a loss of trade secret rights from this disclosure by establishing a contractual relationship between the trade secret owner and the potential licensee and imposing restrictions on use of the disclosed information.

- **License Agreements.** The license may: (i) provide only the right to use specific information (*e.g.*, a formula for a new beverage), (ii) permit access to broad categories of information, or (iii) grant rights, under a patent if and when it issues, in inventions claimed in a pending patent application. A "hybrid license" includes trade secrets and other forms of intellectual property (*e.g.*, a patent license to make and sell a medical device manufactured using the licensor's trade secrets; a trademark license to market a new type of integrated circuit developed with the licensor's trade secrets).

- **Evaluation/Beta Test Agreements.** The trade secret owner may permit another party access to pre-release versions or prototypes of products and related information for purposes of testing or evaluation. The licensee is required to keep the products and information secret and may be required to provide the licensor with information about the product's performance, which information the licensee also must keep confidential.

- **Nondisclosure Agreements.** *See supra* Chapter 4. These agreements are used in a variety of circumstances to create a confidential relationship in which trade secrets are disclosed or exchanged. This may include disclosures or exchanges of information with vendors, independent contractors or potential business partners, such as customers, investors and purchasers. Similar to a secrecy agreement, a nondisclosure agreement protects the confidentiality of the disclosed information and limits the recipient's use of the information and its disclosure to others. Protections and obligations may be bilateral, if information will be exchanged by both parties, or unilateral if only one party will disclose information to the other.

- **Technology/Research Collaboration Agreements.** These agreements memorialize the roles and responsibilities of parties in performing research or development activities and their rights and obligations with respect to trade secrets that are disclosed, exchanged or developed in the course of these relationships. One type of agreement is a "Material Transfer Agreement" in which biological materials, such as cell lines, are provided by one party to the other for research or scientific purposes. The characteristics, protocols and instructions relating to these materials may be trade secrets and the recipient will be required to maintain them in confidence. Another type of agreement is a "Research and Development Agreement" in which information, data, or both, are transferred to enable the recipient to perform specific research activities.

- **Services Agreements.** A party may contract for the storage or processing of its data, which may include trade secrets. These "Cloud Services" or "Software as a Service" (SaaS) agreements typically include a license permitting the service provider to use the customer's data to perform the contracted services and obligations requiring the service provider to maintain the confidentiality and ensure the security of this data. The agreement may provide for the licensor's ownership of data that is generated in the course of the service provider's performance of the services. In turn, the service provider may want the right to analyze the generated data to identify areas of its platform, through which the services are delivered, that may be improved.

- **Implied-In-Fact Licenses.** *See infra* Chapter 25. Occasionally, a trade secret owner discloses confidential information in the absence of a written contract. A contract restricting the recipient's use of the information may be implied from the circumstances in which the information was disclosed. For example, an idea disclosed to another party may be protected against misappropriation by contract and trade secret laws, particularly if the recipient knew or reasonably should have understood that the idea was disclosed in confidence with the intention that the recipient would pay for its use. *Phillips v. Frey*, 20 F.3d 623, 630–32 (5th Cir. 1994); *Pachmayr Gun Works, Inc. v. Olin Mathieson Chem. Corp.*, 502 F.2d 802, 807-08 (9th Cir. 1974), *superseded by statute on other grounds*, Act of Jan. 2, 1975, Pub. L. No. 93-600, § 3, 88 Stat. 1955, *as recognized in Transgo, Inc. v. AJAC Transmission Parts Corp.*, 768 F.2d 1001 (9th Cir. 1985). Another instance in which an implied license may be formed is when an independent contractor develops software for a client and delivers the program without a written license agreement. Ordinarily, a software developer, as the owner of trade secrets contained in computer code he develops, may assert his trade secret rights to prevent others from accessing and using the code. If, however, a developer delivers software to a client without an express intent to retain control over the program's use, the developer may be deemed to have granted the client an unlimited license to use and modify the software, including the trade secrets embodied within the code. *Asset Mktg. Sys., Inc. v Gagnon*, 542 F.3d 748, 758 (9th Cir. 2008).

If, prior to engaging in discussions about a potential business relationship, parties want to ensure that any trade secrets they receive from the other party will not taint their own trade secrets, they may elect to enter into a non-confidential evaluation agreement in an effort to prevent the assertion of misappropriation claims against them. In contrast to a trade secret license or a nondisclosure agreement, a non-confidential evaluation agreement confirms that neither party is responsible for maintaining the confidentiality of any information disclosed by the other party. If the parties later need to exchange confidential information, they may enter into a trade secret license superseding the non-confidential evaluation agreement.

§ 20.04 Fundamental Trade Secret Licensing Terms

Although the circumstances in which trade secrets are licensed vary, giving rise to many different forms of license agreements, these agreements have many terms in common.

A. Licensed Subject Matter

Ordinarily, every trade secret license should include a description of what is being licensed. The definition of the licensed subject matter defines the scope of the licensee's confidentiality obligations and use and disclosure rights.

1. Scope of Licensed Subject Matter

a. Trade Secrets

Licensed subject matter may be confined to trade secrets or may include information that is not protected as a trade secret. Thus, the licensed subject matter should not carelessly be defined as being a "trade secret" when the licensor intends the license to cover non-trade secret information as well since otherwise only information that qualifies as a trade secret under the law governing the agreement will fall within the scope of the license.

In jurisdictions that have adopted the Uniform Trade Secrets Act, such as California, information is a trade secret if it derives independent economic value from not being generally known and is subject to efforts that are reasonable under the circumstances to maintain its secrecy. Cal. Civ. Code § 3426.1(d); *see supra* Chapter 1. In states that have not adopted the Uniform Trade Secrets Act, a trade secret is generally understood to comprise information which is used in the owner's business and provides an advantage over competitors who do not know or use it. Restatement (First) of Torts § 757 cmt. (b) (1939). On occasion, courts look to whether information is "sufficiently valuable and secret to afford an actual or potential economic advantage over others" to determine whether it is a trade secret. Restatement (Third) of Unfair Competition § 39 (1995).

b. Know-How

Licenses may cover information that falls short of satisfying the criteria for a trade secret. One example of such information is "know-how," which may or may not constitute trade secret information. Know-how is information that "enables one to accomplish a particular task or to operate a particular device or process." J. Thomas McCarthy et al., McCarthy's Desk Encyclopedia of Intellectual Property 330 (3d ed. 2004). "[T]he concept of 'know how' is . . . a very fuzzily defined area. . . . It covers a multitude of matters, however, which in the broad sense are not protectable." *Id.* at 237 (quoting *Van Prods. Co. v. Gen. Welding & Fabricating Co.*, 213 A.2d 769, 777 (Pa. 1965)). Know-how may include the licensor's knowledge and skill acquired in developing and using a trade secret and such information may facilitate a licensee's use of the trade secret. "Show-how" is a subset of know-how, which may include technical assistance, training, instruction or consulting to assist a licensee's use of licensed trade secrets.

c. Confidential or Proprietary Information

A license may also cover information that is characterized as "confidential" or "proprietary." Although this information may not qualify as a trade secret under the law governing the license agreement, it may nevertheless have value to the licensee and the licensor may desire to restrict its use. "Confidential" information is information that the licensor has maintained in secrecy, but may or may not satisfy other requirements of trade secret protection. "Proprietary" information is information in which the licensor claims an ownership interest, but may or may not qualify as a trade secret. A license may include the following confidential or proprietary information which may or may not qualify as trade secret under applicable law:

- Pre-release products and prototypes;
- Specifications;
- Products subject to restrictions on reverse engineering and/or disassembly;
- Software algorithms, source code and documentation;
- Product designs, blueprints, drawings and plans;
- Invention disclosures and unpublished patent applications;
- Business information;
- Financial, technical, scientific or research data;
- Business, marketing or product development plans and strategies;
- Business methods and production processes;
- Customer requirements;
- Website or search engine usage data;
- Customer data, including personally identifiable information;
- Identities of vendors and suppliers;
- Pricing and cost data;
- Terms of third party agreements;
- Test plans and testing results;
- Bills of materials;
- Manufacturing and assembly documentation;
- Chemical formulas and recipes; and
- Cell lines and biological materials and substances.

In addition, confidential information may include information relating to the discussions between a prospective licensor and prospective licensee, information relating to the existence and terms of a license agreement the parties enter into and information that the licensee derives from the licensor's confidential information provided in connection with the license agreement.

d. Third Party Licensed Information

Licensed subject matter may include information that the licensor has obtained from third parties under a duty of confidentiality. A licensee receiving such third party information may want to ensure that the licensor has the right to disclose it and sublicense its use to the licensee. Likewise, a licensor providing a third party's trade secrets to a licensee will want to impose on the licensee the same restrictions n use and further disclosure of these trade secrets as imposed on the licensor.

2. Identification of Licensed Subject Matter

The license agreement should effectively identify the trade secrets and any additional proprietary or confidential information (for simplicity, throughout this chapter, such trade secrets and additional proprietary or confidential information are referred to as proprietary information) that the licensor wishes to protect and that the licensee wishes to use. A licensor ordinarily needs to know what proprietary information it has licensed in order to enforce its rights under the agreement. In taking action for misappropriation of trade secrets against a licensee that has violated a license, the licensor generally will need to accurately and adequately describe the trade secrets provided to the licensee. *See Vital State Canada, Ltd. v. DreamPak, LLC*, 303 F. Supp. 2d 516, 523–25 (D.N.J. 2003) (plaintiff failed to show likelihood of success of misappropriation claim by failing to allege details of the misappropriated trade secrets). This usually requires licensors to maintain an accurate inventory of their trade secrets. Maintaining current records of trade secret inventories can be particularly challenging for trade secret owners that continuously innovate. They may wish to perform periodic audits to ensure their license agreements contain accurate descriptions of, and adequately cover, all of the proprietary information provided to licensees.

Licensees have a similar need for clarity concerning the proprietary information they receive from licensors. They need to know what they are licensing in order to avoid confusion as to whether their use of proprietary information is authorized and to isolate licensed information from their own trade secrets to avoid inadvertently tainting future innovations. With a clear understanding of its rights in proprietary information, a licensee can ensure that its use is within the scope of the license and avoid liability for trade secret misappropriation and breach of the license agreement.

To improve clarity as to the scope of a trade secret license, the licensed subject matter may be defined in terms of specific proprietary information that the licensor transfers to the licensee. Yet, it may not always be possible to identify all proprietary information within the scope of the license. As such, the parties may opt to define the licensed subject matter as encompassing a general category or several categories of information.

Sample Clause: "Proprietary Information" means all confidential or proprietary information, whether in written, verbal, graphic, electronic or other form, that becomes known by, or was transmitted or otherwise disclosed directly or indirectly by either party to the other party including, without limitation, business, financial and marketing plans, forecasts, strategies, projections and analyses, data and information that reveals trade secrets, ideas, works of authorship, formulas, designs, methodologies, technology and product roadmaps, present and future product plans, know-how, techniques, data, processes, software source code, algorithms, documentation, architecture, structure and protocols, inventions (whether patentable or not), patent applications, information on strategic partnerships and alliances, supplier and customer relationships, and other technical and business information and other information, which the disclosing party received in confidence from any other person or entity.

The business relationship in which trade secrets are licensed may contemplate the transfer of information to the licensee within either a "closed universe" or an "open universe." A "closed universe" involves a one-time disclosure or periodic disclosures of specific information (*e.g.*, software license or biological material transfer). An "open universe" involves an ongoing exchange of information to fulfill a specified purpose (*e.g.*, joint development or research collaboration activities or discussions relating to a business relationship). As multiple disclosures of proprietary information may occur during the term of a multi-year agreement, the parties should periodically update the description of the proprietary information contained in the license agreement to help ensure the license and the agreement's confidentiality protections cover the disclosed information.

Where trade secrets are disclosed in the form of tangible objects, such as product samples, the licensor will want to include such items within the license agreement's definition of "Proprietary Information."

Sample Clause: All Product Samples disclosed, delivered or made available to Licensee shall be deemed Proprietary Information. As used in this Agreement, "Product Samples" means all goods or products, which incorporate any proprietary information, design, technology, know-how or intellectual property owned or licensed by Licensor, which is generally not known by the public.

Proprietary information may not always be in tangible form and, instead, may be delivered to the licensee orally, electronically or visually. Creating a record of transferred proprietary information can help avoid disputes concerning the licensee's use of this information. In the event of a claim of the licensee's unauthorized use of proprietary information, a record of transferred information could help prove that the licensor was the source of the information at issue or could support a defense that the information was not transferred to the licensee. To provide further clarity as to whether proprietary information is received from a licensor and whether it is subject to a license agreement's restrictions, the licensee may require the licensor to label or otherwise identify each piece of proprietary information the licensor discloses to the licensee.

Sample Clause: "Proprietary Information" means all information disclosed by either party to the other party that is, if disclosed in writing, labeled as "proprietary" or "confidential" or, if disclosed orally, graphically, electronically or visually, is identified as proprietary or confidential at the time of disclosure and is so confirmed in writing within thirty (30) days after the initial disclosure.

The licensor, however, will not want to risk losing protection of proprietary information if it fails to label information before disclosing it to the licensee. In such event, the parties may agree that information will be deemed to be within the license restrictions on use and disclosure if it would be reasonable to assume the information is confidential or proprietary.

Sample Clause: Information shall be deemed to be Proprietary Information if, in the absence of being marked "Proprietary" or with a similar legend, the receiving party should reasonably discern, by objective examination of the disclosure and the surrounding facts and circumstances, the information to be proprietary or confidential in nature.

Trade secret protection can be lost by a licensor failing to comply with a license agreement's requirement to mark as confidential all trade secrets disclosed to the licensee. *Convolve, Inc. v. Compaq Computer Corp.*, 527 Fed. App'x 910, 924, 925 (Fed. Cir. 2013). However, in the absence of a marking requirement, a court may find a trade secret owner's procedures restricting access to sensitive information sufficient to support an inference that the owner took reasonable precautions to protect its trade secrets. See *PQ Labs, Inc. v Qi*, No. 12-0450 CW), 2014 U.S. Dist. LEXIS 11769 (N.D. Cal. Jan. 29, 2014).

B. Identities of the Parties

A license should specifically identify the licensor and the licensee. If the licensed subject matter is owned or in the possession of one or more affiliated companies, the license agreement should define the "licensor" in a manner that includes these companies. A licensee that employs one or more affiliated companies in its operations may need to include these companies under the license if they are responsible for fulfilling the purpose of the agreement. For example, a manufacturer of consumer electronics products may need to share licensed proprietary information with its subsidiaries that need this information to manufacture components and assemble and distribute the products. This may be accomplished by allowing the licensee to sublicense the licensed information to affiliates for specified purposes. Because the licensor does not have privity of contract with the sub-licensees, the licensor may wish to impose conditions upon the licensee for granting sublicenses.

Sample Clause: The sublicense granted to Licensee's subsidiaries shall be subject to the following conditions: (i) Licensee's guarantee of the full compliance of such subsidiaries with all of the restrictions and limitations on the use and disclosure of Proprietary Information set forth herein, (ii) Licensee's agreement that it shall be liable to Licensor for any and all violations by a subsidiary of such restrictions and limitations on the use and disclosure of Proprietary Information and to indemnify Licensor for all damages, liabilities, losses, cost and expenses suffered by Licensor as a result of any such violation by a subsidiary, and (iii) Licensor being made a third party beneficiary of each such sublicense granted by Licensee.

§ 20.05 Trade Secret License Terms and Conditions

This section describes terms and conditions typically found in trade secret license agreements.

A. Recitals

Recitals describe the context and background of an agreement and may evidence the parties' intentions in entering into a trade secret license. If the licensee will receive information that does not qualify as a trade secret, the licensor may want the licensee to acknowledge in the recitals the proprietary nature of this information. Conversely, a licensee may seek to confirm in the recitals that the licensor has taken adequate measures to protect licensed information as a trade secret. In addition, recitals may include a description of the purpose for which licensed information will be used.

Generally, recitals do not create binding obligations. *See Multimedia Games, Inc. v. Network Gaming Int'l Corp.*, No. 98-CV-67-H(M), 1999 U.S. Dist. LEXIS 23369, *15 (N.D. Okla. Sept. 3, 1999). But, recitals are important as they are conclusively presumed to be true as between the parties. Cal. Evid. Code § 622.

B. License Grant

The licensee's right to use licensed proprietary information is usually conditioned upon the licensee's compliance with the license agreement's terms and conditions. If the licensee breaches the agreement, the licensor may bring an action for misappropriation of trade secrets and for breach of contract. *See infra* § 20.05.I.2. The licensor also may have a contractual right to terminate the license.

1. Exclusivity

Unless the licensor reserves rights in licensed proprietary information, granting an exclusive license will preclude the licensor from using the proprietary information and granting additional licenses. An exclusive license granting all substantial rights in a trade secret may constitute a constructive assignment of the licensor's ownership. *Black Clawson Co. v. Kroenert Corp.*, 245 F.3d 759, 765 (8th Cir. 2001). In contrast, a nonexclusive license does not convey all substantial rights and is essentially a covenant by the licensor not to sue the licensee for trade secret misappropriation.

If an exclusive licensee fails to fully exploit licensed proprietary information or use it at all, the licensor may (depending on how the licensor expects to profit from the license) run the risk of being deprived of the full value of its proprietary information. Imposing minimum performance requirements (*e.g.*, achievement of a minimum volume of annual sales of licensed products or payment of a minimum amount of annual royalties) can help ensure a licensee's diligence in commercializing licensed proprietary information and, in turn, increase the licensor's chances of being paid a royalty in the future. A licensee's failure to fulfill the minimum performance requirements may entitle the licensor to terminate the licensee's exclusivity or the entire license.

Sample Clause: In the event Licensee fails to pay Licensor the applicable Minimum Royalty, then, as Licensor's sole remedy, Licensor may elect to terminate Licensee's exclusivity hereunder upon ninety (90) days' prior written notice such that Licensee's rights thereafter shall be nonexclusive.

A licensor may wish to reserve rights under an exclusive license to use and/or disclose licensed proprietary information for a specified purpose, such as its own ongoing research and development activities. Additionally, a licensor may wish to make clear that its grant of an exclusive license does not preclude the licensor's continued use of residuals—information relating to the licensed trade secret that is retained in the memories and mental impressions of the licensor's employees.

2. License Scope

In addition to the right to use the licensed trade secret, licensed rights may include the right to make, have made, use, distribute and sell products made from the licensee's use of licensed proprietary information or products embodying or incorporating the proprietary information. The license may also include the right to disclose the trade secret to others in order to fulfill a specified purpose.

A licensee may need to grant sublicenses to third parties, such as independent contractors, vendors and suppliers, to use licensed proprietary information. The licensor may wish to condition such sublicenses upon its prior written approval and limit the licensee's right to sublicense to only certain types of information or for only certain types of activities or uses.

Sample Clause: Licensee shall not divulge, transfer or sublicense any Proprietary Information or any rights therein, in whole or part, to any third party, except to the extent necessary for third party service providers to perform hosting, back-up and recovery services for Licensee, provided that each such service provider is approved in advance by Licensor and has executed written confidentiality agreement to safeguard the Proprietary Information.

If the licensee is permitted to disclose licensed information to third parties, those third parties should be in privity with the licensor, such as by signing a nondisclosure agreement with the licensor. The license agreement might also require the licensee to indemnify the licensor for any misappropriation committed by a third party to whom the licensee provides licensed information.

The license may limit the licensee's use of the licensed subject matter within a specified territory or a specified application or field of use, or both.

Sample Clause: Subject to all of the terms and conditions of this Agreement, Licensor grants Licensee an exclusive license to install, use, display and perform the Proprietary Information and to integrate the Proprietary Information with Licensee's Technology, all within the Territory and the field of use of Licensee's business.

If the licensee is engaged in developing products or technology that may be competitive with the licensor's products or technology, the licensee will want to make clear that such development efforts do not violate the license. Further, the licensee may wish to be able to refuse receiving proprietary information from the licensor that the licensee believes is similar or equivalent to information it has developed on its own.

Sample Clause: Licensor acknowledges that Licensee is currently developing, internally and/or in conjunction with third parties, products that are similar to or competitive with Licensor's products and that Licensee may develop, now or in the future, information or materials or receive information or materials from third parties that may be similar to the Proprietary Information which Licensor may provide. Nothing in this Agreement will be construed as a representation that Licensee will not develop, communicate, or use technology, information, or products that, without violation of this Agreement, compete with or are the same or similar to the technology, information, or products contemplated by the Proprietary Information. Subject only to compliance with the non-disclosure obligations set forth in this Agreement, nothing in this

Agreement nor in connection with any discussions of the parties or any disclosure of Proprietary Information will in any way be construed as a limitation upon any right or ability of Licensee or any of its employees or agents to continue to pursue such development efforts without obligation or liability to Licensor. Licensee shall have the right to refuse to accept any Proprietary Information prior to its disclosure and, upon Licensor's receipt of such notification, Licensee shall have no obligation hereunder with respect to any such Proprietary Information disclosed by Licensor despite Licensee's refusal.

3. License Restrictions

Trade secret licenses, whether exclusive or nonexclusive or limited to a specified territory or field of use, ordinarily include restrictions on the licensee's ability to disclose and use licensed proprietary information.

Sample Clause: The Proprietary Information provided to Licensee by Licensor is provided solely for use in the Research Program and will not be used for any commercial purpose and not for the benefit of any third party. The Proprietary Information may only be possessed or used by employees of the Licensee who are under the control of the Investigator and bound to the terms of this Agreement, and may not be provided to any other individual, entity or institution, including institutions and entities affiliated or under contract with the Recipient without the prior written consent of Licensor.

Restrictions on a licensee's disclosure of a licensed proprietary information typically do not prohibit disclosure to individuals related to the licensee's fulfillment of the purpose of the license or others who are subject to confidentiality obligations, such as:

- Employees, consultants and independent contractors with a "need to know" licensed information in order to fulfill the purpose for which the information was disclosed. Typically, a licensor will require the licensee to ensure that these individuals have entered into written confidentiality agreements before receiving licensed information and to instruct such individuals to keep licensed information in strict confidence and not disclose it to any third parties. Further, the licensee should be required to immediately disable a terminated employee's access to licensed information.

- The licensee's financial, legal and tax advisors.

- Prospective investors, underwriters, lenders and acquirers of the licensee's stock, business or assets that require access to licensed information to perform due diligence for a specific transaction. A licensor may require these third parties and the licensee to enter into a form of confidentiality agreement that the licensor has approved protecting licensed information.

If licensed information includes personally identifiable information (PII), the licensee may be required to comply with the terms of the licensor's privacy policy. A privacy policy describes the licensor's own restrictions on use and disclosure of information it collects from customers, website visitors, and users of the licensor's mobile software applications. If the licensee fails to comply with the licensor's privacy policy, the licensor may be subject to criminal and civil claims and the licensee may be required to indemnify the licensor for liabilities, losses and damages it suffers.

A licensee that receives sensitive data under a trade secret license may be required to adhere to minimum data security requirements for storing the data. If the data is PII protected by statute or regulation, such as financial information or health information, the licensor may require the licensee to adhere to legal requirements for ensuring the security of this data. *See, e.g.*, Gramm-Leach-Bliley Act, 15 U.S.C. § 6801(b) (2012); Health Insurance Portability and Protection Act of 1996, 42 U.S.C. § 1320d-2 (2012).

Sample Clause: Licensee shall comply with all applicable laws, regulations and ordinances relating to the use of the Proprietary Information and shall establish and maintain administrative, technical and physical safeguards to protect the security, integrity and confidentiality of the Proprietary Information, including protection against contemplated threats or hazards and against any unauthorized or unlawful access to this data.

The licensor may wish to reserve a right to conduct periodic audits of the licensee's data use and security practices to ensure compliance with PII protections and data security requirements. Further, the licensee may be required to perform vulnerability threat assessments of its own Internet operations in which licensed PII is used and to report the results of such tests to the licensor.

Generally, restrictions on a licensee's use of licensed proprietary information limit the license to a specified purpose (*e.g.*, internal use of confidential information by the licensee to evaluate a proposed business relationship with the licensor). However, occasionally license restrictions are employed more broadly to attempt to prevent a licensee from using licensed information to develop competing products.

Sample Clause: Neither party shall make, have made or sell any product or other item using or incorporating any of the other party's Proprietary Information or any derivative works of the other party's Proprietary Information.

A licensee that is subject to such restrictions may want to ensure that its receipt of licensed proprietary information does not taint the licensee's own proprietary information and its ability to use such proprietary information in the future. Further, because a licensee's personnel cannot be forced to forget information to which they have had access, the licensee may wish to exclude from restrictions on its use of licensed proprietary information "residual" knowledge, general knowledge or experience acquired by the licensee's personnel during the course of the project for which licensed information was provided.

Sample Clause: Each party will be free to use for any purpose the Residuals resulting from access to or work with the other party's Proprietary Information, provided that such party shall maintain the confidentiality of the Proprietary Information as provided herein. Neither party shall have any obligation to limit or restrict the assignment of personnel who have had authorized access to the Proprietary Information or to make any payments to the other party for any use of Residuals. The term "Residuals" means generalized knowledge, skill, expertise, know-how or techniques contained in or embodied by the Proprietary Information, which is retained in the memories of personnel (without the aid of notes or other memory aids and without any conscious attempt to memorize for purposes other than those specified herein) by personnel who have had authorized access to the Proprietary Information.

If licensed proprietary information is embodied in software or other products, the licensor may wish to restrict the licensee from reverse engineering or undertaking other efforts to learn the techniques and processes used by the licensor in developing these products.

Sample Clause: Licensee shall not reverse assemble, reverse compile or reverse engineer any software or computer code that is part of the Proprietary Information, or otherwise attempt to derive or discover any source code or underlying trade secrets contained therein, except to the extent permitted by applicable law.

C. Technology and Knowledge Transfer

A licensor that grants a license to use a trade secret has an obligation to disclose the licensed trade secret to the licensee. *See Farnam Cos. v. Stabar Enters.*, No. CV 03-503-PHX-NVW, 2005 U.S. Dist. LEXIS 32509, *22 (D. Ariz. Dec. 12, 2005) (confidentiality agreement that does not include an express obligation of licensor to disclose trade secret does not reserve licensor's right to withhold disclosure). The license agreement may specify mechanisms or procedures for the licensor's delivery of licensed trade secrets to the licensee.

Sample Clause: Upon Licensor's completion of the Scope of Work, it shall present the research results to Licensee in a written report and via videoconference at a mutually agreed upon time, including a description of how the results were achieved and how Licensee can implement the solution developed by Licensor.

To facilitate its use of a trade secret, the licensee may need the licensor to furnish additional information and assistance. The licensee may require access to the licensor's personnel and records, such as technical data, specifications, designs, drawings, engineering information, process or production information, formulas, information on compositions of matter, techniques or methods, proprietary tools, testing methods and specific technology.

The transfer may involve a one-time disclosure and the licensor's performance of specified activities. Alternatively, the licensee may require the licensor to provide ongoing assistance and to transfer all information necessary or useful for the licensee to exploit licensed proprietary information.

Sample Clause: In order to facilitate the exercise of the rights granted hereunder, Licensor shall disclose to Licensee, to the extent reasonably practicable, within ninety (90) days following the Effective Date one copy of all existing documentation (including, without limitation, Licensor's ISO 9001 certification documentation) in Licensor's possession pertaining to Licensor's procedures for operating the equipment used to manufacture the Products and all existing documentation (including, without limitation, engineers' notes, schematics and diagrams) in Licensor's possession describing the trade secrets, manufacturing processes and procedures and know-how, existing on the Effective Date, in use at Licensor's facilities which are applied to the design and construction of tooling and operation of a manufacturing line for the production of the Products or to produce raw material for use in the production of the Products. Licensor covenants and agrees to disclose to Licensee all improvements of the Proprietary Information as soon as reasonably practicable after Licensor's development thereof.

An obligation to transfer technology should be clear as to whether the licensor is required to provide only developments and improvements that the licensor creates in the course of its business or to develop improvements of licensed proprietary information or new technology for the licensee. Any obligation to transfer technology or other materials to a licensee, however, should not require the licensor to disclose information that it is contractually or legally restricted from providing.

D. Ownership of Developments and Improvements

If proprietary information is licensed for use in connection with a research or development project, the parties likely will want to clarify their ownership rights in new information, trade secrets and improvements that result from this use. For example, if a licensor provides proprietary biological materials for use in a scientific research program, the parties will want to specify their respective rights to any research data, pre-clinical and clinical results, techniques, inventions, improvements, materials, discoveries, ideas, processes and know-how arising out of the licensee's use of the proprietary materials.

Absent a contract provision to the contrary (*e.g.*, an assignment of ownership rights in new developments and improvements), the licensee likely will own new trade secrets that it creates from using licensed proprietary information. The licensee, however, must continue to comply with the terms of the license pertaining to the licensor's proprietary information that is embodied within new materials that the licensee creates or that are needed in order for the licensee to exploit these new materials. In exchange for allowing a licensee to retain ownership of such new developments and improvements, the licensor may require a grant-back license of these items.

If proprietary information is licensed for the purpose of evaluating the commercial potential of the licensor's technology, the licensor will want to ensure that the licensee does not use licensed proprietary information to develop new technology that the licensee may wish to commercialize instead. The licensor may require the licensee to transfer its ownership of any new developments created using the licensor's proprietary information.

Sample Clause: Licensee shall not, without the prior written consent of Licensor, acquire, directly or indirectly, from the possession or use of the Proprietary Information any right, title or interest in inventions, improvements, original works of authorship or derivative works derived from or based upon the Proprietary Information ("Improvements"). Nor shall Licensee claim any legal right either by means of patent applications or otherwise with regard to any Improvements. In the event and to the extent Licensee acquires any rights in any Improvements, Licensee agrees to assign, and does hereby irrevocably assign, transfer and convey to Licensor, and its successors and assigns, at no expense, all of Licensee's right, title and interest in and to such Improvements and any and all intellectual property and proprietary rights therein for the maximum terms of protection available anywhere in the world. Licensee shall promptly notify Licensor of any Improvement discovered, conceived of, reduced to practice or developed by or on behalf of Licensee and provide Licensor with a detailed written description of the Improvements. Any and all such Improvements shall be deemed Proprietary Information.

In a services agreement where the customer grants a vendor a license to use data to perform services, the customer will want to secure its ownership of any new data that is generated from the vendor's use of the customer's data.

E. Confidentiality

A trade secret license will require the licensee to maintain the confidentiality of the licensed trade secret because the failure to do so could lead to the loss of trade secret protection. The same confidentiality obligation may be imposed on the licensor, particularly in an exclusive license, because the loss of trade secret protection would be detrimental to the licensee. Moreover, courts may not enforce a licensee's nondisclosure obligations if the licensor itself has failed to use reasonable efforts to protect the confidentiality of the information sought to be protected. *nClosures Inc. v Block & Co.* 770 F.3d 598 (7th Cir. 2014).

A duty of confidentiality may include:

- Holding licensed proprietary information in strict confidence and taking measures to maintain its secrecy, including those used by the licensee to protect the confidentiality of its own sensitive information;
- Restricting the use of licensed proprietary information, other than for the permitted activities to carry out the purpose of the license and its enforcement;
- Restricting the personnel who are given access to licensed proprietary information, such as those who are necessary to carry out the purpose of the license;
- Prohibiting publications or presentations containing licensed proprietary information or information derived from it;
- Requiring documents and information containing licensed proprietary information to be labeled as "confidential"; and
- Requiring written confidentiality agreements with all third parties to whom licensed proprietary information is disclosed.

In addition, the parties should consider including measures (*e.g.*, redaction from public filing in litigation or pursuant to regulatory requirements) to protect the confidentiality of information in the license agreement should the agreement become the subject of litigation or be required to be provided to a government agency. Even if the license agreement does not contain information about the licensor's trade secrets, it may reveal other sensitive information, such as the nature of the licensee's research and development activities or confidential terms of the licensor's licensing program.

A party with confidentiality obligations may be permitted to disclose a licensed trade secret and other confidential or proprietary information to third parties under certain circumstances. A license agreement may include provisions to address these circumstances, such as:

- Disclosure to government agencies (*e.g.*, information contained in filings with the Securities and Exchange Commission) or to obtain regulatory approval (*e.g.*, information contained in applications and requests for approval submitted to the Food and Drug Administration) or intellectual property protection (*e.g.*, information contained in patent applications or other documents filed with the U.S. Patent and Trademark Office). In some cases, a party submitting sensitive information to a government agency may request confidential treatment by the agency to protect the confidentiality of the disclosed information. *See supra* Chapters 18 and 19. The licensor will want to ensure that such treatment will preclude a public release of the information pursuant to a request made under the Freedom of Information Act or the California Public Records Act. Further, although patent application filings may be maintained in secrecy in the U.S. Patent and Trademark Office, this secrecy lasts only until the application is published eighteen months after it is filed.

- Disclosure in order to comply with law, a regulatory requirement or a court order, but the disclosing party should be permitted to disclose only the information necessary for compliance and should be required to cooperate with the licensor's attempt to obtain confidential treatment or a protective order to protect the confidentiality of the information.

- Disclosure to potential investors, acquirers and lenders conducting due diligence in connection with a proposed transaction, if they have signed a confidentiality agreement protecting the disclosed information.

- Disclosure to financial, tax and legal advisors or others who have a duty to maintain the confidentiality of information received from their clients.

The licensor might specify security measures the licensee must employ to safeguard the confidentiality of licensed proprietary information. These may include:

- Administrative, technical and physical security procedures, such as limiting access to specified individuals, password protection and encryption of sensitive data.

- Limiting the number of computers on which proprietary information may be stored and requiring these computers to be isolated from internal and external computer networks.

- Limiting or restricting copying of proprietary information.

- Restricting the licensee's use of proprietary information to one or more specific sites or facilities.

To ensure compliance with these security measures, the licensor may want the right to audit or inspect the licensee's systems and facilities where licensed information is held.

A licensee may inadvertently or unintentionally disclose proprietary information it is required to protect. Although an inadvertent disclosure may be a breach of the trade secret license, the remedy, which may include the licensor's right to revoke the license, may not always be appropriate, such as where the disclosure was due to circumstances beyond the licensee's control (*e.g.*, a security breach caused by a hacker). A licensor may wish to include in the license agreement a provision requiring the licensee to take action, or cooperate with the licensor, to remedy an inadvertent disclosure and conditioning continuation of the license upon the licensee's adoption of measures to prevent a reoccurrence of the disclosure. In the event of a security breach, the agreement may require the licensee to notify the licensor of the breach and to provide the licensor assistance in investigating the breach and seeking available remedies.

Because it may be difficult to measure damages for misappropriation of a trade secret or breach of a license agreement, such as the licensee's inadvertent disclosure due to its failure to provide agreed-upon security measures, the license agreement can specify a liquidated damages remedy if appropriate.

While trade secret licenses are subject to confidentiality obligations, certain information is typically excluded from these obligations, such as:

- Information that was generally available to the public or is part of the public domain at the time of the licensor's disclosure of the same information;
- Information that becomes generally known or available to the public other than through an act or omission by the licensee;
- Information that is received from a third party that does not breach a duty of confidentiality to the licensor and the recipient does not have any restriction on the use or disclosure of this information;
- Information that is already known by the licensee prior to the licensor's disclosure of the same information and the recipient does not have any restriction on the use or disclosure of this information;
- Information that was independently developed by the licensee or its employees who did not have knowledge of the licensor's confidential information; and
- Information that the licensor publicly discloses.

Although a licensee's confidentiality obligations may exclude publicly available information, the licensor may have a proprietary interest in information that is derived from publicly available sources. Combinations of public information from a variety of different sources, when combined in a novel way, can be a trade secret. *O2 Micro Int'l Ltd. v. Monolithic Power Sys., Inc.*, 420 F. Supp. 2d 1070, 1089 (N.D. Cal. 2006) *aff'd*, 221 F. App'x. 996 (Fed. Cir. 2007). A licensor of such information should take care to ensure the licensee is obligated to maintain its confidentiality.

Sample Clause: Any Proprietary Information shared in accordance with this Agreement shall not be deemed to be within any of the exclusions of Licensee's confidentiality obligations hereunder: (a) merely because it is embraced by more general information in the prior possession of Licensee or of others, or (b) merely because it is expressed in public literature in general terms not specifically in accordance with the Proprietary Information, nor shall a combination of features be deemed to be within such exclusions merely because the individual features are within such exceptions.

Often, the license will provide that if the licensee invokes an exclusion, it will have the burden of proving that the exclusion applies. In some cases, the license agreement will require proof of the exclusion based upon documentation created by the licensee in the ordinary course of its business. In other cases, imposition of a higher evidentiary standard may be appropriate, such as requiring the licensee to provide clear and convincing evidence to support the exclusion.

Under the Defend Trade Secrets Act of 2016 (the "DTSA"), an individual who receives a trade secret in his or her capacity as an employee, independent contractor, or consultant of the trade secret owner and discloses the trade secret when reporting unlawful activities to government officials or as part of an anti-retaliation lawsuit will be immunized from liability under certain circumstances. 18 U.S.C. §1833(b)(1)–(2). Notice of this immunity protection must be included in any agreement governing the use of trade secrets by an employee, independent contractor, or consultant. 18 U.S.C. §1833(b)(3)–(4). Failure to comply with this requirement may preclude an employer or licensor from recovering exemplary damages or attorneys' fees in a lawsuit against an employee or contractor for trade secret theft. 18 U.S.C. §1833(b)(3)(C). The DTSA, however, does not preclude a trade secret owner from seeking other remedies, such as breach of contract remedies.

Sample Clause: Notwithstanding Licensee's confidentiality and nondisclosure obligations herein, Licensee is hereby advised as follows pursuant to the Defend Trade Secrets Act of 2016: "An individual shall not be held criminally or civilly liable under any Federal or State trade secret law for the disclosure of a trade secret that (A) is made (i) in confidence to a Federal, State, or local government official, either directly or indirectly, or to an attorney and (ii) solely for the purpose of reporting or investigating a suspected violation of law; or (B) is made in a complaint or other document filed in a lawsuit or other proceeding, if such filing is made under seal. An individual who files a lawsuit for retaliation by an employer for reporting a suspected violation of law may disclose the trade secret to the attorney for the individual and use the trade secret information in the court proceeding, if the individual (A) files any document containing the trade secret under seal; and (B) does not disclose the trade secret, except pursuant to court order."

F. Compensation

A trade secret license often will contain terms requiring the licensee to compensate the licensor for use of licensed proprietary information. Compensation terms vary greatly depending upon how licensed information is used. For example, a one-time or annual license fee may be suitable for use of licensed information in a research or development project. Alternatively, the licensee may be required to pay royalties based upon sales of a product if licensed information will be used in a process to manufacture the product.

The compensation terms of trade secret licenses differ from patent licenses in several respects. Royalties under a trade secret license may be based on the licensee's sales or manufacturing activities anywhere in the world. In contrast, because patents are limited to specific jurisdictions, royalties under a patent licensee will be based upon only the licensee's activities within the jurisdictions where licensed patents have been obtained. Another difference is that trade secret license royalties may be calculated on all revenues from the licensee's exploitation of the trade secret. Patent license royalties, however, are limited to revenues from only the products that fall within the scope of the licensed patent's claims. The duration of a trade secret licensee's payment obligations is another distinction from a patent license. A trade secret licensee's payment obligations may survive indefinitely, even after the trade secret is no longer protectable. In contrast, royalty obligations under a patent license must end upon the patent's invalidity or expiration.

1. License Fees

A trade secret license may require the licensee to pay a license fee.

Sample Clause: In consideration of the license granted herein, Licensee will pay Licensor a nonrefundable license fee in the amount of five hundred thousand dollars ($500,000) within thirty (30) days following Licensor's delivery of the reference design kit to be used in designing the products described in Exhibit "A" hereto.

Under certain circumstances, such as in the event of the licensor's breach or wrongful termination, a licensee will want to have the right to obtain a refund of a license fee that otherwise is nonrefundable. Further, the license agreement may require the payment of royalties in addition to a license fee. In such a case, the licensee may wish to have the license fee (or a portion) credited against royalties that the licensee is required to pay.

2. Royalties

Royalties may be calculated numerous ways. One method is based upon a percentage, or royalty rate, of the proceeds from the use of licensed proprietary information. Another method is based upon a specified amount to be paid for each product sold by the licensee. The amount of the royalty rate varies according to the industry in which licensed information is used. Generally, a higher royalty rate is paid for exclusive licenses than for nonexclusive licenses. Occasionally, the royalty rate may change based upon the licensee's performance. For example, the royalty rate may decrease with increasing volumes of royalty-bearing sales. Alternatively, the royalty rate may change upon the occurrence or nonoccurrence of certain events. For example, the royalty rate may decrease if a patent does not issue from a pending patent application claiming licensed information.

Royalties based upon the proceeds from the use of licensed proprietary information are ordinarily determined by applying the royalty rate to the amount of gross revenues from sales of products made from the use of licensed information. This amount may be subject to a deduction of expenses associated with royalty-bearing product sales.

Sample Clause: As a royalty for the Product, Licensee shall pay Licensor an amount equal to six percent (6%) of Net Sales. "Net Sales" means the gross amount billed or otherwise recognized with respect to the Product sold by Licensee or any related entity (excluding free samples and clinical trial units of the Product), less (to the extent included in the gross amount and to the extent not for promotional purposes): (a) cash discounts actually given; (b) credits or allowances actually given or made on account of price adjustments, rebates (including chargebacks and contractual agreements), or volume reimbursements; (c) separately stated (on customer invoice) taxes on sales (such as sales and use taxes); and (d) separately stated (on customer invoice) delivery charges actually paid to third party carriers (including transportation and insurance costs), all as determined in accordance with generally accepted accounting principles.

Alternatively, royalties based upon a specified per unit amount are determined by multiplying this amount and the quantity of royalty-bearing products sold.

A licensee's obligation to pay royalties under a trade secret license is not extinguished simply because the licensed trade secret becomes publicly available. *Aronson v. Quick Point Pencil Co.*, 440 U.S. 257, 266 (1979). Having early access to a trade secret affords a licensee a head start in the market, even if the trade secret later is no longer secret. The continuing royalty compensates the licensor for providing the licensee with this head start. To attempt to avoid a dispute later on, the licensor may want to include in the license an express acknowledgement by the licensee that its obligation to pay royalties is not extinguished by licensed information becoming publicly available.

A "hybrid" license covering both trade secrets and patent rights may have royalty obligations that extend beyond the term of licensed patents since trade secrets may be protectable indefinitely. Requiring a licensee to pay royalties for a patent license after the patent expires, however, is a misuse of the patent and may give rise to an antitrust violation. To avoid this, hybrid license agreements may impose separate royalty obligations—one set of obligations for the trade secret license and another for the patent license. The licensee's royalty obligations will remain in effect for its continued use of the trade secret after the patent expires if the trade secret and the patent comprise separate and distinct types of intellectual property and do not overlap. *Pitney-Bowes, Inc. v. Mestre*, 517 F. Supp. 52, 61 (S.D. Fla. 1981).

Sample Clause: The royalty rate shall be reduced by fifty percent (50%) with respect to any Net Sales in a particular country of a Licensed Product that incorporates Licensed Trade Secrets and is not covered by a Licensed Patent enforceable in such country.

3. Payment and Reporting

Trade secret license agreements providing for the payment of a license fee and/or royalties typically will specify when the compensation is to be paid and will set forth a mechanism enabling the licensor to ensure that the correct amounts are paid. Royalty payments usually are paid periodically during the license term, such as on a monthly or quarterly basis. Often, these payments are due at the same time as royalty statements reporting sales of royalty-bearing products during the applicable royalty period. The information a licensee is required to include in its royalty statements may be limited to the financial data used to calculate royalties or may include additional sales and market data.

Sample Clause: On or before the last day of each calendar quarter, Licensee shall provide Licensor with a written statement showing, on a country-by-country basis, with respect to such calendar quarter (i) the quantity of Licensed Products shipped, (ii) the quantity of Licensed Products sold, (iii) the calculation of Net Sales in U.S. Dollars, including the calculation for any currency conversions, and (iv) the identity and shipping address of each customer purchasing a Licensed Product.

Because royalty statements may contain sensitive information relating to the licensee's sales and the commercial success of the licensor's trade secrets, the licensor and the licensee may require that this information be kept confidential.

A licensee usually is required to maintain accounting books and records relating to royalty-bearing sales in support of the royalty statements it provides to the licensor. A licensor will want a right to audit and inspect the licensee's books and records to verify that the royalty payments were correct. This audit right may survive termination and expiration of the license agreement because a licensee's royalty obligations often will continue beyond the term of the license. Generally, the party conducting the audit is responsible for paying the cost of the audit. However, if the audit shows that the licensee has underpaid, then the licensee may be required to reimburse the licensor for the cost of the audit. A licensee may want to require the licensor to maintain the information obtained from the audit in confidence, but a licensor should reserve the right to use this information in any legal action to enforce the trade secret license. Also, a licensee may wish to contest the results of an audit and have the right to conduct and offer a second audit to show that its royalty payments were correct.

G. Representations and Warranties

Representations and warranties in connection with a trade secret license serve a due diligence function providing the licensee assurances that the licensor has obtained the necessary clearances for the licensee to use licensed proprietary information. Typically, such assurances confirm that:

- The licensor's disclosure of licensed information is lawful;
- The licensor has maintained the secrecy of licensed information;
- The licensee is entitled to use licensed information;
- Licensed information is protected against unlicensed use by third parties; and
- The licensee's permitted use of licensed information will not give rise to a claim brought by another party.

Because the use of licensed proprietary information could infringe a patent that the licensor does not know exists, particularly if the patent has not issued at the time the licensor makes the representation and warranty, a licensor will want to limit the scope of a representation and warranty of non-infringement from use of licensed information to only infringement claims of which the licensor is on notice or only claims of trade secret misappropriation.

Certain warranties—warranties of merchantability, fitness for a particular purpose and non-infringement—are implied under the California Commercial Code in contracts involving sales of goods, unless these warranties are disclaimed in writing. Cal. Com. Code §§ 2314, 2315 and 2312(3). A license of trade secrets contained in software may be considered to be a contract for the sale of goods for purposes of the California Commercial Code and these warranties may be implied in software license agreements. *See RRX Indus. v. Lab-Con, Inc.*, 772 F.2d 543, 546 (9th Cir. 1985) ("Because software packages vary depending on the needs of the individual consumer, we apply a case-by-case analysis"); *c.f.*, *Sys. Unlimited, Inc. v. Cisco Sys.*, 228 F. App'x. 854, 859 (11th Cir. 2007) (conveyance of intellectual property associated with software was not a transaction in the sale of goods) (applying California law). Yet, courts in other jurisdictions have not applied implied warranties to trade secrets, not even those contained in licensed software. *See Dravo Corp. v. White Consol. Indus.*, 602 F. Supp. 1136, 1140 (W.D. Pa. 1985) (acquisition of assets, the majority of which consisted of drawings and tracings were essentially a conveyance of ideas and not a sale of goods); *Lamle v. Mattel, Inc.*, 394 F.3d 1355, 1359 n.2 (Fed. Cir. 2005) (license of intellectual property is not a sale of goods).

Even though representations and warranties are often combined to provide assurances as to the same matters, the remedies for the breach of a representation differ from those available for the breach of a warranty. A warranty generally is a promise that a proposition of a fact is true. Breach of a warranty ordinarily gives rise to a breach of contract claim under which the claimant may seek to recover the difference in value between what was warranted and what was actually delivered. A representation generally is a statement relating to a past, present or future fact. Breach of a representation can give rise to a claim of misrepresentation or fraud in the inducement. In addition to recovering damages for breach of the contract, the claimant under a claim for breach of a representation may seek to recover its costs in obtaining a substitute product (*i.e.*, "cover") and other costs and expenses it incurred under the contract.

In some cases, such as in connection with a nondisclosure agreement to protect information exchanged during preliminary discussions about a prospective business relationship, the parties may not wish to make any representations or warranties about the information they share.

Sample Clause: The Recipient acknowledges that the Disclosing Party shall not be responsible for and has not made any representation or warranty, express or implied, as to the accuracy, reliability or completeness of any of the Proprietary Information.

H. Indemnification

Indemnification allocates the risks associated with the use of licensed proprietary information between a licensor and a licensee. A licensor may act as a private insurer against liability resulting from the licensee's use of licensed information. Typically, a licensor will indemnify a licensee against the licensor's breach of its representations and warranties, including the breach of a representation and warranty that the licensee's use of licensed information will not violate any third party's intellectual property rights. If the licensee will use licensed information in a process or in components to produce products, the licensor may seek to have the licensee provide reciprocal indemnity protection for claims arising from the licensee's products, but not caused by licensed information, (*e.g.*, claims based upon infringement by the licensee's products of third party intellectual property rights or arising from product defects).

I. Term and Termination

1. Term

The term of a trade secret license usually begins on a date specified in the license agreement, which may correspond to the date one or both parties sign the agreement. If licensed proprietary information was disclosed before the agreement was signed, it may be appropriate for the term to begin on the disclosure date. The license term may be a specified period of time or may end upon completion of the project or purpose for which the trade secret is licensed. In cases in which a trade secret license does not specify its duration, a court may construe the license as terminable by either party at will. *Zee Med. Distrib. Ass'n v. Zee Med., Inc.*, 80 Cal. App. 4th 1, 14 (2000).

If the parties to a trade secret license contemplate an ongoing relationship, they may wish to provide for renewal of the license. Renewal may be automatic until either party decides not to renew or may require either party to elect to renew the license prior to expiration of the license. A party's right to renew may be conditioned upon the satisfaction of specified performance requirements, such as the licensee's payment of minimum royalties during the license term. The parties should consider whether the terms and conditions of the license in effect during the prior term should continue during the renewal term or whether new terms should apply. This is particularly important with respect to compensation terms. The value of a trade secret may change during the license term justifying an adjustment of the royalty rate or license fee during the renewal term.

2. Termination

A trade secret license agreement may provide a right to terminate the license upon the occurrence of specified conditions. This right may be either unilateral or bilateral. For example, the licensee may have the right to terminate the license for convenience by providing the licensor with written notice and the licensor and the licensee each may have a right to terminate if the other party commits a material breach of the license agreement.

Usually, a trade secret license agreement will provide the licensor a right to terminate the license if the licensee materially breaches any of its obligations. Once the licensee is notified of the breach, it may have an opportunity to cure the breach and, if it fails to do so, the licensor may terminate the license. In some cases, a breach cannot be cured, such as where the licensee discloses licensed proprietary information without authorization. The licensee, under these circumstances, may not be given time to attempt to cure the breach before the licensor is permitted to terminate the license. However, if a licensee's use of licensed information is so embedded in its business operations or manufacturing processes or if there are other circumstances such that termination of the license would shut down the licensee's business or cause other significant hardship to the licensee, then the licensee will want to ensure that the license cannot be revoked under any circumstances, even as a remedy for its breach.

A licensor may be able to pursue both a breach of contract claim and a claim for trade secret misappropriation against a licensee that breaches a trade secret license agreement. *See Celeritas Techs. v. Rockwell Int'l Corp.*, 150 F.3d 1354, 1359-60 (Fed. Cir. 1998) (contract claim and damages relating to breach of nondisclosure agreement distinct from trade secret misappropriation claims); *S.O.S. Inc. v. Payday, Inc.*, 886 F.2d 1081, 1090 (9th Cir. 1989) (suggesting a breach of a license agreement may constitute misappropriation); *see also supra* Chapter 2. Under a breach of contract claim, a licensor is entitled to recover the compensation it would have received had the licensee not breached the agreement. Restatement (Second) of Contracts, § 347 (1981). Under a trade secret misappropriation claim, a licensor may recover the licensee's unjust enrichment or the licensor's lost profits from the licensee's use of the trade secret and, at the same time, the licensor may seek an injunction prohibiting the licensee's further use of the trade secret. *See supra* Chapters 12 and 13. If a licensee breaches a condition of the license, then the licensor may be able to rescind the license and pursue both trade secret misappropriation and breach of contact claims. *See Graham v. James*, 144 F.3d 229, 236–37 (2d Cir. 1998).

In addition to claims of misappropriation of trade secrets and breach of contract, a licensee's breach of its confidentiality obligations may give rise to a claim under California Business & Professions Code §§ 17200, *et seq*. *See Spring Design, Inc. v. Barnesandnoble.com, LLC*, No. 09-cv-05185-JW, 2010 WL 5422556, at *9 (N.D. Cal., Dec. 27, 2010). *But see supra* Chapters 8 and 9 (discussions of UTSA preemption).

3. Post-Termination

Once a trade secret license expires or is terminated, certain rights and obligations under the agreement may remain and continue in effect. For example, the licensee may be permitted to sell royalty-bearing products held in inventory after the termination date, subject to paying royalties on these sales. Other rights and obligations that typically survive termination or expiration include:

- Rights to audit the licensee's books and records pertaining to licensed products sales;
- Confidentiality and disclosure restrictions; and
- Representations and warranties and indemnification obligations.

If the agreement does not require the licensee to stop using licensed proprietary information after the agreement ends, then the licensee's rights and obligations concerning the trade secret may be unclear. *See Merck & Co. v. SmithKline Beecham Pharms. Co.*, C.A. No. 15443-NC, 1999 Del. Ch. LEXIS 242, at *124–25 (Del. Ch. Aug. 5, 1999). One court has found that a licensee did not have a continuing duty to maintain the confidentiality of a trade secret after the agreement ended because the agreement failed to impose such a duty. *Expansion Plus Inc. v. Brown-Forman Corp.*, 132 F.3d 1083, 1086 (5th Cir. 1998).

If a licensee is prohibited from using the licensor's proprietary information after the agreement ends, the licensee should be required to return or destroy all materials in its possession containing licensed information or that were created using licensed information, including copies of such materials. Further, a licensor will want to ensure that the licensee destroys all electronic data containing licensed information.

Sample Clause: Upon any termination or expiration of this Agreement, (i) Licensee shall have the right to ship its existing inventory of Licensed Products then in the manufacturing process, (ii) Licensee shall promptly pay Licensor any unpaid amount due as of the date of termination or expiration, and (iii) each party shall cease all use of the other party's Proprietary Information and shall return to the other or destroy all copies of the other party's Proprietary Information within thirty (30) days after the date of termination or expiration and have an officer of such party certify in writing it has complied with this obligation.

The licensee should consider the possibility that data used in the licensee's computer network may be stored in numerous locations and, as a result, the licensee may not be able to easily certify the destruction of all licensed information.

If the licensee refuses to stop using licensed proprietary information, the licensor may seek to enjoin the licensee's continued use and the court may order the licensee to surrender physical embodiments of the trade secret for destruction. Cal. Civ. Code §§ 3426.2(a),(c).

Notwithstanding an obligation to return to the licensor, or destroy, proprietary information in its possession, the licensee may wish to have the right to retain one copy of the proprietary information it received from the licensor solely for use in connection with any future claims relating to the license agreement or in responding to inquiries by regulatory agencies.

Sample Clause: Following expiration or termination of this Agreement, so long as required by any relevant law, governmental or regulatory authority, Licensee may retain one (1) copy of the Proprietary Information in a secure location for the purpose of determining its obligations hereunder and for record-keeping purposes only, subject to the confidentiality obligations and restrictions set forth in this Agreement.

Even if a licensee is prohibited from using the licensor's proprietary information after the license expires or is terminated, agreements often specify how long the licensee's confidentiality obligations will continue. The licensee will not want to be obligated indefinitely to maintain the secrecy of licensed information it may continue to possess (e.g., information that its employees remember). At the same time, the licensor will not want to risk the loss of trade secret protection by not requiring the licensee to continue safeguarding the licensor's proprietary information from inadvertent use or disclosure. Often, the parties will agree upon a specific period of time after the license agreement ends when a post-termination confidentiality obligation will lapse. This time period depends upon the nature of the licensed information and how quickly such information is likely to become obsolete.

Sample Clause: The confidentiality obligations herein shall survive the termination or expiration of this Agreement for a period of five (5) years, except with respect to Confidential Information constituting trade secrets, which shall remain in effect so long as they are protected as trade secrets under applicable law.

§ 20.06 Other Considerations When Drafting Trade Secret Licenses

In addition to the terms and conditions discussed in the preceding sections, it may be helpful to include provisions in trade secret licenses in order to address particular issues, such as: (i) restrictions on the licensee's ability to transfer the license to a third party, (ii) the licensee's rights in licensed trade secrets if the licensor enters bankruptcy, (iii) each party's rights to enforce licensed trade secrets against unauthorized users, (iv) the law to be applied in interpreting the license agreement, (v) the venue where disputes under the agreement must be brought and the procedures to be undertaken for resolving disputes, and (vi) restrictions on use of licensed information outside of the United States.

A. Assignment

Absent an express prohibition in the license agreement or a violation of law or public policy, a licensee may freely assign its rights under a trade secrets license without obtaining the licensor's consent. Restatement (Second) of Contracts, § 317(2) (1981). A licensee's assignment of a trade secret license is an important concern for a licensor that would not want a competitor to gain access to licensed trade secrets through an acquisition of the licensee. To prevent such an outcome, the licensor may restrict the licensee from assigning its license to a third party without the licensor's prior written consent.

B. Licensor's Bankruptcy

What rights does a licensee have to licensed trade secrets if the licensor goes into bankruptcy? In the event of a licensor's bankruptcy, the debtor in possession or the bankruptcy trustee may either affirm and accept, or reject, the licensor's executory contracts, which may include a trade secret license. 11 U.S.C. § 365(a) (2012). In most cases, a trade secret license will be an executory contract because the licensor and the licensee have ongoing performance obligations (*e.g.*, the licensee's compliance with the license restrictions and its payment of royalties and the licensor's transfer of know-how and materials pertaining to licensed trade secrets and its indemnification obligations) under the license agreement. If the debtor in possession or the trustee rejects the trade secret license, the licensee may elect to retain its rights under the license and continue paying royalties or other consideration as it comes due and to continue performing its other obligations under the agreement. 11 U.S.C. § 365(n) (2012). A licensee that elects to retain its rights in licensed trade secrets, however, likely will have no right to any future transfers of technology or materials from the licensor that are called for under the license agreement.

C. Enforcement of Licensed Trade Secrets

Because unauthorized use of a trade secret dilutes the value of a license of the trade secret, particularly if the license is exclusive, the licensee has an interest in taking action to stop the use. The licensor, however, may want to control the outcome of litigation that could impact the validity and enforceability of its trade secret rights.

Which party should be entitled to take action against a theft of licensed trade secrets? This right usually resides with the trade secret owner, unless the licensee has an exclusive license. *See*

Black Clawson Co. v. Kroenert Corp., 245 F.3d 759, 764 (8th Cir. 2001). A nonexclusive licensee may not have standing to sue for trade secret misappropriation. *RMS Software Dev. v. LCS, Inc.*, No. 01-96-00824-CV, 1998 Tex. App. LEXIS 1053, at *10 (Tex. Ct. App. Feb. 19, 1998) (unpublished). *Compare* Appendix A, comments to Jury Instruction 4400 (no California state case addressing whether licensees have standing). Therefore, a nonexclusive trade secret licensee that requires assurance that action will be taken against unauthorized use of licensed trade secrets will want to impose such an obligation upon the licensor in the license agreement. If such action is to be taken by the licensor, the parties will need to consider their respective obligations to fund the action and their respective rights to any damages award.

D. Legal Actions

Which jurisdiction's laws will be used to interpret the terms of a trade secret license? Addressing this issue is particularly important when the licensor and licensee operate in different countries. Even with respect to parties from different states, the application of the laws of one state instead of another can significantly affect the scope of a license to use information defined as a "trade secret."

Generally, courts will enforce the parties' choice of law to interpret the agreement if the choice is reasonable and does not contravene a strong California public policy. Restatement (Second) of Conflicts of Laws, § 187(2) (1971); *Meras Eng'g, Inc. v. CH2O, Inc.*, No. C-11-0389-EMC, 2013 U.S. Dist. LEXIS 5426, at *32 (N.D. Cal. Jan. 14, 2013). In California, generally, parties to a contract involving a transaction of $250,000 or more may specify that the contract will be governed by California law. Cal. Civ. Code § 1646.5.

E. Venue and Dispute Resolution

Courts will usually honor a forum selection clause specifying where disputes must be heard (such as a dispute as to a trade secret license), unless doing so would be unreasonable or unjust. *See Graham Tech. Solutions v. Thinking Pictures, Inc.*, 949 F. Supp. 1427, 1431, 1432-33 (N.D. Cal. 1997). To limit a party's ability to bring and maintain an action in a venue other than the one specified, the license agreement must state that jurisdiction of the specified courts is exclusive. *See, e.g., Pelleport Investors, Inc. v. Budco Quality Theaters, Inc.*, 741 F.2d 273, 279-81 (9th Cir. 1984); *see also Hammes v. AAMCO Transmissions, Inc.*, 33 F.3d 774, 783 (7th Cir. 1994).

In addition to specifying the governing law and forum where disputes will be heard, the parties to a trade secret license may wish to provide for the recovery of attorneys' fees and costs that are incurred in connection with a dispute relating to the license agreement. In general, courts will enforce provisions permitting the prevailing party in litigation to recover its attorneys' fees. *Fineberg v. Niekerk*, 175 Cal. App. 3d 935, 942-43 (2d Dist. 1985). Arbitrators have significant discretion in framing relief, however, so they may not abide by such contractual provisions.

To reduce the risk of consumer class action lawsuits, a licensor may wish to include arbitration provisions in consumer contracts that contain trade secret licenses, such as end user software license agreements, website terms of service agreements and mobile software application end user license agreements. Such provisions in consumer contracts are enforceable under California law.

The U.S. Supreme Court ruled that the Federal Arbitration Act preempts states from imposing restrictions on arbitration agreements. *AT&T Mobility LLC v. Concepcion*, 131 S. Ct. 1740, 1753 (2011) (overruling a prior decision of the California Supreme Court holding class action waivers in consumer contracts to be unconscionable). Yet, arbitration provisions still may be found to be unenforceable, (*e.g.*, as unconscionable) under some circumstances. *See Sanchez v. Carmax Auto Superstores Cal., LLC*, 224 Cal. App. 4th 398, 402 (2014). *Ramos v Superior Court* 28 Cal. App. 5th 1042 (2018) (terms requiring payment of arbitration costs and attorneys' fees, limiting arbitrator's authority to provide relief, and imposing strict confidentiality obligations rendered arbitration provision in law firm's partnership agreement unenforceable as a matter of law).

F. Export Controls

Is licensed proprietary information subject to restrictions on use outside of the United States? If proprietary information will be disclosed to anyone outside the United States or to a foreign national within the United States, the trade secret owner must ensure that the disclosure complies with applicable export controls. The export and re-export of technology and software originating in the United States, including trade secrets, that present a national security risk are regulated through the U.S. Commerce Department Bureau of Industry and Security (BIS). In addition, the U.S. State Department through the International Traffic in Arms Regulations controls defense articles and services that have been designated as having military applications. The applicability of export restrictions and the conditions that must be met before proprietary information consisting of restricted technology may be exported requires an analysis of:

- The nature and classification of the technology;
- The ultimate destination of the technology;
- The recipient of the technology; and
- The end use of the technology.

Export regulations require a written letter from the ultimate recipient of technology controlled for national security reasons to provide the licensor assurance that, unless prior authorization is obtained from the BIS, the recipient will not knowingly re-export the technology to any destination, or export the direct product of the technology. U.S. Export Admin. Regulations, 15 C.F.R. § 748, Supp. 2 (o)(3)(i) (2013). For this reason, any license agreement involving a license of proprietary information consisting of restricted technology should include such an assurance to the licensor.

Chapter 21
TRADE SECRETS CLAIMS AT THE U.S. INTERNATIONAL TRADE COMMISSION

**By: Steven P. Hollman, Esq.
and Michael J. Allan, Esq.**

---

§ 21.01 Trade Secret Misappropriation at the U.S. International Trade Commission

Until relatively recently, trade secret misappropriation cases were seldom filed at the U.S. International Trade Commission ("ITC" or "Commission").[19] Recent filings show that aggrieved owners of trade secrets are more likely to perceive the ITC as a forum for claims of importation of goods made using misappropriated trade secrets. And recognition that the ITC is available even for instances where the misappropriation occurred on foreign soil has contributed to the burgeoning docket of trade secret misappropriation cases in the ITC. California's major role in foreign commerce, particularly as a participant in trade on the Pacific Rim, underscores the need for California practitioners to understand the remedies available in the ITC when trade secret misappropriation involves importation of goods.

In this chapter we explain the ITC's role in investigating alleged unfair trade practices through importation, sale for importation or sale of imported articles produced using misappropriated trade secrets. We address:

- ITC jurisdiction
- Advantages and disadvantages of filing at the ITC
- The ITC process, from filing the complaint through decision
- The post-hearing appeal process
- The procedural and substantive law of trade secrets at the ITC
- The ITC's unique "domestic industry" requirement
- Some practical tips

§ 21.02 The ITC Process

A. The Agency, the Statute, and Institution of an Investigation

The ITC is a quasi-judicial independent agency, based in Washington, D.C., and has nationwide jurisdiction and subpoena power. It is the successor to the U.S. Tariff Commission. The ITC is responsible for administering Section 337 of the Tariff Act of 1930, as amended (19 U.S.C. § 1337), which is commonly referred to as "section 337." Subject matter jurisdiction in trade secret misappropriation is vested in the ITC by 19 U.S.C. § 1337(a)(1)(A), which states in relevant part:

> … the following are unlawful, and when found by the Commission to exist shall be dealt with, in addition to any other provision of law, as provided in this section:
>
> (A) Unfair methods of competition and unfair acts in the importation of articles … into the United States, or in the sale of such articles by the owner, importer or consignee, the threat or effect of which is—

[19] In the 9 years from 2006 through 2015, only 8 investigations were initiated based solely on claims of trade secret misappropriation. In contrast, in the 5 years from 2016 through 2020, 15 such investigations were initiated. USITC, Year in Review, for Fiscal Years 2006–2010; U.S. International Trade Commission FY 2011 At A Glance; U.S. International Trade Commission FY 2012 At A Glance; U.S. International Trade Commission FY 2013 At A Glance; and USITC, 337Info. *See* https://usitc.gov/intellectual_property/337_statistics_types_unfair_acts_alleged_active.htm.

(i) to destroy or substantially injure an industry in the United States;

(ii) to prevent the establishment of such an industry; or

(iii) to restrain or monopolize trade and commerce in the United States.

19 U.S.C. § 1337(a)(1)(A) (2008).

While the basic provision of section 337 governing trade secret misappropriation cases is quoted above, the statute contains 14 subsections that set forth detailed procedures for the conduct of investigations under section 337.

Section 337 cases begin with the filing of a verified complaint by a complainant, although the statute also allows the ITC to initiate an investigation. The complaint is a detailed, fact-based pleading. The complainant must allege an unfair act, importation, the existence of a domestic industry and, in a trade secret case, the threat or effect of injury to the domestic industry. To satisfy standing, the complainant must be the owner (or exclusive licensee) of the intellectual property right at issue.[20] Although the complainant must allege (and ultimately prove) the existence of a U.S. domestic industry, the complainant need not have U.S. citizenship to satisfy this requirement. Rather, the complainant must show sufficient qualifying domestic activity.[21] The complaint also lists the types of imported articles that are affected by the alleged unfair act, and names as respondents the persons/companies believed to be involved in manufacturing, exporting, importing and/or selling after importation, the articles alleged to be imported in violation of the statute. The respondents may be located in the United States or abroad.

Upon receipt of a complaint, the ITC reviews the pleading for sufficiency and consistency with the ITC's Rules of Practice and Procedure. Like most federal agencies, the ITC has promulgated detailed procedural rules. The rules pertaining to section 337 proceedings are found in Title 19 of the Code of Federal Regulations, at Parts 201 (general rules) and 210 (rules specific to section 337, and patterned on the Federal Rules of Civil Procedure). Normally, an investigation is formally instituted within 30 days of the filing of the complaint. While it is unusual for the ITC not to institute an investigation, the process may be delayed pending a response from the complainant for additional information requested by the Commission. The ITC institutes an investigation upon publication of a notice of investigation in the Federal Register. The notice outlines the scope of the investigation and lists the parties involved. Peculiar to section 337 proceedings is the role of the ITC's Office of Unfair Import Investigations ("OUII")—a staff attorney from OUII may participate in any investigation as a full party to protect the public interest. In the past, a staff attorney participated in every case; currently, OUII selectively participates in most investigations.

---

[20] *See Certain Rubber Resins and Processes for Manufacturing Same ("Certain Rubber Resins")*, Inv. No. 337-TA-849, Initial Determination (hereinafter, "ID"), at 44 (June 17, 2013) (*aff'd in relevant part*).

[21] *See Certain Botulinum Toxin Products, Processes for Manufacturing or Relating to Same and Certain Products Containing Same ("Certain Botulinum Toxin Products"), Inv. No. 337-TA-1145, ID*, at 166 (July 6, 2020) (where complainant's "evidence shows that critical operations such as the manufacturing of the API, physician support activities, and nearly all of the R&D activities all occur in the United States," domestic operations were found to be qualitatively significant in comparison to foreign operations and sufficient to satisfy domestic industry requirement).

B. Jurisdiction at the ITC

1. Subject Matter Jurisdiction

Subject matter jurisdiction in an ITC trade secrets matter is established, for example, by a verified allegation in the complaint of an unfair act in the importation of articles produced through misappropriation of one or more valid trade secrets. Jurisdiction exists regardless of the geographic location of the misappropriation and is based upon the importation of the articles. *TianRui Group Co. Ltd. v. International Trade Commission*, 661 F.3d 1322, 1326, 1328-1329 (Fed. Cir. 2011) ("*TianRui*") (section 337 applies to imported goods produced through the misappropriation of trade secrets that occurs abroad).

In *TianRui*, the ITC found that Chinese company TianRui hired nine employees from a licensee of U.S. company Amsted, and these employees disclosed to TianRui their knowledge of Amsted's proprietary process, which TianRui then used to make a competing product. Although that product was imported into the U.S., all of the acts of misappropriation occurred in China. Nonetheless, the ITC issued an exclusion order against TianRui. The Federal Circuit affirmed, holding that section 337 "does not purport to regulate purely foreign conduct" because "of the statute's focus on the act of importation and the resulting domestic injury." 661 F.3d at 1329. The determination in *TianRui* did not turn on whether the trade secrets at issue had been developed and practiced in the United States. Instead, the decision was predicated on the fact that the goods at issue were imported and injured, or could injury, a domestic industry. *Id.* at 1337.

The ITC's broad subject matter jurisdiction over trade secrets developed and misappropriated abroad recently was reaffirmed in the decision of an Administrative Law Judge ("ALJ") rejecting the argument that the ITC's jurisdiction does not "reach alleged misappropriation of a Korean company's Korean trade secrets based on activity solely in Korea by another Korean company."[22] The ALJ's decision reaffirms the ITC's expansive jurisdiction over extraterritorial misappropriation.

2. *In Rem* Jurisdiction

In rem jurisdiction is jurisdiction of the goods alleged to be the fruits of misappropriation of trade secrets and imported into the United States. This jurisdiction provides the authority for any exclusion order that may issue as a result of the ITC investigation.

The importation requirement is modest. In *Certain Trolley Wheel Assemblies*, Inv. No. 337-TA-161, USITC Pub. No. 1065, 0084 WL 951859, Comm'n Determination at *7-8 (Nov. 1984), the Commission found the importation requirement satisfied by the importation of a single product of no commercial value. Similarly, an unreviewed ID in *Certain Purple Protective Gloves*, Inv. No. 337-TA-500, USITC Order No. 17, 2004 WL 2330140, at *3 (Sept. 23, 2004), found "[a] complainant need only prove importation of a single accused product to satisfy the importation element."

---

[22] *See Certain Botulinum Toxin Products*, ID, at 23-18 (finding subject matter jurisdiction based on "the alleged (and in this case proven) importation of products made by misappropriated trade secrets, which has resulted in harm to the domestic industry") (citing *Certain Rubber Resins*, ID, at 16-18).

3. *In Personam* Jurisdiction

In personam jurisdiction is usually established by the personal appearance of a party or its counsel and/or the personal service of the complaint and notice of investigation upon a party named in the investigation. It provides the authority for issuance of a cease and desist order by the Commission. *See, e.g., Certain Miniature Hacksaws*, Inv. No. 337-TA-237, ID, 1986 WL 379287 (Oct. 15, 1986).

C. The Speedy Process Before the Administrative Law Judge

Once initiated, a section 337 investigation in general moves quickly as compared to traditional litigation. The case is immediately assigned to an ALJ, who presides over the investigation during the discovery phase and through issuance of a Final Initial Determination. The ALJ issues two ultimate decisions: an ID as to whether there has been a violation of section 337, and a Recommended Determination ("RD") as to what remedy should be imposed, if any, and what amount of bond should be posted during the 60-day window after a final ITC decision. During this narrow window, the President of the United States has the opportunity to review, and possibly disapprove, the remedy ordered by the ITC. Historically, the President has exercised this authority to disapprove ITC remedial orders in very rare circumstances.

An ALJ frequently issues numerous discovery-related orders during the course of a case, as well as rulings on motions for summary determination and other types of motions. The ALJ will first issue a Protective Order, which covers the submission (via discovery or formal filing) and handling of confidential information during the course of the proceeding. Next, the ALJ typically issues an order notifying the parties of the Ground Rules to be followed during the investigation, which function as procedural rules which supplement the Commission's rules. The ALJ also sets a procedural schedule, which includes a target date for completion of the investigation; the target date normally is no longer than 16 months (a target date of longer than 16 months is permitted, but the ALJ must obtain the Commissioners' approval in such instances). The quick target date is driven by the statute's requirement that section 337 investigations be completed at the earliest practicable time.

Discovery may begin the day after publication of the notice of investigation in the *Federal Register*, a period that is usually four to seven months long. The available discovery tools are the same as in federal district court—interrogatories, requests for documents and things, requests for admissions, depositions, and inspections of land/property, but the turnaround on written discovery requests typically is 10 days, as opposed to the 30 days typically afforded under the Federal Rules of Civil Procedure. Discovery of parties occurs via notice, and of third parties, via subpoena. Discovery of documents located abroad, and of persons domiciled abroad, occurs routinely in section 337 investigations, provided that the discovery is sought from parties to the investigation or their employees. For foreign discovery sought from non-parties, normal Hague Convention or other applicable procedures must be followed. Notable in trade secret cases is the observation that ALJs are not reluctant to order foreign facility inspections, and even forensic examinations, where the only way to obtain relevant and necessary discovery is through such procedures. Failure by a party to cooperate in discovery can result in sanctions and/or adverse inferences.[23]

The ALJ presides over an evidentiary hearing conducted in accordance with the Administrative Procedure Act. Typically, hearings last one to two weeks, during which fact and expert witnesses testify and are subject to cross-examination. Many of the current ALJs prefer that direct testimony be introduced via written witness statements, to conserve hearing time. During the hearing, exhibits are introduced and entered into evidence. As is generally true in administrative hearings, evidence is limited to that which is relevant, material and reliable; but the formal Federal Rules of Evidence do not control. The ALJs generally use the Federal Rules of Evidence as guidelines to help in this process. Nevertheless, reliable hearsay is admissible, and generally the rules for authenticating documents are relaxed unless a real issue arises regarding the authenticity of offered documents. The parties also submit pre-hearing and post-hearing briefs.

D. Decisions by the ALJ and the Full Commission

Usually within two to three months after the hearing, the ALJ issues his or her decision in the form of an ID. The IDs are typically quite long and address all litigated issues. The parties may seek review of the ID by the full Commission. If the ID is unchallenged and the Commission does not review the ID *sua sponte*, the ID becomes the final decision of the Commission on the issue of violation of the statute. If the Commission determines to review the ID, it may review it in whole or in part, and it may adopt, modify, reverse, vacate or take other action it deems appropriate. Commission Rule 210.42(a)(1)(i) requires the ALJ to certify the record and file the ID on violation "no later than four months before the target date" set in the investigation. Thus, by rule, the Commission has four months to complete its review process. The Commission is also responsible for issuing the final decision on remedy and bonding (*see infra* § 21.11), inasmuch as the ALJ's decision on those issues is only a "recommended determination." As discussed below, if a violation of the statute is found, and the statutory public interest factors do not preclude issuance of relief, the remedy may be in the form of a general or limited exclusion order and/or a cease and desist order. Monetary damages are not available in a section 337 investigation (although the ITC may impose monetary penalties for violation of a cease and desist order or in other limited circumstances). Exclusion orders are enforced by U.S. Customs and Border Protection. Cease and desist orders are enforced by the ITC. 19 U.S.C. §§ 1337(d) and (f).

E. Presidential Review and Review by the Federal Circuit

If the ITC orders a remedy, the President (as delegated to the U.S. Trade Representative) has 60 days to review the remedy and disapprove for policy reasons. During the

---

[23] Parties who misappropriate trade secrets often leave a forensic record of the theft, which can make it difficult to defend effectively against the misappropriation charge. In some instances, respondents have been found to have engaged in evidence spoliation to cover their tracks. Such instances can result in significant sanctions, including issuance of default judgment. *E.g., Organik Kimya, San. ve Tic. A.S. v. Int'l Trade Comm'n*, 843 F.3d 994, 1003-04 (Fed. Cir. 2017) (finding that Commission did not abuse its discretion in implementing default judgment sanctions resulting in 25-year limited exclusion order where respondent was found to have engaged in massive spoliation). *See also Certain Balanced Armature Devices, Products Containing Same, and Components Thereof,* Inv. No. 337-TA-1186, ID, (Jan. 14, 2021) (*aff'd on review*); *Certain Lithium Ion Batteries, Battery Cells, Battery Modules, Battery Packs, Components Thereof, and Processes Therefor*, Inv. No. 337-TA-1159, ID, at 131 (Feb. 14, 2020) (*aff'd on review*). See also Chapter 23 (Spoliation).

presidential review period, imports covered by an ITC exclusion order may enter under bond (the bond amount having been determined by the Commission, as discussed above). Presidential disapproval has occurred, but rarely. In 2013, the President disapproved an ITC remedy due to overarching federal policies related to standards essential patents; it was the first disapproval since the Reagan Administration and only the sixth such time the President exercised disapproval.

A final ITC determination is appealable to the U.S. Court of Appeals for the Federal Circuit. 19 U.S.C. § 1337(c). Any party adversely affected by an ITC final determination may ask the Federal Circuit to review the determination. *Id.* The Federal Circuit reviews issues of law *de novo*; issues of fact are reviewed under the substantial evidence standard, based on the record developed before the agency. 19 U.S.C. § 1337(c); 5 U.S.C. § 706; 5 U.S.C. § 706(2)(E).

§ 21.03 Required Elements of Trade Secret Misappropriation

To successfully prosecute an unfair trade practice case at the ITC based upon trade secret misappropriation, a complainant must establish four basic substantive elements by a preponderance of evidence.

- Ownership of the asserted trade secret
- The existence of the trade secret
- Access by respondent(s) to the trade secret
- Use or disclosure of the trade secret by respondent(s) causing injury to the complainant

Certain Cast Steel Railway Wheels, Certain Processes for Manufacturing or Relating to Same and Certain Products Containing Same ("Certain Cast Steel Railway Wheels"), Inv. No. 337-TA-655, 2009 WL 4261206, ID at *36 n.14 (Oct. 16, 2009) (citation omitted) ("*Cast Steel Railway Wheels*"); and *Certain Rubber Resins,* Comm'n Op. at 10 (Feb. 26, 2014).

§ 21.04 Ownership and Standing

Commission Rule 210.12(a)(7) requires that:

> For every intellectual property based complaint (regardless of the type of intellectual property right involved), include a showing that at least one complainant is the owner or exclusive licensee of the subject intellectual property;

19 C.F.R. § 210.12(a)(7). Thus, the Commission Rules require that the complainant own the alleged trade secrets at issue or be the exclusive licensee.

§ 21.05 Existence of Trade Secrets

In *TianRui* the Federal Circuit held that "a single federal standard, rather than the law of a particular state, should determine what constitutes a misappropriation of trade secrets sufficient to establish an 'unfair method of competition' under section 337." 661 F.3d at 1327. Citing, *inter alia*, *Certain Processes for the Manufacture of Skinless Sausage Casings and Resulting Products*, Inv. No. 337–TA–148/169, USITC Pub. 1624 (Dec. 1984), ("*Certain Sausage Casings*"), the Federal Circuit noted that the Commission has long interpreted section 337 to apply to trade secret misappropriation. 661 F.3d at 1326.

A trade secret was defined in *Certain Sausage Casings* as:

> any formula, pattern, device or compilation of information which is used in one's business, and which gives him an opportunity to obtain an advantage over competitors who do not know or use it. It may be a formula for a chemical compound, a process of manufacturing, a treating or preserving materials, a pattern for a machine or other device, or a list of customers. It differs from other secret information in a business . . . in that it is not simply information as to single or ephemeral events in the conduct of the business . . . . A trade secret is a process or device for continuous use in the operation of the business . . . .

Certain Sausage Casings, 1984 WL 273789, ID at *94 (July 31, 1984) (citing The Restatement of the Law of Torts § 757, Comment c). Similarly, the Model Uniform Trade Secret Act (cited with approval by the Federal Circuit in *TianRui*, 661 F.3d at 1327-28) defines a Trade Secret as "information, including a formula, pattern, compilation, program, device, method, technique, or process, that:

> (i) derives independent economic value, actual or potential, from not being generally known to, and not being readily ascertainable by proper means by, other persons who can obtain economic value from its disclosure or use, and (ii) is the subject of efforts that are reasonable under the circumstances to maintain its secrecy."

Model Uniform Trade Secret Act § 1(4) (as amended 1985).

Certain Sausage Casings identified the following six relevant factors to determine whether or not a trade secret exists:

> (1) the extent to which the information is known outside of complainant's business;
>
> (2) the extent to which it is known by employees and others involved in complainant's business;
>
> (3) the extent of measures taken by complainant to guard the secrecy of the information;
>
> (4) the value of the information to complainant and to its competitors;
>
> (5) the amount of effort or money expended by complainant in developing the information; and
>
> (6) the ease or difficulty with which the information could be properly acquired or duplicated by others.

Id. (citing Restatement of Law of Torts, § 757, Comment b (1939)). These factors are not a six-part test that must be met to find a trade secret exists; rather, they are "instructive guidelines for ascertaining whether a trade secret exists." *See, e.g.*, *Learning Curve Toys, Inc. v. PlayWood Toys, Inc.*, 342 F.3d

714, 722 (7th Cir. 2003); *see also Certain Cast Steel Railway Wheels*, 2009 WL 4261206, ID at *94-95.

Information that may be eligible for protection as a trade secret may lose that protection if adequate steps are not taken to maintain secrecy. The burden on a complainant is to establish that reasonable precautions were taken to preserve secrecy to ensure that it would be difficult for others to discover the secret without the use of improper means. *Certain Sausage Casings*, 1984 WL 273789, ID at *94 (citing *Henry Hope X-Ray Prods., Inc. v. Marron Carrell, Inc.*, 216 U.S.P.Q. 762, 764 (9th Cir. 1982).

§ 21.06 Burden to Prove Whether or Not the Trade Secret Is Generally Known

A. Extent to which the Trade Secret Is Known Outside of Complainant's Business

Whether or not information is generally known or readily ascertainable may be considered in determining whether or not a *prima facie* case has been made that a trade secret exists. *See supra* § 21.05. Only secret information can be protected by trade secret law. "Matters of general knowledge in the industry, or those that can be readily discerned are not eligible for trade secret protection." *Certain Sausage Casings*, 1984 WL 273789, ID at *94 (citing *Motorola, Inc. v. Fairchild Camera & Instrument Corp.*, 177 U.S.P.Q. 614, 620-21 (D. Ariz. 1973)).

"Matters disclosed in patents also will destroy any claims of trade secret." *Certain Sausage Casings*, 1984 WL 273789, ID at *94 (citing *Henry Hope X-Ray Products, Inc. v. Marron Carrel, Inc.*, 216 U.S.P.Q. 762, 765 (9th Cir. 1982)). A specific embodiment of general concepts or a combination of elements, some or all of which may be known in the industry may be protectable as a trade secret. *Certain Sausage Casings*, 1984 WL 273789, ID at *94 (citing *Cybertex Computer Prods., Inc. v. Whitfield*, 203 U.S.P.Q. 1020, 1024 (D. Col. 1977)).

Certain Sausage Casings made clear that the complainant bears the burden to establish that a trade secret exists and its secrecy has been adequately protected. *Id.* at *95. The *Certain Sausage Casings* ID explained that the "burden on complainant is to establish that reasonable precautions were taken to preserve secrecy to ensure that it would be difficult for others to discover the secret without the use of improper means." *Id.*

In *Certain Cast Steel Railway Wheels*, the ALJ found that the complainant introduced sufficient evidence in the form of expert testimony that the trade secrets were not "generally known," and the testimony of a third party that the trade secrets at issue were "not generally well known." 2009 WL 4261206, ID at *12-13. Specifically, the ID cited testimony from the expert that although his task was not to compute a numerical value for the trade secrets, in his opinion, "they are valuable for not being generally known." *Id.* at *12. On appeal, the Federal Circuit indicated that the findings in the Final ID were sufficient to establish the elements of trade secret misappropriation under the generally understood law of trade secrets, as reflected in the Restatement, the Uniform Trade Secrets Act, and previous Commission decisions under section 337. *TianRui*, 661 F.3d at 1328.

Once the complainant has met its burden and shown that the trade secret exists, the burden shifts to the respondent to rebut that showing. At the ITC, such a rebuttal can be made with evidence that the trade secret could be produced through reverse engineering or by independent development. *Certain Sausage Casings*, 1984 WL 273789, ID at *95. *See infra* § 21.09.

B. The Extent of Measures Taken by Complainant to Guard the Secrecy of the Information

A complainant has the burden to demonstrate that it took reasonable steps to maintain as confidential the asserted trade secret information. While a company generally needs to take more than one such step, for a small company, it is generally sufficient to demonstrate that only key individuals have access to the information and any disclosure to other outside the company is governed by an agreement to confidentiality. *See Learning Curve Toys*, 342 F.3d at 724-26. More sophisticated parties generally will need to take more rigorous steps to maintain confidentiality. *Id.; see also Certain Rubber Resins*, 2013 WL 4495127, ID at *53 (June 17, 2013) (the ALJ found that the complainant had taken adequate steps to protect its trade secrets when it required employees to sign confidentiality agreements; required third parties, and consultants, suppliers and customers given access to trade secrets to sign confidentiality agreements; limited access to confidential information to an "as needed" basis; changed raw materials names to codes to protect the confidentiality of the identity of the raw materials; stored confidential documents in a secured file room with logged access; and implemented a written document control policy).

§ 21.07 The Trade Secret "Has Value"

Another factor for consideration is whether the information at issue is a valuable trade secret. *See supra* § 21.05. The ITC generally does not require that the complainant assign a specific economic value to the trade secret. Rather, the complainant should provide competent evidence that the trade secret has "some" value. This can be, for example, a showing that the trade secret helps to improve a product or a process for making a product, including making the process less expensive or more effective.

In *Certain Cast Steel Railway Wheels*, the ALJ found that the trade secrets at issue had value because the individual trade secrets were "useful[]" to the manufacture of a cast steel railway wheel and the trade secrets, taken as a whole, have demonstrated value in a qualitative and quantitative sense, as demonstrated by manufacturing licenses for the trade secrets. 2009 WL 4261206, ID at *16.

In *Certain Rubber Resins*, the ALJ found, and the Commission concurred, that despite the fact that some of the individual elements were generally known or readily ascertainable, the overall process was a trade secret. 2013 WL 4495127, ID at *104; Comm'n Op. at 40-41. The ALJ rejected respondents' argument that all of the individual elements were generally known, and therefore the overall combination of the elements was generally known. The ALJ reasoned that, even assuming arguendo that each of the individual elements was not a trade secret (because they were individually disclosed in various references), respondents' expert did not provide any basis to combine these various references together to reach the overall process flow. As a result, the ALJ concluded that the respondents failed to rebut complainant's showing that the overall process flow (the combination of seventeen elements) was not generally known. 2013 WL 4495127, *ID* at *54.

The Commission in *Rubber Resins* approved the ALJ's finding that the combination of trade secrets was valuable, noting that the overall process for producing tackifier products produced a superior tackifier product compared to the complainant's only competition (other than respondents), and that the complainant generated licensing revenue for the trade secrets as a whole, which had a significant present value. Comm'n Op. at 41.

§ 21.08 Misappropriation of Trade Secrets

A. Access

The third element of trade secret misappropriation is "access" by the respondent. *See supra* § 21.03. The complainant may demonstrate access through disclosure of the trade secret to the respondent while in a confidential relationship, or provide evidence that the respondent wrongfully acquired the trade secret by unfair means.

In *Certain Rubber Resins* the ALJ found, and the Commission concurred, that the complainant established that two of the respondents' key employees accessed the trade secrets at issue by virtue of their positions at complainant's manufacturing facilities, and that their access was subject to confidentiality agreements. 2013 WL 4495127, ID at *131; Comm'n Op. at 41-42. The evidence also established that the two employees were recruited by the respondents. 2013 WL 4495127, ID at *131. Evidence of the access included emails showing variations in formulas for the product, process flow and raw materials used. *Id.* at *134.

In *Certain Rubber Resins*, the ALJ also found that the respondents wrongfully acquired complainant's alleged trade secrets by unfair means when the two key employees left complainant to work for respondents and disclosed complainant's alleged trade secrets to the respondents. *Id.* at *131.

The evidence in *Certain Rubber Resins* showed that one of the employees was provided with an email account in respondents' company, and was in communication with them while he was still employed by the complainant, as shown by an email that was retrieved from his laptop during a forensic examination. *Id.* at *136.

The ALJ also relied on inferential evidence—(1) the respondents' lack of success to produce the products prior to November 2006, followed by their use of parameters post-November 2006 that strikingly resemble complainant's parameters without evidence of prior experimentation; and (2) the second employee who had access to the trade secrets began working for the respondents in September 2006. *Id.* at *139.

In addition, the forensic expert testified that he found evidence of a document of the respondent's, in his analysis of the employee's laptop, which was created months before the employee left the complainant's employ. The folder in which the document was found contained what was described as numerous pages of the original handwritten test record for the respondents, which identified a product with the identical title used by the complainant to identify its trade secret process. *Id.* at *136.

While the evidence in *Certain Rubber Resins* did not show a specific document that established that the two employees of complainant had removed the trade secrets, the ALJ found that they had unquestioned access to the trade secrets at issue, and the respondents began using "the exact or strikingly similar parameters" in their production of the accused product starting in November 2006. *Id.* at *138.

B. Use or Disclosure

The final element in section 337 trade secret cases is "use" or "disclosure" of the trade secret. *See Certain Cast Steel Railway Wheels*, 2009 WL 4261206, ID at *36 n.14 (citation omitted). Because section 337 is an unfair trade practice statute, one key requirement is importation of an article produced or sold using the misappropriated trade secret. This requirement thus effectively leads to a departure from a misappropriation claim made under California's trade secret statute (the CUTSA), since the elements of trade secret misappropriation under the CUTSA do not require "use" in order to establish misappropriation. *See* CAL. CIV. CODE § 3426.1(b). Under the CUTSA, a misappropriation may be based on improper acquisition of a trade secret and need not be based on improper use or disclosure. *See id.* as well as Chapter 2. Another difference between proving misappropriation at the ITC and under the CUTSA is that the CUTSA makes threatened misappropriation actionable. *See* CAL. CIV. CODE § 3426.2(a) as well as Chapter 12. A trade secret claim under section 337, however, requires that the trade secret actually has been used or disclosed.

Misappropriation is not necessarily negated by modifications to or deviation from the trade secret. *See Mangren Research & Dev. Corp. v. Nat'l Chem. Co.*, 87 F.3d 937, 944 (7th Cir. 1996) ("... if trade secret law were not flexible enough to encompass modified or even new products that are substantially derived from the trade secret of another, the protections that law provides would be hollow indeed"). Citing *Certain Cast Steel Railway Wheels*, the ALJ in *Rubber Resins* noted that the user of another's trade secret is liable even if he uses it with modifications or improvements upon it effected by his own efforts, so long as the substance of the process used by the actor is derived from the other's secret. In *Certain Rubber Resins*, the ALJ found that any minor modifications made by the respondents that were enabled by using complainant's confidential trade secrets also qualified as "unfair acts" under 19 U.S.C. § 1337(a)(1)(A). 2013 WL 4495127, ID at *149.

In *Certain Rubber Resins*, the ALJ relied on detailed expert testimony contrasting respondents' technology before and after their access to complainant's trade secrets, to conclude the respondents dramatically changed course in their approach to the process for producing the accused tackifier resins. *Id.* at *147-50. The expert had conducted side-by-side comparisons of complainant's formulas and the accused tackifier resins and provided detailed testimony supporting his findings. *Id.* at *149. The expert testimony included opinions that the similarities between complainant's and respondents' formulas and manufacturing processes—considering the access enjoyed by the two employees who left complainant to join respondents—supported the conclusion that respondents used complainant's trade secrets. *Id.* The ALJ also concluded that the strong circumstantial evidence compelled the conclusion that respondents' access to complainant's trade secrets gave them a substantial head start on any minor modifications/derivations. *Id.* at *150.

§ 21.09 Affirmative Defenses of Independent Development or Reverse Engineering

At the ITC, potential defenses to an allegation of misappropriation include that the respondent discovered the secret by reverse engineering a finished product or by independent research. *See, e.g.*, *Certain Sausage Casings*, ID at *95.

Independent development is often asserted; but "when a respondent asserts that his use of the secret process is the product of independent development, respondent bears a heavy burden of persuasion to show that independent development" occurred. *Id.* (citation omitted).

In *Certain Rubber Resins*, the respondents' claim of independent development suffered from "multiple evidentiary gaps." 2013 WL 4495127, ID at *212. Key allegations regarding the respondents' purported independent development were unsupported by credible evidence. *Id.* The respondents demonstrated that they developed minor modifications to the process but only by using the complainant's trade secrets as a starting point. *Id.* at *213. The ALJ found that the respondents' process was not based on their own work, and the respondents' independent development defense failed as a result. *Id.*

One factor that may be considered in connection with this defense is the amount of effort or money expended by complainant in developing the information. In *Certain Sausage Casings*, for example, the ALJ found that the efforts expended by complainants over a period of years increased speed, improved product quality, and overall efficiency of manufacturing operations. The ALJ noted that those results were accomplished by "an extensive and intricate system of drawings, standards and specifications" considered by the complainants to be a necessary aspect of successful operations. In contrast, the ALJ observed, "... the incomplete and seemingly disorganized frame-work of [the respondent's] operations tends to bolster the doubts raised about the independent development of their operations." *Certain Sausage Casings* 1984 WL 273789, ID at *116.

§ 21.10 Domestic Industry

In all cases brought to the ITC, the complainant has the burden to prove what is known as the "domestic industry" requirement. This is an aspect of the case that is unique to the ITC. Failure to prove this element will result in a disposition unfavorable to the complainant, and can result in early termination of the case. As explained below, trade secret-based ITC proceedings use a different domestic industry requirement than ITC proceedings that are based on patents.

Most section 337 cases are patent-based proceedings, and in those cases a complainant must establish that an industry "relating to the articles protected by the patent . . . exists or is in the process of being established" in the United States. 19 U.S.C. § 1337(a)(2). The domestic industry requirements for those cases, which are referred to as "statutory cases," consists of an "economic prong" and a "technical prong." *Certain Data Storage Systems and Components Thereof*, Inv. No. 337-TA-471, ID Granting EMC's Motion No. 471-8 Relating to the Domestic Industry Requirement's Economic Prong (unreviewed) at *3 (Public Version, Oct. 22, 2002). The "economic prong" of the domestic industry requirement is satisfied when it is determined that the economic activities set forth in subsections (A), (B), and/or (C) of 19 U.S.C. § 1337(a)(3) have taken place or are taking place. *Certain Variable Speed Wind Turbines and Components Thereof*, Inv. No. 337-TA-376, USITC Pub.

No. 3003, 1996 ITC LEXIS 556, Comm'n Op. at 21 (Nov. 1996) ("*Certain Wind Turbines*"). To meet the technical prong, the complainant must establish that it practices at least one valid claim of the asserted patent. *Certain Point of Sale Terminals and Components Thereof*, Inv. No. 337-TA-524, Order No. 40 (Apr. 11, 2005).

Unlike "statutory cases," trade secret cases brought pursuant 19 U.S.C. § 1337(a)(1)(A) require different proof related to the domestic industry.

Section 1337(a)(1)(A), which is the subsection that governs trade secrets claims at the ITC, proscribes:

> Unfair methods of competition and unfair acts in the importation of articles (other than articles provided for in subparagraphs (B), (C), (D), and (E)) into the United States, or in the sale of such articles by the owner, importer, or consignee, the threat or effect of which is—
>
> (i) to destroy or substantially injure an industry in the United States;
>
> (ii) to prevent the establishment of such an industry; or
>
> (iii) to restrain or monopolize trade and commerce in the United States.

19 U.S.C. § 1337(a)(1)(A).

There are two major differences between statutory cases and trade secrets cases. First, there is no requirement in a trade secrets case that the complainant prove that the domestic industry currently uses the intellectual property involved. Thus, there is no "technical prong" requirement in a trade secrets case. Second, the complainant must prove that a domestic industry exists that is subject to injury as a result of unfair acts, *i.e.*, "the target of the unfair acts and practices." *See Certain Cast Steel Railway Wheels*, ID, at *31-32; *Certain Nut Jewelry and Parts Thereof*, Inv. No. 337-TA-229, Comm'n Op. at *16-17 (Nov. 1986). This requirement does not exist in a statutory case.

In non-statutory IP investigations, the Commission may consider a broad range of elements in evaluating whether a domestic industry exists beyond those set forth in subsection 337(a)(3). *TianRui*, 661 F.3d at 1335-37; *Certain Hand Dryers and Housings for Hand Dryers* ("*Certain Hand Dryers*"), Inv. No. 337-TA-1015, Comm'n Op. at 4 ("[T]here is no requirement to show investments in the section 337(a)(3) categories to establish a violation of section 337(a)(1)(A)."). For example, the commission has not limited its analysis to investments in manufacturing but has credited investments in R&D as well, including for facilities where R&D is conducted and R&D personnel. *See Certain Rubber Resins*, ID, at 623-24 (crediting investments "in domestic research and development" in a trade secret case). In *Certain Cast Steel Railway Wheels*, a domestic industry was found to exist based in part on investments in three facilities where research and development was conducted, as well as employment of personnel working on research and development. *Certain Cast Steel Railway Wheels*, Unreviewed ID, at 80-81. In that case, the R&D expenditures were not related to the trade secrets that allegedly were misappropriated. *Id.* at 75-81.

"The Commission has a long history ... of looking to 'the realities of the marketplace,' when determining the [existence of a] domestic industry in a trade secrets investigation." *Certain Botulinum Toxin Products*, ID, at 48. "There is no minimum monetary expenditure that a complainant must demonstrate, and there is no need to defined or quantify an industry in absolute mathematical terms." *Id.; see Certain Male Prophylactic Devices,* Inv. No. 337-TA-546, Comm'n Op. at 39 (Aug. 1, 2007) ("[t]here is no mathematical threshold test."). When a complainant conducts operations abroad, a comparative analysis of a complainant's domestic expenditures versus its foreign expenditures, or an analysis of the value added by the domestic activities, is conducted to determine the significance of the domestic activities. *Certain Botulinum Toxin Products*, ID, at 48-49.

A. Existence of Domestic Industry

1. Scope of the Investigation

To establish the existence of a relevant domestic industry, one frequently must determine the scope of the investigation, which is established by the Notice of Investigation issued and published by the Commission. *See, e.g.*, *Certain Telephonic Digital Added Main Line Systems*, Inv. No. 337-TA-400, Order 8 (Dec. 2, 1997); *Certain NOR & NAND Flash Memory Devices & Products Containing Same*, Inv. No. 337-TA-560, Order No. 14 (July 6, 2006); *Certain Inkjet Ink Cartridges with Printheads and Components Thereof ("Certain Inkjet Ink Cartridges")*, Inv. No. 337-TA-723, Order No. 12 (Oct. 5, 2010); 19 C.F.R. § 210.10(b)).

In *Certain Rubber Resins*, for example, the Notice of Investigation ordered that an investigation be instituted to determine:

> [W]hether there is a violation of subsection (a)(1)(B) of section 337 in the importation into the United States, the sale for importation, or the sale within the United States after importation of certain rubber resins and processes for manufacturing same by reason of misappropriation of trade secrets, the threat or effect of which is to destroy or substantially injure an industry in the United States.

Certain Rubber Resins, 2013 WL 4495127, ID at *223.

Based upon the scope defined in the Notice of Investigation in *Certain Rubber Resins*, the ALJ found that the relevant domestic industry at issue is one that includes "rubber resins," and was not limited to "tackifier resins." *Id.*

2. Proof of Existence of the Domestic Industry

In *Certain Cast Steel Railway Wheels*, the respondent, TianRui, argued that the complainant did not satisfy the domestic industry requirement of section 337 because the complainant no longer practiced its process in the United States. Therefore, the respondent argued, there was no "domestic industry" that could be injured by the misappropriation of trade secrets relating to that process.

The Commission found the existence of a domestic industry, upholding the decision of the ALJ who held that it was not essential that the domestic industry use the proprietary process, as long as the misappropriation of that process caused injury to the complainant's domestic industry. In upholding the Commission's determination, the Federal Circuit specifically found that "there is no express requirement in the general provision that the domestic industry relate to the intellectual property involved in the investigation." *TianRui*, 661 F.3d at 1335.

Similarly, in *Certain Rubber Resins*, respondents argued that apportionment of domestic operations to domestic industry in a trade secret case must be to "that portion of complainant's domestic operations devoted to utilization of the confidential and proprietary technology at issue which is the target of the unfair acts or practices." *Certain Rubber Resins*, 2013 WL 4495127, ID at *223. (citing *Certain Sausage Casings*, 1984 WL 273789, ID at *136). The ALJ rejected that argument, citing *TianRui*, and found that the complainant had proven by a preponderance of evidence that a domestic industry in rubber resins exists in the United States. *Id.*

The ALJ noted the unrebutted and corroborated evidence of complainant's expert witness who testified regarding complainant's market share in the relevant industry and the amount of tackifier resins provided in the United States by complainant. This testimony was supported by fact testimony and documents provided by complainant. The evidence also showed a manufacturing site and a research and development site, both of which represented millions of dollars in investment. Complainant also provided related manufacturing and sales figures for its operations in the United States. *Id.* at *224-26. On review, the ALJ's findings were affirmed by the Commission. Comm'n Op. at 60.

B. Injury, Threat of Injury, or Tendency to Substantially Injure the Domestic Industry

Another notable difference between a "statutory" case and an unfair trade practices case involving trade secrets is that a complainant in a trade secrets case must satisfy an "injury component," which requires proof by a preponderance of evidence that the "threat or effect" of a respondent's misappropriation is "to destroy or substantially injure" the domestic industry. 19 U.S.C. § 1337(a)(1)(A); *TianRui*, 661 F.3d at 1335.

1. Actual Injury

The Commission has considered a "broad range of indicia" to determine whether unfair acts have the effect of substantially injuring the domestic industry. These factors include:

(1) the respondent's volume of imports and penetration into the market;

(2) the complainant's lost sales;

(3) underselling by the respondent;

(4) the complainant's declining production, profitability and sales; and

(5) the harm to complainant's goodwill and reputation.

Certain Cast Steel Railway Wheels, 2009 WL 4261206, ID, *at *32 (quoting Certain Electric Power Tools, Battery Cartridges and Battery Chargers*, Inv. No. 337-TA-284, Unreviewed ID, at 246 (1991) ("*Certain Electric Power Tools*")).

When a complainant alleges actual injury, (*i.e.*, effect) there must be a causal nexus between the unfair acts of the respondents and the injury. *Bally/Midway Mfg. Co. v. Int'l Trade Comm'n*, 714 F.2d 1117, 1125 (Fed. Cir. 1983) ("*Bally*").

To prove actual injury, a complainant must prove that the unfair acts by the respondents substantially injured the relevant domestic industry in the United States. Unlike the often complicated and costly damages phase of a district court action, the focus at the ITC is upon the question of whether or not there has been ***any*** damage to the domestic industry, and the Commission need not quantify the amount of that injury.

Consideration of whether or not the accused importations had the effect of substantial injury to the domestic industry necessarily includes the five indicia used by the Commission in *Certain Electric Power Tools* and restated in *Certain Cast Steel Railway Wheels*, described above. It is important to view those indicia in light of the nature and characteristics of the relevant domestic industry.

In *TianRui* the complainant submitted evidence that imported cast steel railway wheels could compete directly with wheels produced by a trade secret owner. The Commission concluded that such competition was sufficiently related to the investigation to constitute an injury to an "industry" within the meaning of section 337(a)(1)(A). *TianRui*, 661 F.3d at 1337. On review, the Federal Circuit upheld the Commission's ruling, holding that "the Commission's conclusion in that regard is based on a proper construction of the statute and that its factual analysis of the effect of TianRui's imports on the domestic industry is supported by substantial evidence." *Id.*

In *Certain Rubber Resins*, the arguments regarding injury were similar to those made in *TianRui*. The complainant argued damages in the form of lost sales and negative impacts upon its contract negotiations with existing customers resulting from the respondents' offers to sell to the complainant's customers. 2013 WL 4495127, ID, at *239. The respondents countered that the complainant's lost sales were de-minimis and that their "offers" to sell to the complainant's customers could not be the basis for a finding of injury. *Id.*

The complainant produced expert testimony that the importation of the accused products was enough to produce approximately 50,000 tires, which were likely to be used or sold in the United States. *Id.* The expert opined that even modest market penetration by a rival, particularly a rival using misappropriated trade secrets, would reduce prices. *Id.* The ALJ found the respondents penetrated the market for rubber resins to a degree that was disproportionate to the actual volume of tackifier resins they imported. *Id.* at *243.

While the respondents admitted that they imported tackifier resins, they argued that the quantity of importations was "miniscule," and therefore respondent's penetration into the market was "negligible." *Id.* The ALJ found otherwise, citing *Certain Trolley Wheel Assemblies*, in which the Commission found that the importation of a single trolley wheel assembly met the requirement for "importation or sale." *Id.* at *20. The Commission so held despite the fact that the trolley wheel assembly was not sold and was imported with the designation "without commercial value." *Id.* at *240 (citing *Certain Trolley Wheel Assemblies*, Comm'n Op. at 7-8). The ALJ in *Certain Rubber Resins* found that the respondents' offer to sell their tackifier resins to one of the complainant's customers, coupled with the importation and resultant qualification of the respondents' tackifier resins for sale to that customer, resulted in actual damages to the complainant's domestic industry. 2013 WL 4495127, ID, at *243. The ALJ concluded that the respondents committed unfair practices in the importation and sale of articles made with misappropriated trade secrets that resulted in actual injury to a domestic industry and that there was a causal nexus between the respondents' unfair acts and the actual injury to the complainant's domestic industry, which violated 19 U.S.C. § 1337(a)(1)(A). *Id.* On review, the Commission affirmed the ALJ's findings on all bases except lost sales. Comm'n Op. at 63.

2. Threat of Injury or Tendency to Injure

An alternative to proving actual damage is for the complainant to prove that a respondent's unfair acts threaten to injure or destroy the complainant's domestic industry. In evaluating whether or not a "threat of substantial injury" exists, Commission consideration includes the following factors:

(1) substantial foreign manufacturing capacity;

(2) ability of imported product to undersell the domestic product;

(3) explicit intention to enter into the U.S. market;

(4) the inability of the domestic industry to compete with the foreign products because of vastly lower foreign costs of production and lower prices; and

(5) the significant negative impact this would have on the domestic industry.

In addition, the threatened injury must be "substantive and clearly foreseen," and the complainant must show a causal connection between the respondent's unfair act and the alleged future injury. *Certain Methods for Extruding Plastic Tubing*, Inv. No. 337-TA-110, 0082 WL 941574, Comm'n Op. at *9 (Sept. 1982); *Certain Digital Multimeters, and Products with Multimeter Functionality*, Inv. No. 337-TA-588, 2010 WL 5642165, Comm'n Op. at *33 (Dec. 2010) ("*Certain Digital Multimeters*"); and *Certain Electric Power Tools* at 247-48.

In *Certain Rubber Resins*, the complainant based its threatened injury case on the respondents' substantial foreign manufacturing capacity, their ability to import product to undersell the complainant's product, an explicit intention to enter into the U.S. market, lower foreign costs of production and lower prices. 2013 WL 4495127, ID, at *228. The respondents did not contest that they had substantial foreign manufacturing capacity, an ability to undersell the complainant, and the explicit intention to enter into the U.S. market. *Id.* at *243.

The focus of the dispute in *Certain Rubber Resins* was whether the legal standard required proof of a foreign cost advantage, or a showing of "vastly" lower production costs. Several cases were cited by the complainant that did not use the word "vastly," (*see, e.g.*, *Certain Digital*

Multimeters, at 17; *Certain Air Impact Wrenches*, Inv. No. 337-TA-311, USITC Pub. 2419 (June 18, 1991), at 138, 139 (May 6, 1991); *Certain Electric Power Tools*, ID, at 248, 249), while other cases used the word "vastly." *Id.* at *244. The ALJ found that the latter cases used "vastly" in reference to the facts proved by the evidence rather than listing "vastly lower production costs" as a requirement. *Id.* (citing, *e.g.*, *Certain Plastic Tubing* at *24, 26, 27.) The ALJ ruled that the "broad range of indicia" used by the Commission to determine whether unfair acts have the tendency substantially to injure the domestic industry does not require a finding of "vastly lowered production costs," and found that respondents' unfair acts had "the effect of substantial injury and a tendency to substantially injure the domestic industry. *Id.*

While the decision in *Certain Rubber Resins* did not use production costs as an indicator, it did include a finding that the complainant's products could not compete with the respondents' products based upon the respondents' lower prices, which respondents admitted were derived in part from lower costs of production. *Id.* at *245. The ALJ found that the evidence also supported a finding that the respondents' lower costs of production arose, at least in part, from costs they were able to avoid as a result of their misappropriation of the complainant's trade secrets instead of actually developing the process necessary to produce a product equal to that of complainant's resins. *Id.* Thus, the ALJ concluded that the respondents' unfair acts had the effect of substantial injury and a tendency substantially to injure the complainant's domestic industry. *Id.* Those findings and conclusions were affirmed by the Commission on review. Comm'n Op. at 66.

Finally, in *Certain Rubber Resins*, the ALJ found that the evidence as a whole demonstrated that the threat to injure or destroy the domestic industry was substantive and clearly foreseen as a result of the respondents' unfair acts. *Id.*

§ 21.11 Remedies and Bonding in Trade Secrets Cases

Pursuant to 19 U.S.C. § 1337(d), the Commission may issue either a limited or a general exclusion order. A limited exclusion order instructs U.S. Customs and Border Protection ("CBP") to exclude from entry into the United States all articles that are produced using the misappropriated trade secret(s) at issue and that originate from a named respondent in the investigation. A general exclusion order instructs CBP to exclude from entry all articles that are produced using the misappropriated trade secret(s), without regard to source.

A. General Exclusion Order

A general exclusion order is permitted in certain limited situations. Specifically, the statute provides:

> (2) The authority of the Commission to order an exclusion from entry of articles shall be limited to persons determined by the Commission to be violating this section unless the Commission determines that—
>
> (A) a general exclusion from entry of articles is necessary to prevent circumvention of an exclusion order limited to products of named persons; or

> (B) there is a pattern of violation of this section and it is difficult to identify the source of infringing products.

19 U.S.C. § 1337(d)(2); *see also Certain Hydraulic Excavators*, Inv. No. 337-TA-582, Comm'n Op. (Feb. 3, 2009) (describing the standard for general exclusion orders). The Federal Circuit has noted that a complainant must meet "the heightened requirements of 1337(d)(2)(A) or (B)" before the Commission can issue a general exclusion order. *Kyocera Wireless Corp.v. Int'l Trade Comm'n*, 545 F.3d 1340, 1358 (Fed. Cir. 2008) ("*Kyocera*"). Because of its considerable impact on international trade, potentially extending beyond the parties and articles involved in the investigation, the Commission exercises caution in issuing general exclusion orders.

1. Circumvention—19 U.S.C. § 1337(d)(2)(A)

This prong of the statute requires a showing that "a general exclusion from entry of articles is necessary to prevent circumvention of an exclusion order limited to products of named persons[.]" 19 U.S.C. § 1337(d)(2)(A).

The standard for a finding under this subsection is difficult to meet. In one example, the Commission upheld a finding that this standard was met and issued a General Exclusion Order, based upon findings that, among other conduct, foreign manufacturers package their products in unmarked, generic or reseller branded packaging that lacks any markings or labels to identify their origin, and many manufacturers and distributors create multiple websites and corporate identities with ease, allowing them to sell infringing products while concealing their true identities. *Certain Inkjet Ink Cartridges*, Comm'n Op. (February, 2013).

2. Pattern of Violation and Difficulty to Identify Source—19 U.S.C. § 1337(d)(2)(B)

This prong requires a showing that "there is a pattern of violation of this section and it is difficult to identify the source of infringing products." *Certain Rubber Resins*, ID, at *268. Proving a violation by only the named respondents in an investigation may not be sufficient to show a pattern of violation and difficulty in identifying the sources of infringing products. *Certain Self-Cleaning Litter Boxes & Components Thereof*, Inv. No. 337-TA-625, Comm'n Op. at 56 (Apr. 28, 2009) (explaining that a "pattern of violation of this section" had not been proven where the evidence showed imports only by the three named respondents), *rev'd on other grounds, Lucky Litter LLC v. Int'l Trade Comm'n*, 403 Fed. App'x. 490 (Fed. Cir. 2010). In another investigation, the Commission found that infringement by four respondents did not establish the "pattern of violation" that warranted a general exclusion order. *Certain Ground Fault Circuit Interrupters & Products Containing Same*, Inv. No. 337-TA-615, Comm'n Op. at 26 (Mar. 26, 2009)), *rev'd in part on other grounds, General Protecht Group, Inc. v. Int'l Trade Comm'n*, 619 F.3d 1303 (Fed. Cir. 2010). However, if numerous respondents are named and proven to be in violation of section 337, and additional evidence is adduced to demonstrate the difficulties in identifying sources for infringing products, this statutory factor may be satisfied.

In *Certain Rubber Resins*, the ALJ found that the complainant failed to demonstrate that it was entitled to a general exclusion order under Section 337(d)(2)(B), because the complainant had not introduced any evidence of importation that was unrelated to one of the respondents. *Certain Rubber Resins*, ID, at *269. The ALJ explained that the Commission has found that complainants failed to show a "pattern of violation" when the complainants "failed to identify a single act of importation that is unrelated to one of the Respondents." *Id.* As a consequence, the ALJ declined to recommend a general exclusion order pursuant to 19 U.S.C. § 1337(d)(2)(B). *Id.*

B. Limited Exclusion Order

The remedy most frequently ordered by the Commission in a section 337 investigation is the limited exclusion order ("LEO"), instructing CBP to exclude from entry all articles that are produced using the misappropriated trade secret at issue and that originate from a named respondent in the investigation. The LEO typically applies to the named respondents as well as all of their affiliated companies, parents, subsidiaries, other related business entities, and their successors or assigns and covers the products that are made using trade secrets misappropriated from a complainant.

An LEO may also include a "certification provision." Certification provisions are generally included in exclusion orders where Customs is unable easily to determine by inspection whether an imported product violates a particular exclusion order, and it gives CBP the authority to accept a certification from the parties that goods being imported are not covered by the exclusion order. *See, e.g.*, *Certain Semiconductor Chips With Minimized Chip Package Size & Products Containing Same*, Inv. No. 337-TA-605, Comm'n Op. (July 29, 2009); *Certain Ground Fault Circuit Interrupters & Products Containing Same*, Inv. No. 337-TA-615, Comm'n Op. (Mar. 26, 2009).

C. Duration of Exclusion Order

The Commission has based the duration of exclusion orders in trade secrets investigations on a "reasonable research and development period," or an "independent development time" for the trade secrets at issue. *See Certain Apparatus for the Continuous Production of Copper Rod*, Inv. No. 337-TA-52, Comm'n Op. at 67 (Nov. 1979); *Certain Sausage Casings*, Comm'n Decision Not to Review ID Finding Violation at *19.

In *Certain Rubber Resins* the ALJ recommended and the Commission ordered the exclusion order run for 10 years from the target date, based upon expert testimony that it would take at least 10 years of devoted research and development to develop the complainant's process. *Certain Rubber Resins*, ID, at *269-70. Similarly, in *Organik Kimya*, the Commission determined that the evidence demonstrated it would have taken Organik Kimya 25 years to develop -- without using Dow's trade secrets -- a commercial opaque polymer comparable to that of complainant Dow Chemical Company. The Commission concluded that 25 years was an appropriate length for an exclusion order. 848 F.3d at 1001. However, the Commission expressly allowed Organik Kimya to bypass the limited exclusion order and import products using opaque polymers into the U.S. prior to the elapse of the 25-year period provided the company could demonstrate to the Commission that it had developed the opaque polymers without the use of Dow's misappropriated trade secrets. *Id.* at 1004-05.

D. Cease and Desist Order

Section 337 permits the Commission to issue a cease and desist order as a remedy for violation of section 337, either in lieu of or in addition to an exclusion order. 19 U.S.C. § 1337(f)(1). Generally, the Commission will issue a cease and desist order directed to a domestic respondent when there is a "commercially significant" amount of a respondent's imported product in inventory in the United States that could be sold, so as to undercut the remedy provided by an exclusion order. *Certain Crystalline Cefadroxil Monohydrate*, Inv. No. 337-TA-293, USITC Pub. 2391, Comm'n Op. on Remedy, the Public Interest and Bonding at 37-42 (June 1991); *Certain Condensers, Parts Thereof and Products Containing Same, Including Air Conditioners for Automobiles*, Inv. No. 337-TA-334, Comm'n Op. at 26-28 (Aug. 20, 1997). The complainant bears the burden of proving that a respondent has a commercially significant inventory in the United States. *Certain Integrated Repeaters, Switches, Transceivers & Products Containing Same*, Inv. No. 337-TA-435, Comm'n Op., 2002 WL 31359028, at *14 (Aug. 16, 2002).

In *Certain Cast Steel Railway Wheels*, the Commission issued a limited exclusion order to last for a period of ten years, and a cease and desist order to last for a like period. 2010 WL 1055967, Comm'n Op. at *1, *5 (Mar. 19, 2010). The cease and desist order prohibited respondents from importing, selling, marketing, advertising, distributing, offering for sale, transferring (except for exportation), soliciting U.S. agents or distributors or aiding or abetting other entities in the importation, sale for importation, sale after importation, transfer (except for exportation), or distribution of cast steel railway wheels and products containing the same manufactured using any of the asserted trade secrets in that case. *Id.*

E. Bonding

Once the Commission finds a violation of section 337, it must determine the amount of a bond to be required of a respondent, pursuant to section 337(j)(3), during the 60-day Presidential review period following the issuance of permanent relief. The purpose of the bond is to protect the complainant from any injury. 19 C.F.R. §§ 210.42(a)(1)(ii), 210.50(a)(3). The complainant has the burden to support any bond amount it proposes. *Certain Rubber Antidegradants, Components Thereof, and Products Containing Same*, Inv. No. 337-TA-533, Comm'n Op. at 19, 2006 ITC LEXIS 591, at *60 (July 21, 2006).

When reliable price information is available, the Commission often has set the bond by eliminating the differential between the domestic product and the imported, infringing product. *See Certain Microsphere Adhesives, Processes for Making Same, and Products Containing Same, Including Self-Stick Repositionable Notes*, Inv. No. 337-TA-366, Comm'n Op. at 24 (1995). In other cases, the Commission has turned to alternative approaches, particularly when the level of a reasonable royalty rate could be ascertained. *See, e.g.*, *Certain Integrated Circuit Telecommunication Chips and Products Containing Same, Including Dialing Apparatus*, Inv. No. 337-TA-337, Comm'n Op. at 41 (1995).

§ 21.12 ITC Investigations v. Court Cases—The Nuts and Bolts

As set forth above, there are a number of differences between ITC investigations and court cases—both in terms of procedure and available remedy. This section highlights some of the primary differences; explains why certain factual scenarios make the ITC an attractive option for enforcing a variety of rights, including trade secret rights; and provides certain practical tips.

A. Speed

ITC investigations are fast, even those that involve complex issues and multiple parties. The average ITC investigation, including trade secret cases, has an average target date of 16 months. The target date is the date by which the Commission will issue its Final Determination and all dates in the investigation work back from the target date. The Commission has four months to review the ALJ's ID, and the ALJ typically has two to three months to issue the ID after the hearing. Thus, an investigation with a 16-month target date will typically be heard by the ALJ eight to nine months after the notice of investigation. All fact and expert discovery, dispositive motions, and all pre-hearing tasks (which are very similar to pre-trial tasks) are compressed into an eight to nine month timeframe.

The speed of ITC investigations – and the fact of moving an investigation from file to trial in only eight or nine months – generally rivals, if not exceeds, any "rocket docket" court. The fast pace, coupled with the numerous unique procedural aspects involved in section 337 administrative proceedings, can provide advantages to all parties in terms of facilitating early settlements and reducing overall litigation spend given the compressed time schedule. Those advantages tend to be magnified for a complainant, who often has a least a several month lead on the respondents by the time the investigation is instituted by the Commission. That typically occurs 30 days after the filing of the complaint, which itself generally happens after the complainant has met with and obtained comments from OUII staff concerning the allegations in the complaint. Complainants often have their experts engaged and their discovery ready to serve at initiation. Given the collapsed time frame for the typical investigation, this head start can give the complainant a tremendous tactical advantage.

B. Jurisdictional Differences

The jurisdictional differences between ITC proceedings and court cases are significant, and they should be considered in connection with any enforcement action. Given the in rem nature of section 337 trade secret (and other) proceedings, litigants are able to assert claims against entities on a worldwide basis in one proceeding. Thus, an ITC complaint may name individuals or entities in, by way of example, China, India, France, California and New York. Assuming each of the named respondents was involved in importing, selling for importation or selling after importation the accused products, those products all would be subject to jurisdiction before the ITC—based in Washington, D.C. There is no requirement or need to establish minimum contacts or otherwise prove personal jurisdiction where an exclusion order is sought. These significant differences between ITC court practice are critically important to note when choosing an enforcement forum. The breadth of subject matter jurisdiction for extra-territorial acts also militate in favor of bringing the action in the ITC. But see Chapter 7 (discussing the extra-territorial reach of the Defend Trade Secrets Act [DTSA]).

C. Procedural Differences and Pleadings

There are a number of important procedural differences between ITC proceedings and court cases, some of which are discussed above. As a general rule, ITC proceedings have a number of procedural requirements that generally are not found in court cases, beginning with the extensive set of "ground rules" set by each ALJ. A firm knowledge of Commission practice and procedure is critical to practicing effectively before the Commission.

Apart from the ground rules, there are a number of discovery differences between ITC and court practice. In general, the timelines for responding to discovery and motions practice are accelerated in an ITC investigation. For example, a party has ten days to respond to interrogatories and requests for production and ten days to respond to a motion in the ITC. In court cases, generally parties have thirty days to respond to discovery requests, and often, it can take much longer for motions to be resolved.

Discovery in court cases generally is more limited than discovery at the ITC. For example, in the ITC, each party may serve 175 interrogatories including discrete subparts. *See* 19 C.F.R. § 210.29(a) (as amended on Apr. 19, 2013). By contrast, in court, the number is far more limited. *See* Fed. R. Civ. P. 33 (maximum number of 25); Cal. Civ. Proc. Code § 2030.030 (maximum number of 35).

In general, the admission of evidence in an administrative proceeding is more relaxed than in a court case. The ITC proceeding does not involve a jury, but rather a seasoned ALJ, well versed in trade secret and other intellectual property rights and also in creating a solid record for evidentiary findings. As an example of the more relaxed treatment of evidence, reliable hearsay evidence is admissible in ITC proceedings. ALJs will consider such hearsay evidence and determine the weight, if any, to ascribe to that evidence. Additionally, it is not necessary to authenticate documents in an ITC investigation, unless there is a genuine issue regarding authenticity. The evidentiary process in court generally is more stringent.

There also exist some differences in pleadings between ITC and court cases. The ITC requires very detailed, fact-based pleadings that go well beyond the typical federal court requirements for notice pleading. In general, a complainant at the ITC has a much more difficult job putting together a complaint than does a court plaintiff.

D. Parties (Including the Staff)

In a court case, the parties are the plaintiff(s) and the defendant(s). In an ITC investigation, the parties are the complainant(s) and respondent(s). In addition, a staff attorney from the ITC's OUII may be assigned to the matter. The staff attorney represents the public's interest in the investigation and participates fully in the investigation (although perhaps not on all issues). For example, the staff attorney may propound discovery to the parties, may submit responses to the private parties' motions, may submit pre- and post-hearing briefs, and may examine or cross-examine witnesses during depositions and at the hearing. Developing a cordial relationship with the staff attorney and being attentive to public interest arguments that may resonate with OUII can give a party a decided advantage in eliciting OUII support for a party's position.

E. Remedies

Monetary damages are not available in ITC proceedings. The ITC can exclude products from being imported into the United States through general and limited exclusions orders. The ITC also can prevent products that have been imported into the United States from being sold in the U.S. market via a cease and desist order. Those remedies, which are tantamount to injunctive relief, do not require the Commission to consider the multi-factor test required in court prior to issuance of an injunction (*see supra* Chapter 12). In contrast, courts are able to award monetary damages as well as award injunctions.

In matters where money damages are an important consideration, complainants may file a parallel court proceeding. In fact, this procedural pattern is a common occurrence—that is, a complainant often files parallel actions before the ITC and in federal district court. Typically, and if the parties and claims are the same, the district court case will be stayed until the faster-moving ITC proceeding is completed. *See* 28 U.S.C. § 1659(a) (the stay is mandatory if the respondent seeks a stay and the statutory requirements are otherwise met). To stay the district court proceeding, a respondent must request such a stay within thirty days after the district court action is filed, or within thirty days after the Notice of Investigation for the section 337 case is published in the *Federal Register*, whichever is longer. Furthermore, the record before the ITC can be used in connection with the district court case. *See* 28 U.S.C. § 1659(b). Thus, the parties are able to litigate one proceeding at a time.

F. Role of Experts

Practice before the ITC requires adherence to a fairly sophisticated array of technical and procedural rules and well developed legal standards. A sizeable cadre of experts have developed, and many make regular appearances in ITC 337 proceedings. Their expertise and assistance can be a sizeable advantage. For trade secret investigations, parties likely will want to consider engaging experts on domestic industry issues, trade secret issues, and injury and remedy issues. Engaging these experts early can fortify a party's discovery plan and facilitate strategic summary determination motions. See also Chapter 24 (use of experts in trade secret litigation).

G. Costs

Where the value of the trade secrets at issue in a proceeding exceed $10 million, it is not unusual for the cost of an ITC trade secret investigation to be $5 million or more. The big difference with a federal district court case is that in district court, that tab would be incurred over the course of 2-1/2 or 3 years, but in the ITC, it may be incurred over 9 to 12 months. A good resource on costs is the biannual AIPLA Report of the Economic Survey. The most recent available survey was conducted in 2019.

Chapter 22
DIGITAL FORENSICS IN TRADE SECRET INVESTIGATIONS

By: James D. Vaughn, Esq.
and Michael Bandemer, Esq.

---

§ 22.01 Introduction

Much of the information generated in the corporate world today, including trade secrets, is created and stored electronically on computers, networks, mobile devices, and/or in the cloud. Because of this, companies spend millions securing their networks and data from outsiders such as thieves, hackers, competitors, and foreign countries. However, the greatest risk of data and trade secret theft often comes from insiders, primarily current employees and trusted contractors, as they typically have authorized access to the information and the means to easily store and transfer the data.

When there are suspicions of a theft or potential threat, computer forensics methodologies are typically employed to uncover evidence of who, what, why, when, and how the theft occurred. This chapter outlines many of the practical considerations of performing a digital forensics examination and some common techniques for uncovering relevant evidence. This chapter addresses the ever-changing technological advances that have occurred in recent years.

A. Computer and Digital Forensics

"Computer forensics" is the science of preserving and analyzing the files and information contained on computers for the purpose of presenting findings or opinions about the use and content of that information in court. While often used interchangeably, the term "digital forensics" has a broader context and may include the analysis of phones, tablets, cloud storage sites, websites, social media sites, audit logs and other digital evidence.

In a trade secret matter, the analysis of evidence obtained from computers, networks, mobile devices, and other electronic storage media has become common. While it is still feasible that a thief could send electronic files to a printer and then walk out the door with a box full of papers, it is much more convenient and efficient to copy electronic documents to an external drive connected through the USB port, to a cloud storage site on the web or other storage device. In fact, it is difficult to think of a modern day scenario involving an allegation of trade secret theft where the preservation and analysis of electronic information would not be necessary or relevant.

Digitally copying electronic documents normally creates a trail like footprints through the sand. The use of digital forensics allows us not only to preserve those footprints, but often to recreate the steps taken by a thief to walk away with valuable company assets.

1. Evolution of Computer Forensics and Related Technologies

The use of computer forensics was once reserved only for those in law enforcement and federal agencies like the Federal Bureau of Investigations (FBI). Those bodies had access to government-developed hardware, software utilities, and applications that would allow them to identify, preserve, analyze, and often recover information stored on computers. In some cases, those tools are still only available to law enforcement. These same tools are useful to investigations of trade secret theft.

Today, there are many commercially available hardware and software products available to the forensics examiner to perform digital forensics on all varieties of personal computers, networks, mobile devices and other electronic devices and media. The products have become very specialized. For instance, there are specific tools designed for analyzing a phone or a tablet, for finding Internet artifacts on a computer, or for collecting and analyzing information in the cloud. Therefore, any comprehensive digital forensics examination will typically employ multiple tools and techniques to properly preserve, collect and analyze available evidence relevant to a trade secret theft investigation.

2. Methodology Time Lag

It is worth noting here that the capabilities of commercially available digital forensic tools can often lag the release of new operating systems or devices. This is because the companies that make digital forensics software and equipment need time to modify and to adapt their products to handle the features and characteristics of the latest operating system and/or device releases. This can be especially true with smartphones and other mobile devices whose manufacturers tend to make frequent releases of new models with changes to the features, operating system, and security settings. Amongst other things, this may impact what information may be extracted from the device, whether deleted information can be recovered or whether the forensic software requires a password to be known to bypass the encryption. Also, forensic software companies are having an increasingly difficult time finding ways to bypass passwords and other protection schemes due to the increased focus on security by mobile device manufacturers. This means it can take weeks or months before an update is available for a forensic tool to accommodate the latest smartphone or notepad.

For instance, when the iPhone 4 was released in the summer of 2010, forensic tools were not able to bypass the password and therefore were unable to preserve and extract the information on the device unless the password was obtained from the custodian. Approximately six months later, technology advancements allowed forensic tools to bypass the password, enabling digital forensics examiners to access and analyze the contents.

Thus, it is important to keep in mind that what is possible using digital forensics technology at any given time often depends on the specific hardware and software of the targeted device and the digital forensics tools that have been made commercially available to handle them. The time lapse with tools being able to perform certain functions as described above has shortened, but with that also comes more frequency that tools need to be updated to keep up with the smartphone's enhanced features. It is also important to consider more traditional ways of obtaining passwords, like interviewing IT personnel and coworkers, building dictionaries of words from other devices the individual may have used, and of course, looking for those sticky notes under the keyboard.

3. The Relationship Between Digital Forensics and E-discovery

E-discovery is primarily concerned with conducting a reasonable and repeatable effort to identify responsive and relevant electronically stored information (ESI) that is not privileged. As defined in the E-discovery reference model (EDRM), E-discovery is the process of identifying, collecting, culling/filtering, reviewing, and producing ESI to a requesting party in litigation or as the result of a regulatory proceeding. There are elements of digital forensics intertwined into E-discovery, especially when it comes to the proper preservation and collection of ESI, where it is common to use digital forensic tools and techniques.

In E-discovery, one must take reasonable steps to maintain chain-of-custody and to avoid spoliation of evidence. These are concerns typically associated with digital forensics. Additionally, while E-discovery is focused primarily on the collection and review of user documents such as those created using Microsoft Office Word or Excel and email, digital forensics is broader (or a deeper dive). A digital forensics examination often includes collecting and analyzing artifacts from the operating system, Internet history, available logs and journals, and when available, unallocated space. Routine E-discovery does not typically delve into questions about the source computer or storage device and ESI, although E-discovery may uncover the need to ask the deeper diving questions. Some examples include the following:

- When was the operating system installed and when was the employee's profile created?
- Were there previous versions of a document that were deleted?
- How did the ESI come to rest in its current state?
- Was ESI copied to an external storage device and, if so, when?
- Did this employee use cloud storage or have online email accounts?
- Can we recover text messages from this employee's phone?

Answering questions of this nature usually requires someone with knowledge, training, and experience in digital forensics to properly preserve, gather, and interpret the evidence.

Thus, the two disciplines are complimentary and overlapping and many matters utilize elements of both E-discovery and digital forensics to reach their investigative and discovery objectives.

4. Challenges Involving Mobile Devices

The widespread popularity and adoption of mobile devices and remote access to corporate resources have added complexity to both E-discovery and digital forensics efforts. While a great source of evidence, smartphones and tablets such as Android Phones, iPhones and iPads require special handling and tools to ensure proper preservation and collection of evidence. Additionally, data stored on these mobile devices is often stored within applications or in the cloud, sometimes making access to ESI problematic without appropriate authority and account credentials. Because of this, relevant ESI for an employee may go unidentified or simply ignored. Another challenge is that many companies allow for employees to bring their own device (BYOD) into the work environment, often resulting in the commingling of personal and work-related information, or companies allow an employee to control the credentials to a corporate issued mobile device with no way to access it upon the departure of the employee.

B. Trade Secrets and ESI

The Ponemon Institute, which has studied data loss risks, found that trade secrets are the most common Intellectual Property ("IP") type stolen, amounting to over 50% of the cases studied. Over 60% of companies polled had experienced attempts to steal their proprietary information. The most frequent perpetrators were current or former employees or others in trusted relationships. Insiders have the means to easily transport information outside the organization using thumb drives and the Internet. There were patterns found for who, what, when, how, and why insiders typically steal IP. In its study of data loss, the Ponemon Institute found the following:

- Employees are moving IP outside the company in all directions;
- When employees change jobs, sensitive business documents often travel with them;
- Employees are not aware they are putting themselves and their companies at risk;
- Employees typically attribute ownership of IP to the person who created it; and
- Organizations are failing to create a culture of security.

See www.ponemon.org.

§ 22.02 Typical Patterns

Various organizations and individuals have attempted to study, understand and report on the behavioral patterns associated with IP thefts. This has led to a better understanding of the motivations and circumstances surrounding the theft as well as enhanced knowledge of how to improve defending and responding to such thefts.

A. Profile of Typical IP Theft

Some of the organizations that have studied and written about the profile of a trade secret theft include The Ponemon Institute; Carnegie Mellon University's (CMU) Computer Emergency Response Team's Insider Threat group; and the Computer Security Institute. In a white paper released years back, but still relevant today, Eric Shaw and Harley Stock compiled the data and summarized the statistical profile of the "who, what, when, how and why" of typical patterns of trade secret theft, as summarized below.

- **Who Takes IP:** The majority of IP theft is committed by current male employees averaging about 37 years of age who serve in mainly technical positions. In about a quarter of these cases, the insider was recruited by an outsider who had targeted the data and about 20 percent of thefts involved collaboration with another insider.

- **What They Steal:** In the CMU study, the insiders stole trade secrets in 52 percent of the cases studied. Business information such as billing information, price lists and other administrative data was stolen in 30 percent, source code in 20 percent, proprietary software in 14 percent, customer information in 12 percent, and business plans in 6 percent.

- **When They Steal:** Unlike other forms of computer crime, most of these IP thefts occur during working hours, at the work site, consistent with the subject's routine authorized access to the information. Most frequently, these thefts were quick attacks—over two-thirds lasted less than a month, consistent with the insiders' need to take the information on their way out and use it at a new job or to start a business.

- **How They Steal:** There were six channels through which insiders stole information: email, removable media, printed materials, remote network access, file transfer, and downloads to laptops. The majority of the thieves (54 percent) used a network—email, a remote network access channel or network file transfer—to remove the stolen data. The balance stole the data from a host computer by placing it on a laptop or some form of removable media, rather than transferring it over the network.

- **Why They Steal:** While insiders stole IP primarily to gain advantage at a new job or to start a business, about a quarter of the sample gave the stolen data to a foreign company or national entity. Common events or problems that preceded the thefts and probably contributed to the thieves' motivation included:

  - Disagreements over ownership of IP
  - Fights over compensation
  - Conflicts over relocation
  - Disagreements over the thief's role after a merger or acquisition
  - Being passed over for promotion
  - General conflict with a supervisor

Eric D. Shaw & Harvey V. Stock, Behavioral Risk Indicators of Malicious Insider Theft of Intellectual Property: Misreading the Writing on the Wall, available at

https://zadereyko.info/downloads/Malicious_Insider.pdf.

B. Common Roles and Responsibilities in Investigations

Most investigations require a team to assess the situation properly and to ensure that the investigation is conducted in a legal, thorough, and defensible manner. The team's objectives include:

- Coordinating incident response logistics and team efforts
- Creating a primary events timeline
- Identifying key players and data sources
- Ensuring appropriate preservation of evidence
- Providing guidance to the response team on legal rights and responsibilities
- Communicating with company personnel and outsiders
- Examination of evidence and presentation of findings

Generally, a response team is made up of both internal corporate representatives and outside professional services. A typical team might be comprised of the following roles and responsibilities:

- Outside counsel – Provide legal, investigative guidance and coordination, key player interviews and communication, data privacy.
- Senior Business Unit/Department executive – Provide business background information related to business, key players and data sources. Identify proprietary information, storage locations and naming conventions.
- Inside counsel – Strategic decisions, coordination of team members, report to executive management, authorizations for access and privileges, key player interviews.
- Human resources – Employee interviews, employment information, corrective actions.
- Information Technology personnel – Custody and control of information systems and custodian data sources.
- Forensics Consultant/Expert – Collection and examination of electronic evidence.

C. Overview of the Steps in a Forensic Investigation of Trade Secret Theft

If a company has electronically stored proprietary or confidential information, the theft of trade secrets is a real possibility. While there are affirmative measures that can be taken to minimize the leakage of this information outside the organization, it is essentially impossible in most corporate environments to put in place enough measures to eliminate all risks. Therefore, companies should consider taking steps to increase the probability of success for any internal investigation into trade secret theft. These may include:

- Establishing the response team ahead of time and understanding legal rights to take necessary steps outlined in a playbook.
- Creating a playbook that outlines standard protocols, check lists and company best practices for the response team to follow in the event of a data theft.
- Developing a data map that details where the company stores trade secrets and who in the company has access to them.
- Reviewing IT/HR procedures for departing employees and the proper handling of their equipment to ensure there is a reasonable opportunity for the company to preserve any and all evidence in the event of an investigation.
- Documenting ways to identify company trade secrets. This may be accomplished by knowing folder locations, file names, certain embedded file metadata (such as company, author, title, etc…) or unique content.

In the unfortunate event that the company experiences a data or trade secret theft, the following steps are typically involved in a digital forensics investigation:

- Identifying and scoping
- Preservation and Collection (as soon as reasonably possible)
- Analysis
- Reporting

Several of these steps (identification and scoping, preservation and collection, and analysis) are described more fully in the sections that follow.

§ 22.03 Identifying and Scoping of ESI Data Sources and Key Evidence

To conduct an investigation effectively, one must identify and understand all of the potential data sources that may yield key evidence. What this means in any given case is dependent on the specifics of the situation.

The first goal should be to understand the company's infrastructure and how users might access data within that infrastructure. Beyond the traditional laptop or desktop, the information can also reside in locations unknown to the company's IT personnel. Some helpful approaches include:

- Interviewing IT personnel to gain understanding of how the servers are accessed by users, what types and frequencies of backups exist, and what logs may exist that cannot be found on the workstation or servers.
- Gaining an understanding of what systems are standard and those that are not. Will the collection of data require a customized approach? Are systems decommissioned or inoperable that may provide evidence?
- Understanding the use and access of third-party repositories such as outsourced email, company cloud services, and online backup programs.
- When possible, understanding the user's routine activity on the computer including websites visited, usage of removable devices, and file usage activity.
- Understanding what level of security a user had so as to determine what he or she could have accessed. This should include not only security rights on the user's workstation, but also on company servers and other repositories such as document management systems.

§ 22.04 Preservation/Collection

The preservation and collection phase of the investigation is by far the most important step when working with digital evidence, yet often it is treated with little importance when the data is gathered. Unlike traditional E-discovery cases, trade secret investigations rely on large amounts of metadata that can be altered. If data is not gathered in a way that preserves this metadata, or in a timely manner, significant evidence may be lost.

A. Collection Methods

There are various ways a forensic expert will collect data, including forensic imaging or a targeted collection. It should also be noted that with today's technology, remote collections can be performed for not only cloud based systems, but also for mobile devices, laptops and many other physical devices.

1. Forensic Image

A forensic image is made and verified by using forensically accepted hardware or software to capture the entire contents of media while the source is in "read only" mode. When speaking in generalities, some attorneys or forensic experts may refer to this forensic image as a "bit stream copy" or a "mirror image."

2. Targeted Collection

A targeted collection involves using a forensically accepted tool or technique to capture and to verify selected active files and folders from media. For example, collecting certain sub-folders from a laptop computer would be a targeted collection.

There are distinct differences between a full forensic image and a targeted collection, so it is important to understand the differences before deciding which approach might work best for a given matter. For example, if one were looking for deleted files from a laptop hard drive, then a forensic image would be the preferred method instead of a targeted collection. The described targeted collection above would only allow for active files to be collected, while a forensic image would allow you to search for, and potentially recover, deleted items since it is a copy of the entire hard drive.

3. Cloud Collection

Cloud collections typically involve gaining user credential for the account and then using third party software to extract data and metadata from the account or by using the cloud service provider's built-in retrieval platform. For example, Google and Apple's iCloud allow an authenticated user to first request and then download all email, files activity metadata etc. from an account using one simple process. This can then easily be ingested into an eDiscovery processing platform.

B. Documentation and Chain of Custody

Good documentation is important for many reasons, such as to produce evidence, to prove credibility as a witness and to do so showing that industry standards were used. Forensic consultants working within industry standards should advocate for usage of forms and other documentation that will allow the expert to testify to what was done, how it was done, and when. Examples of documentation include:

- The make and serial number of the device being imaged
- The date and time of the computer being imaged as it is routinely maintained, in contrast to the actual date and time
- The software or hardware used to capture the data

- The date the data was captured
- How the targeted collection or forensic image was verified
- The chain of custody for the collected data (who had it at all times throughout the life of the project)
- Photos of the device.

C. Encryption/Password Considerations

It is very common to encounter data sources that are either password-protected or encrypted. How to deal with this varies from device to device, and possibly from one encryption program to another. For example, data on a laptop that has full drive encryption cannot be read until the laptop is decrypted. Depending on the situation, the decryption may occur before or after the data is collected. In some cases, forensic software can be used first to image the drive and then to decrypt it using credentials subsequently fed to it. In other cases, it may be necessary either to have the laptop decrypted prior to imaging the drive, or to perform what is called a "live image." A live image simply means that the examiner will power on the computer, log in as the user or administrator, and use a forensic software tool to image the hard drive while it is in a decrypted state.

Password-protected devices may not have encrypted data, but instead simply require a password to access the device. For traditional laptops and desktops, today's technology allows a forensic examiner to bypass that password when creating a forensic image. For other devices such as a smartphone, the examiner may or may not be able to create a forensic image without first obtaining the password (or "pass code").

D. Metadata

Metadata is generally described as "data about data." It is the underlying information about documents, such as when a file was created or modified, who authored a document, when a document was printed, or when a file was copied or deleted. The forensic community commonly references two types of metadata: file system metadata and document metadata. The important thing to remember is that when conducting digital forensics, both types of metadata may play a significant role.

File system metadata is metadata that is created by the operating system (e.g., Windows or Mac). For example, when a user inserts a removable device to a Mac or Windows laptop and copies a file from the device onto the computer, the operating system recognizes the arrival of this new file and begins to track it by assigning it a creation date, among other things. Although the type of information tracked may vary between Windows and Mac, the operating system tracks this information independently: it does not matter what type of file it is or what program might be needed to open the file.

Document metadata, also known as embedded metadata, is metadata that is embedded within a particular document, and is placed there by the program used to create, to modify, or to save the document. For example, if a user opens a Word document called tradesecrets.docx, makes changes to it, prints it, saves it, then closes it, several pieces of embedded metadata could be affected, such as the author of the document, who last saved it, the print date, revision number, editing time and, if the feature was used, a history of changes made to the document. It should also be noted that certain "event logs" may record portions of this activity as well, such as a change being made to a document.

E. Practice Tip – Social Media

While social media itself might not be the vehicle for the theft of a trade secret, it may be valuable to show artifacts of things like communications with certain individuals, patterns of behavior, or raiding of corporate employees through solicitation. There are forensic tools available for capturing data from social media sites while preserving metadata. Social media examples for which these tools are available include Facebook, Instagram, LinkedIn, and Twitter.

§ 22.05 Analysis

A. Data Reliability/User Activity

Upon the proper preservation, collection and back-up of evidence, analysis can begin. It is recommended that the examiner perform analysis on a working copy of the computer image or collected data. In the beginning phases of analysis, it is prudent to ensure that the evidence being analyzed is relevant to the expected user/timeframe and reliable before delving deeper into the forensic examination. Understanding the reliability of the information on the computer or phone may also cause the examiner to reconsider the potential forensic value of the information contained on the computer as well as to realign priorities with what may reasonably be learned from the computer.

While there are many procedures an examiner may take to evaluate relevance and reliability, common steps include:

- Reviewing the operating system to determine when the operating system was installed or upgraded and what version is currently installed. A recent installation of the operating system may indicate that the computer is new or may indicate that there was an inadvertent or deliberate reinstallation of the operating system causing the deletion of all previously existing user profiles and information. The version of the operating system will also provide the examiner an indication of what evidence may be available and how it should be interpreted.

- Determining the user profiles that have been created on the computer and the first and last login dates and times.

- Reviewing the system for attempts to obfuscate data on the computer. Indications of this may be found by reviewing the operating system files for installed and executed applications that have the ability to wipe or clean the system of typical sought-after artifacts such as Internet history, external storage devices connected or recently opened documents.

- Lastly, collecting and sorting a listing of relevant and/or commonly used files (such as Microsoft Office documents, spreadsheets, and PDF's) including file system Created, Accessed and Last Modified dates and times to understand whether there is use of the computer during the relevant time period. This will also assist in determining if there are patterns such as spikes in the use of the computer that may be indicators of mass deletion, copying or uploading of files. This information may also be correlated with other forensic artifacts discussed throughout this chapter.

B. Communication

Communication can come in many forms as it pertains to forensic analysis on a user's device. It can be used to steal trade secrets through webmail, corporate mail, cloud storage or transfer, and more. Further, it can look different from one device to another depending on a number of factors.

C. Movement of Data

When conducting the forensic analysis, the goal is to find evidence of the movement of the data to either support, disprove or show inconclusiveness that data has been exfiltrated. Depending on the case specifics, movement tracking may be done through several means, including Internet history, corporate and/or personal email usage, cloud storage, mobile devices and backups, removable devices, short cuts and registry files. Following are some issues to consider for each of these means of moving data.

1. Internet History

    - What websites were visited and when?
    - What files were accessed and when?
    - Were online repositories accessed?
    - Was webmail accessed?
    - What searches were performed?

2. Webmail/Corporate Mail/Instant Messaging

    - Was personal email (also known as "webmail") used?
    - Were any emails and/or attachments opened?
    - Were any company attachments sent to a non-business email address?
    - Were any chat or instant message applications used to communicate about activities or to attach files?

3. Cloud Storage

    - Were any software backup/synchronization programs installed (e.g., Carbonite, Acronis)?

- Were any software programs for cloud storage installed (e.g., Dropbox, SugarSync)?
- Is there any evidence of FTP (File Transfer Protocol) usage?

4. Mobile Devices and Phone Back-Ups

- Is this mobile device a unique repository?
- What apps are installed?
- Are there third party-editing programs?
- When was the device backed up? Backups may be snapshots from different intervals.
- Consider the various forms of instant communications on a mobile device such as texts, iMessages, SMS, MMS and app-based messenger programs

5. Removable Devices

- When was the device connected for the first time?
- When was it connected the last time?
- Identifying particular devices that were used on the computer
- What gets recorded on these devices and what does not?
- Were any files opened from connected devices?
- Is there any reason to infer a mass copy to removable devices?

6. Audit Logs

- Does the company use cloud-based email that will allow audit logs to be produced?
- Does the company have a data loss prevention (DLP) system in place?
- Does the company use VPN to connect to their network, and if so, keep audit logs?

7. Searching of ESI

Sometimes searching various data repositories using keywords or other search mechanisms can be very useful to identify unknown activity or to identify additional activity related to what has already been discovered during the analysis. Some of the considerations related to searching include the following:

- Whether searching is necessary and, if so, what to look for in the data.
- Understanding the difference between searching active files versus deleted or "unallocated" files. For example, metadata may be present for recovered files and folders, but may not be for other data in the unallocated space.
- The quality of the keywords used to search (for example, one can often reduce false hits by using connectors or longer terms).
- Does the device contain journals or snapshots made on the computer from earlier points in time that can also be searched or analyzed?

§ 22.06 Practice Tip - Considerations When Collecting Mac Data

There are distinct differences between the collection and analysis of Mac data as compared to PC data. Depending on the case specifics, the following may be important:

- Imaging considerations – On a Mac, sometimes the hard drive cannot be removed. This can be more common on certain brands of PCs as well.
- USB devices – The Apple operating system's log of USB storage devices is significantly more volatile over time when compared with a Windows operating system which is designed to keep a log of every-time a storage device is plugged in.
- LNK files – The Mac does not create temporary link files (also known as "shortcuts" or "pointers").
- Deletions – on a Mac, a deleted file is often unrecoverable.
- Internet History – on a Mac, Internet history is stored in one contiguous file and is limited compared to a PC's Internet history.

§ 22.07 Considering an Expert

If you conduct a digital forensics investigation, you need to make sure you have the right people to do it. You want to make sure they know what they are doing and that they will be able to testify if needed. When considering a digital forensics expert, many variables may come into play. Some general guidelines for these variables include:

A. Company Resources

- Does the company have either internal resources or a network of qualified personnel to assist, given the size and timing of the project?

- If so, what, if anything, would be handled by an outside contractor (e.g., imaging out of state to save on travel costs)?

B. Qualifications and Experience

- What qualifications does the proposed consultant have, individually or as an organization? For example, do they maintain any professional certifications?
- Are the certifications relevant to the assistance you need?
- How many other similar matters has the consultant worked on?
- Can the consultant describe to your satisfaction the relevant matters they worked on?

C. Testimony Experience

- Federal court
- State court
- Arbitration
- Deposition
- Jury trial

§ 22.08 Considerations When Selecting a Neutral

Sometimes parties to a dispute agree to select a neutral forensic examiner to perform analysis on behalf of each party, or collectively among the parties, and sometimes the court selects a neutral. To the extent parties have input on the neutral, there are several issues to consider.

A. Selection

One important point for selecting a neutral examiner is that "neutral" should really mean just that. While a neutral might be inclined to provide information outside the scope of his or her engagement, unless asked to do so as part of the agreement he or she should not provide opinions.

Similar to selecting your own consultant, some considerations that may be helpful in selecting a neutral examiner may include:

- How many times have they served as a neutral?
- What were the relevant matters for which they served as a neutral?
- Can they provide referrals from clients who have retained them as a neutral?

- Have they provided written expert reports or testimony as part of their role as a neutral?

B. Protocol and Reporting

While a protocol may not be necessary, it can be quite valuable when working with a neutral. The steps of a protocol can also be comparable to your own forensic consultant's role. If the role of the neutral is simply to execute tasks and provide information in response, the clearer the directions are, the better the results will be for all concerned parties. Digital forensics sometimes can be described as a "scientific art." In other words, examiners may vary in their approach as to how to accomplish the same tasks. A protocol can be helpful to prevent misinterpretation of what the parties expect. While certainly not a complete list, some of the following items may be considered:

- Specific devices to be imaged/analyzed
- Devices to be returned to the custodian during analysis
- Date parameters
- Types of files to be analyzed (e.g., have files also been renamed)
- Analysis tasks (e.g., what analysis will be performed)
- Reporting requirements
- Format of data productions
- Parameters for case closeout and return/destruction of data
- Remediation/removal of sensitive of data, if applicable –
    - Typically, most situations will require some form of remediation which will require a different perspective and handling. Forensic and eDiscovery methodologies do not address the deletion of discovered data so software tools used for collection, analysis and review will likely not work for this phase. Additionally, deleting sometimes thousands of files manually can be a time consuming and costly process. Thankfully there are developing tools that are designed to identify and purge responsive files. Methods to consider may include software that can be remotely deployed and managed to inventory data on laptops or desktops and then purge specific files. If you have specific files to be remediated from an Office 365 cloud instance this can be achieved remotely using the Security and Compliance center, or other third-party tools. In summary there are many options available for the remediation phase, however considering all the different repositories of data in use today this does require some creative thinking and verification of results.

Chapter 23
SPOLIATION SANCTIONS IN TRADE SECRETS CASES

By: Rebecca ("Bec") Edelson, Esq.
and Mikela T. Sutrina, Esq.

---

§ 23.01 Introduction and Background

Preservation of electronically stored information and other potentially relevant evidence can be critical in trade secrets cases. Failure to comply with preservation obligations may have devastating consequences, including the issuance of sanctions.

Here, we address the duty to preserve potentially relevant evidence, the scope of that duty, what constitutes spoliation, the scope of possible sanctions, and the importance of this issue as it relates to trade secrets cases. Finally, we offer for consideration some potential measures to reduce the risk of spoliation.

§ 23.02 The Duty to Preserve Potentially Relevant Evidence

A. California Law

Although there is a larger, more developed body of federal case law addressing the preservation duty, California state law also recognizes a duty to refrain from spoliation. *See, e.g., Cedars-Sinai Med. Ctr. v. Sup.Ct.,* 18 Cal. 4th 1, 12 (1998) (destroying evidence in response to, or in anticipation of, a discovery request "would surely be a misuse of discovery" within meaning of Discovery Act).

"Spoliation occurs when evidence is destroyed or significantly altered or when there is a failure to preserve property for another's use as evidence in current or future litigation." *Strong v. State of Cal.*, 201 Cal.App.4th 1439, 1458 (2011) (refusing to recognize as a tort cause of action a claim for negligent spoliation); *see also* William v. Russ, 167 Cal. App. 4th 1215 (2008) (holding that the evidence was sufficient to support a finding that the litigant acted intentionally, not negligently, in destroying the subject file).

That spoliation was unintentional does not mean the court is without the ability to impose a remedial sanction. *See, e.g., Puritan Ins. Co. v. Sup. Ct*, 171 Cal. App. 3d 877, 885-886 (1985) (affirming the exclusion of the plaintiff's expert's testimony about the subject shaft where the shaft was negligently lost before the defendant's expert could examine it) (decided under the former discovery act).

B. Federal Law

Under federal law, there is a general duty to preserve potentially relevant evidence once a party "reasonably anticipates litigation." *See Zubulake v. UBS Warbug LLC*, 220 F.R.D. 212, 217-18 (S.D.N.Y. 2003); *see also First Fin. Sec., Inc. v. Freedom Equity Grp., LLC*, No. 15-CV-1893-HRL, 2016 WL 5870218, at *3 (N.D. Cal. Oct. 7, 2016) ("The duty to preserve evidence begins when litigation is pending or reasonably foreseeable.").

According to a district court in the Ninth Circuit, "there is no question that the duty to preserve relevant evidence may arise before litigation is formally commenced." *Apple Inc. v. Samsung Elecs. Co.*, 888 F. Supp. 2d 976, 990 (N.D. Cal. 2012). Thus, receiving a demand letter, a government agency charge, or a records subpoena may trigger a preservation duty, regardless of whether an actual lawsuit is filed.

§ 23.03 What Is Spoliation?

"A party's destruction of evidence qualifies as willful spoliation if the party has 'some notice that the documents were *potentially* relevant to the litigation before they were destroyed.'" *Leon v. IDX Sys. Corp.*, 464 F.3d 951, 959 (9th Cir. 2006) (quoting *United States v. Kitsap Physicians Serv.*, 314 F.3d 995, 1001 (9th Cir. 2002)) (emphasis in original). Intentional destruction can take the form of shredding hard-copy documents, deleting emails, texts, or other messages, overwriting operating systems or system-wide servers, and "wiping" or permanently deleting files or even entire hard drives. Further, concealing, altering, or modifying evidence (including metadata) also constitutes spoliation and can subject a party to sanctions.

However, spoliation, may also extend to the negligent destruction or loss of evidence (*e.g.*, due to improperly implemented preservation protocols, failure to promptly recognize a duty to preserve, or a belief that certain evidence was not "relevant"). *See Al Otro Lado, Inc. v. Wolf*, No. 3:17-cv-02366-BAS-KSC, 2021 U.S. Dist. LEXIS 30450, at *3, *8 (S.D. Cal. Feb. 18, 2021) ("The Court may impose sanctions for spoliation even in the absence of bad faith"; "the requisite culpable state of mind for purposes of spoliation [includes] a party's 'conscious disregard' of its preservation obligations.") (citation omitted; brackets added); *Lewis v. Ryan*, 261 F.R.D. 513, 521 (S.D. Cal. 2009) (the required culpable state of mind "includes negligence."); *see also U.S. E.E.O.C. v. Wedco, Inc.*, No. 3:12-cv-00523-RCJ-VPC, 2014 WL 4635678, at *5 (D. Nev. Sept. 15, 2014) (declining to find bad faith where witness "shredded his handwritten notes" because he viewed them as a "draft" and the "important information" was transferred to the final document, but still imposing adverse inference sanction); *Clark Const. Grp., Inc. v. City of Memphis*, 229 F.R.D. 131, 136 (W.D. Tenn. 2005) (granting request for rebuttable adverse inference instruction based upon a finding the defendant acted negligently in destroying documents it claimed "were reasonably viewed as garbage . . . that a reasonable person would consider not to be relevant").

The duty may also impose the obligation to take affirmative steps to avoid spoliation. *See Zubulake*, 220 F.R.D. at 217-18 (stating that "once a party reasonably anticipates litigation, it must suspend its routine document retention/destruction policy and put in place a litigation hold to ensure the preservation of relevant documents").

§ 23.04 The Scope of Possible Sanctions

A. Federal Law

Federal courts may issue sanctions under two Federal Rules of Civil Procedure: Rules 37(b) and 37(e). Further, some courts have observed that the court has "inherent power" to "levy sanctions in response to abusive litigation practices," outside of Rule 37. *Leon*, 464 F.3d at 958.

Rule 37(b) specifically provides for the following sanctions for failure to obey a court order regarding discovery and/or preservation of documents:

- An "issue" sanction, directing that the matters embraced in the order or other designated facts be taken as established for purposes of the action, as the prevailing party claims;

- An "evidence" sanction, prohibiting the disobedient party from supporting or opposing designated claims or defenses, or from introducing designated matters in evidence;

- Striking pleadings in whole or in part;

- Staying further proceedings until the order is obeyed;

- Dismissing the action or proceeding in whole or in part;

- Rendering a default judgment against the disobedient party; or

- Treating as contempt of court the failure to obey any order except an order to submit to a physical or mental examination.

See Fed. R. Civ. P. 37(b)(2)(A).

Further, Rule 37(b)(2)(C) provides that "instead of or in addition to the orders [set forth in Rule 37(b)(2)(A)], the court must order the disobedient party, the attorney advising that party, or both to pay the reasonable expenses, including attorneys' fees, caused by the failure, unless the failure was substantially justified or other circumstances make an award of expenses unjust." Fed. R. Civ. P. 37(b)(2)(C).

Separately (or, in addition to, under certain circumstances), Rule 37(e), provides for the following possible sanctions for a party's reasonable failure to preserve electronically stored information ("ESI") "only upon finding that the party acted with the intent to deprive another party of the information's use in the litigation" and if the information cannot be restored or replaced by other means:

- A presumption that the lost information was unfavorable to the party;

- An instruction to the jury that it may or must presume the information was unfavorable to the party; or

- Dismissal of the action or entry of a default judgment.

See Fed. R. Civ. P. 37(e).

B. California Law

California Code of Civil Procedure Section 2023.030 authorizes sanctions for misuses of discovery: (1) monetary sanctions, (2) issue or adverse inference sanctions, (3) evidence sanctions,

(4) terminating sanctions ranging from orders to strike pleadings, default judgment, or dismissal, and/or (5) contempt sanctions.

Depending on the circumstances before it, the court may be able to rely on its inherent powers to attempt to remedy perceived injustice created by a spoliation incident. For example, courts have an inherent power to preclude evidence to prevent abuses of the litigation process. *Peat, Marwick, Mitchell & Co. v. Sup.Ct. (People)*, 200 Cal. App. 3d 272, 287, 289 (1988) (observing that the court has inherent power to exclude evidence based on destruction of evidence).

However, "...absent exceptional circumstances, the court shall not impose sanctions on a party or any attorney of a party for failure to provide electronically stored information that has been lost, damaged, altered, or overwritten as the result of the routine, good faith operation of an electronic information system [provided that] [t]his subdivision shall not be construed to alter any obligation to preserve discoverable information." Cal. Civ. Proc. Code § 2023.030(f).

§ 23.05 Standards For Imposing Sanctions For Spoliation

A. Federal Law

In determining whether spoliation occurred, federal courts may consider a three-part test: "(1) that the party having control over the evidence had an obligation to preserve it at the time it was destroyed; (2) that the records were destroyed with a 'culpable state of mind;' and (3) that the evidence was 'relevant' to the party's claim or defense such that a reasonable trier of fact could find that it would support that claim or defense." *Apple*, 888 F. Supp. 2d at 989-90 (citing cases).

If a federal district court determines a party spoliated evidence, its "discretion in selecting the form of a spoliation sanction is broad, and can range from comparatively minor sanctions, such as awarding attorneys' fees, to more severe sanctions, such as dismissal." *Rockman Co. (USA), Inc. v. Nong Shim Co., Ltd.*, 229 F. Supp. 3d 1109, 1121 (N.D. Cal. 2017). In exercising this discretion, courts generally consider "(1) the degree of fault of the party who altered or destroyed the evidence; (2) the degree of prejudice suffered by the opposing party; and (3) whether there is a lesser sanction that will avoid substantial unfairness to the opposing party." *Id.* at 1122. Further, "a party's motive or degree of fault is relevant to what sanction, if any, is imposed." *In re Napster*, 462 F. Supp. 2d 1060, 1066-67 (N.D. Cal. 2006). However, "courts should choose the least onerous sanction corresponding to the willfulness of the destructive act and the prejudice suffered by the victim." *Id.*

A district court's "inherent powers" may also permit it to "award sanctions in the form of attorneys' fees against a party or counsel who acts 'in bad faith, vexatiously, wantonly, or for oppressive reasons.'" *Leon*, 464 F.3d at 961 (quoting *Primus Auto. Fin. Servs., Inc. v. Batarse*, 115 F.3d 644, 648 (9th Cir. 1997)). The court must make an "express finding" that the party's "behavior 'constitutes or was tantamount to bad faith.'" *Id. See also Toppan Photomasks, Inc. v. Park*, No. 13-cv-03323-MMC, 2014 US. Dist. LEXIS 74063, at *36 (N.D. Cal. May 29, 2014) (awarding attorneys' fees in trade secret misappropriation case where party "continued to delete or overwrite files" after the court issued an order regarding preservation of evidence and thus acted "willfully and with varying degrees of fault, including bad faith").

Courts in the Ninth Circuit may consider the following factors when determining whether to levy sanctions against a party under Rule 37 or under their inherent powers: "(1) the public's interest in expeditious resolution of litigation; (2) the court's need to manage its dockets; (3) the risk of prejudice to the party seeking sanctions; (4) the public policy favoring disposition of cases on their merits; and (5) the availability of less drastic sanctions." *Leon*, 464 F.3d at 958.

B. California Law

A California state court may find that "[s]poliation occurs when evidence is destroyed or significantly altered or when there is a failure to preserve property for another's use as evidence in current or future litigation." *Strong v. State of Cal.*, 201 Cal.App.4th 1439, 1458 (2011).

"[S]anctions should be tailored to serve [a] remedial purpose, should not put the moving party in a better position than he would otherwise have been had he obtained the requested discovery, and should be proportionate to the offending party's misconduct." *Williams v. Russ*, 167 Cal. App. 4th 1215, 1223 (2008).

California courts have considered the egregiousness of a party's actions and whether a party's actions were intentional or negligent. *See Williams*, 167 Cal. App. 4th at 1224-1225 (considering whether Plaintiff acted negligently or intentionally by allowing relevant files to be destroyed); *New Albertsons, Inc. v. Sup. Ct*, 168 Cal. App. 4th 1403, 1426 (2008) ("[I]f it is sufficiently egregious, misconduct committed in connection with the failure to produce evidence in discovery may justify the imposition of nonmonetary sanctions even absent a prior order compelling discovery, or its equivalent").

§ 23.06 Examination of Representative Trade Secrets Cases

Spoliation sanction claims may arise in virtually any type of litigation, including but not limited to trade secret misappropriation litigation. Below we explore a few trade secret cases where spoliation sanctions were addressed.

A. *E.I. du Pont de Nemours & Co. v. Kolon Indus., Inc.*, 803 F. Supp. 2d 469 (E.D. Va. 2011).

In *E.I. du Pont de Nemours & Co. v. Kolon Industries, Inc.*, the court considered whether to grant the plaintiff, E.I. du Pont de Nemours & Co.'s ("E.I.") motion for sanctions for spoliation of evidence against the defendant, Kolon Industries, Inc. ("Kolon"). 803 F. Supp. 2d 469, 476 (E.D. Va. 2011). While reviewing Kolon's discovery production in relation to E.I.'s misappropriation of trade secrets claim, E.I. found screenshots taken by Kolon's employees of emails in Kolon's employees' email accounts with instructions such as "Delete," "Need to Delete," "Remove All," and "Get Rid Of." *Id.* Kolon did not respond to E.I.'s letter outlining its concerns and requesting that Kolon advise E.I. of any known destruction or attempted destruction of documents or emails by Kolon's employees. *Id.* As a result, E.I. filed a motion for spoliation sanctions. *Id.* E.I. engaged a digital forensics firm to perform a forensic analysis of Kolon's servers and employees' personal computers. *Id.* at 477. The forensics firm ultimately determined Kolon's employees deleted a total of 17,811 emails and files. *Id.* at 480. Further, 9,010 of the emails were found to be responsive to certain keywords identified in the litigation, and 991 of the electronic files were deemed to likely be relevant to the litigation. *Id.*

Because Kolon's key employees deleted files and email items related to the litigation from their personal computers in the days after E.I. filed its lawsuit, the court concluded Kolon breached its duty to preserve. *Id.* Further, based on key employees *intentionally* deleting relevant documents, files, and emails from their computers upon learning E.I. filed its litigation, the court presumed relevant the unrecoverable files. *Id.* at 505.

The court ruled, "Having found both bad faith and intentional deletion of relevant materials, the [c]ourt will inform the jury that certain Kolon executives and employees, after learning that [E.I.] had sued Kolon, deleted much electronically stored information that would have been available to [E.I.] for use in presenting its case." *Id.* Further, the court imposed attorneys' fees, expenses, and costs associated with E.I.'s motion for sanctions as an additional sanction against Kolon. *Id.* at 510.

Thereafter, the jury that had been instructed that Kolon deleted evidence awarded E.I. $919,900,000.00. *E.I. du Pont de Nemours & Co. v. Kolon Indus., Inc.*, No. 3:09CV58, 2014 WL 792137, at *1 (E.D. Va. Feb. 25, 2014), vacated (June 12, 2014). The award was later reduced to $275,000,000.00 via agreement between the parties. *See Kolon Industries Inc. Pleads Guilty For Conspiring To Steal Dupont Trade Secrets Involving Kevlar Technology*, 2015 WL 1938810, DOJ 15-537 (Apr. 30, 2015). But, the *Kolon* case illustrates how a jury instruction addressing a party's spoliation potentially can potentially influence the outcome of litigation.

B. *Roadrunner Transp. Servs., Inc. v. Tarwater*, 642 F. App'x 759 (9th Cir. 2016).

In *Roadrunner Transportation Services, Inc. v. Tarwater*, Defendant, Tarwater ("Tarwater") appealed the district court's entry of default judgment in favor of Plaintiff, Roadrunner Transportation Services, Inc. ("Roadrunner"). 642 F. App'x 759, 759 (9th Cir. 2016). The court held the district court did not abuse its discretion by entering default judgment as a sanction for Tarwater's deletion of data from his laptop computers. *Id.*

Specifically, the court determined "there was ample evidence that Tarwater deleted emails and files on his laptops after receiving multiple preservation demands from Roadrunner, and even after the court explicitly ordered Tarwater to preserve 'all data' on his electronic devices." *Id.* A computer expert testified that files on one of Tarwater's devices had been deleted and overwritten during litigation. *Id.* The court reasoned that the district court did not err in finding that Tarwater willfully destroyed evidence, that Roadrunner had been deprived of evidence of Tarwater's alleged misappropriation, and that a less drastic sanction could not adequately rectify the damage to Roadrunner's case. *Id.* at 759-60.

C. *WeRide Corp. v. Kun Huang*, No. 5:18-cv-07233-EJD, 2020 WL 1967209 (N.D. Cal. Apr. 24, 2020).

In *WeRide Corp. v. Kun Huang*, Plaintiffs, WeRide Corp. and WeRide Inc. (collectively, "WeRide"), moved the court to issue sanctions against Defendants in response to Defendants' alleged spoliation of evidence. No. 5:18-cv-07233-EJD, 2020 WL 1967209, at *1 (N.D. Cal. Apr. 24, 2020).

WeRide claimed Defendants, who were WeRide's previous employees, and AllRide, a direct competitor, spoliated evidence by destroying emails, tampering with five different categories of source code, and destroying evidence through other means. *Id.* at *3. WeRide claimed Defendants destroyed emails by: (1) setting AllRide's email servers to automatically delete all emails older than 90 days, despite knowing that litigation was imminent, and after the litigation was filed, and (2) deleting email accounts after WeRide filed the original complaint and the court issued the preliminary injunction. *Id.* Further, WeRide argued Defendants spoliated five categories of source code relevant to WeRide's claims of trade secret misappropriation. *Id.* at *5. Lastly, WeRide alleged Defendants destroyed evidence through other means as a result of one of the Defendants deleting ESI on two WeRide issued computers and his own personal laptop. *Id.* WeRide also alleged that Allride began using DingTalk, an application that automatically deletes messages after they have been sent and read in an effort to further cover up spoliation activity. *Id.* at *7-8.

WeRide sought sanctions under Federal Rules of Civil Procedure 37(b) and 37(e) as well as the court's "inherent powers" to sanction. *Id.* at *8. The court determined that because it would issue terminating sanctions under Rules 37(b) and 37(e), it did not need to consider whether it should sanction Defendants under its inherent power. *Id.* The court applied the *Leon v. IDX System Corp.* factors in determining whether to issue sanctions under Rule 37(b) and Rule 37(e). *Id.* at *10. Further, the court noted that under *Leon* "a finding of willfulness, fault, or bad faith is required for dismissal to be proper." *Id.*

In considering the *Leon* factors, the court found Defendants' admitted violations of the preliminary injunction and failure to inform the court or WeRide of the auto-deletion function on its email servers until the eve of a discovery hearing, two months after Defendants alleged they found out about this function, met the first two *Leon* factors. *Id.* The court examined the third *Leon* factor, finding "[Defendants'] mass spoliation of its internal emails [to have been] highly prejudicial to WeRide." *Id.* at *11. The court further found the prejudice to WeRide was so great as to outweigh the fourth *Leon* factor. *Id.* Lastly, the court determined the fifth *Leon* factor also weighed in favor of terminating sanctions because other lesser sanctions were "far too mild and vague to sufficiently cure the prejudice to WeRide." *Id.* As a result, the court issued terminating sanctions against Defendants under Rule 37(b). *Id.* at *12.

The court also found Defendants failed to preserve ESI in violation of Rule 37(e) by destroying specific email accounts and performing a mass deletion of emails from its servers, including after Defendants knew about the litigation and the preliminary injunction order. *Id.* at *12. Thus, the court issued terminating sanctions against Defendants under Rule 37(e). *Id.*

The court also ultimately determined Defendants acted in bad faith by implementing the auto-delete setting on AllRide's email server, using DingTalk, and maintaining a policy of deleting email accounts and wiping the computers of former employees *after* the court ordered the preliminary injunction. *Id.* at *10. The court noted, "[t]his practice of destroying potentially discoverable material shows both willfulness and bad faith." *Id.* Accordingly, in addition to terminating sanctions, the court ordered Defendants to pay WeRide's reasonable fees and costs incurred in relation to 1) their motion for sanctions, 2) all discovery related to Defendants' spoliation of evidence, and 3) discovery motion practice before a judge. *Id.* at *16. Though it appears this case later settled, Defendants faced devastating damages as a result of the court's order and their spoliation actions.

D. *Keating v. Jastremski*, No. 3:15-CV-00057-L-AGS, 2020 WL 1809139 (S.D. Cal. Apr. 9, 2020).

In *Keating v. Jastremski*, the court considered whether to adopt the Special Master's Report and Recommendation granting Defendant, John A. Jastremski, and Defendant-Counterclaimant, the Retirement Group's (collectively "TRG") motion for terminating sanctions against Counter-Defendants, Lloyd J. Silvers, Steven Dalton, and Ardent Retirement Planning, LLC (collectively "Ardent"). No. 3:15-CV-00057-L-AGS, 2020 WL 1809139, at *1 (S.D. Cal. Apr. 9, 2020). TRG claimed members of Ardent Retirement Planning, LLC, an investment company composed of past TRG employees, downloaded TRG's proprietary information and then intentionally destroyed evidence of such information. *Id.* at *1-2. The court adopted the Special Master's finding that Ardent formed a deliberate plan to destroy evidence after reviewing testimony from a recruiter hired by Ardent claiming Ardent had internal discussions concerning downloading TRG's information, Ardent deliberately decided to communicate via conference calls as to avoid creating documents that could be used against it in the future, and Ardent instructed employees to wipe data from their devices. *Id.* at *3-4. The court found the recruiter's testimony was corroborated by conference call agendas, as well as defendant Dalton's email messages. *Id.* at *5.

Further, the court adopted the Special Master's determination that Ardent deleted extensive electronic evidence after reviewing testimony from a computer forensic expert finding Ardent deleted or destroyed thousands of emails, multiple USB flash drives, and a hard drive potentially related to TRG's proprietary information. *Id.* at *6-12. Based on the testimony the court reviewed, the court determined Ardent "intentionally destroyed evidence in anticipation of and during litigation with knowledge that the evidence may be potentially relevant to TRG's prosecution of its counterclaims against [Ardent]." *Id.* at *12. Additionally, the court found implementing less drastic sanctions did not apply where a party destroyed evidence before the court had "an opportunity to order less drastic sanctions or issue a warning," as was the case with Ardent. *Id.* at *13. Finally, the court determined that while the public policy favoring disposition of cases on the merits generally weighs against terminating sanctions, this fact alone did not outweigh the court's conclusions. *Id.* at *14. Thus, under federal courts' inherent authority to sanction a party who engages in spoliation of evidence, the court adopted the Special Master's Recommendation and granted TRG's motion for terminating sanctions and entered default judgment. *Id.*

E. *Capstone Logistics Hldgs., Inc. v. Navarette*, 2020 WL 3429775 (S.D.N.Y. June 23, 2020).

In *Capstone Logistics Hldgs., Inc. v. Navarette*, the court granted Plaintiff's motion for summary judgment on their trade secret misappropriation claims, holding the record was "full of evidence that the . . . Defendants wrongfully retained and misused" the Plaintiff's trade secrets and confidential information. 2020 WL 3429775, at *5 (S.D.N.Y. June 23, 2020). Significantly, as it relates to spoliation, the court noted that although there was not "direct evidence" with respect to one Defendant, the Defendant's spoliation of evidence relating to the trade secret claim provided sufficient circumstantial evidence upon which to grant summary judgment. *Id.* at *5 n. 9. Specifically, the Defendant at issue was working for a competitor before his last day of employment with Plaintiff, created a spreadsheet of contacts for the competitor prior to returning his work computer, and deleted all content from his work computer before returning it to Plaintiff. *Id.* As a result, and in combination with allegations the Defendant had poached Plaintiff's clients for his new employer, the court found it was a "reasonable conclusion" to infer from the Defendant's spoliation that he had deleted evidence of misappropriation. *Id.*

F. *Ajaxo, Inc. v. E*Trade Fin. Corp.*, 48 Cal. App. 5th 129, 261 Cal. Rptr. 3d 583 (2020).

In *Ajaxo, Inc. v. E*Trade Fin. Corp.*, a jury found Defendant liable for trade secret misappropriation and breach of contract, but did not award damages as to trade secret misappropriation. 48 Cal. App. 5th 129, 139 (Cal. App. 2020). After a second jury found no damages, the trial court denied Plaintiff's request to seek a reasonable royalty as compensatory damages. *Id.* After a second appeal, the appellate court remanded, directing the trial court to exercise its discretion to determine whether Plaintiff was entitled to a reasonable royalty. *Id.*

At the second trial regarding Plaintiff's request for a reasonable royalty, the trial court declined to award any royalty, largely due to Plaintiff's spoliation of the "items needed to establish the nature of the trade secret for purposes of the royalty analysis.". *Id.* at 171. The court found "all printed copies of the source code . . . were destroyed, and all copies erased, lost or destroyed" by Plaintiff. *Id.* at 171 (internal citation omitted). The trial court further found Plaintiff acted in "bad faith." *Id.* Plaintiff appealed this decision, arguing it presented sufficient evidence in the second trial for a reasonable royalty determination. *Id.* at 145. Specifically, Plaintiff argued its own spoliation of evidence did not prevent a reasonable royalty determination, because the spoliation issue and Defendant's "unclean hands" affirmative defense (relating to the spoliation) had been fully adjudicated and rejected in the first trial. *Id.* at 145, 164. Therefore, according to Plaintiff, the court's consideration of Plaintiff's spoliation in conducting its reasonable royalty analysis was erroneous. *Id.*

The appellate court disagreed, holding that the trial court's rejection Defendant's affirmative defense of unclean hands and spoliation argument in relation to damages from unjust enrichment did not determine the substantive effect of Plaintiff's spoliation of the evidence on unrelated issues. *Id.* at 172. That is, the appellate court determined the issue of Plaintiff's spoliation of evidence was properly assessed in the second trial as it related to the royalty determination. *Id.* Because Plaintiff had a duty to prove the value and amount of any royalty claimed, Plaintiff's spoliation of the exact evidence needed to establish the nature of the trade secret for purposes of the royalty analysis was relevant to the court's decision. *Id.* The court declined to overturn the trial court's reasonable royalty determination. *Id.*

§ 23.07 Reducing The Risk Of Spoliation and/or Devastating Spoliation Sanctions

A potential litigant should confer with qualified litigation counsel to consider appropriate steps to try to prevent spoliation (intentional or otherwise). Although what are appropriate steps may depend on the particular circumstances, below we offer a few potential measures for consideration. They are not exhaustive. *See also* Chapter 22 for related material.

A. Consider In Advance Implementing Protocols That May Facilitate Preservation In The Future

Proactively implement protocols regarding data preservation, including protocols that are easy to modify if and when litigation is a possibility. For example, if a business uses an auto-deletion program, it should consider disabling and/or deactivating auto-deletion programs upon learning of *potential* litigation.

Additionally, consider protocols concerning where employees may maintain records and requiring the company to track who maintains particular types of company documents (or things such as prototypes) and where and how they are maintained. Especially in a work-from-home world, such policies can aid in avoiding spoliation and immediately implementing preservation instructions in the event of potential litigation.

B. Distribute Litigation Holds

When litigation becomes reasonably foreseeable, contact counsel to assist the company to develop an appropriate preservation plan in light of the particular circumstances.

A prompt litigation hold memorandum is a common step towards preservation. A properly issued and implemented litigation hold memorandum instructing key employees to preserve potentially relevant evidence may be critical in avoiding spoliation or even defending against a spoliation sanctions motion. Litigation holds should be clear and easy to understand, but also comprehensive in identifying what the company considers categories of potentially relevant evidence and/or other litigants (or the judge) may assert are categories of potentially relevant evidence.

Additionally, identify who should receive the litigation hold memo (*e.g.*, custodians of the categories of potentially relevant evidence). Identify a key point of contact for employee questions and confirm receipt of and compliance with the litigation hold. Further, if the scope of the litigation and claims at issue changes, update the litigation hold appropriately. Consider reminders and follow-up to confirm the litigation hold is being followed.

Distribute the litigation hold memo to key IT personnel so that auto-delete programs are deactivated and other technical systems which could impact data preservation are properly addressed.

C. Consider Making A Forensic Image

Creating a forensic image of electronic data subject to the litigation hold may reduce the risk of devastating spoliations sanctions (*e.g.*, if employees do not abide by the litigation hold and potentially relevant evidence is lost, the company will have a forensic copy to present in its place). Although it may cause the company to incur expense in the short term (paying a qualified forensic consultant to make appropriate forensic images), such measure may reduce expense for the company in the longer term.

§ 23.08 Conclusion

Spoliation sanctions may be devastating to a party in litigation, especially in trade secrets cases. These sanctions may be the reason a party cannot prove its case or the reason it cannot defend itself in high-stakes litigation. Spoliation sanctions can injure the litigant's credibility and reputation and also can result in significant monetary awards, including attorneys' fees awards. Proactively and promptly attempting to address preservation may reduce the risk of spoliation and crushing sanctions.

Chapter 24
WORKING WITH EXPERTS IN TRADE SECRETS CASES

By: Bradley C. Graveline, Esq.
and Kent R. Raygor, Esq.

Expert analysis and testimony relating to liability and damages is critical in most trade secrets cases under California's Uniform Trade Secret Act ("CUTSA") and the Federal Defend Trade Secrets Act ("DTSA"). This chapter analyzes the use of expert witnesses in both federal and state courts in California. Careful planning of expert analysis and preparation for expert testimony is important to the presentation of a successful trade secret misappropriation case or defense thereof.

§ 24.01 Identification And Retention Of Experts

The first step in working with an expert in a trade secrets case is to identify: (1) the issues that might be aided by expert testimony; and (2) the experts who might be able to opine on those issues. In many cases, it is appropriate to identify and retain experts early in the case. A litigant may wish to consider retaining multiple experts to provide for flexibility as issues in the case become more fully developed.

There are several ways to go about identifying experts. First, consider seeking recommendations from colleagues who might have represented clients in cases with similar issues. Second, conduct independent research to identify experts in a particular field. Look for persons with the right academic and professional credentials who seem to be thought leaders in the field at issue in your case. Third, you might wish to seek assistance from a firm that specializes in finding technical consultants and expert witnesses. Keep in mind that these firms charge a fee for their services, typically in the form of a percentage of the hourly rate.

Regardless of how you retain the expert, it is important to research the expert's background before incurring any significant expert fees on behalf of your client. In particular, look for anything the expert has written that might contradict the positions he or she might take in your case. Look for prior court decisions that mention your expert, focusing on any cases in which the expert's analysis or credibility has been called into question by a court. In many cases, it is advantageous to retain an expert with past testifying experience, but it is important to understand the expert's prior cases and testimony.

Once you have identified an appropriate expert, it is important to enter into a written engagement letter with him or her. Expert engagement letters commonly include provisions that:

- The expert will be paid at a specified hourly rate;
- The expert is being retained by the client and will take direction from counsel for the client;
- The expert is to maintain the confidentiality of all confidential client material received in connection with the case as well as all communications with counsel;
- The client is responsible for payment of expert expenses;
- The expert is not to undertake any work except approved by counsel.

Many law firms have policies and procedures relating to the retention of experts. If you work for such a firm, consider such policies and procedures.

§ 24.02 Legal Standard For Admissibility Of Expert Testimony

The admissibility of an expert's potential opinion should be considered as soon as you begin working with the expert. Federal Rule of Evidence ("FRE") 702 sets forth the standard for the admissibility of expert testimony. It provides that a qualified expert may testify if "(a) the expert's scientific, technical, or other specialized knowledge will help the trier of fact to understand the evidence or determine a fact in issue; (b) the testimony is based on sufficient facts or data; (c) the testimony is the product of reliable principles and methods; and (d) the expert has reliably applied the principles and methods to the facts of this case." Fed. R. Evid. 702. In California state courts, the Evidence Code provides the framework for the admissibility of expert opinion evidence. "If a witness is testifying as an expert, his testimony in the form of an opinion is limited to such opinion as is: [¶](a)[r]elated to a subject that is sufficiently beyond common experience that the opinion of an expert would assist the trier of fact; and [¶](b) [b]ased on matter (including his special knowledge, skill, experience, training, and education) perceived by or personally known to him at or before the hearing, whether or not admissible, that is of a type that reasonably may be relied upon by an expert in forming an opinion upon the subject to which his testimony relates, unless an expert is precluded by law from using such matter as a basis for his opinion." Cal. Evid. Code § 801. An opinion based in whole or in part on improper matter may be excluded. *Id.* at § 803. To determine the admissibility of an expert's opinion evidence, the court may in its discretion require examination of an expert "concerning the matter upon which his opinion is based" before the expert is allowed to testify. *Id.* at § 802.

In *Daubert v. Merrell Dow Pharmaceuticals, Inc.*, 509 U.S. 579, 589 (1993), the Supreme Court held that FRE 702 requires the district court to act as a gatekeeper to "ensure that any and all scientific testimony or evidence admitted is not only relevant, but reliable." In *Kumho Tire Co., Ltd. v. Carmichael*, 526 U.S. 137, 147 (1999), the Supreme Court clarified that the "basic gatekeeping obligation" articulated in *Daubert* applies not only to scientific testimony but to all expert testimony, including damages testimony. The Supreme Court also made clear that the reliability inquiry is a flexible one, and "whether *Daubert's* specific factors[24] are, or are not, reasonable measures of reliability in a particular case is a matter that the law grants the trial judge broad latitude to determine." *Id.* at 153. So long as an expert's methodology is sound and her opinions satisfy the requirements of FRE 702, underlying factual disputes and how much weight to accord the expert's opinion are questions for the jury. *Primiano v. Cook*, 598 F.3d 558, 565 (9th Cir. 2010). Trial courts should screen "unreliable nonsense opinions, but not exclude opinions merely because they are impeachable." *City of Pomona v. SQM N. Am. Corp.*, 750 F.3d 1036, 1044 (9th Cir. 2014).

Daubert set forth the following non-exclusive factors to assist the district court in determining the reliability of an expert's methodology and analytical approach:

- whether it "can be (and has been) tested";
- whether it "has been subjected to peer review and publication";
- whether it poses a high "known or potential rate of error" when applied;

[24] The *Daubert* factors are set forth below.

- whether there are "standards controlling [its] operation"; and
- whether it enjoys "general acceptance" within a "relevant scientific community."

Daubert, 509 U.S. at 592–94.

In *Sargon Enterprises, Inc. v. University of Southern California*, 55 Cal. 4th 747, 771–72 (2012), California's Supreme Court held that "under Evidence Code sections 801, subdivision (b), and 802, the trial court acts as a gatekeeper to exclude expert opinion evidence that is (1) based on matter of a type on which an expert may not reasonably rely, (2) based on reasons unsupported by the material on which the expert relies, or (3) speculative." *Sargon* further explained "[t]his means that a court may inquire into, not only the type of material on which an expert relies, but also whether that material actually supports the experts reasoning. 'A court may conclude there is simply too great an analytical gap between the data and the opinion proffered.'" *Id.* at 771. When assessing whether an expert's opinion is admissible, the trial court's role "does not involve choosing between competing expert opinions." Rather, the court's focus "must be solely on principles and methodology, not on the conclusions that [the experts] generate. *Id.* Although *Sargon* involved expert opinion evidence presented at trial, its holding was not limited to that particular context. Courts have applied *Sargon* to declarations submitted in connection with motions for summary judgment, summary adjudication, and class certification. *See e.g.*, *Sanchez v. Kern Emergency Med. Transp. Corp.*, 8 Cal. App. 5th 146, 156 (2017); *Shiffer v. CBS Corp.*, 240 Cal. App. 4th 246, 253 (2015); *Apple, Inc. v. Sup. Ct.*, 19 Cal. App. 5th 1101 (2018).

The Ninth Circuit has declared that the "inquiry envisioned by Rule 702 is . . . a flexible one," and trial courts should not automatically apply every *Daubert* factor. *See Hangarter v. Provident Life and Acc. Ins. Co.*, 373 F.3d 998, 1017 (9thCir. 2004) ("Concerning the reliability of non-scientific testimony such as [plaintiff's expert], the *Daubert* factors . . . are simply not applicable to this kind of testimony, whose reliability depends heavily on the *knowledge and experience* of the expert, rather than the methodology behind it."). *See also Mfg. Automation and Software Sys. Inc. v. Hughes, et al.*, No. 2:16-cv-08962-CAS (KSx), 2018 WL 3197696 (C.D. Cal. 2018) (holding that the determination of the reliability of expert testimony is within the court's broad discretion).

Pursuant to the standards set forth in FRE 702, Cal. Evid. Code § 801 and § 802, *Sargon* and *Daubert,* courts addressing trade secret misappropriation claims have allowed experts in trade secrets cases to testify on topics such as:

- whether particular information constitutes a trade secret;[25]
- whether the alleged trade secret is readily ascertainable;[26]
- the reasonableness of efforts taken by a company to protect a trade secret;[27]

---

[25] *See GSI Tech., Inc. v. United Memories, Inc.*, No. 5-13-cv-01081-PSG, 2015 WL 12942201 (N.D. Cal. Oct. 14, 2015). The determination of whether particular information constitutes a trade secret is discussed in Chapter 1.

[26] *See Copart, Inc. v. Sparta Consulting, Inc.*, 277 F. Supp. 3d 1127, 1154 (E.D. Cal. 2017).

[27] *See Weride Corporation v. Huang*, 379 F. Supp. 3d 834, 847 (N.D. Cal. 2019).

- a comparison of allegedly misappropriated information with the company's trade secret;[28] and
- the amount of damages due to a plaintiff.[29]

§ 24.03 Use Of Experts In Preliminary Injunction Proceedings

Many trade secret cases involve preliminary injunction motions, whereby a plaintiff seeks to enjoin a defendant from misappropriation of the claimed trade secrets at issue. In order to obtain a preliminary injunction, a plaintiff generally must establish: (1) the likelihood of its success on the merits; (2) the possibility of irreparable harm to if relief not granted; and (3) the extent to which the balance of hardships favors the respective parties. *See* Chapter 12. Expert testimony often is a critical part of injunction proceedings. For example, in *Cutera, Inc. v. Lutronic Aesthetics, Inc.*, No. 2-20-cv-00235-KJM-DB, 444 F. Supp. 3d 1198 (E.D. Cal. 2020), the plaintiff sought a temporary restraining order barring defendants' continued misappropriation of its trade secrets following the departure of thirteen individuals from plaintiff's to defendant's employ. *Id.* at 1202. In support of its motion, plaintiff relied on the analysis conducted by its forensic expert which showed that certain of plaintiff's former employees had either shortly before or after departing plaintiff's employ: 1) attached external hard drives to their laptop but then employed "artifacts" making impossible to know which files or folders had been transferred to the external drives; 2) synchronized several documents from the laptops to an online iCloud account, including files titled "Copy of Dec Level 5 Deal 1.13.xlsx," "Cutera 2015 Product Pricing Matrix 9 19 14 w Candela.xlsx," "Cutera 2015 Product Pricing Matrix 9 19 14.xlsx," "NA ASM TM 2019 Plan.pdf," "Copy of sales demo June wpricing.xlsx.icloud," and "Budget 2020 $' v1-22-20.xlsc.icloud:"; 3) deleted 116 gigabytes of data from a laptop; and 4) copied twenty folders from a laptop to an external hard drive, including folders titled, "2019 Price List & Commissions," "2019 rep info," "Coolsculpting accounts," "marketing," "pitches," "presentations," "region business plans," "top leads," "Cutera Lasers Year End Discount," and "Greenway pitch." *Id.* at 1202–03. Based on when these events occurred, either at the time of employee's departure from Cutera or shortly thereafter, the court determined the evidence strongly suggested an intent by the former Cutera employees to use this information in their employment with the defendant Lutronic and sufficient to show plaintiff's likelihood of success on the merits of its misappropriation claims. *Id.* at 1208. This same evidence gave rise "to a reasonable inference that the former Cutera Employees intended to use this information to benefit their new employer," and to Plaintiff's detriment, establishing irreparable harm. *Id.* at 1209. In large part owing to the forensic expert's analysis, contained in a declaration, the court granted plaintiff's motion for a temporary restraining order.

Similarly, in *Pyro Spectaculars North, Inc. v. Souza*, No. CIV S-12-0299 GGH, 861 F. Supp. 2d 1079 (E.D. Cal. 2012), the plaintiff, PSI, sought a preliminary injunction to prohibit its former employee from using its trade secrets to benefit a competitor. Through its forensic expert, plaintiff was able to establish that the defendant had, on the date of his resignation, transferred over 60 files containing plaintiff's client information regarding from his PSI-assigned laptop to an external hard drive. Plaintiff's forensics expert was also able to establish that defendant tried to cover up this

---

[28] *See Mattel, Inc. v. MGA Entertainment, Inc.*, 782 F. Supp. 2d 911, 956-958 (C.D. Cal. 2011).

[29] *Mattel, Inc. v. MGA Entertainment, Inc.*, No. cv 04-9049 DOC (RNBx), 2011 WL 836418 (C.D. Cal. 2011). Calculation of damages in trade secrets cases is discussed in Chapter 11.

transfer by subsequently deleting these files from his PSI-assigned laptop. *Id.* at 1085. In addition, plaintiff's forensics expert's review of defendant's personal computer established that he had sent numerous proposals, some of which were similar to plaintiff's previous proposals, which offered the same products at a lower price than offered by plaintiff. *Id.* Faced with such evidence, defendant did not dispute that he downloaded and retained PSI documents and provided them to his new employer but instead contested their status as a trade secret. *Id.* at 1087. The court ultimately determined that the plaintiff was likely to succeed on the claim that the information defendant downloaded was a trade secret, and given the forensic reports showing their misappropriation, granted the preliminary injunction. *Id.* at 1090.

While injunction proceedings seek emergency relief and therefore are, by their nature, very fast paced, careful preparation of expert analysis and testimony can be key to success. Depending on the court and the nature of the dispute, a judge may allow limited discovery, including expert declarations and depositions, or even live expert testimony, in connection with a preliminary injunction hearing. Accordingly, it might be necessary to prepare an expert declaration and prepare your expert for a deposition or live testimony in a compressed time period. You also might need to prepare for and take the deposition and/or cross-examination of your opponent's expert in very short order.

Keep in mind that, regardless of the outcome of injunction proceedings, any weaknesses in expert analysis during injunction proceedings can be exploited by your opponent during later proceedings in the case, particularly if you use the same expert at trial. In some situations, a court may strike expert testimony at trial where it is inconsistent with prior opinions the expert has rendered in the case. *See Bonds v. Roy*, 20 Cal. 4th 140, 148 (1999) (excluding an expert's testimony where the proffered opinion was one the expert had expressly disavowed at his deposition, also citing the rule that a party must disclose "the general substance of an expert's expected testimony . . . . ").

As an additional form of injunctive relief, the DTSA allows owners of misappropriated trade secrets to submit ex parte applications, in extraordinary circumstances, for the court to "issue an order providing for the seizure of property necessary to prevent the propagation or dissemination of the trade secret that is the subject of the action." 18 U.S.C.A. § 1836(b)(2)(A)(i). A federal law enforcement officer shall serve the civil seizure order and carry out the seizure pursuant to the order. The applicant may not participate in the seizure. If needed, a technical expert unaffiliated with the applicant may assist the law enforcement officer with the seizure. For a technical expert to assist, the court must determine that the expert will aid the efficient execution of the seizure and minimize the burden of the seizure. *Id.* at § 1836(b)(2)(E).

§ 24.04 Use Of Expert Opinions In Summary Judgment Motions

Expert opinion is frequently used to support and oppose motions for summary judgment. There are a number of factors litigants should consider in preparing and opposing motions supported by expert opinion.

A. Questions Of Fact

The use of expert opinions in support of a summary judgment motion might seem a bit counterintuitive, as summary judgment is proper only if there are no material questions of fact. *See* Chapter 14. When filing or opposing a motion for summary judgment, the initial consideration should be whether the introduction of an expert opinion will raise a question of fact, particularly when there are expert opinions on both sides of the issues. Nevertheless, there are circumstances when expert analysis can be used to establish the absence of a question of fact and the propriety of summary judgment. Some trade secret misappropriation cases in which courts have granted and denied motions for summary judgment based on questions of material fact are discussed below.

In *Business Solutions, LLC v. Ganatra*, No. SA CV 18-1426-DOC (KESx, 2020 WL 1279209 (C.D. Cal. 2020), plaintiff alleged a former employee stole screen shots containing customer information from its CRM and then provided the same to his current employer and defendant. From these screenshots, plaintiff argued defendant was able to learn its pricing strategies, program offerings, and social media strategies and subsequently used them to (a) perform in-house analyses; (b) add social media services to its offerings which competed with plaintiff (which it previously did not offer); and (c) get to market much quicker than it would have without the stolen screenshots. *Id.* at **1, 4. Defendant moved for summary judgment, arguing plaintiff failed to allege any damages in connection with its claims and that it failed to present any evidence on which to base a reasonably royalty award. The court disagreed and denied defendant's motion for summary judgment. In doing so, the court cited plaintiff's expert report which stated the screenshots "provide key information about the length of the sales cycle, and line-by-line analysis of these dates would help a competitor's sales team to improve forecasting" which "would contribute to contribute to lower costs, a better win rate, and higher sales at BrandRep." *Id.* at *5. Plaintiff's expert further quantified its lost revenues (from the stolen screen shots) between $360,000 and $1,300,000. *Id.* Based on this information, the court found "[p]laintiff has provided sufficient evidence of damages to survive summary judgement" and that a "jury should decide whether to accept the expert's testimony." *Id.*

In *Prostar Wireless Group, LLC v. Domino's Pizza, Inc.*, 360 F. Supp. 994 (N.D. Cal. 2018), plaintiff spent years developing a custom global positioning service ("GPS") driver tracking system for defendant's franchises (the "Solution"). After approximately eight years of collaboration, defendant told plaintiff it would not be using plaintiff's Solution. Plaintiff subsequently learned defendant was working to create its own solution. As a result, plaintiff sued defendant for, among other things, misappropriation of its trade secrets which it alleged resulted in $170 million in lost profits. Defendant moved for summary judgment, arguing that, as a new business, plaintiff could not calculate anticipated profits with any degree of certainty. *Id.* at 1019. The court began by noting California's general rule that new businesses cannot recover damages for anticipated future profits because "their occurrence is uncertain, contingent and speculative." *Id.* at 1020. Anticipated future profits, however, "are allowed where their nature and occurrence can be shown by reasonable reliability." *Id.* Reasonable reliability can be established through evidence including "expert testimony, economic and financial data, market surveys and analysis, business records of similar enterprises and the like." *Id.* The court determined that plaintiff could not establish with reasonable certainty either the occurrence or the extent of its alleged lost profits. *Id.* at 1021. As to the extent of lost profits, the court noted that plaintiff's damages expert relied on "no specific economic or financial data, market survey, or analysis based on the business records or operating histories of similar enterprises" thereby making plaintiff's claims of lost profits "uncertain, contingent and speculative." *Id.* Because plaintiff's expert could not establish a question of material fact, the court granted defendant's motion for summary judgment on lost profits.

B. Make Sure Your Experts' Opinions Are Based On Valid Scientific Methodology

As discussed above, a court may reject expert analysis that is not based on scientific methodology. Courts have discretion to make this determination at the summary judgment stage of the case, if expert analysis is interjected into the motion or opposition. In *QR Spex, Inc. v. Motorola, Inc.*, No. CV 03-6284-JFW (FMOx), 2004 WL 5642907 (C.D. Cal. Oct. 28, 2004), the defendant filed a motion to exclude the expert report of Dr. Goodman, plaintiff's expert, because it did not meet the standards for admissibility under FRE 702. The court determined that Dr. Goodman was unqualified to render his opinion as to whether plaintiff's Bluetooth trade secret was in the public domain as of October 31, 2002. In so holding, the court rendered its decision based on Dr. Goodman's admission at this deposition that "I don't know anything about trade secrets." *Id.* at *10. Further, it was undisputed that Plaintiff's Bluetooth trade secret was a trade secret prior to October 31, 2002. As a result, Dr. Goodman's opinion was not relevant to any disputed issues before the Court. *Id.* The court also determined that Dr. Goodman's opinions did not meet the standards for relevance and reliability as required by FRE702 and *Daubert,* because he did not do things he testified it would have been helpful to do and because he admitted he had no evidence supporting aspects of his opinions. *Id.* at *8.

In *FLIR Systems, Inc. v. Parrish*, 174 Cal. App. 4th 1270 (2009), the Court of Appeals affirmed the trial court's judgment for the defendant former employees (awarding attorneys' fees and costs) who had been sued by their former employer for trade secret misappropriation. Prior to trial, the court denied defendants' motion for summary judgment, which plaintiffs opposed by submitting a declaration from their expert. The declaration indicated there was a way to predict the likelihood of trade secret misappropriation. Although the trial court found defendants made a compelling argument for summary judgment, it was concerned "the concepts in this action are highly technical" and denied defendants' motion for summary judgment to see what would develop at trial. *Id.* at 1282. At trial, however, plaintiffs' experts admitted there no valid scientific methodology to predict trade secret misuse and agreed that no trade secrets were, in fact, misappropriated. *Id.* at 1283. In affirming the trial court's judgment, the Court of Appeals reasoned that under the CUTSA, sanctions "may be awarded for the bad faith filing *or* maintenance of a groundless action" and held the trial court reasonably inferred there was no misappropriation or threatened misappropriation of trade secrets before the summary judgment motion was argued. *Id.* Plaintiffs argued that, since the court denied defendants' motion for summary judgment, the court was estopped from finding that plaintiffs brought the litigation in bad faith. *Id.* at 1282. The court rejected this argument, declaring "[i]f the rule were otherwise, a trade secrets plaintiff could file sham declarations to successfully oppose a summary judgment motion and immunize itself from sanctions." *Id.* at 1283.

In *Manufacturing Automation and Software Systems, Inc. v. Hughes, et al.*, No. 2:16-cv-08962-CAS(KSx), 2018 WL 3197696 (C.D. Cal. 2018), plaintiff alleged that defendants, former employees of plaintiff, copied its software to produce, market, and sell a counterfeit version to plaintiff's current or potential customers. *Id.* at *1. Defendants moved to exclude plaintiff's expert, Erik Laykin, and asked that the court strike Laykin's declaration filed in support of plaintiff's opposition to defendants' motion for partial summary judgment. Defendants argued that Laykin was not qualified under FRE 702 because he was not a computer programmer, could not read source code and lacked the requisite qualifications to assist the trier of fact. *Id.* at *5. Defendants also argued that the court should exclude Laykin's opinions as a sanction for his alleged violations of the Protective Order (*e.g.*, he permitted his team to review defendant's source code designated "Highly Confidential – Source Code" and reviewed the source code on paper, as opposed to on a secure computer as required by the Protective Order). *Id.* The court declined to exclude the expert's opinions, reasoning that 1) Laykin and his team had examined thousands of pages of database code to resolve intellectual property disputes, 2) Laykin has been retained as an expert in numerous cases involving trade secret theft, 3) Laykin's experience as an expert witness required him to compare and opine on software products—including source code—of competitive firms, and 4) Laykin has experience and skill in the area of computer forensics. *Id.* The court concluded that wholesale exclusion of Laykin's opinion "appears unwarranted" and instead could be challenged through "cross-examination, contrary evidence and attention to the burden of proof, not exclusion." *Id.*

C. Experts May Not Provide Legal Opinions

It is often disputed whether an expert opinion constitutes an impermissible legal opinion or conclusion. In the context of trade secrets cases, this dispute sometimes hinges on whether an expert may opine that particular information is or is not trade secret.

For example, in *Highmark Digital, Inc. v. Casablanca Design Centers, Inc.*, No. CV 18-18-06105 SJO (JPR), 2020 WL 2114940 (C.D. Cal. 2020), the defendants moved to exclude from the opinion of plaintiff's expert, Derek Huisjen, that plaintiff's conversion software and certain files were trade secrets. The court stated that it is well-established that expert testimony regarding legal conclusion is inadmissible, but "the law is unsettled on whether an expert is permitted to conclude that certain technology constitutes a trade secret." *Id.* at *7. Ultimately, the court held that Huisjen could not offer the legal conclusion that plaintiff's source code and files constitute trade secrets but held Huisjen could still offer his opinions as to the value of plaintiff's conversion software and files, how the conversion software functions, what information is contained in the subject files, the reason that the files, and plaintiff's source code are valuable. *Id.* at *8. In so holding, the court cited *GSI Tech., Inc. v. United Memories, Inc.*, No. 5-13-cv-01081-PSG, 2015 WL 12942201 at *4 (N.D. Cal. 2015), a case permitting testimony on whether the technology at issue possessed independent economic value and whether the party undertook reasonable efforts to main the technology's secrecy. *Id.* at *8.

Similarly, in *CDA of America, Inc. v. Midland Life Ins. Co.,* No. 01-CV-837, 2006 WL 5349266, at *5 (S.D. Ohio 2006), the defendant sought to exclude the testimony of plaintiff's expert, Timothy A. Pfeifer, on whether the insurance conversation program at issue constituted a trade secret. Specifically, defendant argued Pfeifer's testimony was nothing more than legal conclusions. *See Aguilar v. Int'l Longshoremen's Union,* 966 F.2d 443, 447 (9th Cir. 1992). The court found Pfeifer had significant experience in insurance conservation and permitted his testimony on that basis. *CDA* at *5. In doing so, however, the court cautioned that "[a]t trial, however, Defendants must ensure that Pfeifer's testimony does not turn to the issue of whether or not CDA's insurance conversation program constituted a "trade secret," as that would, as a matter of law, encroach upon the province of the jury in breach of FRE704." *Id.* at *6.

§ 24.05 Motions In Limine/Daubert Motions

Prior to trial, consider filing motions attacking your opponent's experts, with the goal of limiting or eliminating their testimony at trial. Such motions may be directed to the legal and/or factual sufficiency of the expert opinions. They also can be based on failure to properly disclose expert opinions in expert reports and/or expert depositions. Your opponent also may file similar motions, so you should be prepared to both attack and defend expert opinions prior to and during trial.

A. Full Disclosure Of Expert Opinions

Courts may strike expert opinions that are not properly disclosed in expert reports or depositions. If it appears that your opponent plans to try to elicit expert testimony at trial that was not disclosed previously, consider filing a motion to exclude such opinions at trial.

In *Space Data Corporation v. Alphabet Inc.*, No. 16-cv-03260-BLF, 2019 WL 2603285 (N.D. Cal. June 25, 2019), plaintiff, Space Data, sought to exclude defendant's damages expert, Dr. Ingberman, from offering opinions on trade secret misappropriation because, as an economist, plaintiff's expert did not have any foundation to argue what is and is not improper trade secret or confidential information misuse. The court held that defendant's damages expert could testify on the "value of the trade secrets in question and may build in and discuss the assumptions on which he relies" but that he could not "testify that a given trade secret has no value because it is not a trade secret—such testimony falls outside the purview of damages." *Id.* at *4. Regarding plaintiff's financial trade secrets, defendant argued that Dr. Ingberman was qualified "as to what is and what is not a financial trade secret." In its decision, the court noted that it found Dr. Ingberman "generally qualified to opine on whether financial trade secrets are in fact trade secrets." *Id.* Defendant's failure to disclose Dr. Ingberman for this purpose, however, resulted in the court barring Dr. Ingberman from offering any testimony on plaintiff's financial trade secret (or technical trade secrets) "where the testimony concerns whether the asserted trade secret is or is not a trade secret." *Id.*

In *Ajaxo, Inc. v. E*Trade Financial Corporation*, 48 Cal. App. 5th 129 (2020), Ajaxo sued E*Trade for trade secret misappropriation and breach of a confidentiality agreement. Ajaxo's founder and inventor of its "wireless proxy" technology, Sing Koo, and Ajaxo's damages expert, testified there were three models that could determine a royalties award: 1) the enterprise direct use model; 2) the end-user subscription model; and 3) the value added developer distribution model. E*Trade objected to Koo's testimony about the royalty models, arguing he did not disclose those opinions or his basis for them in his expert disclosure or deposition before trial. The trial court overruled the objection without prejudice to a later motion to strike. On cross-examination, Koo agreed that his royalty opinions based on the end-user subscription and enterprise direct use models were not included in his expert report or deposition testimony. Further, Koo admitted: 1) his royalty calculations did not rely on positions taken by the parties during the negotiations; 2) he did not consider the financial terms of E*Trade's actual service agreement for the alleged misappropriate wireless proxy technology; and 3) he did not consider evidence regarding E*Trade's actual usage of the wireless trading platform. Instead, he relied on E*Trade's total accounts as reported in their 10-K filings. At the conclusion of the trial, the court found that Koo did not timely disclose his enterprise direct use and subscription royalty models and granted defendant's motion to strike Koo's expert testimony related to both models. On appeal, Ajaxo challenged the trial court's exclusion of these two royalty theories. The court found no abuse of discretion by the trial court where his expert report only disclosed the value-added developer distribution model. *Id.* at *182.

B. Consider Whether Expert Is Offering Appropriate Expert Opinion

As noted above, courts generally will not allow opinions that fail to meet the requirements of FRE 702 and Cal. Evid. Code §§ 801 and 802. A party may bring a motion in limine to bar expert testimony for failure to comply with those code sections.

For example, in *Waymo LLC v. Uber Technologies, Inc.*, No. C 17-00939 WHA, 2017 WL 6887043 (N.D. Cal. 2017), the court granted defendant's motion to exclude the testimony and opinions of plaintiff's damages expert, Michael Wagner, because his testimony did not qualify as expert testimony under FRE 702 and because his testimony would be "substantially more prejudicial than probative under FRE 403." *Id.* at *2. The court found that Wagner brought "no specialized knowledge to the table" because he was not an economist, but instead, "merely an inactive CPA and inactive lawyer." *Id.* at *5. The court found that Wagner had "simply adopted the opinions of others and performed grade-school arithmetic counsel can do on an easel." *Id.* The court found that the evidence Wagner relied on "can speak for itself," and Wagner's only contribution "would be to pile on a misleading façade of expertise." *Id.* "Straightforward application of grade-school arithmetic to uncomplicated numbers is well within the ken of an average juror. There is no reason for Wagner to serve as a mouthpiece for arguments that Waymo's lawyers can make." *Id.* citing *United States v. Morales*, 108 F.3d 1031, 1038 (9th Cir. 1997) (expert witness testimony is admissible under [FRE] 702 if the subject matter at issue is "beyond the common knowledge of the average layman . . . . ").

C. Compliance With The Requirements Of FRCP 26(a)(2)(B)

A party may move to strike an expert report for failure to meet the disclosure requirement of Federal Rule of Civil Procedure ("Rule") 26(a)(2)(B) which provides that an expert's written report must contain, among others things, "(ii) the facts or data considered by the witness in forming them." For example, in *Atmel Corp. v. Information Storage Devices.*, 189 F.R.D. 410 (N.D. Cal. 1999), the court prohibited plaintiff's expert, George Kern, from testifying on direct examination to certain opinions expressed in his expert report "because those conclusions were based, at the time rendered, on an unreliable methodology." *Id.* at 411. Specifically, Kern submitted his initial expert report in which he opined that seventeen of plaintiff's trade secrets were not generally known or published several years ago in the semi-conductor industry and that these same seventeen pieces of information constituted trade secrets. Although Kern had thirty years of practical experience in the semiconductor industry, he admitted that in preparing his expert report he did not search out or review any technical articles or consult with colleagues knowledgeable about the matter in forming his opinion that plaintiff's trade secrets were not generally known during a three-year period beginning ten years before trial, *i.e.*, 1989–1992. Instead, Kern admitted that he chose to rely on his unrefreshed recollection. The court excluded as unreliable Kern's proposed testimony that alleged trade secrets were not "generally known" in the semiconductor industry at that time or published during a particular time. *Id.* at 416–17.

In *Yeti by Molly Ltd. v. Deckers Outdoor Group*, 259 F.3d 1101 (9th Cir. 2001), defendant appealed the district court's decision to exclude the testimony of its only damages expert,

Dan Vuckovich. Although defendant disclosed Vuckovich's identity to plaintiffs on August 1, 1997, it failed to provide his expert report until twenty-eight days before trial which was almost two years after discovery had closed and one year after plaintiff's damages expert had last supplemented his report. *Id.* at 1105. It attempted to justify its failure by noting that Vuckovich would be used only as a rebuttal witness, and that an expert report would be disclosed if defendant decided to have him testify. *Id.* The court began its analysis by noting Rule 26(a)(2)(B) "requires the parties to disclose the identity of each expert 'accompanied by a written report prepared and signed by the witness.'" *Id.* at 1106. Further, Rule 37(c)(1) forbids the "use at trial of any information required to be disclosed by Rule 26(a) that is not properly disclosed," unless one of two exceptions applies: the failure to disclose is either: 1) substantially justified; or 2) harmless. *Id.* Reviewing the district court's decision under an abuse of discretion standard, the Court of Appeals affirmed the district court's determination that neither of those exceptions applied. *Id.* Defendant's failure was not "substantially justified" where the only reason they offered was their mistaken impression was plaintiff's damages report would be supplemented again and they were waiting for that before disclosing Vukovich's report. *Id.* Even if that were the case, the court found that defendant's should have issued a preliminary report (as required by Rule 26(a)(2)(B)) or alternatively asked for an extension of the discovery deadline. *Id.* at 1107. Nor did the court agree the delay was harmless where it occurred one month before a complex trial was set to begin and would have required plaintiff's to depose Vukovich in order to prepare to question him at trial. *Id.* Consequently, the Ninth Circuit affirmed the district court's decision to exclude Vukovich's testimony.

D. Experts Are Allowed to Use Proxies Where There Is No Defined Methodology For Allocating Damages Among Trade Secrets

In cases in which there is no defined methodology for valuing trade secrets, California courts have allowed experts to use some degree of creativity in determining trade secret damages based on the number or value of related factors.

In *Live Person, Inc. v. [24]7.ai, Inc.*, No. 17-cv-01268-JST, 2019 WL 3254226 (C.D. Cal. July 19, 2019), plaintiff's damages expert, Dr. William Choi, calculated damages by assigning a value to each trade secret based on the number of predictive information or rules contained within each trade secret. The greater the number of rules associated with each trade secret, the more valuable the trade secret. *Id.* at *3. Defendant moved to exclude Dr. Choi's opinion because he provided no reason for his assumption that each rule within a trade secret had the same value and further argued Dr. Choi's methodology was contrary to the court's prior admonition that "[s]ome trade secrets are more valuable than others." *Id.* In denying defendant's motion, the court noted that "other courts have approved calculations of damages employing similar per-unit methodologies" and cited *VIA Techs., v. ASUS Comput. Int'l*, No. 14-cv-03586-BLF, 2017 WL 3051048 at *6 (N.D. Cal. 2017) as precedent for an expert using "surface area as a proxy for design effort much as Dr. Choi uses the number of rules as a proxy for the effort to construct a trade secret." *Id.* at *4. The court also noted that defendant's own damages expert conceded at her deposition that there was no defined methodology for allocating damages among trade secrets and that she herself would have applied Dr. Choi's methodology to allocate damages for the lost profits associated with a particular customer. *Id.* Based on this concession and the *VIA* holding, the court held Dr. Choi's opinion was sufficiently reliable and could be admitted at trial.

Nevertheless, it is important to carefully consider potential *Daubert* challenges in the event your expert finds it necessary to value trade secrets via the use of a proxy.

E. Factual Foundation For Expert Opinions

An expert ordinarily should be prepared to point to the facts upon which his or her opinion is based. In *BladeRoom Group Ltd. v. Facebook, Inc.*, No. 5-15-cv-01370-EJD, 2018 WL 1611835 (N.D. Cal. 2018) at *5, the court excluded as unreliable the lost profits opinion of defendant's damages expert because she did not cite any facts to support her opinion. In addition, the court determined the record evidence contradicted the expert's opinion. As a result, the court found the expert's opinion would not "assist the jury because it is too speculative to serve as a reliable method of assessing [plaintiff's] lost profits." *Id.*

§ 24.06 Trial And Related Practice Tips

A successful misappropriation of trade secrets case requires careful preparation, including diligent work with your experts to prepare them for direct and cross examinations, preparation of direct examination outlines for your experts and preparation of detailed cross examination outlines for your opponent's experts. It also can be important for the expert to think about and prepare for possibilities, such as not all alleged trade secrets at issue will be adjudicated to be misappropriated or part of the expert's opinion or its foundation or demonstrative will be excluded. To the extent possible, the expert's opinions or contemplated testimony should take into account such possibilities.

The following cases illustrate the potential importance of expert testimony at trial. In many cases, the expert testimony can be a key factor appellate courts consider in upholding or reversing a trade secret monetary award.

In *Yeti by Molly Ltd. v. Deckers Outdoor Group*, 259 F.3d 1101 (9th Cir. 2001), plaintiff sued defendant for, among other things, trade secret misappropriation, and received a jury verdict in its favor. Defendant appealed, arguing there was insufficient evidence to support the damages finding. The Court of Appeals affirmed and noted it must "uphold the jury's finding of the amount of damages unless the amount is grossly excessive or monstrous, clearly not supported by the evidence, or based only on speculation or guesswork." *Id.* at 1107. In finding that the evidence supported the jury's verdict, the court cited plaintiff's damages expert, Paul Polzin, who testified that plaintiffs suffered $8,062,099 in lost opportunities. Polzin came to this figure by calculating royalties plaintiff could have made by licensing their trade secrets to other footwear manufacturers. *Id.* The court dismissed defendant's attempts to discredit Polzin by noting they "made the same arguments to the jury and failed to carry the day. Because there is substantial evidence in the record, we affirm the jury's compensatory damages awards." *Id.* at 1108.

In *Management and Engineering Technologies Intern. v. Information Systems Support Inc.*, 490 Fed. Appx. 30 (9th Cir. 2012), plaintiff sued defendant for misappropriation of trade secrets and obtained a jury verdict in its favor. On appeal, the court held that jury's finding of trade secret misappropriation was supported by sufficient evidence but the amount of damages was not. Its decision to vacate the jury's damages award rested on the testimony of plaintiff's damages expert, Mark Peterson. In particular, the court noted that, at trial, Peterson failed to "apportion value among the legally valid and the legally invalid alleged trade secrets." *Id.* at 34. Instead, he testified about the "hypothetical negotiated price that [defendant] would have paid for *all* of the information alleged to be trade secrets." *Id.* Further, Peterson admitted the damages amount would need to be reduced if some of plaintiff's trade secret theories were legally insufficient. *Id.* As a result, the court found the evidence was insufficient to support the damages award and vacated and remanded for further proceedings.

A. Preparing An Expert Witness For Trial

Thoroughly preparing an expert witness for trial is usually critical to success, particularly if the expert has limited testifying experience. In general, it is best to work with your expert to prepare an outline of questions and answers, and then to practice the direct examination with the expert multiple times before the expert testifies. Make sure the witness understands the logistics and arrangement of the courtroom, and make the practice direct examinations as close as possible to what the witness will actually experience at trial. If possible, you may wish to designate your colleagues to serve the roles of opposing counsel and judge, so that the expert will get a realistic sense of how his or her testimony will proceed at trial. In the event your expert will be testifying remotely due to COVID concerns or other issues, make sure you devote sufficient time to ensuring the witness fully understands all necessary technology and that the witness's technology is compatible with the court's technology. Do as many dry runs as possible with the technology in advance of trial, including in the courtroom if the court allows this (in our experience, most do). Make sure the witness has appropriate audio, proper lighting, and a professional looking background that is free of distractions. Virtual backgrounds are not preferred unless that is the only option, and, if it is, use a plain background.

It is best to devote at least as much time—if not more time—to preparing your expert witness for cross examination. Try to ask your witness in advance what you believe are the most difficult questions he or she is likely to be asked, and practice answers in advance of trial. Make sure the witness understands the judge may ask questions as well.

Make sure your expert understands her primary role: to break down complex information so that the jury (or judge, if a bench trial) understands what happened in a manner that is consistent with your theory of the case. The expert's role is not tell the jury everything she knows about the subject but to give them enough understanding of the specific issue(s) to find for your client. Second, make sure your expert uses plain English instead of specialized jargon (if possible) and answers your questions in sound bites, as opposed to prolonged lectures. Rambling answers risk the jury not understanding what the expert is saying and may result in undermining the expert's credibility. Third, get your expert to use demonstratives to illustrate and supplement their answers. The jury will appreciate seeing visual aids that show what the expert did, how she did it, and why. Where possible, have the expert use examples and analogies from everyday life that will be readily accessible to the jury. Visual aids and real-life examples can make complex information much easier to comprehend. Fourth, make sure your expert comes across as self-confident and decisive when answering questions. Experts typically fall into the habit of hedging their answers because they know they will cross-examined and don't want to be boxed into a particular answer that can be used to impeach them. While this is a natural concern for any witness, expert or fact, responding in a tentative manner has two drawbacks: a) it makes their answer harder to understand; and b) it is less persuasive in helping the jury understand your theory of the case. Credibility is key. Jurors will believe the experts they understand and trust. For that reason (and others), it is ordinarily important that the expert knows their expert opinion and is comfortable with it and does not believe it overreaches.

B. Direct Examination Of An Expert At Trial

Direct examinations should be structured in a manner that makes the expert's testimony clear and meets the jurors' (or judge's) needs. A typical structure for a direct examination is 1) introduction; 2) education, formal training and experience; 3) what the expert did and why; 4) the expert's opinions; 5) basis for the expert's opinions and explanations; and 6) repeat the conclusions (framed differently in order to avoid an objection directed at cumulative evidence).

The introduction has two components: 1) nonverbal; and 2) verbal. The nonverbal component is particularly important if your expert has little experience testifying before a jury. Ordinarily, make sure your expert dresses in either a suit or non-controversial, non-distracting apparel that is appropriate for a courtroom. Also, ensure your expert is familiar with the courtroom prior to testifying so they know where to sit and otherwise how to conduct herself on the stand. Decide in advance what materials she will need, *e.g.*, the expert report or visual aids and how she will access them. The verbal component should begin immediately and address the jurors' needs: who is the expert, what was their task and why. It may be helpful to provide the expert, the court and opposing counsel with binders containing paper copies of the exhibits the expert will use during their direct examination.

The next step is to qualify the expert by asking questions about their professional background. Your main task here is to convince the jury (and/or judge) that the expert has the qualifications and experience to give an opinion on the particular subject and that the expert's judgment is sound and their opinion is correct. You will want to bring out the expert's education training and experience but only those portions that are relevant to the issues in the case. Spending time on qualifications that are not relevant to the expert's opinion risks losing the jury's attention and/or drawing relevance objections from opposing counsel. You will also want to humanize the expert. Satisfy the jurors' curiosity by asking questions about how they got into their chosen profession. If the expert has any unique or impressive credentials, such as winning a Nobel peace prize, writing a well-known book, or inventing a commonly known pharmaceutical, be sure to bring those out on direct. Doing so makes your expert's opinion that much more persuasive.

Next, you will want to bring out what the expert did, how they did it and why. If possible, break up your questions so that the expert can answer in one or two sentences so their answer is clear to the jury. If what the expert did is complicated or involved several steps, use visual aids to discretely break out each step. Your goal is to turn what the expert did into an interesting story that can be easily followed.

Next, you want to discuss the expert's opinion. Because an expert is ordinarily permitted to testify on matters within their "knowledge, skill, experience, training, or education," you must ensure the expert's testimony falls within their area of expertise to render opinions on the subject matter. If the expert provided several opinions, consider using a PowerPoint that summarizes each opinion. As always, be sure to practice the direct examination many times with the expert prior to trial so that the expert knows what will be asked and responds with an answer that is consistent with your theory of the case. Also, do not ask any open-ended questions such as "what happened next?" While the expert is on your side, doing so might confuse the expert, resulting in an unexpected and possibly harmful answer. With enough practice, the expert should easily be able to anticipate your questions, be familiar with your phrasing of the questions, and know the appropriate way to respond.

Finally, your expert should explain the reasons for their opinion. This is where you want your expert to assume the teacher role. Your expert can create the classroom setting by leaving the stand and writing on an easel and speaking directly to the jury. Having your expert assume the teacher mantle allows the jury to see the facts in a manner consistent with your theory of the case. When done effectively, it may also dispel any notion that the expert's opinion is for sale to the highest bidder. The expert should explain how they reached their opinion by giving short, easy to understand answers to your questions accompanied with visual aids. Again, your expert only needs to explain how they reached their opinion(s). This is not the time for the expert to show-off all of their knowledge on the subject. Doing so risks irritating the jury and/or losing their attention.

C. Cross Examination Of An Expert At Trial

Before you can plan your cross-examination, you need to do your research. The first step is to become knowledgeable about the subject matter on which the expert will opine. Read the leading treatises and articles and make sure you understand them. Use your own expert to explain anything you do not understand. The point is not to become as knowledgeable as the expert, but must you know enough about the subject to effectively cross-examine an expert. Your research also should include investigating the expert's background and prior writings. Find everything the expert has ever published. You may uncover an article or book she has authored that is contrary to their opinion in this case. Find out the expert's involvement in litigation and obtain copies of the expert's reports in those cases, if possible. Has the expert's opinions or methodology ever been excluded or otherwise discredited in a judge's opinion? If so, you will want to bring this out on cross examination. You also will want your expert to review the opposing expert's report, resume and deposition transcripts to identify areas for impeachment.

One area of attack is the expert's qualifications. Do they have the highest degree or certification in the field? If not, bring this out to create doubt as to the basis for the expert's opinions. Of course, if your expert suffers from the same issue, or has less credentials that the opposing expert, leave this alone. What about the expert's experience in the field? Is it limited to academia? If yes, it can be helpful to get the expert to admit that they do not have any hands-on experience. Alternatively, if the expert has numerous credentials and expertise but not in the same area involved in the trial, this should be brought out so that it is clear to the jury the expert's expertise is irrelevant to facts in this case.

Another way to impeach an expert witness is to show the jury that their full-time job is testifying as a professional witness. For example, if the witness only testifies for plaintiffs and they are doing so here, this creates the impression that they are biased and can only see the evidence through one lens. Be sure, however, that your expert is not vulnerable to the same attack before proceeding.

Sometimes an expert will rely on certain predicate facts in rendering their opinion without making an independent effort to verify them. In the trade secrets arena, the plaintiff's damages expert will usually assume their client's information is a) a trade secret; and 2) has been misappropriated when calculating damages. This can be a high-yield area for cross-examination if you can call into question the accuracy of those predicate facts. If the expert's assumptions are unreliable or plain wrong, then their whole opinion should be discredited. Also, getting the expert to admit they just assumed things can make the expert look incompetent in jury's eyes.

Probably the most fertile cross-examination topic is using the expert's prior, inconsistent statements against them. If the expert said one thing at their deposition and gives a contrary answer at trial, the question in the jury's mind becomes, were they lying then or are they lying now? You can achieve the same effect using the expert's prior publications, expert reports and deposition transcripts from other trials which are inconsistent with the expert's opinion in the current case.

§ 24.07 Conclusion

Working with experts in a trade secrets case requires careful and thorough preparation at every step, from retaining the expert, to disclosing the expert's opinions, to preparing declarations for use in preliminary injunction or summary judgment proceedings, to preparing for and presenting the expert at trial. It also requires exploring and exploiting any of your opposing expert's weaknesses, including lack of appropriate qualifications, bias, failure to disclose opinions in full, failure to follow accepted scientific methodologies, and credibility questions based on prior statements or writings. By carefully and thoroughly preparing for your expert's and your opponent's expert's testimony, you will maximize your client's chance of success in the case.

Chapter 25
PROTECTING IDEAS WITH IMPLIED-IN-FACT CONTRACTS
By: Randall E. Kay, Esq.

---

§ 25.01 Introduction

Some say that ideas are as "free as air." Juries say otherwise. Juries have found that protectable ideas can have tremendous value:

- Mattel and MGA battled over the ideas for the name, concept, prototypes and preliminary drawings for the Bratz female fashion dolls, resulting in a $100 million jury verdict in Mattel's favor in the 2008 trial. The Ninth Circuit reversed. On retrial, Mattel lost on its idea-based claim and MGA won an $88.5 million verdict on its trade secret claim against Mattel. The Ninth Circuit again reversed, vacating the award to MGA.

- A jury found that Fisher-Price misappropriated ideas for a backpack component to its Rescue Heroes action figure toys, and awarded the concept-developing plaintiff $1.7 million as unpaid royalties.

- A jury awarded $30 million to two marketing executives who claimed that Taco Bell Corp. used their idea for a talking Chihuahua advertising campaign ("Yo quiero Taco Bell").

- A jury awarded $240 million to All Pro Sports Camp Inc., who claimed Disney used its idea for the Wide World of Sports complex at Disney World.

- A jury awarded $8.2 million to a man who said his lawyers stole his idea for a golf-themed restaurant.

- A jury found 20th Century Fox liable for $19 million for the ideas for the film "Jingle All the Way" starring Arnold Schwarzenegger, finding that Fox used ideas from a high school biology teacher's script in making the film.

- A jury found that Walt Disney Co. stole ideas to create Radio Disney after it backed out of a contract, and awarded the plaintiff $20 million. After the verdict was dismissed and a new trial ordered, a different jury awarded the plaintiff $9.5 million.

- A jury awarded $7.3 million to a man who claimed MCA and Universal City Studios stole the ideas in his screenplay to create the television series "Northern Exposure."

Idea protection takes many forms as shown by the examples above. While many of the reported decisions in idea claim cases involve scripts and screenplays, the claim has applicability to submissions involving technology and scientific submissions as well. See, e.g., *JBF Interlude 2009 Ltd., v. Quibi Holdings LLC*, Nos. 2:20-cv-02299-CAS (SKx), 2:20-cv-02250-CAS (SKx), 2020 WL 6203555 (N.D. Cal. October 19, 2020); *Canter v. West Pub. Co, Inc.*, 31 F. Supp. 2d 1193, 1203 (N.D. Cal. 1999). This chapter addresses idea protection in California under principles of contracts implied-in-fact.

§ 25.02 Distinctions Between Trade Secret and Idea Claims

A claim for trade secret misappropriation requires the existence of trade secret information. As detailed *supra* in Chapter 1, to show the existence of a protectable trade secret, one must have proof of (1) information; (2) economic value; (3) value from not being generally known; and (4) reasonable secrecy efforts. Cal. Civ. Code § 3426.1(d). An idea can constitute a trade secret when it has economic value from not being generally known and it has been kept secret. *Altavion, Inc. v. Konica Minolta Sys. Lab.*, 226 Cal. App. 4th 26, 53-56 (2014).

In certain circumstances, California contract law will protect ideas that do not qualify as trade secrets. Contractual idea claims and trade secret claims have different requirements. Idea claims under California's "implied-in-fact contract law" require proof of (1) access, (2) promise to pay, (3) use, and (4) damages.

Idea claims do not require three elements of a trade secret claim:

- Idea claims do not require proof that the idea derives "economic value" from not being generally known (although without economic value a plaintiff may have difficulty proving damages).
- Idea claims do not require proof that the ideas were not generally known. For example, an idea to make a movie regarding the sinking of the Titanic would have been generally known during most of the Twentieth Century so it would not constitute a trade secret. The ingenuity of the idea to make a movie about the Titanic could, though, have been the basis for a claim over an idea if the idea-holder had strategic reasons why such a film might have commercial success at a given point in time. *See Blaustein v. Burton*, 9 Cal. App. 3d 161 (1970) (idea claim over motion picture version of Shakespeare's "Taming of the Shrew" despite the fact that this play already had been made into a movie decades earlier).
- Idea claims do not require proof of reasonable efforts to maintain secrecy of the idea. Rather, the analogous element in an idea case is whether the idea purveyor struck his bargain prior to disclosing the idea to the defendant.

Despite the differences between protection of trade secrets and ideas, similarities exist that warrant discussion of idea claims in a trade secret treatise. Both types of claims can arise from a setting where the defendant gained access to the plaintiff's intellectual property through a disclosure between the parties. Both types of claims can result from a potential collaboration that stalled or failed for one reason or another. In both types of claims, the party making the disclosure may want to seek legal recourse when it discovers that the other party unilaterally commercialized the subject of the disclosure. Clients and lawyers assessing claims arising from failed collaborations should evaluate the applicability of an idea claim as well as a trade secret claim. Given that different proof supports the two claims, failure of proof for a trade secret claim does not necessarily harm the viability of an idea claim.

§ 25.03 Legal Principles for Contracts Implied-in-Fact

Claims of contracts implied-in-fact arise most frequently in the entertainment area ("that movie was my idea" or "that television show was my idea"). Contracts implied-in-fact exist in all industries, though, including technology, advertising, and consumer products.

A. Elements of Proof of an Implied-in-Fact Contract

California law recognizes legal protection for "ideas" under a contract implied-in-fact in the following circumstances:

(1) the plaintiff disclosed the idea making it accessible to the recipient;

(2) the recipient voluntarily accepted the disclosure knowing the conditions on which it was tendered (i.e., the recipient must have had the ability to reject the disclosure if the conditions were unacceptable);

(3) the recipient used the work; and

(4) the plaintiff can prove damages in the form of the reasonable value of the work.

Proof of these elements demonstrates a viable claim for breach of contract implied-in-fact. *Desny v. Wilder*, 46 Cal. 2d 715, 739 (1956); *Donahue v. Ziv Television Programs, Inc.*, 245 Cal. App. 2d 593, 609 (1966).

In the seminal California idea case, *Desny v. Wilder*, the court stated the principles of a contract implied-in-fact:

> [I]n the absence of an express contract, when the service is requested and rendered the law does not hesitate to infer or imply a promise to compensate for it . . . . The person who can and does convey a valuable idea to a producer who commercially solicits the service or who voluntarily accepts it knowing that it is tendered for a price should likewise be entitled to recover . . . . [T]he idea purveyor cannot prevail in an action to recover compensation for an abstract idea unless (a) before or after disclosure he has obtained an express promise to pay, or (b) the circumstances preceding and attending disclosure, together with the conduct of the offeree acting with knowledge of the circumstances, show a promise of the type usually referred to as 'implied' or 'implied-in-fact.'

Desny, 46 Cal. 2d at 733-38. In *Desny*, the court held that "the law itself, to prevent fraud and unjust enrichment, will imply a promise to compensate." *Id* at 739.

If the defendant *requested* that the plaintiff disclose an idea, most courts will find that the request or solicitation implies a promise to pay for the idea if the defendant uses it. In *Yadkoe v. Fields*, 66 Cal. App. 2d 150 (1944), defendant W.C. Fields wrote to the plaintiff regarding a proposed submission of ideas for jokes for a radio show:

> [I]f you would like to submit a couple of scripts gratis and I am able to use them, who knows, both parties being willing, we might enter into a contract. My reason for injecting the vile word "gratis" is that we get so many letters from folks who if we even answer in the negative, immediately bring suit for plagiarism. Whilst we have never had to pay off, they sometimes become irritating no end.

Id. at 154. Ironically, W.C. Fields ran into the precise situation he tried to avoid. Despite the use of the word "gratis," the court permitted recovery by plaintiff on an implied contract theory, holding that the requested disclosure, followed by use of the ideas, supported an implied contract claim. *Id.* at 161.

The Ninth Circuit articulated the elements of an implied-in-fact contract claim in the context of a screenplay submission as: (1) submission of the screenplay for sale to the defendants (2) conditioning the use of the screenplay on payment; (3) the defendants knew or should have known of the condition; (4) the defendants voluntarily accepted the screenplay; (5) the defendants actually used the screenplay; and (6) the screenplay had value. *Jordan-Benel v. Universal City Studios, Inc.*, 859 F.3d 1184 (9th Cir. 2017), citing *Benay v. Warner Bros., Entm't, Inc.*, 607 F.3d 620, 629 (9th Cir. 2010).

Protectability under copyright law is not required for an implied-in-fact contract claim. *Ryder v. Lightstorm Entm't, Inc.*, 246 Cal. App. 4th 1064, 1073 (2016). In fact, if a copyright registration covers a work – whether for a manuscript or software – a claim for breach of contract implied-in-fact may not survive a copyright preemption defense. *Design Data Corp., v. Unigate Enterprise, Inc.*, 105 U.S.P.Q.2d 1718 at *6-7 (N.D. Cal. 2013).

B. Unsolicited Submissions

Under California law, even an unsolicited submission voluntarily received by the defendant can result in an implied contract. *See Desny*, 46 Cal. 2d at 738-39. The California view in effect regards failure to reject as a negative form of solicitation. In essence, the person to whom an idea is disclosed has an affirmative duty to act to avoid an inference that he promises to pay for the idea if used.

However, a California appellate court found that an implied-in-fact contract was not created when a plaintiff, based upon information contained in a writer's market guide, sent an unsolicited script to an agent for a film company. *See Grosso v. Miramax Film Corp.*, No. B193872, 2007 WL 2585053 (Cal. App. Ct. Sep. 10, 2007). The court stated that the excerpt from the writer's guide was not a solicitation from the defendant to the general public accompanied by a promise to pay. The court noted that the plaintiff simply had mailed off his script after reading in the guide that the agent accepted unsolicited material, he had never received a response from the agent, and he never had any communications with either the agent or the film company. *Id.* at *9.

C. Concreteness Requirement

Ideas subject to protection under California law must have sufficient "concreteness" to constitute protectable property. Copyright law protects the author's expression of ideas and not the ideas themselves. An implied-in-fact contract claim requires "concreteness" of ideas. The court in

Yadkoe explained: "While we recognize that an abstract idea as such may not be the subject of a property right, yet, when it takes upon itself the concrete form which we find in the instant case, it is our opinion that it then becomes a property right subject to sale." *Yadkoe*, 66 Cal. App. 2d at 159. In *Yadkoe*, where the plaintiff submitted jokes for use by the defendant entertainer, the court found the material sufficiently concrete to warrant recovery by the plaintiff. *Id.* at 161. More recently, in an unpublished opinion, the court in *Concept Chaser Co., Inc. v. Pentel of America, Ltd.*, Nos. B241929 and B243330, 2014 WL 2197619 at *8 (Cal. App. Ct. May 27, 2014), posited that abstract ideas may be subject to a contract implied-in-fact.

D. Novelty Not Required

California courts have eliminated "novelty" from the requirements for implied-in-fact contracts. *Donahue v. Ziv Television Programs, Inc.*, 245 Cal. App. 2d 593, 600 (1966). One court explained that the courts should not arbitrarily inject a novelty requirement into an implied-in-fact contract but, instead, should permit the parties to contract with each other as they see fit. *Chandler v. Roach*, 156 Cal. App. 2d 435, 443 (1957). In another case, the court stated: "Whether novelty, therefore, is relevant to attempted recovery under an implied contract theory is a question of law. California has answered that question of law. The answer is 'no'." *Haglund v. Dow Chemical Co.*, 218 U.S.P.Q. 55, 62 (E.D. Cal. 1982).

E. Summary Judgment in Idea Cases

Disputed issues of fact often exist regarding formation of an implied-in-fact contract. *See Blaustein v. Burton*, 9 Cal. App. 3d 161, 184 (1970) (whether parties entered contract for compensation if defendants used producer's idea for particular motion picture adaptation of "Taming of the Shrew" constituted question of fact precluding summary judgment). Whether the defendant used the plaintiff's idea, breaching the implied contract, generally constitutes a question of fact. *Desny*, 46 Cal. 2d. at 749 (seminal idea law case finding use of plaintiff's idea inappropriate for summary judgment). Access, similarity and use constitute questions of fact for the jury in the absence of undisputed evidence compelling a result for one side. *Mann v. Columbia Pictures, Inc.*, 128 Cal. App. 3d 628, 648 (1982).

Case law confirms that—with appropriate proof of undisputed facts—either plaintiffs or defendants can prevail at summary judgment in implied-in-fact contract cases. For instance, in *Hollywood Screentest of Am., Inc. v. NBC Universal*, 151 Cal. App. 4th 631, 647-48 (2007), the appellate court affirmed the trial court's grant of summary judgment for the defendant on the basis that the undisputed evidence established independent creation of the television show "Next Action Star." Similarly, in *Spinner v. American Broadcasting Cos.*, 215 Cal. App. 4th 172 (2013), the appellate court affirmed a grant of summary judgment in the defendant's favor because uncontroverted evidence of independent creation negated the "use" element in the plaintiff's cause of action over the creation of the television show "Lost." *Id.* at 185. The appellate court in *Spinner* also held that even assuming an inference of use on the part of the defendant, summary judgment was warranted because the plaintiff failed to provide adequate proof of access to the plaintiff's work. *Id.* at 189 (finding that the plaintiff showed "only a bare possibility of access based on speculation, supposition, and guess work").

In *Landsberg v. Scrabble Crossword Game Players, Inc.*, the court affirmed summary judgment in the plaintiff's favor by finding no material dispute that defendants copied from plaintiff's manuscript. 802 F.2d 1193, 1195-97 (9th Cir. 1986). *See also Aliotti v. R. Dakin & Co.*, 831 F.2d 898, 902-03 (9th Cir. 1987) (affirming summary judgment for defendant based on plaintiff's failure of proof that she struck her deal prior to disclosing her ideas to the defendant).

F. Comparison with Other Types of Contracts

1. Express Contracts

The distinction between an implied-in-fact contract and an express contract is that, in the former, the promise is implied from the promisor's conduct, rather than being expressed in words. Under a contract implied-in-fact, the required proof is essentially the same as in an express contract, with the exception that conduct from which the promise may be implied must be proved. *Weitzenkorn v. Lesser*, 40 Cal. 2d 778, 794 (1953); *Gorlach v. The Sports Club Co.*, 209 Cal. App. 4th 1497, 1507 (2012) (noting that the difference between implied and express contracts under California Civil Code section 1621 is "the mere mode of proof by which they are to be respectively established").

2. Contracts Implied-in-Law

Litigants, lawyers and even courts confuse contracts implied-in-fact with contracts implied-in-law. The simplest distinction is that a contract implied-in-law is not a contract at all. Instead, it is a court-imposed equitable obligation—or a "quasi-contract"—also known as a claim for quantum meruit. *Hedging Concepts, Inc. v. First Alliance Mortgage*, 41 Cal. App. 4th 1410, 1419 (1996); *Donahue*, 245 Cal. App. 2d at 605. This form of quantum meruit claim allows for recovery of reasonable value of services rendered to avoid unjust enrichment. *Hedging Concepts*, 41 Cal. App. 4th at 1419.

§ 25.04 Demonstrating Use of an Idea

Establishing that the defendant copied from the plaintiff is a universally recognized prerequisite to recovery in idea cases. The court in *Whitfield v. Lear*, 751 F.2d 90 (1984) described the use requirement as follows:

> We conclude that the communications in question and the allegation of custom in the industry are sufficient to withstand a motion for summary judgment on this point . . . . The correspondence between the parties, brief as it was, has some of the attributes of bargaining . . . . To support recovery on an implied-in-fact contract, he must show not only access but also that the appellees actually used his ideas by demonstrating "some substantial similarity" between the ideas and themes of the two programs.

Id. at 93-94.

Courts look to many factors to determine whether substantial similarity exists between works of a plaintiff and a defendant. In *Weitzenkorn v. Lesser*, 40 Cal. 2d 778 (1953), the California Supreme Court compared the form and manner of expression of the works, their basic dramatic core, existence of a similar moral message, the combination of characters, the locale, the use of a myth as an element, whether such items as the combination of characters, locale or mythical element were used for the same purpose, and the divergence in characterizations, description, and events. *Id.* at 791-92.

In *Desny v. Wilder*, 46 Cal. 2d. 715 (1956), the court reversed summary judgment on grounds that substantial fact issues existed regarding defendants' alleged use of plaintiff's ideas. *Desny*, 46 Cal. 2d at 746-52. Desny contended that the defendants used his synopsis and composition in making a motion picture photoplay. *Id.* at 744. Desny had presented Paramount with ideas for a photoplay regarding a real life incident from the 1920's involving a man's entrapment in an underground cave. *Id.* Factors the court considered in evaluating use of Desny's ideas included similarities in selection of historical data, as well as similarities of fictional material. *Id.* at 746-49. The court recited more than a dozen similarities between Desny's synopsis and Paramount's photoplay regarding events, locations, character development and storyline. *Id.* As a result, the court held that determination of defendants' use of Desny's ideas could not be made at summary judgment. *Id.*

In *Minniear v. Tors*, 266 Cal. App. 2d 495, 505 (1968), through a number of striking similarities in basic plot ideas, themes, sequences, and dramatic "gimmicks" in the Sea Hunt TV series, the plaintiff proved sufficient use to submit the facts to a jury.

The case of *Teich v. Gen. Mills, Inc.*, 170 Cal. App. 2d 791 (1959), presents an example of a court rejecting a claim that the defendant used the plaintiff's idea. In *Teich*, the plaintiff submitted an idea for a sun-picture kit (for inclusion in children's cereal boxes) to one of defendant's employees in California. *Teich*, 170 Cal. App. 2d at 795. The employee (along with several others) met with plaintiff, discussed the idea, and admitted at trial that, had defendant used the idea, it would have been obligated to pay plaintiff. *Id.* However, the court found sufficient evidence (correspondence and testimony) to support the defense that the sun-picture kit included in the cereals was developed by another company and proposed to the defendant's Minneapolis head office, which had no contact with the California employees who knew of plaintiff's idea. *Id.* at 798-802. The evidence of independent development defeated the implied contract claim. *Id.* at 803-06. Accordingly, the appellate court upheld the trial court's post-trial ruling for defendant (despite the jury's award of $35,000 to plaintiff). *Id.* at 806.

§ 25.05 Defense of Failure to Prove Basic Elements of Claim

The failure of proof of any single element constitutes a complete defense to an implied-in-fact contract claim:

(1) Access: In some cases the basic threshold issue—the defendant's access to the plaintiff's work—cannot be shown by any direct evidence. At times, circumstantial evidence of access combined with striking similarity of ideas may suffice. For example, in *Spinner v. American Broadcasting Cos.*, 215 Cal. App. 4th 172 (2013), the court determined that the plaintiff's access theory failed because it relied only on "a bare possibility of theoretical access premised on mere speculation." *Id.* at 187. In other instances, though, plaintiffs have filed meritless

idea lawsuits in entertainment cases on the eve of a film debut in an effort to obtain publicity or a quick settlement.

(2) Agreement to pay upon use: For an agreement to bind a defendant, the parties must have struck their bargain prior to the plaintiff's disclosure. As the court in *Desny* wrote, "The idea man who blurts out his idea without having first made his bargain has no one but himself to blame for the loss of his bargaining power." *Desny v. Wilder*, 46 Cal. 2d. 715, 739 (1956).

(3) Use: The determination whether the defendant used the plaintiff's work consumes the most time and resources in implied-in-fact contract disputes. Proof of this element involves fact-intensive documentary evidence and witness testimony from both percipient and expert witnesses.

(4) Proof of reasonable value of the work: While damages constitute a required element of proof, plaintiffs rarely suffer a complete failure of proof for this element. Because plaintiffs often can testify to the value of their own ideas, plaintiffs typically have at least some proof of a damage claim. *See Donahue v. Ziv Television Programs, Inc.*, 245 Cal. App. 2d 593, 609 (1966) ("[W]e see no reason why the person who conceives an idea which may be the subject of contract, should not be competent to testify to its value or, perhaps more accurately, to the value of his services in disclosing it.").

§ 25.06 Defense of Independent Development

In practice, defendants most frequently challenge idea claims on grounds of independent development. Independent development constitutes a complete defense to an idea claim. *Teich* 170 Cal. App. 2d at 802-03. In *Teich*, the court noted that a plaintiff's showing of access and similarity raises an inference of copying. *Id.* at 797. The appellate court further noted, though, that the trial court properly ruled that the defendant overcame that inference with satisfactory proof of independent creation. *Id.* at 802-03. In the *Teich* case, a third party performed the independent creation. *Id.* at 801. More commonly in idea cases, though, the defendant relies on proof of its own independent development of the claimed ideas.

In *Mann v. Columbia Pictures, Inc.*, 128 Cal. App. 3d 628, 650 (1982), the plaintiff asserted that Columbia Pictures used her outline in creating the film "Shampoo." Following a $185,000 verdict in the plaintiff's favor, the trial court ruled in the defendant's favor on a post-trial motion on grounds of independent development. *Id.* at 631. The appellate court confirmed that evidence of independent development provided a complete defense to plaintiff's claims of access and use. *Id.* at 650.

More recently, the court in *Hollywood Screentest of Am., Inc, v. NBC Universal*, 151 Cal. App. 4th 631, 646-47 (2007) cited the *Teich* case at length and reiterated that direct evidence of independent creation can overcome inferences of use presented by the plaintiff. Inference of use can be overcome as a matter of law if the evidence "conclusively demonstrates" that the defendant independently created its product. *Spinner,* 215 Cal. App. 4th at 187 (citing *Teich*, 170 Cal. App. 2d at 799).

§ 25.07 Other Defenses

While other defenses to claims of breach of contract implied-in-fact are beyond the scope of this chapter, a couple of the more common defenses merit mention:

- Copyright preemption. For those implied-in-fact contract claims that arise from alleged use of manuscripts, source code or other written material, counsel should evaluate the applicability of a copyright preemption defense. In *Montz v. Pilgrim Films & Television, Inc.*, 649 F.3d 975, 977 (9th Cir. 2011), the appellate court held *en banc* that copyright law does not preempt an implied contractual claim to compensation for use of a submitted idea. Copyright preemption may result, though, if the work at issue falls within the scope of copyright and if the plaintiff's implied-in-fact contract claim asserts rights equivalent to rights protected exclusively by copyright. *See* 17 U.S.C. § 301(a) (2014).

- Statute of limitations. Many implied-in-fact contract cases involve statute of limitation defenses. This results from the time passage that often exists between the idea purveyor's disclosure and the recipient's product release. The two-year statute of limitations for oral contracts governs contracts implied-in-fact. *NBCUniversal Media, LLC v. Superior Court*, 225 Cal. App. 4th 1222, 1230 (2014); Cal. Civ. Proc. Code § 339(1). Related issues include (1) whether a claim based on a "napkin writing" could fall under the longer four-year statute of limitations for written contracts; and (2) whether a court will toll the statute of limitations during the nonpublic period of alleged access to or use of the plaintiff's idea.

§ 25.08 Remedies—What Is an Idea Worth?

No single rule governs how prevailing plaintiffs in idea cases are compensated. In fact, compensation can range from a calculation of actual profits realized as a result of using the idea, to a more subjective valuation based on what the plaintiff believes the idea is worth.

In *Landsberg v. Scrabble Crossword Game Players, Inc.*, 802 F.2d 1193 (9th Cir. 1986), the court awarded far more than simply the reasonable value of the services:

> If the implied contract between Landsberg and S&R provided merely for the payment of the reasonable value by S&R for the use of Landsberg's manuscript, then the grant of the total profits of S&R and Crown Publishers would exceed the amount Landsberg would have received in the absence of breach. He would be entitled only to the market value of S&R's use of the manuscript . . . . Landsberg was therefore entitled under the terms of the implied contract to more than the fair value of S&R's use. He was entitled to deny S&R permission to use it at all, and to exploit his work through another means.

> Because S&R's breach resulted in Landsberg's losing the opportunity to market his work as he saw fit, the profits from S&R's exploitation of it are both the best measure of his losses due to the breach, and are consistent with § 3358's limitation. To read the contract as requiring anything less than both compensation and permission would be to sanction a forced exchange.

Id. at 1198.

Most courts hold that a plaintiff is competent to testify as to the value of his services in disclosing his idea. *See Donahue v. Ziv Television Programs, Inc.*, 245 Cal. App. 2d 593, 609 (1966).

The following chart summarizes the remedies awarded in a sampling of California idea cases, including descriptions of formulas and factors:

Case	Idea	Award/Formula/Result
Donahue v. Ziv Television Programs, Inc., 245 Cal. App. 2d 593, 609 (1966).	Idea for television series "Sea Hunt."	Jury awarded $250,000; plaintiff testified to value of submission at $1 million; trial court overturned verdict; appellate court affirmed order granting new trial.
Landsberg v. Scrabble Crossword Game Players, Inc., 802 F.2d 1193 (9th Cir. 1986).	Idea for book of winning strategies for playing Scrabble.	Approximately $1 million representing all profits from sale of book (because plaintiff lost opportunity to market his work), attorneys' fees, costs, prejudgment interest, and $200,000 in punitive damages (punitive damages awarded under law subsequently rejected in this context).
Mann v. Columbia Pictures, Inc., 128 Cal. App. 3d 628 (1982).	Idea for movie "Shampoo."	$185,000 awarded by jury; overturned by trial court and affirmed on appeal.
Stanley v. Columbia Broadcasting Sys., 35 Cal. 2d 653 (1950).	Idea for radio program.	$35,000 jury verdict. Plaintiff and expert testified as to value of idea, lack of value to plaintiff once defendant used idea, and customary royalty payments in radio industry.
Teich v. Gen. Mills, Inc., 170 Cal. App. 2d 791 (1959).	Idea for sun-picture kit to include in boxes of children's cereal.	$35,000 jury verdict; overturned by trial court and affirmed on appeal.

Veith v. MCA, Inc., No. B090339, 1997 Cal.App. Unpub. LEXIS 1 (1997).	Idea for television show "Northern Exposure."	$7.3 million jury verdict; upheld on appeal.
Yadkoe v. Fields, 66 Cal. App. 2d 150 (1944).	Ideas for jokes that W.C. Fields could use on radio show.	$8,000 jury verdict. Plaintiff testified to value of idea; jury could consider lack of value once used by defendant.

§ 25.09 Conclusion

Idea claims can protect against misuse of all types of concepts, inventions and discoveries. California law will protect ideas under an implied-in-fact contract if the recipient had the ability to reject a submission and knew compensation would be sought, the recipient used the idea, and the plaintiff proves the reasonable value of the idea.

Idea claims boil down to the basic concepts of access, promise to pay, use and damages. In California, idea protection stands as a viable alternative to trade secret law in many situations.

Chapter 26
RICO
By: Cary D. Sullivan, Esq.

---

§ 26.01 Introduction

With the passage of the DTSA in 2016, Congress confirmed that DTSA claims qualify as predicate conduct for purposes of civil liability under the Racketeer Influenced and Corrupt Organizations Act ("RICO"). *See* 18 U.S.C. § 1961(1) (cross-referencing 18 U.S.C. § 1832). RICO prohibits "racketeering activity," and the RICO statute defines which predicate conduct qualifies as racketeering activity. Since 2016, that includes DTSA violations.

RICO can be a powerful tool for trade secret plaintiffs because it provides for broad liability and treble damages, creates claims that are difficult to dismiss at the pleading stage, and can generate publicity. But these benefits do not come without cost. RICO has particular, and sometimes heightened, pleading requirements, and courts seem to have increasingly skepticism of RICO claims given perceived overuse.

This chapter provides a brief background on RICO and discusses potential benefits and risks associated with pleading civil RICO claims based on predicate DTSA violations. This chapter also discusses the small handful of California cases in which DTSA violations have been alleged as predicate conduct for RICO claims.

§ 26.02 RICO Background

RICO was enacted as Title IX of the Organized Crime Control Act of 1970 ("OCCA") to prevent organized crime from infiltrating legitimate business. Congress passed the OCCA in response to a series of highly-publicized investigations and congressional hearings regarding "La Cosa Nostra." Indeed, after the OCCA was passed, prosecutors consistently wielded RICO to pursue some of the highest-profile mob families, including the Gambinos and Bonannos. Congress defined a broad range of "racketeering activity" in an effort to encompass a broad range of organized crime operations. In doing so, Congress shaped a law that would ensnare not only mob families but also corporations, Ponzi schemes, and even prominent political figures. Congress also created a civil RICO cause of action, opening the floodgates to civil litigation against alleged racketeering enterprises.

Nowadays, civil RICO claims are most commonly brought against businesses that are allegedly engaged in some form of fraud. *See Klehr v. A.O. Smith Corp.*, 521 U.S. 179, 191 (1997) (noting that a "high percentage" of civil RICO claims allege fraud). Since the enactment of the DTSA, trade secret plaintiffs can use RICO claims as another weapon in their arsenal.

In recent years, splits have emerged between and among federal circuits regarding several aspects of civil RICO claims that are particularly relevant in the trade secret context, including the following:

- Whether injunctive relief is available to private plaintiffs.[30]

---

[30] *Compare Religious Tech. Ctr. v. Wollersheim*, 796 F.2d 1076, 1082–89 (9th Cir. 1986) (holding that injunctive relief is not available to private RICO plaintiffs), *with Nat'l Org. for Women, Inc. v. Scheidler*, 267 F.3d 687, 695–700 (7th Cir. 2001), *rev'd on other grounds*, 537 U.S. 393 (2003) (holding that injunctive relief is available to private RICO plaintiffs).

- How to calculate the date of claim accrual for limitations purposes. Various federal circuits apply three different rules: the "injury-discovery" rule,[31] the "injury and pattern discovery" rule,[32] and the "last predicate act" rule.[33]
- Whether RICO provides a basis for nationwide jurisdiction and service of process when a defendant lacks minimum contacts with a particular forum.[34]
- How to determine whether an injury is "domestic," as statutorily required, when it is based at least in part on extraterritorial conduct.[35]

§ 26.03 RICO Violations

The RICO statute prohibits four types of activities: (1) using or investing income of an enterprise, (2) acquiring an interest of an enterprise, (3) conducting or participating in the conduct of an enterprise's affairs, and (4) conspiring to commit any of the first three types of activity. 18 U.S.C. § 1962(a)–(d). Because it can be difficult for plaintiffs to establish injury through the first two types of activities (racketeering investment and acquisition), civil RICO claims are generally brought under the third and fourth categories.

18 U.S.C. § 1962(c) prohibits conducting or participating in an enterprise's pattern of racketeering activity. The elements of a 1962(c) action are: (1) conduct, (2) of an enterprise, (3) through a pattern, (4) of racketeering activity, (5) causing injury to the plaintiff's "business or

---

[31] Under the injury-discovery rule, the limitations period begins to run when a plaintiff knows or has reason to know of an injury. The First, Second, Fourth, Fifth, Seventh, and Ninth Circuits apply this rule. *See Rodriguez v. Banco Cent.*, 917 F.2d 664, 665–66 (1st Cir. 1990); *Bankers Trust Co. v. Rhoades*, 859 F.2d 1096, 1102 (2d Cir. 1988); *Pocahontas Supreme Coal Co. v. Bethlehem Steel Corp.*, 828 F.2d 211, 220 (4th Cir. 1987); *Rotella v. Wood*, 147 F.3d 438, 440 (5th Cir. 1998); *Bontkowski v. First Nat'l Bank of Cicero*, 998 F.2d 459, 461 (7th Cir. 1993); *Grimmett v. Brown*, 75 F.3d 506, 510–12 (9th Cir. 1996).

[32] Under the injury and pattern discovery rule, the limitations period begins to run when a plaintiff knows or has reason to know both that an injury occurred and that the injury is part of a pattern of racketeering activity. The Sixth, Eighth, Tenth, and Eleventh Circuits apply this rule. *See Caproni v. Prudential Sec.*, 15 F.3d 614, 619–20 (6th Cir. 1994); *Granite Falls Bank v. Henrikson*, 924 F.2d 150, 154 (8th Cir. 1991); *Bath v. Bushkin, Gaims, Gaines & Jonas*, 913 F.2d 817, 820 (10th Cir. 1990); *Bivens Gardens Office Bldg., Inc. v. Barnett Bank*, 906 F.2d 1546, 1552–54 (11th Cir. 1990).

[33] The Third Circuit applies the last predicate act rule, which provides that the limitations period begins to run when a plaintiff knows, or has reason to know, of the last injury or predicate act that is part of a pattern of racketeering activity. *See Keystone Ins. Co. v. Houghton*, 863 F.2d 1125, 1126 (3rd Cir. 1988).

[34] *Compare Butcher's Union Local No. 498 v. SDC Inv., Inc.*, 788 F.2d 535, 539 (9th Cir. 1986) ("[T]he court must have personal jurisdiction over at least one of the participants in the alleged multidistrict [RICO] conspiracy and the plaintiff must show that there is no other district in which a court will have personal jurisdiction over all of the alleged co-conspirators.") *with Lisak v. Mercantile Bancorp, Inc.*, 834 F.2d 668, 671 (7th Cir. 1987) (finding that a federal court can exercise jurisdiction over RICO defendant in the absence of minimum contacts with the forum because RICO cases are governed by federal question jurisdiction).

[35] *Compare Bascuñan v. Elsaca*, 874 F.3d 806, 820–21 (2nd Cir. 2017) (holding that the domestic injury requirement is satisfied where the physical property or monetary assets at issue are located in the U.S.), *and Armada (Singapore) PTE, Ltd. v. Amcol International Corp.*, 885 F.3d 1090, 1094–95 (7th Cir. 2018) (holding that the domestic injury requirement with respect to intangible assets is only satisfied when the intangible assets are located in the U.S.), *with Humphrey v. GlaxoSmithKline PLC*, 905 F.3d 694, 707 (3rd Cir. 2018) (applying a multi-factor test to determine the domestic injury requirement). The Ninth Circuit has not yet addressed this issue. *See Harmoni Int'l Spice, Inc. v. Wenxuanbai,* 2:16-cv-00614, 2019 WL 4194306, at *7 (C.D. Cal. July 2, 2019).

property" by the conduct constituting the violation. *See Living Designs, Inc. v. E.I. Dupont de Nemours & Co.*, 431 F.3d 353, 361 (9th Cir. 2005). Racketeering activity is defined to include more than fifty types of federal and state offenses. 18 U.S.C. § 1961(1).

18 U.S.C. § 1962(d) prohibits any conspiracy to violate any of the subsections. A RICO conspiracy requires only an agreement to commit a substantive RICO violation. *Oki Semiconductor Co. v. Wells Fargo Bank*, 298 F.3d 768, 774–75 (9th Cir. 2002). Conspiracy defendants must have been "aware of the essential nature and scope of the enterprise and intended to participate in it." *Howard v. Am. Online Inc.*, 208 F.3d 741, 751 (9th Cir. 2000). But there is no requirement that a conspirator actually participate in the predicate acts. *See Salinas v. United States*, 522 U.S. 52, 65 (1997) ("The interplay between [RICO] subsections (c) and (d) does not permit us to excuse from the reach of the conspiracy provision an actor who does not himself commit … the two or more predicate acts requisite to the underlying offense.").

§ 26.04 Potential Benefits of Pleading RICO Claims Based on Predicate DTSA Violations

RICO claims offer several potential benefits to trade secret plaintiffs.

A. Treble Damages

RICO claims can potentially lead to lucrative awards. The RICO statute mandates that prevailing plaintiffs be awarded treble damages plus reasonable costs and attorneys' fees. *See Bridge v. Phoenix Bond & Indem. Co.*, 553 U.S. 639, 647 (2008) ("RICO provides a private right of action for treble damages to any person injured in his business or property"). Courts in some jurisdictions also can issue private injunctions, as noted above.

B. "Sticky" Claims

RICO claims encompass a wide range of predicate conduct over a long period of time, and even different types of predicate conduct within a single claim. By way of example, predicate conduct includes trade secret misappropriation, bribery, witness tampering, mail and wire fraud,[36] violations of the Controlled Substances Act, securities fraud, embezzlement, and certain forms of counterfeiting and copyright infringement. 18 U.S.C. § 1961(1). Plaintiffs can even assert potential derivative liability where a defendant is not directly involved in the alleged wrongdoing.

---

[36] Wire fraud and trade secret misappropriation are often asserted together as RICO predicate conduct because trade secret misappropriation often occurs through the use of electronic communications. "The elements of wire fraud are: (1) the existence of a scheme to defraud; (2) the use of wire, radio, or television [or other electronic communications] to further the scheme; and (3) a specific intent to defraud." *United States v. Jinian*, 725 F.3d 954, 960 (9th Cir. 2013). Thus, where a plaintiff asserts that a defendant misappropriated trade secrets through an electronic medium such as email, the plaintiff could assert both wire fraud and DTSA violations as predicate conduct for a RICO claim. The Central District of California emphasized the connection between trade secret misappropriation and wire and mail fraud in *Bryant v. Mattel, Inc.*, CV 04–9049, 2010 WL 3705668 (C.D. Cal. Aug. 2, 2010). "Trade secret misappropriation can be fraudulent, unlike copyright infringement and patent infringement," for example where "[t]he employer discloses trade secret materials to the employee pursuant to the employee's promise to keep that information confidential, and the employee may commit mail fraud or wire fraud by betraying that trust through the use of the mails or wires." *Id.* at *6 (citations omitted).

Plaintiffs can encompass predicate conduct occurring over a very long period of time because acts occurring within ten years of each other may be used to establish a "pattern" of racketeering. *See* 18 U.S.C. § 1961(5). For example, notwithstanding RICO's four-year limitations period, *see Agency Holding Corp. v. Malley-Duff & Assocs., Inc.*, 483 U.S. 143 (1987), if a defendant committed a predicate act once a year for ten years, a court may admit evidence of each of those acts to establish a "pattern" of predicate conduct. In other words, so long as a plaintiff can establish that some predicate conduct occurred within the limitations period, evidence of other predicate acts extending back well beyond that period may also be admitted. This allows plaintiffs to establish a chain of predicate acts going back a decade or more.

Plaintiffs can also establish a chain of predicate acts projecting into the future, because the "threat of . . . continuing racketeering activity" also constitutes predicate conduct. *See H. J. Inc. v. Northwestern Bell Tel. Co.*, 492 U.S. 229, 240 (1989). Thus, RICO allows plaintiffs to bring claims based on a wide range of conduct over a long period of time, even where the individual acts might be time-barred. All of this combines to create claims that often prove difficult to dismiss at the pleading stage.

C. Liability for All Conspirators and Members of the Enterprise

RICO conspirators may be liable even where they do not participate in the predicate conduct. RICO also provides for recovery against members of a RICO enterprise in unique situations. For example, where claims were previously adjudicated in arbitration against certain members of a RICO enterprise, but other members of the enterprise were not subject to the arbitration, RICO claims may be brought against those other members. *Uthe Tech. Corp. v. Aetrium, Inc.*, 808 F.3d 755 (9th Cir. 2015). As the Ninth Circuit explained, because RICO provides for treble damages, which are generally not available in arbitration, arbitration generally cannot fully compensate a RICO plaintiff, even if the predicate claims were fully satisfied. *Id.*

D. Publicity

RICO claims can generate significant publicity. It is no trivial thing to be labeled a racketeer or to be identified as part of a racketeering enterprise. Those eye-catching labels are generally associated with criminal conduct.[37] The attendant publicity, or even the threat of it, can create additional advantages for plaintiffs.

---

[37] *See, e.g.*, Peter J. Henning, RICO Offers a Powerful Tool to Punish Executives for the Opioid Crisis, N.Y. TIMES (May 23, 2019), https://www.nytimes.com/2019/05/23/business/dealbook/rico-insys-opioid-executives.html; Ben Foldy & Nora Naughton, New Charge in UAW Corruption Investigation Specifies Racketeering, WALL ST. J. (Jan. 6, 2020), https://www.wsj.com/articles/new-charge-in-uaw-corruption-investigation-specifies-racketeering-11578352253; Talia Kaplan, Rep. Nunes calls for racketeering investigation into Amazon, Apple, Google following Parler ban, FOX NEWS (Jan. 10, 2021), https://www.foxnews.com/politics/nunes-racketeering-investigation-amazon-apple-google-parler-ban; Lucy Bayly & Paul A. Eisenstein, GM files racketeering lawsuit against Fiat Chrysler for conspiring with labor union, NBC NEWS (Nov. 20, 2019), https://www.nbcnews.com/business/autos/gm-files-racketeering-lawsuit-against-fiat-chrysler-conspiring-labor-union-n1087051.

§ 26.05 Potential Risks of Pleading RICO Claims Based on Predicate DTSA Violations

There are also several risks or difficulties that trade secret plaintiffs should consider before bringing a RICO claim.

A. Increased Scrutiny

Because judges may be skeptical of RICO claims given perceived overuse, there is often increased scrutiny of RICO claims, particularly where pled without a well-developed factual basis. As the Ninth Circuit observed, "[g]iven the resulting proliferation of civil RICO claims and the potential for frivolous suits in search of treble damages, greater responsibility will be placed on the bar to inquire into the factual and legal bases of potential claims or defenses prior to bringing such suit or risk sanctions for failing to do so." *Pioneer Lumber Treating, Inc. v. Cox*, 5 F.3d 539 (9th Cir. 1993); *see also, e.g.*, *Preferred Commc'ns v. City of L.A.*, 91-56018, 1994 U.S. App. LEXIS 760, at *1–4 (9th Cir. Jan. 7, 1994) (affirming district court's imposition of Rule 11 sanctions on plaintiff's counsel because RICO allegations "were not well grounded in fact," especially "[g]iven the district court's explicit finding that the claims were factually unsupportable, along with [the plaintiff's] failure to come forward with any evidence of racketeering"); *Religious Tech. Ctr. v. Gerbode*, CV 93-2226, 1994 U.S. Dist. LEXIS 6432, at *8–10 (C.D. Cal. May 2, 1994) (imposing Rule 11 sanctions for frivolous RICO claims because reasonable inquiry would have disclosed recent Supreme Court case negating claims).

B. Particular Pleading Requirements

Plaintiffs must be mindful of certain requirements to plead a RICO claim successfully. To begin, RICO claims are dependent on viable underlying predicate conduct. If a trade secret plaintiff cannot plead a viable DTSA violation, for example, the RICO claim (if only based on DTSA violations) likewise will not be viable. Where predicate conduct is fraud-based, Rule 9(b)'s heightened pleading standard requires that the plaintiff plead the who, what, when, and where for each predicate act of fraud. *Alan Neuman Prods., Inc. v. Albright*, 862 F.2d 1388, 1392–93 (9th Cir. 1988).

1. "Person" Distinct From "Enterprise"

A RICO plaintiff must plead that a "person" conducts or participates in, but is separate from, a RICO "enterprise." *Cedric Kushner Promotions, Ltd. v. King*, 533 U.S. 158, 160 (2001). In other words, the person and the enterprise must be distinct. A RICO enterprise can consist of "any individual, partnership, corporation, association, or other legal entity, and any union or group of individuals associated in fact although not a legal entity." 18 U.S.C. § 1961(4). But the "person" must be separate and distinct from individuals comprising the enterprise.

2. Pattern of Racketeering Activity

A RICO plaintiff must plead a "pattern of racketeering activity," consisting of at least two separate acts of racketeering conduct within ten years of each other. 18 U.S.C. § 1961(5). However, "while two acts are necessary, they may not be sufficient" to establish a pattern. *Sedima v. Imrex Co.*, 473 U.S. 479, 496 n.14 (1985). Where a plaintiff alleges fewer predicate acts, he must do more to demonstrate that the acts constitute a "pattern" than if he alleges many acts forming a more obvious pattern. The acts must also be related to each other and must "amount to or pose a threat of continued criminal activity." *H.J. Inc. v. Nw. Bell Tel. Co.*, 492 U.S. 229, 239 (1989). "[P]roof of a single scheme can be sufficient so long as the predicate acts involved are not isolated or sporadic." *Turner v. Cook*, 362 F.3d 1219, 1229 (9th Cir. 2004). Racketeering acts are sufficiently related where they "have the same or similar purposes, results, participants, victims, or methods of commission, or otherwise are interrelated by distinguishing characteristics and are not isolated events." *H.J. Inc.*, 492 U.S. at 240.

3. Injury and Damages

RICO requires a concrete injury to a protected "business or property" interest. *Canyon Cty. v. Syngenta Seeds, Inc.*, 519 F.3d 969, 975 (9th Cir. 2008). In the trade secret context, losses cannot be "mere injury to a valuable intangible property interest." *Chaset v. Fleer/Skybox Int'l, LP*, 300 F.3d 1083, 1087 (9th Cir. 2002). Thus, it is insufficient to allege merely the loss of intellectual property. A plaintiff must also allege financial harm. Courts have found concrete financial losses where, for example, plaintiffs have lost profits, contracts, or specific corporate opportunities. *E.g.*, *Bryant v. Mattel, Inc.*, CV 04-9049, 2010 WL 3705668, at *12 (C.D. Cal. Aug. 2, 2010); *Attia v. Google LLC*, 17-CV-06037, 2018 WL 2971049, at *14 (N.D. Cal. June 13, 2018). Courts have also considered investigatory costs, like the cost of a forensic auditor, as concrete losses. *Bryant*, 2010 WL 3705668, at *11–12.

While RICO does not allow for punitive damages, the Ninth Circuit and some other circuits have held that plaintiffs may seek both RICO treble damages and state law punitive damages for the same predicate conduct. *See, e.g.*, *Neibel v. Trans World Assur. Co.*, 108 F.3d 1123, 1131 (9th Cir. 1997) *overruled on other grounds by United States v. Fernandez*, 388 F.3d 1199, 1230 (9th Cir. 2004); *Avery Dennison Corp. v. Four Pillars Enter. Co.*, 45 F. App'x 479, 488 (6th Cir. 2002) (following the Ninth Circuit's reasoning in *Neibel*); *Craig Outdoor Advert., Inc. v. Viacom Outdoor, Inc.*, 04-0074-CV, 2005 WL 8165819, at *4 (W.D. Mo. Dec. 14, 2005), *aff'd in relevant part*, 528 F.3d 1001 (8th Cir. 2008).[38]

C. RICO Case Statement

Perhaps most notably, some courts require that RICO plaintiffs file a separate case statement, along with the complaint, setting forth particularized facts supporting the RICO claim.[39] In those courts, the case statement is considered along with the complaint in determining the sufficiency

---

[38] These opinions generally rely on the Supreme Court's majority opinion in *PacifiCare Health Systems, Inc. v. Book*, interpreting RICO treble damages awards as "on different points along the spectrum between purely compensatory and strictly punitive awards." 538 U.S. 401, 405 (2003). Thus, the RICO treble damages award did not result in double recovery with state law punitive damages. *See Avery Dennison Corp.*, 45 F. App'x at 488. *But see Morley v. Cohen*, 888 F.2d 1006, 1013 (4th Cir. 1989) (finding that state law punitive damages need to be reduced in light of treble damages under single satisfaction rule and Maryland Joint-Tortfeasors Act).

[39] Although the form and substance of RICO case statements vary by court, they generally seek additional details regarding the following types of information: 1) associated individuals or entities and their alleged roles and functions in the RICO enterprise; 2) specific benefits the enterprise allegedly received from the racketeering activities; 3) specific predicate acts; and 4) concrete harm allegedly resulting from the actions of the enterprise.

of the pleading when facing a motion to dismiss. *See, e.g.*, *Walter v. Drayson*, 538 F.3d 1244, 1247 (9th Cir. 2008); *L.A. Turf Club, Inc. v. Horse Racing Labs, LLC*, 15-cv-09332, 2016 WL 6823493, at *2 n.2 (C.D. Cal. May 2, 2016). Case statements are designed to ensure that the plaintiff has conducted a sufficient factual investigation prior to filing a RICO claim. They also serve to educate the court on the factual and legal disputes at issue. Circuit courts have affirmed dismissal of RICO claims with prejudice for failure to comply with standing orders requiring particularized supporting facts in a case statement. *See, e.g.*, *Figueroa Ruiz v. Alegria*, 896 F.2d 645, 648–49 (1st Cir. 1990).

District courts may require a case statement either by local rule or chambers rule. *Miranda v. Ponce Federal Bank*, 948 F.2d 41, 44 n.3 (1st Cir. 1991) (standing order); *City of N.Y. v. ESmokes, Inc.*, 03 CV 10091, 2005 WL 372044 (S.D.N.Y. Feb. 16, 2005) (local rule); *RedMeatMedia v. Strategic Am., Inc.*, SA-13-CA-347, 2013 WL 12131904, at *20 (W.D. Tex. Nov. 21, 2013) (noting that trial courts in each federal district in Texas require case statements as part of plaintiff's duty to conduct "reasonable inquiry" before signing complaint). In California district courts, there currently are no local or chambers rules requiring RICO case statements, but occasionally individual judges have required them. *See, e.g.*, *Sy v. Stewart Fin. Inc.*, CV 12-2098, 2012 WL 12895706, at *1 (C.D. Cal. Apr. 16, 2012) (dismissing a RICO claim after the plaintiff failed to comply with the court's order to file a case statement); *Keehan v. United Law Grp., Inc.*, 10-CV-00484, 2010 WL 11508959, at *4 (S.D. Cal. June 23, 2010) (ordering the plaintiff to file a case statement "[b]ecause Plaintiff's Complaint [did] not adequately allege a cause of action under RICO" on its own).

§ 26.06 California Cases Involving RICO Claims Based on Predicate DTSA Violations

As of this writing, only six published decisions in California district courts or the Ninth Circuit address RICO claims based on predicate DTSA violations. As discussed below, these cases focus on the need to establish a sufficient pattern of racketeering activity and the requirement of a concrete financial loss.[40]

A. Pattern of Racketeering Activity: Attia, Cutera, and SolarCity

The Ninth Circuit and two California district courts have addressed patterns of racketeering activity in the context of trade secret misappropriation. These cases demonstrate the importance of alleging multiple predicate acts that are sufficiently connected and continuous.[41]

---

[40] District courts outside the Ninth Circuit have focused on other RICO requirements in cases involving predicate DTSA violations. For example, several courts have analyzed the existence, or lack thereof, of an enterprise. *See, e.g.*, *Marina Dist. Dev. Co. LLC v. AC Ocean Walk LLC*, 20-cv-15719, 2021 WL 1526552, at *6–7 (D.N.J. Apr. 19, 2021); *Brand Energy & Infrastructure Servs. v. Irex Contracting Grp.*, 16-2499, 2017 WL 1105648, at *9–10 (E.D. Pa. Mar. 23, 2017).

[41] District courts outside the Ninth Circuit have also emphasized the importance of alleging multiple predicate DTSA violations in establishing a pattern of racketeering activity. *See, e.g.*, *Sorensen v. Polukoff*, 18-CV-67, 2020 WL 1692815, at *4–5 (D. Utah Apr. 7, 2020) (dismissing RICO claim partially because plaintiff failed to establish a pattern of racketeering conduct and instead asserted a "closed-ended series of predicate acts constituting a single scheme . . . to accomplish a discrete goal . . . directed at a finite group of individuals . . . with no potential to extend to other persons or entities") (internal quotations omitted); *C-Ville Fabricating, Inc. v. Tarter*, 18-cv-379, 2019 WL 1368621, at *19 (E.D. Ky. Mar. 26, 2019) (finding that plaintiff adequately established a pattern of racketeering activity by alleging multiple victims, multiple schemes, and multiple resulting injuries); *Brand Energy*, 2017 WL 1105648, at *12 (finding that plaintiff

1. *Attia v. Google LLC*

In *Attia v. Google LLC*, 983 F.3d 420, 423 (9th Cir. 2020),[42] an architect entered into a partnership with Google to pursue a venture based on architecture technology. The plaintiff, Attia, brought DTSA and RICO claims, based on predicate DTSA violations. *Id.* Attia alleged that Google disclosed his trade secrets in a 2012 patent application, before the 2016 enactment of the DTSA. *Id.* While the DTSA does not apply to pre-enactment conduct, Attia alleged that Google continued to use his trade secrets post-enactment. *Id.*

The Ninth Circuit held that "misappropriation of a trade secret prior to the enactment of the DTSA does not preclude a claim arising from post-enactment misappropriation or continued use of the same trade secret." *Id.* at 425. The court noted, however, that "disclosure of a trade secret in a patent application extinguishes the information's trade secret status." *Id.* at 426. Given that the 2012 patent disclosure destroyed the information's trade secret status, the court held that Attia did not state a viable DTSA claim. *Id.*

The court then turned to the RICO claim, addressing whether Attia had adequately pled a pattern of racketeering activity. *Id.* at 427. To establish a pattern, Attia cited other, similar complaints against Google, on the theory that Google had engaged in a pattern of disclosing trade secrets in patent applications. *Id.* It is not clear why the court addressed the pattern of racketeering activity after it already held that Attia did not have a protectable trade secret. In any event, the court held that the cited complaints were not sufficiently related to the allegations in the complaint to form the requisite pattern of racketeering activity, and dismissed the RICO claim as well. *Id.*

2. *Cutera, Inc. v. Lutronic Aesthetics, Inc.*

In *Cutera, Inc. v. Lutronic Aesthetics, Inc.*, 2:20-cv-00235, 2020 WL 4937129, at *6 (E.D. Cal. Aug. 24, 2020), the plaintiff alleged that the defendant targeted and hired key employees and induced those employees to bring the plaintiff's trade secrets to the defendant. The court dismissed the RICO claim for failing to sufficiently plead a pattern of racketeering activity. *Id.* The court noted that a RICO plaintiff must allege that the predicate acts have a certain "degree of continuity." *Id.* The court explained that the complaint did not contain allegations showing that the defendant was likely to continue using the plaintiff's trade secrets, and it dismissed the RICO claim without prejudice. *Id.* The plaintiff subsequently filed an amended complaint which asserted that the employees who took the trade secrets were continuing to use them and would continue to use them in the future. The defendant did not challenge the amended complaint.

---

adequately alleged a pattern of racketeering activity by alleging "dozens of DTSA violations" with respect to plaintiff's trade secrets, and by establishing that defendant would likely continue to use the trade secrets in the future).

[42] To date, *Attia* is the only case in which the Ninth Circuit has addressed DTSA violations as RICO predicate conduct.

3. *SolarCity Corp. v. Pure Solar Co.*

SolarCity Corp. v. Pure Solar Co., 16-cv-01814, 2016 WL 11019989, at *2, 7 (C.D. Cal. Dec. 27, 2016), involved claims brought under both RICO and the DTSA, although DTSA violations were not pled as predicate conduct. The DTSA claims were premised on the theft of confidential customer information by a former employee. *Id.* at *1, 4. The RICO claims were premised on predicate acts of mail and wire fraud. *Id.* at *7. The court confirmed that trade secret misappropriation can be committed via mail or wire fraud. *Id.* Where a "Plaintiff alleges that the members of an enterprise have stolen Plaintiff's trade secrets and thereby defrauded it, a RICO claim based on mail or wire fraud may lie." *Id.*

Relevant here, the defendants challenged certain of the RICO elements. First, the defendants argued that the complaint failed to sufficiently allege a RICO enterprise. *Id.* at *6. The court agreed as to two of the defendants because the complaint did not allege any facts indicating that they participated in the operation of the enterprise. *Id.*

Second, the defendants challenged the alleged pattern of racketeering activity. *Id.* at *6. According to the allegations, one defendant regularly provided his username and password so that another defendant could access the plaintiff's customer information. *Id.* at *7. Given that this was alleged as their "regular way of doing business," the court found it sufficiently pled that the conduct would continue into the future. *Id.*

B. Concrete Injury Requirement: *Micron*, *MedImpact*, and *MD Helicopters*

Three California district courts have addressed the concrete injury requirement in the context of trade secret misappropriation. These cases demonstrate the importance of alleging a concrete financial loss that is caused—both actually and proximately—by the alleged misconduct.[43]

1. *Micron Tech., Inc. v. United Microelectronics Corp.*

In *Micron Tech., Inc. v. United Microelectronics Corp.*, 17-cv-06932, 2019 WL 1959487, at *1 (N.D. Cal. May 2, 2019), the plaintiff alleged that the defendants recruited and hired certain key employees and induced them to bring the plaintiff's trade secrets to the defendants. In moving to dismiss, the defendants argued that the plaintiffs had not alleged a "concrete financial loss." *Id.* at *12.

The court agreed, explaining that it is insufficient to use conclusory phrases like "caused . . . considerable harm" or "will continue to cause . . . irreparable and substantial injury." *Id.*

---

[43] Some district courts outside the Ninth Circuit have addressed the concrete injury requirement in cases involving DTSA-based predicate conduct in the context of standing—that is, whether the alleged injuries were sufficient to confer standing to bring a RICO claim. *See, e.g.*, *Joe Schroeder Legacy, LLC v. Serv. 247 of Ill., Inc.*, 20 C 3201, 2021 WL 170729, at *5 (N.D. Ill. Jan. 19, 2021) (finding that plaintiffs lacked standing to bring RICO claim because they failed to establish adequate RICO injury "aside from conclusory statements that they have been harmed"); *Li v. Gelormino*, 18-cv-442, 2019 WL 1957539, at *7 (D. Conn. May 2, 2019) (finding that plaintiff lacked standing to bring RICO claim because plaintiff did not allege any facts to support her assertion that she suffered financial loss).

The court dismissed the RICO claim with leave to amend. *Id.* The plaintiff subsequently filed an amended complaint detailing injuries suffered as a result of the misconduct, namely substantial investigatory costs (including hundreds of hours of employee labor), computer forensic costs (including the use of third-party computer forensics consultants), and increased operational costs. The court has not yet ruled on the sufficiency of the amended complaint.

2. *MedImpact Healthcare Sys., Inc. v. IQVIA Inc.*

In *MedImpact Healthcare Sys., Inc. v. IQVIA Inc.*, 19-cv-1865, 2020 WL 5064253 (S.D. Cal. Aug. 27, 2020), the plaintiffs alleged that the defendants purchased a joint venture partner under false pretenses in order to misappropriate the plaintiff's trade secrets. The plaintiffs alleged as predicate conduct DTSA violations as well as mail and wire fraud. *Id.* at *22. In moving to dismiss, the defendants did not directly challenge the DTSA predicate conduct, but they did challenge the allegations of causation and injury. *Id.* at *24–25.

With respect to causation, RICO requires a "showing that the defendant's violation not only was a 'but for' cause of his injury, but was the proximate cause as well." *See Holmes v. Sec. Investor Protection Corp.*, 503 U.S. 258, 268 (1992). The proximate cause requirement "demand[s] . . . some direct relation between the injury asserted and the injurious conduct alleged." *Id.* In *MedImpact*, the court held that the complaint sufficiently alleged causation because it alleged that the RICO enterprise stole the plaintiffs' customers and caused price erosion, both of which caused plaintiffs to lose revenue. *MedImpact*, 2020 WL 5064253, at *24. The court explained that "'California recognizes a property interest in the confidentiality and exclusive use of trade secret information'; therefore, Plaintiffs' allegation of trade secret misappropriation resulted in loss of business or property." *Id.* at *25 (citation omitted). The court also noted that the plaintiffs had alleged the loss of specific contracts as a result of the misappropriation, which satisfied the concrete injury requirement. *Id.*

3. *MD Helicopters, Inc. v. Aerometals, Inc.*

In *MD Helicopters, Inc. v. Aerometals, Inc.*, 16-cv-02249, 2021 WL 978953, at *1 (E.D. Cal. Mar. 16, 2021), the plaintiff alleged that the defendant used the plaintiff's manufacturer drawings to unfairly compete in the airplane parts market. The plaintiff sought leave to amend its complaint to add new claims under the DTSA and RICO, based on DTSA predicates. *Id.* The defendant argued that the new claims would be futile, in part, because the plaintiff purportedly failed to allege a concrete financial loss. *Id.* at *2, 6. The court disagreed, finding that the following allegations sufficiently pled a concrete financial loss: 1) the defendant made sales that would have otherwise been made by the plaintiff; and 2) the plaintiff had been injured by price erosion. *Id.* at *6.

§ 26.07 Practical Advice

While RICO claims based on DTSA predicate violations are still relatively new, the developing case law provides guidance.

For plaintiffs, even if there is no local requirement to file a RICO case statement, it is a good idea to include in the complaint the level of specificity required in case statements. This will help ensure that the complaint withstands pleading challenges, particularly given the increased level of scrutiny some courts may apply. In addition, alleging multiple types of predicate conduct, over an extended period of time, not only will increase the viability of the claim, it also will open additional avenues of discovery should the case proceed beyond the pleading stage.

For defendants, when preparing pleading challenges, particular attention should be paid to conclusory allegations as well as the pattern and relatedness, or lack thereof, of predicate conduct, including whether the plaintiff has sufficiently demonstrated that the pattern is likely to continue in the future. In addition, there may be early summary judgment opportunities where the plaintiff fails to establish a concrete financial loss that is both proximately and actually caused by the predicate conduct.

Appendix A
COMMENTARY ON THE CALIFORNIA TRADE SECRETS JURY INSTRUCTIONS
By: Dylan W. Wiseman, Esq.

---

§ A.01 Introduction

Under California Rules of Court, Rule 2.1050(a), the stated goal of the Judicial Council of California Civil Jury Instructions ("CACI") "[i]s to improve the quality of jury decision making by providing standardized instructions which accurately state the law in a way that is understandable to the average juror."

The CACI 4400 series of instructions, which pertain to actions under the California Uniform Trade Secrets Act ("CUTSA"), were approved in December 2007.

This Appendix reproduces the CACI 4400 series instructions (as approved at the Judicial Council's Rules Committee October 2020 Meeting and Judicial Council November 2020 Meeting), including the "Directions for Use," "Sources and Authority" and "Secondary Sources" provided by the Judicial Council. The CACI jury instructions are available online at http://www.courts.ca.gov/partners/317.htm, and are reprinted on the following pages with the permission of the Judicial Council. Readers should check the website to determine if there has been an update by the Judicial Council after November 2020.

Following each instruction (including the Judicial Council's stated Directions for Use and Sources and Authority), we offer some "Comments" about the instruction. The Comments are enclosed in gray boxes so they may be easily identified as our Comments, not the Judicial Council's. The "Comments" are intended for consideration by trial lawyers, whether they are presenting cases for plaintiffs or defendants.

Juries often struggle with the concept of a "trade secret," how it is defined, how it can be misappropriated, and what resulting damages may be. Trade secret trials often involve technical information or business information, such as customer lists and pricing. Given that juries may be unfamiliar with these matters, having clear and accurate jury instructions can be very important.

For civil claims under the federal Defend Trade Secrets Act (18 U.S.C. 1831-39) ("DTSA"), in 2017, the United States Court of Appeals for the Eleventh Circuit has approved a set of pattern jury instructions, which can be found at: https://www.ca11.uscourts.gov/pattern-jury-instructions. Likewise, in 2017, United States Court of Appeals for the Ninth Circuit approved a set of criminal pattern jury instructions for counts under the Economic Espionage Act of 1996 (18 U.S.C. 1831), as amended by the Defend Trade Secrets Act. The Ninth Circuit's pattern criminal jury instructions can be found at: https://www.ce9.uscourts.gov/jury-instructions/node/727. Unless otherwise stated, we do not address in this Appendix the Ninth or Eleventh Circuits' pattern instructions.

CACI Series 4400

Judicial Council of California Civil Jury Instructions (CACI) > Series 4400 TRADE SECRETS

Series 4400 TRADE SECRETS

4400 Misappropriation of Trade Secrets—Introduction

4401 Misappropriation of Trade Secrets—Essential Factual Elements

4402 "Trade Secret" Defined

4403 Secrecy Requirement

4404 Reasonable Efforts to Protect Secrecy

4405 Misappropriation by Acquisition

4406 Misappropriation by Disclosure

4407 Misappropriation by Use

4408 Improper Means of Acquiring Trade Secret

4409 Remedies for Misappropriation of Trade Secret

4410 Unjust Enrichment

4411 Punitive Damages for Willful and Malicious Misappropriation

4412 "Independent Economic Value" Explained

4413 Reserved for Future Use

4420 Affirmative Defense—Information Was Readily Ascertainable by Proper Means

4421 Affirmative Defense—Statute of Limitations—Three-Year Limit (Civ. Code, § 3426.6)

4422–4499 Reserved for Future Use

CACI 4400

Judicial Council of California Civil Jury Instructions (CACI) > Series 4400 TRADE SECRETS

4400 Misappropriation of Trade Secrets—Introduction

[*Name of plaintiff*] **claims that [he/she/***nonbinary pronoun***/it] [is/was] the [owner/licensee] of** [*insert general description of alleged trade secret[s]*]**.**

[*Name of plaintiff*] **claims that [this/these]** [*select short term to describe, e.g., information*] **[is/are] [a] trade secret[s] and that** [*name of defendant*] **misappropriated [it/them]. "Misappropriation" means the improper [acquisition/use/ [or] disclosure] of the trade secret[s].**

[*Name of plaintiff*] **also claims that** [*name of defendant*]**'s misappropriation caused [[him/her/***nonbinary pronoun***/it] harm/ [or]** [*name of defendant*] **to be unjustly enriched].**

[*Name of defendant*] **denies** [*insert denial of any of the above claims*]**.**

[[*Name of defendant*] **also claims** [*insert affirmative defenses*]**.]**

New December 2007; Revised December 2010

Directions for Use

This instruction is designed to introduce the jury to the issues involved in a case involving the misappropriation of trade secrets under the California Uniform Trade Secrets Act. (See Civ. Code, § 3426.1 et seq.) It should be read before the instructions on the substantive law.

In the first sentence, provide only a general description of the alleged trade secrets. Then in the second sentence, select a short term to identify the items, such as "information," "customer lists," or "computer code." The items that are alleged to be trade secrets will be described with more specificity in CACI No. 4401, *Misappropriation of Trade Secrets—Essential Factual Elements.*

Select the appropriate term, "owner" or "licensee," to indicate the plaintiff's interest in the alleged trade secrets. No reported California state court decision has addressed whether a licensee has a sufficient interest to assert a claim of trade secret misappropriation. These instructions take no position on this issue. The court should make a determination whether the plaintiff has the right as a matter of substantive law to maintain a cause of action for misappropriation of trade secrets if that issue is disputed.

Civil Code section 3426.1(b)(1) defines "misappropriation" as improper "[a]cquisition" of a trade secret, and subsection (b)(2) defines it as improper "[d]isclosure or use" of a trade secret. In some cases, the mere acquisition of a trade secret, as distinguished from a related disclosure or use, will not result in damages and will only be relevant to injunctive relief. Because generally the jury should be instructed only on matters relevant to damage claims, do not select "acquiring" in the second paragraph unless there is evidence that the acquisition resulted in damages, other than damages from related disclosure or use.

To avoid confusion, instruct the jury only on the particular theory of misappropriation applicable under the facts of the case. For example, the jury should not be instructed on misappropriation through "use" if the plaintiff does not assert that the defendant improperly used the trade secrets. Nor should the jury be instructed on a particular type of "use" if that type of "use" is not asserted and supported by the evidence.

In the third paragraph, select the nature of the recovery sought, either damages for harm to the plaintiff or for the defendant's unjust enrichment, or both.

Include the last paragraph if the defendant asserts any affirmative defenses.

Sources and Authority

- Uniform Trade Secrets Act: Definitions. Civil Code section 3426.1.

- "[W]e agree with the federal cases applying California law, which hold that section 3426.7, subdivision (b), preempts common law claims that are 'based on the same nucleus of facts as the misappropriation of trade secrets claim for relief.' Depending on the particular facts pleaded, the statute can operate to preempt the specific common claims asserted here: breach of confidence, interference with contract, and unfair competition." (*K.C. Multimedia, Inc. v. Bank of America Technology & Operations, Inc. (2009) 171 Cal.App.4th 939, 958–959 [90 Cal.Rptr.3d 247]*, internal citation omitted.)

- " ' "Trade secret law promotes the sharing of knowledge, and the efficient operation of industry; it permits the individual inventor to reap the rewards of his labor by contracting with a company large enough to develop and exploit it." [Citation.]' 'Trade secret law also helps maintain "standards of commercial ethics … ." [Citation.] … By sanctioning the acquisition, use, and disclosure of another's valuable, proprietary information by improper means, trade secret law minimizes "the inevitable cost to the basic decency of society when one … steals from another." [Citation.] In doing so, it recognizes that " 'good faith and honest, fair dealing, is the very life and spirit of the commercial world.' " ' " (*Altavion, Inc. v. Konica Minolta Systems Laboratory, Inc. (2014) 226 Cal.App.4th 26, 42 [171 Cal.Rptr.3d 714]*, internal citations omitted.)

- "[W]e find no support for [a current-ownership] rule in the text of the CUTSA, cases applying it, or legislative history. Nor do we find any evidence of such a rule in patent or copyright law, which defendants have cited by analogy. Defendants have offered no persuasive argument from policy for our adoption of such a rule." (*Jasmine Networks, Inc. v. Superior Court (2009) 180 Cal.App.4th 980, 986 [103 Cal.Rptr.3d 426].*)

- "[T]he only California authority [defendant] cited for the asserted requirement [that a trade-secrets plaintiff must own the trade secret when the action is filed] was the official California pattern jury instructions—whose 'first element,' [defendant] asserted, 'requires the plaintiff to be either the owner or the licensee of the trade secret. See CACI Nos. 4400, 4401.' [Defendant] did not quote the cited instructions—for good reason. The most that can be said in favor of its reading is that the broader and less specific of the two instructions uses the present tense to refer to the requirement of ownership. That instruction, whose avowed purpose is 'to introduce the jury to the issues involved' in a trade secrets case (Directions for Use for CACI No. 4400), describes the plaintiff as claiming that he 'is' the owner/licensee of the trade secrets underlying the suit. (CACI No. 4400.) The second instruction, which enumerates the actual *elements* of the plaintiff's cause of action, dispels whatever weak whiff of relevance this use of the present tense might have. It requires the plaintiff to prove that he 'own*ed*' or 'was a licensee o*f*' the trade secrets at issue. (CACI No. 4401, italics added.) Given only these instructions to go on, one would suppose that past ownership—i.e., ownership at the time of the alleged misappropriation—is sufficient to establish this element." (*Jasmine Networks, Inc., supra, 180 Cal.App.4th at p. 997*, original italics.)

Secondary Sources

13 Witkin, Summary of California Law (11th ed. 2017) Equity, § 83

Gaab & Reese, California Practice Guide: Civil Procedure Before Trial—Claims & Defenses, Ch. 10(II)-A ¶ 10:250 (The Rutter Group)

1 Milgrim on Trade Secrets, Ch. 1, Definitional Aspects, § 1.01 (Matthew Bender)

3 Levy et al., California Torts, Ch. 40, Fraud and Deceit and Other Business Torts, § 40.50 et seq. (Matthew Bender)

49 California Forms of Pleading and Practice, Ch. 565, Unfair Competition, § 565.103 (Matthew Bender)

1 Zamore, Business Torts, Ch. 17, *Trade Secrets*, § 17.05 et seq. (Matthew Bender)

Edelson & Kay, eds., Trade Secret Litigation and Protection in California (State Bar of California 2009) Chs. 1, 2, 6, 12

Comments. If appropriate, consider proposing a special instruction that the plaintiff is claiming the defendant's unjust enrichment as a measure of its actual damages. *See Klamath-Orleans Lumber, Inc. v. Miller*, 87 Cal.App.3d 458, 466 (1978); *see also* Chapter 13 (monetary remedies).

CACI 4401

Judicial Council of California Civil Jury Instructions (CACI) >
Series 4400 TRADE SECRETS

4401 Misappropriation of Trade Secrets—Essential Factual Elements

---

[*Name of plaintiff*] claims that [*name of defendant*] has misappropriated a trade secret. To succeed on this claim, [*name of plaintiff*] must prove all of the following:

- **That [*name of plaintiff*] [owned/was a licensee of] [the following:][*describe each item claimed to be a trade secret that is subject to the misappropriation claim*];**
- **That [this/these] [*select short term to describe, e.g., information*] [was/were] [a] trade secret[s] at the time of the misappropriation;**
- **That [*name of defendant*] improperly [acquired/used/ [or] disclosed] the trade secret[s];**
- **That [[*name of plaintiff*] was harmed/ [or] [*name of defendant*] was unjustly enriched]; and**
- **That [*name of defendant*]'s [acquisition/use/ [or] disclosure] was a substantial factor in causing [[*name of plaintiff*]'s harm/ [or] [*name of defendant*] to be unjustly enriched].**

New December 2007; Revised December 2010, December 2014

Directions for Use

In element 1, specifically describe all items that are alleged to be the trade secrets that were misappropriated. (*See Altavion, Inc. v. Konica Minolta Systems Laboratory, Inc.* (2014) 226 Cal.App.4th 26, 43 [171 Cal.Rptr.3d 714].) If more than one item is alleged, include "the following" and present the items as a list. Then in element 2, select a short term to identify the items, such as "information," "customer lists," or "computer code."

In element 1, select the appropriate term, "owned" or "was a licensee of," to indicate the plaintiff's interest in the alleged trade secrets. No reported California state court decision has addressed whether a licensee has a sufficient interest to assert a claim of trade secret misappropriation. These instructions take no position on this issue. The court should make a determination whether the plaintiff has the right as a matter of substantive law to maintain a cause of action for misappropriation of trade secrets if that issue is disputed.

Read also CACI No. 4402, "Trade Secret" Defined, to give the jury guidance on element 2.

Civil Code section 3426.1(b)(1) defines "misappropriation" as improper "[a]cquisition" of a trade secret, and subsection (b)(2) defines it as improper "[d]isclosure or use" of a trade secret. In some cases, the mere acquisition of a trade secret, as distinguished from a related disclosure or use, will not result in damages and will only be relevant to injunctive relief. Because generally the jury should be instructed only on matters relevant to damage claims, do not select "acquired" in element 3 or "acquisition" in element 5 unless there is evidence that the acquisition resulted in damages, other than damages from related disclosure or use.

To avoid confusion, instruct the jury only on the particular theory of misappropriation applicable under the facts of the case. For example, the jury should not be instructed on misappropriation through "use" if the plaintiff does not assert that the defendant improperly used the trade secrets. Nor should the jury be instructed on a particular type of "use" if that type of "use" is not asserted and supported by the evidence.

Give also CACI No. 4409, Remedies for Misappropriation of Trade Secret.

Sources and Authority

- Uniform Trade Secrets Act: Definitions. Civil Code section 3426.1.
- Trade Secrets Must Be Identified With Reasonable Particularity. Code of Civil Procedure section 2019.210.
- "A trade secret is misappropriated if a person (1) acquires a trade secret knowing or having reason to know that the trade secret has been acquired by 'improper means,' (2) discloses or uses a trade secret the person has acquired by 'improper means' or in violation of a nondisclosure obligation, (3) discloses or uses a trade secret the person knew or should have known was derived from another who had acquired it by improper means or who had a nondisclosure obligation or (4) discloses or uses a trade secret after learning that it is a trade secret but before a material change of position." (*Ajaxo Inc. v. E*Trade Group Inc.* (2005) 135 Cal.App.4th 21, 66 [37 Cal.Rptr.3d 221].)
- "A cause of action for monetary relief under CUTSA may be said to consist of the following elements: (1) possession by the plaintiff of a trade secret; (2) the defendant's misappropriation of the trade secret, meaning its wrongful acquisition, disclosure, or use; and (3) resulting or threatened injury to the plaintiff. The first of these elements is typically the most important, in the sense that until the content and nature of the claimed secret is ascertained, it will likely be impossible to intelligibly analyze the remaining issues." (*Silvaco Data Systems v. Intel Corp.* (2010) 184 Cal.App.4th 210, 220 [109 Cal.Rptr.3d 27], internal citations omitted.)
- "A cause of action for misappropriation of trade secrets requires a plaintiff to show the plaintiff owned the trade secret; at the time of misappropriation, the information was a trade secret; the defendant improperly acquired, used, or disclosed the trade secret; the plaintiff was harmed; and the defendant's acquisition, use, or disclosure of the trade secret was a substantial factor in causing the plaintiff harm." (*AMN Healthcare, Inc. v.*

Aya Healthcare Services, Inc. (2018) 28 Cal.App.5th 923, 942 [239 Cal.Rptr.3d 577] [citing CACI].)

- "It is critical to any [UTSA] cause of action—and any defense—that the information claimed to have been misappropriated be clearly identified. Accordingly, a California trade secrets plaintiff must, prior to commencing discovery, 'identify the trade secret with reasonable particularity.' " (*Altavion, Inc., supra*, 226 Cal.App.4th at p. 43.)

- "We find the trade secret situation more analogous to employment discrimination cases. In those cases, as we have seen, information of the employer's intent is in the hands of the employer, but discovery affords the employee the means to present sufficient evidence to raise an inference of discriminatory intent. The burden of proof remains with the plaintiff, but the defendant must then bear the burden of producing evidence once a prima facie case for the plaintiff is made. [¶] We conclude that the trial court correctly refused the proposed instruction that would have shifted the burden of proof." (*Sargent Fletcher, Inc. v. Able Corp.* (2003) 110 Cal.App.4th 1658, 1674 [3 Cal.Rptr.3d 279], internal citation omitted.)

- "[W]e find no support for [a current-ownership] rule in the text of the CUTSA, cases applying it, or legislative history. Nor do we find any evidence of such a rule in patent or copyright law, which defendants have cited by analogy. Defendants have offered no persuasive argument from policy for our adoption of such a rule." (*Jasmine Networks, Inc. v. Superior Court* (2009) 180 Cal.App.4th 980, 986 [103 Cal.Rptr.3d 426].)

- "[T]he only California authority [defendant] cited for the asserted requirement [that a trade-secrets plaintiff must own the trade secret when the action is filed] was the official California pattern jury instructions—whose 'first element,' [defendant] asserted, 'requires the plaintiff to be either the owner or the licensee of the trade secret. See CACI Nos. 4400, 4401.' [Defendant] did not quote the cited instructions—for good reason. The most that can be said in favor of its reading is that the broader and less specific of the two instructions uses the present tense to refer to the requirement of ownership. That instruction, whose avowed purpose is 'to introduce the jury to the issues involved' in a trade secrets case (Directions for Use for CACI No. 4400), describes the plaintiff as claiming that he 'is' the owner/licensee of the trade secrets underlying the suit. (CACI No. 4400.) The second instruction, which enumerates the actual elements of the plaintiff's cause of action, dispels whatever weak whiff of relevance this use of the present tense might have. It requires the plaintiff to prove that he 'owned' or 'was a licensee of' the trade secrets at issue. (CACI No. 4401, italics added.) Given only these instructions to go on, one would suppose that past ownership—i.e., ownership at the time of the alleged misappropriation—is sufficient to establish this element." (*Jasmine Networks, Inc., supra*, 180 Cal.App.4th at p. 997, original italics.)

Secondary Sources

Gaab and Reese, California Practice Guide: Civil Procedure Before Trial—Claims & Defenses, Ch. 10(II)-A ¶ 10:250 (The Rutter Group)

1 Milgrim on Trade Secrets, Ch. 1, Definitional Aspects, § 1.01 (Matthew Bender)

Zamore, Business Torts, Ch. 17, Trade Secrets, § 17.05 et seq. (Matthew Bender)

3 Levy et al., California Torts, Ch. 40, Fraud and Deceit and Other Business Torts, § 40.51 (Matthew Bender)

49 California Forms of Pleading and Practice, Ch. 565, Unfair Competition, § 565.103[4] (Matthew Bender)

Edelson & Kay, eds., Trade Secret Litigation and Protection in California (State Bar of California 2009) Chs. 1, 2, 6, 10, 11, 12

***Comments*.**

If appropriate, consider proposing a special instruction that the plaintiff is claiming the defendant's unjust enrichment as a measure of its actual damages. *See Klamath-Orleans Lumber, Inc. v. Miller*, 87 Cal.App.3d 458, 466 (1978); *See also* Chapter 13 (monetary remedies).

Consider proposing, if appropriate, that CACI 4401 be given with CACI No. 430 regarding substantial factor causation.

Under Civil Code § 3426.1(b)(2)(B)(i)-(iii), an employer can be found liable where it knew or "had reason to know" of the wrongdoing by an employee. *But see also* Chapter 2 at Section 2.04 (addressing cases applying *respondeat superior* liability to employer defendants accused of trade secret misappropriation).

See also Chapter 8 for a discussion of pleading the requisite elements of a trade secret misappropriation claim.

CACI 4402

Judicial Council of California Civil Jury Instructions (CACI) >
Series 4400 TRADE SECRETS

4402 "Trade Secret" Defined

To prove that the [*select short term to describe, e.g., information*] [was/were] [a] trade secret[s], [*name of plaintiff*] must prove all of the following:

- That the [*e.g., information*] [was/were] secret;
- That the [*e.g., information*] had actual or potential independent economic value because [it was/they were] secret; and
- That [*name of plaintiff*] made reasonable efforts to keep the [*e.g., information*] secret.

New December 2007; Revised April 2008

Directions for Use

Give also CACI No. 4403, Secrecy Requirement, if more explanation of element 1 is needed. Give CACI No. 4412, "Independent Economic Value" Explained, if more explanation of element 2 is needed. Give CACI No. 4404, Reasonable Efforts to Protect Secrecy, if more explanation of element 3 is needed.

Sources and Authority

- "Trade Secret" Defined. Civil Code section 3426.1(d).
- " 'Trade secrets are a peculiar kind of property. Their only value consists in their being kept private.' Thus, 'the right to exclude others is central to the very definition of the property interest. Once the data that constitute a trade secret are disclosed to others, or others are allowed to use those data, the holder of the trade secret has lost his property interest in the data.' " (*DVD Copy Control Assn., Inc. v. Bunner* (2003) 31 Cal.4th 864, 881 [4 Cal.Rptr.3d 69, 75 P.3d 1], internal citations omitted.)
- "The 'test for a trade secret is whether the matter sought to be protected is information (1) that is valuable because it is unknown to others and (2) that the owner has attempted to keep secret. [Citation.] … [I]n order to qualify as a trade secret, the information "must be secret, and must not be of public knowledge or of a general knowledge in the trade or business." ' " (*AMN Healthcare, Inc. v. Aya Healthcare Services, Inc.* (2018) 28 Cal.App.5th 923, 943 [239 Cal.Rptr.3d 577].)

- "[A]ny information (such as price concessions, trade discounts and rebate incentives) disclosed to [cross-complainant's] customers cannot be considered trade secret or confidential." (*Whyte v. Schlage Lock Co.* (2002) 101 Cal.App.4th 1443, 1455 [125 Cal.Rptr.2d 277].)

- " '[A] trade secret … has an intrinsic value which is based upon, or at least preserved by, being safeguarded from disclosure.' Public disclosure, that is the absence of secrecy, is fatal to the existence of a trade secret. 'If an individual discloses his trade secret to others who are under no obligation to protect the confidentiality of the information, or otherwise publicly discloses the secret, his property right is extinguished.' A person or entity claiming a trade secret is also required to make 'efforts that are reasonable under the circumstances to maintain its secrecy.' " (*In re Providian Credit Card Cases* (2002) 96 Cal.App.4th 292, 304 [116 Cal.Rptr.2d 833], internal citations omitted.)

- "The requirement that a customer list must have economic value to qualify as a trade secret has been interpreted to mean that the secrecy of this information provides a business with a 'substantial business advantage.' In this respect, a customer list can be found to have economic value because its disclosure would allow a competitor to direct its sales efforts to those customers who have already shown a willingness to use a unique type of service or product as opposed to a list of people who only might be interested." (*Morlife, Inc. v. Perry* (1997) 56 Cal.App.4th 1514, 1522 [66 Cal.Rptr.2d 731], internal citations omitted.)

- "The sine qua non of a trade secret, then, is the plaintiff's possession of information of a type that can, at the possessor's option, be made known to others, or withheld from them, i.e., kept secret. This is the fundamental difference between a trade secret and a patent. A patent protects an idea, i.e., an invention, against appropriation by others. Trade secret law does not protect ideas as such. Indeed a trade secret may consist of something we would not ordinarily consider an idea (a conceptual datum) at all, but more a fact (an empirical datum), such as a customer's preferences, or the location of a mineral deposit. In either case, the trade secret is not the idea or fact itself, but information tending to communicate (disclose) the idea or fact to another. Trade secret law, in short, protects only the right to control the dissemination of information." (*Silvaco Data Systems v. Intel Corp.* (2010) 184 Cal.App.4th 210, 220–221 [109 Cal.Rptr.3d 27], original italics.)

- "[I]f a patentable idea is kept secret, the idea itself can constitute information protectable by trade secret law. In that situation, trade secret law protects the inventor's 'right to control the dissemination of information'—the information being the idea itself—rather than the subsequent use of the novel technology, which is protected by patent law. In other words, trade secret law may be used to sanction the misappropriation of an idea the plaintiff kept secret." (*Altavion, Inc. v. Konica Minolta Systems Laboratory, Inc.* (2014) 226 Cal.App.4th 26, 55–56 [171 Cal.Rptr.3d 714], original italics, internal citations omitted.)

- "[T]he doctrine has been established that a trade secret can include a system where the elements are in the public domain, but there has been accomplished an effective, successful and valuable integration of the public domain elements and the trade secret gave the claimant a competitive advantage which is protected from misappropriation." (*Altavion, Inc., supra*, 226 Cal.App.4th at p. 48.)

Secondary Sources

13 Witkin, Summary of California Law (11th ed. 2017) Equity, §§ 89, 90

Gaab & Reese, California Practice Guide: Civil Procedure Before

Trial—Claims & Defenses, Ch. 10(II)-A ¶ 10:250 (The Rutter Group)

Trade Secrets Practice in California (Cont.Ed.Bar 2d ed.) §§ 4.8–4.10

1 Milgrim on Trade Secrets, Ch. 1, Definitional Aspects, § 1.01 (Matthew Bender)

3 Levy et al., California Torts, Ch. 40, Fraud and Deceit and Other Business Torts, § 40.52 (Matthew Bender)

49 California Forms of Pleading and Practice, Ch. 565, Unfair Competition, § 565.103[4][a] (Matthew Bender)

Edelson & Kay, eds., Trade Secret Litigation and Protection in California (State Bar of California 2009) Ch. 1

Comments.

The provision in CACI No. 4402

"[t]hat the [e.g., information] [was/were] secret;" does not appear anywhere in the statutory definition of a "trade secret". (Civil Code § 3426.1(d).) Therefore, if appropriate, practitioners may wish to consider requesting that the statutory definition of a "trade secret" be used instead in the instruction read to the jury. However,

- Section 3426.1(d) does refer to a trade secret's "secrecy" and requires that the information not be "generally known," and "secret" is included in the term "trade secret," and

- CACI No. 4403 does explain that absolute secrecy is not required, and CACI No. 4404 does reflect that only reasonable steps to maintain secrecy are required.

In addition, if this is the first use of the term "independent economic value," practitioners may wish to consider asking the judge to give CACI No. 4412 with CACI No. 4402.

See also Chapter 1 (What Is a Trade Secret?) for ideas as to potential special instructions about what is and what is not a trade secret, depending upon the circumstances of a particular lawsuit going to trial. For example:

- Trade secrets must consist of information, and not "general knowledge, skill and experience acquired in his or her former employment." *The Retirement Group v. Galante* 176 Cal.App.4th 1226, 1237 (2009) (citing Continental *Car-Na-Var Corp. v. Mosely* 24 Cal.2d 104, 110 (1944).)

- Trade secrets can be embodied in hard copy records, electronic records, or information which is memorized or learned. (*Morlife, Inc. v. Perry* 56 Cal.App.4th 1514, 1523 (1997) [66 Cal.Rptr. 2d 731].)

CACI 4403

Judicial Council of California Civil Jury Instructions (CACI) > Series 4400 TRADE SECRETS

4403 Secrecy Requirement

The secrecy required to prove that something is a trade secret does not have to be absolute in the sense that no one else in the world possesses the information. It may be disclosed to employees involved in [*name of plaintiff*]'s use of the trade secret as long as they are instructed to keep the information secret. It may also be disclosed to nonemployees if they are obligated to keep the information secret. However, it must not have been generally known to the public or to people who could obtain value from knowing it.

New December 2007

Directions for Use

Read this instruction with CACI No. 4402, "Trade Secret" Defined, to give the jury additional guidance on the secrecy requirement of element 1 of that instruction.

Sources and Authority

- " 'Trade secrets are a peculiar kind of property. Their only value consists in their being kept private.' Thus, 'the right to exclude others is central to the very definition of the property interest. Once the data that constitute a trade secret are disclosed to others, or others are allowed to use those data, the holder of the trade secret has lost his property interest in the data.' " (*DVD Copy Control Assn., Inc. v. Bunner* (2003) 31 Cal.4th 864, 881 [4 Cal.Rptr.3d 69, 75 P.3d 1], internal citations omitted.)

- "[T]he test for a trade secret is whether the matter sought to be protected is information (1) that is valuable because it is unknown to others and (2) that the owner has attempted to keep secret. … [I]n order to qualify as a trade secret, the information 'must be secret, and must not be of public knowledge or of a general knowledge in the trade or business.' " (*DVD Copy Control Assn., Inc. v. Bunner* (2004) 116 Cal.App.4th 241, 251 [10 Cal.Rptr.3d 185], internal citations omitted.)

- "The secrecy requirement is generally treated as a relative concept and requires a fact-intensive analysis. Widespread, anonymous publication of the information over the Internet may destroy its status as a trade secret. The concern is whether the information has retained its value to the creator in spite of the publication." (*DVD Copy Control Assn., Inc., supra*, 116 Cal.App.4th at p. 251, internal citations omitted.)

- "[A]ny information (such as price concessions, trade discounts and rebate incentives) disclosed to [cross-complainant's] customers cannot be considered trade secret or confidential." (*Whyte v. Schlage Lock Co.* (2002) 101 Cal.App.4th 1443, 1455 [125 Cal.Rptr.2d 277].)

- " '[A] trade secret … has an intrinsic value which is based upon, or at least preserved by, being safeguarded from disclosure.' Public disclosure, that is the absence of secrecy, is fatal to the existence of a trade secret. 'If an individual discloses his trade secret to others who are under no obligation to protect the confidentiality of the information, or otherwise publicly discloses the secret, his property right is extinguished.' A person or entity claiming a trade secret is also required to make 'efforts that are reasonable under the circumstances to maintain its secrecy.' " (*In re Providian Credit Card Cases* (2002) 96 Cal.App.4th 292, 304 [116 Cal.Rptr.2d 833], internal citations omitted.)

- " '[R]easonable efforts to maintain secrecy have been held to include advising employees of the existence of a trade secret, limiting access to a trade secret on 'need to know basis,' and controlling plant access.' " (*Courtesy Temporary Service, Inc. v. Camacho* (1990) 222 Cal.App.3d 1278, 1288 [272 Cal.Rptr. 352].)

Secondary Sources

13 Witkin, Summary of California Law (11th ed. 2017) Equity, §§ 89, 90

Gaab & Reese, California Practice Guide: Civil Procedure Before

Trial—Claims & Defenses, Ch. 10(II)-A ¶ 10:250 (The Rutter Group)

Trade Secrets Practice in California (Cont.Ed.Bar 2d ed.) §§ 4.2–4.10

1 Milgrim on Trade Secrets, Ch. 1, Definitional Aspects, § 1.03 (Matthew Bender)

3 Levy et al., California Torts, Ch. 40, Fraud and Deceit and Other

Business Torts, § 40.52 (Matthew Bender)

49 California Forms of Pleading and Practice, Ch. 565, Unfair Competition, § 565.103[4] (Matthew Bender)

Edelson & Kay, eds., Trade Secret Litigation and Protection in California (State Bar of California 2009) § 1.03(3), (4)

Comments. See Comments in connection with CACI No. 4402.

CACI 4404

Judicial Council of California Civil Jury Instructions (CACI) > Series 4400 TRADE SECRETS

4404 Reasonable Efforts to Protect Secrecy

To establish that the [*select short term to describe, e.g., information*] [is/are] [a] trade secret[s], [*name of plaintiff*] must prove that [he/she/*nonbinary pronoun*/it] made reasonable efforts under the circumstances to keep it secret. "Reasonable efforts" are the efforts that would be made by a reasonable [person/business] in the same situation and having the same knowledge and resources as [*name of plaintiff*], exercising due care to protect important information of the same kind. [This requirement applies separately to each item that [*name of plaintiff*] claims to be a trade secret.]

In determining whether or not [*name of plaintiff*] made reasonable efforts to keep the [*e.g., information*] secret, you should consider all of the facts and circumstances. Among the factors you may consider are the following:

- Whether documents or computer files containing the [*e.g., information*] were marked with confidentiality warnings;]
- Whether [*name of plaintiff*] instructed [his/her/*nonbinary pronoun*/its] employees to treat the [*e.g., information*] as confidential;]
- Whether [*name of plaintiff*] restricted access to the [*e.g., information*] to persons who had a business reason to know the information;]

[d. Whether [*name of plaintiff*] kept the [*e.g., information*] in a restricted or secured area;]

[e. Whether [*name of plaintiff*] required employees or others with access to the [*e.g., information*] to sign confidentiality or nondisclosure agreements;]

[f. Whether [*name of plaintiff*] took any action to protect the specific [*e.g., information*], or whether it relied on general measures taken to protect its business information or assets;]

[g. The extent to which any general measures taken by [*name of plaintiff*] would prevent the unauthorized disclosure of the [*e.g., information*];]

[h. Whether there were other reasonable measures available to [*name of plaintiff*] that [he/she/*nonbinary pronoun*/it] did not take;]

[i. *Specify other factor(s).*]

The presence or absence of any one or more of these factors is not necessarily determinative.

New December 2007

Directions for Use

Give this instruction with CACI No. 4402, "Trade Secret" Defined, to guide the jury with regard to element 3 of that instruction, that the plaintiff made reasonable efforts to keep the information secret. Read only the factors supported by the evidence in the case. Use factor i to present additional factors.

Sources and Authority

- "Reasonable efforts to maintain secrecy have been held to include advising employees of the existence of a trade secret, limiting access to a trade secret on 'need to know basis,' and controlling plant access. [¶] ... Requiring employees to sign confidentiality agreements is a reasonable step to ensure secrecy." (*Whyte v. Schlage Lock Co.* (2002) 101 Cal.App.4th 1443, 1454 [125 Cal.Rptr.2d 277, internal citations omitted.)

- "A person or entity claiming a trade secret is also required to make 'efforts that are reasonable under the circumstances to maintain its secrecy.' A leading treatise has collected the cases of successful and unsuccessful claims of secrecy protection; among the factors repeatedly noted are restricting access and physical segregation of the information, confidentiality agreements with employees, and marking documents with warnings or reminders of confidentiality." *(In re Providian Credit Card Cases* (2002) 96 Cal.App.4th 292, 304 [116 Cal.Rptr.2d 833], referring to Trade Secrets Practice in California (Cont.Ed.Bar 2d ed.) §§ 4.9–4.10.)

- "In addition to possessing actual or potential economic value, the other part of the definition of a trade secret is that the information must have been protected by 'efforts that are reasonable under the circumstances to maintain its secrecy.' [W]hether a party claiming a trade secret undertook reasonable efforts to maintain secrecy is a question of fact, and it may be implicit in a determination that the information does not qualify as a trade secret, also a question of fact." (*In re Providian Credit Card Cases, supra*, 96 Cal.App.4th at p. 306, internal citations omitted.)

Secondary Sources

Advising California Employers and Employees (Cont.Ed.Bar) Ch. 11, Reasonable Effort to Maintain Secrecy, § 11.6

Trade Secrets Practice in California (Cont.Ed.Bar 2d ed.) §§ 4.9–4.10

1 Milgrim on Trade Secrets, Ch. 1, Definitional Aspects, §§ 1.03–1.05 (Matthew Bender)

3 Levy et al., California Torts, Ch. 40, Fraud and Deceit and Other Business Torts, § 40.52 (Matthew Bender)

Edelson & Kay, eds., Trade Secret Litigation and Protection in California (State Bar of California 2009) § 1.03(4)

Comments.

If appropriate, a practitioner may ask the court for the deletion of inapplicable circumstances from the instruction (e.g., if no computer information is at issue or if the plaintiff has no employees, the practitioner may seek to have those portions of the instruction omitted to avoid jury confusion).

Similarly, if there is a concern that this instruction will place undue significance on the order in which the factors are presented, the practitioner may ask that the court add to the instruction something like: "The order in which I read the factors to you is not significant. The factors I read first are not necessarily more important than the ones I read at the end of this instruction."

In addition, if the following are applicable to the case, a practitioner may -- if appropriate – consider asking that they be explained:

[f. Whether [name of plaintiff] took any action to protect the specific [e.g., information], or whether it relied on general measures taken to protect its business information or assets;]

[g. The extent to which any general measures taken by [name of plaintiff] would prevent the unauthorized disclosure of the [e.g., information];]

[h. Whether there were other reasonable measures available to [name of plaintiff] that [he/she/nonbinary pronoun/it] did not take;]

For example, with respect to f. and g., there may be concern that the jury will not know what is meant by "general measures" (e.g., they are to be contrasted with heightened measures to protect trade secret information). Similarly, if appropriate, the practitioner may seek to have "business information or assets" clarified for the jury.

In addition, with respect to h., the practitioner representing the trade secret plaintiff may – if appropriate -- seek a clarification of that portion of the instruction (e.g., that there were other reasonable protective measures available but not taken does not necessarily make the measures taken insufficient – the measures that were taken may be reasonable under the circumstances).

Further, defense counsel may -- if appropriate and applicable under the circumstances of the case – seek a clarifying instruction that the defendant may rebut that the plaintiff's measures were reasonable even if the plaintiff took the measures listed in the instruction (e.g., regardless of what protective measures the plaintiff took, *other* actions or omissions by the plaintiff could render the protective measures for the information unreasonable as a whole).

See also Comments in connection with CACI No. 4402 as well as Chapter 1 for other potential ideas for requested modifications (if appropriate).

CACI 4405

Judicial Council of California Civil Jury Instructions (CACI) > Series 4400 TRADE SECRETS

4405 Misappropriation by Acquisition

[*Name of defendant*] **misappropriated** [*name of plaintiff*]**'s trade secret[s] by acquisition if** [*name of defendant*] **acquired the trade secret[s] and knew or had reason to know that [he/she/***nonbinary pronoun***/it/[***name of third party***]] used improper means to acquire [it/them].**

New December 2007

Directions for Use

Read this instruction with CACI No. 4401, *Misappropriation of Trade Secrets—Essential Factual Elements,* if the plaintiff claims that the defendant's acquisition of the information alleged to be a trade secret is a misappropriation. Give also CACI No. 4408, *Improper Means of Acquiring Trade Secret.*

Civil Code section 3426.1(b)(1) defines "misappropriation" as improper "[a]cquisition" of a trade secret, and subsection (b)(2) defines it as improper "[d]isclosure or use" of a trade secret. In some cases, the mere acquisition of a trade secret, as distinguished from a related disclosure or use, will not result in damages and will only be relevant to injunctive relief. Because generally the jury should only be instructed on matters relevant to damage claims, this instruction should not be given unless there is evidence that the acquisition resulted in damages, other than damages from related disclosure or use.

Sources and Authority

- "Misappropriation" Defined. Civil Code section 3426.1(b)(1).
- "Defendants … obtained these secrets improperly. Their tortious acts resulted from a breach of confidence by [defendant] in copying or stealing plans, designs and other documents related to [plaintiff]'s products which defendants themselves wanted to produce in competition with [plaintiff]. The protection which is extended to trade secrets fundamentally rests upon the theory that they are improperly acquired by a defendant, usually through theft or a breach of confidence." (*Vacco Indus. v. Van Den Berg* (1992) 5 Cal.App.4th 34, 50 [6 Cal.Rptr.2d 602].)

- "One does not ordinarily 'acquire' a thing inadvertently; the term implies conduct directed to that objective. The choice of that term over 'receive' suggests that inadvertently coming into possession of a trade secret will not constitute acquisition. Thus one who passively receives a trade secret, but neither discloses nor uses it, would not be guilty of misappropriation. We need not decide the outer limits of acquisition as contemplated by CUTSA, however, for there is no suggestion here of acquisition even in the broadest sense, i.e., that [defendant] ever came into possession of the source code constituting the claimed trade secrets. Indeed [plaintiff] does not directly argue that [defendant] acquired the trade secrets at issue but only that, under the terms of the statute, it could have done so without itself having 'knowledge' of them. We doubt the soundness of this suggestion, but assuming it is correct, it remains beside the point unless [defendant] came into possession of the secret. Since there is no basis to find that it did, the mental state required for actionable acquisition appears to be academic." (*Silvaco Data Systems v. Intel Corp.* (2010) 184 Cal.App.4th 210, 223 [109 Cal.Rptr.3d 27], internal citations omitted.)

Secondary Sources

3 Levy et al., California Torts, Ch. 40, Fraud and Deceit and Other Business Torts, § 40.53[1][a] (Matthew Bender)

49 California Forms of Pleading and Practice, Ch. 565, Unfair Competition, § 565.103[4][c] (Matthew Bender)

Edelson & Kay, eds., Trade Secret Litigation and Protection in California (State Bar of California 2009) Chs. 2, 6, 12

Comments.

The Directions for Use advise,

"Because generally the jury should only be instructed on matters relevant to damage claims, this instruction should not be given unless there is evidence that the acquisition resulted in damages, other than damages from related disclosure or use."

This instruction may be sought, among other situations, where a plaintiff seeks to impute liability to an employer who "knew or had reason to know" that its employee or agent had acquired the alleged trade secret by improper means. This instruction also may be sought where a plaintiff seeks to hold liable an individual corporate officer or director who knew or had reason to know of the misappropriation by improper acquisition by an employee. *See PMC, Inc v. Kadisha*, 78 Cal.App.4th 1368, 1383 (2000); *see also* Chapter 2 for a discussion of imputed, vicarious, or joint liability for misappropriation.

Constructive knowledge is addressed by Civil Code section 19:

"Every person who has actual notice of circumstances sufficient to put a prudent man upon inquiry as to a particular fact, has constructive notice of the fact itself in all cases in which, by prosecuting such inquiry, he/she/it might have learned such a fact."

If this instruction is the first instance in which "improper means" is addressed, consider (if appropriate) proposing that CACI No. 4405 and CACI No. 4408 be presented together.

See also Chapter 2 for a discussion of misappropriation by acquisition and, in turn, ideas for proposing special instructions (if appropriate under the particular circumstances of the litigation).

CACI 4406

Judicial Council of California Civil Jury Instructions (CACI) >
Series 4400 TRADE SECRETS

4406 Misappropriation by Disclosure

[*Name of defendant*] **misappropriated** [*name of plaintiff*]**'s trade secret[s] by disclosure if** [*name of defendant*]

- disclosed [it/them] without [*name of plaintiff*]'s consent; and
- [did any of the following:]

  [insert one or more of the following:]

  [acquired knowledge of the trade secret[s] by improper means][./; or]

  [at the time of disclosure, knew or had reason to know that [his/her/nonbinary pronoun**/its] knowledge of** [name of plaintiff]**'s trade secret[s] came from or through** [name of third party]**, and that** [name of third party] **had previously acquired the trade secret[s] by improper means][./; or]**

  [at the time of disclosure, knew or had reason to know that [his/her/nonbinary pronoun**/its] knowledge of** [name of plaintiff]**'s trade secret[s] was acquired** [insert circumstances giving rise to duty to maintain secrecy]**, which created a duty to keep the** [select short term to describe, e.g., information] **secret][./; or]**

  [at the time of disclosure, knew or had reason to know that [his/her/nonbinary pronoun**/its] knowledge of** [name of plaintiff]**'s trade secret[s] came from or through** [name of third party]**, and that** [name of third party] **had a duty to** [name of plaintiff] **to keep the** [e.g., information] **secret][./; or]**

  [before a material change of [his/her/nonbinary pronoun**/its] position, knew or had reason to know that [it was/they were] [a] trade secret[s] and that knowledge of [it/them] had been acquired by accident or mistake.]**

New December 2007; Revised December 2010

Directions for Use

Read this instruction with CACI No. 4401, *Misappropriation of Trade Secrets—Essential Factual Elements,* if the plaintiff claims that the defendant's disclosure of the information alleged to be a trade secret is a misappropriation.

If consent is at issue, CACI No. 1302, *Consent Explained,* and CACI No. 1303, *Invalid Consent,* may also be given.

In element 2, select the applicable statutory act(s) alleged to constitute misappropriation by disclosure. (See Civ. Code, § 3624.1(b)(2).) If only one act is selected, omit the words "did any of the following."

If either of the first two acts constituting misappropriation by disclosure is alleged, give also CACI No. 4408, *Improper Means of Acquiring Trade Secret.*

Sources and Authority

- "Misappropriation" Defined. Civil Code section 3426.1(b)(2).
- Constructive Notice. Civil Code section 19.
- "The fact that [defendant]'s postings were not of the 'entire secret,' and included only portions of courses, does not mean that [defendant]'s disclosures are not misappropriations. While previous partial disclosures arguably made public only those parts disclosed, [defendant]'s partial disclosures of non-public portions of the secrets may themselves be actionable because they constitute 'disclosure … without … consent by a person who … knew or had reason to know that his … knowledge of the trade secret was … [either] derived from or through a person who had utilized improper means to acquire it [or] acquired under circumstances giving rise to a duty to maintain its secrecy or limit its use.' " (*Religious Tech. Ctr. v. Netcom On-Line Commun. Servs.* (N.D. Cal. 1995) 923 F.Supp. 1231, 1257, fn. 31.)
- "Under the UTSA, simple disclosure or use may suffice to create liability. It is no longer necessary, if it ever was, to prove that the purpose to which the acquired information is put is outweighed by the interests of the trade secret holder or that use of a trade secret cannot be prohibited if it is infeasible to do so." (*Morlife, Inc. v. Perry* (1997) 56 Cal.App.4th 1514, 1527 [66 Cal.Rptr.2d 731].)
- "[N]othing in the UTSA requires that the defendant gain any advantage from the disclosure; it is sufficient to show 'use' by disclosure of a trade secret with actual or constructive knowledge that the secret was acquired under circumstances giving rise to a duty to maintain its secrecy." (*Religious Tech. Ctr., supra*, 923 F.Supp. at p. 1257, fn. 31.)

- "Liability under CUTSA is not dependent on the defendant's 'comprehension' of the trade secret but does require 'knowledge' of it." (*Silvaco Data Systems v. Intel Corp.* (2010) 184 Cal.App.4th 210, 229 [109 Cal.Rptr.3d 27].)

- " 'Knowledge,' of course, is '[t]he fact or condition of knowing,' … and in this context, '[t]he fact of knowing a thing, state, etc. …' (8 Oxford English Dict., supra, p. 517.) To 'know' a thing is to have information of that thing at one's command, in one's possession, subject to study, disclosure, and exploitation. To say that one 'knows' a fact is also to say that one possesses information of that fact. Thus, although the Restatement Third of Unfair Competition does not identify knowledge of the trade secret as an element of a trade secrets cause of action, the accompanying comments make it clear that liability presupposes the defendant's 'possession' of misappropriated information." (*Silvaco, supra*, 184 Cal.App.4th at pp. 225–226, original italics.)

- "The record contains no evidence that [defendant] ever possessed or had knowledge of any source code connected with either [software product]. So far as the record shows, [defendant] never had access to that code, could not disclose any part of it to anyone else, and had no way of using it to write or improve code of its own. [Defendant] appears to have been in substantially the same position as the customer in the pie shop who is accused of stealing the secret recipe because he bought a pie with knowledge that a rival baker had accused the seller of using the rival's stolen recipe. The customer does not, by buying or eating the pie, gain knowledge of the recipe used to make it." (*Silvaco, supra*, 184 Cal.App.4th at p. 226.)

- "When a competitor hires a former employee of plaintiff who is likely to disclose trade secrets, '[i]t is a question of fact whether the competitor had constructive notice of the plaintiff's right in the secret.' " (*Ralph Andrews Productions, Inc. v. Paramount Pictures Corp.* (1990) 222 Cal.App.3d 676, 682–683 [271 Cal.Rptr. 797], internal citation omitted.)

Secondary Sources

3 Levy et al., California Torts, Ch. 40, Fraud and Deceit and Other Business Torts, § 40.53[1][b] (Matthew Bender)

49 California Forms of Pleading and Practice, Ch. 565, Unfair Competition, § 565.103[4][c] (Matthew Bender)

Edelson & Kay, eds., Trade Secret Litigation and Protection in California (State Bar of California 2009) Chs. 2, 6, 12

Gaab & Reese, California Practice Guide: Civil Procedure Before Trial—Claims & Defenses, Ch. 10(II)-A ¶ 10:250 (The Rutter Group)

Comments. The consent element under Civil Code § 3426.1(b)(2) is express or implied consent. If consent is at issue, consider proposing that CACI No. 1302, *Consent Explained*, and CACI No. 1303, *Invalid Consent*, be given.

See also Comments on CACI No. 4407 as well as Chapter 2 for a discussion of imputed, vicarious, or joint liability for misappropriation as well as of misappropriation by disclosure and, in turn, ideas for proposing special instructions (if appropriate under the particular circumstances of the litigation).

Consistent with the purpose of the CACI instructions, practitioners should consider proposing (if appropriate) a more simplified instruction. For example:

"A misappropriation by use can make liable not only the defendant if [he/she/it] improperly obtained and then disclosed the alleged trade secret, but also other defendants if, at the time they disclosed the trade secret, they knew or should have known that the alleged trade secret had been wrongfully obtained."

If this instruction is the first instance in which "improper means" is addressed, consider (if appropriate) proposing that CACI No. 4405 and CACI No. 4408 be presented together.

CACI 4407

Judicial Council of California Civil Jury Instructions (CACI) >
Series 4400 TRADE SECRETS

4407 Misappropriation by Use

[*Name of defendant*] **misappropriated** [*name of plaintiff*]**'s trade secret[s] by use if** [*name of defendant*]

- used [*it/them*] without [*name of plaintiff*]'s consent; and
- **[did any of the following**:]

  [insert one or more of the following:]

  [acquired knowledge of the trade secret[s] by improper means][./; or]

  [at the time of use, knew or had reason to know that [his/her/nonbinary pronoun**/its] knowledge of** [name of plaintiff]**'s trade secret[s] came from or through** [name of third party]**, and that** [name of third party] **had previously acquired the trade secret[s] by improper means][./; or]**

  [at the time of use, knew or had reason to know that [his/her/nonbinary pronoun**/its] knowledge of** [name of plaintiff]**'s trade secret[s] was acquired under circumstances creating a legal obligation to limit use of the** [select short term to describe, e.g., information]**][./; or]**

  [at the time of use, knew or had reason to know that [his/her/nonbinary pronoun**/its] knowledge of** [name of plaintiff]**'s trade secret[s] came from or through** [name of third party]**, and that** [name of third party] **had a duty to** [name of plaintiff] **to limit use of the** [e.g., information]**][./; or]**

  [before a material change of [his/her/nonbinary pronoun**/its] position, knew or had reason to know that [it was/they were] [a] trade secret[s] and that knowledge of [it/them] had been acquired by accident or mistake.]**

New December 2007; Revised December 2010

Directions for Use

Read this instruction with CACI No. 4401, *Misappropriation of Trade Secrets—Essential Factual Elements,* if the plaintiff claims that the defendant's use of the information alleged to be a trade secret is a misappropriation.

If consent is at issue, CACI No. 1302, *Consent Explained,* and CACI No. 1303, *Invalid Consent,* may also be given.

In element 2, select the applicable statutory act(s) alleged to constitute misappropriation by use. (See Civ. Code, § 3624.1(b)(2).) If only one act is selected, omit the words "did any of the following."

If either of the first two acts constituting misappropriation by disclosure is alleged, give also CACI No. 4408, *Improper Means of Acquiring Trade Secret.*

Sources and Authority

- "Misappropriation" Defined. Civil Code section 3426.1(b)(2).
- Constructive Notice. Civil Code section 19.
- "Under the plain terms of the Uniform Trade Secrets Act, defendants may be personally liable if: they used, through the corporation, [plaintiff]'s trade secrets; at the time of the use of the confidential information they knew or had reason to know that knowledge of the trade secrets was derived from or through a person who had improperly acquired the knowledge, or the secrets were obtained by a person who owed a duty to plaintiffs to maintain the secrecy. Employing the confidential information in manufacturing, production, research or development, marketing goods that embody the trade secret, or soliciting customers through the use of trade secret information, all constitute use. Use of a trade secret without knowledge it was acquired by improper means does not subject a person to liability unless the person receives notice that its use of the information is wrongful." (*PMC, Inc. v. Kadisha* (2000) 78 Cal.App.4th 1368, 1383 [93 Cal.Rptr.2d 663], internal citations omitted.)
- "Under the UTSA, simple disclosure or use may suffice to create liability. It is no longer necessary, if it ever was, to prove that the purpose to which the acquired information is put is outweighed by the interests of the trade secret holder or that use of a trade secret cannot be prohibited if it is infeasible to do so." (*Morlife, Inc. v. Perry* (1997) 56 Cal.App.4th 1514, 1527 [66 Cal.Rptr.2d 731].)
- "One clearly engages in the 'use' of a secret, in the ordinary sense, when one directly exploits it for his own advantage, e.g., by incorporating it into his own manufacturing technique or product. But 'use' in the ordinary sense is not present when the conduct consists entirely of possessing, and taking advantage of, something that was made using the secret. One who bakes a pie from a recipe certainly engages in the 'use' of the latter; but one who eats the pie does not, by virtue of that act alone, make 'use' of the recipe

in any ordinary sense, and this is true even if the baker is accused of stealing the recipe from a competitor, and the diner knows of that accusation. Yet this is substantially the same situation as when one runs software that was compiled from allegedly stolen source code. The source code is the recipe from which the pie (executable program) is baked (compiled). Nor is the analogy weakened by the fact that a diner is not ordinarily said to make 'use' of something he eats. His metabolism may be said to do so, or the analogy may be adjusted to replace the pie with an instrument, such as a stopwatch. A coach who employs the latter to time a race certainly makes 'use' of it, but only a sophist could bring himself to say that coach 'uses' trade secrets involved in the manufacture of the watch." (*Silvaco Data Systems v. Intel Corp.* (2010) 184 Cal.App.4th 210, 224 [109 Cal.Rptr.3d 27].)

- "Liability under CUTSA is not dependent on the defendant's 'comprehension' of the trade secret but does require 'knowledge' of it. So far as the record shows, [defendant] did not know and had no way to get the information constituting the trade secret. It therefore could not, within the contemplation of the act, 'use' that information." (*Silvaco Data Systems, supra*, 184 Cal.App.4th at p. 229.)

- " 'Knowledge,' of course, is '[t]he fact or condition of knowing,' … and in this context, '[t]he fact of knowing a thing, state, etc. …' (8 Oxford English Dict., supra, p. 517.) To 'know' a thing is to have information of that thing at one's command, in one's possession, subject to study, disclosure, and exploitation. To say that one 'knows' a fact is also to say that one possesses information of that fact. Thus, although the Restatement Third of Unfair Competition does not identify knowledge of the trade secret as an element of a trade secrets cause of action, the accompanying comments make it clear that liability presupposes the defendant's 'possession' of misappropriated information." (*Silvaco Data Systems, supra*, 184 Cal.App.4th at pp. 225–226, original italics.)

- "When a competitor hires a former employee of plaintiff who is likely to disclose trade secrets, '[i]t is a question of fact whether the competitor had constructive notice of the plaintiff's right in the secret.' " (*Ralph Andrews Productions, Inc. v. Paramount Pictures Corp.* (1990) 222 Cal.App.3d 676, 682–683 [271 Cal.Rptr. 797], internal citation omitted.)

- "Our Supreme Court has previously distinguished solicitation—which is actionable—from announcing a job change—which is not: 'Merely informing customers of one's former employer of a change of employment, without more, is not solicitation. Neither does the willingness to discuss business upon invitation of another party constitute solicitation on the part of the invitee. Equity will not enjoin a former employee from receiving business from the customers of his former employer, even though the circumstances be such that he should be prohibited from soliciting such business.' " (*Hilb v. Robb* (1995) 33 Cal.App.4th 1812, 1821 [39 Cal.Rptr. 2d 887], internal citation omitted; but see Morlife, Inc., supra, 56 Cal.App.4th at p. 1527, fn. 8 ["we need not decide whether the 'professional announcement' exception … has continued vitality in light of the expansive definition of misappropriation under the UTSA"].)

- "[T]o prove misappropriation of a trade secret under the UTSA, a plaintiff must establish (among other things) that the defendant improperly 'used' the plaintiff's trade secret. Thus, under Evidence Code sections 500 and 520, the plaintiff bears the burden of proof on that issue, both at the outset and during trial." (*Sargent Fletcher, Inc. v. Able Corp.* (2003) 110 Cal.App.4th 1658, 1668 [3 Cal.Rptr.3d 279], internal citation omitted.)

- "[I]nformation relative to customers (e.g., their identities, locations, and individual preferences), obtained by a former employee in his contacts with them during his employment, may amount to 'trade secrets' which will warrant his being enjoined from exploitation or disclosure after leaving the employment. [¶] It is equally clear, however, that the proscriptions inhibiting the ex-employee reach only his use of such information, not to his mere possession or knowledge of it." (*Golden State Linen Service, Inc. v. Vidalin* (1977) 69 Cal.App.3d 1, 7–8 [137 Cal.Rptr. 807], internal citations omitted.)

- "Since these 'Marks' likely encompass any trade secrets, it is reasonable to conclude that one party's use of the trade secrets that affects the other party's rights in the mark would constitute the misappropriation of the trade secrets 'of another.' " (*Morton v. Rank Am., Inc.* (C.D. Cal. 1993) 812 F.Supp. 1062, 1074 [one can misappropriate trade secret jointly owned with another].)

Secondary Sources

3 Levy et al., California Torts, Ch. 40, Fraud and Deceit and Other Business Torts, § 40.53[1][b] (Matthew Bender)

49 California Forms of Pleading and Practice, Ch. 565, Unfair Competition, § 565.103[4][c] (Matthew Bender)

Edelson & Kay, eds., Trade Secret Litigation and Protection in California (State Bar of California 2009) Chs. 2, 6, 12

Gaab & Reese, California Practice Guide: Civil Procedure Before Trial—Claims & Defenses, Ch. 10(II)-A ¶ 10:250 (The Rutter Group)

Comments.

Civil Code § 3426.1(b)(2)(A) imposes liability upon the person who acquired the trade secret by improper means and then used the alleged trade secret. In contrast, Civil Code § 3426.1(b)(2)(B) imposes liability upon those persons who used or disclosed the trade secret and "knew or should have known" that their knowledge of the disclosed trade secret was the product of wrongdoing. If appropriate, consider proposing to the judge that CACI No. 4407 be tailored to clarified to make this distinction (rather than inviting a finding of a misappropriation by disclosure based on "any of the following."). Similarly, if appropriate, consider proposing to the judge that CACI No. 4407 (as well as other instructions) be tailored to delete circumstances which are not claimed to have occurred or be supported by evidence).

Consistent with the purpose of the CACI instructions, practitioners should consider proposing (if appropriate) a more simplified instruction. For example:

"A misappropriation by use can make liable not only the defendant if [he/she/it] improperly obtained and then used the alleged trade secret, but also other defendants if, at the time they used the trade secret, they knew or should have known that the alleged trade secret had been wrongfully obtained."

Practically speaking, most misappropriation claims involve the acquisition by improper means (i.e., breach of a duty to maintain confidentiality) followed by use or disclosure. Further, if a defendant acquires the alleged trade secret by improper means, and consequently avoids incurring the expense of extensive research and development, the acquisition by improper means may result in the defendant being unjustly enriched and/or the plaintiff's damages.

For constructive knowledge, Civil Code section 19 provides: "Every person who has actual notice of circumstances sufficient to put a prudent man upon inquiry as to a particular fact, has constructive notice of the fact itself in all cases in which, by prosecuting such inquiry, he/she/it might have learned such a fact."

Also, the consent element under Civil Code § 3426.1(b)(2) is express or implied consent. If consent is at issue, CACI No. 1302, Consent Explained, and CACI No. 1303, Invalid Consent, should also be given.

See also Chapter 2 for a discussion of imputed, vicarious, or joint liability for misappropriation as well as of misappropriation by use and, in turn, ideas for proposing special instructions (if appropriate under the particular circumstances of the litigation).

If this instruction is the first instance in which "improper means" is addressed, consider (if appropriate) proposing that CACI No. 4405 and CACI No. 4408 be presented together.

CACI 4408

Judicial Council of California Civil Jury Instructions (CACI) >
Series 4400 TRADE SECRETS

4408 Improper Means of Acquiring Trade Secret

Improper means of acquiring a trade secret or knowledge of a trade secret include, but are not limited to, [theft/bribery/misrepresentation/breach or inducing a breach of a duty to maintain secrecy/ [or] wiretapping, electronic eavesdropping, [or] [*insert other means of espionage*]].

[However, it is not improper to acquire a trade secret or knowledge of the trade secret by [any of the following]:

1. **Independent efforts to invent or discover the information;]**
2. **Reverse engineering; that is, examining or testing a product to determine how it works, by a person who has a right to possess the product;]**
3. **Obtaining the information as a result of a license agreement with the owner of the information;]**
4. **Observing the information in public use or on public display;] [or]**
5. **Obtaining the information from published literature, such as trade journals, reference books, the Internet, or other publicly available sources.]]**

New December 2007

Directions for Use

In the first paragraph, include only those statutory examples of "improper means" supported by the evidence. (See Civ. Code, § 3426.1(a).) The option for "wiretapping, eavesdropping, [or] [insert other means of espionage]" expresses the statutory term "espionage."

Include the optional last paragraph if any of those methods of obtaining the information are supported by the evidence. Omit any methods that are not at issue. If only one is at issue, omit "any of the following."

Sources and Authority

- "Improper Means" Defined. Civil Code section 3426.1(a).
- Electronic Eavesdropping. Penal Code section 630.
- "*The Restatement of Torts, Section 757, Comment* (f), notes: 'A complete catalogue of improper means is not possible,' but Section 1(1) includes a partial listing. Proper means include: 1. Discovery by independent invention; 2. Discovery by "reverse engineering," that is, by starting with the known product and working backward to find the method by which it was developed. The acquisition of the known product must of course, also be by a fair and honest means, such as purchase of the item on the open market for reverse engineering to be lawful; 3. Discovery under a license from the owner of the trade secret; 4. Observation of the item in public use or on public display; 5. Obtaining the trade secret from published literature. … [T]he assertion that a matter is readily ascertainable by proper means remains available as a defense to a claim of misappropriation. Information is readily ascertainable if it is available in trade journals, reference books, or published materials." (Civ. Code, § 3426.1, Legis. Comm. Comment (Senate), 1984 Addition.)

Secondary Sources

13 Witkin, Summary of California Law (11th ed. 2017) Equity, § 83

Gaab & Reese, California Practice Guide: Civil Procedure Before Trial—Claims & Defenses, Ch. 10(II)-A ¶ 10:250 (The Rutter Group)

3 Levy et al., California Torts, Ch. 40, Fraud and Deceit and Other Business Torts, § 40.53[1][b] (Matthew Bender)

49 California Forms of Pleading and Practice, Ch. 565, Unfair Competition, § 565.103[4][b] (Matthew Bender)

Edelson & Kay, eds., Trade Secret Litigation and Protection in California (State Bar of California 2009) § 2.01(D)

Comments.

The definition of "improper means" found in Civil Code § 3426.1(a) includes "theft, bribery, misrepresentation, breach or inducement of a breach of a duty to maintain secrecy, or espionage through electronic or other means." Section 3426.1(a) further provides "Reverse engineering or independent derivation *alone* shall not be considered improper means." (Emphasis added.)

The phrase "alone" in Section 3426.1(a) may be significant. If the defendant engages in a misappropriation by stealing the information or breaches a confidentiality agreement and also attempts to reverse engineer or derive independently the alleged trade secret, there still may exist the potential for the acquisition by "improper means." *See* Chapter 2 for a discussion of reverse engineering.

CACI No. 4408 contains several provisions which are not found in Civil Code § 3426.1(a). For example, "[3. Obtaining the information as a result of a license agreement with the owner of the information;] [4. Observing the information in public use or on public display;] [or] [5. Obtaining the information from published literature, such as trade journals, reference books, the Internet, or other publicly available sources.]]." (Civ. Code, § 3426.1, Legis. Comm. Comment (Senate), 1984 Addition.)

In addition, that matter is readily ascertainable by proper means is a potential defense to a claim of misappropriation. (Civ. Code, § 3426.1, Legis. Comm. Comment (Senate), 1984 Addition.)

For a discussion on the scope of the "defense to a claim of misappropriation," please review *Comments* to CACI No. 4420.

Consistent with CACI No. 4408, the federal Defend Trade Secrets Act specifically excludes from the definition of "acquisition by improper means" the following: "reverse engineering, independent derivation, or any other lawful means of acquisition." (18 U.S.C. § 1839(6)(b).)

CACI 4409

Judicial Council of California Civil Jury Instructions (CACI) > Series 4400 TRADE SECRETS

4409 Remedies for Misappropriation of Trade Secret

If [*name of plaintiff*] proves that [*name of defendant*] misappropriated [his/her/*nonbinary pronoun*/its] trade secret[s], then [*name of plaintiff*] is entitled to recover damages if the misappropriation caused [[*name of plaintiff*] to suffer an actual loss/ [or] [*name of defendant*] to be unjustly enriched].

[If [*name of defendant*]'s misappropriation did not cause [[*name of plaintiff*] to suffer an actual loss/ [or] [*name of defendant*] to be unjustly enriched], [*name of plaintiff*] may still be entitled to a reasonable royalty for no longer than the period of time the use could have been prohibited. However, I will calculate the amount of any royalty.]

New December 2007

Directions for Use

Give this instruction with CACI No. 4401, *Misappropriation of Trade Secrets—Essential Factual Elements*, in all cases.

Select the nature of the recovery sought; either for the plaintiff's actual loss or for the defendant's unjust enrichment, or both. If the plaintiff's claim of actual injury or loss is based on lost profits, give CACI No. 3903N, *Lost Profits (Economic Damage)*. If unjust enrichment is alleged, give CACI No. 4410, *Unjust Enrichment*.

If neither actual loss nor unjust enrichment is provable, Civil Code section 3426.3(b) provides for a third, alternate remedy: a reasonable royalty for no longer than the period of time the use could have been prohibited. Both the statute and case law indicate that the question of a reasonable royalty should not be presented to the jury. (See Civ. Code, § 3426.3(b) [*the court may order the payment of a reasonable royalty*]; *Unilogic, Inc. v. Burroughs Corp.* (1992) 10 Cal.App.4th 612, 628 [12 Cal.Rptr.2d 741]; *See also* Civ. Code, § 3426.2(b) [court may issue an injunction that conditions future of a trade secret on payment of a reasonable royalty].) However, no reported California state court case has directly held that "reasonable royalty" issues should not be presented to the jury. (But see *Unilogic, Inc., supra*, 10 Cal.App.4th at p. 627.) Include the optional second paragraph if the court wants to advise the jury that even if it finds that the plaintiff suffered no actual loss and that the defendant was not unjustly enriched, the plaintiff may still be entitled to some recovery.

For simplicity, this instruction uses the term "damages" to refer to both actual loss and unjust enrichment, even though, strictly speaking, unjust enrichment may be considered a form of restitution rather than damages.

Sources and Authority

- Remedies for Misappropriation of Trade Secret. Civil Code section 3426.3.

- "Under subdivision (a), a complainant may recover damages for the actual loss caused by misappropriation, as well as for any unjust enrichment not taken into account in computing actual loss damages. Subdivision (b) provides for an alternative remedy of the payment of royalties from future profits where 'neither damages nor unjust enrichment caused by misappropriation [is] provable.' " (*Ajaxo Inc. v. E*Trade Group Inc. (2005) 135 Cal.App.4th 21, 61 [37 Cal.Rptr.3d 221].*)

- "[B]ased on the plain language of the statute, the Court—not the jury—determines if and in what amount a royalty should be awarded. See Cal. Civ. Code section 3416.3(b) ('the Court may order payment of a reasonable royalty')." (*FAS Techs. v. Dainippon Screen Mfg.* (N.D. Cal. 2001) 2001 U.S. Dist. LEXIS 15444, **9–10.)

- "To adopt a reasonable royalty as the measure of damages is to adopt and interpret, as well as may be, the fiction that a license was to be granted at the time of beginning the infringement, and then to determine what the license price should have been. In effect, the court assumes the existence *ab initio* of, and declares the *equitable* terms of, a supposititious license, and does this *nunc pro tunc*; it creates and applies retrospectively a compulsory license." (*Altavion, Inc. v. Konica Minolta Systems Laboratory, Inc. (2014) 226 Cal.App.4th 26, 68 [171 Cal.Rptr.3d 714]*, original italics.)

- "Nor was it necessary to submit the liability issue to the jury in order to allow the trial court thereafter to determine a reasonable royalty or to impose an injunction. Just as [cross complainant] presented no evidence of the degree of [cross defendant]'s enrichment, [cross complainant] likewise presented no evidence that would allow the court to determine what royalty, if any, would be reasonable under the circumstances." (*Unilogic, Inc. supra, 10 Cal.App.4th at p. 628.*)

- "It is settled that, in fashioning a pecuniary remedy under the CUTSA for past use of a misappropriated trade secret, the trial court may order a reasonable royalty only where 'neither actual damages to the holder of the trade secret nor unjust enrichment to the user is provable.' 'California law differs on this point from both the [Uniform Act] and Federal patent law, neither of which require[s] actual damages and unjust enrichment to be unprovable before a reasonable royalty may be imposed.' " (*Ajaxo Inc. v. E*Trade Financial Corp. (2010) 187 Cal.App.4th 1295, 1308 [115 Cal.Rptr.3d 168]*, internal citations omitted.)

- "[W]here a defendant has not realized a profit or other calculable benefit as a result of his or her misappropriation of a trade secret, unjust enrichment is not provable within the meaning of section 3426.3, subdivision (b), whether the lack of benefit is determined as a matter of law or as a matter of fact. To hold otherwise would place the risk of loss on the wronged plaintiff, thereby discouraging innovation and potentially encouraging corporate thievery where anticipated profits might be minimal but other valuable but nonmeasurable benefits could accrue." (*Ajaxo Inc., supra, 187 Cal.App.4th at p. 1313* [jury's finding that defendant did not profit from its misappropriation of trade secrets means that unjust enrichment is not "provable" within the meaning of section 3426.3(b)].)

Secondary Sources

13 Witkin, Summary of California Law (11th ed. 2017) Equity, §§ 92–93

Gaab & Reese, California Practice Guide: Civil Procedure Before Trial—Claims & Defenses, Ch. 10(II)-E ¶¶ 10:370–10:372 (The Rutter Group)

1 Milgrim on Trade Secrets, Ch. 15, Trial Considerations, § 15.02 (Matthew Bender)

3 Levy et al., California Torts, Ch. 40, Fraud and Deceit and Other Business Torts, § 40.54 (Matthew Bender)

49 California Forms of Pleading and Practice, Ch. 565, Unfair Competition, § 565.103[6], [7] (Matthew Bender)

Edelson & Kay, eds., Trade Secret Litigation and Protection in California (State Bar of California 2009) Ch. 11

Comments.

Section 3426.3(b) of the California Civil Code actually states:

(b) If neither damages nor unjust enrichment caused by misappropriation are *provable*, the court may order payment of a reasonable royalty for no longer than the period of time the use could have been prohibited.

Emphasis added. Thus, if appropriate and important, practitioner may wish to ask the court to modify the instruction given accordingly. Further, if appropriate, practitioners may consider asking the court not to give at all the portion of the instruction concerning a royalty (e.g., if the practitioner is concerned that including the instruction would make the jury more likely not to award damages for unjust enrichment).

Also, if expert testimony is going to be offered in connection with damages issues or unjust enrichment issues, practitioners should also consider seeking the issuance of CACI Nos. 219, 220, and 221.

See also Chapter 13 for a discussion of monetary remedies.

CACI 4410

Judicial Council of California Civil Jury Instructions (CACI) > Series 4400 TRADE SECRETS

4410 Unjust Enrichment

[*Name of defendant*] was unjustly enriched if [his/her/*nonbinary pronoun*/its] misappropriation of [*name of plaintiff*]'s trade secret[s] caused [*name of defendant*] to receive a benefit that [he/she/*nonbinary pronoun*/it] otherwise would not have achieved.

To decide the amount of any unjust enrichment, first determine the value of [*name of defendant*]'s benefit that would not have been achieved except for [his/her/*nonbinary pronoun*/its] misappropriation. Then subtract from that amount [*name of defendant*]'s reasonable expenses[, including the value of the [*specify categories of expenses in evidence, such as labor, materials, rents, interest on invested capital*]]. [In calculating the amount of any unjust enrichment, do not take into account any amount that you included in determining any amount of damages for [*name of plaintiff*]'s actual loss.]

New December 2007

Directions for Use

Give this instruction with CACI No. 4409, *Remedies for Misappropriation of Trade Secrets*, if unjust enrichment is alleged and supported by the evidence. If it would be helpful to the jury, specify the categories of expenses to be allowed to the defendant. Include the last sentence if both actual loss and unjust enrichment are alleged.

Sources and Authority

- Remedies for Misappropriation of Trade Secret. Civil Code section 3426.3.
- "In general, '[a] person who has been unjustly enriched at the expense of another is required to make restitution to the other.' (*Rest., Restitution, § 1.*) 'Ordinarily the benefit to the one and the loss to the other are co-extensive, and the result … is to compel the one to surrender the benefit which he has received and thereby to make restitution to the other for the loss which he has suffered.' [¶] 'In other situations, a benefit has been received by the defendant but the plaintiff has not suffered a corresponding loss or, in some cases, any loss, but nevertheless the enrichment of the defendant would be unjust. In such cases, the defendant may be under a duty to give to

the plaintiff the amount by which he has been enriched.' " (*Unilogic, Inc. v. Burroughs Corp. (1992) 10 Cal.App.4th 612, 627–628 [12 Cal.Rptr.2d 741]*.)

- "A defendant's unjust enrichment is typically measured by the defendant's profits flowing from the misappropriation. A defendant's profits often represent profits the plaintiff would otherwise have earned. Where the plaintiff's loss does not correlate directly with the misappropriator's benefit, … the problem becomes more complex. There is no standard formula to measure it. A defendant's unjust enrichment might be calculated based upon cost savings or increased productivity resulting from use of the secret. Increased market share is another way to measure the benefit to the defendant. Recovery is not prohibited just because the benefit cannot be precisely measured. But like any other pecuniary remedy, there must be some reasonable basis for the computation." (*Ajaxo Inc. v. E*Trade Financial Corp. (2010) 187 Cal.App.4th 1295, 1305 [115 Cal.Rptr.3d 168]*, footnote and internal citations omitted.)

- "[W]here a defendant has not realized a profit or other calculable benefit as a result of his or her misappropriation of a trade secret, unjust enrichment is not provable within the meaning of section 3426.3, subdivision (b), whether the lack of benefit is determined as a matter of law or as a matter of fact." (*Altavion, Inc. v. Konica Minolta Systems Laboratory, Inc. (2014) 226 Cal.App.4th 26, 66 [171 Cal.Rptr.3d 714]*.)

- "Another crucial point is that unjust enrichment, as the phrase is used here, is, in effect, synonymous with restitution. ' " 'The phrase "unjust enrichment" is used in law to characterize the result or effect of a failure to make restitution of or for property or benefits received under such circumstances as to give rise to a legal or equitable obligation to account therefor.' " ' " (*Ajaxo Inc., supra, 187 Cal.App.4th at p. 1305*, internal citations omitted.)

- *Restatement of Restitution, section 1, comment a*, states: "A person is enriched if he has received a benefit (see Comment b). A person is unjustly enriched if the retention of the benefit would be unjust (see Comment c)."

- *Restatement of Restitution, section 1, comment b*, states: "*What constitutes a benefit*. A person confers a benefit upon another if he gives to the other possession of or some other interest in money, land, chattels, or choses in action, performs services beneficial to or at the request of the other, satisfies a debt or a duty of the other, or in any way adds to the other's security or advantage. He confers a benefit not only where he adds to the property of another, but also where he saves the other from expense or loss. The word 'benefit,' therefore, denotes any form of advantage. The advantage for which a person ordinarily must pay is pecuniary advantage; it is not, however, necessarily so limited, as where a physician attends an insensible person who is saved subsequent pain or who receives thereby a greater chance of living."

- *Restatement of Restitution, section 1, comment c*, states: "*Unjust retention of benefit*. Even where a person has received a benefit from another, he is liable to pay therefor only if the circumstances of its receipt or retention are such that, as between the two persons, it is unjust for him to retain it. The mere fact that a person benefits another is not of itself sufficient to require the other to make restitution therefor. Thus, one who improves his own land ordinarily benefits his neighbors to some extent, and one who makes a gift or voluntarily pays money which he knows he does not owe confers a benefit; in neither case is he entitled to restitution. The Restatement of this Subject states the rules by which it is determined whether or not it is considered to be just to require restitution."

Secondary Sources

13 Witkin, Summary of California Law (11th ed. 2017) Equity, § 93

1 Milgrim on Trade Secrets, Ch. 13, Issues Prior to Commencement of Action, § 13.03[2][a] (Matthew Bender)

3 Levy et al., California Torts, Ch. 40, Fraud and Deceit and Other Business Torts, § 40.54[4] (Matthew Bender)

49 California Forms of Pleading and Practice, Ch. 565, Unfair Competition, § 565.103[7][b] (Matthew Bender)

Edelson & Kay, eds., Trade Secret Litigation and Protection in California (State Bar of California 2009) § 11.03

Comments.

If expert testimony is going to be offered in connection with the unjust enrichment issue, practitioners should also consider seeking the issuance of CACI Nos. 219, 220, and 221.

See also Chapter 13 for a discussion of monetary remedies.

CACI 4411

Judicial Council of California Civil Jury Instructions (CACI) > Series 4400 TRADE SECRETS

4411 Punitive Damages for Willful and Malicious Misappropriation

---

If you decide that [*name of defendant*]'s misappropriation caused [*name of plaintiff*] harm, you must decide whether that conduct justifies an award of punitive damages. The purposes of punitive damages are to punish a wrongdoer for the conduct that harmed [*name of plaintiff*] and to discourage similar conduct in the future.

In order to recover punitive damages, [*name of plaintiff*] must prove [by clear and convincing evidence] that [*name of defendant*] acted willfully and maliciously. You must determine whether [*name of defendant*] acted willfully and maliciously, but you will not be asked to determine the amount of any punitive damages. I will calculate the amount later.

"Willfully" means that [*name of defendant*] acted with a purpose or willingness to commit the act or engage in the conduct in question, and the conduct was not reasonable under the circumstances at the time and was not undertaken in good faith.

"Maliciously" means that [*name of defendant*] acted with an intent to cause injury, or that [*name of defendant*]'s conduct was despicable and was done with a willful and knowing disregard for the rights of others. "Despicable conduct" is conduct so vile, base, or wretched that it would be looked down on and despised by ordinary decent people. [*Name of defendant*] acted with knowing disregard if [he/she/*nonbinary pronoun*/it] was aware of the probable consequences of [his/her/*nonbinary pronoun*/its] conduct and deliberately failed to avoid those consequences.

New December 2007

Directions for Use

Give this instruction if there is evidence that the defendant acted willfully and maliciously, so as to support an award of punitive damages. (See Civ. Code, § 3426.3(c).)

No reported California state court case has addressed whether the jury or the court should decide whether any misappropriation was "willful and malicious," and if so, whether the finding must be made by clear and convincing evidence rather than a preponderance of the evidence. In *Ajaxo Inc. v. E*Trade Group Inc. (2005) 135 Cal.App.4th 21, 66 [37 Cal.Rptr.3d 221]*, the court affirmed a jury's finding by clear and convincing evidence that the defendant's misappropriation was willful and malicious. If the court decides to require the "clear and convincing" standard, include the bracketed language in the first paragraph and also give CACI No. 201, *Highly Probable—Clear and Convincing Proof.*

Once the jury finds "willful and malicious" conduct, it appears that the court should decide the amount of punitive damages. (See *Robert L. Cloud & Assocs. v. Mikesell (1999) 69 Cal.App.4th 1141, 1151, fn. 8 [82 Cal.Rptr.2d 143].*). This would be consistent with the Uniform Trade Secrets Act, on which the California Uniform Trade Secrets Act is based. (See Uniform Trade Secrets Act § 3, 2005 com. ["This provision follows federal patent law in leaving discretionary trebling to the judge even though there may be a jury, compare 35 U.S.C. Section 284 (1976)"].)

Sources and Authority

- Exemplary Damages for Willful and Malicious Misappropriation. Civil Code section 3426.3(c).
- Attorney Fees and Costs. Civil Code section 3426.4.
- "The court instructed the jury that 'willful' means 'a purpose or willingness to commit the act or engage in the conduct in question, and the conduct was not reasonable under the circumstances then present and was not undertaken in good faith.' Further, the court instructed the jury that 'malice' means 'conduct which is intended by the defendant to cause injury to the plaintiff or despicable conduct which is carried on by the defendant with a willful and conscious disregard for the rights of others when the defendant is aware [of] the probable consequences of its conduct and willfully and deliberately fails to avoid those consequences. Despicable conduct is conduct which is so vile and wretched that it would be looked down upon and despised by ordinary decent people.' In addition, the court instructed the jury that a finding of willful and malicious misappropriation must be supported by clear and convincing evidence. [¶] Our Supreme Court has recognized that malice may be proven either expressly by direct evidence probative of the existence of hatred or ill will, or by implication from indirect evidence from which the jury may draw inferences." (*Ajaxo Inc., supra,* 135 Cal.App.4th at pp. 66–67, internal citations and footnote omitted.)
- "The limitation on punitive damages under the UTSA to twice the compensatory damages does not create an equivalency between an award of punitive damages under the UTSA and an award of treble damages under another statutory scheme. … While an award of treble damages is equally punitive in its effect, the computation of the penalty is strictly mechanical. In contrast, an award of punitive damages under the UTSA is subject to no fixed standard; the statute merely sets a cap on the amount of the award. The trial court retains wide discretion to set the amount anywhere between zero and two times the actual loss. (§ 3426.3, subd. (c).) Thus, evidence of the defendant's financial condition remains essential for evaluating whether the amount of punitive damages actually awarded is appropriate." (*Robert L. Cloud & Assocs. supra, 69 Cal.App.4th at p. 1151, fn. 8.*)

- "In order to justify [attorney] fees under Civil Code section 3426.4, the court must find that a 'willful and malicious misappropriation' occurred. That requirement is satisfied, in our view, by the jury's determination, upon clear and convincing evidence, that defendants' acts of misappropriation were done with malice. This finding was necessary to the award of punitive damages which was made by the jury." (*Vacco Industries, Inc. v. Van Den Berg (1992) 5 Cal.App.4th 34, 54* [*6 Cal.Rptr.2d 602]*.)

Secondary Sources

13 Witkin, Summary of California Law (11th ed. 2017) Equity, § 93

Gaab & Reese, California Practice Guide: Civil Procedure Before Trial—Claims & Defenses, Ch. 10(II)-E ¶¶ 10:385–10:388 (The Rutter Group)

1 Milgrim on Trade Secrets, Ch. 15, Trial Considerations, § 15.02[3][i] (Matthew Bender)

3 Levy et al., California Torts, Ch. 40, Fraud and Deceit and Other Business Torts, § 40.54[5] (Matthew Bender)

49 California Forms of Pleading and Practice, Ch. 565, Unfair Competition, § 565.103[7][c] (Matthew Bender)

Edelson & Kay, eds., Trade Secret Litigation and Protection in California (State Bar of California 2009) § 11.05

Comments.
See Chapter 13 for a discussion of monetary remedies.

CACI 4412

Judicial Council of California Civil Jury Instructions (CACI) > Series 4400 TRADE SECRETS

4412 "Independent Economic Value" Explained

[*Select short term to describe, e.g., Information*] **has independent economic value if it gives the owner an actual or potential business advantage over others who do not know the** [*e.g., information*] **and who could obtain economic value from its disclosure or use.**

In determining whether [*e.g., information*] **had actual or potential independent economic value because it was secret, you may consider the following:**

- **The extent to which** [*name of plaintiff*] **obtained or could obtain economic value from the** [*e.g., information*] **in keeping [it/them] secret;**
- **The extent to which others could obtain economic value from the** [*e.g., information*] **if [it were/they were] not secret;**
- **The amount of time, money, or labor that** [*name of plaintiff*] **expended in developing the** [*e.g., information*]**;**
- **The amount of time, money, or labor that [would be/was] saved by a competitor who used the** [*e.g., information*]**;**
- [*Insert other applicable factors*]**.]**

The presence or absence of any one or more of these factors is not necessarily determinative.

New April 2008

Directions for Use

Give this instruction to further explain element 2 of CACI No. 4402, *"Trade Secret" Defined.* Inapplicable factors may be omitted.

Sources and Authority

- "Trade Secret" Defined. Civil Code section 3426.1(d).

- "[I]t is not true that evidence of 'some' helpfulness or usefulness, if credited, would compel a finding of independent economic value. The Restatement defines trade secret as business or technical information 'that is sufficiently valuable and secret to afford an actual or potential economic advantage over others.' (Rest.3d, Unfair Competition, § 39.) The advantage 'need not be great,' but must be 'more than trivial.' (Rest.3d, Unfair Competition, § 39, com. e, p. 430.) Merely stating that information was helpful or useful to another person in carrying out a specific activity, or that information of that type may save someone time, does not compel a factfinder to conclude that the particular information at issue was 'sufficiently valuable … to afford an … economic advantage over others.' (Rest.3d, Unfair Competition, § 39.) The factfinder is entitled to expect evidence from which it can form some solid sense of *how* useful the information is, e.g., *how much* time, money, or labor it would save, or at least that these savings would be 'more than trivial.' (Rest.3d., Unfair Competition, § 39, com. e.)" (*Yield Dynamics, Inc. v. TEA Systems Corp. (2007) 154 Cal.App.4th 547, 564–565 [66 Cal.Rptr.3d 1]*, original italics.)

- "[T]he focus of the inquiry regarding the independent economic value element is 'on whether the information is generally known to or readily ascertainable by business competitors or others to whom the information would have some economic value. [Citations.] Information that is readily ascertainable by a business competitor derives no independent value from not being generally known. [Citation.]' " (*Altavion, Inc. v. Konica Minolta Systems Laboratory, Inc. (2014) 226 Cal.App.4th 26, 62 [171 Cal.Rptr.3d 714]*.)

- "Moreover, it seems inherent in the requirement of value, as codified, that it is relevant to ask to *whom* the information may be valuable. The statute does not speak of value in the abstract, but of the value that is '[d]eriv[ed] … *from not being generally known to the public or to other persons who can obtain economic value* from its disclosure or use … .' In other words, the core inquiry is the value to the owner in *keeping the information secret* from persons who could *exploit it to the relative disadvantage of the original owner.*" (*Yield Dynamics, Inc., supra, 154 Cal.App.4th at p. 568*, original italics, internal citation omitted.)

- " '[C]ourts are reluctant to protect customer lists to the extent they embody information which is "readily ascertainable" through public sources, such as business directories. … . On the other hand, where the employer has expended time and effort identifying customers with particular needs or characteristics, courts will prohibit former employees from using this information to capture a share of the market. Such lists are to be distinguished from mere identities and locations of customers where anyone could easily identify the entities as potential customers. … . As a general principle, the more difficult information is to obtain, and the more time and resources expended by an employer in gathering it, the more likely a court will find such information constitutes a trade secret.' " (*San Jose Construction, Inc. v. S.B.C.C., Inc. (2007) 155 Cal.App.4th 1528, 1539–1540 [67 Cal.Rptr.3d 54]*, internal citation omitted.)

- "The requirement that a customer list must have economic value to qualify as a trade secret has been interpreted to mean that the secrecy of this information provides a business with a 'substantial business advantage.' In this respect, a customer list can be found to have economic value because its disclosure would allow a competitor to direct its sales efforts to those customers who have already shown a willingness to use a unique type of service or product as opposed to a list of people who only might be interested." (*Morlife, Inc. v. Perry (1997) 56 Cal.App.4th 1514, 1522 [66 Cal.Rptr. 2d 731]*, internal citations omitted.)

- " 'The value of information claimed as a trade secret may be established by direct or circumstantial evidence. Direct evidence relating to the content of the secret and its impact on business operations is clearly relevant. Circumstantial evidence of value is also relevant, including the amount of resources invested by the plaintiff in the production of the information, the precautions taken by the plaintiff to protect the secrecy of the information …, and the willingness of others to pay for access to the information.' " (*Altavion, Inc., supra, 226 Cal.App.4th at p. 62.*)

Secondary Sources

1 Milgrim on Trade Secrets, Ch. 1, Definitional Aspects, § 1.01 (Matthew Bender)

49 California Forms of Pleading and Practice, Ch. 565, Unfair Competition, §§ 565.103–565.105 (Matthew Bender)

Edelson & Kay, eds., Trade Secret Litigation and Protection in California (State Bar of California 2009) Ch. 1

Comments.

CACI No. 4412 was added a year after the other definitional instructions. Practitioners should seek to have it given after CACI No. 4402.

See also Chapter 1 for a discussion of the meaning of the term "trade secret."

CACI 4420

Judicial Council of California Civil Jury Instructions (CACI) > Series 4400 TRADE SECRETS

4420 Affirmative Defense—Information Was Readily Ascertainable by Proper Means

---

[*Name of defendant*] **did not misappropriate** [*name of plaintiff*]**'s trade secret[s] if** [*name of defendant*] **proves that the** [*select short term to describe, e.g., information*] **[was/were] readily ascertainable by proper means at the time of the alleged [acquisition/use/ [or] disclosure].**

There is no fixed standard for determining what is "readily ascertainable by proper means." In general, information is readily ascertainable if it can be obtained, discovered, developed, or compiled without significant difficulty, effort, or expense. For example, information is readily ascertainable if it is available in trade journals, reference books, or published materials. On the other hand, the more difficult information is to obtain, and the more time and resources that must be expended in gathering it, the less likely it is that the information is readily ascertainable by proper means.

New December 2007; Revised December 2009

Directions for Use

Give also CACI No. 4408, Improper Means of Acquiring Trade Secret.

One case has suggested in a footnote that in order for the defense to apply, the defendant must have actually obtained plaintiff's secrets through readily ascertainable means rather than improperly. (See *ABBA Rubber Co. v. Seaquist (1991) 235 Cal.App.3d 1, 21–22, fn. 9 [286 Cal.Rptr. 518].*) Such a requirement would not constitute an affirmative defense but rather would be a denial of the improper-means element of the plaintiff's claim. (See 5 Witkin, California Procedure (4th ed. 1996) Pleadings, § 1081 [affirmative defense admits the truth of the essential allegations of the complaint].) Because the advisory committee believes that this is an affirmative defense, no such requirement has been included in this instruction. (See *San Jose Construction, Inc. v. S.B.C.C., Inc. (2007) 155 Cal.App.4th 1528, 1542–1543 [67 Cal.Rptr.3d 54]* [triable issue of fact as to whether information was readily ascertainable, that is, whether defendant *could have* replicated it within short period of time].)

Sources and Authority

- "Trade Secret" Defined. Civil Code section 3426.1(d)(1).

- "The Legislative Committee Comment [to Civ. Code, § 3426.1] further explains the original draft defined a trade secret in part as 'not being readily ascertainable by proper means' and that 'the assertion that a matter is readily ascertainable by proper means remains available as a defense to a claim of misappropriation. Information is readily ascertainable if it is available in trade journals, reference books, or published materials.' " (*DVD Copy Control Assn., Inc. v. Bunner (2003) 31 Cal.4th 864, 899]*, conc. opn. of Werdegar, J.; see Legis. Comm. Comment (Senate), 1984 Addition.)

- "The focus of the first part of the statutory definition is on whether the information is generally known to or readily ascertainable by business competitors or others to whom the information would have some economic value. Information that is readily ascertainable by a business competitor derives no independent value from not being generally known." (*Syngenta Crop Protection, Inc. v. Helliker (2006) 138 Cal.App.4th 1135, 1172 [42 Cal.Rptr.3d 191]*, internal citations omitted.)

- "With respect to the general availability of customer information, courts are reluctant to protect customer lists to the extent they embody information which is 'readily ascertainable' through public sources, such as business directories. On the other hand, where the employer has expended time and effort identifying customers with particular needs or characteristics, courts will prohibit former employees from using this information to capture a share of the market. Such lists are to be distinguished from mere identities and locations of customers where anyone could easily identify the entities as potential customers. As a general principle, the more difficult information is to obtain, and the more time and resources expended by an employer in gathering it, the more likely a court will find such information constitutes a trade secret." (*Morlife, Inc. v. Perry (1997) 56 Cal.App.4th 1514, 1521–1522 [66 Cal.Rptr.2d 731]*, internal citations omitted.)

- "[Defendant] argues that even if reverse engineering … did not actually occur, the binder contents were not trade secrets because they could have been reverse engineered—that is, they were readily ascertainable. … Considering the length of time that each proposal took to create and finalize and the urgency with which four of the project owners impressed upon the prospective contractors to begin the work, we cannot overlook the possibility that the information was not readily ascertainable in the circumstances presented. … Thus, a triable issue of fact exists as to whether the entire proposal for each project was indeed readily ascertainable—that is, whether [defendant] could have replicated each offer within the short period it claimed to have needed." (*San Jose Construction, Inc., supra, 155 Cal.App.4th at pp. 1542–1543*, footnote omitted.)

- "While ease of ascertainability is irrelevant to the definition of a trade secret, 'the assertion that a matter is readily ascertainable by proper means remains available as a defense to a claim of misappropriation.' Therefore, if the defendants can convince the finder of fact at trial (1) that 'it is a virtual certainty that anyone who manufactures' certain types of products uses rubber rollers, (2) that the manufacturers of those products are easily identifiable, and (3) that the defendants' knowledge of the plaintiff's customers resulted from that identification process and not from the plaintiff's records, then the defendants may establish a defense to the misappropriation claim. That defense, however, will be based upon an absence of misappropriation, rather than the absence of a trade secret." (*ABBA Rubber Co., supra, 235 Cal.App.3d at pp. 21–22, fn. 9*, internal citations omitted.)

- "[T]he evidence established that [plaintiff]'s customer list and related information was the product of a substantial amount of time, expense and effort on the part of [plaintiff]. Moreover, the nature and character of the subject customer information, i.e., billing rates, key contacts, specialized requirements and markup rates, is sophisticated information and irrefutably of commercial value and not readily ascertainable to other competitors. Thus, [plaintiff's] customer list and related proprietary information satisfy the first prong of the definition of 'trade secret' under section 3426.1." (*Courtesy Temporary Serv., Inc. v. Camacho (1990) 222 Cal.App.3d 1278, 1288 [272 Cal.Rptr. 352].*)

- "In viewing the evidence presented in the light most favorable to the prevailing party, it is difficult to find a protectable trade secret as that term exists under Civil Code section 3426.1, subdivision (d). While the information sought to be protected here, that is lists of customers who operate manufacturing concerns and who need shipping supplies to ship their products to market, may not be generally known to the public, they certainly would be known or readily ascertainable to other persons in the shipping business. The compilation process in this case is neither sophisticated nor difficult nor particularly time consuming. The evidence presented shows that the shipping business is very competitive and that manufacturers will often deal with more than one company at a time. There is no evidence that all of appellant's competition comes from respondents' new employer. Obviously, all the competitors have secured the same information that appellant claims and, in all likelihood, did so in the same manner as appellant—a process described herein by respondents." (*American Paper & Packaging Prods., Inc. v. Kirgan (1986) 183 Cal.App.3d 1318, 1326 [228 Cal.Rptr. 713].*)

Secondary Sources

1 Milgrim on Trade Secrets, Ch. 1, Definitional Aspects, § 1.07[1] (Matthew Bender)

3 Levy et al., California Torts, Ch. 40, Fraud and Deceit and Other Business Torts, §§ 40.52[1], 40.53[1][b] (Matthew Bender)

49 California Forms of Pleading and Practice, Ch. 565, Unfair Competition, § 565.103[4][a] (Matthew Bender)

Comments.

CACI No. 4420 has been the subject of at least three challenges to the Judicial Council on the grounds that "readily ascertainable by proper means" should not be denoted as an affirmative defense, which would excuse wrongdoing if the elements of trade secret misappropriation are proven. Rather, some courts view it as a way for a defendant to negate the element of a misappropriation of trade secret claim. *See, e.g., ABBA Rubber Co. v. Seaquist*, 235 Cal.App.3d 1, 21–22, fn. 9 (1991) (quoted in the Sources and Authority section above). *See also IMAX Corp. v. Cinema Technologies, Inc.*, 152 F.3d 1161, 1168 (9th Cir. 1998) (on scope of defense of showing reverse engineering); *SEIU v. Rosselli*, 2009 WL 1382259, *4 (N.D. Cal. May 14, 2009) (defense based "on the absence of a misappropriation."); *Brescia v. Angelin*, 172 Cal.App.4th 133, 147 (2009) (The defense of independent derivation is a defense to the element of misappropriation.).)

That some courts refer to a "defense" may have caused some to assume that the courts meant an affirmative defense. However, an affirmative defense is a defense for which the defendant has the burden of proof and if established would negate liability even if it is proven the defendant committed the alleged acts. In contrast, if a defendant claims it did not engage in a misappropriation, but rather engaged in reverse engineering or derived independently the alleged trade secret, practitioners should seek CACI No. 4408.

It should also be noted that:

The phrase "and not being readily ascertainable by proper means by" was included in the section as originally proposed by the National Conference of Commissioners of Uniform State Laws. It was *removed* from this section in favor of the phrase 'the public or to.' This change was made because the original language was *viewed as ambiguous in the definition of a trade secret*. However, the assertion that a matter is readily ascertainable by proper means remains available as a defense to a claim of misappropriation. (Civ. Code, § 3426.1, Legis. Comm. Comment (Senate), 1984 Addition.)" (Emphasis added).

See also ABBA Rubber Co. v. Seaquist, 235 Cal.App.3d 1, 21 (1991) ("That deletion apparently resulted from arguments that conditioning the scope of a trade secret on the extent to which the information was not readily ascertainable would 'mudd[y] the meaning of the term trade secret' and 'invite[] the various parties to speculate on the time needed to discover a secret.'") Whether information is "readily ascertainable by proper means" is not part of the CUTSA definition of a "trade secret."

In contrast, under the federal Defend Trade Secrets Act, whether information "not being generally known to, and not being readily ascertainable through proper means," is an element of definition of a "trade secret." (18 U.S.C. § 1839(3)(b).) Thus, while California's Legislature removed the "readily ascertainable by proper means" standard from its statutory definition of a "trade secret," Congress kept "not being readily ascertainable through proper means" as part of the statutory definition of a "trade secret." Therefore, if appropriate, practitioners should consider seeking separate instructions if asserting CUTSA and DTSA claims.

As set forth above, CACI No. 4408 addresses the standard for independent derivation or reverse engineering to disprove that a "misappropriation" occurred. Consistent with CACI No. 4408, the DTSA specifically excludes from the definition of "acquisition by improper means" the following: "reverse engineering, independent derivation, or any other lawful means of acquisition." (18 U.S.C. § 1839(6)(b).)

Like all affirmative defenses, the purported affirmative defense addressed by CACI No. 4420 is waived if not asserted in the defendant's answer. If a defendant is permitted to assert the subject information is "readily ascertainable" as an affirmative defense and the circumstances warrant giving the CACI No. 4420 instruction, until such time that the Judicial Council changes its view that "readily ascertainable" is an affirmative defense or the controlling appellate court holds that it is not an affirmative defense, practitioners should consider requesting that the instruction be given. Further, depending on the circumstances, if CACI No. 4420 is to be given, practitioners may consider requesting that an instruction clarifying the parties' respective burdens of proof be given if there is concern that the jury would otherwise be confused.

CACI 4421

Judicial Council of California Civil Jury Instructions (CACI) >
Series 4400 TRADE SECRETS

4421 Affirmative Defense—Statute of Limitations—Three-Year Limit (Civ. Code, § 3426.6)

[*Name of defendant*] **claims that** [*name of plaintiff*]**'s lawsuit was not filed within the time set by law. To succeed on this defense,** [*name of defendant*] **must prove that the claimed misappropriation of** [*name of plaintiff*]**'s trade secrets occurred before** [*insert date three years before date of filing*]**.**

However, the lawsuit was still filed on time if [*name of plaintiff*] **proves that before** [*insert date three years before date of filing*]**,** [**he/she/***nonbinary pronoun***/it**] **did not discover, nor with reasonable diligence should have discovered, facts that would have caused a reasonable person to suspect that** [*name of defendant*] **had misappropriated** [*name of plaintiff*]**'s** [*select short term to describe, e.g., information*]**.**

New April 2009

Directions for Use

Give this instruction if the California Uniform Trade Secrets Act statute of limitations is at issue. (See Civ. Code, § 3426.6.) In an action in which the defendant is or was a customer of the initial misappropriator, modifications may be required. (See *Cypress Semiconductor Corp. v. Superior Court (2008) 163 Cal.App.4th 575 [77 Cal.Rptr.3d 685].*)

It is not necessary that the plaintiff know the identity of the defendant in order to trigger the duty to discover. (*Cypress Semiconductor Corp., supra, 163 Cal.App.4th at p. 587.*) Therefore, "[*name of defendant*]" in the last sentence will need to be modified if inquiry notice may have been triggered against an actual, but unidentified, misappropriator. (See *Cypress Semiconductor Corp., supra, 163 Cal.App.4th at p. 585.*)

This instruction places the burden on the plaintiff to prove that it did not know nor have any reason to suspect the misappropriation earlier than three years before filing. (See Civ. Code, § 3426.6.) This is the rule for the burden of proof under the nonstatutory delayed-discovery rule. (See *Glue-Fold, Inc. v. Slautterback Corp. (2000) 82 Cal.App.4th 1018, 1030 [98 Cal.Rptr.2d 661]*; CACI No. 455, *Statute of Limitations—Delayed Discovery.*) Certain statutes that have their own delayed discovery language (as does Civil Code section 3426.6) have been construed to place the burden on the defendant to prove that the plaintiff knew or should have suspected the facts giving rise to the cause of action earlier than the limitation date. (See, e.g., *Samuels v. Mix (1999) 22 Cal.4th 1, 8–10 [91 Cal.Rptr.2d 273, 989 P.2d 701]* [construing Code Civ. Proc., § 340.6 on legal malpractice]; CACI No. 610, *Affirmative Defense—Statute of Limitations—Attorney Malpractice—One-Year Limit.*) No court has construed Civil Code section 3426.6 to transfer the burden of proof on delayed discovery to the defendant, so presumably the burden of proof remains with the plaintiff under the nonstatutory rule.

Sources and Authority

- Statute of Limitations. Civil Code section 3426.6.
- "The unanimous conclusion of courts considering the issue—i.e., from federal courts construing section 3426.6—is that it is the first discovered (or discoverable) misappropriation of a trade secret which commences the limitation period." (*Glue-Fold, Inc., supra, 82 Cal.App.4th at p. 1026.*)
- "The statute is triggered when the plaintiff knows or has reason to know the third party has knowingly acquired, used, or disclosed its trade secrets." (*Cypress Semiconductor Corp., supra, 163 Cal.App.4th 585.*)
- "[T]he misappropriation that triggers the running of the statute is that which the plaintiff suspects, not that which may or may not actually exist." (*Cypress Semiconductor Corp., supra, 163 Cal.App.4th at p. 587.*)
- "[A] plaintiff may have more than one *claim* for misappropriation, each with its own statute of limitations, when more than one defendant is involved. This is different from saying that each *misappropriation* gives rise to a separate claim, which is what section 3426.6 precludes." (*Cypress Semiconductor Corp., supra, 163 Cal.App.4th at p. 583*, original italics.)
- "A *misappropriation* within the meaning of the UTSA occurs not only at the time of the initial acquisition of the trade secret by wrongful means, but also with each misuse or wrongful disclosure of the secret. But a *claim* for misappropriation of a trade secret arises for a given plaintiff against a given defendant only once, at the time of the initial misappropriation, subject to the discovery rule provided in section 3426.6. Each new misuse or wrongful disclosure is viewed as augmenting a single claim of continuing misappropriation rather than as giving rise to a separate claim." (*Cadence Design Systems, Inc. v. Avant! Corp. (2002) 29 Cal.4th 215, 223 [127 Cal.Rptr.2d 169, 57 P.3d 647]*, original italics.)
- "It [is appropriate] to construe section 3426.6 as meaning that a cause of action for misappropriation against a third party defendant accrues with the plaintiff's discovery of that defendant's misappropriation. Any continuing misappropriation by that defendant constitutes a single claim." (*Cypress Semiconductor Corp., supra, 163 Cal.App.4th at p. 583.*)

- "If someone steals a trade secret and then sells it to a third party, when does the statute of limitations begin to run on any misappropriation claim the trade secret owner might have against the third party? … We conclude that with respect to the element of knowledge, the statute of limitations on a cause of action for misappropriation begins to run when the *plaintiff* has any reason to suspect that the third party knows or reasonably should know that the information is a trade secret. The third party's actual state of mind does not affect the running of the statute." (*Cypress Semiconductor Corp., supra, 163 Cal.App.4th at p. 579*, original italics.)

- "We conclude that the trial court erred in ruling, under the stipulated facts, that the statute of limitations did not begin to run until August 2003, when [defendant] actually learned that the DynaSpice program contained [plaintiff]'s trade secrets. Rather, the question is: When did [plaintiff] first have any reason to suspect that a … customer [of the initial misappropriator] had obtained or used DynaSpice knowing, *or with reason to know,* that the software contained [plaintiff]'s trade secrets?" (*Cypress Semiconductor Corp., supra, 163 Cal.App.4th at p. 588*, original italics.)

- "[I]t is not necessary that the plaintiff be able to identify the person or persons causing the harm. Since the identity of the defendant is not an element of a cause of action, the failure to discover the identity of the defendant does not postpone accrual of the cause of action. ' "Although never fully articulated, the rationale for distinguishing between ignorance" of the defendant and "ignorance" of the cause of action itself "appears to be premised on the commonsense assumption that once the plaintiff is aware of" the latter, he "normally" has "sufficient opportunity," within the "applicable limitations period," "to discover the identity" of the former.' In this case, therefore, the statute began to run when [plaintiff] had any reason to suspect that the CSI customers knew or should have known that they had acquired [plaintiff]'s trade secrets." (*Cypress Semiconductor Corp., supra, 163 Cal.App.4th at p. 587*, internal citations omitted.)

Secondary Sources

13 Witkin, Summary of California Law (11th ed. 2017) Equity, § 91

Gaab & Reese, California Practice Guide: Civil Procedure Before Trial—Claims & Defenses, Ch. 11(I)-D ¶¶ 11:250–11:252 (The Rutter Group)

3 Levy et al., California Torts, Ch. 40, Fraud and Deceit and Other Business Torts, § 40.55 (Matthew Bender)

49 California Forms of Pleading and Practice, Ch. 565, Unfair Competition, § 565.274 (Matthew Bender)

Matthew Bender Practice Guide: California Unfair Competition and Business Torts, Ch. 8, Trade Secrets, 8.28

Comments.

The DTSA also has a three-year statute of limitations, triggered by a "discovered or should have discovered" standard for accrual of the claim:

A civil action under subsection (b) may not be commenced later than 3 years after the date on which the misappropriation with respect to which the action would relate is discovered or by the exercise of reasonable diligence should have been discovered. For purposes of this subsection, a continuing misappropriation constitutes a single claim of misappropriation.
18 U.S.C. § 1836(d).

See Chapter 9 for a discussion of the statute of limitation defense.

Appendix B
MODEL NON-DISCLOSURE AGREEMENT

By: David Almeling, Esq.
and Angelique Kaounis, Esq.

---

§ B.01 Introduction

The Trade Secrets Interest Group of the Intellectual Property Section of the California Lawyers Association is pleased to provide the following updated Model Third Party Non-Disclosure Agreement for adaption and use when parties share confidential information in furtherance of a proposed transaction, relationship, and/or other joint activity.

DISCLAIMER: This model agreement is intended to serve as a starting point only, and should be tailored to meet your specific requirements. For example, the circumstances of your proposed business arrangement may make it appropriate to have provisions specifically designed for dealing with software source code in lieu of or in addition to the provisions of this model agreement. There are bracketed "optional" provisions, and occasionally explanations within the model agreement (usually in footnotes for ease of reference). The document should not be construed as legal advice for any particular facts or circumstances or generally. If you are not a lawyer, please consult a lawyer. You are accepting this document "as is," without warranty of any kind, expressed or implied, including, but not limited to, the implied warranties of merchantability and fitness for a particular purpose, and all liability for damages resulting from its use is disclaimed.

This Model Agreement is subject to copyright and licensed under the Creative Commons type license cc-by-sa-3.0 (attribution share-alike), which states, in summary:

You are free:

- **to Share**—to copy, distribute and transmit the work

- **to Remix**—to adapt the work

Under the following conditions:

- **Attribution**—You must attribute the work in the manner specified by the author or licensor (but not in any way that suggests that they endorse you or your use of the work).

- **Share Alike**—If you alter, transform, or build upon this work, you may distribute the resulting work only under the same or similar license to this one.

With the understanding that:

- **Waiver**—Any of the above conditions can be **waived** if you get permission from the copyright holder.

- **Public Domain**—Where the work or any of its elements is in the **public domain** under applicable law, that status is in no way affected by the license.

- **Other Rights**—In no way are any of the following rights affected by the license:

- Your fair dealing or **fair use** rights, or other applicable copyright exceptions and limitations;

- The author's **moral** rights;

- Rights other persons may have either in the work itself or in how the work is used, such as **publicity** or privacy rights.

- **Notice**—For any reuse or distribution, you must make clear to others the license terms of this work. That notice must be on the final page, or the page before the court's execution / signature line, and must be as follows:

"Model Third Party Non-Disclosure Agreement © 2014 and licensed under the Creative Commons type license cc-by-sa-3.0 (attribution share-alike) (http://creativecommons.org/licenses/by-sa/3.0/) by the California Lawyers Association, IP Section, Trade Secrets Interest Group (ipsection.org), principal authors David Almeling and Angelique Kaounis, assisted by Neil Olson, David Morales, and Danielle Hesse. This entire notice, with links, in quotes must always be reproduced *as is* in 8pt font or larger, on the final page of the Model Non-Disclosure Agreement."

The full license terms, which you are deemed to have read and agreed to if you use any portion of this Model Protective Order, are available here: https://creativecommons.org/licenses/by-sa/3.0/legalcode.

The Trade Secrets Interest Group wishes to thank the following members for their time and knowledge in drafting this Model Agreement: David Almeling and Angelique Kaounis, assisted by Neil Olson, David Morales, and Danielle Hesse.

Suggested revisions and examples of custom-tailored provisions are welcome. Email those to the Chair of the Trade Secrets Interest Group, whose email address may be found at https://calawyers.org/section/intellectual-property-law/ip-interest-groups/.

§ B.02 Model Non-Disclosure Agreement

The Model Non-Disclosure Agreement is reprinted on the following pages.

NON-DISCLOSURE AGREEMENT[44]

This Non-Disclosure Agreement ("Agreement") is entered into as of [insert date] (the "Effective Date") by and between [insert Company A] and [insert Company B] (Company A and Company B shall be referred to singly as a "Party" and collectively as the "Parties"). In consideration of the mutual obligations, covenants, and warranties herein, the Parties agree as follows:

BACKGROUND AND DEFINITIONS

1. This Agreement is made for the purpose of [insert purpose] (the "Purpose").

2. "Confidential Information" shall mean all confidential, proprietary[45] and trade secret information and materials, whether in written, oral, visual, electronic, or another format (including, for example, demonstrations, models or prototypes, software, computer tapes, audio or video tapes or recordings, and other media), and whether intentionally disclosed or observed inadvertently, including, but not limited to, the following: [insert specific description if possible]; research, product plans or other information regarding the disclosing Party's (the "Disclosing Party") products or services and markets therefor, customer lists and customers, software, developments, inventions, processes, formulas, technology, designs, drawings, engineering, hardware configuration information, marketing, finances, pricing, or other business information;[46] information of a confidential, sensitive, non-public, or personal nature, including information belonging to a third party for which the Company owes a duty of confidentiality; any other Company proprietary or confidential information, including but not limited to any materials or any oral and written communications between the parties marked "confidential," "proprietary" or similarly marked;[47] or any materials which a reasonable person would recognize from the surrounding facts and circumstances to be proprietary or confidential. When Confidential

---

[44] The importance of adhering to the terms of an NDA was highlighted in the case of *Convolve, Inc. v. Compaq Computer Corp.*, 527 Fed.App'x. 910, 925, 2013 WL 3285331 (Fed. Cir. July 1, 2013). As the court there explained, "[t]he CUTSA states that misappropriation occurs when a trade secret is acquired under circumstances giving rise to a duty to maintain its secrecy. Cal. Civ. Code § 3426.1(b)." *Id.* In that case, "Convolve disclosed its alleged trade secrets to Seagate pursuant to the provisions of [an] NDA." *Id.* Therefore, the court held that "the 'circumstances' giving rise to a duty to maintain the secrecy of the disclosed information [wa]s dictated by the terms of the NDA." *Id.* Because "Convolve did not follow the procedures set forth in the NDA to protect the shared information," the court concluded that "no duty ever arose to maintain secrecy of that information." *Id.*

[45] A recent case in the employment context discusses the proprietary nature of information that may be protected under an NDA. *See Hamilton v. Juul Labs, Inc.*, 2020 WL 5500377 (N.D. Cal. Sept. 11, 2020). For a discussion of NDAs in the employment context, please see Chapter 4.

[46] One court recently has held that "business information" must still be inherently confidential in nature, and a non-disclosure agreement which facially extends to non-confidential information may be deemed an invalid restraint on employee mobility. *See, e.g.*, *Brown v. TGS Mgmt. Co., LLC*, 57 Cal. App. 5th 303, 317–318 (2020).

[47] One court has observed that "[p]ertinent [California] case law teaches that a purported trade secret owner cannot meet its burden merely by showing that its alleged proprietary information was the subject of a confidentiality agreement or labeled 'secret' or 'confidential' because such labels, without more, 'do not establish anything.'" *Pollara v. Radiant Logistics Inc.*, 2014 WL 12585781, at *1 (C.D. Cal. June 6, 2014) (addressing customer lists and quoting *Thompson v. Impaxx, Inc.*, 113 Cal.App.4th 1425, 1430 (2003)); *see also Hamilton*, 2020 WL 5500377 at *5-6 (observing that a clause providing that "***Company Confidential Information also includes all information of which the unauthorized disclosure could be detrimental to the interests of Company, whether or not such information is identified as Confidential Information***" "is arguably an ambiguous, catch-all phrase that could encompass more than proprietary information") (emphasis in original).

Information is disclosed in a form other than in writing, the Disclosing Party shall [may] (i) identify the material as Confidential Information at the time of disclosure; and (ii) confirm in writing the transmission of the Confidential Information by summarizing the content of the disclosure within 14 days of the disclosure taking place.[48] "Confidential Information" does not include any of the foregoing items which have become publicly known or made available to the Receiving Party through no breach of this agreement or other wrongful act [by the Receiving Party].

CONDITIONS ON USE AND DISCLOSURE OF CONFIDENTIAL INFORMATION

3. All Confidential Information disclosed by any Party shall remain the property of the Disclosing Party.

4. Each Party receiving Confidential Information (the "Receiving Party") shall use the Confidential Information solely for the Purpose and shall not use the Confidential Information for any other purpose without the prior written consent of the Disclosing Party.[49]

5. The Receiving Party and those of its employees, officers, agents and affiliates permitted access hereunder will hold the Confidential Information in confidence and will take all necessary steps to preserve the confidential and proprietary nature of the Confidential Information. Without limiting the foregoing, the Receiving Party will (1) not disclose any Confidential Information to persons within its organization who do not have a need to know in order for the Receiving Party to engage in the Purpose; (2) not disclose any Confidential Information to any person outside of its organization unless such person has a need to know in order for the Receiving Party to engage in the Purpose, and such person is bound by fiduciary or contractual duties of confidentiality to the Receiving Party that are at least as stringent as those contained in this Agreement; (3) if reasonably required, cause each of the Receiving Party's employees, officers, agents, affiliates and attorneys who have access to the Confidential Information to sign a confidentiality and non-disclosure agreement, for the benefit of the Disclosing Party, containing terms at least as stringent as those contained in this Agreement, and, in any event, advise all of its employees, officers, agents, and affiliates of the confidential and proprietary nature of the Confidential Information; and (4) in all instances, exercise at least the same degree of care to maintain the secrecy of the Confidential Information as the Receiving Party exercises to protect its own most valuable trade secrets, but in no case less than reasonable care. A list of individuals authorized to receive Company A's Confidential Information is attached hereto as Schedule __. A list of

---

[48] The preceding sentence is included to remind parties of the option of marking documents as confidential (insofar as such markings may be relevant to whether reasonable efforts were taken to maintain the secrecy of information at issue), understanding that this option may not always be practical or possible.

[49] A Disclosing Party may wish to include a clause prohibiting the Receiving Party from improperly attempting to "reverse engineer" the Confidential Information as received. *But see* Civ. Code § 3426.1(a) ("Reverse engineering . . . alone shall not be considered improper means.").

individuals authorized to receive Company B's Confidential Information is attached hereto as Schedule[50] __.

6. If the Receiving Party is required by order of any court or other government or regulatory agency to disclose any Confidential Information belonging to any Disclosing Party, it shall provide all Parties with prompt written notice within 3 business days of any such requirement so that the Parties whose Confidential Information is at risk may seek a protective order or take other appropriate action. Upon the request and at the expense of the requesting Party, the other Parties will reasonably cooperate with the requesting Party to obtain an appropriate protective order or other reliable assurance that confidential treatment will be accorded the Confidential Information. Subject to the foregoing requirements, it shall not be a breach of this Agreement for a Receiving Party to disclose Confidential Information if such disclosure is: (a) in response to a valid order of a court or governmental body of the United States or any political subdivision thereof; (b) otherwise required by law; or (c) necessary to establish the Disclosing Party's rights under this Agreement.

7. In the event of a demonstrable breach of this Agreement by either Party, the non-breaching Party shall have the right to (1) compensation from the breaching Party for any and all [reasonably foreseeable] damages or losses sustained or incurred by reason of such breach, including reasonable attorneys' fees and costs; and (2) apply to a court for the immediate entry of an order restraining and/or enjoining the breach of this Agreement and otherwise to specifically enforce the terms of this Agreement.

8. No license or other rights to Confidential Information or any intellectual property rights (including patents, trademarks, copyrights, and/or trade secrets) are granted or implied hereby and the Disclosing Party retains all of its rights therein. [The fact that a Party discloses its Confidential Information to the Receiving Party shall not be deemed to constitute any representation, warranty, assurance, guarantee or inducement by the Disclosing Party to the other of any kind with respect to the Confidential Information, including without limitation, that use thereof will not infringe any trademarks, patents, copyrights, or any other intellectual property rights, or other rights of third persons or of the Disclosing Party.]

9. Nothing in this Agreement requires or shall be construed as a representation that the Receiving Party will not develop or acquire information that is the same as or similar to the Disclosing Party's Confidential Information, or obligate either Party to discontinue any of its individual activities, including for example, any product (or service) development or offering or internal systems development, as long as the Receiving Party does not do so in breach of this Agreement. [Each Party agrees that this Agreement will not restrict the right of the other to enter into agreements with other parties [for the same or similar efforts, or] [to make, have made, use, sell, buy, develop, market, or otherwise transfer any technology, products or services now or in the future]. Moreover, this Agreement does not constitute, create, give effect to, or otherwise imply a joint venture, pooling agreement, partnership, or

---

[50] The option of including a list of individuals to whom the Confidential Information may be disseminated can serve as a method of limiting the disclosure.

formal business arrangement of any kind, nor shall it constitute, create, give effect to, or otherwise imply an agreement to agree, or an obligation on the part of either Party to submit a proposal to perform or enter into a contract with the other Party with regard to the Purpose or any other proposed transactions, relationships and/or joint activities.]

GENERAL TERMS AND CONDITIONS

10. **Warranties**. Each Party warrants that it is authorized to enter into this Agreement and that its affiliates, subsidiaries, agents, attorneys, employees, officers, directors and representatives will conform to the terms and conditions of this Agreement. Each Party further represents and warrants that the execution of this Agreement and the performance of its obligations hereunder will not breach or be in conflict with any other agreement to which that Party is a party or is bound, and that the Party is not subject to any covenants or similar restrictions or any court order or other legal obligation or limitation that would affect the performance of his or their duties hereunder. [*May require modification where regulatory approval is required for a contemplated transaction.*]

11. **Export**. Both Parties agree to comply with all applicable export and import control laws and regulations. Each Party also agrees that it shall not knowingly export or re-export, directly or indirectly, to any country, any of the Confidential Information (or any product, process or service resulting directly therefrom) without first having obtained all necessary approvals thereof.

12. **Assignment**. Neither Party shall transfer or assign any rights or delegate any obligations herein, in whole or in part, whether voluntarily or by operation of law, without the prior written consent of the other Party, which shall not be unreasonably withheld. Notwithstanding the above, either Party shall have the right to assign this Agreement and the obligations hereunder to any successor-in-interest by way of a merger, acquisition, or sale of all or substantially all of that Party's assets on condition that the assignee of this Agreement will assume all obligations and liability of the assignor under or in connection with this Agreement and agrees to be bound by the terms and conditions of this Agreement.

13. **Governing Law and Venue**. This Agreement shall be construed and enforced in accordance with the laws of the State of [insert], without regard to choice of laws principles. The exclusive venue for any dispute relating to or arising from this Agreement shall be [insert].

14. **Severability**. In the event any provision of this Agreement is deemed unenforceable, the validity of the remaining provisions hereof shall not be affected.

15. **Term**. This Agreement applies to any Confidential Information that may have been provided by either Party before or after the Effective Date, and will continue to govern all disclosures of Confidential Information, until terminated by thirty (30) days written notice by either Party to the other, *except that each Party's obligations relating to Confidential*

Information disclosed prior to termination will continue for so long as the Confidential Information remains confidential and proprietary. [*Consider the following in lieu of the italicized text*: Notwithstanding the foregoing, for a period of __ years/months from the date of termination of this Agreement, each Party agrees to use the same care and discretion to avoid disclosure, publication, or dissemination of any Confidential Information disclosed by the other Party as it employs with similar information of its own which it does not desire to have published, disclosed, or disseminated.] [*Also consider*: Following the period of confidentiality specified in the foregoing sentence, no obligation is assumed by, or is to be implied against the Receiving Party with respect to the Disclosing Party's Confidential Information and such information will be considered non-confidential.]

16. **Return or Destruction of Documents**. Within ten business days of receipt of a written request from the Disclosing Party, the Receiving Parties shall return to the requesting Disclosing Party, or destroy (and confirm the same in writing) any and all written Confidential Information disclosed to the Receiving Party, including all tangible and electronic copies thereof, as well as all notes, analyses, summaries or any other work product created by the Receiving Party or its representatives which are based on or derived from the Disclosing Party's Confidential Information. However, the Receiving Party [or its counsel] may retain one archival copy of the Confidential Information that it may use only in case of a dispute concerning this Agreement.[51]

17. **No Oral Modification**. No amendment, modification, or waiver of any provision of this Agreement shall be binding or enforceable unless and until memorialized in a written document signed by the Parties.

18. **Entire Agreement**. This Agreement contains the entire understanding of the Parties regarding the subject matter hereof and supersedes any and all prior or contemporaneous communications, understandings or agreements with respect to the subject matter hereof.

19. **Binding Effect**. This Agreement shall bind the Parties and the Parties' successors and assigns.

20. **Counterparts**. This Agreement may be executed in one or more counterparts, each of which shall be an original but all of which shall collectively constitute a single instrument.

21. **Headings and Interpretation**. The headings and captions in this Agreement are for convenience only, and in no way define or describe the scope or content of any provision of this Agreement. Each Party acknowledges that it has been represented by counsel of its choice in connection with this Agreement [and the transaction[s] contemplated by this Agreement]. Accordingly, any rule of law or any legal decision that would require interpretation of any claimed ambiguities in this Agreement against the drafting Party has no application and is expressly waived.

---

[51] Parties may also consider the inclusion of an inspection right permitting the disclosing party to confirm (to the extent feasible) that its confidential information is no longer in the possession of the receiving party.

IN WITNESS WHEREOF, the Parties hereby execute this Agreement as of the Effective Date.

____________________	____________________
Company A	Company B
By: ____________________	By: ____________________
Its: ____________________	Its: ____________________
Address:	Address:
____________________	____________________
____________________	____________________
Email: ____________________	Email: ____________________

Appendix C
MODEL PROTECTIVE ORDER
By: Robert B. Milligan, Esq.

Some state and federal courts in California have developed protective orders for use by the parties. The protective orders are often an excellent starting point for counsel to customize a protective order appropriate for specific trade secret cases.

The Northern District of California model protective orders can be found on the Court's website at https://cand.uscourts.gov/forms/model-protective-orders/. The Court has a specific custom protective order entitled Model Protective Order for Litigation Involving Patents, Highly Sensitive Confidential Information and/or Trade Secrets. Several magistrate judges in the Central District have also made protective orders available on their Judges' Procedures and Schedules pages at https://www.cacd.uscourts.gov/judges-schedules-procedures.

Some state courts have model protective orders available on their websites. The Los Angeles Court protective order can be found at
http://www.lacourt.org/division/civil/pdf/FormProtectiveOrder1Confidential_1.pdf.

The Santa Clara Court protective order in complex cases can be found at
https://www.scscourt.org/court_divisions/civil/complex/Model%20Protective%20Order.pdf

The Alameda Court protective order in complex cases can be found at
http://www.alameda.courts.ca.gov/dept17/Model%20Protective%20Order%20-%20Complex.pdf

Several legal organizations have published helpful articles on protective orders and specifically protective order considerations in trade secret cases. For a good overview of the topic, please see the following articles:

The Sedona Conference Commentary on Protecting Trade Secrets in Litigation About Them, June 2021 Public Comment Version

The Sedona Conference, The Sedona Guidelines: Best Practices Addressing Protective Orders, Confidentiality & Public Access in Civil Cases, 8 SEDONA CONF. J. 141 (2007)

TABLE OF AUTHORITIES

Page(s)

Cases

Statutes

State

Federal

www.ingramcontent.com/pod-product-compliance
Lightning Source LLC
LaVergne TN
LVHW060013210926
848481LV00013B/3700
9781735907420